Analytical and Practical Aspects of Drug Testing in Hair

FORENSIC SCIENCE SERIES

Series Editor

Robert Gaensslen, Ph.D.

Professor and Director
Graduate Studies in Forensic Science
University of Illinois at Chicago
Chicago, Illinois, U.S.A.

Analytical and Practical Aspects of Drug Testing in Hair, edited by Pascal Kintz

Bitemark Evidence, edited by Robert B. J. Dorion

Forensic Computer Crime Investigation, edited by Thomas A. Johnson

Analytical and Practical Aspects of Drug Testing in Hair

Edited by
Pascal Kintz

Taylor & Francis
Taylor & Francis Group
Boca Raton London New York

CRC is an imprint of the Taylor & Francis Group,
an informa business

CRC Press
Taylor & Francis Group
6000 Broken Sound Parkway NW, Suite 300
Boca Raton, FL 33487-2742

Printed in the United States of America on acid-free paper
10 9 8 7 6 5 4 3 2 1

International Standard Book Number-10: 0-8493-6450-7 (Hardcover)
International Standard Book Number-13: 978-0-8493-6450-1 (Hardcover)

Library of Congress Cataloging-in-Publication Data

Kintz, Pascal.
Analytical and practical aspects of drug testing in hair / Pascal Kintz.
p. cm.
Includes bibliographical references and index.
ISBN 0-8493-6450-7 (alk. paper)
1. Hair--Analysis. 2. Drugs--Analysis. 3. Chemistry, Forensic. I. Title.

RB47.5.K56 2006
363.25'62--dc22 2006044577

Visit the Taylor & Francis Web site at
http://www.taylorandfrancis.com

and the CRC Press Web site at
http://www.crcpress.com

Foreword

Given the limitations of self-reports on drug use, testing for drugs of abuse is important for most clinical and forensic toxicological situations, both for assessing the reality of the intoxication and for evaluation of the level of drug impairment.

It is generally accepted that chemical testing of biological fluids is the most objective means of diagnosis of drug use. The presence of a drug analyte in a biological specimen can be used to document exposure. The standard in drug testing is the immunoassay screen, followed by the gas chromatographic-mass spectrometric confirmation conducted on a urine sample. In recent years, remarkable advances in sensitive analytical techniques have enabled the analysis of drugs in unconventional biological specimens such as hair. The advantages of this sample over traditional media, like urine and blood, are obvious: collection is noninvasive, relatively easy to perform, and in forensic situations it can be achieved under close supervision of law enforcement officers to prevent adulteration or substitution. Moreover, the window of drug detection is dramatically extended to weeks, months, or even years when testing hair. It appears that the value of alternative-specimens analysis for the identification of drug users is steadily gaining recognition. This can be seen from its growing use in preemployment screening, in forensic sciences, in traffic medicine, in clinical applications, and for doping control.

Since the first edition of the book *Drug Testing in Hair* was published in 1996, numerous advances have been introduced in this specific topic of science. The years 1995–1996 were those of cannabis detection. The 1997–1998 period was the golden time for benzodiazepines detection, followed by 1999–2000 and the applications in doping control. With the development of liquid chromatography-tandem mass spectrometry (LC-MS/MS), the most recent period (2003–2005) is characterized by the detection in hair of a single exposure and the related applications in drug-facilitated crimes. This revised edition, *Analytical and Practical Aspects of Drug Testing in Hair*, reviews all of these developments as well as the validation of analytical procedures and the interpretation of data.

After the International Association of Forensic Toxicologists (TIAFT) workshop in Abu Dhabi in 1995, it was decided to create the Society of Hair Testing. This was done late in December 1995 in Strasbourg, France, and, since that date, the society has organized both scientific and practical meetings each year. It is also responsible for proposing to its members an annual quality control procedure on authentic hair specimens. Various consensuses have also been published in the scientific literature. Under the leadership of the successive presidents (Hans Sachs, Christian Staub, and now Carmen Jurado), the society has contributed to major progress in the field.

Special thanks must go to all of the international authors who have agreed to write a chapter to what, I hope, is a worthwhile book. As was the case in the first edition, various opinions, sometimes controversial or contradictory, have emerged among the different authors. I find it helpful to define the areas of agreement among the active investigators and what issues require further efforts to reach a consensus.

Pascal Kintz
TIAFT President

Preface

"Where have you been? I can hardly recognize you," might be the greeting of a mentor to an infrequent visit from a junior colleague. This would have been very appropriate 25 years ago were hair analysis under discussion. Few analytical toxicologists then considered hair as a desirable specimen for routine analyses. Some very few dabbled with Beethoven's or Napoleon's hairs, but they were the exceptions. Obtaining the samples was not the problem. These could be obtained easily. How to get acceptable results was the challenge.

The analytical techniques then in use (thin-layer chromatography [TLC], gas chromatography [GC], high-performance liquid chromatography [HPLC]) were quite adequate for their current use but were much too insensitive if hair was to be analyzed. The advent of immunoassays changed the analytical scene markedly. The increased sensitivity they provided made hair analysis feasible. Applying immunoassays to hair analysis soon revealed another limitation and deficiency. Although sensitivity became realistic, specificity was lacking. Creative investigators then recognized that the esoteric mass spectrometry (MS) that was coming into greater use could provide the desired sensitivity and specificity.

As practitioners developed expertise and funding became more available, they moved forward with hyphenated mass-spectrometric procedures — GC-MS, GC-MS/MS, and HPLC-MS/MS. Applying these techniques to hair analysis ensured the desired sensitive and specific results. The pursuit of zero began.

Routine analysis of hair became a reality when incorporation of automated sample-handling equipment became realistic. "Look, Ma, no hands!" was now commonplace. Few toxicologists recognize that this now-robotic procedure is a real threat to their professional existence.

As the technology of hair analysis has grown, so has its applications. Readers of this volume will find authors' suggestions that will resolve many questions. Has the patient been taking his medication? How often is this omitted? Are unborn children harmed when pregnant women use drugs? Does the use of drugs enhance an athlete's performance? Are females more susceptible to sex that might otherwise be unwelcome because they are surreptitiously given a drug? How do drugs affect criminals? When and for how long have drugs influenced work performance? Answers to these and ever so many other questions can be provided by hair analyses.

Very accomplished practitioners pass on their expertise to readers of this volume. Theirs is not the last word, but they do reflect the present state of the art, which is ever changing. Without a doubt, there will be progress as time goes by. However, it is comforting to have the easy access to the current status that this volume provides the reader.

Irving Sunshine, Ph.D.

Contributors

Francis Billault
Laboratoire TOXLAB
Paris, France

Thomas Cairns
Psychemedics Corporation
Culver City, California

Marjorie Chèze
Laboratoire TOXLAB
Paris, France

Vincent Cirimele
Laboratoire ChemTox
Illkirch, France

Rafael de la Torre
Institut Municipial d'Investigació (IMIM)
and
Universitat Pompeu Fabra
Barcelona, Spain

Mark Deveaux
Laboratoire TOXLAB
Paris, France

Henrik Druid
Department of Forensic Medicine
Karolinska Institutet
Stockholm, Sweden

Gaëlle Duffort
Laboratoire TOXLAB
Paris, France

Óscar García-Algar
Pediatric Service, URIE
Hospital del Mar
and
Universitat Autònoma
Barcelona, Spain

Jean-Pierre Goullé
Laboratoire de Pharmacocinetique et de Toxicology Cliniques
Group Hospitalier du Havre
Havre, France

Virginia Hill
Psychemedics Corporation
Culver City, California

Carmen Jurado
Ministerio de Justicia
Seville, Spain

David A. Kidwell
Naval Research Laboratory
Washington, D.C.

Pascal Kintz
X'pertise Consulting
Laboratoire ChemTox
Illkirch, France

Robert Kronstrand
National Board of Forensic Medicine
Department of Forensic Genetics and Forensic Chemistry
Linköping, Sweden

Manfred R. Moeller
Saarland University Hospital
Homburg, Germany

Gilbert Pepin
Laboratoire TOXLAB
Paris, France

Simona Pichini
Department of Drug Research and Evaluation
Istituto Superiore di Sanità
Rome, Italy

Fritz Pragst
Institut für Rechtsmedizin
Department of Toxikologische Chemie
Berlin, Germany

Hans Sachs
Forensisch Toxikologisches Centrum
GmbH Muenchen
Sekretariat BeateThieme
Munich, Germany

Michael Schaffer
Psychemedics Corporation
Culver City, California

Karen Scott
Forensic Toxicology
Anglia Ruskin University
Cambridge, U.K.

Frederick P. Smith
Forensic Science Program
University of New Haven
West Haven, Connecticut

Michael Uhl
Bavarian State Criminal Police Office
Munich, Germany

Marion Villain
Laboratoire ChemTox
Illkirch, France

Robert Wennig
Laboratoire National de
Santé—Toxicologie
Université de Luxembourg
Limpertsberg, Luxembourg

Michel Yegles
Laboratoire National de
Santé—Toxicologie
Université de Luxembourg
Limpertsberg, Luxembourg

Table of Contents

1 Drug Incorporation into Hair

Robert Kronstrand and Karen Scott

CONTENTS

1.1 HAIR PHYSIOLOGY

1.1.1 Structure and Growth of Human Hair

Hair is a complex epidermal outgrowth, synthesized in the hair follicle. It is composed of 65 to 95% proteins, 1 to 9% lipids, 0.1 to 5% pigments (melanin), and small amounts of trace elements, polysaccharides, and water [1]. Human hair contains at least two cell types: the cuticle composed of overlapping scale cells and the cortex composed of spindle-shaped cortical cells. In the core of the cortex there may be condensed cells forming the medulla, which might be continuous or interspersed with air spaces [2]. The main features of the hair follicle are shown in Figure 1.1.

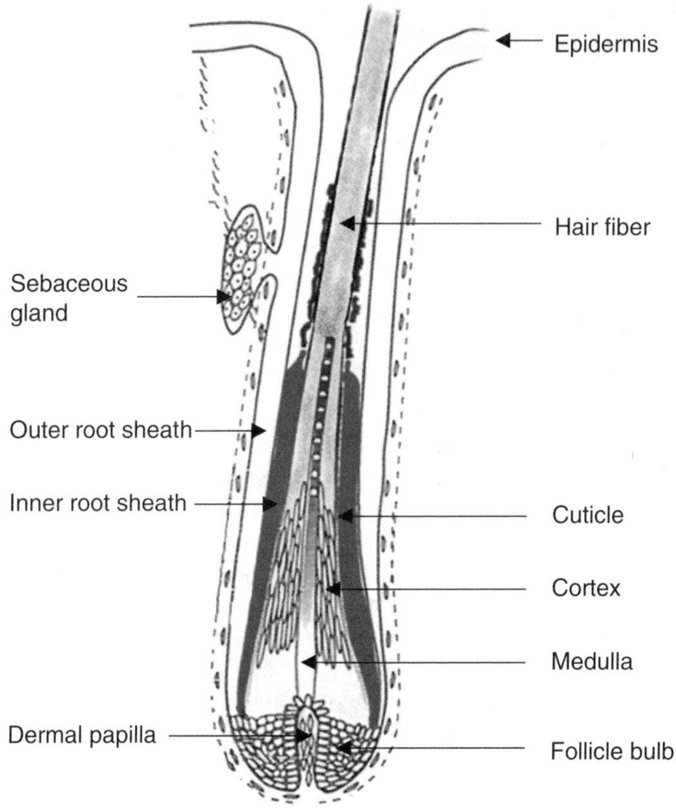

FIGURE 1.1 Schematic diagram of the hair follicle. The cells in the follicle bulb move upward to be part of either the cortex, the cuticle, or the inner root sheath, and if present, the medulla. When the growing hair is dehydrated and keratinizes, the inner root sheath degrades. (Modified from Powell, B.C. and Rogers, G.E., in *Formation and Structure of Human Hair*, Jollès, P., Zahn, H., and Höcker, H., Eds., Birkhäuser Verlag, Basel, 1997, pp. 59–148. Published with the kind permission of Birkhäuser Verlag.)

The follicle consists of several cell layers. As a part of the epidermis, the outer root sheath (ORS) surrounds the other layers. The inner root sheath (IRS) encases the growing hair fiber. The extensive mitotic activity in the hair follicle bulb gives rise to a stream of cells moving upward to form the body of the hair fiber and the IRS. The melanocytes, located at the apex of the dermal papilla, synthesize melanin in organelles called melanosomes, and then transfer these to the migrating cells from the hair follicle bulb. The growth rate of human scalp hair is approximately 0.35 mm per day for both males and females [3], but can vary greatly. Pötsch [4] found a variation between 0.07 and 0.78 mm/day, with 82% of the examined population between 0.32 and 0.46 mm/day.

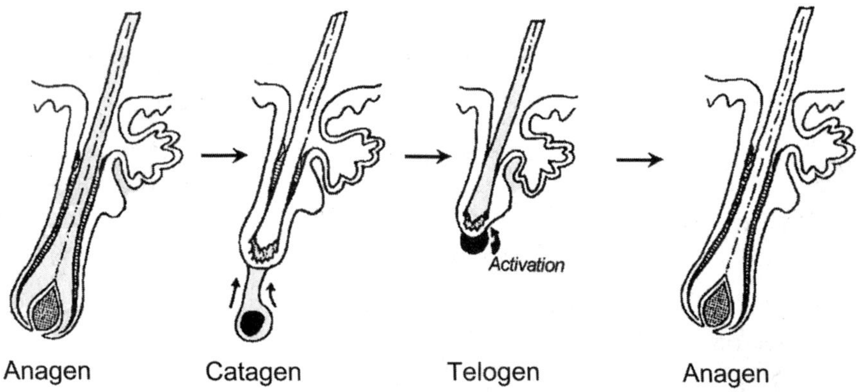

FIGURE 1.2 The different stages of the hair growth cycle. The human hair cycle starts with the anagen phase, during which the follicle develops and hair is produced. Catagen is the phase of regression where the activity of the follicle bulb stops and the dermal papilla contracts as the follicle approaches the resting phase, telogen. After the telogen phase, another growth cycle commences. (Modified from Powell, B.C. and Rogers, G.E., in *Formation and Structure of Human Hair*, Jollès, P., Zahn, H., and Höcker, H., Eds., Birkhäuser Verlag, Basel, 1997, pp. 59–148. Published with the kind permission of Birkhäuser Verlag.)

The hair growth cycle consists of periods of growth and dormancy. In humans, each hair follicle has its own cycle independent of its neighbors. The human hair cycle starts with the *anagen* (or growing) phase, during which the follicle develops and the hair is produced. The duration of the anagen phase varies greatly and usually continues between 7 to 94 weeks but may last several years, depending on anatomical region [5]. *Catagen* is the phase of regression, where the activity of the follicle bulb ceases and the dermal papilla contracts as the follicle approaches the resting phase, *telogen*. See Figure 1.2. After the telogen phase, another growth cycle commences.

1.1.2 Pigmentation

Melanins in mammals are formed in specialized cells called melanocytes, which enclose distinct cytoplasmic organelles known as melanosomes. Pigment formation (follicular melanogenesis) takes place in the melanosomes in four stages [6]. In the first stage, the basic structural unit consists of tyrosinase and protein, which is then followed by formation of an inner membranous structure in which melanin is biosynthesized and accumulates. Finally, the melanosome then transforms into a uniformly dense melanin particle. The melanized melanosome is then transferred into cortical and medulla keratinocytes, which then form the pigmented hair shaft. This activity is regulated by a series of enzymes, structural and regulatory proteins, transporters, and receptors and their ligands during the anagenic stage of the hair growth cycle [7]. The hair bulb is the only site of pigment formation for the hair shaft. The active melanocytes, which exist in the upper hair matrix of the anagen hair follicle, transfer melanin mainly to the hair shaft cortex, to a lesser extent to the medulla, and only rarely to the hair cuticle. A partial scheme of the melanin

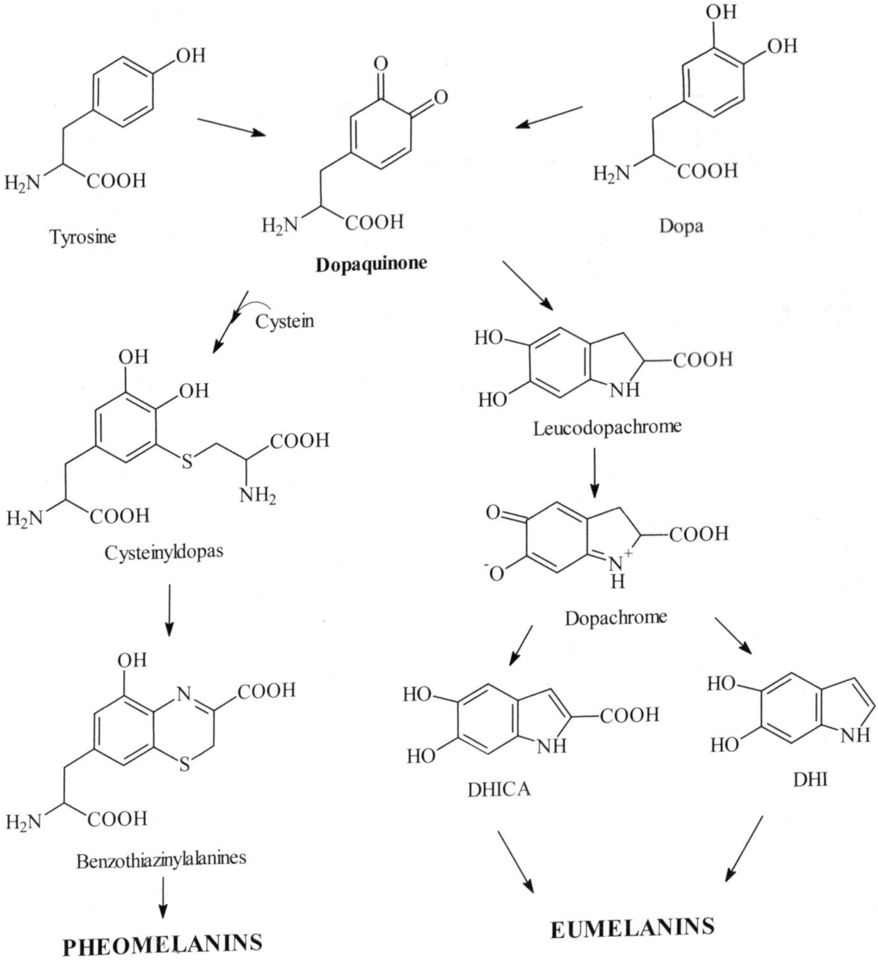

FIGURE 1.3 Simplified scheme illustrating *in vivo* biosynthesis of eumelanins and pheomelanins.

synthesis is presented in Figure 1.3. Early studies by Nicolaus et al. [8] and Swan and Waggott [9] revealed that eumelanins are heterogeneous polymers consisting of 5,6-dihydroxyindole (DHI) and 5,6-dihydroxyindole-2-carboxylic acid (DHICA) units. The structural components of pheomelanins are benzothiazine, benzothiazole, and isoquinoline units. In the initial stages, cysteine is required for the synthesis of pheomelanin but not for eumelanin [10, 11].

Hair color is genetically controlled and is among the most diverse of the pigmentation phenotypes. Previously it was believed that two chemically distinct types of melanin pigments existed. The dark eumelanins and the yellow-to-red pheomelanins, with the color of human hair and skin mostly determined by the quantity of these two melanins [12]. Now, four types of melanin are thought to be responsible for this diversity, namely eumelanin, oxyeumelanin, pheomelanin, and oxypheomelanin [13]. Oxyeumelanin and oxypheomelanin are formed as oxidative products of the pigment

TABLE 1.1
Classification of Human Hair Pigmentation by Its Content of Oxidative Breakdown Products

Class	Pigmentation	Color	PTCA (ng/mg)	BTCA (ng/mg)	TTCA (ng/mg)
I	eumelanic	black to dark brown	100–300	—	—
II	oxyeumelanic	brown/chestnut	50–80	—	≥200
III	pheomelanic	fiery/carroty red	—	1000–2500	—
IV	oxypheomelanic	other red hues	—	—	100–300

Note: PTCA = pyrrole-2,3,5-tricarboxylic acid; BTCA = benzothiazolecarboxylic acid; TTCA = thiazole-2,3,5-tricarboxylic acid.

Source: Modified from Prota, G., *Pigment Cell Res.*, 13, 283–293, 2000.

monomer units. In his paper on melanins, melagenesis, and melanocytes published in 2000, Prota [13] states that most of the traditional concepts regarding the variety of human hair colors must be reconsidered. He presents a four-class system for defining hair color as shown in Table 1.1.

In this respect, black to dark brown hair contains virtually intact eumelanin. As the intensity of brown coloration lightens, the hair is found to contain more of an oxidative breakdown product of eumelanin, namely oxyeumelanin. The oxidative process is induced by the presence of hydrogen peroxide. Hair containing large amounts of oxyeumelanin is blond. This study showed the traditional view of mixed-type melanins created from the same melanocyte in chestnut/brown hair to be incorrect, as only eumelanin and oxyeumelanin were detected. Thus, the broad spectrum of hair color variations in Caucasians can be attributed to two pigments, eumelanin and pheomelanin, but at different stages of structural integrity.

1.2 DRUG INCORPORATION ROUTES

Several studies have been carried out to explain the factors that influence the incorporation of drugs from the bloodstream [4, 14–25]. The pathways for incorporation of drugs into hair and the mechanisms by which they bind to hair constituents have been much discussed in the scientific literature. A schematic view of pathways for incorporation of drugs into hair is shown in Figure 1.4. Three models for incorporation have been proposed: drugs can enter the hair through (1) active or passive diffusion from the bloodstream feeding the dermal papilla, (2) diffusion from sweat and other secretions bathing the growing or mature hair fiber, or (3) external drug from vapors or powders that diffuse into the mature hair fiber. Indeed, a combination of these routes is probably the most realistic model to choose. Still, the relative importance of the different routes is not yet clarified and may vary greatly between

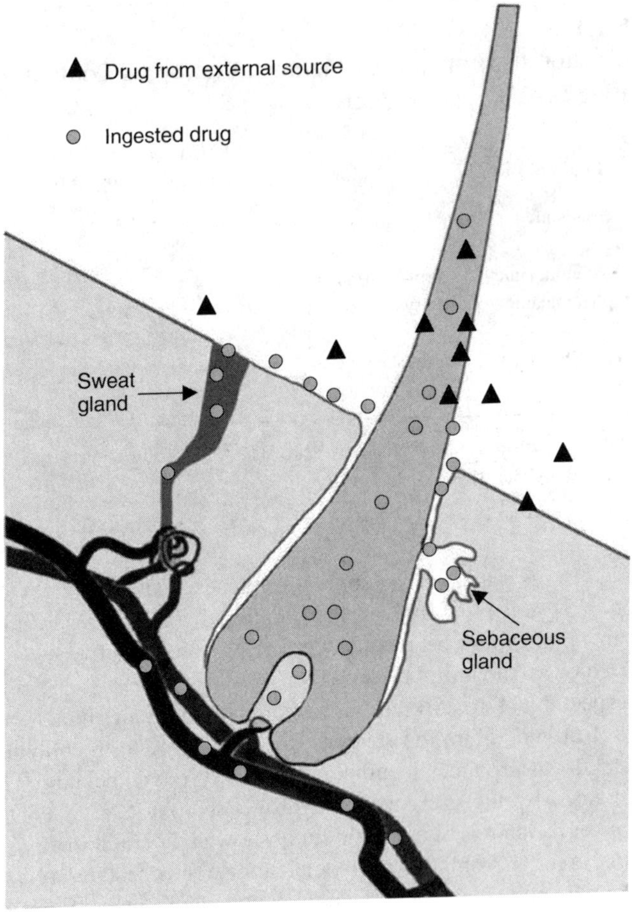

FIGURE 1.4 Three models of drug incorporation. Ingested drugs can enter the hair from the bloodstream feeding the dermal papilla as well as by sweat and sebum bathing the mature hair fiber. External drug from vapors or powders may also incorporate into the mature hair fiber.

substances and individuals. From an interpretive viewpoint, the most important route is via the bloodstream, for example when we are interested in answering questions about the time of intake or even the dose taken.

1.2.1 Incorporation from the Bloodstream

Due to rapid cell division in the cells forming hair, the hair follicle is provided with a good blood supply. Drugs circulating in the blood will thus also be delivered to the hair follicle. For a drug to enter the matrix cells of the growing hair, it first has to diffuse across the cell membrane. The rate of this transport, where only drug molecules not bound to protein may participate, is related to the lipid solubility of the drug. Also, the pH gradient between the plasma and the cell is important for the transport. Many drugs are either weak bases or weak acids that can be ionized by

FIGURE 1.5 Photograph of hair strands containing bands of incorporated rhodamine. (Published with the kind permission of Dr. James Ruth, University of Colorado, Health Sciences Center, and Dr. Peter Stout, RTI, International Center for Forensic Sciences.)

protonation or deprotonation. The pH of plasma is 7.3, whereas the pH of the keratinocytes and melanocytes is lower, varying between 3 and 6 [26]. Therefore, the assumption that basic drugs, in contrast to acidic drugs, may accumulate in keratinocytes and melanocytes seems likely, as the diffusion into the cell is favored by the pH gradient, and once in the cell cytosol, the molecule will be protonated and not be able to diffuse back into the plasma. The binding of drugs to the cell proteins may also enhance this effect, as the drug concentration in the cytosol decreases when the molecules are associating with structures within the cell. (See also Section 1.3, Mechanisms of Binding.) A well-designed series of experiments evaluating incorporation mechanisms was performed by Stout and Ruth [27] using the dyes rhodamine and fluorescein. These compounds are structurally similar, but rhodamine is a cation, whereas fluorescein is an anion. After intraperitoneal administration of the dyes on 3 consecutive days during 2 weeks, they observed distinct bands of rhodamine in the mature hair representing each daily dose, as shown in Figure 1.5. The *in vivo* deposition was mainly in the cortex and the medulla. Fluorescein was also present in the matrix cells during formation but not in the keratinized hair. This was considered an effect of an efflux of the anion fluorescein from the cell before the keratinization occurs because of the favorable conditions for acids to reenter the plasma.

Borges et al. [28] specifically observed this influx and efflux using amphetamine and a nonbasic analog (N-acetylamphetamine) in pigmented and nonpigmented melanocytes as well as keratinocytes (*in vitro*). The neutral N-acetylamphetamine was not taken up by any of the cells, whereas amphetamine was taken up by both pigmented and nonpigmented cells. These data suggest that there is a specific cellular transport process operating for amphetamine but not for the neutral-structure analog. The same group [14] dosed LE-rats with amphetamine and N-acetylamphetamine and found both substances in newly grown hair. Thus, even though the *in vitro* influx of N-acetylamphetamine could not be distinguished from the background signal, it was found to incorporate into hair *in vivo*. Gygi et al. [17] administered the weak base codeine and the weakly acidic phenobarbital to rats and compared their incorporation into nonpigmented hair. When accounting for the differences in plasma area under the curve, codeine showed 15 times higher concentration than phenobarbital. This is also in agreement with the hypothesis of active transport of drugs that are positively charged at physiological pH. Nakahara et al. [19, 29] studied the incorporation of cocaine and its metabolite benzoylecgonine (BE) into rat hair after administration of cocaine, and found that although the plasma concentration of BE was approximately four times higher than that of cocaine, its concentration in hair was ten times lower. Evidently, the plasma concentration was not the major factor for drug incorporation into hair. Indeed, when dosing the animals with BE, no or very little BE could be found in hair. BE, with its physical properties as a zwitterion (structure including both a carboxylic acid and a basic nitrogen) might exhibit the same efflux from the cytosol as reported for fluorescein. The origin of the BE present in hair after cocaine administration was investigated, and they concluded that a conversion of cocaine already present in the hair shaft was degraded to BE. Again, the physicochemical properties of the drugs seem more important than their plasma concentrations.

1.2.2 Incorporation from Sweat and Other Secretions

It is well known that drugs and their metabolites are excreted in sweat [30–33], and several papers have addressed this issue in the context of drug incorporation into hair. Henderson et al. [34] reported that deuterated cocaine was found in multiple segments after a single dose, supporting sweat or other secretions as a route for drug deposition in hair. Raul et al. [35] suggested that cortisol and cortisone incorporates into hair not through the bloodstream, but mainly through diffusion from sweat. Both cortisone and cortisol are neutral substances and should incorporate at approximately the same rate; still, the ratio in hair is opposite that of blood. An explanation for this is that cortisol is converted to cortisone by type 2 HSD (11-beta-hydroxysteroide-dehydrogenase) in sweat before its incorporation, thus explaining the difference in ratio.

Stout and Ruth [25] evaluated the incorporation of cocaine, flunitrazepam, and nicotine and demonstrated insignificant deposition of the drugs onto the hair from sebum. They also concluded that the more lipophilic the substance, the higher is its accumulation in hair, owing to a greater ability to pass through the cell membranes. Even though incorporation from sweat represents the deposition of ingested drugs, it may complicate or preclude the results from multiple segments of hair, as it tends to broaden the band of positive hair from a single (or multiple) dose. The incorporation of lipophilic drugs from deep compartments in skin has also been suggested [36].

1.2.3 Incorporation from External Contamination

Efforts to differentiate between deposition from internal or external sources have been made both *in vitro* and *in vivo*, for example by using the fluorescent compounds rhodamine and fluorescein. Pötsch and Moeller [21] found that after soaking hair in rhodamine solution the dye penetrated the hair at the cuticle scale junctions and further along the nonkeratinous cell membrane complex. Both Stout and Ruth [27] and DeLauder and Kidwell [37] observed differences in the binding of fluorescein and rhodamine when externally applying the dyes. The deposition of fluorescein was highly pH dependent and less compared with rhodamine, which showed no pH dependence. Stout and Ruth also performed *in vivo* studies on mice and found that the deposition of both fluorescein and rhodamine was markedly different from the *in vitro* results. The *in vivo* deposition was mainly in the cortex and the medulla as compared with the cuticle junctions observed when soaking the hair. Independent of the route of deposition the dyes could not be removed by extensive washing. This suggests that even though the endogenous and exogenous deposition of these model compounds could be distinguished, the analytical result after extraction still remains difficult to interpret. Schaffer et al. (2005) and Cairns et al. (2004) recently reported the use of new decontamination procedures that distinguished between external and endogenous deposition [38–40]. These issues are discussed in depth in other parts of this book.

1.3 MECHANISMS OF BINDING

Several hair components have been suggested as possible molecular sites for drug binding and interaction. Of these, keratin and melanin have been investigated in some detail to assess the mechanisms by which the binding occurs. The binding of drugs to melanin was first published more than four decades ago [41]. Since that time, a substantial number of studies have been carried out on a variety of drugs with a wide range of physicochemical properties to evaluate this binding. These studies have shown that both neutral and charged species have the ability to bind to melanin, highlighting the efficiency of melanin as an absorber of *in vivo* toxins. The binding of drugs to keratin has been much less widely investigated, with only a few papers concentrating solely on this route. The remarkable capacity of melanin to bind various chemicals has emerged as one of the strongest retention mechanisms of the body [42]. The physiological function of this binding is not fully understood. Neither are the binding mechanisms clearly elucidated. Melanin could function as a local regulator that binds and releases endogenous and exogenous substances, or act as protective chemical filters, since melanins are present in very sensitive tissues (close to receptors in the eye, ear, and brain). The binding of certain drugs and inorganic cations to melanin has been thoroughly studied both *in vitro* and *in vivo* [43–49]. The general conclusion is that the binding and accumulation of these chemicals in pigmented tissue is one of the most pronounced retention mechanisms of the body, but the affinities vary widely between different ions and compounds. Organic amines and metal ions have high melanin affinity (e.g., Ni^{2+} with $K_1 = 5.2 \times 10^6 M^{-1}$). These substances are positively charged at physiological pH and interact through the melanin polymer by electrostatic forces between their cationic groups and the anionic carboxylic groups on the surface of the melanin polymer. The electrostatic binding of the substances is strengthened by van der Waals forces between aromatic indole rings in the melanin polymers and aromatic rings of the organic amines. Melanin may also be involved in charge-transfer reactions when electron-donating complexes interact with the melanin. Hydrophobic interactions with aliphatic molecules are extensive owing to the hydrophobic core of the melanin polymer. However, covalent binding has been suggested to explain the strong and partly irreversible binding of chlorpromazine and chloroquine to melanin [49].

1.3.1 *In Vitro* Binding Studies to Melanin and Keratin

Several groups [46, 50–53] have made headway in evaluating the mechanisms of binding of drugs to hair through *in vitro* experiments. These methodologies include both direct and indirect experimentations to evaluate how and to what extent different drugs bind. By comparing these *in vitro* results with *in vivo* experiments using the same drugs, the extent to which melanin plays a role in drug incorporation into hair can be estimated. Drugs that have been evaluated in this way include chlorpromazine and other phenothiazines, clenbuterol, salbutamol, chloroquine, haloperidol, tricyclic antidepressants, benzodiazepines, and amphetamines.

Initially, Scatchard analysis was the method of choice for the interpretation of surface interactions. Although this method still has uses in the interpretation of the binding nature (e.g., upward concavity is indicative of negative cooperativity), its use in the determination of binding parameters such as number of binding sites and equilibrium constants is limited. Stepien and Wilczok [54] studied the effects of pH, ionic strength, and organic solvent on the interaction of chloroquine with synthetic dopa-melanin to evaluate the mechanism of drug binding to melanin. The results indicate that electrostatic, hydrophobic, and van der Waals forces participate in the formation of a chloroquine-melanin complex. The Scatchard method of data interpretation showed that two classes of binding sites take part in the complex formation. The stronger of the two binding sites with the association constant K_1 on the order of 10^5 were thought to involve both hydrophobic interactions and electrostatic attractions between the protonated ring system of chloroquine and the ortho-semiquinone groups of melanin. The weaker binding sites with K_2 on the order of 10^4 were thought to involve ionic bonds between the protonated aliphatic nitrogen of the chloroquine molecule and carboxyl groups of melanin. Van der Waals forces occurring at the conjunctions of the aromatic rings of the drug and the aromatic indole-nuclei of the melanin were also thought to contribute to the weaker binding.

Larsson's group also used the Scatchard method to study the *in vitro* binding of chlorpromazine, chloroquine, paraquat, and Ni^{2+} to melanin [46]. Scatchard analysis showed that more than one binding class must be implicated in the binding of both the organic substances and Ni^{2+} to melanin. The clear influence of the ionic environment on the ability of the substrate to bind to melanin was noted, indicating that electrostatic forces between the cationic forms of the substances and anionic sites on the melanin polymer are important for complex formation. Several agreements were found between the data for paraquat- and Ni^{2+}-binding, indicating a dominant influence of electrostatic forces for the melanin binding of paraquat. However, several indications were found that nonelectrostatic contributions must be added to form the binding sites for chlorpromazine and chloroquine. Again, these contributions are though to be provided by van der Waals forces occurring at the conjunctions of the aromatic rings in the substances and the aromatic indole nuclei of the melanin. Experiments with chlorpromazine indicated that the positive ion radical of the substance had a very high melanin affinity, suggesting that melanin may be able to oxidize chlorpromazine to a positive ion radical, resulting in firm binding of the substance to melanin.

The presently accepted structural model for melanin is based on a hierarchical organization of basic molecules (including DHI and DHICA), which covalently bind and interact to form irregular particles with large and complex surface areas [55]. The surface absorption of neutral molecules can therefore be evaluated using the classical Langmuir isotherm. In 2005, Bridelli et al. [50] investigated the binding of three physically, chemically, and structurally different drugs (gentamicin [mwt 462, water soluble, basic], methotrexate [mwt 454, practically insoluble in water, acidic], and chlorpromazine [mwt 319, water solubility 0.4 g/ml, pKa 9.3]) to assess how best to interpret drug-melanin surface binding [50]. The Brunauer classification system categorizes melanin adsorption isotherms as type I. Following this, four types of binding isotherms were studied, namely Langmuir, Freundlich, Tempkin, and Dubinin-Radushkevich. In short, the Langmuir isotherm assumes that sorption takes place at specific homogeneous sites; the Freundlich isotherm is used for heterogeneous sites; the Tempkin isotherm considers the effects of indirect adsorbate/adsorbate interactions on adsorption isotherms; and the Dubinin-Radushkevich isotherm describes adsorption of various substances on different surfaces.

It was found that the binding of different drugs was best analyzed using different models, indicating that the physicochemical or the geometrical characteristics of the interacting molecules play an essential role in the mechanisms of interaction. Gentamicin (basic) showed the highest amount of binding of the three drugs and fitted best with the Freundlich isotherm. Methotrexate fitted best with both the Langmuir isotherm and the Dubinin-Radushkevich isotherm, with the Langmuir isotherm agreeing with conclusions drawn by analyzing the data using the Scatchard method. Finally, chlorpromazine was best fitted with both Langmuir and Tempkin isotherms.

1.3.2 Evaluation of Binding Parameters

Testorf et al. [53] investigated the time course of [^{3}H]-flunitrazepam binding to melanin and found a rapid initial binding followed by a slowly increasing binding after approximately 10 min of incubation. These data fitted well to theoretical curves composed of a diffusion-limited term with the square root of time and a Langmuir binding term, as shown in Figure 1.6. Displacement experiments by the same group were carried out using 0.04 mg/ml of melanin incubated for 60 min with 5n*M* [^{3}H]-flunitrazepam and increasing quantities of unlabeled displacement drug (Figure. 1.7). The results showed that the benzodiazepines diazepam and nitrazepam both displace [^{3}H]-flunitrazepam in a very similar way to flunitrazepam itself, indicating similar binding characteristics. In contrast, although the tranquillizers zopiclone and zolpidem also displace [^{3}H]-flunitrazepam, a lower degree of displacement was observed. The weakly acidic drug phenobarbital was found to have a significantly lower ability to displace [^{3}H]-flunitrazepam. These latter results indicate a lower binding affinity of less basic and acidic drugs to melanin, as previously discussed.

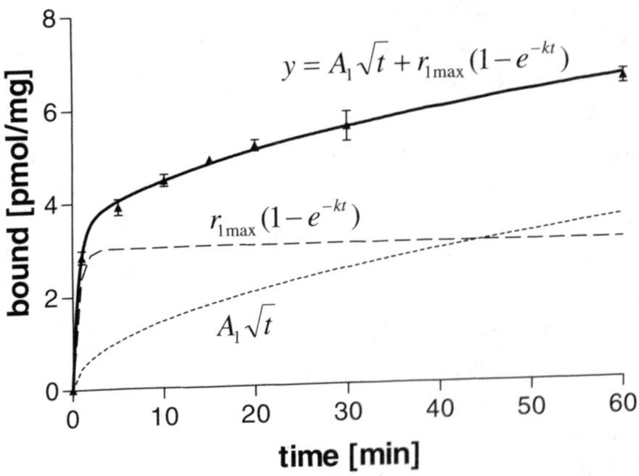

FIGURE 1.6 Binding of 5n*M* [^{3}H]-flunitrazepam to melanin with different incubation times (n = 3, mean ± s.e.m). Nonlinear regression was used to fit the curve (solid line) and resulted in $A_1 = 0.45$, $r_{1max} = 3.03$, and $k_1 = 1.57$. The contributions from the two terms of this curve are shown separately (dashed line = Langmuir binding term and dotted line = diffusion term). The estimated amount of melanin-associated drug was 15 pmol/mg after incubating 20n*M* of [^{3}H]-flunitrazepam with 0.04 mg/ml of melanin for 60 min at room temperature.

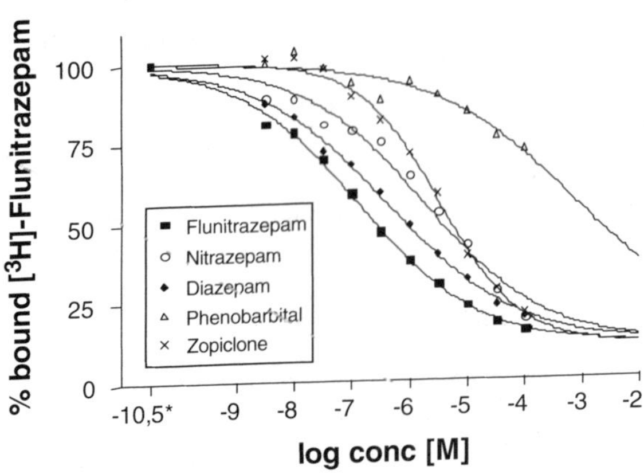

FIGURE 1.7 Binding of 5n*M* [^{3}H]-flunitrazepam to melanin (0.04 mg/ml) with different displacing drugs in the incubation medium (n = 6, mean ± s.e.m.). (*) x-value −10.5 is 100% [^{3}H]-flunitrazepam without displacing drug. Sigmoidal dose-response curves (solid lines) were fitted to the data.

Work by Gautam et al. [51] shows a similar fast initial binding followed by a slowly increasing binding for amphetamine. The binding of amphetamine and methamphetamine to sepia melanin is depicted in Figure 1.8. The initial rapid binding

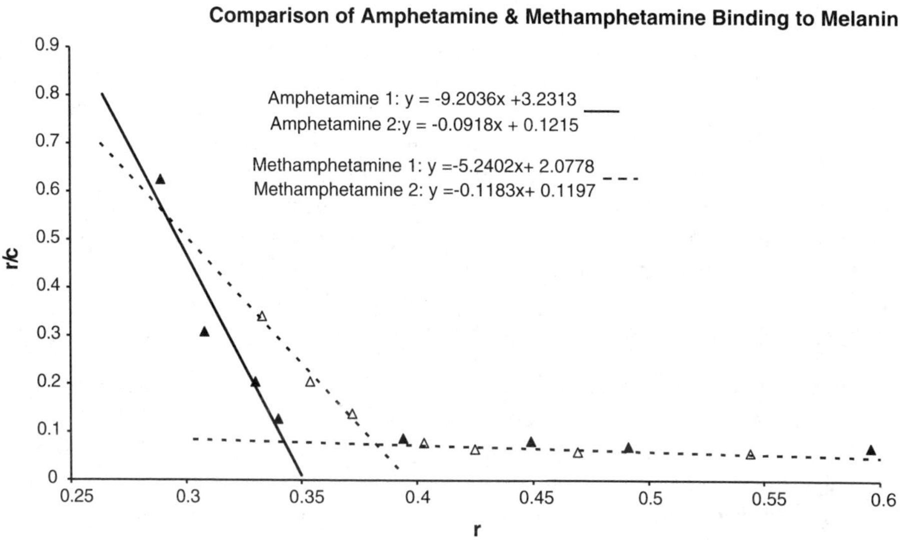

FIGURE 1.8 Scatchard comparison of the binding of amphetamine and methamphetamine to sepia melanin. (Modified from Gautam, L. et al., *J. Anal. Toxicol.*, 29, 339–344, 2005 and unpublished data.)

(amphetamine 1 and methamphetamine 1) is followed by a slower but higher degree of binding (amphetamine 2 and methamphetamine 2). Bearing in mind the limitations of calculations by Scatchard analysis, the calculated Kd:s shows that amphetamine associates with the initial site almost twice as strongly as methamphetamine; however, the degree of association to the second site is approximately the same for both drugs. (Gautam et al., unpublished results). The stronger initial binding for amphetamine can be explained by stronger ionic interactions between the primary amine and melanin than between melanin and a secondary one.

1.3.3 Effects of Melanin Type

Borges et al. [56] carried out a series of experiments to determine the *in vitro* binding of cocaine, benzoylecgonine, amphetamine, and N-acetylamphetamine to synthetic melanin subtypes. The melanins studied included two black eumelanin subtypes (5,6-dihydroxyindole [DHI] and 5,6-dihydroxyindole-2-carboxylic acid [DHICA] derived melanins), a reddish-brown pheomelanin (from 5-cysteinyl-S-Dopa [5-CysDOPA]), and two mixed eu-/pheomelanin copolymers. Results indicated that the more basic drugs (cocaine and amphetamine) bind to eumelanins and mixed eu-/pheomelanins to varying degrees, but not to pure pheomelanin. Benzoylecgonine and N-acetylamphetamine, both of which are net-neutral molecules, did not bind to any type of melanin. In addition to the determination of the extent of binding, the eumelanin chemical functional groups were investigated to determine which groups bind the drugs. Using amphetamine as a target and tandem mass spectrometry, a noncovalent adduct with dimerized oxidized catechol was determined. Similar functional groups on the eumelanin polymer may represent important drug-binding sites. In summary, melanin types were found to differ in their extent of drug binding, which may help explain why hair-color biases exist. Mårs and Larsson [57] evaluated the binding of chloroquine and chlorpromazine to pheomelanin both *in vivo* and *in vitro* and found that the drugs accumulated in the hair follicles and the dermal melanocytes. The binding in yellow mice was comparable with that in black mice. Their *in vitro* studies showed that the binding kinetics to pheomelanin was, in principle, comparable with the binding to eumelanin, but with lower association constants (chlorpromazine with $K_1 = 2.16 \times 10^4 M^{-1}$ compared with 7.3×10^6).

1.3.4 Drug Binding during Melanogenesis

In vitro studies of the types discussed above demonstrate surface binding of drugs to melanin. The relative affinities of the drugs allow predictions to be made as to the likelihood of detecting a particular drug during routine analysis. In carrying out a digestion of a hair sample, the analyst is merely breaking the ionic and hydrogen bond and disrupting the van der Waals forces that attract and attach drugs to the melanin granule once it has formed.

Pötsch et al. [23] compared the binding of tritiated cocaine to melanin granules and human hair *in vitro*. They found that the adsorption of ^{3}H-cocaine on melanin follows a Langmuir adsorption isotherm type I, and concluded that even if drugs adsorb on the surface of melanin granules, this only accounts for part of the drug-melanin interaction *in vivo* and that the binding and entrapment of drugs in melanin during melanogenesis appears to have a role. Similarly, Larsson et al. [58] found that fetal eye melanin in pigmented mice showed a fivefold greater accumulation of injected [*N*-methyl-^{14}C] nicotine-*d*-bitartrate than maternal eye melanin. These results may be due to a structural resemblance of nicotine to the main precursor of melanin, indole-5,6-quinone, allowing the nicotine to be accepted as a precursor in the formation of new melanin. Harrison et al. [59] studied the incorporation of radiolabeled amphetamine in animal hair. Despite exhaustive digestion, between 25 and 80% of the radiolabeled drug remained, indicating that the amphetamine may have been biosynthetically incorporated into the melanin during melanogenesis.

Sodium sulfide removed significantly more radioactivity from pigmented hair than did sodium hydroxide. Claffey and coworkers [60] investigated the removal of flunitrazepam and nicotine in pigmented hair using either sodium hydroxide or sodium sulfide. Sodium sulfide solubilized 35 and 74% of the flunitrazepam- and nicotine-associated radioactivity, respectively. Of this, 12 and 43%, respectively, could be partitioned into ethyl acetate. This also suggests that part of the incorporated drug is covalently bound to hair. As drugs bound in this way must be introduced to the melanin during its biosynthesis, the contribution of passive drug and so-called environmental exposure routes is much less than with surface-bound drug, i.e., drug bound through sebaceous excretions and through the cuticle. In addition, these drugs would not be as easily removed through processes such as hygienic washing and chemical treatments. Several groups have made headway in this respect. Palumbo et al. [61, 62] have isolated and identified a 2-thiouracil adduct of a melanin intermediate during *in vitro* synthesis of melanin in the presence of thiouracil. The formation of the adduct was found to be dependent on enzymatically generated dopaquinone. Evidence was also provided for the ability of the drug to affect melanogenesis by interaction with biosynthetic intermediates beyond the dopaquinone stage, suggesting other possible modes for its chemical binding to the growing pigment. Dehn et al. [63] used MALDI-TOF MS

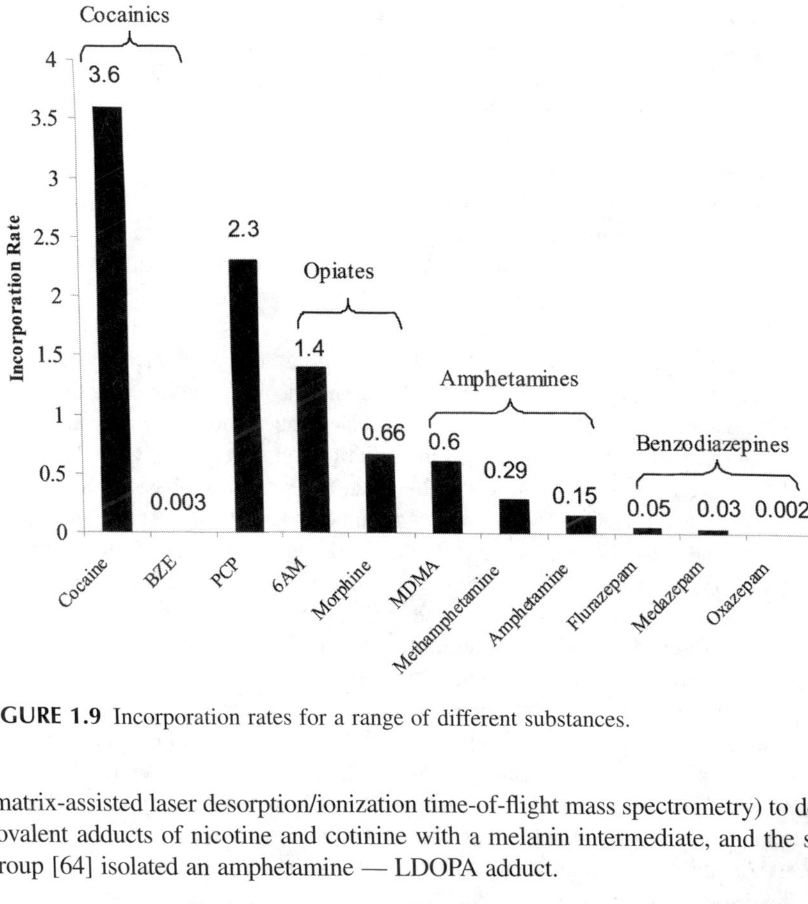

FIGURE 1.9 Incorporation rates for a range of different substances.

(matrix-assisted laser desorption/ionization time-of-flight mass spectrometry) to detect covalent adducts of nicotine and cotinine with a melanin intermediate, and the same group [64] isolated an amphetamine — LDOPA adduct.

1.3.5 *In Vivo* Studies on Binding of Drugs to Hair

The Japanese research group at the Institute of Health Science in Tokyo, Japan, has carried out several *in vivo* experiments using dark-agouti (DA) rats to evaluate drug incorporation solely from the bloodstream (DA rats have no sweat glands). Nakahara et al. [19] studied the incorporation of cocaine and its metabolite benzoylecgonine (BE) into rat hair and found that, although the plasma concentration of BE was approximately four times higher than that of cocaine, its concentration in hair was ten times lower [19]. Evidently, the plasma concentration was not the major factor for drug incorporation into hair. Rather, the physicochemical properties of the drugs seemed more important. Cocaine is a weak base, whereas BE is a zwitterion, because the structure includes a carboxylic acid in addition to the basic nitrogen. This was the beginning of a large series of animal experiments performed by investigators from Japan where the concept of incorporation rate (ICR) was introduced. Thus, ICR is defined as the drug concentration in hair divided by the area under the concentration-time curve for plasma.

In 1995 the same research group determined the melanin affinity and lipophilicity of 20 drugs with different physicochemical properties [20]. Figure 1.9 highlights the degree of variation seen between a variety of drugs and their metabolites.

In 1996, Nakahara and Kikura [18] evaluated the ICRs of 32 structural analogs of amphetamine. Their major findings can be summarized as follows:

1. The longer the N-alkyl chain, the higher is the ICR.
2. Triple bonds on the alkyl-chain reduced the ICR.
3. N-benzene rings increased the ICR.
4. Adding groups to the nitrogen atom to remove basicity resulted in nearly zero ICRs.

All these experiments were performed on DA pigmented rats, so the conclusions cannot be extrapolated to nonpigmented hair. The melanin contained within DA rat hair is eumelanin. Therefore, as human hair has a much more complex and diverse pigmentation, conclusions regarding human hair cannot necessarily be drawn from this data. Nevertheless, the relationship between ICRs and drug basicity and melanin affinity formed the basis for other *in vivo* studies on both pigmented and nonpigmented animals [14, 17, 22, 24, 25, 60, 65–67]. Drugs such as amphetamine and its analogs — PCP, codeine, phenobarbital, cocaine, methadone, and nicotine — were used to evaluate these relationships. In all these papers, the results demonstrated that *basic drugs* showed a binding preference for pigmented rather than nonpigmented hair. In addition, Gygi et al. [17] evaluated the distribution of a weak acid (phenobarbital) in hair and found no difference between pigmented and nonpigmented hair in the same animal. Borges et al. [14] studied the incorporation of amphetamine and the nonbasic analog, N-acetylamphetamine, in the rat. The average concentrations in pigmented and nonpigmented hair for amphetamine were 6.44 ± 1.31 and 2.04 ± 0.58 ng/mg hair, respectively, whereas for N-acetylamphetamine they were, respectively, 0.87 ± 0.08 and 0.83 ± 0.15 ng/mg hair, supporting the proposed binding preference of basic drugs to pigmented hair.

1.3.6 Keratin

Data from *in vitro* studies on the binding of drugs to the hair proteins are scarce, although a paper by Appelgren et al. [68] addresses this question. After having detected clenbuterol in both pigmented and white hair from cattle, they performed a comparison of the binding of ^{3}H-clenbuterol to eumelanin and keratin. Scatchard analysis showed more than one binding class for melanin, but only one for keratin. The analysis also showed that the association constant for keratin was of the same order as the second binding class for melanin, with $K_1 = 2.0 \times 10^4 M^{-1}$ for melanin and $K_1 = 8.1 \times 10^2 M^{-1}$ for keratin. The results supported the assumption that keratin binds clenbuterol and supports the hypothesis that keratin plays a role in the mechanism of binding drugs to hair.

TABLE 1.2
Methamphetamine and Amphetamine Concentrations in Senile White and Pigmented Hair from Gray-Haired Persons

	Pigmented Hair		White Hair			
Subject	MA (ng/mg)	A (ng/mg)	MA (ng/mg)	A (ng/mg)	Ratio Pigmented/White Methamphetamine	Ratio Pigmented/White Amphetamine
1	0.25	0.15	0.10	0.07	2.50	2.14
2	3.65	1.43	0.89	0.37	4.10	3.86
4	1.90	0.6	0.46	0.18	4.13	3.33
7	2.64	0.65	0.33	0.12	8.00	5.42
8	1.05	0.32	0.28	0.11	3.75	2.91
10	0.31	0.09	0.11	0.03	2.82	3.00
12	0.85	0.25	0.20	0.11	4.25	2.27
14	1.25	0.46	0.68	0.26	1.84	1.77
15	1.62	0.52	0.88	0.28	1.84	1.86
Mean ± SD					3.69 ± 1.88	2.95 ± 1.16

Source: Data from Kronstrand et al., *J. Anal. Toxicol.*, 27, 135–141, 2003. With permission.

Banning and Heard [69] investigated the binding of doxycycline to keratin and melanin. Dose-dependent binding of doxycycline to keratin and melanin was observed and was of similar magnitude for each. Studies in human subjects with gray hair have also shown that various drugs are detectable in both the colored (melanin rich) and white (melanin free) hair shafts of these individuals. Again, this supports the proposition that keratin and hair proteins play an important role in the binding of drugs in hair. Further studies in people with gray hair have shown that chlorpromazine [70], cocaine [71], amitriptyline [72], and methamphetamine [73] are found in significantly higher concentrations in pigmented hair strands than in senile white hair strands. This preference for binding to pigmented hair may be attributed to a strong ionic interaction between the positively charged drugs and the polyanionic melanin polymer that is absent in white hair. However, as the drugs could be detected in white hair, pigmentation was not the only factor involved. Binding to hair protein (e.g., keratin) may account for a significant part of the drug accumulation in hair, as previously discussed. Kronstrand et al. [73] evaluated the results of amphetamine and methamphetamine extracted from pigmented and non-pigmented hair from nine subjects and found that the concentrations were always higher in the pigmented portion of the hair (Table 1.2). Student's t-test showed that the concentrations in pigmented and white hair differed significantly for both methamphetamine ($p < 0.01$) and for amphetamine ($p < 0.02$).

1.4 GENERAL DISCUSSION

1.4.1 ROUTES

There are three main routes by which drugs can enter the hair; the bloodstream, the sebaceous and eccrine secretions, and external contamination. Drugs deposited in hair directly from the bloodstream result in distinct bands of drug that can be correlated to the time of ingestion. Although drugs deposited onto the external surfaces of the hair are removed by analytical washing procedures, it has been shown that a fraction of these drugs are able to access the inner compartments of the hair shaft and therefore obscure the results of hair testing. As a result, although there exists a dose-concentration relationship within subjects, the many factors influencing drug incorporation weaken this possible relationship when comparing individuals. Drugs have different abilities to enter cells from the blood, and recent research has shown that the mechanism of passive diffusion does not always apply to drugs crossing the cell membranes. Therefore, a high area under the curve in plasma does not necessary result in a high incorporation rate.

1.4.2 BINDING

In vitro binding studies have shown that drugs associate with both keratins and melanins, with eumelanin as the structure providing the highest binding. Positively charged ions have a greater affinity to melanin than neutral or negatively charged ones. The *in vitro* binding of flunitrazepam, amphetamine, and methamphetamine to melanin has been characterized, and the kinetics of this binding revealed information about the binding mechanisms.

The results from variation of incubation time show a rapid binding initially followed by an almost linear slope depicting slowly increasing drug binding. A solely electrostatic attraction to the surface would decrease as more of the drug was bound, up to the point of saturation. In fact, the excellent fit of these data to the curve, composed of one term containing the square root of time added to one Langmuir binding term, suggests the mechanisms of binding (see Figure 1.6). At first, the Langmuir binding dominates and may reflect a superficial binding to the surface of the melanin granule. This is followed by a binding that is limited by diffusion, as suggested by the fit to the square root of time. This binding may reflect the diffusion of drug molecules into the matrix of melanin deeper in the granule.

Pötsch [4] suggested that the most important association of drugs with melanin was that which occurred during synthesis of melanin, i.e., the entrapment of drug molecules within the melanin polymer. They concluded that surface binding was of minor importance. The experiments of Testorf et al. [53] show that molecules may not only be bound to the surface of the preformed melanin, but might also migrate into the granule. The exponential relationships obtained in some papers also suggest that several mechanisms are involved when drugs associate with melanin in the melanocytes [74, 75]. Incorporation of basic drugs into hair has shown positive relationships to melanin. The increase in drug incorporation at elevated melanin contents may be explained by a threshold melanin content in the hair melanocyte, providing an intracellular moiety that favors drug retention, in addition to the strong ionic interaction between positively charged drugs and the polyanionic melanin. Thus, the incorporation of drugs into hair may relate to the melanin content in the melanocyte, even though the direct binding to melanin explains only a part of the retention mechanism.

Displacement experiments demonstrate that several benzodiazepines displace [^{3}H]-flunitrazepam in a way very similar to flunitrazepam itself, indicating similar binding characteristics. Phenobarbital, on the other hand, which is a weak acid, had a significantly lower ability to displace [^{3}H]-flunitrazepam (Figure 1.7). This is consistent with the results of Gygi et al. [17], who found no difference in phenobarbital incorporation between pigmented and albino hair in the rat. These findings agree with the theory that the electrostatic forces that bind drugs to melanin favors the binding of positively charged ions.

Melanin is not the only hair component responsible for the accumulation of drugs in hair. Other structures are much more abundant within hair, and melanin represents only a few percent of the total hair mass. Paired results from the analysis of pigmented and white hair from gray-haired subjects confirmed the preference for binding to pigmented hair. However, drugs could also be detected in white hair, proving that binding to hair protein or association with other hair matrix accounts for a significant part of drug accumulation in hair. The results demonstrate that interpretation of hair drug concentrations is complicated by the extent of hair pigmentation. This effect of melanin on the incorporation of drugs into human hair must be considered when evaluating results of hair analysis quantitatively. The attractions of drugs to melanin and subsequent entrapment of drugs during melanogenesis has to be further evaluated.

1.5 CONCLUDING REMARKS

As discussed, there are several ways by which drugs can enter the hair. From an interpretative viewpoint, the most important route is via the bloodstream, for example when we are interested in answering questions about the time of drug intake. Unfortunately, the reality is that other routes exist, and the distinct bands created via the bloodstream become blurred. Therefore, to make unlimited use of the interpretative value of hair analysis, a great deal more research is required to develop our understanding of the biological mechanisms involved.

REFERENCES

1. Harkey, M.R., Anatomy and physiology of hair, *Forensic Sci. Int.*, 63, 9–18, 1993.
2. Powell, B.C. and Rogers, G.E., The role of keratin proteins and their genes in the growth, structure and properties of hair, in *Formation and Structure of Human Hair*, Jollès, P., Zahn, H., and Höcker, H., Eds., Birkhäuser Verlag, Basel, 1997, pp. 59–148.
3. Pecoraro, V. and Astore, I.P.L., Measurement of hair growth under physiological conditions, in *Hair and Hair Disease*, Orphanos, C.E. and Happle, R., Eds., Springer Verlag, Berlin, 1990, p. 237.
4. Pötsch, L., A discourse on human hair fibers and reflections on the conservation of drug molecules, *Int. J. Legal Med.*, 108, 285–293, 1996.

5. Castanet, J. and Ortonne, J.-P., Hair melanin and hair color, in *Formation and Structure of Human Hair*, Jollès, P., Zahn, H., and Höcker, H., Eds., Birkhäuser Verlag, Basel, 1997, pp. 209–225.
6. Prota, G., The role of peroxidase in melanogenesis revisited, *Pigment Cell Res.*, Suppl. 2, 25–31, 1992.
7. Slominski, A., Wortsman, J., Plonka, P.M., Schallreuter, K.U., Paus, R., and Tobin, D.J., Hair follicle pigmentation, *J. Invest. Dermatol.*, 124, 13–21, 2005.
8. Nicolaus, R.A., Prota, G., Santacrose, C., Scherillo, G., and Sica, D., Struttura e biogenesi della feomelanine, nota VII: sulla struttura delle tricosiderine, *Gazzetta Chimica Italiana*, 99, 323–350, 1967.
9. Swan, G.A. and Waggott, A., Studies related to the chemistry of melanins, X: quantitative assessment of different types of units present in dopa-melanin, *J. Chem. Soc. Perkin Trans. I*, 10, 1409–1418, 1970.
10. Prota, G., Structure and biogenesis of pheomelanins, in *Pigmentation: Its Genesis and Biological Control*, Riley, V., Ed., Appleton Century Crofts, New York, 1972, pp. 615–630.
11. Thomson, R.H., The pigments of reddish hair and feathers, *Angewandte Chemie Int. Ed.* (in English), 13, 305–312, 1974.
12. Ozeki, H., Ito, S., and Wakamatsu, K., Chemical characterization of melanins in sheep wool and human hair, *Pigment Cell Res.*, 9, 51–57, 1996.
13. Prota, G., Melanins, melanogenesis and melanocytes: looking at their functional significance from the chemist's viewpoint, *Pigment Cell. Res.*, 13, 283–293, 2000.
14. Borges, C.R., Wilkins, D.G., and Rollins, D.E., Amphetamine and N-acetylamphetamine incorporation into hair: an investigation of the potential role of drug basicity in hair color bias, *J. Anal. Toxicol.*, 25, 221–227, 2001.
15. Gygi, S.P., Joseph, R.E., Jr., Cone, E.J., Wilkins, D.G., and Rollins, D.E., Incorporation of codeine and metabolites into hair: role of pigmentation, *Drug Metab. Dispos. Biol. Fate Chem.*, 24, 495–501, 1996.
16. Gygi, S.P., Wilkins, D.G., and Rollins, D.E., Distribution of codeine and morphine into rat hair after long-term daily dosing with codeine, *J. Anal. Toxicol.*, 19, 387–391, 1995.
17. Gygi, S.P., Wilkins, D.G., and Rollins, D.E., A comparison of phenobarbital and codeine incorporation into pigmented and nonpigmented rat hair, *J. Pharm. Sci.*, 86, 209–214, 1997.
18. Nakahara, Y. and Kikura, R., Hair analysis for drugs of abuse, XIII: effect of structural factors on incorporation of drugs into hair: the incorporation rates of amphetamine analogs, *Arch. Toxicol.*, 70, 841–849, 1996.
19. Nakahara, Y., Ochiai, T., and Kikura, R., Hair analysis for drugs of abuse, V: the facility in incorporation of cocaine into hair over its major metabolites, benzoylecgonine and ecgonine methyl ester, *Arch. Toxicol.*, 66, 446–449, 1992.
20. Nakahara, Y., Takahashi, K., and Kikura, R., Hair analysis for drugs of abuse, X: effect of physicochemical properties of drugs on the incorporation rates into hair, *Biol. Pharm. Bull.*, 18, 1223–1227, 1995.
21. Pötsch, L. and Moeller, M.R. On pathways for small molecules into and out of human hair fibers, *J. Forensic Sci.*, 41, 121–125, 1996.
22. Pötsch, L., Skopp, G., and Moeller, M.R., Influence of pigmentation on the codeine content of hair fibers in guinea pigs, *J. Forensic Sci.*, 42, 1095–1098, 1997.
23. Pötsch, L., Skopp, G., and Rippin, G., A comparison of 3H-cocaine binding on melanin granules and human hair *in vitro*, *Int. J. Legal Med.*, 110, 55–62, 1997.

24. Stout, P.R., Claffey, D.J., and Ruth, J.A., Incorporation and retention of radiolabeled S-(+)-and R-(−)-methamphetamine and S(+)- and R(−)-N-(n-butyl)-amphetamine in mouse hair after systemic administration, *Drug Metab. Dispos. Biol. Fate Chem.*, 28, 286–291, 2000.
25. Stout, P.R. and Ruth, J.A., Deposition of [3H]cocaine, [3H]nicotine, and [3H]flunitrazepam in mouse hair melanosomes after systemic administration, *Drug Metab. Dispos. Biol. Fate Chem.*, 27, 731–735, 1999.
26. Robbins, C.R., *Chemical and Physical Behavior of Human Hair*, Springer Verlag, Berlin, 1994.
27. Stout, P.R. and Ruth, J.A., Comparison of *in vivo* and *in vitro* deposition of rhodamine and fluorescein in hair, *Drug Metab. Dispos.*, 26, 943–948, 1998.
28. Borges, C.R., Martin, S.D., Meyer, L.J., Wilkins, D.G., and Rollins, D.E., Influx and efflux of amphetamine and N-acetylamphetamine in keratinocytes, pigmented melanocytes, and nonpigmented melanocytes, *J. Pharm. Sci.*, 91, 1523–1535, 2002.
29. Nakahara, Y. and Kikura, R., Hair analysis for drugs of abuse, VII: the incorporation rates of cocaine, benzoylecgonine and ecgonine methyl ester into rat hair and hydrolysis of cocaine in rat hair, *Arch Toxicol.*, 68, 54–59, 1994.
30. Cone, E.J., Hillsgrove, M.J., Jenkins, A.J., Keenan, R.M., and Darwin, W.D., Sweat testing for heroin, cocaine, and metabolites, *J. Anal. Toxicol.*, 18, 298–305, 1994.
31. Kacinko, S.L., Barnes, A.J., Schwilke, E.W., Cone, E.J., Moolchan, E.T., and Huestis, M.A., *Clin. Chem.*, 51, 2085–2094, 2005.
32. Kintz, P., Excretion of MBDB and BDB in urine, saliva, and sweat following single oral administration, *J. Anal. Toxicol.*, 21, 570–575, 1997.
33. Kintz, P., Tracqui, A., and Mangin, P., Sweat testing for benzodiazepines, *J. Forensic Sci.*, 41, 851–854, 1996.
34. Henderson, G.L., Harkey, M.R., Zhou, C., Jones, R.T., and Jacob P., Incorporation of isotopically labeled cocaine and metabolites into human hair, part 3: 1, dose-response relationships, *J. Anal. Toxicol.*, 20, 1–12, 1996.
35. Raul, J.S., Cirimele, V., Ludes, B., and Kintz, P., Detection of physiological concentrations of cortisol and cortisone in human hair, *Clin. Biochem.*, 37, 1105–1111, 2004.
36. Pragst, F., Rothe, M., Spiegel, K., and Sporkert, F., Illegal and therapeutic drug concentrations in hair segments: a timetable of drug exposure? *Forensic Sci. Rev.*, 10, 81–111, 1998.
37. DeLauder, S.F. and Kidwell, D.A., The incorporation of dyes into hair as a model for drug binding, *Forensic Sci. Int.*, 107, 93–104, 2000.
38. Cairns, T., Hill, V., Schaffer, M., and Thistle, W., Removing and identifying drug contamination in the analysis of human hair, *Forensic Sci. Int.*, 145, 97–108, 2004.
39. Schaffer, M., Hill, V., and Cairns, T., Hair analysis for cocaine: the requirement for effective wash procedures and effects of drug concentration and hair porosity in contamination and decontamination, *J. Anal. Toxicol.*, 29, 319–326, 2005.
40. Schaffer, M.I., Wang, W.L., and Irving, J., An evaluation of two wash procedures for the differentiation of external contamination versus ingestion in the analysis of human hair samples for cocaine, *J. Anal. Toxicol.*, 26, 485–488, 2002.
41. Potts, A.M., The concentration of phenothiazines in the eye of experimental animals, *Invest. Ophthalmol.*, 1, 522–530, 1962.
42. Larsson, B.S., Interaction between chemicals and melanin, *Pigment Cell Res.*, 6, 127–133, 1993.
43. Larsson, B., Oskarsson, A., and Tjalve, H., Binding of paraquat and diquat on melanin, *Exp. Eye Res.*, 25, 353–359, 1977.

44. Larsson, B., Oskarsson, A., and Tjalve, H., On the binding of the bisquaternary ammonium compound paraquat to melanin and cartilage *in vivo*, *Biochem. Pharmacol.*, 27, 1721–1724, 1978.
45. Larsson, B. and Tjalve, H., Studies on the melanin-affinity of metal ions, *Acta Physiol. Scand.*, 104, 479–484, 1978.
46. Larsson, B. and Tjalve, H., Studies on the mechanism of drug-binding to melanin, *Biochem. Pharmacol.*, 28, 1181–1187, 1979.
47. Tjalve, H., Nilsson, M., Henningsson, A.C., and Henningsson, S., Affinity of putrescine, spermidine and spermine for pigmented tissues, *Biochem. Biophys. Res. Commun.*, 109, 1116–1122, 1982.
48. Tjalve, H., Nilsson, M., and Larsson, B., Binding of 14C-spermidine to melanin *in vivo* and *in vitro*, *Acta Physiol. Scand.*, 112, 209–214, 1981.
49. Tjalve, H., Nilsson, M., and Larsson, B., Studies on the binding of chlorpromazine and chloroquine to melanin *in vivo*, *Biochem. Pharmacol.*, 30, 1845–1847, 1981.
50. Bridelli, M.G., Ciati, A., and Crippa, Binding of melanins re-examined: Adsorption of some drugs to the surface of melanin particles, P.R., *Biophys. Chem.*, Jan. 20, 119(2), 137–145, 2006.
51. Gautam, L., Scott, K.S., and Cole, M.D., Amphetamine binding to synthetic melanin and Scatchard analysis of binding data, *J. Anal. Toxicol.*, 29, 339–344, 2005.
52. Koeberle, M.J., Hughes, P.M., Wilson, C.G., and Skellern, G.G., Development of a liquid chromatography-mass spectrometric method for measuring the binding of memantine to different melanins, *J. Chromatogr. B Biomed. Appl.*, 787, 313–322, 2003.
53. Testorf, M.F., Kronstrand, R., Svensson, S.P., Lundstrom, I., and Ahlner, J., Characterization of [3H]flunitrazepam binding to melanin, *Anal. Biochem.*, 298, 259–264, 2001.
54. Stepien, K.B. and Wilczok, T., Studies of the mechanism of chloroquine binding to synthetic DOPA-melanin, *Biochem. Pharmacol.*, 31, 3359–3365, 1982.
55. Clancy, C.M. and Simon, J.D., Ultrastructural organization of eumelanin from Sepia officinalis measured by atomic force microscopy, *Biochemistry*, 40, 13353–13360, 2001.
56. Borges, C.R., Roberts, J.C., Wilkins, D.G., and Rollins, D.E., Cocaine, benzoylecgonine, amphetamine, and N-acetylamphetamine binding to melanin subtypes, *J. Anal. Toxicol.*, 27, 125–134, 2003.
57. Mars, U. and Larsson, B.S., Pheomelanin as a binding site for drugs and chemicals, *Pigment Cell Res.*, 12, 266–274, 1999.
58. Larsson, B.S., Olsson, S., Szutz, T., and Ullberg, S., Incorporation of 14C-nicotine into growing melanin, *Toxicol. Lett.*, 4, 199–203, 1979.
59. Harrison, W.H., Gray, R.M., and Solomon, L.M., Incorporation of D-amphetamine into pigmented guinea-pig hair, *Br. J. Dermatol.*, 91, 415–418, 1974.
60. Claffey, D.J., Stout, P.R., and Ruth, J.A., A comparison of sodium hydroxide and sodium sulfide digestion of mouse hair in the recovery of radioactivity following systemic administration of [3H]-nicotine and [3H]-flunitrazepam, *J. Anal. Toxicol.*, 24, 54–58, 2000.
61. Palumbo, A., d'Ischia, M., Misuraca, G., Iannone, A., and Prota, G., Selective uptake of 2-thiouracil into melanin-producing systems depends on chemical binding to enzymically generated dopaquinone, *Biochim. Biophys. Acta*, 1036, 221–227, 1990.
62. Palumbo, A., Napolitano, A., De Martino, L., Vieira, W., and Hearing, V.J., Specific incorporation of 2-thiouracil into biological melanins, *Biochim. Biophys. Acta*, 1200, 271–276, 1994.
63. Dehn, D.L., Claffey, D.J., Duncan, M.W., and Ruth, J.A., Nicotine and cotinine adducts of a melanin intermediate demonstrated by matrix-assisted laser desorption/ionization time-of-flight mass spectrometry, *Chem. Res. Toxicol.*, 14, 275–279, 2001.

64. Claffey, D.J. and Ruth, J.A., Amphetamine adducts of melanin intermediates demonstrated by matrix-assisted laser desorption/ionization time-of-flight mass spectrometry, *Chem. Res. Toxicol.*, 14, 1339–1344, 2001.
65. Gerstenberg, B., Schepers, G., Voncken, P., and Völkel, H., Nicotine and cotinine accumulation in pigmented and unpigmented rat hair, *Drug Metab. Dispos. Biol. Fate Chem.*, 23, 143–148, 1995.
66. Green, S.J. and Wilson, J.F., The effect of hair color on the incorporation of methadone into hair in the rat, *J. Anal. Toxicol.*, 20, 121–123, 1996.
67. Slawson, M.H., Wilkins, D.G., and Rollins, D.E., The incorporation of drugs into hair: relationship of hair color and melanin concentration to phencyclidine incorporation, *J. Anal. Toxicol.*, 22, 406–413, 1998.
68. Appelgren, L.E., Larsson, B.S., and Torneke, K., Clenbuterol in hair: *in vitro* studies on its binding to melanin and keratin, *J. Vet. Pharmacol. Ther.*, 20, 305–306, 1997.
69. Banning, T.P. and Heard, C.M., Binding of doxycycline to keratin, melanin and human epidermal tissue, *Int. J. Pharmaceutics*, 235, 219–227, 2002.
70. Sato, H., Uematsu, T., Yamada, K., and Nakashima, M., Chlorpromazine in human scalp hair as an index of dosage history: comparison with simultaneously measured haloperidol, *Eur. J. Clin. Pharmacol.*, 44, 439–444, 1993.
71. Reid, R.W., O'Connor, F.L., Deakin, A.G., Ivery, D.M., and Crayton, J.W., Cocaine and metabolites in human graying hair: pigmentary relationship, *J. Toxicol. Clin. Toxicol.*, 34, 685–690, 1996.
72. Rothe, M., Pragst, F., Thor, S., and Hunger, J., Effect of pigmentation on the drug deposition in hair of grey-haired subjects, *Forensic Sci. Int.*, 84, 53–60, 1997.
73. Kronstrand, R., Ahlner, J., Dizdar, N., and Larson, G., Quantitative analysis of desmethylselegiline, methamphetamine, and amphetamine in hair and plasma from Parkinson patients on long-term selegiline medication, *J. Anal. Toxicol.*, 27, 135–141, 2003.
74. Kronstrand, R., Andersson, M.C., Ahlner, J., and Larson, G., Incorporation of selegiline metabolites into hair after oral selegiline intake, *J. Anal. Toxicol.*, 25, 594–601, 2001.
75. Kronstrand, R., Forstberg-Peterson, S., Kagedal, B., Ahlner, J., and Larson, G., Codeine concentration in hair after oral administration is dependent on melanin content, *Clin. Chem.*, 45, 1485–1494, 1999.

2 Passive Exposure, Decontamination Procedures, Cutoffs, and Bias: Pitfalls in the Interpretation of Hair Analysis Results for Cocaine Use

David A. Kidwell and Frederick P. Smith

CONTENTS

2.1 INTRODUCTION

The devil is in the details, and there are many details concerning the analysis of hair for drugs of abuse and the interpretation of the analytical result. Several controversies have arisen over the years surrounding a number of these details on analysis. The controversies have focused on three broad areas: (1) the mechanisms for appearance and binding to hair of drugs of abuse, (2) removal of external contamination, and (3) bias. The conclusions reached in these three areas and the weight given to the scientific facts greatly color the interpretation of any hair analysis result. This review outlines the historical evidence accumulated in these three areas of research and discusses how the interpretation of these data has led to two dissimilar models of incorporation and removal of drugs from hair. Also, new data are presented to clarify areas of controversy and show how some of the variables of cutoffs, bias, passive exposure, and decontamination are closely related. An understanding of the data and its interpretation is critical to the proper application of hair analysis results.* This review focuses on cocaine as the most known and studied drug and with the greatest potential to contaminate hair due to its presence in the environment. As methamphetamine becomes more widely abused and smoked** and as heroin smoking increases, these drugs will contaminate environments, much like cocaine. Considering the mechanism for drug binding to hair, other amine-containing drugs (PCP, amphetamines, and opiates) should behave similarly to cocaine.

2.2 HISTORICAL CONCERNS FOR PASSIVE EXPOSURE IN HAIR ANALYSIS

The human body has the ability to cleanse itself of drugs by metabolism and excretion. Thus, any exposure to a drug must be recent for the drug to be detected in blood, saliva, sweat, or urine. On the other hand, hair is a unique matrix because no active metabolism/excretion is present to remove drugs once deposited. There are two major removal mechanisms for drugs in hair: replacement/cutting of hair, with a time frame of months to years, and the slow hygienic removal of bound substances. For widespread use of hair analysis, this is both good news and bad news. The good news is

* In this chapter, all concentrations of drugs have been converted to nanograms of drug per milligram of hair (ng/mg), as recommended in the 2nd International Conference on Hair Testing held in Genova, Italy, June 1994 and published [1]. Attention must be given to the units of measure of the results presented here when a comparison is made to the results of other authors. Many commercial companies used units of pg/mg or ng/10 mg. When these units are discussed with the chief scientists of those companies, they readily admit that these units are used to make the numbers look bigger. Units are *not* just semantics. The size of a number is more important in legal proceedings in an adversarial legal system, such as in the U.S., because a jury or judge is unlikely to understand units. In court trials, where I have been an expert witness for the defense and where reasonable scenarios for passive exposure have been put forth, it is much harder to convince the jury that large numbers could result from passive exposure. They may agree that 0.0005 μg cocaine/mg hair or even 0.5 ng cocaine/mg could be due to inadvertent exposure and acquit the defendant. However, 500 pg cocaine/mg of hair seems too much for passive exposure, even though all three are the same amounts.

** Smoking of methamphetamine appears to be increasing in the western and midwestern U.S.

that, if drugs enter the hair exclusively as a result of ingestion, they can be detected for long periods of time. The bad news is that, if drugs become bound to hair, even partially by other mechanisms such as passive (accidental) exposure, they may be difficult to remove and distinguish from actual use. This has been a problem for analysis of trace metals in hair. Additionally, although acute exposure can be a random event, if the uptake of drugs by hair is rapid and release by hygiene slow, then one could not discern acute from chronic exposure. Essentially, hair would act as an integrator of drug exposure, i.e., if segmental analysis were done on that hair sample, then the drug would be throughout the hair rather than in discrete bands. An analogy is dying of hair. An individual may dye his or her hair at a random time; the uptake of dye takes minutes, and the release of dye takes months. Sometime after the initial dying, the individual may repeat the dying process to achieve a uniform color (dying of the roots), thus integrating the color over time. Another analogy is the slow metabolism of tetrahydrocannabinol (THC) in marijuana. Because THC is fat soluble, uptake is rapid into the fat of the body, but release from that fat and eventual metabolism is slow. Thus, a single use (analogous to hair exposure of any material) to THC produces a slow metabolism (analogous to decontamination of hair by hygiene) and thereby a long detection window.

As early as 1978, Lenihan [2] pointed out that hair "is a mirror of the environment." Additionally, many investigators have noted that, while in some cases blood/urinary concentrations of trace metals are associated with elevated hair concentrations, this is not always true. Numerous other authors have discussed the problems of trace metal analysis with respect to passive exposure from the environment [3–7]. A detailed discussion of the literature on hair analysis for heavy metals is beyond the scope of this chapter, but one can be found in Chatt and Katz [8], and a brief review can be found in Manson and Zlotkin [9]. Chatt and Katz [8] state three factors that prevent the use of hair analysis for assessment of heavy-metal and mineral ingestion. These are: (1) a difficulty in differentiating external deposition of trace metals from ingestion; (2) an inability to define normal ranges of trace metal concentrations in hair; and (3) a dearth of information on mechanisms of the incorporation of trace elements into hair. Likewise, Harkey and Henderson [10] have contrasted hair testing for drugs of abuse with hair testing for nutritional status and noted many similarities. Some scientists have dismissed using hair testing for nutritional status as pure quackery [11, 12].

Other authors have argued that trace metals and drugs of abuse are not comparable because trace metals are ubiquitous in the environment, trace metals bind to the sulfhydryl groups of the keratin proteins, and trace metals diffuse faster than drugs [13]. These arguments are spurious. Drugs exist in many environments (see below) and, even if not ubiquitous, that does not rule out occasional contact. Drugs bind to functionalities in proteins such as aspartic and glutamic acids. In addition, drugs bind through van der Waals interactions, which ions cannot do [14]. Both binding mechanisms can be quite strong. Drugs (and other substances) can enter hair though diffusion. Diffusion through a chemical gradient (more later) is difficult to model and depends only partially on the diffusion constant. Ignoring the complication of a chemical gradient, which would be equally applicable to metals, the diffusion constants of drugs should be similar to the *hydrated* radius of metal ions (realistic in solutions). Even if the diffusion constants of drugs were slower, just a short delay would be needed to get an equivalent diffusion length. Additionally, diffusion of small molecules into hair depends on prior cosmetic treatment. For example, the diffusion of sodium dodecyl sulfate (a charged, large, organic molecule) is ten-fold higher into bleached hair versus untreated hair [7]. Thus, trace metal detection in hair makes a good model for drugs, and the known problems that plague trace metal analysis remain unresolved and will also plague drug testing.

The potential for environmental exposure and the difficulty in distinguishing ingestion from external sources has greatly diminished the value of hair analysis for heavy metals as a tool to gather information about blood levels vs. time. However, estimating the extent of exposure to heavy metals, or more importantly lack of exposure, via hair analysis is still a valuable use for the technique. One may ask: are drugs uniquely different from heavy metals in terms of their binding mechanisms, removal mechanisms, or presence in the environment? Or, are metal ions comparable to drugs? The evidence supports the conclusion that drugs are similar to heavy metals, and the literature on heavy metal analysis of hair must be weighed when evaluating hair analysis data for drugs of abuse.

In 1986, I initiated several studies with the goal of validating hair analysis as a useful forensic tool. The results of these initial studies were surprising [15] and led to alternative explanations of the incorporation of drugs into hair [16, 17]. Hypotheses developed from these studies suggested that drugs were incorporated into hair via sweat and that external contamination had to be considered in data interpretation. To our knowledge, sweat as a mechanism of transfer of drugs of abuse into hair was not considered prior to these reports, although deposition of heavy metals in hair from sweat had been published prior to this time [14]. This concept has polarized the hair-testing community. More recent findings from this laboratory and those of other investigators have given support to my original hypothesis [14, 18].

2.3 MECHANISMS FOR INCORPORATION OF DRUGS INTO HAIR

2.3.1 Why Consider Mechanisms of Drug Incorporation?

A model for drug incorporation guides ones interpretation of the analytical result and the procedures used to reach this result. Most often, the forensic scientist seeks to determine, "Did this individual *use* drugs?" and not, "Did this individual come into contact with drugs?" Hair analysis (as is frequently practiced today) is only valuable if the drugs that are measured in hair arise from ingestion rather than from other sources. Therefore, it is imperative that drugs arising from the external environment be removed prior to analysis. If this cannot be accomplished, the forensic scientist must find other proof of use level, such as finding the presence of unique compounds derived only from *in vivo* metabolism. To evaluate whether or not passive exposure can contribute to drugs in hair, the mechanisms of appearance and binding of drugs to hair both from external (passive) sources and ingestion must be understood. Furthermore, an understanding of these mechanisms may give clues for differentiation between the different modes of drug deposition.

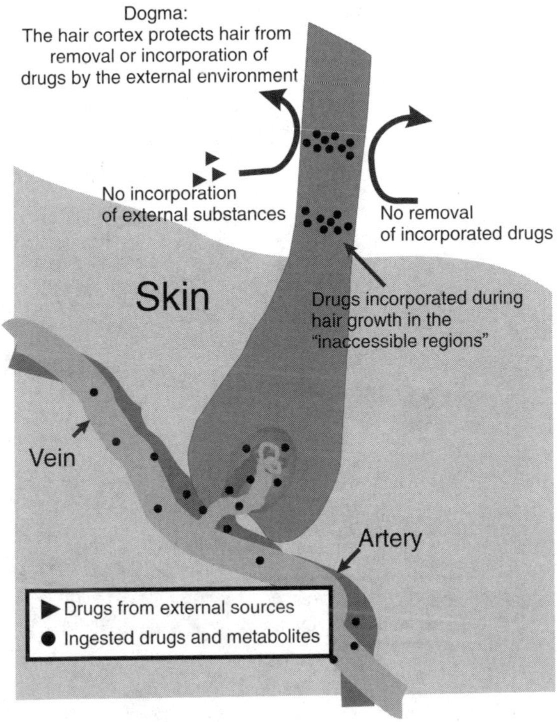

FIGURE 2.1 The entrapment model of drug incorporation into hair. Drugs are incorporated into hair at the root from the bloodstream during the hair growth phase. Their concentration in hair reflects that present in the bloodstream. A central dogma of the entrapment model is that once incorporated, the drugs are resistant to removal or insertion by the environment.

2.3.2 Models for Drug Incorporation

An early theoretical position explaining the incorporation of drugs into hair has been given much attention [19]. In this model (termed the entrapment model), drugs in the bloodstream are claimed to be entrapped by inaccessible regions of the hair during the hair growth process (Figure 2.1). After the hair emerges from the scalp, these drugs form bands that are in direct proportion to the concentrations present when the hair was formed. The entrapped drugs are protected by the hair matrix so that they cannot be removed or changed by the external environment. Because hair grows at a relatively constant rate, this model predicts that hair analysis would provide a history of drug consumption in both time and amount. There is little or no direct evidence in support of this hypothetical construct of inaccessible regions in hair. To the contrary, there is considerable evidence that inaccessible regions do not exist. The entrapment model is therefore to be considered purely hypothetical at this time.

Based on unexpected results for simple exposure studies, this early hypothesis on incorporation of drugs was questioned. Evidence supported an alternative proposal for drug incorporation [20]. In this alternative model (Figure 2.2), some drugs

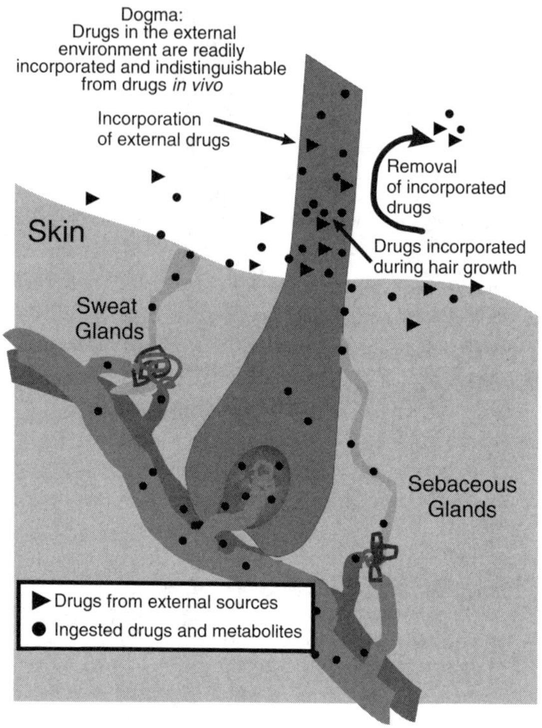

FIGURE 2.2 Sweat model for drug incorporation. Drugs are incorporated into hair from two sources: blood and sweat. Because the sweat is external, it can be contaminated with external sources of drugs. Once incorporated, the source of drugs — internal or external — is lost. A central dogma of the sweat model is that drugs in hair are not resistant to removal or incorporation by the environment.

are incorporated during hair growth from the compounds present in the bloodstream. In addition, water-soluble drugs excreted into sweat/sebum, which bathe the hair, are incorporated after the hair emerges from the skin. In this model, drugs can come from three sources. The first source is the blood, as described above in Figure 2.1. The second source is excretion of the drug or metabolites into sweat and subsequent incorporation into the hair. The third source of drugs in hair is from passive exposure of the hair to the drug, either from vapor phase (e.g., smoke) or solid-phase contact (e.g., drugs on furniture or clothing or skin-to-hair contact) followed by dissolution of the drug into drug-free sweat or other aqueous media. Because both of the latter two sources of drugs are in aqueous solution, they are indistinguishable after they are incorporated into the hair.

The model depicted in Figure 2.2 is called the "sweat model" to emphasize the contribution of drugs from external, aqueous media of moderate ionic strength (wet hair). The sweat model predicts that few or no regions in the hair are inaccessible to the external environment. A model similar to that of the sweat model for drugs of abuse has been proposed for heavy metal ions, where a substantial fraction of the heavy metal ions detected in the hair come from an external source such as sweat [6].

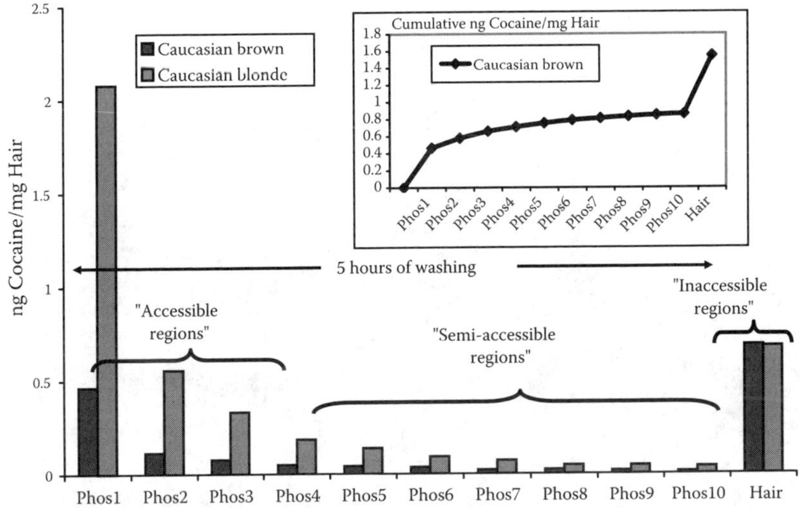

FIGURE 2.3 Example of data that prompted the entrapment model for drug incorporation in hair. In this case, two hair samples were externally contaminated with a solution of cocaine and extensively washed with an exchange of buffer every 30 min. The loss of cocaine into the wash solutions is exponential (the key observation for the entrapment model). After the hair is analyzed, a greater amount is found in the hair than in many of the wash steps. The naming of the regions is somewhat arbitrary. Frequently, these data are presented as a cumulative curve (inset). However, a cumulative curve makes the steps more difficult to observe and will not be used in this chapter.

2.3.3 Basis for the Models Depicted in Figure 2.1 and Figure 2.2

It may be helpful to review the data that prompted the entrapment model and see how these data came to be misinterpreted. The main support for the entrapment model comes from extraction kinetics, covered in more detail below. When hair from a drug user is extracted with solvents, such as phosphate buffer in water, drug is removed in an exponential manner, illustrated in Figure 2.3. Baumgartner et al. [13] interpreted this exponential decrease to arise from drugs being removed from various regions of the hair. These regions were given the names: accessible, semiaccessible, and inaccessible. Baumgartner et al. considered the inaccessible region to be inaccessible from the outside environment, so that if drugs are entrapped in this region during hair formation, they are not removable by washing. Furthermore, drugs from the external environment cannot penetrate into that area.

To further bolster this concept, Baumgartner et al. [13] invoke the structure of hair as containing microfibrils (which hair certainly does) and claim that these represent the inaccessible regions of hair (see Figure 2.4). The concept of inaccessible regions can be tested on the atomic level. Microfibrils are protein strands mostly bonded through van der Waals interactions rather than cross-linked though chemical bonds. Because these strands are composed of proteins, and proteins are composed of amino acids, this gives a unique way to determine how accessible the whole hair structure is to the external environment. Amino acids contain amide bonds

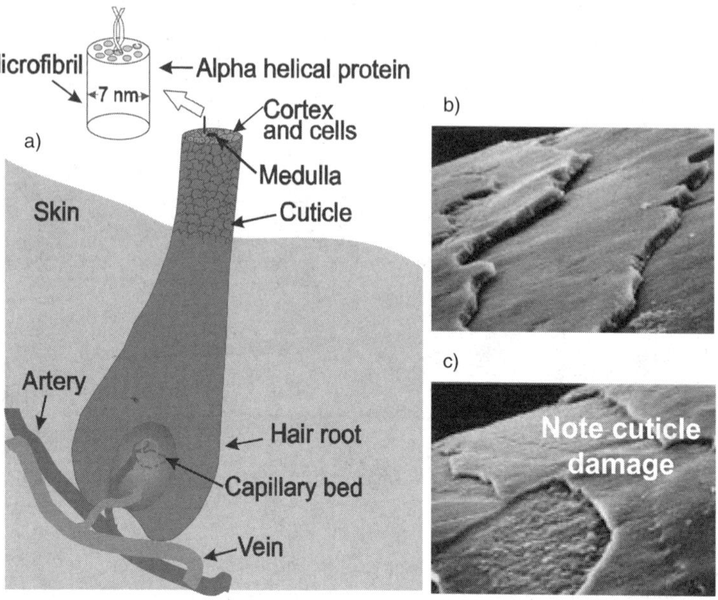

FIGURE 2.4 (a) Schematic model of the interior of hair showing the microfibrils. (b) Photograph of the cuticle on normal hair. (c) Photograph of the cuticle on hair that has been damaged by combing when wet. The cuticle is also very important in protecting the hair from contamination. The scales on the cuticle rise in the presence of moisture, which allows readier access to the interior and provides a vehicle for diffusion. (The hair cuticle photographs are from *Science News*, 160, 124, 2001 and used with permission of K. Ramaprasad, TRI/Princeton, Princeton.)

(see Figure 2.5), which have a unique infrared (IR) signature and are exchangeable. Upon exposing hair to deuterated water, these amide hydrogens exchange for deuterium and shift the IR absorption frequency from ca. 3300 cm to ca. 2416 cm [21]. Greater than 90% of the amide hydrogens in hair [22] can be exchanged.* This access at the atomic level shows that inaccessible regions absolutely do not exist.

An alternative way to understand the example illustrated in Figure 2.3 is to consider diffusion through a limited volume and a chemical gradient. Holmes [23] has modeled mathematically this concept for the commercially important process of dying of wool. Such mathematics are beyond the scope of this review, but the process can be understood schematically. Hair has weak binding sites for cationic molecules such as drugs. Because of these binding sites, coupled with restricted diffusion, one could envision washout kinetics without evoking "inaccessible regions." Drugs in hair are thought to bind though ionic and van der Waals interactions with the protein

* We independently repeated the work of Bendit [21], followed the H-D exchange by FTIR, and showed a large exchange of amide hydrogens for deuterium atoms. However, somewhat drastic conditions of time, temperature, and acid are required to exchange amide hydrogens (even in dissolved proteins such as bovine serum albumin [BSA]). Our preliminary work was never published because these exchange conditions would not be faced in ordinary hygiene, and therefore proponents of inaccessible regions could still claim that they remain inaccessible under "normal" conditions.

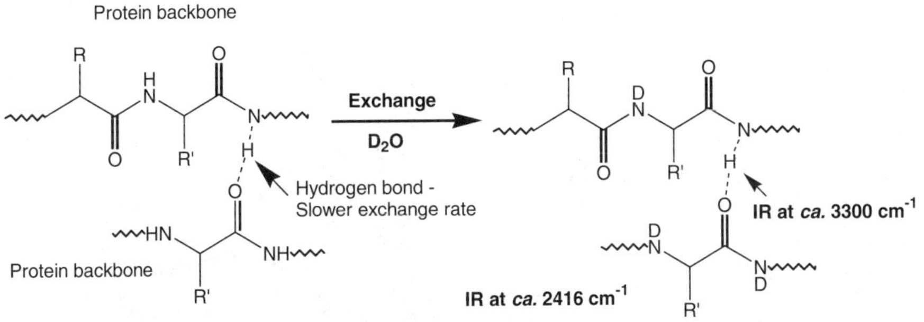

FIGURE 2.5 Schematic of the exchange of amide hydrogens for deuterium. Because many amide hydrogens are involved in hydrogen bonding, acid media and high temperature are required for their exchange. The rate of exchange could provide information on the involvement of the amide bond in hydrogen bonding. This exchange will go both ways, with the deuterium exchanging back for protium when the deuterated protein is placed in water. Exchange reactions require care, as deuterated water is quickly contaminated with moisture in the air and that absorbed on surfaces, making 100% deuteration difficult.

chain. These interactions are modeled as antibodies in the dialysis illustration, but an ion-exchange resin could serve the same purpose. A simple example of limited diffusion though a chemical gradient is shown schematically in Figure 2.6 [24]. In this case, consider a dialysis bag containing excess drugs. If the dialysis bag is placed in a large volume of water, the excess drugs will diffuse from the bag. If that water is changed at time intervals and the drugs measured, one would observe an exponential decrease in the amount of drug released with time. This is simple diffusion though the pores of the bag: the smaller the pores, the slower the rate. This rate will also be affected by changing the surface area, the number of pores, the thickness of the bag (the pore length), temperature, etc. After time, all the free drug (that not bound to the antibodies, the binding element) will have been released from the bag. At that point, the removal rate will slow and be proportional to the binding constant of the antibody *and* the factors affecting simple diffusion, listed above. In no case, would a reasonable scientist consider this porous bag to contain "inaccessible regions," yet the empirical results are identical to what one observes from decontaminating the hair of a drug user or exposed hair (compare Figure 2.6 with Figure 2.3).

Diffusion is proportional to a number of factors, concentration of the species and others, that are fixed due to the nature of the object (pore size, area, etc.). Concentration can be arbitrarily changed with larger concentrations meaning faster diffusion. Because environmental amounts of drugs can be millions of times greater than that found in hair, diffusion can be quite rapid.* Figure 2.6b can also illustrate how easily

* Consider that typical concentrations for cocaine in hair are on the order of 1 ng cocaine/mg hair. Contrast that with a single dose of cocaine of 50 to 100 mg and the fact that many drug users use several doses of cocaine. This potential 100 millionfold or more difference (of course not all the dose would be placed on the hair!) for a single exposure (multiple exposures are possible, such as repeated contact with contaminated hands) allows diffusion *into* negative hair to be rapid. On the other hand, diffusion *out* of the hair is slow because of binding of drug to the hair, and the concentration gradient of the drug from the hair to the environment is much smaller because of lower concentrations in the hair.

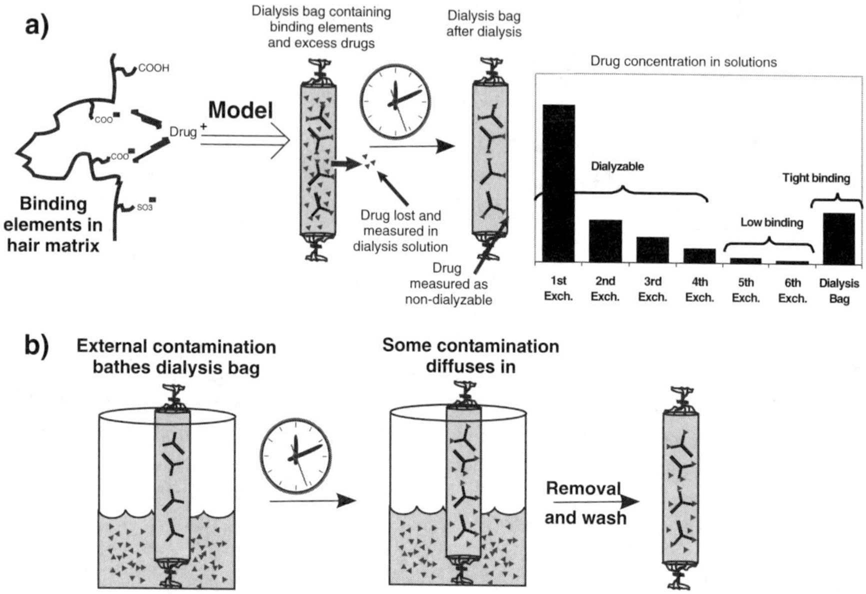

FIGURE 2.6 (a) Diffusion model for generating "inaccessible domains" in hair. (b) Example of how external drugs may the dialysis bag. Drugs bind via ionic and van der Waals interactions with the hair matrix. The cuticle (Figure 2.4b) and cortex provide a barrier to diffusion. This diffusion through a restricted environment can be modeled as a dialysis bag containing binding elements and excess drugs. (Figure modeled from DeLauder, S.F. and Kidwell, D.A., The incorporation of dyes into hair as a model for drug binding, *Forensic Sci. Int.*, 107, 39, 2000.)

this bag can be contaminated from the external environment. If this dialysis bag were placed in a concentrated solution of drugs, the drugs would quickly diffuse into the bag, producing the initial picture discussed above. Then that larger external source of drugs can be removed and, in the absence of water, that dialysis bag would retain those drugs indefinitely, waiting for analysis at some time in the future.

A schematic model for sources of drugs in hair is shown in Figure 2.7. As Figure 2.7 further illustrates, there usually is some passage of time between ingestion or exposure and hair analysis. During that time, drugs loosely bound to the surface of the hair could be washed away by normal hygienic hair care. This part of the process, normal hygiene, eviscerates the conclusions from decontamination kinetics. The removal of drugs will depend upon several variables, not the least of which are the characteristics of the solutions used to wash or treat the hair. In fact, one might visualize hygienic practices as an *in vivo* extraction of drugs of abuse and compare them with laboratory decontamination/extraction procedures. The cleansing of hair by an individual before the sample is taken for hair analysis greatly complicates the classification of external contamination. How personal hygiene affects hair analysis will be discussed in detail in the theoretical framework section of this chapter.

There is empirical evidence that sweat contributes to drug incorporation into hair. When Henderson et al. [26] administered deuterated cocaine to a number of

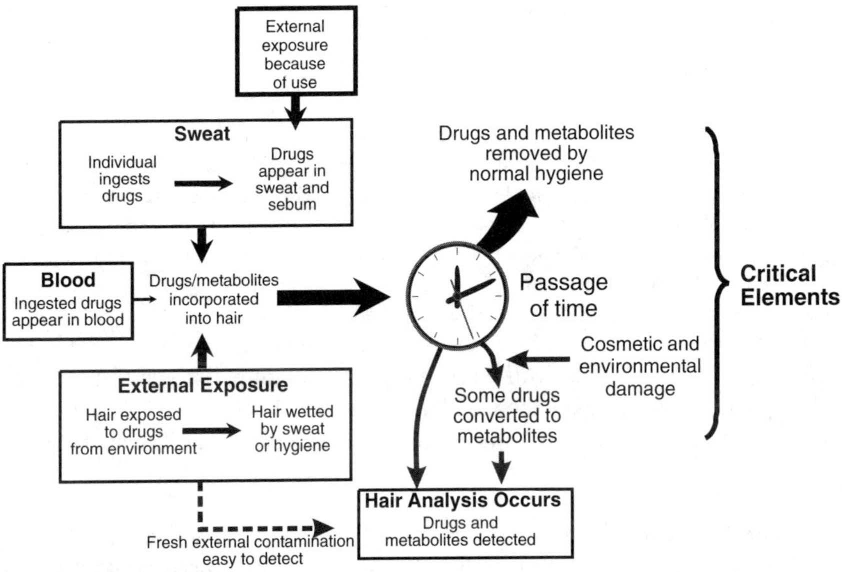

FIGURE 2.7 Framework for the incorporation and removal of drugs into and out of hair. The passage of time and hygiene are important components for contamination. Freshly contaminated hair is more readily detected as contaminated than is hair that has been rinsed because of the high concentration of drugs on the outside (Figure 2.6b). Over time, the loosely bound drugs on the surface can migrate into the interior and become more tightly bound. Additionally, hygiene removes the surface-bound drugs. (Figure taken from Blank, D.L. and Kidwell, D.A., in *Drug Testing in Hair*, Kintz, P., Ed., CRC Press, Boca Raton, FL, 1996, p. 17.)

subjects, they found that the distribution of the deuterated cocaine in the hair frequently did not appear in tight bands. In some cases, it appears throughout the hair. Additionally, they had subjects hold negative hair in their hands and induced sweat though exercise. The negative hair became positive with deuterated cocaine.

Cone [27] studied the time frame of drugs appearing in hair. He administered codeine to several subjects and found that some drug appeared in the hair after 24 h. This time is too short for initial formation of the hair in the root and for that hair to emerge above the skin (generally considered 10 to 14 days). A later but larger bolus of codeine did appear in the correct time frame, which would be more supportive of the binding during hair formation. While administering the drug, sweat would contain the highest concentrations. Because most drug administration studies are conducted under medical supervision, they are unlikely to intentionally cause sweating of the subject, such as real-life labor occupation or vigorous exercise. Furthermore, most clinical studies administer drugs in a manner (intravenous, tablets, or special smoking devices) to reduce or eliminate the possibility of externally contaminating the subject. An important route by which drugs get into sweat is through external contamination; the drug user is inexperienced at controlling contamination and contaminates him/herself during or after use. This external contamination on the skin will increase the concentration of the drug in sweat to high, arbitrary values, enhancing the diffusion discussed above.

Proponents of the inaccessible-region hypothesis will readily admit that hair can be contaminated externally with drugs in a laboratory and that hair will mimic hair from drug users [28], stating:

> We also discovered that the extended soaking of hair in concentrated drug solutions could be adapted for the preparation of control samples which would meet all of the criteria characterizing hair samples from drug users. However, the severe conditions necessary for the production of such control specimens cannot by the farthest stretch of the imagination be viewed as mimicking realistic contamination scenarios, either by sweat or by any other means.

Therefore, at least under certain conditions, even proponents of inaccessible regions agree that contaminated hair will mimic hair from drug users. It is just that there is a disagreement on the likelihood of that occurring. Elsewhere [13], these same proponents have indicated that some of these circumstances are not that uncommon by stating:

> With respect to a determination of contamination but no drug use, it is possible to further subdivide such a finding into: (a) trivial contamination; and (b) extensive contamination. Trivial contamination is characterized by contamination levels which exceed the endogenous exposure cut-off values … by an empirically determined small margin. … In our experience, this type of contamination may arise when a nondrug-using individual is constantly in the company of drug users. In contrast to this, extensive contamination is characterized by a level of contamination exceeding the endogenous cut-off level by a large margin. Contamination of this type has been found in individuals who are heavily involved in the drug culture such as a nondrug-using drug dealer or drug manufacturer.

These statements clearly imply that some hair samples from nondrug users can become contaminated and pass all the criteria (exceed the various cutoff levels) for a drug user's hair sample. What contributes to this misidentification is normal hygiene: people wash their hair. By removing the surface contamination, hair washed after contamination will generate a result indistinguishable from that generated by hair from a drug user (compare Figure 2.3 with Figure 2.6) and in a manner analogous to contaminating the dialysis bag, as discussed above.

In summary, there is little support for inaccessible regions in hair. The data that are the basis for this model can readily be explained by diffusion through a chemical barrier. Because of the porous nature of hair, which varies due to cosmetic treatments and genetics, hair can entrap drugs quickly from the environment, and the drugs will not readily be removed. After normal hygiene, these entrapped drugs will look like those from a drug user to any wash kinetic procedure. Interpretation of a positive result must be made with caution to account for drugs that may be present in the environment of a nondrug user.

2.4 DRUGS IN THE ENVIRONMENT

Environmental surveys are difficult to conduct because: the environment is so varied, access is limited, and it is challenging to survey large numbers of individuals

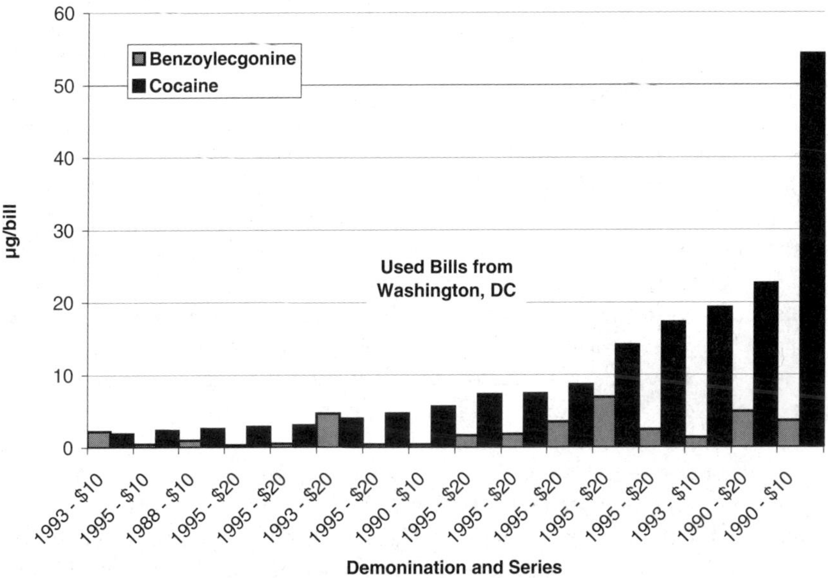

FIGURE 2.8 Levels of cocaine and benzoylecgonine on older U.S. Currency. \$10 and \$20 bills were extracted with 0.1*M* HCl and the extracts analyzed by GC-MS (gas chromatography-mass spectrometry). (Data from Kidwell, D.A. and Gardner, W.P., ONDCP International Technology Symposium, Washington, DC, 1999, p. 21-1. With permission.)

for exposure while excluding illicit drug use. However, one measure of public exposure to illicit drugs comes from monitoring currency [26–29]. Paper money is known to accumulate drugs, especially cocaine, probably from connection with the drug trade or from transfer of sweat by drug-using individuals. A survey of 55 randomly picked, older currency bills (selected to appear handled) from a local financial institution revealed widely varying levels of cocaine (Figure 2.8). Only brand-new currency appeared to be cocaine free. We also analyzed \$1 bills with the thought that these are more frequently handled than higher denominations.* For the \$1 bills, we used currency from different areas of the country to look for regional differences in contamination.

Although the amounts of cocaine present are substantially lower than what would be expected after handling drugs, could one get contamination from money? To test this scenario, two individuals vigorously rubbed currency between their dry hands for 30 sec [32]. Skin wipes were taken of their hands between each test. The currency was also analyzed to determine the extent of contamination. In 16 attempts, less than 15 ng of cocaine were transferred from the currency to the hands. Because liquids enhance transfer of drugs, transfer of drugs from currency to hands was also tested after spraying the hands with simulated sweat [33]. After spraying the hands, the currency was then tightly held for 30 sec. Simulated sweat enhanced

* One-dollar bills have an average lifetime of 22 months before needing replacement compared with 9 years for \$100 bills (see: http://www.moneyfactory.gov/document.cfm/18/2232).

cocaine transfer. In 11 attempts, up to 197 ng of cocaine was transferred. In both sets of experiments, the ratio of benzoylecgonine (BE, a metabolite of cocaine) to cocaine that was transferred correlated to the concentrations found on the currency, but the total amounts transferred did not. Because both experimental protocols likely were unusual handling of currency, we concluded that the transfer of appreciable amounts of cocaine to the hands of a nondrug-using individual from currency is unlikely but nevertheless possible when hands or bills are damp and bills are more highly contaminated.

An interesting aspect of contamination is that it is not uniform in the environment. For example, Figure 2.9a shows the concentration of cocaine on $1 bills from various locations in the U.S. There is a marked difference from inner-city Washington, DC, and its suburbs. Part of this difference is where the banks receive their currency. The inner-city Washington, DC, bank received its currency from the Federal Reserve in Baltimore, MD, whereas the suburban bank received its currency from the Federal Reserve in Richmond, VA. Baltimore is known to have a high *per capita* cocaine use. Additionally, the notes were screened for other drugs such as methamphetamine. Notes from Las Vegas, NV, had high methamphetamine levels compared with those in Washington, DC, and surrounding areas (Figure 2.9b). At the time this study was undertaken, methamphetamine abuse was concentrated in the southwestern U.S.

Besides money, people handle many other objects where drugs can accumulate, in part because their volatility is very low. We wanted to see if individuals living in an inner-city neighborhood would have greater contact with cocaine than those in a suburban neighborhood. To reduce the risk that we were examining environments where drug use was ongoing, we evaluated contamination on the desks of elementary school children. Given the ages of these children (<9 years old), willing cocaine use was unlikely, as was active cocaine use in the classrooms. Cocaine concentrations on the desks of the inner-city school children were much greater than those from the more affluent suburbs (Figure 2.10). Furthermore, benzoylecgonine was found, sometimes in levels higher than cocaine. While cocaine appeared in higher concentrations in the inner city schools, the much lower concentration on the suburban desks revealed more benzoylecgonine than cocaine. Perhaps this reflects more decomposition of the cocaine on the suburban objects, as contamination events may be less frequent, or cleaning that is more chemically destructive.

In situations where drugs are known to be present in the environment, it is easy to demonstrate that passive exposure can produce positive hair analysis results. In Haley and Hoffmann's study [34] of the nicotine and cotinine concentrations in the hair of smokers and nonsmokers, there appeared to be a higher average of nicotine in the unwashed hair of smokers (average 8.75 ng/mg). However, nonsmokers also had appreciable levels (average 2.42 ng/mg) that overlapped those of smokers. In addition, cotinine (the nicotine metabolite) does appear to be a marker of tobacco use in the smoker population. Kintz and coworkers [35] proposed a cutoff level of 2 ng of nicotine/mg of hair to identify smoking individuals, but even at this level, not all nonsmokers in their study would be negative. This demonstrates that monitoring unique metabolites (if present) and carefully chosen cutoff levels can be helpful in reducing false positives but does not eliminate them.

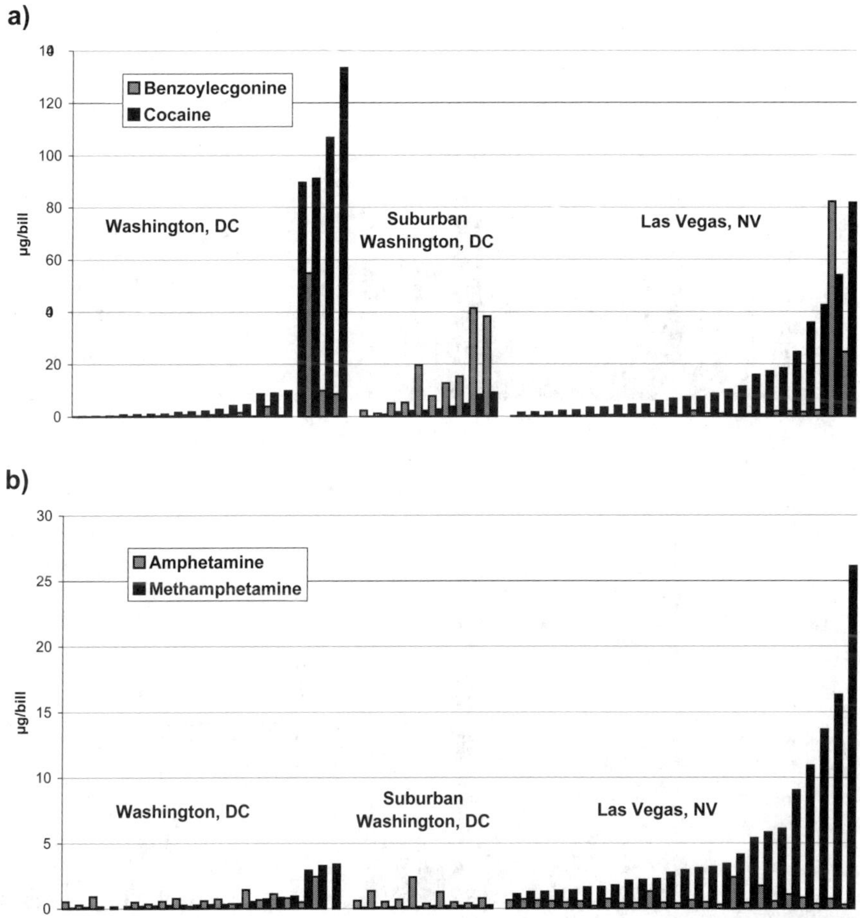

FIGURE 2.9 (a) Levels of cocaine and benzoylecgonine on used U.S. $1 bills. (b) Levels of methamphetamine on used U.S. $1 bills. The currency was extracted as described in Figure 2.8 and analyzed by electron impact-GC-MS (EI-GC-MS). The inner-city Washington, DC, bank received its currency from the Federal Reserve in Baltimore, MD. The suburban bank received its currency from the Richmond VA Federal Reserve. The differences in drug levels are very evident. Similarly, differences were noted in regional drug preferences, with methamphetamine being more prevalent in the southwestern U.S. than in the eastern coast. (Unpublished data obtained by the authors and Graham Beaber.)

One could argue that nonsmokers breathe in cigarette smoke as evidenced by nicotine and cotinine sometimes present in their urine [36]. This could be one source of the hair positives. One might not expect similar levels of nicotine and cotinine in the hair of nonsmokers versus smokers because it is inconceivable that the nonsmoker could get the same amount of smoke in themselves for the same length of time as a smoker who is intentionally inhaling. Many individuals have observed that just being near a smoker for a short period of time contaminates their clothing or the room where the smoking has occurred. Thus, the hair of the nonsmoker could

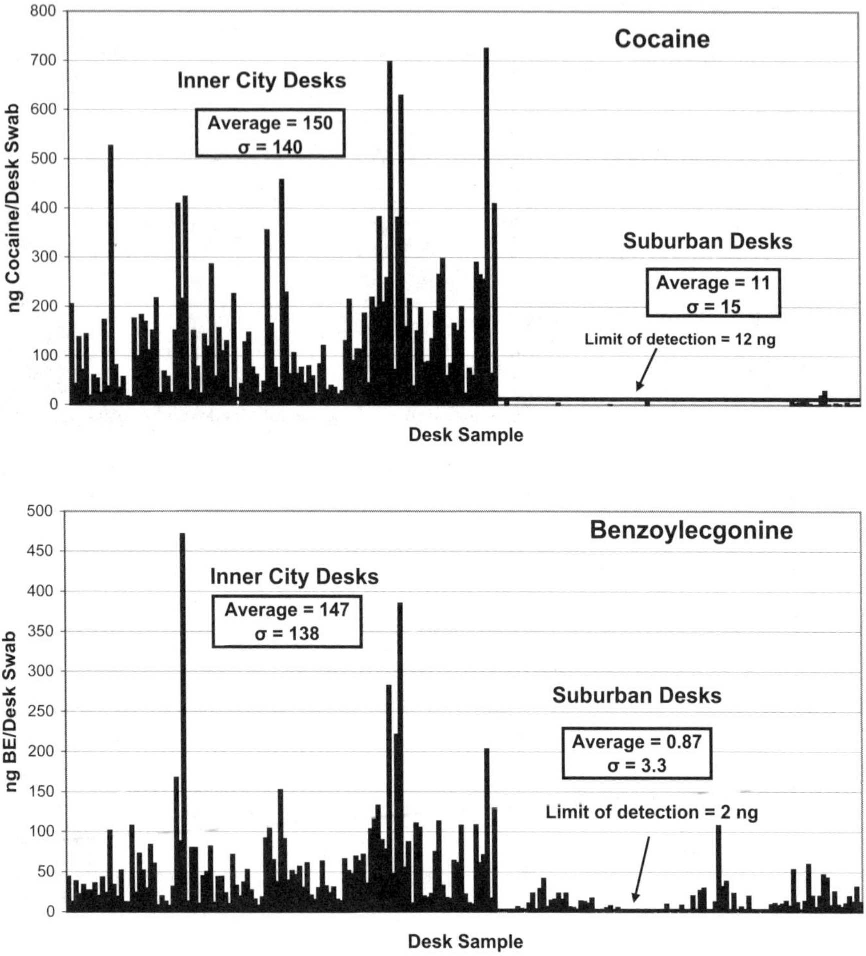

FIGURE 2.10 Levels of cocaine and benzoylecgonine on the desks of school children. A substantial difference between the levels of cocaine and benzoylecgonine on the desks of school children in the inner city and the suburbs is apparent. The desks were wiped with alcohol pads, and the pads were dried, extracted, and analyzed as for sweat wipes (see Kidwell et al. [82]). Benzoylecgonine apparently comes either from cocaine decomposition or the sweat of drug users. A difference in cleanliness between the two school systems was noted. (Unpublished data obtained by the authors and Janelle Baldwin.)

be contaminated with smoke transferring nicotine. Additionally, if the smoker and nonsmoker had close physical contact, cotinine could transfer via sweat and therefore explain how the nicotine metabolite was present in the hair of nonsmokers.

In two separate studies, Smith and Kidwell [34] examined the children and spouses of cocaine users. In these studies, the children lived in a family where cocaine was used and thereby was present in the environment. The quantity present in the environment was not known. This study assumed that children 1 to 13 years of age are unlikely to be self-administering cocaine, so that any cocaine in the hair of the children must

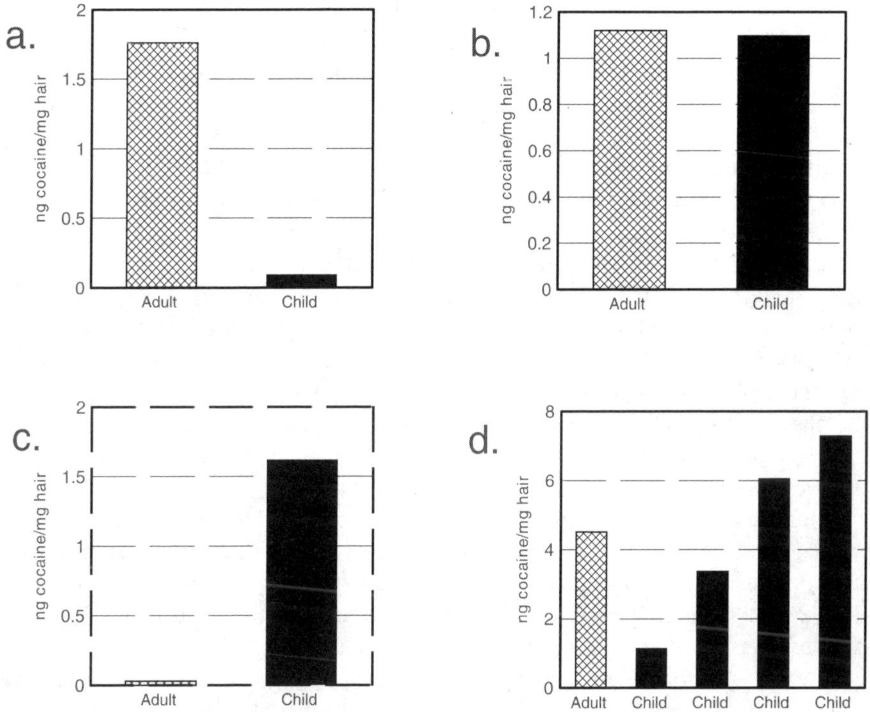

FIGURE 2.11 Concentrations of cocaine in the hair of family groups. Cocaine was used by all adults and presumably not by the children. (Figure from Smith, F.P. and Kidwell, D.A., *Forensic Sci. Int.*, 83, 179, 1996. With permission.)

have come from passive exposure. Skin wipes were obtained from the children by swiping their foreheads with a cotton swab to assess external exposure. All of the skin wipes in the experimental population (n = 29) were positive for cocaine, indicating extensive surface contact with cocaine. In the active adult using population, 80% were positive for cocaine in their hair, and 85% of the children in this study were positive for cocaine. The distribution of the concentrations of cocaine in the hair of these two groups was also similar. Analysis of the data showed that several children of cocaine users had both cocaine and benzoylecgonine in their hair in varying quantities compared with the adult users. These amounts were less than, greater than, or equal to that of the drug-using parent (Figure 2.11). The concentrations of cocaine within a family group varied greatly, which is consistent with passive exposure being a random event (Figure 2.11d). Therefore, no simple cutoff level could distinguish between the adult users and the young children living in that environment. Furthermore, this study demonstrates that certain metabolites, such as benzoylecgonine, may not be an indicator of drug use. The presence of benzoylecgonine in the environment and in hair has been noted before [38]. Alternatively, it may be produced by degradation of the cocaine once the cocaine is incorporated into the hair [39].

Smith and Kidwell are not the only group to study children living in a drug-using environment. Lewis et al. [40] tested hair from children living in a drug-using environment to help assess their exposure to drugs and possibly remove the children from that environment. Unfortunately, Lewis et al. did not report the concentrations that they found in the hair samples. Besides finding drugs in the hair, a disparity among the races of the individuals and the percentages of positive results was noted. This is covered in more detail below. Additionally, De Giorgio and coworkers [41] reported on one case where a child had a positive hair sample. Because of other evidence, they concluded that the positive result was from ingestion of cocaine rather than exposure.

In summary, based on the presence of benzoylecgonine, some drugs in money appear to be transferred from the hands of individuals handling drugs. This is a human-to-an-inanimate-object transfer and fits the model of drugs transferred from contaminated hands to the hair of a nondrug user. In the reverse (inanimate-object-to-human transfer), sweat facilitated the transfer of drugs from money to a human, reinforcing the observation that liquids are important in drug contamination studies. From these two examples of transfer from individuals to inanimate objects and the reverse, it is easy to see how someone living in an environment where cocaine use is occurring (past or present) may be at greater risk of contamination. Likewise, drug transfer to the hair from the environment has been demonstrated from studying children living in a drug-using or contaminated environment. As shown in Figure 2.11 and later analyzed in Table 2.3 below, some of these children pass all commercial criteria for drug use yet are urine negative. Furthermore, from the study with the desks of school children, it is reasonable to conclude that individuals living in the inner city may have a higher risk of cocaine exposure than those in the suburbs. Thus, risk of contamination may reflect where one lives as well as one's choices and associations. For an integrating medium such as hair, this risk is greatly magnified because the time window for incorporation is great and, once incorporated, the removal of drug is slow.

2.5 DECONTAMINATION PROCEDURES

Drugs that are placed on hair when it is dry or in organic solvents are readily removed [42, 43]. This early work may have provided a false sense of security that hair could be effectively decontaminated. In contrast to dry or organic solvents, when hair is exposed to aqueous solutions of drugs, the hair readily incorporates the drugs, and the hair is difficult to decontaminate (Figure 2.3). Water is an important part of this process because it provides a medium for diffusion of the drugs into the hair, and it expands the cuticle and the proteins in the hair, facilitating hair permeability.

Data such as shown in Figure 2.3 led us to conclude in the early 1990s that no wash process would be 100% effective in removing external contamination in almost any contamination scenario [44, 45]. Eventually, Schaffer et al. [46, 47] reached the same conclusion that 100% removal of external contamination was not possible, but did not become concerned. In more recent work, Schaffer and coworkers [48] concluded that their contamination experiments "far exceed any likely real-life contamination scenarios" based on what drug concentration could be found in Pharmchek™ sweat patches from individuals administered controlled doses of cocaine. This is the wrong comparison. Sweat patches only sample a limited area (about 14 cm^2), are frequently placed on areas of the skin, such as the upper arm, where sweating is less than the palms of the hands, and do not truly integrate the drugs in the sweat. Furthermore, the sweat patch is partially protected from external contamination by the membrane layer and therefore would greatly underestimate the amount of drugs found in sweat from the hands of a drug user due to contamination. This comparison might be valid if, for example, the drugs were transferred from the hands of a drug user to the hair of a nonuser through sweat (such as from intimate contact) *and* the sweat *only* had contribution of drugs from the bloodstream of the drug user. Unfortunately, drug users often contaminate themselves during drug use (that is why their hair is contaminated) so that they may have *any* amount on their hands available for transfer to the nondrug user. The extent of contamination would be exacerbated if the drug user had used the drugs shortly before intimate contact with the nondrug user (to adjust his/her mood) rather than hours or days before, when normal hygiene could remove some of that external contamination. Some drug users conceal their drug habits even from intimate partners.

2.5.1 Decontamination Solvents

No standard decontamination methods for hair have gained wide acceptance [49]. Several authors use methanol for both decontamination and extraction of the drug from the hair [43, 50]. Generally, the less polar and less aqueouslike the solvent, the less that solvent swells the hair and the poorer is the removal of externally applied drugs [49]. Therefore, in going from water to methanol to higher alcohols to methylene chloride (or other nonhydrogen-bonding solvents), one could expect poorer removal of external contamination. Schaffer et al. [46] compared their commercial phosphate buffer procedure with a methanol procedure used by several other authors. Methanol worked fairly well compared with phosphate buffer in removing external contamination and may have an advantage for lipophilic drugs such as THC. On average, methanol removed 48% (n = 14, SD = 18) of cocaine from externally contaminated hair, and three phosphate buffer washes removed 88% (n = 14, SD = 4.6). Interestingly, when aliquots of hair were washed with more phosphate buffer for a total of 5 h, very little additional cocaine was removed (92% total, n = 10, SD = 4.6). In no case was all the cocaine removed from these externally contaminated hair samples, even though a commercial procedure was being employed. This is discussed in more detail below.

Decontamination must be employed to remove potential external environmental contamination, as the amount of drug present in hair is low compared with that available from the environment. In general, the larger the number of discriminating criteria during the decontamination process, the better chance that a given decontamination procedure has in distinguishing contamination from use [51]. One of the better decontamination procedures is that of Baumgartner and Hill, which has been used commercially. This procedure has the advantage that several criteria must be met before a sample is considered positive. The technique has evolved over the years, and a brief description of some of the published wash procedures is given in Table 2.1. It is apparent from Table 2.1 that the procedures have varied substantially over the years, frequently without adjusting any of the cutoffs for the various wash criteria. Many times, other authors have tried to test these procedures, but they have been criticized by individuals associated with commercial testing for not following the exact procedures, which seem to change frequently. One of the major criticisms is that most authors do not digest the hair in the same manner as Baumgartner and Hill, and thereby do not quantitate the amount of drug correctly. This criticism appears to be unjustified. Any procedure that does not digest the hair, should only *underestimate* the amount of drug remaining in the hair; after all, it is not expected that the analytical procedures *produce* cocaine. Examining how the criteria work from Table 2.1 (for example, Rew), one can see that underestimating the amount of cocaine present in the hair would tend to make Rew smaller and bias it toward being a contaminated hair sample rather than hair from a cocaine user. Thus, if a researcher, using testing procedures outlined in Table 2.1, finds a false positive due to environmental contamination, that finding cannot be criticized for detecting too little cocaine in the hair.

Enough studies of exposure have been done and the hair decontaminated by commercial procedures to use their data to evaluate their wash criteria rather than trying to reproduce the method exactly and be critiqued for not taking an inconsequential step. Schaffer et al. [46] exposed 14 hair samples to cocaine at 1 μg/ml for 1 h. These hair samples were then decontaminated with either isopropanol and then three 30-min phosphate washes* (Method D in Table 2.1, but at 40°C**), or three methanol rinses, or isopropanol with three 30-min phosphate washes followed by two 1-h phosphate washes for a select ten samples (Method E, Table 2.1, but at 40°C). They report that the methanol removed 16.7 to 77%, phosphate (Method D) removed 76 to 93%, and phosphate (Method E) 82.9 to 97.2% of the contamination. As pointed out previously [25], it is not the percentage of cocaine removed during decontamination but the amount remaining that matters. Cocaine was present after washing in all 38 hair samples. More importantly, benzoylecgonine (a purportedly definitive metabolite) was present in some samples, having been generated during the washing procedure. Although all of the hair samples washed with phosphate buffer were below the 0.5 ng/mg cutoff commonly used to determine a positive sample, this would be expected given the low exposure level to cocaine. Higher or longer exposure would be expected to produce higher amounts of remaining drugs in the hair and thereby defeat the cutoff criterion. In our early work, we showed that the higher the concentration of the cocaine exposure solution or the longer the exposure, the more drug was incorporated [14]. Schaffer et al. [48] recently reconfirmed the linear nature of the length of exposure and the amount of drug.

Baumgartner and Hill initially defined three wash criteria (termed Rc, Rsz, and Rew) by which one could distinguish external contamination from drug use during routine analysis [13]. Later, they added one more criterion (termed Resz) for more forensic or questioned samples. These criteria are defined in Table 2.2. The curvature

---

* Schaffer et al. [46, 48] report in several places that they use 0.5*M* phosphate at pH 6.0 for washing the hair. This appears to be a misprint, and the more standard 0.01*M* phosphate is assumed. If this were correctly reported, then this is yet another change in the procedure. A higher salt concentration may further weaken any ionic bonding of the drugs with the hair and increase the removal rate.

** Schaffer et al. [45, 47] report using 40°C to maintain the temperature inside the extraction tubes at 37°C. Although plastic may allow slower temperature equilibrium with the inner extraction solvent and the water bath than glass, higher temperatures are not used for glass tubes. If this were a great concern, simply prewarming the extraction buffer would solve this problem.

TABLE 2.1
Summary of the Decontamination Procedures of Baumgartner et al.

Method Designation	Procedure	Comments	Reference
A	10-min shampoo and ten distilled-water rinses; hair extracted; extracts analyzed by radioimmunoassay (RIA)	earliest description of hair decontamination; refluxing for 4 h in ethanol was used for the cocaine extraction; only used RIA for cocaine analysis	Baumgartner et al. [52]
B	15-min ethanol wash; two 30-min phosphate washes; hair digested; digests analyzed by RIA	earliest description of hair decontamination with phosphate buffer; 10m*M* phosphate (pH 7) at 37°C; 5–10 mg of hair was used in 1 ml of solvent; the ethanol must be "dry"; only Rew calculated and must be above 5[a]; only used RIA on the digest	Baumgartner and Berka [53]
C	15-min ethanol wash; three 30-min phosphate washes; hair digested, and digests analyzed by GC-MS	10m*M* phosphate (pH 5.6, later 5.5) at 37°C using shaking at 100 rpm; however, the shaking rate has varied among researchers; 25 mg of hair was used in 2 ml of solvent; this amount has varied down to 12 mg; the ethanol must be "dry"	Baumgartner, Hill, and Blahd [19]
D	15-min isopropanol wash; three 30-min phosphate washes	isopropanol substituted for ethanol because of concern for forming cocaethylene during analysis, a more definitive "metabolite" of cocaine; this procedure was presumably for routine analysis; the isopropanol must be "dry"	Baumgartner and Hill [13]
E	15-min isopropanol wash; three 30-min phosphate washes; two 1-h phosphate washes	extended wash criteria employed for questioned samples; alleged to decontaminate the "semiaccessible domain" of hair; Resz now used	Baumgartner and Hill [54]
F	15-min isopropanol wash; three 30-min phosphate washes; two 1-h phosphate washes; hair digested, and digests analyzed by LC-MS/MS	procedure appears similar to the previous procedure, except BSA (0.01%) was added to the phosphate buffer (now pH 6) and about 12 mg of hair must be used[b]; only the last phosphate wash is analyzed, so that Rc, Rsz, and Resz cannot be calculated; instead a new criterion is substituted (Rnc), wherein 5 times the concentration of the last phosphate wash (measured by RIA) is subtracted from the hair (measured by LC-MS/MS)[c]; if result is above the cutoff, then the sample is considered positive	Cairns et al. [47]

[a] Sometimes Rew is referred to as Rtew for truncated extended wash ratio.

[b] The addition of BSA should be explored further. If drugs are in equilibrium during washing with the buffer and binding sites on the hair, any binding element in solution can shift that equilibrium. BSA can bind drugs, therefore its addition can increase the decontamination rate. Activated charcoal or ion exchange resins are alternative choices and may have advantages as they can be physically removed and tested separately to measure removal rates.

TABLE 2.1 (continued)

[c] Apparently the washes are measured using an immunoassay and that value is subtracted from the hair measured by a specific assay such as LC-MS/MS. The scientific validity of this subtraction cocaethylene and not for BE, which is present in lower amounts than is the cocaine. Without the exact immunoassay it will be impossible to reproduce their method. Likewise, if the immunoassay is changed, a different lot may produce a slightly different result.

Note: The procedures have been modified by a number of authors over the years. Method F appears to be the procedure currently used commercially.

Note: The addition of BSA is interesting and should be explored further. If drugs are in equilibrium during washing with the buffer and binding sites on the hair, any binding element in solution can shift that equilibrium. BSA can bind drugs. Hence, its addition may increase the decontamination rate. Activated charcoal or ion-exchange resins are alternative choices and may have advantages, as they can be physically removed and tested separately to measure removal rates.

TABLE 2.2
Decontamination Criteria from Baumgartner and Hill

Criterion	Symbol	Mathematical Definition	Cutoff Value
Curvature ratio	Rc	amount of drug in the three phosphate washes = 3 × (amount of drug in last phosphate wash)	1.3
Extended wash ratio	Rew[1]	amount of drug in hair = amount of drug in last phosphate wash	10
Safety zone ratio	Rsz	amount of drug in hair = amount of drug in all phosphate washes	0.33
Extended safety zone ratio	Resz	amount of drug in hair = amount of drug in all phosphate washes	0.25
New criterion	Rnc	amount of drug in hair = 5 × (amount of drug in last phosphate wash)	0.5

Note: The Rc, Rew, and Rsz criteria were for production work and assumed three 30-min phosphate washes. The Resz criterion was used for forensic samples and required a further 2 h of washing. For a positive, all criteria must be met. The new criterion is applicable for Method F and is given the symbol Rnc for this chapter.

ratio is basically a measure of surface contamination. The higher the contamination, the higher is this number. The extended wash ratio and safety zone ratios are basically a measure of the extent of removal of the drug by the decontamination process.

We evaluated the curvature ratio, extended wash ratio, and safety zone ratio on 110 externally contaminated hair samples from nondrug users [14]. Essentially all exposed hair samples passed these criteria, with many by wide margins, indicating to us that these methods were insufficient in distinguishing external contamination. We also found that of all the criteria, the curvature ratio eliminated the most samples

TABLE 2.3
Blind Hair Samples Sent to a Commercial Laboratory

Hair Sample	Results	Commercial Result	Comments
Lab. prep	0.35	negative	below cutoff
Lab. prep	0.47	undetermined	use vs. contamination unknown
Lab. prep	0.44	negative	below cutoff
Lab. prep	2.1	1.1	should have been negative
Lab. prep	0.54	negative	negative by special procedures, probably no BE present
Known cocaine user in drug rehab	1.5	3.8	—
Known cocaine user 1	0.847	undetermined	insufficient hair to determine contamination or use
Child 1	5.58	40.6	—
Known cocaine user 2	0.089	negative	below cutoff
Child 2	0.08	negative	below cutoff
Child 2b	0.092	negative	below cutoff
Known cocaine user 3	0.137	undetermined	use vs. contamination unknown
Child 3	14.4 (103)	100.3	initial analysis was low; upon reanalysis, using a modified procedure, 103 ng cocaine/mg hair was found
Child 6	0.238	undetermined	use vs. contamination unknown
Child 6b	2.27	undetermined	use vs. contamination unknown
Known cocaine user 4	0.572	undetermined	use vs. contamination unknown

Note: These samples consisted of negative hair, hair from known cocaine users, hair from the children of cocaine users, and negative hair exposed in the laboratory. All of the negative hair samples were negative and are not listed. The results are reported as ng cocaine/mg hair, with a positive cutoff level of 0.5 ng cocaine/mg hair.

because these laboratory-prepared positives were not highly contaminated and this ratio relies upon fresh contamination. Fresh contamination is more representative of a consistent drug user, where time has not elapsed for personal hygiene to remove the loosely bound surface contamination.

Our early work was criticized for not following the exact procedures specified, with the implication being that if only the procedures had been followed exactly, these contaminated hair samples would have been determined as contaminated [28]. We believe that the important parts of the published procedures were followed and that any minor modifications would not change the result [55]. To more fully evaluate wash kinetics and remove any doubt that proper procedures were being followed, we sent (in a blind fashion) negative hair samples, hair from known drug users, hair from the children of drug users, and negative hair exposed to drugs in our laboratory to a commercial laboratory for analysis. The results are shown in Table 2.3. Many of the hair samples from the users came back as contaminated (which was surprising) or as "use cannot be determined." However, one of the four negative hair samples, exposed in the laboratory, was reported as positive.

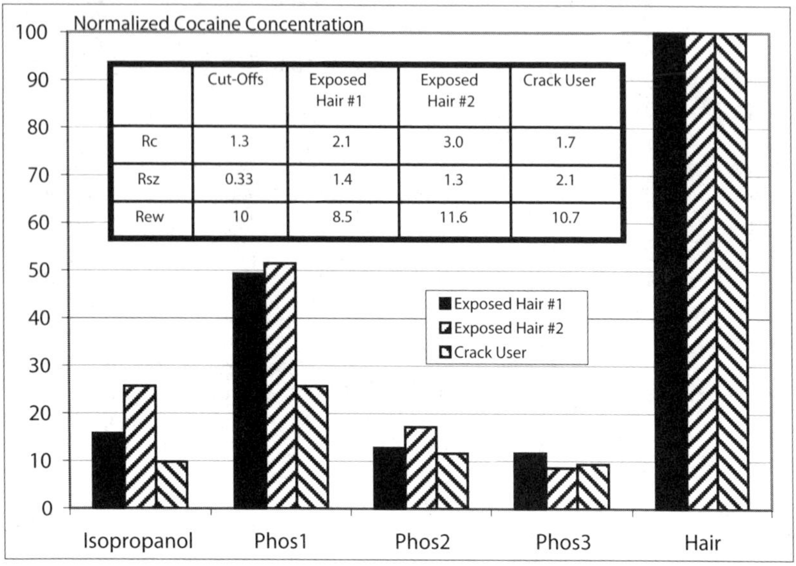

FIGURE 2.12 Normalized plots for two exposed hair samples and one from a cocaine user. The inset shows the calculated kinetic criteria. Only exposed sample 1 fails the Rew criterion. Visually, one would be hard-pressed to distinguish exposed sample 2 from the hair of the real cocaine user. (Data calculated from Mieczkowski, T., Distinguishing passive contamination from active cocaine consumption: assessing the occupational exposure of narcotics officers to cocaine, *Forensic Sci. Int.*, 84, 87–111, 1997. With permission.)

As part of controls for another study, Mieczkowski [56] sent exposed hair samples and a real user sample to a commercial laboratory for evaluation. Mieczkowski did not report the results (negative, positive, or contaminated). However, the values for the various wash solutions were provided, allowing one to perform the calculations. Figure 2.12 shows a normalized plot for the three control samples. Because the samples had differing amounts of drugs, the data were normalized to present a better visual pattern of how the drugs were washed out of the hair. One of the two externally exposed control samples would have passed all of the kinetic wash criteria in place at that time. In fact, the values are more positive than the hair from the real cocaine user.

Fresh contamination is easier to detect though wash kinetics. As depicted in Figure 2.7, time often passes after the contamination event before a hair test is taken. This time interval allows decontamination of the surface to occur though normal hygiene and degradation of the drug to potential "metabolites" (benzoylecgonine in the case of cocaine) through hydrolysis. Cairns et al. [47] contaminated six hair samples by exposing them to 10 μg/ml of cocaine for only 10 min. After exposure, the hair was stored for 3 days then decontaminated by shampooing intermittently. Analyses were performed at 1, 3, 8, and 16 days. The results for the four kinetic wash criteria are shown in Figure 2.13. Most of the specimens fail extended wash ratio (Rew), but Rew can be increased by increasing the exposure time. Even with the unreasonably brief exposure (10 min) used to contaminate these samples, one sample passed all the older wash criteria and still quantitated above the cutoff level

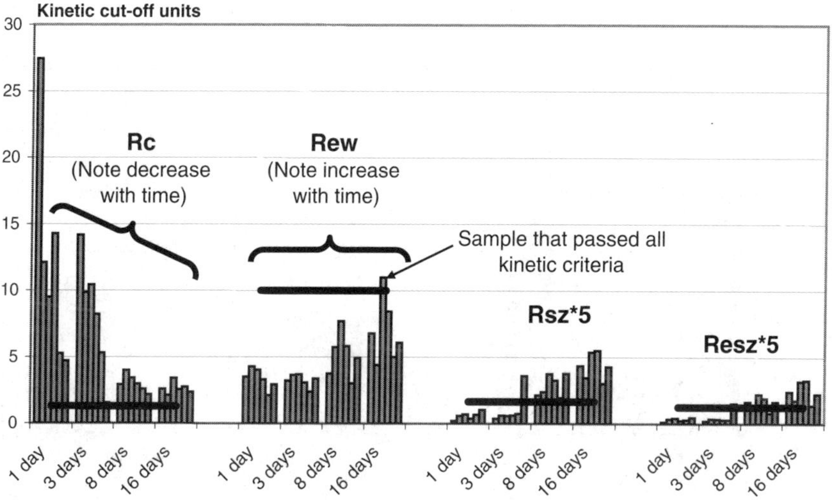

FIGURE 2.13 Calculated Rc, Rew, and Rsz for six cut-hair samples exposed to 10 μg/ml of cocaine for only 10 min. The results of the truncated kinetic analysis are presented by reconstructing the data. After 8 days the hair was shampooed three times, and after 16 days a total of six times. For the first 3 days, no hygiene was performed. Note that as time passes and more hygiene occurs, Rew and Rsz increase and approach a positive hair sample (the cutoff values are represented by the solid lines). Rc, which measures contamination, decreases with time and hygiene but is always above the cutoff value. The cutoff levels for Rsz and Resz were multiplied by 5 to place them on scale. (Data calculated from Cairns, T. et al., *Forensic Sci. Int.*, 145, 97, 2004. With permission.)

of 0.5 ng/mg. This specimen should then be called positive.* Surprisingly, many samples would *pass* the cutoff criteria of 0.5 ng/mg of hair if a cutoff *alone* were the determining factor, reinforcing that multiple criteria are helpful.**

To further evaluate the concept that time and personal hygiene are important factors in any attempt to distinguish contaminated hair from that of a drug user, Romano and coworkers [39] looked at decontamination vs. time after intentionally externally contaminating the hair of four subjects. Figure 2.14a shows the amount of drug remaining in the hair of four nondrug-using subjects after exposure to cocaine and after decontamination with methylene chloride and phosphate buffer. One procedure was that of Kintz and Mangin [57] using methylene chloride as the decontamination solvent and the other was similar to Method F in Table 2.1. Methylene chloride appears to only remove the loosely adhering cocaine. As time passes, normal hygiene also removes drug, leaving less for the methylene chloride to remove in absolute terms. The percent removed by the three methylene chloride washes compared with the amount remaining is shown in Figure 2.14b. Methylene chloride

* This sample would fail the new criterion (Rnc, Method F) by failing the cutoff level test. Some commercial testing, such as the Safety Net testing, uses the limit of detection (LOD) as the cutoff. For this analysis 0.02 ng/mg is the LOD, and several samples *will* pass this single criterion.

** Recall that the uptake in hair of drugs from solution is proportional to time and concentration, so increasing either would allow a greater incorporation of drug.

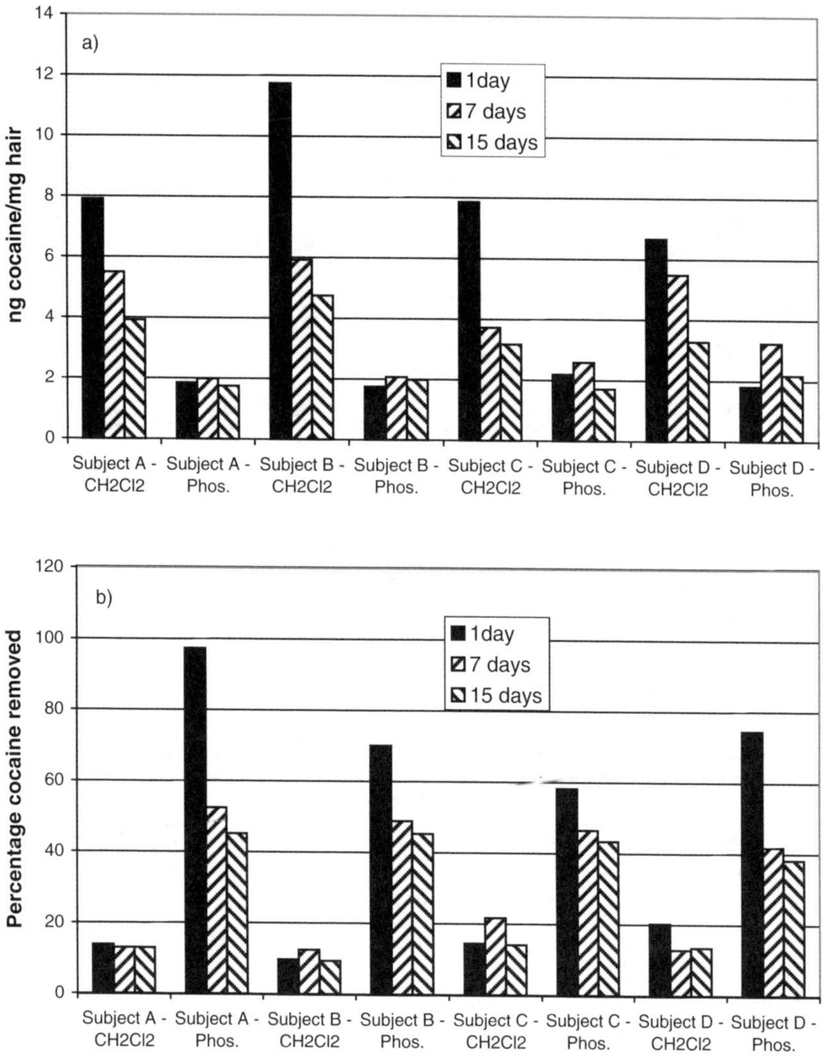

FIGURE 2.14 (a) Amount of cocaine in the hair of four externally contaminated subjects after washing with either methylene chloride or phosphate buffer. (b) The percent removed compared with the total for each procedure. The hair was originally contaminated by having four drug-free subjects place 10 mg of cocaine HCl (1/10 of a dose) on their hands and rub their hair. Hair was collected after various times. The hairs were decontaminated with either three methylene chloride washes or multiple phosphate washes (a total of eight). (Data calculated from Romano, G. et al., *Forensic Sci. Int.*, 123, 119, 2001. With permission.)

appears to be equally as effective as the phosphate buffer in removing the loosely bound drug. In contrast, phosphate buffer appears to remove all the loosely bound drug and some of the more tightly bound material. As time passes and as the individual washes his or her hair repeatedly, the amount of loosely bound drug diminishes and the effectiveness of phosphate buffer decreases (Figure 2.14b). This is also evident in the amount of cocaine left after the phosphate buffer washes appear to plateau (reaching a remarkably consistent value), reflecting the higher binding of the cocaine to the inner hair, possibly to the melanin. A similar effect for phosphate buffer can be seen in Figure 2.13, where the lower value for Rc with time reflects the poorer ability of phosphate buffer to remove external contamination.

Romano et al. [39] have been criticized for not following the proper procedures [47] in three areas. (1) The use of too many wash solutions. Their use of too many wash solutions appears to be because they were trying to replicate an older procedure and is not a fatal error. Romano provided quantitation on all the solutions. Because drugs not extracted by a given wash solution must be left in the hair, the values for the extra wash solutions can be combined to reproduce many of the wash procedures outlined in Table 2.1. (2) Improper temperature for decontamination. Romano reported using 45°C for the extraction procedure. Although this temperature better approximates warm water used for personal hygiene than does 37°C, a higher temperature could increase the extraction rate. I inquired if this was an error in the publication, and the coauthor Barbera replied that the temperature was actually 37°C, which is the temperature required. Furthermore, as evident in Table 2.1, that temperature is not set in stone. (3) Too much hair was used relative to the wash solution. Historically (see Table 2.1), up to 25 mg of hair had been extracted with 2 ml of buffer. Romano reported 100 mg in 5 ml of buffer. It is highly unlikely that this small difference can turn a positive sample negative, as the concentration of drugs in the hair is very small relative to the buffer volume. Therefore, the criticisms of Romano et al. are inconsequential.

In summary, hair can be contaminated with solutions of drugs such that these externally incorporated drugs are not removed with any decontamination procedure. Many of the arbitrary criteria have been foiled when contaminated hair is aged with time and hygiene. Certainly samples can be prepared in a laboratory that pass all relevant criteria. It is insufficient to only define where a given decontamination method works; you also need to know where it fails. Many more contamination/decontamination experiments must be performed before the precise envelope in which a certain procedure works and fails is known. These experiments need to be carried out even if the contamination scenarios are not relevant to preconceived notions about real-life conditions.

2.6 CUTOFFS AND WHY THEY MATTER

Cutoff levels for drugs in hair are a crucial part of the hair-testing process. A cutoff level is a number (concentration) at or above which a sample is called positive. Slightly below this level a sample must be reported as negative, even though a drug may be present. Cutoff levels are often arbitrarily set based on:

1. *Instrumental factors*: In routine testing, the performance of the test must be reproducible on a day-to-day basis. Setting a cutoff level too low will cause batch failures because the quality controls in a given batch will not quantitate properly.
2. *Regulatory requirements*: The Substance Abuse and Mental Health Services Administration (SAMHSA, the U.S. government agency tasked with regulating some aspects of drug testing) requires that a testing laboratory be

able to quantitate a sample at 40% of the cutoff level. Setting a requirement to be able to analyze a specimen below the cutoff level ensures that the laboratory has the required sensitivity and precision to detect and quantitate drugs at the cutoff level. Because of this 40% rule, setting a cutoff level at the limit of detection (LOD) is scientifically impossible.

3. *Policy*: Drug testing is frequently cited as being a deterrent to use rather than to identify drug users and to eliminate them from the workforce. Often, a drug-testing program is implemented because of a perceived problem in the workforce. An employer may resist firing substantial numbers of employees, opting instead to eliminate the most egregious drug users. Cutoff levels are one method to identify those frequent users of drugs because the higher amount of drug present in the biological matrix may correlate with more substantial use. This concept has some merit for an integrator of drug use, such as hair, but is less meaningful for self-cleaning matrices such as urine because the time of ingestion of the drug is unknown.
4. *Scientific and protective considerations*: Higher cutoff levels reduce the risk of environmental exposure and false positives from the presence of drugs rather than active use. However, higher cutoff levels are often balanced with the increased risk of missing infrequent or low-use individuals.

Historically, both analytical equipment and immunoassay screening have improved, so that lower cutoff levels now could be justified if the instrumental criterion were the sole determinant. With lower cutoff levels, more drug users would be identified but at the risk of identifying more passively exposed individuals. Cutoff levels should not be lowered arbitrarily without scientific support. SAMHSA, after consulting mainly with commercial hair-testing companies, has proposed the cutoff levels for hair testing that are listed in Table 2.4. The Society of Hair Testing [58] has proposed somewhat different cutoff levels,* and their criteria are also given in Table 2.4.

Ideally a cutoff level should be set only for scientific purposes. It should be set sufficiently low such that the majority of individuals using drugs are detected and sufficiently high that nonusing individuals in the presence of drugs are not identified as positive. All too often, when developing a new technology, cutoff levels are set for the above reasons 1, 2, and 3 because the required false-positive data (reason 4) has not been obtained. In contrast, drug levels are measured in individuals known to be ingesting drugs or who were purposely given drugs in an experimental setting. These levels from drug users are then used to set the cutoff levels ignorant of the contamination levels faced by individuals in many real-life environments.

One alternative to controlled-dose studies (which are expensive and limited in the number of subjects) is to examine the drug level in a given matrix in the general population (such as data from employment drug screens). Where passive exposure is possible, this approach cannot be used. For example, say that the drug, ethyl alcohol, was an illicit substance (as it was during Prohibition in the U.S. in the 1920s, which regulated drinking alcohol but not products with <0.5% alcohol, products containing

* A considerable amount of discussion at the Third European Conference on Hair Analysis, Crete, October 6–8, 2003, went into these cutoff levels, as some research argued that they were not sufficiently high to protect against passive exposure, while others argued that they were too high to measure exposure.

TABLE 2.4
Proposed Cutoff Levels for Various Drugs in the Confirmation Assay

Drug	Analyte	SAMHSA[a] Cutoff Level (ng drug/mg hair)	SOHT[b] Cutoff Level (ng drug/mg hair)	Comments
Marijuana	delta-9-tetrahydro-cannabinol-9-carboxylic acid	0.05	0.0002 (THC-COOH) 0.05 (THC)	Although this is a specific metabolite, it is recommended that delta-9 THC be measured to determine contamination levels and external removal; achieving these trace levels requires extraction of a considerable amount of hair
Cocaine	cocaine	0.5	0.5	BE/cocaine ratio must be greater than 5%, or CE or NC must be present; the SOHT does not make a recommendation as to the BE/cocaine ratio
	benzoylecgonine (BE)	>5% of cocaine level	0.05	
	cocaethylene (CE)	0.05	0.05	
	norcocaine (NC)	0.05	0.05	
Opiates	morphine	0.2	0.2	Morphine must be present if 6-MAM is detected
	codeine	0.2	0.2	
	6-acetylmorphine (6-MAM)	0.2	0.2	
PCP	PCP	0.3	No data	—
Amphetamines	amphetamine	0.3	0.2	Amphetamine must be also present in hair from a methamphetamine user; a *d,l* analysis can be done; see: Nystrom et al. [59]
	methamphetamine	0.3	0.2	
	MDMA	0.3	0.2	
	MDA	0.3	0.2	
	MDEA	0.3	0.2	

[a] The proposed SAMHSA (Substance Abuse and Mental Health Services Administration) levels are from: Proposed Revisions to Mandatory Guidelines for Federal Workplace Drug Testing Programs, *Federal Register*, 69, no. 71, 19673–19732 (13 April 2004).

[b] The SOHT levels are from the Society of Hair Testing, Recommendations for hair testing in forensic cases, *Forensic Sci. Int.*, 145, 83–84, 2004.

denatured alcohol, or wine used for religious purposes, among other things) and the vast information on its presence in the human body was unknown. Also, suppose that you had just invented a breath test for alcohol and wished to detect alcohol abusers. You might test the breath of many people and find that the levels vary widely. Because you were confident in the instrumentation, you believed that you could reliably detect alcohol at 10 mg/dl blood equivalents in breath, and therefore you set the cutoff level at this value. Would you have tested sufficient numbers of people to distinguish the few mouthwash users, the few sacramental wine drinkers, or the few individuals with natural alcohol levels due to food consumption at this level? Probably not. And even if you did, how could you distinguish these few individuals from those who intentionally consumed sufficient alcohol to get drunk — a group that your breath test can clearly detect — if the samples were being sent to a distant laboratory for analysis? You cannot. Although studying populations to measure levels and get a distribution of possible values has merit, studying populations to demonstrate that a drug test has validity is clearly wrong, because you cannot know the source of the positive result when passive exposure can occur. In the case of alcohol, your test would have been used to identify people intentionally consuming alcohol rather than inadvertently consuming trace amounts. A large distinction between this hypothetical example and a hair test for drugs is that individuals in the breath test would have needed to consume alcohol in some manner (even though the three sources of alcohol given above were allowed during Prohibition), and therefore some physiological effect could be claimed. In the case of hair testing, an individual only needs to be in the presence of drugs for passive exposure to occur and a false positive generated. No physiological effect, even a small one, can be claimed based on surface contamination.

From the above example, it is clear that even if a cutoff level were set after extensive clinical trials and exhaustive analytical work, that cutoff may not protect certain individuals from falsely being labeled as an alcohol user because the passive-exposure amounts and severity would be unknown.

Because alcohol needed to be consumed for a positive test, controlled studies could define the minimum level of consumption (with large uncertainty) to reach that cutoff value. If this level is sufficiently removed from normal dietary sources of alcohol, then that cutoff level would provide some protection from false accusation of drug use. This approach has been taken for opiate analysis in urine, where poppy seeds can contribute to a false positive. Early in the Department of Defense (DoD) urinalysis program, it was thought that the morphine contained in poppy seeds was present in too small an amount to generate an opiate positive. In fact, testing the urine of several individuals who consumed poppy seeds failed to detect opiates. The morphine cutoff level was set at 300 ng/ml for many of the reasons set forth above. For reasons still unknown, an increase in the number of opiate positives was observed in 1986. Not only did the individuals deny use, but their stories were credible. Later it was learned that some kinds of poppy seeds contain large amounts of opiates, depending upon the country of origin, thoroughness of seed cleaning, and method of preparation. For an individual to be positive, these poppy seeds must be eaten in sufficient quantities by an individual with a high absorption rate for opiates and shortly before a urine test is administered. As a result of these false positives, procedures were put in place for a medical review officer to evaluate each positive opiate urinalysis for supporting evidence of opiate use, while the cutoff level for morphine remained at 300 ng/ml. A sufficient number of reviews needed to occur such that demands were placed on the suspected drug users (to travel for a face-to-face medical review and the stigma attached), their commands (to find job replacements while the review took place), and the medical community (to supply the trained reviewers) to cause concern. The cutoff level was then raised substantially to 4000 ng/ml. Even at this level, it was shown scientifically that one could reach this cutoff by ingesting poppy seeds. However, this higher cutoff level reduced the burden on the medical review process such that it is now infrequent. Note that in this example for urinalysis, the cutoff level was adjusted to reduce false positives even though some individuals who illicitly used opiates *would go undetected.*

In the case of hair testing, the conditions under which drugs may be incorporated from the environment in real-world settings remain unknown, largely unstudied, and hard to model in experimental settings. As discussed in greater detail in other sections, some factors have been identified from laboratory-exposure studies that increase the drug uptake in hair. Besides the presence of a drug, what is especially important is the presence of moisture either during the exposure or after. Moisture allows the hair proteins to swell (opening holes in the cuticle shell) and provides a transport vehicle for movement of the drug into hair through diffusion. Both the timing and amount of moisture from sweat, hygiene, and humidity is so variable that no experimental studies could entail all possibilities. Several attempts have been made to mimic exposure under somewhat real-world conditions. In two sets of experiments, Romano et al. [39] placed either cocaine or heroin on the hands of subjects and had them rub their hair with their contaminated hands. The hair was tested frequently for the drugs and metabolites. In the case of cocaine, four subjects were studied, and after 70 days, all had measurable levels of cocaine (range 0.8 to 2.5 ng/mg) as well as benzoylecgonine (range 0 to 0.9 ng/mg), which increased with time, presumably from natural degradation, as only pure cocaine was initially present. The amounts decreased in an exponential manner due to hygienic removal and new hair growth (Figure 2.15). In the case of heroin, heroin was applied to six subjects. After 99 days, morphine and 6-MAM were detectable at levels ranging from 0.15 to 1.2 ng/mg. Like cocaine, the drug concentrations decreased in an exponential manner with time. These two studies conclusively demonstrate that fractions of a single dose of drugs can produce, for extended periods of time, positive hair results that greatly exceed the cutoff levels listed in Table 2.4.

Studies like that of Romano et al. [39] should be considered to define the amount of drugs where passive exposure will be a concern (10 mg will definitely cause concern). Studies like that of Smith et al. [37] should be considered to measure exposure in drug-containing environments and also in the general population using skin swabs. One cannot easily determine if a surveyed individual has drugs on their skin, because they could be a drug user, and a urine test would be required. Furthermore, just surveying individuals using hair testing may run the risk that a portion of the drugs in the hair can come from external exposure.

Not all positive hair analysis results are due to passive exposure. Many positive hair analysis results are due to ingestion of drugs. The discussion in this section clearly illustrates that interpretation of the data must take passive exposure into consideration to determine the source of drugs in any one positive result; cutoffs alone are insufficient, even in decontaminated hair.

2.7 BIAS IN HAIR TESTING

2.7.1 Definition of Bias

Of considerable concern in the U.S. is the equal treatment of racial/ethnic groups, especially those that have been at an historical disadvantage. Bias in drug testing can be defined as an increased likelihood of detecting one group of individuals over

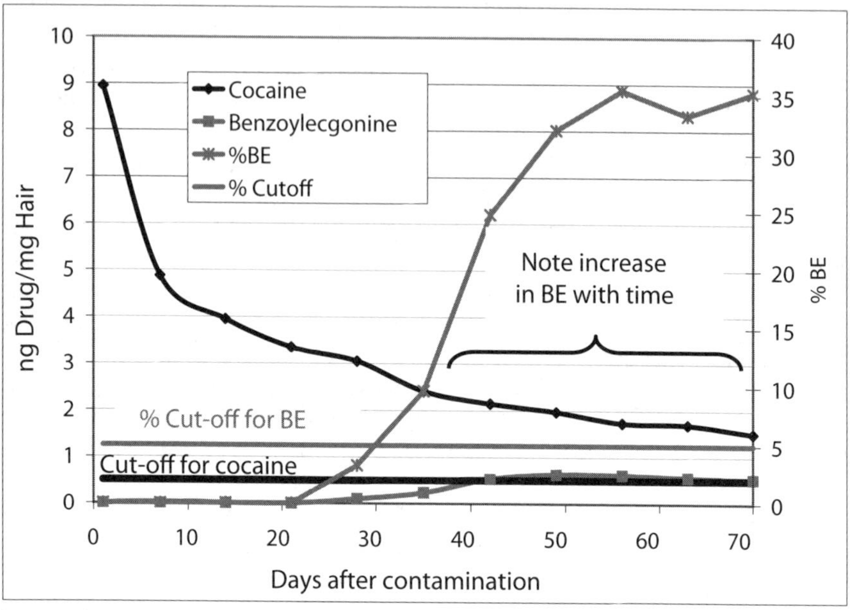

FIGURE 2.15 Average cocaine and benzoylecgonine concentrations in hair of four externally contaminated subjects. Normal hygiene is part of the decontamination process. Therefore, rigorous decontamination in the lab analysis is not as critical. One subject routinely washed his/her hair with vinegar, and no benzoylecgonine formed. Cocaine is known to be more stable in acidic environments. It is possible that either the vinegar removed the BE or that the acid conditions slowed the cocaine hydrolysis. (Would this happen in real drug users?) This subject was excluded from the BE average line. All subjects would have been positive for at least 70 days after exposure under the proposed SAMHSA cutoff for cocaine only, and all would have been positive for the last 40 days if the 5% BE rule were in effect. (Data obtained from Romano, G. et al., *Forensic Sci. Int.*, 123, 119, 2001. With permission.)

another when both have comparable use or exposure. Bias in hair testing can come in two disguises: (1) Two individuals ingest the same amount of drug but, due to biological or genetic reasons, one individual does not incorporate as much of that drug into his/her hair. Upon testing, that lower-incorporating individual escapes detection. (2) Two individuals are not drug users but are exposed to drugs from their living conditions. Due to biological, cultural, or genetic reasons, one individual incorporates drugs into their hair more readily from the environment and retains them longer compared with the other individual. Upon testing, that individual with the higher rate of incorporation is accused of drug use when he/she was actually passively exposed.

Several researchers have demonstrated that different hair samples, when exposed under identical *in vitro* conditions, incorporate diverse amounts of drugs [14, 20, 25, 61–63]. As shown in Figure 2.16, incorporation of cocaine varies among individual hair samples. Generally, the hair of Caucasian males or females incorporates much less drugs than the hair of many African Americans. When the *in vitro* results similar

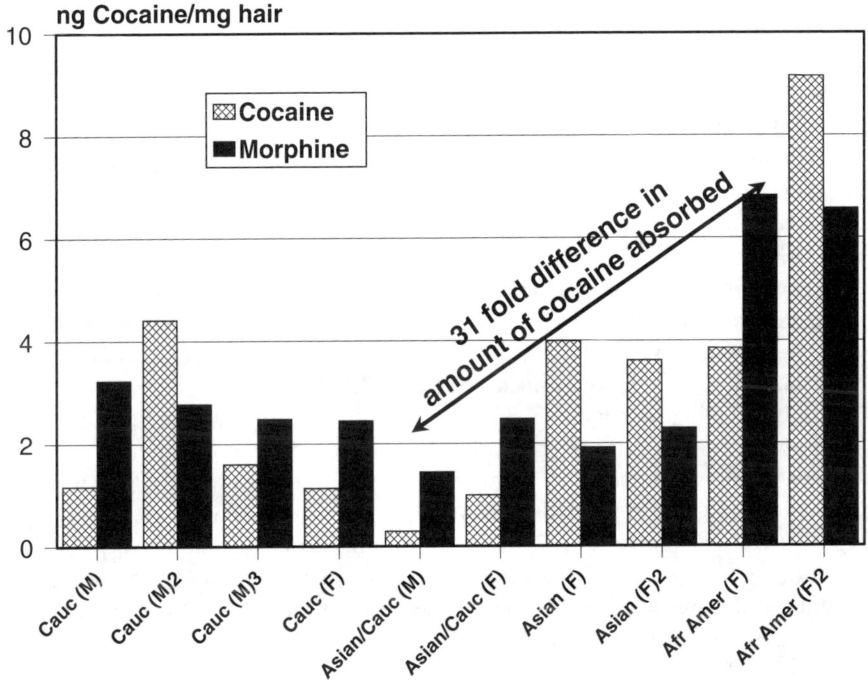

FIGURE 2.16 Incorporation of cocaine into hair of different types. The hair samples were exposed to 5 μg/ml cocaine containing a tritiated tracer for 1 h at 37°C in phosphate buffer at pH 5.6. After decontamination with ethanol and three phosphate buffer washes, the hair was digested and the radioactivity measured. (Figure from Kidwell, D.A. et al., *Forensic Sci. Int.*, 107, 93, 2000. With permission.)

to Figure 2.16 were first presented, numerous authors concluded incorrectly that drug incorporation was correlated with hair color [65–70]. In a limited sample, we observed that the incorporation of cocaine and morphine is not well correlated to hair color. For example, the black hair from the Asian-Caucasian male absorbed much less cocaine or morphine than the black hair from the African-American female, yet the colors were similar on inspection.

Khumalo et al. [71] compared black African hair with those from Caucasians and Asians and noted morphological differences. Some of these differences may account for differential drug binding. For example, light microscopic and scanning electron microscopic examination of over 2000 black African hair samples revealed a tightly interwoven mat of hair shafts. Participants' hair had not been cut for at least one year, and they had used no chemical treatments, limiting grooming to shampooing, drying, and combing. Examination of the African hairs showed that many shafts were knotted (10 to 16% vs. 0.15%) and appeared broken in comparison with hair from Caucasians and Asians. In addition, African hairs exhibited interlocking features. Combing, washing, and brushing cause physical degradation of the hair, as does exposure to weathering (see the example of the damage to the cuticle from wet-combing in Figure 2.4c) [72]. Hair-shaft breakage observed among black Africans is well documented in the cosmetic literature [73], in that each twist is a stress point prone to structural damage. Joseph et al. [63] observed that dark Africoid hair had 5 to 43 times more binding capacity than light Caucasoid hair, which they attributed to melanin-binding sites. Part of this observation may hinge on hair-shaft damage, which was not characterized. Hair-shaft damage increases drug binding because drugs must first penetrate the cuticle, and this penetration is aided by the damage.

The very characteristics of African hair that make it more susceptible to damage from combing, brushing, washing, etc., make it more susceptible to damage from cosmetic treatments and chemicals as well, such as hot-curl straightening [74], perming, swimming pool water, bleaching, and dyeing [72, 75]. Damage from perming is known to increase cocaine uptake [48]. Formulas for chemical straightening or relaxing hair include sodium hydroxide solutions, salts of thioglycolic acid/hydrogen peroxide, and guanidine hydroxide [76]. Straightening or perming of hair requires that the disulfide bonds in the proteins be broken with a reducing agent (thioglycolic acid) and reformed in a different pattern with an oxidizing agent (hydrogen peroxide) [77]. Only some of these disulfide bonds re-form when the hair is reoxidized in the perming process (the rest tend to be oxidized to sulfinic and sulfonic acids). For these chemical reasons, inaccessible regions that have been argued to exist before the cosmetic treatment certainly do not exist afterward [33].

Other severe treatments to hair include bleaching and dyeing chemicals, which contain 6% hydrogen peroxide. Permanent hair dye containing hydrogen peroxide causes extensive cuticular detachment and holes of various sizes in the endocuticle [78]. Chemical straightening also disrupts the hair's protective cuticle and makes hair more porous and permeable [79]. The resulting damage from all of these cosmetic treatments to black African hair requires the use of ethnic hair conditioners, petrolatum, and similar products, which retail stores stock on entire ethnic-product aisles due to their popularity among African Americans, to whom they are extensively marketed [80]. Many of these products can dissolve drugs, such as cocaine, or provide a softening of the hair to enhance drug penetration. Surface treatments would make external contamination more problematic with treated black African hair, as the ethnic conditioners trap and concentrate the drugs on the surface, effectively providing a long-term exposure after only a brief contamination. Additionally, African Americans frequently do not wash their hair as often as others because of potential cosmetic damage and a lower production of sebum that needs removal [14]. So in general for African Americans, there are four factors that can combine to increase the bias for passive exposure. They are: (1) high melanin content that aids cocaine binding, (2) damaged hair that allows access to the sites for binding, (3) hair surface treatments that enhance the transfer of drugs from the environment to the surface of the hair and within, and (4) less frequent removal of contamination by normal hygiene.

We originally referred to the observed bias shown in Figure 2.16 as "matrix bias" or "hair-type bias" due to hair color and texture differences [81]. Other authors then reinterpreted this bias by the more inflammatory term of "racial bias"

[66], which in the context of U.S. policy has strong implications [82].* In a general scheme, we have proposed that the uptake and retention of drugs by hair has at least four components that may differ among cultural groups: (1) permeability and other characteristics of the hair due to genetic influences, (2) use of cosmetic hair treatments and hair-care habits (which may be culturally influenced), (3) removal of drugs during personal hygiene, and (4) route of administration of the drugs (intravenous, internasal, oral, or smoking), with associated passive exposure to the drugs from the environment and during use. Many of these components are influenced by the personal habits of groups of individuals rather than genetic characteristics. Therefore, a better term for the differences in uptake and retention of drugs is "cultural bias" rather than racial or matrix bias, reflecting the likely contributions of the various components [64]. As mentioned above, many of these factors *can* combine (depending on the scenario for a given individual) to disfavor African Americans.

For bias to be observed in hair analysis of drug users, two criteria must be present: (1) low-dose/exposure (at high doses all samples are positive) and (2) different incorporation rates of drugs and different binding capacities for drugs in various hair samples. Figure 2.17a and Figure 2.17b give theoretical distributions of two populations, arbitrarily distinguished as light hair and dark hair, and demonstrate how bias can be generated. In Figure 2.17a, assume that the population is a low-use-rate population and that the dark-haired population incorporates drug into their hair at twice the rate as the light-haired population. Depending upon the cutoff level (concentration where a sample is considered positive), virtually no bias (0.5%) to complete bias (100% bias) is observed. Figure 2.17b presents theoretical distributions of a high-use population where the mean values of the dark hair are

* An example of the appearance of racial bias and the controversy that it engendered can be found in the sentencing guidelines for crack cocaine. In 1986 the U.S. Congress passed legislation adopting mandatory sentencing guidelines for the possession of crack cocaine in the wake of widespread media attention on the crack cocaine problem. A first-time offender with a conviction of possession with intent to distribute 5 g or more of crack cocaine faced a 5-year mandatory minimum sentence, whereas the same sentence for powdered cocaine would be reached at 500 g. This 1:100 disparity in amounts has caused much public concern. The result of a complex interaction of statutes and sentencing guidelines is that crack cocaine defendants are more likely to be sentenced to prison and, on average, receive much longer sentences than powder cocaine offenders. There is a racial disparity in cocaine use patterns, with blacks preferring crack cocaine and whites preferring powder cocaine.
The United States Sentencing Commission noted:

> In 1993, Whites account for 30.8 percent of all convicted federal drug offenders, Blacks 33.9 percent, and Hispanics 33.8 percent. Sentencing patterns for some drugs show high concentrations of a particular racial or ethnic group. Most strikingly, crack cocaine offenders are 88.3 percent Black. Conversely, methamphetamine offenders are 84.2 percent White. Powder cocaine cases involve sizeable proportions of Whites (32.0%), Blacks (27.4%), and Hispanics (39.3%). Among defendants convicted of simple possession, 58 percent of powder defendants were White, 26.7 percent were Black, and 15 percent were Hispanic. Among crack defendants, 10.3 percent were White, 84.5 percent were Black, and 5.2 percent were Hispanic.

Public dismay over this apparent racial disparity in law enforcement reached a high enough level such that U.S. Congress directed the U.S. Sentencing Commission to reexamine the sentencing guidelines. The result of this study was a reduced distinction between, but not an elimination of, sentencing for the two forms of cocaine. For a much more detailed discussion of this issue, see [74].

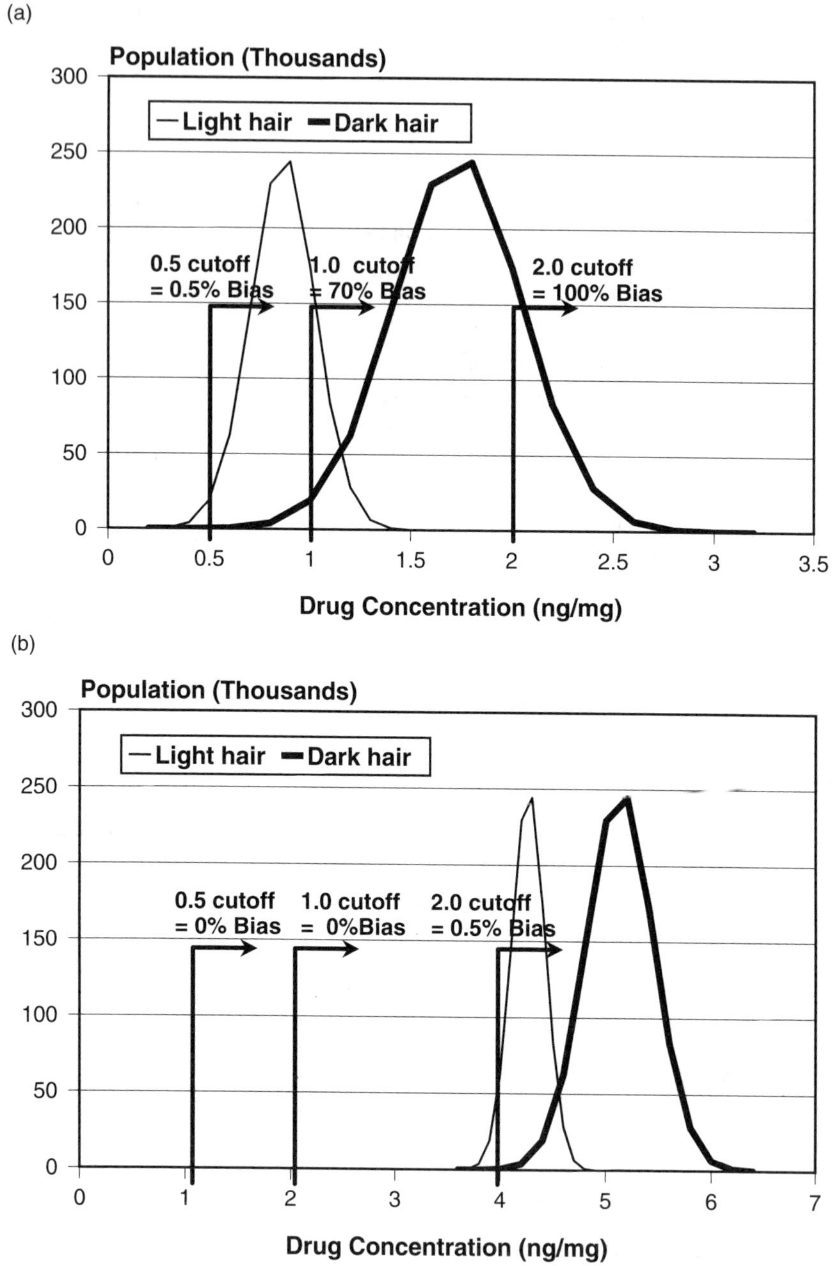

FIGURE 2.17 How bias occurs. The cutoff level interacts with the hair uptake rate to generate apparent bias. Theoretical plots representing (a) low-use/exposure individuals with dark hair levels showing incorporation at 2× light hair levels and (b) high-use/exposure individuals with dark hair levels only 16% greater than light hair levels. The percentage bias is calculated from the equation: (1 − [% light positive]/[% dark positive]) × 100. (Figure plotted from Kidwell, D.A. et al., *Forensic Sci. Int.*, 107, 93, 2000. With permission.)

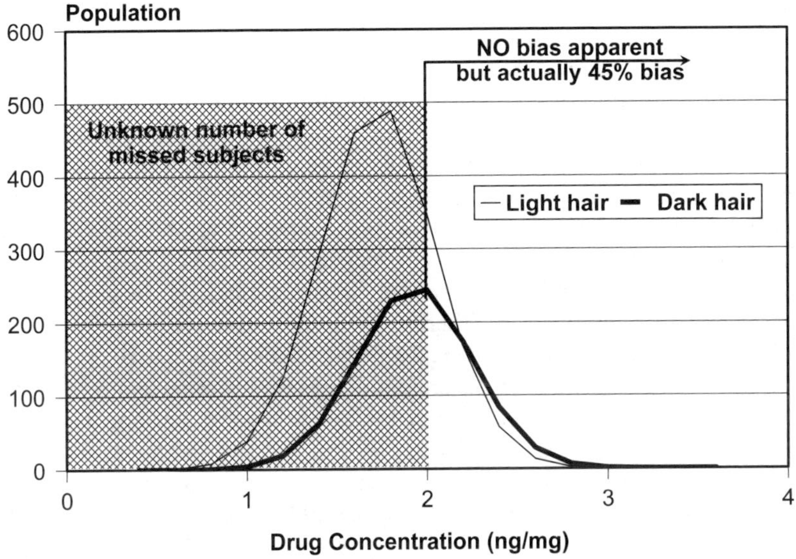

FIGURE 2.18 Theoretical distribution illustrating how the complete distribution of drug concentrations is necessary to determine bias. The light-haired population was twice that of the dark-haired population and was assumed to have a 12% lower mean concentration. Both groups have the same Gaussian distributions and standard deviation. However, any distributions with different shapes can introduce bias. (Figure plotted from Kidwell, D.A. et al., *Forensic Sci. Int.*, 107, 93, 2000. With permission.)

only 16% greater than the light hair. Bias would not be observed in Figure 2.17b because most individuals would be above any of the cutoff levels specified.

Some authors have compared only hair samples above the cutoff level and their distributions to prove the absence of bias from cocaine use [83]. However, such a comparison can be misleading. The number of individuals that used drugs, but were not detected, is unknown. Figure 2.18 illustrates two theoretical distributions with the mean of the dark-haired population 12% greater than the mean of the light-haired population. Because the number of drug users being undetected (under the shaded area) would be unknown, no bias would be apparent. However, if these missing individuals were included in the calculation, the bias increases to 45%. Unless the number of drug users can be verified in a controlled study and the uptake amount into hair determined, absolute bias cannot be calculated.

The cutoff level plays an important role in generating bias only if the two populations have a different drug incorporation rate and different binding capacities for drugs. To avoid this type of bias, the cutoff level must be set so that *all* drug users are detected. Unfortunately, the cutoff level cannot be made arbitrarily low without detecting an increased number of passively exposed individuals — individuals in mere contact with drugs rather than actively ingesting them [37, 84–88]. Thus, the cutoff level must be adjusted to reduce identification of passively exposed individuals and yet identify a substantial number of drug users. By having a cutoff level above zero (or arbitrarily low), bias may be inherent in most technologies where different drug concentrations are detected from the same use. However, this does not appear to be the case for cocaine detection in urine [89].*

Alternatively, one might hypothesize that what appears as "bias" in hair testing could be due to use patterns rather than the analytical procedure, i.e., the dark-haired population having similar incorporation rates as the light-haired population but using twice as much drug. In this example, no bias should be claimed because the difference is potentially due to a factor under the control of the individual (the amount of his/her drug use). There are no data showing differing use rates (as opposed to differing use preferences) among differing populations based on race.

Another hypothesis for any observed bias in populations might be the preferences of drug administration routes by differing groups. For example, if the black-haired populations in Figure 2.18a and Figure 2.18b hypothetically preferred crack cocaine whereas the light-haired individuals preferred powdered cocaine hydrochloride *and* if there were a difference in incorporation rates and binding capacity based on the chemical form of the drug, then a bias may be observed, even at the same dose rates. However, there is no evidence that crack cocaine incorporates into hair any differently than powdered cocaine due to its bioavailability. To the contrary, when studying different routes of administration of cocaine, Henderson et al. [26] found that cocaine levels in hair do not correlate well with bioavailability of the drug.

2.7.2 Bias is Not Observed in Convenience Studies

Mieczkowski et al. [92–94] found no bias in their convenience studies.** However, in their analysis, they use data from a commercial company that provided no clear and objective measure of color despite Mieczkowski's analysis requiring accurate hair color. Furthermore, hair color is only tangentially related to race. In a more recent paper, Kelley and coworkers [83] attempted to address this criticism by obtaining the race of the donor. No racial or hair-color differences were found. They did observe a drug preference in their study, where the Caucasian individuals tended to favor use of amphetamines and the African-American individuals favored the use of cocaine. However, this also was a nonrandom sample of individuals, as only when individuals did not have a photo ID present during the drug test was a picture recorded from which the race and hair color were discerned. Again in this study, it appears that hair color was not objectively measured. For example, dyed hair would

* Some have argued that, because females can have different metabolism rates for cocaine than males (see: Kouri, E.M., et al., Effects of oral contraceptives on acute cocaine response in female volunteers, *Pharmacol. Biochem. Behav.*, 74, 173, 2002; see also: Lukas, S.E., et al., Sex differences in plasma cocaine levels and subjective effects after acute cocaine administration in human volunteers, *Psychopharmacology*, 125, 346, 1996), urine tests also may show bias. This ignores the cutoff level in determining bias. A better choice for bias could be that of laboratories ratioing drug concentrations to creatinine to account for physiological dilution. This could be biased against females (dividing by a smaller number) who, on average, have lower urine creatinine levels than males.

** A convenience study is a sociological term referring to data obtained for other purposes or a group of individuals not selected in a controlled manner. An example of this would be selecting everyone who walks though the door of a supermarket for some survey and then trying to extrapolate that sample to the general population. Such sampling can be biased, as illustrated by the famous newspaper headline "Dewey Wins" (against Harry Truman in the 1948 U.S. presidential race).

skew the results. Another explanation for the failure of these authors to detect bias may be that the individuals undergoing testing use considerable amounts of drugs, and therefore all tests are positive. Many of these samples were from individuals who were either recently arrested or undergoing a preemployment screen. In both cases, it would be a very unlucky individual who was arrested on his or her first drug use or could not stop using drugs before a known preemployment drug-test. Logically, these are frequent drug users, and under those circumstances, a sufficiently low cutoff level will not detect bias (Figure 2.18). Therefore, the conclusion from these studies that racial bias in hair testing does not occur is questionable.

2.7.3 Bias Is Observed in Controlled-Dose Studies

In contrast to these convenience studies, a number of controlled-dose studies have been performed. Animal studies have shown differential incorporation of drugs into the hair of the animals based on color [95–98]. These studies have been ignored by some authors because animal hair is slightly different than human hair [99]. Drug users in outpatient maintenance have been examined, and significantly higher levels of cocaine in African-American subjects compared with Caucasian subjects have been reported [100, 101]. Henderson et al. [18, 102, 103] have completed *in vivo*, controlled-dosage studies with isotopically labeled cocaine on humans. When the average incorporated amounts are compared, Henderson et al. [102] concluded that there was a statistically significant difference between the mean amount of d5-cocaine incorporated into the non-Caucasian hair samples and the Caucasian hair samples (when one non-Caucasian was excluded from the data set). However, due to the limited number of individuals, coupled with the individual variability, the differences in race have been statistically weak. Others, looking at the same data set and using different mathematics, do not see a significant statistical association with race [93, 94]. For other drugs, a clear indication that hair color plays a role has been noted in controlled-dose studies [104–106].

2.7.4 Bias Due to Exposure

Hypothetically consider two people, say an African-American female and a Caucasian male. They both use drugs, and because of differential uptake in conjunction with cutoff levels, the African-American female is identified in a hair test as a drug user, whereas the Caucasian male is not. Contrast this with the situation where the same two individuals are in the *presence* of drugs (maybe unknowingly), get the same exposure, and again due to the differential uptake in conjunction with cutoff levels, the African-American female is identified in a hair test as a drug user, whereas the Caucasian male is not. The first scenario, use, is certainly unfair (but a drug user does get identified), and if it happens often enough, this is possible grounds for not using hair testing. However, the latter scenario, exposure, is a tragedy that should never happen because an innocent individual has her life, liberty, or livelihood at risk.

The issue of bias in exposure has never been studied in so-called large N studies, but it has been studied in laboratory situations. One form of bias is evident from Figure 2.16, where different hair "types" incorporate widely varying amounts of cocaine. In physical chemistry there are two concepts that apply to hair-exposure experiments: kinetics (rate of a reaction) and equilibrium (the product-reactant ratio at an infinite time). The requirements for hair to become contaminated are that drugs must first diffuse into the hair and then they must bind. Experiments in Figure 2.16 are really a rate measurement rather than an equilibrium measurement, because the time for exposure is short and the diffusion rate slow. An example of rate was discussed in Figure 2.3. If diffusion were rapid, Kidwell and Blank [17] and Schaffer et al. [48] would never have seen a linear increase in drug uptake with time. Instead, with a rapid rate, the amount of drug incorporated would plateau, with the plateau corresponding to the equilibrium binding capacity of the hair. Studies by Joseph et al. [107] reported a statistically significant difference between hair types, with African-American hair binding substantially more cocaine (ca. 2×) than Caucasian hair *at equilibrium*. More important is Joseph's observation that the *rate* of uptake in African-American hair is *faster*. Kinetics and equilibrium both have a direct bearing on bias [98]*.

We have postulated several factors — genetics, hair color, and cosmetic treatment (among others) — to account for the bias observed in Figure 2.16. To cause a hair positive for drugs, first there must be the opportunity for contamination to occur. Then the drugs must penetrate the cuticle and enter the cortex, which contains the melanin granules. Although melanin, and therefore hair color, plays a role in the final amount of binding (if equilibrium is reached), the first step is getting past the cuticle. As mentioned above, water (or sweat) is important in swelling the cuticle, which facilitates penetration of the drugs into the hair. Additionally, prior cosmetic treatment damages the cuticle (see Figure 2.4c) and reduces the requirement for water [108].** Some of the cosmetic treatments that are placed on cosmetically straightened hair to add shine and prevent breaking can enhance transfer and binding of drugs. This is practiced frequently by African-American females [109]. Most often, these treatments contain oil and glycerol. Glycerol serves as a replacement for water and is known to aid in drug transfer from keratin to an inert object [110].*** Furthermore, oil absorbs cocaine. Thus, those applying such materials to their hair have a ready system for hair contamination: the oil absorbs and concentrates cocaine from the environment; the glycerol swells the hair and provides a vehicle for drug transfer; the conditioning treatment is not replaced frequently, providing lengthy exposure times (such as 48 to 72 h); the damaged hair is less resistant to drug transfer; and binding of the drugs occurs inside the cortex, with melanin playing a role, as discussed below.****

* Joseph et al. [107] measured both the rate and the equilibrium level. African-American females took up drugs far faster than Caucasian females with the same hair color. This is likely due to cosmetic damage and what we termed "cultural bias." For most exposures, the equilibrium level would never be reached, as it takes days.

** Interestingly, Sagal [108] observed that treated African-American hair (with straightening agents) had more acid bind capability than untreated hair, but Caucasian hair had no similar differences.

*** In this case, drugs were transferred from skin, which contains similar proteins to hair, to a pad placed on the surface. This transfer was approximately twofold better with glycerol in the pad than sweat alone. Part of the reason is that glycerol remains (does not dry out), whereas the presence of sweat is transient. In a yet-unpublished study, we have confirmed that this transfer happens on a larger group of individuals in a real-life setting.

**** Most authors, including us, remove this cosmetic treatment before laboratory contamination experiments are done. This is partly to control the procedure better. Different laboratory pretreatments of the hair can account for differences in the uptake of drugs into hair. Additionally, hair is not available to provide standards, making comparisons between laboratories difficult.

TABLE 2.5
Incorporation of Cocaine into Melanin after Various Digestion Techniques

	Sodium Hydroxide Digestion		Enzyme Digestion	
Matrix	Asian Black Hair	Caucasian Brown Hair	Asian Black Hair	Caucasian Brown Hair
Hair digest without melanin	0.998	0.6	0.75	0.61
Melanin fraction alone	0.069	1.03	0.015	1

Note: Cocaine was incorporated by exposure for 1 h. Values are measured by radioisotope techniques and are in units of ng cocaine/mg hair. Little cocaine is associated with the melanin fraction.

Source: Data from Kidwell, D.A. and Blank, D.L., in Hair Testing for Drugs of Abuse: International Workshop on Standards and Technology, Cone, E.J. et al., Eds., National Institutes of Health, Publ. 95-3727, U.S. Government Printing Office, Washington, DC, 1995, p. 19.

We have proposed two methods to rank hair on its damage and possibly correct for drug uptake in some hair types [64]. One method involves exposing the hair during the wash process to drug surrogates (such as deuterated drugs or halogenated derivatives) in the wash solutions. The surrogates would be incorporated into the hair in a similar fashion to the drug exposure experiments discussed above. During the analysis, the surrogate would be quantitated, and thereby some measure of porosity and binding capability of that hair type could be determined. This procedure would have the advantage of being readily incorporated into commercial screening systems. The other procedure is more involved and measures the uptake of dyes under controlled conditions. Interestingly, commercial laboratories have had a methylene blue staining technique to measure cosmetic damage for at least 15 years but do not appear to use it routinely.* [65]

Although a number of studies have shown selective binding of drugs to melanin, Baumgartner et al. [28, 111] have argued that (1) drugs do not preferentially bind to melanin, (2) even if they bind, melanin is a minor component of hair, (3) even if they bind, the melanin is removed before analysis, and (4) researchers are not testing the right kind of melanin. This laboratory, and others, have observed cocaine binding to melanin [25, 107, 112]. However, when the hair is digested with the enzyme proteinase K in the presence of sodium dodecyl sulfate, the bound drug is released, and very little drug remains in the melanin fraction (Table 2.5). The point that is often overlooked is that if melanin binds cocaine and the cocaine is released during hair processing, then removal of the melanin component would not reduce the bias from the melanin binding. The cocaine that was released will be presented for analysis rather than removed with the melanin. Anionic proteins (which could allow association of cocaine via ionic interactions) may be associated with human hair melanin. Digestion of the keratin matrix with proteinase K would also digest the

* The exact procedure has never been specified. For example, how the uptake is qualified under a microscope appears to be somewhat subjective. A general outline is given in: Baumgartner, W.A. and Hill, V.A., Hair analysis for drugs of abuse: decontamination issues, in *Recent Developments in Therapeutic Drug Monitoring and Clinical Toxicology*, Sunshine, I., Ed., Marcel Dekker, New York, 1992, p. 577.

associated proteins and release cocaine from both pools. Extraction of the hair with solvents or buffers (as is frequently done [49]) in theory may reduce the bias because it leaves the melanin-protein component intact.

Concerning bias, in summary, individuals should be treated fairly and equally. Yet, bias remains an unresolved issue with hair testing. Drugs must have the opportunity to bind (defined by *rate*) and the tenacity to bind (defined by *equilibrium*) for contamination to be problematic. Different hair "types" have different rates of contamination from the environment. Cosmetically treated hair, because of damage and residual chemicals, absorbs drugs at a faster rate than untreated hair. Once inside the hair, the drugs must bind or they will be removed during hygiene or decontamination during the hair-testing process. Melanin or proteins associated with melanin facilitate that binding. To the extent that African Americans and other individuals treat their hair, for cultural or other reasons, they are more susceptible to environmental contamination and the resulting false positives from that contamination. Therefore, bias caused by false positives is of utmost concern.

2.8 CONCLUSIONS

Past and current data show that cocaine is readily incorporated into hair from environmental exposure and not removed by common decontamination techniques. Several authors have proposed wash ratios as one criterion to distinguish active from passive exposure. When tested against contaminated samples that have undergone normal hygienic washing, several hair samples pass all the relevant criteria and appear to be from drug users, even though they were passively exposed. Metabolites in hair may distinguish active use from passive exposure for some drugs. However, for cocaine, benzoylecgonine is produced by degradation in the environment, and other metabolites may come from contaminants in cocaine or the sweat of a drug user. The evidence from this laboratory and from others reviewed in this chapter reinforces and amplifies the serious concern that external contamination of hair by drugs of abuse can occur easily. Environmental contamination is not uniform, so that one group may experience more exposure episodes or higher acute exposure than another and increase the chance for inadvertent contamination of their hair. Any interpretation of hair analysis data should evaluate the prospect that the sample was externally contaminated.

Although a single cutoff level in hair testing can help set the balance between identifying drug users and misidentifying drug-exposed individuals, drug use cannot be defined rigidly. Setting the cutoff level too high will miss many users (false negatives). Setting the cutoff level too low will falsely accuse too many contaminated individuals (false positives). Because external contamination can exist in any amount and can *vary* depending on one's lifestyle and hair type, no cutoff level will suffice for a varied population. Until lifestyle questions are better answered, a higher cutoff level is more ethically defensible.

The pharmacokinetics of the incorporation of drugs into many tissues has been well elaborated. Most scientists accept at least part of the sweat hypothesis for the incorporation of drugs into hair. However, the percentages of the three pools (blood, sweat, and environmental) are not clear and certainly vary among individuals. The lack of a firm scientific basis was partially responsible for the 1990 consensus opinion of the Society of Forensic Toxicology (SOFT) that stated "Hair may be a useful specimen in forensic investigations when supported by other evidence of drug use." SOFT has never revoked its reservations on hair testing.

A familiar American proverb says that "the devil is in the details." Numerous details concerning hair analysis are still unanswered. Commercial companies should address important details — such as hair type, concentration, time, etc., where various criteria fail due to passive exposure — through large-scale validation studies where exposure is controlled. Other details, such as exposure rate and differential binding among populations, will take considerably more work. It is time to pay the devil his due and address these details before hair testing is validated by government regulations to the detriment of certain individuals.

ACKNOWLEDGMENTS

I would like to thank all the individuals who have contributed to the data sets summarized here. I would especially like to thank Janelle Baldwin for her excellent work on sampling the desk of students and Graham Beaber for his analysis of the $1 bills. This work was partially funded by a grant from the National Institutes of Justice administered by the Naval Surface Warfare Center. The opinions expressed here may not reflect the views of the Department of the Navy or the U.S. government.

REFERENCES

1. Anonymous, Society of Hair Testing, *Forensic Sci. Int.*, 84, 3, 1997.
2. Lenihan, J., *Measuring and Monitoring the Environment*, Lenihan, J. and Fletcher, W.W., Eds., Academic Press, New York, 1978, p. 66.
3. Wilhelm, M., Ohnesore, F.K., Lombeck, I., and Hafner, D., Uptake of aluminum, cadmium, copper, lead, and zinc by human scalp hair and elution of the adsorbed metals, *J. Anal. Toxicol.*, 13, 17, 1989.
4. Valkovi, V., *Human Hair Fundamentals and Methods for Measurement of Elemental Composition*, Vol. I, CRC Press, Boca Raton, FL, 1988.
5. Valkovi, V., *Human Hair Trace Element Levels*, Vol. II, CRC Press, Boca Raton, FL, 1988.
6. Hopps, H.C., The biologic basis for using hair and nail for analysis of trace elements, *Sci. Total Environment*, 7, 71, 1977.
7. Breuer, M.M., The binding of small molecules and polymers to keratin and their effects on the physicochemical and surface properties of hair fibers, in *Hair Research Status and Future Aspects*, Orfanos, C.E., Montahna, W., and Stuttgen, G., Eds., Springer-Verlag, New York, 1981, p. 96.
8. Chatt, A. and Katz, S.A., *Hair Analysis: Applications in the Biomedical and Environmental Sciences*, VCH Publishers, New York, 1988, pp. 14 and 77.
9. Manson, P. and Zlotkin, S., Hair analysis: a critical review, *J. Can. Med. Assoc.*, 133, 186, 1985.
10. Harkey, M.R. and Henderson, G.L., Hair analysis for drugs of abuse, *Adv. Anal. Toxicol.*, 2, 298, 1989.
11. Barrett, S., Commercial hair analysis: science or scam? *JAMA*, 254, 1041, 1985.

12. Hambridge, K.M., Hair analysis: worthless for vitamins, limited for minerals, *Am. J. Clin. Nutr.*, 36, 943, 1982.
13. Baumgartner, W.A. and Hill, V.A., Sample preparation techniques, *Forensic Sci. Int.*, 63, 121, 1993.
14. Blank, D.L. and Kidwell, D.A., External contamination of hair by drugs of abuse: an issue in forensic interpretation, *Forensic Sci. Int.*, 63, 145, 1993.
15. Kidwell, D.A., Analysis of drugs of abuse in hair by tandem mass spectrometry, in *Proceedings of the 36th American Society of Mass Spectrometry Conference on Mass Spectrometry and Allied Topics*, San Francisco, June 6-10, 1988, p. 1364.
16. Blank, D.L. and Kidwell, D.A., Screening of hair for drugs of abuse: is passive exposure a complication? 41st Annual Meeting of the American Academy of Forensic Sciences, Las Vegas, NV, Feb. 1989.
17. Kidwell, D.A. and Blank, D.L., Deposition of drugs of abuse into human hair, Society of Forensic Toxicology Conference on Hair Analysis, May 26, 1990.
18. Henderson, G.L., Harkey, M.R., and Jones, R., Hair analysis for drugs of abuse, final report on grant NIJ 90-NIJ-CX-0012 to National Institutes of Justice, Sept. 1993.
19. Baumgartner, W.A., Hill, V.A., and Blahd, W.H., Hair analysis for drugs of abuse, *J. Forensic Sci.*, 34, 1433, 1989.
20. Kidwell, D.A. and Blank, D.L., Mechanisms of incorporation of drugs into hair and the interpretation of hair analysis data, in *Hair Testing for Drugs of Abuse: International Workshop on Standards and Technology*, Cone, E.J., Welch, M.J., and Grigson Babecki, M.B., Eds., National Institutes of Health Publ. 95-3727, Superintendent of Documents, U.S. Government Printing Office, Washington, DC, 1995, p. 19.
21. Fogolari, F., Esposito, G., Viglino, P., Briggs, J.M., and McCammon, J.A., pKa shift effects on backbone amide base-catalyzed hydrogen exchange rates in peptides, *J. Am. Chem. Soc.*, 120, 3735, 1998.
22. Bendit, E.G., Infrared absorption spectrum of keratin 2: deuteration studies, *Biopolymers*, 4, 561, 1966.
23. Holmes, A.W., Some aspects of diffusion into human hair, in *Proceedings 3rd International Wool Research Conference*, Paris, 3, 79, 1965.
24. DeLauder, S.F. and Kidwell, D.A., The incorporation of dyes into hair as a model for drug binding, *Forensic Sci. Int.*, 107, 39, 2000.
25. Blank, D.L. and Kidwell, D.A., Environmental exposure: the stumbling block of hair testing, in *Drug Testing in Hair*, Kintz, P., Ed., CRC Press, Boca Raton, FL, 1996, p. 17.
26. Henderson, G.L., Harkey, M.R., and Jones, R., Hair analysis for drugs of abuse, final report on grant NIJ 90-NIJ-CX-0012 to National Institutes of Justice, Sept. 1993.
27. Cone, E.J., Testing human hair for drugs of abuse, 1: individual dose and time profiles of morphine and codeine in plasma, saliva, urine, and beard compared to drug-induced effects on pupils and behavior, *J. Anal. Toxicol.*, 14, 1, 1990.
28. Baumgartner, W.A. and Hill, V.A., Comments on the paper by D.L. Blank and D.A. Kidwell: external contamination of hair by cocaine: an issue in forensic procedures, *Forensic Sci. Int.*, 63, 157, 1993.
29. Hudson, J.C., Analysis of currency for cocaine contamination, *Can. Soc. Forensics J.*, 22, 203, 1989.
30. Oyler, J., Darwin, W.D., and Cone, E.J., Cocaine contamination of United States paper currency, *J. Anal. Toxicol.*, 20, 213, 1996.
31. Ulvick, S., Cui, J., Kunz, T., Demirgian, J., Hwang, E., Tani, B., Roche, C., Su, C., and Rigdon, S., Cocaine contamination on currency, in *Proceedings of the Counter Drug Law Enforcement: Applied Technology for Improved Operational Effectiveness International Technology Symposium*, Office of Nation Drug Control Policy, Executive Office of the President, Part 2, Oct. 24–27, 1995, Nashua, NH, p. 9-49.

32. Kidwell, D.A. and Gardner, W.P., Testing for illicit drugs via sweat and saliva analysis: application to the detection of body packers, 1999 ONDCP International Technology Symposium, March 8–10, Washington, DC.
33. Skopp, G., Pötsch, L., and Moeller, M.R., On cosmetically treated hair: aspects and pitfalls of interpretation, *Forensic Sci. Int.*, 84, 43, 1997.
34. Haley, N.J. and Hoffmann, D., Analysis for nicotine and cotinine in hair to determine cigarette smoker status, *Clinical Chem.*, 31, 1598, 1985.
35. Kintz, P., Ludes, B., and Mangin, P., Evaluation of nicotine and cotinine in human hair, *J. Forensic Sci.*, 37, 72, 1992.
36. Sepkovic, D.W., Haley, N.J., and Hoffmann, D., Elimination from the body of tobacco products by smokers and nonsmokers, *JAMA*, 256, 863, 1986.
37. Smith, F.P. and Kidwell, D.A., Cocaine in hair, saliva, skin swabs, and urine of cocaine users' children, *Forensic Sci. Int.*, 83, 179, 1996.
38. Janzen, K., Concerning norcocaine, ethylbenzoylecgonine, and the identification of cocaine use in human hair, *J. Anal. Toxicol.*, 16, 402, 1992.
39. Romano, G., Barbera, N., and Lombardo, I., Hair testing for drugs of abuse: evaluation of external cocaine contamination and risk of false positives, *Forensic Sci. Int.*, 123, 119, 2001.
40. Lewis, D., Moore, C., Morrissey, P., and Leikin, J., Determination of drug exposure using hair: application to child protective cases, *Forensic Sci. Int.*, 84, 123, 1997.
41. De Giorgio, F., Strano-Rossi, S., Rainio, J., and Chiarotti, M., Cocaine found in a child's hair due to environmental exposure? *Int. J. Legal Med.*, 118, 310, 2004.
42. Welch, M.J., Sniegoski, L.T., Allgood, C.C., and Habram, M., Hair analysis for drugs of abuse: evaluation of analytical methods, environmental issues, and development of reference materials, *J. Anal. Toxicol.*, 17, 389, 1993.
43. Koren, G., Klein, J., Forman, R., and Graham, K., Hair analysis of cocaine: differentiation between systemic exposure and external contamination, *J. Clinical Pharmacol.*, 32, 671, 1992.
44. Kidwell, D.A. and Blank, D.L., Hair analysis: techniques and potential problems, in *Recent Developments in Therapeutic Drug Monitoring and Clinical Toxicology*, Sunshine, I., Ed., Marcel Dekker, New York, 1992, p. 555.
45. Kidwell, D.A. and Blank, D.L., Mechanisms of incorporation of drugs into hair and the interpretation of hair analysis data, in *Hair Testing for Drugs of Abuse: International Workshop on Standards and Technology,* Cone, E.J., Welch, M.J., and Grigson Babecki, M.B., Eds., National Institutes of Health Publ. 95-3727, Superintendent of Documents, U.S. Government Printing Office, Washington, DC, 1995, p. 19.
46. Schaffer, M., Wang, W.-L., and Irving, J., An evaluation of two wash procedures for differentiation of external contamination versus ingestion in the analysis of human hair samples for cocaine, *J. Anal. Toxicol.*, 26, 485, 2002.
47. Cairns, T., Hill, V., Schaffer, M., and Thistle, W., Removing and identifying drug contamination in the analysis of human hair, *Forensic Sci. Int.*, 145, 97, 2004.
48. Schaffer, M., Hill, V., and Cairns, T., Hair analysis for cocaine: the requirement for effective wash procedures and effects of drug concentration and hair porosity in contamination and decontamination, *J. Anal. Toxicol.*, 29, 319, 2005.
49. Wang, W.-L. and Cone, E.J., Testing human hair for drugs of abuse, IV: environmental cocaine contamination and washing effects, *Forensic Sci. Int.*, 70, 39, 1995.
50. Chiarotti, M., Overview on extraction procedures, *Forensic Sci. Int.*, 63, 161, 1993.
51. Kidwell, D.A. and Riggs, L.A., Comparing two analytical methods: minimal standards in forensic toxicology derived from information theory, *Forensic Sci. Int.*, 145, 85, 2004.

52. Baumgartner, W.A., Black, C.T., Jones, P.F., and Blank, W.H., Radioimmunoassay of cocaine in hair: Concise communication, *J. Nuclear Med.*, 23, 1982, p. 790–792.
53. Baumgartner, W.A. and Berka, C., American Association for Clinical Chemistry, Inc. – In service Training and Continuing Education, 10, 7, 1989.
54. Baumgartner, W.A. and Hill, V.A., Hair analysis for organic analytes: Methodology, reliability issues, and field studies, in *Drug Testing in Hair*, Kintz, P., Ed., CRC Press, Boca Raton, FL, 1996, pp. 224–265.
55. Kidwell, D.A. and Blank, D.L., Comments on sample preparation techniques, *Forensic Sci. Int.*, 63, 137, 1993.
56. Mieczkowski, T., Distinguishing passive contamination from active cocaine consumption: Assessing the occupational exposure of narcotics officers to cocaine, *Forensic Sci. Int.*, 84, 87, 1997.
57. Kintz, P and Mangin, P., What constitutes a positive result in hair analysis: Proposal for the establishment of cut-off values, *Forensic Sci. Int.*, 70, 3, 1995.
58. Anon., Society of Hair Testing, Recommendation for hair testing in forensic cases, *Forensic Sci. Int.*, 145, 83, 2004.
59. Nystrom, I., Trygg, T., Woxler, P., Ahlner, J., and Kronstrand, R., Quantitation of R-(–)- and S-(+)- amphetamine in hair and blood by gas chromatography-mass spectrometry? An application to compliance monitoring in adult-attention deficit hyperactivity disorder treatment, *J. Anal. Toxicol.*, 29, 682–688, 2005.
60. Kidwell, D.A., Analysis of phencyclidine and cocaine in human hair by tandem mass spectrometry, *J. Forensic Sci.*, 38, 272, 1993.
61. Blank, D.L. and Kidwell, D.A., Decontamination procedures for drugs of abuse in hair: are they sufficient? *Forensic Sci. Int.*, 70, 13, 1995.
62. Joseph, R.E., Jr., Su, T.-P., and Cone, E.J., *In vitro* binding studies of drugs to hair: influence of melanin and lipids on cocaine binding to Caucasoid and Africoid hair, *J. Anal. Toxicol.*, 20, 338, 1996.
63. Joseph, R.E., Jr., Tsai, W.-J., Tsao, L.-I., Su, T.-P., and Cone, E.J., *In vitro* characterization of cocaine binding sites in human hair, *J. Pharm. Exp. Ther.*, 282, 1228, 1997.
64. Kidwell, D.A., Lee, E.H., and DeLauder, S. F., Evidence for bias in hair testing and procedures to correct bias, *Forensic Sci. Int.*, 107, 93, 2000.
65. Baumgartner, W.A. and Hill, V.A., Hair analysis for drugs of abuse: no evidence for racial bias, technical memorandum to the National Institutes of Justice, June 1991; Hair analysis for drugs of abuse: forensic issues, in *Proceedings of the International Symposium on Forensic Toxicology*, Federal Bureau of Investigation, Quantico, VA, June 15–19, 1992, p. 75.
66. Mieczkowski, T. and Newel, R., An evaluation of patterns of racial bias in hair assays for cocaine: black and white arrestees compared, *Forensic Sci. Int.*, 63, 85, 1993.
67. Cone, E.J., Mechanisms of drug incorporation into hair, *Ther. Drug Monit.*, 18, 438, 1996.
68. Gygi, S.P., Joseph, R.E., Jr., Cone, E.J., Wilkins, D.G., and Rollins, D.E., Incorporation of codeine and metabolites into hair: role of pigmentation, *Drug Metab. Dispos.*, 24, 495, 1996.
69. Mieczkowski, T. and Newel, R., An analysis of the racial bias controversy in the use of hair assays, in *Drug Testing Technology: Assessment of Field Applications*, Mieczkowski, T., Ed., CRC Press, Boca Raton, FL, 1999, p. 313.
70. Slawson, M.N., Wilkins, D.G., and Rollins, D.E., The incorporation of drugs into hair: relationship of hair color and melanin concentration to phencyclidine incorporation, *J. Anal. Toxicol.*, 22, 406, 1998.
71. Khumalo, N.P., Doe, P.T., Dawber, R.P., and Ferguson, D.J., What is normal black African hair? A light and scanning electron-microscopic study, *J. Am. Acad. Dermatol.*, 45, 814, 2000.

72. Mitu, A.M., Damage Assessment of Human Hair by Electrophoretical Analysis of Hair Proteins, doctoral dissertation, German Wool Research Institute, RSTH Aachen University, Germany, 2004.
73. Love, T., *The World of Wigs, Weaves, and Extensions*, Thomas Learning, Albany, NY, 2002.
74. LoPresti, P., Papa, C.M., and Kligman, A.M., Hot comb alopecia, *Arch. Dermatol.*, 98, 234, 1968.
75. Scott, D.A., Disorders of the hair and scalp in blacks, *Dermatol. Clin.*, 6, 387, 1988.
76. Hatton, L. and Hatton, P., *Perming and Straightening: A Salon Handbook*, Longman Publishing Group, London, 1993.
77. Corbett, J.F., The chemistry of hair-care products, *J. Soc. Dyers Colour*, 92, 285, 1976.
78. Hyund, J.A. and Lee, W.-S., An ultrastructural study of hair fiber damage and restoration following treatment with permanent hair dye, *Int. J. Dermatol.*, 41, 88, 2002.
79. Wickett, R.R., Permanent waving and straightening of hair, *Cutis: Cutaneous Med. Practitioner*, 39, 496, 1987.
80. Holloway, V.L., Ethnic cosmetic products, *Dermatol. Clin.*, 21, 743, 2003.
81. Kidwell, D.A. and Blank, D.L., Hair Analysis: Techniques and Potential Problems, paper presented at the Conference on Hair Analysis, Society of Forensic Toxicology, May 27–29, 1990, Washington, DC.
82. Anon., special report to the Congress: Cocaine and Federal Sentencing Policy, Feb. 1995; available on-line at: http://www.ussc.gov/crack/exec.htm.
83. Kelly, R.C., Mieczkowski, T., Sweeney, S.A., and Bourland, J.A., Hair analysis for drugs of abuse: hair color and race differentials or systematic differences in drug preferences? *Forensic Sci. Int.*, 107, 63, 2000.
84. Cone, E.J., Yousefnejad, D., Darwin, W.D., and Maguire, T., Testing human hair for drugs of abuse, II: identification of unique cocaine metabolites in hair of drug abusers and evaluation of decontamination procedures, *J. Anal. Toxicol.*, 15, 250, 1991.
85. Cone, E.J., Yousefnejad, D., Hillsgrove, M.J., Holicky, B., and Darwin, W.D., Passive inhalation of cocaine, *J. Anal. Toxicol.*, 19, 399, 1997.
86. Wang, W.-L. and Cone, E.J., Testing human hair for drugs of abuse, IV: environmental cocaine contamination and washing effects, *Forensic Sci. Int.*, 70, 39, 1995.
87. Goldberger, B.A., Caplan, Y.H., Maguire, T., and Cone, E.J., Testing human hair for drugs of abuse, III: identification of heroin and 6-acetylmorphine as indicators of heroin use, *J. Anal. Toxicol.*, 15, 226, 1991.
88. Kidwell, D.A., Blanco, M.A., and Smith, F.P., Cocaine detection in a university population by hair analysis and skin swab testing, *Forensic Sci. Int.*, 84, 75, 1997.
89. Preston, K.L., Goldberger, B.A., and Cone, E.J., Occurrence of cocaine in urine of substance-abuse treatment patients, *J. Anal. Toxicol.*, 22, 580, 1998.
90. Kouri, E.M., Lundahl, L.H., Borden, K.N., McNeil, J.F., and Lukas, S.E., Effects of oral contraceptives on acute cocaine response in female volunteers, *Pharmacol. Biochem. Behav.*, 74(1), 173, 2002.
91. Lukas, S.E., Sholar, M., Lundahl, L.H., Lamax, X., Kouri, E., Wines, J.D., Kragie, L., and Mendelson, J.H. Sex differences in plasma cocaine levels and subjective effects after acute cocaine administration in human volunteers, *Psychopharmacology*, 125(4), 346, 1996.
92. Mieczkowski, T. and Newel, R., An evaluation of patterns of racial bias in hair assays for cocaine: Black and white arrestees compared, *Forensic Sci. Int.*, 63 (1993) 85–98.
93. Mieczkowski, T. and Newel, R., Statistical examination of hair color as a potential biasing factor in hair analysis, *Forensic Sci. Int.*, 107, 13, 2000.
94. Mieczkowski, T., Assessing the potential of a "color effect" for hair analysis of 11-nor-9-carboxy-9-tetrahydrocannabinol: analysis of a large sample of hair specimens, *Life Sciences*, 74, 463, 2003.

95. Nakahara, Y. and Kikura, R., Hair analysis for drugs of abuse, VII: the incorporation rates of cocaine, benzoylecgonine and ecgonine methyl ester into rat hair and hydrolysis of cocaine in rat hair, *Arch. Toxicol.*, 68, 54, 1994.
96. Nakahara, Y., The effects of physiochemical factors on incorporation of drugs into hair and behavior of drugs in hair root, in *Drug Testing Technology: Assessment of Field Applications*, Mieczkowski, T., Ed., CRC Press, Boca Raton, FL, 1999, p. 49.
97. Wilkins, D.G., Valdez, A.S., Nagasawa, P.R., Gygi, S.P., and Rollins, D.E., Incorporation of drugs for the treatment of substance abuse into pigmented and nonpigmented hair, *J. Pharm. Sci.*, 87, 435, 1998.
98. Hubbard, D.L., Wilkins, D.G., and Rollins, D.E., The incorporation of cocaine and metabolites into hair: effects of dose and hair pigmentation, *Drug Metab. Disposition*, 28, 1464, 2000.
99. Baumgartner, W.A., Hill, V.A., and Kippenberger, D., Workplace drug testing by hair analysis: advantages and issues, in *Drug Testing Technology: Assessment of Field Applications*, Mieczkowski, T., Ed., CRC Press, Boca Raton, FL, 1999, p. 283.
100. Cone, E.J., Darwin, W.D., and Wang, W.-L., The occurrence of cocaine, heroin and metabolites in hair of drug abusers, *Forensic Sci. Int.*, 63, 55, 1993.
101. Cone, E.J. and Joseph, R.E., Jr., The potential for bias in hair testing for drugs of abuse, in *Drug Testing in Hair*, Kintz, P., Ed., CRC Press, Boca Raton, FL, 1996, p. 69.
102. Henderson, G.L., Harkey, M.R., Zhou, C., Jones, R.T., and Jacob, P., III, Incorporation of isotopically labeled cocaine into human hair: race as a factor, *J. Anal. Toxicol.*, 22, 156, 1998.
103. Henderson, G.L., Harkey, M.R., Zhou, C., Jones, R.T., and Jacob, P., III, Incorporation of isotopically labeled cocaine and metabolites into human hair, 1: dose-response relationships, *J. Anal. Toxicol.*, 20, 1, 1996.
104. Borges, C.R., Wilkins, D.G., and Rollins, D.E., Amphetamine and N-acetylamphetamine incorporation into hair: an investigation of the potential role of drug basicity in hair color bias, *J. Anal. Toxicol.*, 25, 221, 2001.
105. Rollins, D.E., Wilkins, D.G., Krueger, G.G., Augsburger, M.P., Mizuno, A., O'Neal, C., Borges, C.R., and Slawson, M.H., The effect of hair color on the incorporation of codeine into human hair, *J. Anal. Toxicol.*, 27, 545, 2003.
106. Wilkins, D.G., Mizuno, A., Borges, C.R., Slawson, M.H., and Rollins, D.E., Ofloxacin as a reference marker in hair of various colors, *J. Anal. Toxicol.*, 27, 149, 2003.
107. Joseph, R.E., Tsao, W.-J., Su, T.-P., and Cone, E.J., *In vivo* characterization of cocaine binding sites in human hair, *J. Pharmacol. Exp. Ther.*, 282, 1241, 1997.
108. Sagal, J., Acid and base binding behavior of white and pigmented hair, *Textile Res. J.*, 35(7), 672, 1965.
109. Rocafort, C.A., Formulating for the ethnic marketplace, *Soap Cosmetics*, 76, 72, 2000.
110. Kidwell, D.A. and Smith, F.P., Susceptibility of PharmChek™ drugs of abuse patch to environmental contamination, *Forensic Sci. Int.*, 116, 89, 2001.
111. DuPont, R.L. and Baumgartner, W.A., Drug testing by urine and hair analysis: complementary features and scientific issues, *Forensic Sci. Int.*, 70, 63, 1995.
112. Nakahara, Y., Takahashi, K., and Kikura, R., Hair analysis for drugs of abuse, X: effect of physicochemical properties on incorporation rates into hair, *Bio. Chem. Bull.*, 18, 1223, 1995.
113. Baumgartner, W.A., Black, C.T., Jones, P.F., and Blahd, W.H., Radioimmunoassay of cocaine in hair: concise communication, *J. Nucl. Med.*, 23, 790, 1982.

3 Opioids Testing in Hair

Michel Yegles and Robert Wennig

CONTENTS

3.1 INTRODUCTION

Opioid is a generic term for natural or synthetic substances that bind to specific opioid receptors in the central nervous system (CNS). Although the term opiate is often used for all morphinelike drugs, it is more properly limited to the natural opium alkaloids and the semisynthetics derived from them (see Table 3.1, modified from Kintz[1]).

TABLE 3.1
Opioids

Natural opium alkaloids	morphine	agonists
	codeine	
Semisynthetic opiates	heroin	agonists
	pholcodine	
	codethyline	
Semisynthetic opioids	buprenorphine	agonist-antagonist
	naloxone	antagonist
	naltrexone	antagonist
Synthetic opioids	methadone	agonist
	dextropropoxyphene	agonist (weak antagonist)
	dextromoramide	agonist
	pethidine	agonist
	phenoperidine	agonist
	fentanyl	agonist
	alfentanil	agonist
	sufentanyl	agonist
	remifentanil	agonist
	LAAM	agonist
	pentazocine	agonist-antagonist
	nalbuphine	agonist-antagonist

Source: Table modified from Kintz, P., Toxicologie et pharmacologie médicolégales, in *Collection option Bio, Editions scientifiques et médicales*, Elsevier, New York, 1998. With permission.

Narcotic agonists include natural opium alkaloids and semisynthetics. Mixed agonist-antagonist drugs present agonist activity at some receptors and antagonist activity at other receptors; also included are the partial agonists. Narcotic antagonists do not have agonist activity at any of the opioid receptor sites. Antagonists block the opioid receptor, inhibit pharmacological activity of the agonist, and precipitate withdrawal in opioid-dependent patients.

Four types of opiate receptors have been identified: μ including $\mu 1$, receptors, exert their action on spinal and supraspinal analgesia; $\mu 2$ on respiratory depression, euphoria, vomiting, inhibition of gut motility, and physical dependence; δ on spinal analgesia; κ on spinal analgesia and supraspinal analgesia; and σ on dysphoria, hallucination, and cardiac stimulation.

Opioids have long been used to treat acute pain. They are also very useful in palliative care to ease the chronic and severe pain of cancer patients. In recent years there has been an increased use of opioids in the management of nonmalignant chronic pain.

Some opioids are widely abused for their euphoria-producing properties when administered orally, intravenously, intranasally, or when smoked. The euphoria is one of the principal reasons behind the development of psychological dependence. Tolerance rapidly develops to this effect, and rapid dose increases are required by users seeking to achieve the euphoric state. A relatively small dose of a fast-acting opioid may produce intense euphoria in an “opioid naive” user, but once tolerance has been developed, even very large doses may produce none at all.

3.2 OPIATES

3.2.1 Metabolism of Opiates

Heroin is readily absorbed mainly following injection. It undergoes important first-pass effects in the liver. It is rapidly hydrolyzed to 6-monoacetylmorphine (6-MAM) in blood and then more slowly metabolized to morphine, which is the major active metabolite. Small amounts of codeine may be seen in addicts’ urine, but this is thought to be due to the presence of acetylcodeine in illicit heroin samples. All metabolites can be conjugated with glucuronic acid. Up to 80% of a dose is excreted in the urine in 24 h, mainly as morphine-3-glucuronide, with about 5 to 7% of the dose as free morphine, 1% as 6-MAM, 0.1% as unchanged drug, and trace amounts of other metabolites; after inhalation, 14 to 20% of the dose appears in the urine; morphine metabolites are excreted in the bile.[2]

Codeine is well absorbed after oral administration, with peak plasma levels occurring after 1 h. Later, codeine is metabolized in the liver by *O*-demethylation involving CYP2D6 to form morphine by *N*-demethylation to form norcodeine involving CYP3A4, and by conjugation to form glucuronides and sulfates of both unchanged drug and its metabolites. After an oral dose, about 86% is excreted in the urine in 24 h; of the excreted material, 40 to 70% is free or conjugated codeine, 5 to 15% is free or conjugated morphine, 10 to 20% is free or conjugated norcodeine, and trace amounts may be free or conjugated normorphine. Small amounts of hydrocodone, dihydrocodeine, and hydromorphone have also been detected in urine.[1,3]

3.2.2 Hair Analysis

Most illicit heroin samples also contain acetylcodeine. Consequently, codeine with its metabolite morphine can also be detected in cases of heroin abuse. However, after codeine consumption, codeine and morphine may also be detected. Therefore, the ratio of both drugs was proposed to differentiate between codeine and heroin abuse using hair analysis.[4] Thus, if the codeine hair concentration is higher than that of morphine, it can be assumed that codeine had been ingested. However, to definitively discriminate between heroin users and individuals exposed to other sources of morphine alkaloids, heroin or 6-MAM has to be identified in hair.[5–7]

3.2.2.1 Testing Methods

The analysis of hair for opiates, as for other drugs, is performed in four steps: decontamination, extraction, cleanup, and analysis. Several authors have already reviewed this subject,[8,9] thus, only an overview of these different steps will be presented.

3.2.2.1.1 Hair Decontamination

As normal hygienic practices do not sufficiently remove externally deposited drugs, there is a consensus that hair specimens have to be treated by decontamination procedures in the laboratory before extraction and analysis of drugs.[10,11] Among the agents used for cleaning hair are detergents[12,13] and organic solvents such as acetone,[14] methanol,[15,16] ethanol,[17] and dichloromethane[18,19] during various contact times. As the decontamination with organic solvents does not produce hair swelling, such as water or methanol, there is a possibility that not all of the external incorporated drugs will be removed.

However, in a study comparing different washing procedures on morphine content in hair, no single procedure could be recommended.[20] A compromise should be made between intensive washing and the risk of extracting incorporated drugs.

3.2.2.1.2 Extraction

To quantify the amount of a drug that remains in hair after washing, it is necessary to release the incorporated drugs from the hair matrix. This release must be done such that the analytes are not altered or lost by preventing, in the case of opiates, the conversion of 6-MAM to morphine.

The hair sample can be pulverized in a ball-mill prior to testing, or cut into segments of about 1 mm, or the entire hair can be treated for extraction. Incubation of hair specimens in an aqueous buffer is used particularly for immunological techniques like radioimmunoassay (RIA).[12] Incubation in a water bath was also proposed by Kronstrand et al. at 37°C for 18 h,[21] whereas Romolo et al.[16] propose phosphate buffer 0.1*N* at pH 5. Methanol incubation involves treatment of hair specimens in an ultrasound methanol bath at 45°C for several hours.[5,6,22–27] Eser et al.[28] pointed out that methanol incubation was a good extraction method because methanol produces a swelling of hair, thus facilitating drug release from the hair. Two types of enzymatic hair treatments have been used: protease[29] or glucuronidase arylsulfatase.[14] Several authors have also proposed overnight acid hydrolysis using HCl 0.1*M*.[18,19,30,31] Incubation of hair in sodium hydroxide is a good extraction method, principally because the protein matrix is completely destroyed. However, this hair treatment is not suitable for chemically unstable compounds such as 6-MAM.

An evaluation of incubation procedures was discussed in a study by Balikova et al.[32] The methods using 1*M* NaOH or 0.1*M* HCl yielded higher recoveries of morphine or codeine, whereas the incubation in Soerensen buffer did not change the ratio of labile metabolites or parent compounds in an original sample.

3.2.2.1.3 Cleanup

The following extractions methods have been proposed for the quantification of opiates in hair: liquid/liquid extraction[5,18,19,33] and solid-phase extraction using different kind of columns.[13,14,22,26,27,29–32,34–36] After methanolic extraction,[5,6,22–25] methanol is evaporated to dryness and residues can be directly analyzed if the selectivity of the analytical method is sufficient.[37] However, to improve the signal-to-noise ratio, a sample cleanup procedure might be necessary. Supercritical fluid extraction with carbon dioxide has also been used for the cleanup.[38,39] The advantages of this extraction technique include the high speed of the extraction (30 min) and the potential to be connected on-line with gas chromatography-mass spectrometry (GC-MS). Recently, a surfactant-enhanced liquid-phase microextraction (SE-LPME) was proposed.[40]

3.2.2.1.4 Analytical Techniques

Opiates were first detected by RIA in hair of heroin abusers by Baumgartner et al.[12] Since then, various methods using immunoassays (RIA or ELISA [enzyme-linked immunosorbent assay]) or chromatographic techniques have been published. Immunoassays are used as screening tests because of their relative sensitivity, speed, and convenience. However, quantification by immunoassay is difficult to achieve, as the specificity of most kits is directed to a group of drugs and drug metabolites rather than to a single substance. Therefore, presumptively detected analytes by immunoassays have to be identified by a chromatographic method or any other independent technique providing equivalent specificity. Chromatographic procedures have proved to be powerful tools for identifying and quantifying drugs in hair due to the separation ability and the detection sensitivity and specificity, particularly when coupled with MS.

RIAs are the most common screening test for hair. Kits, generally designed for urine, are used at pH values above 7. In a study in which hair specimens from known heroin abusers were analyzed for morphine by a specific RIA,[41] a high specificity for morphine was shown. In a comparative study by Sachs et al.,[4] a large degree of qualitative and quantitative parity was observed for the RIA and GC-MS for levels above 1 ng/mg of morphine in hair. The use of an RIA kit to detect 6-MAM showed good correlation between the GC-MS and RIA results for the hair samples tested.[42] Furthermore, the results from a fluorescence polarization immunoassay (Abbott FPIA TDX) appeared to be correlated with those from GC-MS analyses.[43] In a study by Segura et al.,[44] a screening by a simple ELISA methodology to detect opiates was followed up by GC-MS analysis of the analytes in positive samples with satisfactory results. Cooper et al.[45] compared Cozart microplate ELISA, the microplate enzyme immunoassay (EIA), with GC-MS for opiates in hair using a cutoff of 200 pg/mg hair with a 20-mg hair sample. The results had a sensitivity of 98 ± 2% and a specificity of 92.7 ± 3.5% versus GC-MS. The automated ELISA tests have proved to be valid screening procedures for the detection of opiates in hair, as confirmed by GC-MS.[46] The ELISA methodology using Oral Fluid Micro-Plate Enzyme Immunoassays (Orasure Technologies, Inc.) provided rapid and inexpensive automated pretest procedures to detect drugs in hair or other matrices.

Chromatographic methods such as high-performance liquid chromatography (HPLC), GC-MS, GC-MS/MS, or LC-MS/MS have been used as screening and confirming tests. Moreover, they allow quantification of the drugs and drug metabolites. These methods have been reviewed by Sachs and Kintz.[47]

The most commonly used chromatographic method is gas chromatography coupled to mass spectrometry (GC-MS). To achieve the necessary sensitivity, the analysis is generally done in the selected-ion monitoring (SIM) mode. Various derivatization procedures have been used, including pentafluoropropionic anhydride (PFP)-pentafluoropropanol (PFPOH),[14,26] heptafluorobutyric anhydre (HFBA-HFPOH),[18] BSTFA-1% TMCS,[19,22,24,34] and methoxime-BSTFA.[27] Moreover, the tandem mass spectrometry (MS/MS) represents a very powerful technique due to its excellent selectivity and sensitivity, thus needing no sophisticated sample preparation.[25,48] A direct treatment of methanol-washed hair with a silylating solution has been proposed to extract heroin, 6-MAM, morphine, acetylcodeine, and codeine,

TABLE 3.2
Cutoff for Opiate Consumption

Method	6-MAM Cutoff (ng/mg)	References
GC-MS	presence	Goldberger et al. (1991)[5]
GC-MS	presence	Moeller et al. (1993)[7]
GC-MS	0.5	Kintz and Mangin (1995)[58]
GC-MS	0.5	Pepin and Gaillard (1997)[59]
RIA	0.1	Tagliaro et al. (1997)[55]
GC-MS/MS	0.5	Uhl (2000)[52]
GC/MS	0.1	Montagna et al. (2000)[30]
ELISA	0.2	Cooper et al. (2003)[45]
Chromatographic methods	0.2	SOHT (2004)[10]

obtaining the simultaneous derivatization of the hydroxylated metabolites and thus reducing potential sample contamination.[48] GC-MS/MS has proved to be a highly sensitive and specific technique for the detection of very low concentrations of drugs in hair.[24,49–52] Ion spray LC-MS/MS also shows high sensitivity, is easy to perform, and seems to be appropriate for screening for drugs of abuse.[21,53]

HPLC methods with fluorometry and coulometry detectors have shown to have sufficient sensitivity to enable the detection of low drug concentrations.[47] Capillary zone electrophoresis has been proposed for the quantitative determination of morphine in hair.[54,55] Moreover, additional use of field-amplified sample stacking provided an increase in sensitivity.[56,57]

3.2.2.2 Interpretation of Results

3.2.2.2.1 Cutoff

Cutoff is an important but controversial point in hair analysis. Table 3.2 summarizes the cutoffs for opiate consumption in the literature.

In hair specimens from 20 documented heroin users, 6-MAM was detected predominantly over heroin, morphine, and codeine.[5] Mean concentrations were 0.90 ng/mg (6-MAM), 0.17 ng/mg (heroin), 0.26 ng/mg (morphine), and 0.18 ng/mg (codeine). 6-MAM was considered as a proof for heroin consumption and was usually in higher concentrations than morphine and codeine.

To confirm heroin use, Moeller et al.[7] suggested that morphine/codeine ratios necessary to determine heroin use should be set at 5:1 for low morphine concentrations (<1 ng/mg hair) and 2:1 for concentrations above 1 ng/mg hair. Additionally, the authors suggest that the distinction can be done using 6-MAM. Thus, the ratio of 6-MAM versus morphine should vary between 1.3 and 10.

Gaillard and Pepin[60] also found higher concentrations for 6-MAM than for morphine. The authors proposed that the ratios of 6-MAM/morphine and 6-MAM/codeine should be greater than 7.14 and 50, respectively, to document heroin abuse. In a study by Kauert and Röhrich,[23] which analyzed 141 hair specimens of individuals

TABLE 3.3
6-MAM Concentrations vs. Frequency of Consumption

Classes of Consumption of Heroin (g/week)	6-MAM Concentration in Hair (ng/mg)							
<1	0.8	0.9	1					
1–3	1.1	1.9	3.6	5.4				
3–10	0.8	1.2	2.0	3.9	5.6	6.1	17.2	26.2
>10	25.6	27.6	29.9	30.9	35.6	43.2		

Source: From Pepin, G. and Gaillard, Y., *Forensic Sci. Int.*, 84, 37–41, 1997. With permission.

TABLE 3.4
Proposed Interpretation of 6-MAM Level Found

Conclusion	Absence	Positive		
Consumption	negative	low	medium	high
6-MAM (ng/mg)	<0.5	<2	2–10	>10

Source: From Pepin, G. and Gaillard, Y., *Forensic Sci. Int.*, 84, 37–41, 1997. With permission.

with presumed drug abuse, 6-MAM was determined at a mean concentration of 5.46 ng/mg, whereas morphine was at 0.86 ng/mg. The consumption behavior also was evaluated: a 6-MAM concentration below 1 ng/mg indicates a weekly use, concentrations between 1 and 10 ng/mg correspond to a weekly to daily use, whereas concentrations above 10 ng/mg suggest a multiple daily use or extremely high doses.

In 135 cases involving forensic expertise, an average 6-MAM concentration of 11.3 ng/mg was determined.[59] By retrospective questioning, the measured levels in hair of 6-MAM were compared with the habitual use declared by the consumers[59] (Table 3.3).

These data led the authors to propose three levels (low, medium, high) of consumption in relation to the concentration of the 6-MAM marker found in hair for the consumption of heroin (Table 3.4).

In its first recommendation, the Society of Hair Testing (SOHT)[61] proposed that heroin consumption has to be assumed when the ratio of 6-MAM and morphine is greater than 1.3. In a more recent SOHT statement,[10] the society recommends that heroin use has to be differentiated from codeine or morphine use by the presence of 6-MAM in hair, with a recommended limit of quantification of 0.2 ng/mg hair using chromatographic techniques.

Kintz et al.[62] evaluated the use of acetylcodeine (AC), which is an impurity of illicit heroin synthesis, as a specific marker of illicit heroin in human hair. Fifty hair specimens of persons who had died from a fatal opiate overdose were analyzed. AC was found in 22 samples, with a mean concentrations of 1.04 ng/mg. 6-MAM was also present in these samples at a mean concentration of 7.79 ng/mg. Of the 28 specimens negative for AC, 21 were found positive for 6-MAM. A positive relationship was found between AC concentrations and 6-MAM concentrations ($r = 0.915$, $p = 0.001$). In the same study, neither AC nor codeine was identified in hair specimens collected from 20 subjects taking part in a heroin-maintenance program in Switzerland and receiving daily pure pharmaceutical heroin hydrochloride. The authors concluded that although AC is indicative of illicit heroin use, this substance would not make a suitable biomarker in place of 6-MAM because of its low concentration in hair compared with that of 6-MAM and its absence in about 50% of the specimens tested positive for 6-MAM.

In a study by Girod and Staub,[63] AC was detected in 92% of hair specimens from heroin abusers ($n = 73$) and in only 12% of hair specimens from subjects who had participated in a heroin-maintenance program ($n = 43$). In the group of illicit heroin users, a median 6-MAM concentration of 3.3 ng/mg was determined, whereas median AC concentration was at 0.3 ng/mg. The authors concluded that AC can be considered as a suitable marker together with 6-MAM.

However, in a study by Musshoff et al.,[64] after controlled intravenous administration of pharmaceutical heroin-HCl, AC was found in 10.9% of the samples ($n = 46$) after 12 months of a heroin-maintenance program, whereas in samples from opiate-associated fatalities, AC was found in only 16.7% of the samples ($n = 24$). The authors conclude that the lack of AC in the majority of the opiate-associated deaths questions its applicability as a characteristic marker of the consumption of illicit heroin.

3.2.2.2.2 Dose/Hair Concentration Relationship

The relationship between intake dose and hair concentration is also a critical question in hair analysis. Thus, in cases of chronic abuse, daily doses may vary significantly from day to day, and the establishment of a dose–response relationship requires a large amount of data to take individual differences into account.

In a study by Kintz et al.,[65] hair specimens were collected from 20 subjects taking part in a heroin-maintenance program. Subjects were administered, under controlled conditions, heroin hydrochloride in two or three doses per day intravenously, with self-administered heroin doses ranging between 30 and 800 mg/day. In all cases, a 4-cm segment from the proximal zone (root) was analyzed, corresponding to about 100 days of hair growth. No correlation between the doses of administered heroin and the concentrations of total opiates in hair was observed ($r = 0.346$). However, when considering a single analyte, it was observed that the correlation coefficient seemed to be linked to its plasma elimination half-life.

Girod and Staub[63] confirmed that there is no relationship between daily heroin dose and the 6-MAM-concentration ($r = 0.01$). However, Musshoff et al.[64] found, after controlled heroin administration, a correlation between the dose and the total opiate concentration in hair ($r = 0.66$). They also showed that this correlation is influenced by the plasma elimination half-lives of the analytes.

3.2.2.2.3 Cosmetic Treatment

An important issue of concern for drug analysis in hair is the change in drug concentration induced by the cosmetic treatment of hair. Under normal conditions, the intact

TABLE 3.5
Effect of a Perming Agent on Opiate Content in Hair

	Decrease (%)		
	Morphine	**Codeine**	**Dihydrocodeine**
Spiked hair	79	79	70
Original opiate-positive hair	100	94	100

TABLE 3.6
Effect of Bleaching on Opiate Concentration in Hair

Decrease (%)			
Codeine	**6-MAM**	**Morphine**	**References**
75	86	89	69
94	—	94	67
69	66	81	68
57	89	67	35

cuticle is a strong barrier against the loss of drugs. However, some cosmetic treatments may damage the cuticle, change molecular structure of the hair pigment, or degrade incorporated drugs. Generally, this leads to a decrease of drug content in hair.

Repeated shampooing was found to have no significant action on the drug content of hair.[66] Pötsch and Skopp[67] treated *in vitro* spiked hair and original opiate-positive hair with a commercial perming product (Poly Lock®). Morphine, codeine, and dihydrocodeine concentrations decreased after hair treatment; the reduction was more apparent in the original hair than in the spiked hair (Table 3.5).

Jurado et al.[68] compared dyed hair segments with untreated hair segments from drug users. In dyed hair segments, a decrease of concentrations for codeine, 6-MAM, and morphine (29.5, 41.3, and 61.2 % respectively) was found.

The effect of bleaching on drug concentration in hair for opiates is presented in Table 3.6. Codeine, 6-MAM, and morphine concentrations all decreased after hair bleaching.

Tanaka et al.[70] showed that hydrogen peroxide can also change the chemical structure of drugs. Codeine and morphine were converted to hydroxycodeine and hydroxymorphine after peroxide (30%) treatment.

Finally, the different studies on cosmetic treatment in hair show that it is important to consider cosmetic treatment, particularly dyeing, bleaching, and perming. These hair treatments may drop the original drug concentration below the limit of detection of the analytical methods, thus generating false-negative results.

3.2.3 Methadone

Methadone (MTD) is a synthetic opioid used as an analgesic drug with pharmaceutical properties similar to those of morphine. It was primarily used for the relief of pain and is nowadays mainly employed in maintenance treatment of heroin addicts. The selection of methadone for use in substance-abuse treatment programs is based in part on its relatively long duration of action in suppressing withdrawal compared with other opiates. The main metabolic pathway is *N*-demethylation, resulting in a compound that spontaneously cyclizes to form the major metabolites, 2-ethylidene-1,5-dimethyl-3,3-diphenylpyrrolidine (EDDP) and 2-ethyl-5-methyl-3,3-diphenyl-1-pyrrolidine (EMDP), neither of which are active. Most methods described the quantification in hair of MTD and its metabolite EDDP and, more rarely, the secondary metabolite EMDP.

3.2.3.1 Testing Methods

3.2.3.1.1 Decontamination

Among the agents used for cleaning hair are water followed by acetone,[14,71–74] methanol,[5,75] dichloromethane,[76] dichloromethane followed by water and methanol,[31] water followed by petrol ether and dichloromethane,[77] and hexane followed by methanol and acetone,[52] all for various contact times.

3.2.3.1.2 Extraction

A variety of hair-extraction procedures have been described, including β-glucuronidase/arylsulfatase in pH 7.6 phosphate buffer,[14,73] pronase E in Tris Buffer,[71] methanol incubation,[5,52,75,76,78] phosphate buffer,[74] 0.01 M HCl,[31] and NaOH incubation.[72,77,79]

3.2.3.1.3 Cleanup

A variety of extraction procedures have been described, including solid phase extraction (SPE),[5,31,74,75] liquid/liquid extraction (L/L) using chlorobutane and acetonitrile,[79] solid-phase dynamic extraction (SPDE),[77] solid-phase microextraction (SPME),[71,72,80] and surfactant enhanced liquid-phase microextraction (SE-LPME).[40]

3.2.3.1.4 Analysis

GC-MS is, as for opiates, the golden standard for determination of MTD and its metabolites in hair. Thus GC-MS SIM,[5,14,71,72,75,76,78,81] positive chemical ionization ion trap MS[79,82] and GC-MS/MS[52,77] are commonly used. RIA techniques have also been used[83–85] as well as HPLC with an electrochemical coulometric array. To separate the enantiomers of methadone, LC-MS with a chiral column[73,86] or capillary electrophoresis equipped with a photodiode array detector employing DIMEB as cyclodextrin[74,87] have been used.

3.2.3.2 Methadone Findings in Hair

In 15 segmented hair samples from five subjects of a MTD treatment program ($n = 96$), 95% were positive for MTD (mean value of 10.9 ng/mg) and 76% for the metabolite EDDP (mean value of 1.2 ng/mg).[14] Wilkins et al.[79] found concentrations for two subjects with ranges of 10.1–21 and 21 ng/mg for MTD and 2.6 ng/mg for EDDP, respectively. In another study by Goldberger et al.,[75] disposition of MTD and its metabolites was investigated in head-hair samples collected from heroin users ($n = 20$). Eighteen positive hair specimens were found with concentration up to

15 ng/mg; EDDP was found in 13 specimens in traces, whereas EMDP was found in one specimen. Lucas et al.[71] analyzed hair from eight patients of a MTD maintenance program. The concentration of MTD in hair ranged from 2.45 to 78.10 ng/mg, and for EDDP from 0.98 to 7.76 ng/mg of hair. In 19 cases of 26 cases of drug fatalities, MTD was positive, with concentration ranges of 0.36 to 11.8 ng/mg for MTD and 0.19 to 10.8 ng/mg for EDDP. EMDP was found in only two cases, with concentrations of 0.18 and 0.84 ng/mg.[72]

In hair specimens of 26 patients of a MTD maintenance program, MTD could be determined in every hair specimen, with a mean concentration of 8.2 ng/mg (range: 0.7 to 43.0).[82] The authors could not establish a relation between MTD dose and the concentrations found in hair. Quantification of EDDP in hair was only possible in about 50% of the cases. The authors conclude that the determination of MTD and EDDP in hair is not sufficient to confirm compliance with the treatment. Paterson et al.[78] confirmed that no correlation exists between prescribed dose and concentration of MTD in hair from 60 patients receiving long-term MTD maintenance.

Because the (R)-enantiomer is pharmacologically more active than the (S)-enantiomer, several studies have been published describing methods for the stereoselective determination of MTD. Frost et al.[87] determined the (R)-MTD in hair of one patient following (R)-MTD treatment by capillary electrophoresis. Kintz et al.[73] used LC-MS/MS with an α1-acid glycoprotein column to determine MTD and EDDP enantiomers in nine hair specimens from patients under a racemic MTD treatment program. Concentration ranges were 0.58 to 10.22, 1.89 to 9.53, 0.42 to 1.73, and 0.40 to 2.10 ng/mg for (R)-MTD, (S)-MTD, (R)-EDDP, and (S)-EDDP, respectively. Their results demonstrated the predominance of the (R)-enantiomer. These results were confirmed by Berens et al.[74] in hair specimens from five patients from a MTD treatment program using capillary electrophoresis. (R)-MTD was predominant in three of five cases, with a mean ratio of 1.25 (0.87 to 1.70). Kelly et al.[86] also confirmed this result in hair specimens from 20 patients from a MTD treatment program. Using LC-MS/MS with an α-glycoprotein (AGP) column, a predominance of R-MTD was shown in every specimen.

3.2.4 Buprenorphine

Following intramuscular injection, buprenorphine (BUP) rapidly reaches peak plasma concentration. It is metabolized mainly by N-dealkylation via cytochrome P450 CYP3A4 to N-dealkylbuprenorphine (norbuprenorphine [nBUP]) and by conjugation. It is eliminated mainly in the feces, with a small proportion excreted in the urine as metabolites. Buprenorphine undergoes intensive first-pass metabolism following oral administration; therefore, buprenorphine is administered as a sublingual tablet.

3.2.4.1 Testing Methods

Methods and concentration ranges for the buprenorphine determination in hair and its metabolite norbuprenorphine are described in Table 3.7.

TABLE 3.7
Summary of Methods for the Quantification and Concentration Ranges for Buprenorphine and Its Metabolite in Hair

Decontamination	Extraction	Cleanup	Detection	Concentration Ranges (ng/mg)	Refs.
Dichloromethane	HCl 0.1*N*	L/L	HPLC-coulometric detector	*n* = 3 BUP: 0.48–0.59 nBUP: 0.06–0.15	88
Dichloromethane	HCl 0.1*N*	L/L	RIA HPLC-coulometric detector GC-MS	*n* = 14 BUP: 0.02–0.59 nBUP: 0.02–15	89
Dichloromethane	HCl 0.1*N*	SPE	GC-MS after silylation	*n* = 5 BUP: 0.47–2.4 nBUP: 0.03–0.72	90
Dichloromethane	HCl 0.1*N*	L/L	LC-MS	*n* = 6 BUP: 0.004–0.140 nBUP: 0–0.167	91
Not mentioned	NaOH 1*N*	L/L	LC-MS	*n* = 12 BUP: 0.003–0.124 nBUP: 0.005–1.518	92
Dichloromethane	HCl 0.1*N*	L/L	LC-MS	*n* = 1 BUP: 23 pg/mg nBUP: <LOD	93
Dichloromethane	Soerensen buffer	L/L	One-Step™ ELISA test LC-MS	*n* = 18 BUP: 0.04–0.36	94

Note: L/L = liquid-liquid extraction; SPE = solid-phase extraction.

3.2.4.2 Buprenorphine Findings in Hair

In hair samples from 14 subjects admitted 2 or 3 months previously to a detoxification center, concentration ranges were 0.02 to 0.59 ng/mg for buprenorphine and 0.02 to 0.15 ng/mg for nBUP.[89] Whereas buprenorphine could be identified in all the hair specimens, its metabolite nBUP could not be determined in three specimens. These results suggest that a dose-response relationship exists between the concentration of buprenorphine in hair and the administered dose.

In 12 subjects receiving 8 mg sublingual buprenorphine for a maximum of 180 days, nBUP was present in higher concentrations in hair than the parent compound, with one exception.[92] Buprenorphine concentrations in hair segments ranged from 3.1 to 123.8 pg/mg, whereas nBUP concentrations ranged from 4.8 to 1517.8 pg/mg. Furthermore, in some subjects, buprenorphine and nBUP were detected in hair segments that did not match to the period of drug treatment, indicating that drug movement may have occurred by diffusion in sweat and other mechanisms. The data from this study also suggest that there is a high degree of intersubject variability in measured concentration of buprenorphine

TABLE 3.8
Summary of Methods for the Quantification and Concentration Ranges for Fentanyl, Sufentanyl, and Alfentanil in Hair

Decontamination	Extraction	Cleanup	Detection	Concentration Ranges (ng/mg)	Ref.
		Fentanyl			
EtOH	diluted HCl	L/L	GC-NPD GC-MS	$n = 1$ 0.02	96
MeOH	phosphate buffer	SPE	GC-MS	$n = 5$ (mouse hair) 0.025–0.050	97
		Fentanyl –Sufentanyl			
MeOH	MeOH	no indication	RIA	$n = 13$ fentanyl 0.013–0.048	95
MeOH acetone	phosphate buffer	SPE	GC-MS/MS	$n = 2$ about 0.10	98
MeOH acetone	phosphate buffer	SPE	GC-MS/MS	$n = 1$ fentanyl 0.10 sufentanyl 0.01	25
		Fentanyl, Sufentanyl, Alfentanil			
dichloromethane	phosphate buffer	L/L	GC-MS/MS	$n = 4$ fentanyl 0.008–0.64 sufentanyl 0.002 alfentanil 0.002–0.030	99

Note: L/L = liquid-liquid extraction; SPE = solid-phase extraction; NPD = nitrogen-phosphorus detector.

and BUP in hair segments, even when subjects receive the same dose for an equivalent number of treatment days.

3.2.5 Fentanyl and Congeners

Fentanyl is rapidly metabolized in the liver. Two metabolites, norfentanyl and despropionylfentanyl, have been detected in plasma at concentrations similar to those of fentanyl. About 70% of the dose is excreted in the urine within 72 h, mostly as metabolites, with about 10 to 20% being excreted as unchanged drug within 48 h. About 9% of a dose is eliminated in the feces.

The different methods (RIA,[95] GC-MS,[96,97] and GC-MS/MS[25,98,99]) and the concentration ranges for the determination of fentanyl, sufentanyl, and alfentanil are described in Table 3.8.

Wang et al.[95] determined fentanyl in head-hair samples obtained from 13 surgery patients who received fentanyl during anesthesia. Fentanyl was analyzed by radioimmunoassay (Coat-A-Count Fentanyl assay). The elapsed time after drug administration ranged from 7 to 273 days. Eight of the fentanyl patients' hair samples contained fentanyl concentrations of 0.013 to 0.048 ng/10 mg of hair in proximal hair. No correlation between hair fentanyl concentration and administered dose was found.

In a study by Kintz et al.,[99] fentanyl derivatives were analyzed by GC-MS/MS. The following cases were described: Case 1: 50-year-old anesthetist, positive for fentanyl (644 pg/mg); Case 2: 42-year-old anesthetist, positive for fentanyl (101 pg/mg) and sufentanyl (2 pg/mg); Case 3: 40-year-old anesthetist, positive for alfentanil (30 pg/mg); Case 4: 46-year-old nurse, found dead, positive for alfentanil (2 pg/mg) and fentanyl (8 pg/mg).

3.2.6 Other Opioids

Methods and concentration ranges for the determination of hydrocodone, hydromorphone, and oxycodone,[27] 1-a-acetylmethadol (LAAM),[100] pholocodine,[111] pentazocine,[14,101] dextropropoxyphene,[102,103] tramadol,[25,104–107] piritramide,[108] pethidine,[101] dextromoramide,[109] nalbuphine,[110] and tilidine[104] are described in Table 3.9. Most of the techniques used were chromatographic methods (GC-MS and LC-MS). In general, there is scant data about the concentration ranges of these opioids in hair. For most of the cases, only a few cases reports were described except for dextropropoxyphene and tramadol.

3.3 CONCLUSIONS

This review has shown that, regarding opioids, hair analysis was principally focused on the determination of opiates, particularly morphine, 6-MAM, and codeine.

Several methods and concentration ranges in hair have been published for methadone, buprenorphine, and some fentanyl congeners. However, for some opiods like LAAM and propoxyphene, very few studies were published.

For some opioids like some fentanyl congeners, no methods or cases reports have been published. Besides these opioid agonists, it would also be interesting to investigate in hair the antagonists such as naloxone as well as the newer substances under experimental animal investigation, which are potent, long-lasting, and selective antagonists of morphine-mediated antinociception.[113–115]

Recent developments of increasingly sensitive and specific techniques like GC-MS/MS and LC-MS/MS may help to identify further opioids in hair in the near future.

Table 3.9
Summary of Methods for the Quantification of Some Opioids in Hair

Decontamination	Extraction	Cleanup	Detection	Concentration Ranges (ng/mg)	Ref.
			Hydrocodone, hydromorphone, and oxycodone		
not mentioned	phosphate buffer	SPE	GC-MS methoxime/BSTFA derivatization	qualitative result	27
			LAAM		
different washes tested	protease type VIII	L/L	GC-MS PCI	*n* = 6 (rat hair) 0.88–1.27	100
			Pholcodine		
Acetone	phosphate buffer	L/L	RIA GC-MS	head hair (*n* = 1) 0.5–0.6 beard hair (*n* = 1) 0.6–1.7	111
			Pentazocine		
water/acetone	β–glucuronidase arylsulfatase	SPE	GC-MS	200	7
water/acetone	phosphate buffer	SPE	LC-MS/MS	*n* = 1 0.057	101
			Dextropropoxyphene (DPX) –Norpropoxyphene (DPX)		
water/acetone	β–glucuronidase arylsulfatase	SPE	HPLC-UV	*n* = 11 DPX: 1.2–26.6 NPX: 2.6–71.0	102
dichloromethane phosphate buffer	HCl 0.1*N*	SPE	GC-MS	*n* = 13 DPX: 0.2–27.4 NPX: 0.3–68.0	103
			Tramadol		
MeOH/acetone	phosphate buffer	SPE	GC-MS/MS CI	residue	25
water/acetone	β–glucuronidase arylsulfatase	SPE	GC-MS	*n* = 1 Segment 0–3 cm: 3.7 Segment 3–6 cm: 0.3	104
water/acetone petrol	MeOH	SPE	GC-MS	*n* = 1 80	105
water/acetone	HS-SPME with alkaline digestion	not mentioned	GC-MS	*n* = 2 0.78 and 1.14	106
SDS/MeOH	HCl 3*M*	SPE	GC-MS	*n* = 11 0.18–16.30	107
			Piritamide		
not mentioned	MeOH	not mentioned	LC-MS/MS	*n* = 2 0.64 and 0.004	108

Table 3.9 (continued)
Summary of Methods for the Quantification of Some Opioids in Hair

Decontamination	Extraction	Cleanup	Detection	Concentration Ranges (ng/mg)	Ref.
		Pethidine			
not mentioned	HCl 0.1*M*	SPE	GC-MS	*n* = 1 1.9	112
acetone/water	phosphate buffer	SPE	LC-MS/MS	*n* = 1 0.017	101
		Dextromoramide			
dichloromethane	HCl 0.1*M*	L/L	GC-MS	*n* = 1 1.09–1.48	109
		Nalbuphine			
not mentioned	phosphate buffer	L/L	LC-MS	*n* = 1 three segments 5.07–7.06	110
		Tilidine			
water/acetone	ß-glucuronidase arylsulfatase	SPE	GC/MS	n = 1 Segment 0–3 cm: 5.6 Segment 3–6 cm: 9.1	104

Note: L/L = liquid-liquid extraction; SPE = solid-phase extraction; BSTFA = bis(trimethylsilyl)trifluoroacetamide, SDS = sodium dodecyl sulphate.

REFERENCES

1. Kintz, P., Toxicologie et pharmacologie médicolégales, in *Collection option Bio, Editions scientifiques et médicales*, Elsevier, New York, 1998.
2. Moffat, A., Osselton, M., and Widdop, B., *Clarke's Analysis of Drugs and Poisons*, Pharmaceutical Press, London, 2003.
3. Kolber, I., Labarthe, A., Schneider, S., Yegles, M., and Wennig, R., LC/MS/MS and GC/MS Determination of Codeine Disposition in Classical and Alternative Biological Matrices, communication at TIAFT Meeting , Paris, 2002.
4. Sachs, H. and Arnold, W., Results of comparative determination of morphine in human hair using RIA and GC/MS, *J. Clin. Chem. Clin. Biochem.*, 27, 873–877, 1989.
5. Goldberger, B.A., Caplan, Y.H., Maguire, T., and Cone, E.J., Testing human hair for drugs of abuse, III: identification of heroin and 6-acetylmorphine as indicators of heroin use, *J. Anal. Toxicol.*, 15, 226–231, 1991.
6. Nakahara, Y., Takahashi, K., Shimamine, M., and Saitoh, A., Hair analysis for drugs of abuse, IV: determination of total morphine and confirmation of 6-acetylmorphine in monkey and human hair by GC/MS, *Arch. Toxicol.*, 66, 669–674, 1992.
7. Moeller, M.R., Fey, P., and Sachs, H., Hair analysis as evidence in forensic cases, *Forensic Sci. Int.*, 63, 43–53, 1993.
8. Kintz, P., *Drug Testing in Hair*, CRC Press, Boca Raton, FL, 1997.
9. Madea, B. and Musshoff, F., *Haaranalytik*, Deutscher Aerzte-Verlag, Köln, 2003.

10. Anon., Recommendations for hair testing in forensic cases, *Forensic Sci. Int.*, 145, 83–84, 2004.
11. Garside, D.G.B., *Determination of Cocaine and Opioids in Hair*, CRC Press, Boca Raton, FL, 1996.
12. Baumgartner, A.M., Jones, P.F., Baumgartner, W.A., and Black, C.T., Radioimmunoassay of hair for determining opiate-abuse histories, *J. Nucl. Med.*, 20, 748–752, 1979.
13. Nakahara, Y., Kikura, R., and Takahashi, K., Hair analysis for drugs of abuse, VIII: effective extraction and determination of 6-acetylmorphine and morphine in hair with trifluoroacetic acid-methanol for the confirmation of retrospective heroin use by gas chromatography-mass spectrometry, *J. Chromatogr. B Biomed. Appl.*, 657, 93–101, 1994.
14. Moeller, M.R., Fey, P., and Wennig, R., Simultaneous determination of drugs of abuse (opiates, cocaine and amphetamine) in human hair by GC/MS and its application to a methadone treatment program, *Forensic Sci. Int.*, 63, 185–206, 1993.
15. Goldberger, B.A., Cone, E.J., Grant, T.M., Caplan, Y.H., Levine, B.S., and Smialek, J.E., Disposition of heroin and its metabolites in heroin-related deaths, *J. Anal. Toxicol.*, 18, 22–28, 1994.
16. Romolo, F.S., Rotolo, M.C., Palmi, I., Pacifici, R., and Lopez, A., Optimized conditions for simultaneous determination of opiates, cocaine and benzoylecgonine in hair samples by GC-MS, *Forensic Sci. Int.*, 138, 17–26, 2003.
17. Kintz, P., Tracqui, A., and Mangin, P., Detection of drugs in human hair for clinical and forensic applications, *Int. J. Legal Med.*, 105, 1–4, 1992.
18. Jurado, C., Gimenez, M.P., Menendez, M., and Repetto, M., Simultaneous quantification of opiates, cocaine and cannabinoids in hair, *Forensic Sci. Int.*, 70, 165–174, 1995.
19. Kintz, P. and Mangin, P., Simultaneous determination of opiates, cocaine and major metabolites of cocaine in human hair by gas chromatography/mass spectrometry (GC/MS), *Forensic Sci. Int.*, 73, 93–100, 1995.
20. Marsh, A., Carruthers, M.E., Desouza, N., and Evans, M.B., An investigation of the effect of washing upon the morphine content of hair measured by a radioimmunoassay technique, *J. Pharm. Biomed. Anal.,* 10, 89–93, 1992.
21. Kronstrand, R., Nystrom, I., Strandberg, J., and Druid, H., Screening for drugs of abuse in hair with ion spray LC-MS-MS, *Forensic Sci. Int.*, 145, 183–190, 2004.
22. Cone, E.J., Darwin, W.D., and Wang, W.L., The occurrence of cocaine, heroin and metabolites in hair of drug abusers, *Forensic Sci. Int.*, 63, 55–68, 1993.
23. Kauert, G. and Röhrich, J., Concentrations of delta 9-tetrahydrocannabinol, cocaine and 6-monoacetylmorphine in hair of drug abusers, *Int. J. Legal Med.*, 108, 294–299, 1996.
24. Pichini, S., Pacifici, R., Altieri, I., Pellegrini, M., and Zuccaro, P., Determination of opiates and cocaine in hair as trimethylsilyl derivatives using gas chromatography-tandem mass spectrometry, *J. Anal. Toxicol.*, 23, 343–348, 1999.
25. Uhl, M., Determination of drugs in hair using GC/MS/MS, *Forensic Sci. Int.*, 84, 281–294, 1997.
26. Skender, L., Karacic, V., Brcic, I., and Bagaric, A., Quantitative determination of amphetamines, cocaine, and opiates in human hair by gas chromatography/mass spectrometry, *Forensic Sci. Int.*, 125, 120–126, 2002.
27. Jones, J., Tomlinson, K., and Moore, C., The simultaneous determination of codeine, morphine, hydrocodone, hydromorphone, 6-acetylmorphine, and oxycodone in hair and oral fluid, *J. Anal. Toxicol.*, 26, 171–175, 2002.
28. Eser, H.P., Pötsch, L., Skopp, G., and Moeller, M.R., Influence of sample preparation on analytical results: drug analysis (GC/MS) on hair snippets versus hair powder using various extraction methods, *Forensic Sci. Int.*, 84, 271–279, 1997.

29. Hold, K.M., Wilkins, D.G., Rollins, D.E., Joseph, R.E., Jr., and Cone, E.J., Simultaneous quantitation of cocaine, opiates, and their metabolites in human hair by positive ion chemical ionization gas chromatography-mass spectrometry, *J. Chromatogr. Sci.*, 36, 125–130, 1998.
30. Montagna, M., Stramesi, C., Vignali, C., Groppi, A., and Polettini, A., Simultaneous hair testing for opiates, cocaine, and metabolites by GC-MS: a survey of applicants for driving licenses with a history of drug use, *Forensic Sci. Int.*, 107, 157–167, 2000.
31. Girod, C. and Staub, C., Analysis of drugs of abuse in hair by automated solid-phase extraction, GC/EI/MS and GC ion trap/CI/MS, *Forensic Sci. Int.*, 107, 261–271, 2000.
32. Balikova, M.A. and Habrdova, V., Hair analysis for opiates: evaluation of washing and incubation procedures, *J. Chromatogr. B Anal. Technol. Biomed. Life Sci.*, 789, 93–100, 2003.
33. Cingolani, M., Scavella, S., Mencarelli, R., Mirtella, D., Froldi, R., and Rodriguez, D., Simultaneous detection and quantitation of morphine, 6-acetylmorphine, and cocaine in toenails: comparison with hair analysis, *J. Anal. Toxicol.*, 28, 128–131, 2004.
34. Wang, W.L., Darwin, W.D., and Cone, E.J., Simultaneous assay of cocaine, heroin and metabolites in hair, plasma, saliva and urine by gas chromatography-mass spectrometry, *J. Chromatogr. B Biomed. Appl.*, 660, 279–290, 1994.
35. Yegles, M., Marson, Y., and Wennig, R., Influence of bleaching on stability of benzodiazepines in hair, *Forensic Sci. Int.*, 107, 87–92, 2000.
36. Montagna, M., Polettini, A., Stramesi, C., Groppi, A., and Vignali, C., Hair analysis for opiates, cocaine and metabolites: evaluation of a method by interlaboratory comparison, *Forensic Sci. Int.*, 128, 79–83, 2002.
37. Chiarotti, M., Overview on extraction procedures, *Forensic Sci. Int.*, 63, 161–170, 1993.
38. Edder, P., Staub, C., Veuthey, J.L., Pierroz, I., and Haerdi, W., Subcritical fluid extraction of opiates in hair of drug addicts, *J. Chromatogr. B Biomed. Appl.*, 658, 75–86, 1994.
39. Brewer, W.E., Galipo, R.C., Sellers, K.W., and Morgan, S.L., Analysis of cocaine, benzoylecgonine, codeine, and morphine in hair by supercritical fluid extraction with carbon dioxide modified with methanol, *Anal. Chem.*, 73, 2371–2376, 2001.
40. Sarafraz-Yazdi, A. and Es'haghi, Z., Surfactant enhanced liquid-phase microextraction of basic drugs of abuse in hair combined with high-performance liquid chromatography, *J. Chromatogr. A*, 1094, 1–8, 2005.
41. George, S. and Braithwaite, R.A., The measurement of morphine in the hair of heroin abusers, *Ann. Clin. Biochem.*, 34, 375–383, 1997.
42. Moeller, M.R. and Mueller, C., The detection of 6-monoacetylmorphine in urine, serum and hair by GC/MS and RIA, *Forensic Sci. Int.*, 70, 125–133, 1995.
43. Tagliaro, F., Marigo, M., Dorizzi, R., and Rigolin, F., Detection of morphine in the hair of opiate addicts with the Abbott TDx: a note of caution, *Clin. Chem.*, 34, 1365–1366, 1988.
44. Segura, J., Stramesi, C., Redon, A., Ventura, M., Sanchez, C.J., Gonzalez, G., San, L., and Montagna, M., Immunological screening of drugs of abuse and gas chromatographic-mass spectrometric confirmation of opiates and cocaine in hair, *J. Chromatogr. B Biomed. Sci. Appl.*, 724, 9–21, 1999.
45. Cooper, G., Wilson, L., Reid, C., Baldwin, D., Hand, C., and Spiehler, V., Validation of the Cozart microplate ELISA for detection of opiates in hair, *J. Anal. Toxicol.*, 27, 581–586, 2003.
46. Lachenmeier, K., Musshoff, F., and Madea, B., Determination of opiates and cocaine in hair using automated enzyme immunoassay screening methodologies followed by gas chromatographic-mass spectrometric (GC-MS) confirmation, *Forensic Sci. Int.*, in press.

47. Sachs, H. and Kintz, P., Testing for drugs in hair: critical review of chromatographic procedures since 1992, *J. Chromatogr. B Biomed. Sci. Appl.*, 713, 147–161, 1998.
48. Polettini, A., Groppi, A., and Montagna, M., Rapid and highly selective GC/MS/MS detection of heroin and its metabolites in hair, *Forensic Sci. Int.*, 63, 217–225, 1993.
49. Curcuruto, O., Guidugli, F., Traldi, P., Sturaro, A., Tagliaro, F., and Marigo, M., Ion-trap mass spectrometry applications in forensic sciences, I: identification of morphine and cocaine in hair extracts of drug addicts, *Rapid Commun. Mass Spectrom.*, 6, 434–437, 1992.
50. Gambelunghe, C., Rossi, R., Ferranti, C., Rossi, R., and Bacci, M., Hair analysis by GC/MS/MS to verify abuse of drugs, *J. Appl. Toxicol.*, 25, 205–211, 2005.
51. Traldi, P., Favretto, D., and Tagliaro, F., Ion trap mass spectrometry, a new tool in the investigation of drugs of abuse in hair, *Forensic Sci. Int.*, 63, 239–252, 1993.
52. Uhl, M., Tandem mass spectrometry: a helpful tool in hair analysis for the forensic expert, *Forensic Sci. Int.*, 107, 169–179, 2000.
53. Klys, M., Rojek, S., Kulikowska, J., Bozek, E., and Scislowski, M., Usefulness of multi-parameter opiate analysis in hair of drug users and victims of fatal poisonings. *Przegl Lek*, 62, 585–590, 2005.
54. Tagliaro, F., Poiesi, C., Aiello, R., Dorizzi, R., Ghielmi, S., and Marigo, M., Capillary electrophoresis for the investigation of illicit drugs in hair: determination of cocaine and morphine, *J. Chromatogr.*, 638, 303–309, 1993.
55. Tagliaro, F., De Battisti, Z., Lubli, G., Neri, C., Manetto, G., and Marigo, M., Integrated use of hair analysis to investigate the physical fitness to obtain the driving licence: a casework study, *Forensic Sci. Int.*, 84, 129–135, 1997.
56. Tagliaro, F., Manetto, G., Crivellente, F., Scarcella, D., and Marigo, M., Hair analysis for abused drugs by capillary zone electrophoresis with field-amplified sample stacking, *Forensic Sci. Int.*, 92, 201–211, 1998.
57. Manetto, G., Tagliaro, F., Crivellente, F., Pascali, V.L., and Marigo, M., Field-amplified sample stacking capillary zone electrophoresis applied to the analysis of opiate drugs in hair, *Electrophoresis*, 21, 2891–2898, 2000.
58. Kintz, P. and Mangin, P., What constitutes a positive result in hair analysis: proposal for the establishment of cut-off values, *Forensic Sci. Int.*, 70, 3–11, 1995.
59. Pepin, G. and Gaillard, Y., Concordance between self-reported drug use and findings in hair about cocaine and heroin, *Forensic Sci. Int.*, 84, 37–41, 1997.
60. Gaillard, Y. and Pepin, G., Simultaneous solid-phase extraction on C18 cartridges of opiates and cocainics for an improved quantitation in human hair by GC-MS: one year of forensic applications, *Forensic Sci. Int.*, 86, 49–59, 1997.
61. Anon., Statement of the Society of Hair Testing concerning the examination of drugs in human hair, *Forensic Sci. Int.*, 84, 3–6, 1997.
62. Kintz, P., Jamey, C., Cirimele, V., Brenneisen, R., and Ludes, B., Evaluation of acetylcodeine as a specific marker of illicit heroin in human hair, *J. Anal. Toxicol.*, 22, 425–429, 1998.
63. Girod, C. and Staub, C., Acetylcodeine as a marker of illicit heroin in human hair: method validation and results of a pilot study, *J. Anal. Toxicol.*, 25, 106–111, 2001.
64. Musshoff, F., Lachenmeier, K., Wollersen, H., Lichtermann, D., and Madea, B., Opiate concentrations in hair from subjects in a controlled heroin-maintenance program and from opiate-associated fatalities, *J. Anal. Toxicol.*, 29, 345–352, 2005.
65. Kintz, P., Bundeli, P., Brenneisen, R., and Ludes, B., Dose-concentration relationships in hair from subjects in a controlled heroin-maintenance program, *J. Anal. Toxicol.*, 22, 231–236, 1998.

66. Baumgartner, W. and Hill, V., *Hair Analysis for Drugs of Abuse: Decontamination Issues*, Marcel Dekker, New York, 1992, p. 577–597.
67. Pötsch, L. and Skopp, G., Stability of opiates in hair fibers after exposure to cosmetic treatment, *Forensic Sci. Int.*, 81, 95–102, 1996.
68. Jurado, C., Kintz, P., Menendez, M., and Repetto, M., Influence of the cosmetic treatment of hair on drug testing, *Int. J. Legal Med.*, 110, 159–163, 1997.
69. Cirimele, V., Kintz, P., and Mangin, P., Drug concentrations in human hair after bleaching, *J. Anal. Toxicol.*, 19, 331–332, 1995.
70. Tanaka, S., Iio, R., Chinaka, S., Takayama, N., and Hayakawa, K., Analysis of reaction products of morphine and codeine with hydrogen peroxide by high-performance liquid chromatography/mass spectrometry, *Anal. Sci.*, 19, 163–165, 2003.
71. Lucas, A.C., Bermejo, A.M., Tabernero, M.J., Fernandez, P., and Strano-Rossi, S., Use of solid-phase microextraction (SPME) for the determination of methadone and EDDP in human hair by GC-MS, *Forensic Sci. Int.*, 107, 225–232, 2000.
72. Sporkert, F. and Pragst, F., Determination of methadone and its metabolites EDDP and EMDP in human hair by headspace solid-phase microextraction and gas chromatography-mass spectrometry, *J. Chromatogr. B Biomed. Sci. Appl.*, 746, 255–264, 2000.
73. Kintz, P., Eser, H.P., Tracqui, A., Moeller, M., Cirimele, V., and Mangin, P., Enantioselective separation of methadone and its main metabolite in human hair by liquid chromatography/ion spray-mass spectrometry, *J. Forensic Sci.*, 42, 291–295, 1997.
74. Berens, G., Yegles, M., and Wennig, R., Study of the methadone and EDDP enantiomeric ratio in hair, urine and serum by capillary electrophoresis, *Proceedings TIAFT*, Paris, Aug. 26–30, 2003.
75. Goldberger, B.A., Darraj, A.G., Caplan, Y.H., and Cone, E.J., Detection of methadone, methadone metabolites, and other illicit drugs of abuse in hair of methadone-treatment subjects, *J. Anal. Toxicol.*, 22, 526–530, 1998.
76. Paterson, S., McLachlan-Troup, N., Cordero, R., Dohnal, M., and Carman, S., Qualitative screening for drugs of abuse in hair using GC-MS, *J. Anal. Toxicol.*, 25, 203–208, 2001.
77. Lachenmeier, D.W., Kroener, L., Musshoff, F., and Madea, B., Application of tandem mass spectrometry combined with gas chromatography and headspace solid-phase dynamic extraction for the determination of drugs of abuse in hair samples, *Rapid Commun. Mass Spectrom.*, 17, 472–478, 2003.
78. Paterson, S., Cordero, R., McPhillips, M., and Carman, S., Interindividual dose/concentration relationship for methadone in hair, *J. Anal. Toxicol.*, 27, 20–23, 2003.
79. Wilkins, D.G., Nagasawa, P.R., Gygi, S.P., Foltz, R.L., and Rollins, D.E., Quantitative analysis of methadone and two major metabolites in hair by positive chemical ionization ion trap mass spectrometry, *J. Anal. Toxicol.*, 20, 355–361, 1996.
80. Gentili, S., Cornetta, M., and Macchia, T., Rapid screening procedure based on headspace solid-phase microextraction and gas chromatography-mass spectrometry for the detection of many recreational drugs in hair, *J. Chromatogr. B Anal. Technol. Biomed. Life Sci.*, 801, 289–296, 2004.
81. Balabanova, S., Arnold, P.J., Brunner, H., Luckow, V., and Wolf, H.U., Detection of methadone in human hair by gas chromatography/mass spectrometry, *Z. Rechtsmed.*, 102, 495–501, 1989.
82. Girod, C. and Staub, C., Methadone and EDDP in hair from human subjects following a maintenance program: results of a pilot study, *Forensic Sci. Int.*, 117, 175–184, 2001.
83. Balabanova, S. and Wolf, H.U., Determination of methadone in human hair by radioimmunoassay, *Z. Rechtsmed.*, 102, 1–4, 1989.

84. Marsh, A. and Evans, M.B., Radioimmunoassay of drugs of abuse in hair, part 1: methadone in human hair, method adaptation and the evaluation of decontamination procedures, *J. Pharm. Biomed. Anal.*, 12, 1123–1130, 1994.
85. Marsh, A., Evans, M.B., and Strang, J., Radioimmunoassay of drugs of abuse in hair, part 2: the determination of methadone in the hair of known drug users, *J. Pharm. Biomed. Anal.*, 13, 829–839, 1995.
86. Kelly, T., Doble, P., and Dawson, M., Chiral analysis of methadone and its major metabolites (EDDP and EMDP) by liquid chromatography-mass spectrometry, *J. Chromatogr. B Anal. Technol. Biomed. Life Sci.*, 814, 315–323, 2005.
87. Frost, M., Köhler, H., and Blaschke, G., Enantioselective determination of methadone and its main metabolite 2-ethylidene-1,5-dimethyl-3,3-diphenylpyrrolidine (EDDP) in serum, urine and hair by capillary electrophoresis, *Electrophoresis*, 18, 1026–1034, 1997.
88. Kintz, P., Determination of buprenorphine and its dealkylated metabolite in human hair, *J. Anal. Toxicol.*, 17, (7), 443-4, 1993.
89. Kintz, P., Cirimele, V., Edel, Y., Jamey, C., and Mangin, P., Hair analysis for buprenorphine and its dealkylated metabolite by RIA and confirmation by LC/ECD, *J. Forensic Sci.*, 39, 1497–1503, 1994.
90. Vincent, F., Bessard, J., Vacheron, J., Mallaret, M., and Bessard, G., Determination of buprenorphine and norbuprenorphine in urine and hair by gas chromatography-mass spectrometry, *J. Anal. Toxicol.*, 23, 270–279, 1999.
91. Tracqui, A., Kintz, P., and Mangin, P., HPLC/MS determination of buprenorphine and norbuprenorphine in biological fluids and hair samples, *J. Forensic Sci.*, 42, 111–114, 1997.
92. Wilkins, D.G., Rollins, D.E., Valdez, A.S., Mizuno, A., Krueger, G.G., and Cone, E.J., A retrospective study of buprenorphine and norbuprenorphine in human hair after multiple doses, *J. Anal. Toxicol.*, 23, 409–415, 1999.
93. Kintz, P., Villain, M., Tracqui, A., Cirimele, V., and Ludes, B., Buprenorphine in drug-facilitated sexual abuse: a fatal case involving a 14-year-old boy, *J. Anal. Toxicol.*, 27, 527–529, 2003.
94. Cirimele, V., Etienne, S., Villain, M., Ludes, B., and Kintz, P., Evaluation of the One-Step ELISA kit for the detection of buprenorphine in urine, blood, and hair specimens, *Forensic Sci. Int.*, 143, 153–156, 2004.
95. Wang, W.L., Cone, E.J., and Zacny, J., Immunoassay evidence for fentanyl in hair of surgery patients, *Forensic Sci. Int.*, 61, 65–72, 1993.
96. Selavka, C.M., Mason, A.P., Riker, C.D., and Crookham, S., Determination of fentanyl in hair: the case of the crooked criminalist, *J. Forensic Sci.*, 40, 681–685, 1995.
97. Stout, P.R., Claffey, D.J., and Ruth, J.A., Fentanyl in hair: chemical factors involved in accumulation and retention of fentanyl in hair after external exposure or *in vivo* deposition, *Drug Metab. Dispos.*, 26, 689–700, 1998.
98. Sachs, H., Uhl, M., Hege-Scheuing, G., and Schneider, E., Analysis of fentanyl and sufentanil in hair by GC/MS/MS, *Int. J. Legal Med.*, 109, 213–215, 1996.
99. Kintz, P., Villain, M., Dumestre, V., and Cirimele, V., Evidence of addiction by anesthesiologists as documented by hair analysis, *Forensic Sci. Int.*, 153, 81–84, 2005.
100. Wilkins, D.G., Valdez, A.S., Krueger, G.G., and Rollins, D.E., Quantitative analysis of l-alpha-acetylmethadol, l-alpha-acetyl-N-normethadol, and l-alpha-acetyl-N,N-dinormethadol in human hair by positive ion chemical ionization mass spectrometry, *J. Anal. Toxicol.*, 21, 420–426, 1997.
101. Yegles, M., unpublished data, 2005.

102. Mersch, F., Yegles, M., and Wennig, R., Quantification of dextropropoxyphene and its metabolite by HPLC in hair of overdose cases, *Forensic Sci. Int.*, 84, 237–242, 1997.
103. Gaillard, Y. and Pepin, G., Gas chromatographic-mass spectrometric quantitation of dextropropoxyphene and norpropoxyphene in hair and whole blood after automated on-line solid-phase extraction: application in twelve fatalities, *J. Chromatogr. B Biomed. Sci. Appl.*, 709, 69–77, 1998.
104. Asselborn, G., Yegles, M., and Wennig, R. Chronic multiple drugs abuse with suicidal endpoints: Hair and Tissue Findings. Proceedings TIAFT Padova, Aug. 24–28, 1997, pp. 56–59.
105. Rickert, A. and Daldrup, T., Nachweis von Tramadol in Haaren, in *Proceedings GTFCH Mosbach, Germany*, April 22–24, 1999, pp. 308–314.
106. Sporkert, F. and Pragst, F., Use of headspace solid-phase microextraction (HS-SPME) in hair analysis for organic compounds, *Forensic Sci. Int.*, 107, 129–148, 2000.
107. Hadidi, K.A., Almasad, J.K., Al-Nsour, T., and Abu-Ragheib, S., Determination of tramadol in hair using solid phase extraction and GC-MS, *Forensic Sci. Int.*, 135, 129–136, 2003.
108. Sachs, H., Thieme, D., and Anielski, P., LC-MS-MS Screening auf Piritramid und andere Opiode in Haaren, in *Proceedings GTFCH Mosbach, Germany*, April 03–05, 2003, pp. 392–396.
109. Kintz, P., Cirimele, V., Edel, Y., Tracqui, A., and Mangin, P., Characterization of dextromoramide (Palfium) abuse by hair analysis in a denied case, *Int. J. Legal Med.*, 107, 269–272, 1995.
110. Vinner, E., Klinzig, F., Brassart, C., Houdain, E., Houdret, N., and Lhermitte, M., Dosage de la nalbuphine dans les cheveux par LC/MS, communication at 3e Journées Internationales de Toxicologie Hospitalière, Liège, Nov. 24–25, 2005.
111. Maurer, H.H. and Fritz, C.F., Toxicological detection of pholcodine and its metabolites in urine and hair using radio immunoassay, fluorescence polarisation immunoassay, enzyme immunoassay, and gas chromatography-mass spectrometry, *Int. J. Legal Med.*, 104, 43–46, 1990.
112. Gaillard, Y. and Pepin, G., Screening and identification of drugs in human hair by high-performance liquid chromatography-photodiode-array UV detection and gas chromatography-mass spectrometry after solid-phase extraction: a powerful tool in forensic medicine, *J. Chromatogr. A*, 762, 251–267, 1997.
113. Barrett, A.C., Smith, E.S., and Picker, M.J., Use of irreversible antagonists to determine the relative efficacy of mu-opioids in a pigeon drug discrimination procedure: comparison of beta-funaltrexamine and clocinnamox, *J. Pharmacol. Exp. Ther.*, 305, 1061–1070, 2003.
114. Broadbear, J.H., Sumpter, T.L., Burke, T.F., Husbands, S.M., Lewis, J.W., Woods, J.H., and Traynor, J.R., Methocinnamox is a potent, long-lasting, and selective antagonist of morphine-mediated antinociception in the mouse: comparison with clocinnamox, beta-funaltrexamine, and beta-chlornaltrexamine, *J. Pharmacol. Exp. Ther.*, 294, 933–940, 2000.
115. Kogel, B., Christoph, T., Strassburger, W., and Friderichs, E., Interaction of mu-opioid receptor agonists and antagonists with the analgesic effect of buprenorphine in mice, *Eur. J. Pain*, 9, 599–611, 2005.

4 Hair Analysis for Cocaine

Carmen Jurado

CONTENTS

4.1 INTRODUCTION

Cocaine is the most potent of the naturally occurring stimulants of the central nervous system. Therefore, it has a long history of use and abuse.

If we study the evolution in the type of drugs of abuse consumed by drug addicts over time, there are two different behaviors. On the one hand, noticeable changes can be observed for some drugs. For example, heroin consumption has decreased considerably over the last few years; at the same time, the use of a new generation of synthetic amphetamines or "designer drugs" has increased dramatically. On the other hand, the consumption of other drugs has been more or less homogeneous, and substantial changes have not been observed. This is the case for cannabis and cocaine, for example; the latter is the drug of abuse that centers the interest of this chapter.

As cocaine has been and continues to be one of the drugs of abuse most extensively consumed, many researchers on hair analysis have focused their studies and experiments on this substance. As a consequence, a large body of literature related to cocaine in hair samples has been published to date.

The aim of this chapter is to review, summarize, and discuss all of the aspects related to the analysis of cocaine in hair specimens. The first topic addressed in this chapter is the different methodologies for the analysis of cocaine in hair samples. These analyses have progressed to the point where nearly all of the laboratories can adequately analyze hair samples; nevertheless, new analytical challenges continue to appear and require major discussion.

In addition to the analytical challenges, equal or greater challenges exist in the interpretation and implications of the results produced in the laboratories. When a positive result for cocaine is obtained in hair analysis, the first questions are, "What does it mean?" and "Are there any circumstances that can affect these results?" Both of these questions must be taken into account before reporting the final result.

Finally, quality assurance and quality control are inevitable and appropriate topics, since they significantly impact the way we practice our analyses and the reliability of our results.

4.2 ANALYTICAL METHODOLOGIES

One of the main disadvantages of hair analysis when compared with the analysis of other biological fluids, such as urine or blood, is the complexity and laboriousness of the analytical procedures. The analysis of any substance, including cocaine, in hair samples involves the following steps:

- Decontamination or washing of the hair sample to eliminate any possible external contamination.
- Extraction of the drugs and their metabolites. In this step, the drug is released from the hair matrix and then purified and concentrated.
- Instrumental analysis. A large variety of detection methods can be used, including screening techniques and those applied for confirmation and quantitation.

The quality of the results depends on the correct performance of each one of these steps, which are summarized in Table 4.1 and will be thoroughly discussed below, on the basis of published papers and with special emphasis on comparing the efficacies of different methods. Because a very substantial amount of literature can be found on hair analysis for cocaine, only the papers published after 1996 are reviewed in this chapter. Another contributing factor is that the studies performed before 1996 were extensively reviewed by Garside and Goldberger in the chapter devoted to cocaine and opioids in hair[1] that was included in the preceding book about drug testing in hair.[2]

Table 4.1
Summary of Analytical Methodologies for the Analysis of Cocaine in Hair Samples

Ref.	Washing	Extraction	Purification	Derivatization	Analysis
3	MeOH	MeOH, 37°C, 18h	SFE	no	GC-MS-EI
19	$CH_2Cl_2 + H_2O + CH_2Cl_2$	0.1*M* HCl, 56°C, 15h	SFE Isolute Confirm HCX	no	HPLC-FL
36	—	proteinase K tris buffer, pH 6.5	SFE	MSHBA, MBHFBA, TMSIM	GC-MS-PCI
7	CH_2Cl_2	MeOH, 56°C, 18 h	no	BSTFA	GC-MS-EI
6	CH_2Cl_2	MeOH:TFA (9:1), 37°C, overnight	SPE BondElut	HFBA+HFPIOH	GC-MS-EI
28	—	SFE	no	—	—
33	not reported	0.1*M* HCl, 45°C, overnight	SPE Clean Screen	TFA+HFPIOH	GC-MS/MS
15	SDS + acetone	phosphate buffer, pH 6.0	SPE Chromabond-Drug	TFA+HFPIOH	GC-MS-EI
17	$CH_2Cl_2 + H_2O$ + MeOH	0.01*M* HCl, 60°C, 12 h	Automated SPE	Py + PAA	GC-MS-EI and CI
14	Hexane + acetone	MeOH, son., 1 h, 40°C + stand overnight	no	PFPA + HFPIOH	GC-MS/MS
4	MeOH	0.1*M* HCl, 45°C, overnight	SPE BondElut	MSTFA	GC-MS-EI
35	Tween + H_2O	0.12*M* HCl, 45°C, overnight	Toxi-Tube A	no	RIA, HPLC-Fl, CE
34	—	0.1*M* HCl, shaking water bath overnight at r.t.	SPE BondElut	no	HPLC/MS
13	H_2O + MeOH	SFE	—	PFPA	GC-MS-EI
8	CH_2Cl_2	MeOH, 45°C, 18 h	no	MTBSTFA	GC-MS-EI
21	isopropanol + 0.01*M* phosphate buffer	proteinase-K, dithiothreitol, and detergent	Isolute™ SPE	no	HPLC-MS/MS
9	CH_2Cl_2	MeOH, 40°C, 18 h	SPE BondElut	Py + PAA	GC-MS-EI
10	CH_2Cl_2	MeOH 50°C, 18 h	HS-SPME	Acetonitrile + Py + butylchloroformate	GC-MS-EI
5	MeOH	Phosphate buffer, pH 5, 45°C, 18 h	SPE BondElut	MSTFA/TMCS	GC-MS-EI
22	2-propanol + 0.01*M* phosphate buffer + 2-propanol	acetonitrile:MeOH:20m*M* formate buffer, pH 3, 37°C, 18 h	no	no	LC-MS/MS
11	CH_2Cl_2	HCl 37%, 100°C, 30 min	SPE, BondElut Certify	PAA	GC-MS-EI
16	H_2O + acetone	1*M* HCl, 60°C, 60 min	HS-SPME	no	GC-MS-EI
37	—	MeOH, son., 37°C, 3 h	SPE Clean Screen	no	LC-APCI-MS/MS
18	$CH_2Cl_2 + H_2O$ + MeOH	0.01*M* HCl, 60°C, 12 h	Automated SPE	Py + PAA	GC-CI-MS/MS
12	CH_2Cl_2	MeOH, 2-h son. + 56°C overnight	no	MSTFA:NH_4I:DTE	GC-MS/MS

Note: Table 4.1 includes only works published after 1996.

4.2.1 Decontamination Procedures

Hair, being on the exterior of the body, is subject to environmental contact and hence contamination. It is quite possible that certain drugs such as cocaine can contaminate a nonuser's hair. For this reason, the potential for evidentiary false positives caused by environmental contamination of human hair has generated a great deal of controversy regarding the ability of laboratories to reliably differentiate endogenous from exogenous sources of drugs in hair. Consequently, it is of paramount importance to wash the hair samples extensively with appropriate solutions. Laboratories engaged in drug testing of hair currently employ a wide variety of operationally defined decontamination procedures that attempt to remove environmental contamination from the surface of the hair.

Since the beginning of hair analysis, various authors have proposed several decontamination procedures. They include, among others, washings with methanol[3–5] and dichloromethane (CH_2Cl_2).[6–12] Other authors apply sequential washes of water and methanol[13] or washes with acetone followed by n-hexane,[14] sodium dodecyl sulfate,[15] or water.[16] Sequential washes with CH_2Cl_2, water, and methanol[17,18] or with CH_2Cl_2 followed by water and CH_2Cl_2 once again[19] have also been used. More complicated was the washing procedure proposed by Baumgartner,[20] which consisted of a first washing with ethanol followed by three sequential washes with 0.5*M* phosphate buffer. This method has also been used by other authors.[21,22] Variants of these procedures have been employed by many analytical laboratories to remove external environmental drug contaminant from the hair sample prior to digestion. However, the significance and effectiveness of these decontamination procedures have been the subject of much debate.[23–26]

Several authors focused their experiments on studying the efficiency of different decontamination procedures. For example, Schaffer et al.[21] compared the efficacy of three washing methods to differentiate external contamination versus ingestion for the analysis of cocaine in hair. For that purpose they soaked blank hair with a highly concentrated solution of cocaine (1000 ng/ml) and separated three aliquots. One of them was washed with methanol three times, another aliquot was sequentially washed with isopropanol and with 0.01*M* phosphate buffer (pH 6) three times, while the last aliquot was subjected to a wash procedure consisting of isopropanol followed by five phosphate buffer washes. On the one hand, they found that methanol washes removed from 16.7 to 77.5% of the cocaine, with the amount of cocaine remaining ranging from 0.12 to 2.42 ng/mg, thus confirming the results previously obtained by Wang and Cone.[24] On the other hand, the other procedures were able to remove 76.0 to 93% and 82.9 to 97.2% of cocaine when washing three or five times, respectively, with the buffer; and the cocaine in the hair was reduced below the cutoff of 0.5 ng/mg in both cases, demonstrating that the two additional washes were unnecessary. They recognized the unrealistically severe conditions of their contamination procedure, but they concluded that washing methods effective with this degree of contamination would likely be more than sufficient for a less severe contamination.

During the development of a decontamination process for the analysis of all types of drugs of abuse in hair samples, including cocaine, it is necessary to evaluate not only the amount of contaminant removed from the surface of the hair, but also the amount of incorporated drug removed from the hair by this process. Ideally, washing procedures would allow incorporated drugs to remain in place and not be removed from the hair during the decontamination.

Studies on the influence of the decontamination protocol in the final recovery of drugs were performed by Segura et al.[6] in six hair samples from two volunteers who consumed opiates, cocaine, and benzodiazepines. After washing with dichloromethane, only 1.36 ± 0.22% of the internal cocaine was extracted.

Paulsen et al.[27] evaluated the effect of four simple laboratory washing procedures on quantitative measurement of cocaine and metabolites in hair from rats who had been administered cocaine. They compared four washing methods: A: three times with methanol; B: three times with 0.1*M* phosphate buffer (pH 6); C: three times with 0.1*M* phosphate buffer (pH 8); and D: isopropanol followed by three washes with 0.1*M* phosphate buffer (pH 5.5). Cocaine concentrations decreased from the control by 18%, 14%, and 37% when using methods B, C, and D, respectively, while wash A showed an increase of 13%. The metabolites norcaine and ecgonine methyl ester (EME) presented similar profiles. The authors explain the increase in cocaine concentrations when using wash A as due to a higher extraction efficiency of the acid digestion when the hair is previously treated with methanol.

Morrison and coworkers[28,29] evaluated supercritical fluid extraction (SFE) with pure carbon dioxide as a decontamination method for removal of vapor-deposited cocaine from hair before the extraction of cocaine compounds from the hair matrix by the same procedure, SFE. They compared this method with other decontamination procedures, including washes with methanol and ethanol, six times each, and a modified version of the washing protocol reported by Baumgartner and Hill,[20] which consists of one wash with ethanol followed by three sequential washes with 0.01*M* phosphate buffer at pH 6. SFE proved to be superior to all of the liquid washing methods in terms of decontamination efficiency, which for SFE was 84%, followed by 76% efficiency of methanol wash, 62% for the buffer protocol, and 58% for ethanol.

In 1997 the Society of Hair Testing (SoHT)[30] recommended a sequential washing procedure with organic solvent, followed by water or aqueous buffer and finally with an organic solvent once again. In cases where high contamination is suspected, the washes should be analyzed for the drug that is under investigation. Later, the SoHT, in a recommendation for hair testing in forensic cases,[31] was more specific and explained that external contamination must be addressed through various methodologies and cannot be solved with the application of one single approach. Avoiding a possible contamination in the working areas before and during analysis is recommended. With respect to the decontamination strategy, it must include an initial wash with organic solvent to remove oils, followed by aqueous solutions. These washes should be stored in case a later analysis is required. When the hair sample is especially dirty, such as in autopsy or exhumation cases, additional pretreatment of the hair may be necessary.

4.2.2 Extraction

Following the decontamination steps, various extraction methods are employed to release "matrix-bound" drug from the hair.[32] The extraction of drugs from the hair matrix is, without any doubt, the most difficult, the most complicated, and the most time-consuming step in any method of hair analysis for drugs of abuse. Once drugs are incorporated into hair, a stable complex is formed, as demonstrated by the long detection time for chemically labile compounds. The hair components involved in binding and entrapping drugs are proteins, melanin, and lipids. Obviously, the drugs of interest have to be isolated from all of these bindings before the analysis.

A large variety of methodological approaches have been proposed for the extraction of cocaine compounds from the hair matrix. These can be summarized as follows:

- Treatment with acids at various concentrations, but not very acidic. For example 0.1*M* HCl[4,19,33–35] and 0.01*M* HCl[17,18] have been used by several authors. However, higher concentration of HCl leads to the hydrolysis of cocaine to benzoylecgonine (BE) and EME.
- Treatment with enzymes like pronase, proteinase,[21,36] glucuronidase, etc. They are adequate for all the compounds. The inconvenience is the price of the enzymes in comparison with the other methods. In addition, Clauwaert et al.[19] observed that two different enzymatic digestion approaches (proteinase and pronase) performed very well in dissolving the hair, but the chromatograms obtained after high-performance liquid chromatography with fluorescence detector analysis (HPLC-FL) showed large interfering peaks through the whole run.
- Treatment with solvents such as methanol[3,7–10,12,14,37] or buffer solutions.[5,15] They are also able to extract all types of drugs, but the recoveries are lower when we compare them with the other extraction procedures. The addition of trifluoroacetic acid (TFA) to methanol improves the extraction recovery. This procedure was first introduced by Nakahara et al.[38] for the analysis of opiates. Other authors[6] expanded the method to cocaine, methadone, and benzodiazepines. They observed that the mean extractability of cocaine with methanol (MeOH) was only 41 ± 14.7% when compared with MeOH/TFA.

Treatments with alkali should be avoided for the extraction of cocaine, since it is hydrolyzed in such alkaline conditions.

A problem of hair analysis is whether drugs are quantitatively extracted or not from real hair samples. To investigate this, several authors have compared the efficiency of different extraction procedures.

Cirimele and coworkers[39] investigated the efficiencies of four different procedures for the extraction of cocaine, heroin, and their metabolites. They extracted 19 hair samples from drug abusers under various conditions: A: acid incubation with 0.1*M* HCl for 16 h at 56°C; B: alkaline incubation with 1*N* NaOH for 10 min at 100°C; C: enzymatic hydrolysis with phosphate buffer containing ß-glucuronidase arylsulfatase for 2 h at 40°C; D: direct methanol extraction by sonicating with MeOH for 5 h at 45°C. The results showed that for cocaine, acid incubation obtained five times higher concentrations and enzymatic hydrolysis only one time higher. For BE, methods A, C, and D were similar. The higher differences in extraction recoveries

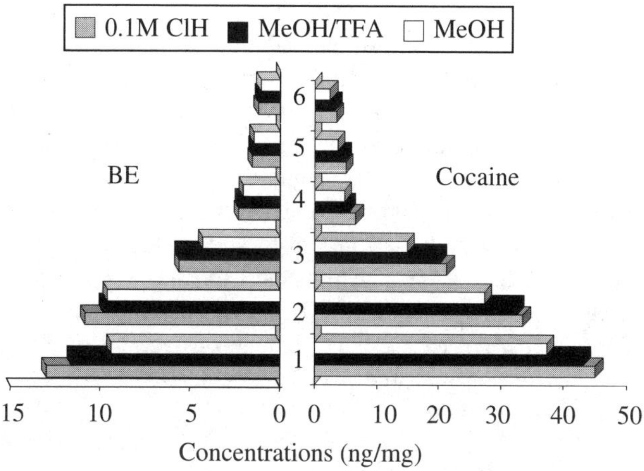

FIGURE 4.1 Distribution of cocaine and benzoylecgonine concentrations in six hair samples after applying three different extraction procedures.

were observed when drug concentrations were elevated. In these cases, methods A and C always showed higher concentrations compared with method D.

Romolo et al.[5] investigated the yield of extraction for four incubation media in authentic hair samples obtained from cocaine and heroin abusers. The samples were incubated in the following conditions: methanol, 0.1*M* phosphate buffer pH 5 and 6, at 45°C overnight, and MeOH/TFA (9:1) at room temperature overnight. The latter method (MeOH/TFA) provided the highest recoveries (100%); buffer pH 5 resulted in very good recoveries for cocaine (98.5%) and BE (96.2%); but with buffer pH 6, the recoveries decreased to 84.7% and 82.7% for cocaine and BE, respectively. The incubation with methanol inhibits the undesired hydrolysis of compounds, but the recoveries were lower for all of the analytes, as reported in many papers.[6,14,40]

In our laboratory, we also compared the efficiency of three different procedures for the extraction of cocaine and opiate compounds from hair. The study was performed with six hair samples obtained from consumers of heroin and cocaine. The three methods we applied were: A: a mild acidic extraction with 0.1*M* HCl at 45°C overnight; B: sonication for 1 h with a mixture of MeOH/TFA (9:1) maintained at room temperature overnight; and C: sonication with methanol for 1 h and maintenance of the solution at room temperature overnight. With respect to the efficacy of the three methods, as shown in Figure 4.1, in the case of cocaine, the extraction with 0.1*M* HCl gave the highest recoveries, but they were very close to those obtained with the mixture of MeOH/TFA. Perhaps, in some cases, concentrations obtained with both methods are the same, while MeOH provided the lowest recoveries in all the samples.

The stability of some analytes may be affected during the extraction step. For example cocaine is easily chemically hydrolyzed to BE and EME, especially at alkaline pH. Consequently, a balance is required during the extraction procedure. On the one hand, the extraction conditions have to make possible the extraction of 100%

of the compounds present in the sample; on the other hand, the extraction procedure has to be performed without significant degradation of the molecules of interest.

Romolo and coworkers[5] also studied the stability of cocaine and 6-monoacetylmorphine (6-MAM) in nine different incubation media: MeOH, 0.1*M* HCl, 0.01*M* HCl, 0.1*M* phosphate buffer solutions (pH 5, 6, 7, 8), carbonate/bicarbonate buffer at pH 9, and MeOH/TFA (9:1). All the samples were incubated at 45°C overnight, and the last mixture was also incubated at room temperature. The results demonstrated that the degradation was very low, from 1.3 to 4.2% when using MeOH or buffer pH 5 and 6. With respect to the aqueous acidic media, a significant degradation (12.1%) occurred with 0.1*M* HCl, while 0.01*M* HCl only degraded 3.0% of cocaine. For buffer solutions at pH 7 to 9, the percentage of degradation was very high at 44.9 to 100% and increased with the pH. No degradation (1.4%) was found with MeOH/TFA at room temperature.

4.2.2.1 Supercritical Fluid Extraction

Supercritical fluid extraction (SFE) has generated considerable interest in the last 15 years as an alternative to traditional extraction techniques. It represents a new technique for the extraction of drugs from human hair. The favorable mass transport properties and timetable solvation power of supercritical fluids have prompted researchers to investigate SFE as an alternative to currently used liquid-solvent-based procedures for drug testing in hair.[41,42]

Cirimele and coworkers[43] extracted cocaine and cannabinoids simultaneously with opiates by using an SFE procedure developed for opiate compounds. Drugs were extracted with supercritical carbon dioxide and a modifier solution of methanol-triethylamine-water (MeOH/TEA/water) (2:2:1).

Morrison et al.[28] investigated SFE as an alternative to the chemical methods for the extraction of cocaine and its principal metabolite BE from hair, and at the same time, they evaluated the reliability of the technique for distinguishing environmental contamination from active drug use. First, they compared the extraction ability of supercritical carbon dioxide (CO_2) modified with water/TEA (85/15) versus acid incubation with 0.1*M* HCl. The results revealed that, while SFE recoveries of cocaine were 80 to 90% relative to acid extraction, the SFE recoveries for BE were poor, around 11% of the values obtained by acid hydrolysis, a deficiency in turn suggested to be a result of poor solubility under the extraction conditions or of an inability to desorb BE from hair under these conditions. These same authors[28] suggested the possibility of differentiating cocaine present at different binding domains in the hair matrix based on differences in SFE behavior. Cocaine spiked on the surface of hair could be recovered using pure CO_2, while isolation of cocaine from noncontaminated drug-user hair required addition of the TEA/water modifier. For these reasons, the SFE protocol includes a preextraction with pure CO_2 followed by two sequential extractions with CO_2 modified with TEA/water. The authors hypothesized that the CO_2-extractable fraction represents physisorbed cocaine present on the surface due to environmental contamination, while the CO_2/TEA/water fraction is believed to represent cocaine chemisorbed at active sites within the hair matrix. Preextraction of hair samples with pure CO_2 is also useful for removing surface oils and waxes that may interfere with subsequent chromatographic analysis.

Brewer et al.[13] employed CO_2-modified methanol in their SFE method for the extraction of cocaine from human hair. They compared the recoveries of cocaine from fortified hair standards extracted with 0.1*M* HCl versus SFE. They found that, under the conditions employed, about twice the amount of cocaine was detected following SFE (800 pg/mg) than following acid extraction (350 pg/mg), thus demonstrating the SFE method to be more efficient than 0.1*M* HCl, even though the extraction time was much shorter (75 min compared with 24 h). They also validated their SFE method with the NIST (National Institutes of Standards and Technology, Gaithersburg, MD) hair standard, and their quantitative results (cocaine: 4.74 ± 0.36 ng/mg; BE: 4.32 ± 0.65 ng/mg) were consistent with NIST values (cocaine: 5.40 ± 0.44 ng/mg; BE: 5.40 ± 0.41 ng/mg).

4.2.2.2 Purification

Solutions containing the analytes of interest, obtained after the extraction of the drugs from the hair matrix, are generally dirty, and an additional purification step is generally required to eliminate possible substance interference, to concentrate and stabilize the analytes present in the sample, and finally to take the sample to the optimal conditions for instrumental analysis, especially when GC-MS is going to be performed. This purification step can be performed by adapting any of the well-known procedures applied in the laboratories for the extraction of cocaine and metabolites from other biological matrices, such as urine.

At first, liquid-liquid extraction (LLE) was applied to isolate cocaine and metabolites from the aqueous solutions. Some laboratories continue applying this approach in the routine analysis of cocaine in hair samples.[44] The introduction of solid-phase extraction (SPE) for the extraction of organic compounds from biological matrices has demonstrated several advantages over the traditional LLE. They include cleaner extracts, higher selectivity, greater reproducibility, and the avoidance of emulsion formation. As a consequence, a large number of toxicological laboratories have implemented this procedure in their routine analyses. In fact, as shown in Table 4.1, the majority of the analytical procedures of cocaine in hair samples utilize SPE in the purification step. The most common extraction column includes Bond Elut Certify™,[4–6,9,11,17,18,34] but Isolute™,[21] Isolute Confirm HCX,[19] Clean Screan,[33,37] and Chromabond-Drug[15] have also been used. Clauwaert et al.[19] found that the use of Bond Elut Certify columns resulted in major interferences in the chromatograms when instrumental analysis was performed by HPLC-FL. When these columns were substituted with Isolute Confirm HCX columns, the final purity of the extracts substantially improved.

More recently, solid-phase microextraction (SPME), a relatively new technique, has gained considerable interest in the field of toxicological analysis. It consists of the direct adsorption of the analytes from the sample onto a fused-silica fiber that is coated with an appropriate stationary phase. During the process, the fiber is inserted into the sample solution (SPME) or into the headspace above the sample

(HS-SPME). The fiber is subsequently placed into the injection port of the gas chromatograph, where it is heated so that the analytes can be thermally desorbed.

The advantages of this technique over SPE are that fewer solvents are used; consequently, fewer residues are generated, and the time of analysis is shorter. Both circumstances are of great value in analytical toxicology. SPME has been applied by several authors for the analysis of volatile and nonvolatile compounds from biological samples, mainly fluids, urine, and blood. The application in hair analysis has been shorter; nevertheless, several authors have applied SPME for the cleanup of their extracts before the analysis of cocaine in hair by GC-MS. Two authors performed the SPME by dipping the fiber into the hydrolysates of hair. Strano-Rossi and Chiarotti[45] performed an enzymatic digestion of the hair with pronase and subsequently SPME. As no derivatization was performed, only cocaine and ethyl benzoylecgonine (EBE) were detected. To confirm positive results, the authors suggested extracting and derivatizing the remaining solution to determine the main metabolites BE and EME. In an effort to detect not only the parent, but also the metabolites, de Toledo et al.[10] used butylchloroformate as the derivatization reagent to convert BE in butylbenzoylecgonine, a less polar compound, prior to the SPME, which was performed by directly dipping a polydimethylsiloxane fiber into the derivatized solution.

A rapid screening procedure based on HS-SPME was developed by Gentili and coworkers[16] for the analysis of cocaine, amphetamine-related compounds, ketamine, and methadone. After acidic extraction with 1*M* HCl, potassium carbonate was added and the vial was sealed. Then the SPME fiber was exposed to the headspace for 5 min at 90°C. Because no derivatization was performed, as in the above-mentioned approach,[45] only cocaine was detected, but not the polar metabolites.

4.2.3 Instrumental Analysis

Many of the laboratories analyzing hair samples for drugs of abuse go directly to the GC-MS analysis, without any previous screening. In fact, in the proficiency tests annually organized by the Society of Hair Testing, only 18 to 20% of the participants perform a screening. For example, in 2003, only 4 out of 22 participants applied previous RIA (one lab) or ELISA (three labs) screening techniques. Nevertheless, a correct procedure of toxicological analysis involves two different steps: screening and confirmation. The first allows for a preliminary monitoring of a large number of samples in a reduced period of time, while the confirmation provides the required specificity.

4.2.3.1 Screening Methods

The purpose of screening methods is primarily to rapidly and with low cost dismiss many negative samples in a vast amount of samples, thus saving time and money. For this reason, these methods are mainly applied in the commercial laboratories that perform workplace or epidemiological analyses, where a large number of samples are analyzed daily; these tests are not so profitable and, consequently, they are not utilized very often in forensic laboratories. Another purpose of the screening methods is to increase the quality of the results by using two independent methods before reporting positive results.

Immunoassays have a firm place in the routine screening methods for the analysis of drugs in hair samples. They can be used by the smallest or largest laboratories, making possible the analysis of thousands of samples per day. Immunological methods must satisfy three requirements:[46]

1. Specificity and cross-reactivity with parent drug and lipophilic metabolites actually found in hair. The primary analyte found in hair after cocaine use is the parent drug, cocaine. As a result, an immunoassay for the analysis of cocaine must be highly specific for cocaine itself.
2. Matrix interference. One important requirement is that the solution obtained after the extraction of the analytes from the hair matrix must not denature the antibody proteins of the immunoassay reagents.
3. Analytical sensitivity and cutoff. These techniques have to be sensitive and specific enough to detect the drugs in the hair, which are in the range of 1 pg/mg to 100 ng/mg. But the cutoffs should not be set at the limit of detection of the assay, because that would produce a very large incidence of false positives. In 2004, two organizations, SAMHSA (Substance Abuse and Mental Health Services Administration) and SoHT (Society of Hair Testing), agreed to establish a cutoff value of 0.5 ng of cocaine per milligram of hair for screening methods of cocaine in hair samples.

Immunoassays whose antibodies are bound to a solid support, such as coated-tube radioimmunoassay or coated-plate ELISA tests, experience less matrix interference than those that use other means of separation of bound and free fractions. Historically, radioimmunoassays (RIA) were the first techniques used for detecting cocaine in hair,[47–49] and they continue to be used by large commercial laboratories with very good results. RIA is a common, sensitive, and reliable immunological technique, but the use of radioactively labeled material prevents it from being performed out of safe areas. Consequently, nonradioactive methodologies are often preferred. Currently, enzyme-linked immunosorbent assay (ELISA) and microplate enzyme immunoassay (EIA) are being routinely employed, since they are good alternatives, being safe, simple, inexpensive, and very sensitive.

Segura et al.[6] compared the efficacy of ELISA tests with a confirmation analysis by GC-MS in selected samples obtained from drug addicts. Given the semiquantitative nature of ELISA measurements, the concentrations were grouped in classes corresponding to 0 to 0.5, 0.5 to 5, 5 to 10, and >10 ng/mg of cocaine equivalents. All samples with high GC-MS concentrations were correctly included in the high-concentration ELISA group, and the decreasing GC-MS concentrations were also classified within their respective ELISA classes. These results demonstrated that ELISA was not only a good screening method, but also that it was able to perform an accurate semiquantitative analysis.

Moore et al.[50] compared the efficacy of two immunoassays for the detection of cocaine in hair: the microplate immunoassay (EIA) and the fluorescence polarization immunoassay (FPIA) using GC-MS as the indicator of true positivity and true negativity. In general, EIA was more sensitive (75%), specific (97.4%), and efficient (91.4%) than the corresponding FPIA, which showed 67.8, 80.5, and 77.1% of sensitivity, specificity, and efficiency, respectively. The authors attribute these differences to the cross-reactivity toward the parent drug cocaine. FPIA was designed for urine analysis, and the cross-reactivity is primarily with BE (100%) while it decreased to 1.0% for cocaine. EIA was designed for oral fluid assay and consequently had a higher cross-reactivity with the parent cocaine of 102 and 100% for the main metabolite BE. An additional advantage of EIA is that it can be easily automated for the simultaneous analysis of multiple plates, including the steps of incubation, washing, reading, and printing.

Up to now, only one paper has reported a screening procedure by a chromatographic method before the confirmation by GC-MS. Kronstrand et al.[22] developed an LC-MS/MS method for the simultaneous analysis of several drugs of abuse (opiates, cocainics, benzodiazepines, amphetamine related compounds, and nicotine) in hair as an alternative to the immunological methods. Drugs were extracted from the hair matrix by incubating 10 to 50 mg of hair with the mobile phase (acetonitrile:methanol:20m*M* formate buffer pH 3). An aliquot was injected into the LC-MS/MS. Positive results for cocaine were confirmed by GC-MS in a new set of samples.

In general, screening methods are used because they provide rapid, inexpensive, and automated procedures for separating negative samples from the positives. But, as the Society of Hair Testing recommended,[30] all positive screening tests should be confirmed by alternative methods, for example by GC-MS or any other technology of comparable or greater specificity and selectivity.

4.2.3.2 Confirmation Methods

The gold standard for confirming the results obtained in screening methods and for performing an adequate quantitative analysis of the drugs present in a hair sample is mass spectrometry, which can be coupled to a gas chromatograph (GC-MS) or, more recently, to a liquid chromatograph (LC-MS). Another possibility lies in the tandem techniques using MS/MS or even MS/MS/MS.

Since 1996 —the time frame for the literature that is of interest to us in this chapter — all of the authors have used MS instrumentation. Only a few exceptions must be considered, such as Tagliaro et al.,[35] who proposed a diagnostic strategy based on screening by RIA and confirmation by HPLC-FL to investigate chronic exposure to drugs of abuse in applicants for a driving license. The hair samples were screened for opiates, cocaine, and ecstasy by RIA, and all positive samples and about 10% of negatives were confirmed by HPLC-FL. Only in complicated cases, when drug consumption was persistently denied and positive results were found, was further confirmation carried out by capillary electrophoresis.[51,52]

A similar HPLC-FL assay was proposed by Clauwaert et al.[19] for the routine analysis of cocaine, BE, and EBE in hair. Hair samples were hydrolyzed with 0.1*M* HCl, and a cleanup was performed by SPE. The residue was dissolved in the HPLC eluent and injected into the HPLC-FL system. But because an unequivocal confirmation is mandatory in toxicological analysis, they validated the results by injecting the same sample into an LC/ESI-MS/MS, and at the same time, they had a complementary confirmation of the presence of cocaine and metabolites in the sample, in case it should be required.

As mentioned above, the procedures published since 1996 have performed the analysis by using an MS- based technique, and more specifically GC-MS, as reflected in Table 4.1. A disadvantage of GC-MS is that a derivatization step is required for polar compounds to make them amenable to chromatographic analysis. Consequently, whereas cocaine and EBE do not need and cannot undergo any derivatization procedure, in the case of other more polar metabolites, such as BE or EME, the derivatization is an unavoidable requirement before GC-MS analysis. Among the several types of derivatization procedures, reviewed by Segura et al.,[53] the formation of trimethylsilyl or perfluorated derivatives has proved to be the most extensively used.

Silylation is the most widely used derivatization procedure for GC-MS analysis. These derivatives combine thermal and chemical stability and high volatility; they are also easy to prepare and show excellent GC behavior.[53] Several silylating reagents have been used, including, *N,O*-bis(trimethylsilyl)trifluoroacetamide (BSTFA),[7] *N*-methyl-*N*-trimethylsilyltrifluoroacetamide (MSTFA),[5,4,12] and *N*-methyl-*N*-*tert*,-butyldimethylsilyltrifluoroacetamide (MTBSTFA).[8]

Acylation and alkylation with perfluorated anhydrides and alcohols are other commonly used derivatization methods. Usually a combination of perfluorated alcohol, which derivatizes acidic functional groups, and perfluorated anhydride, which derivatizes alcoholic functional groups, is used to ensure that all of the compounds containing either carboxylic or alcoholic groups in their molecules are subjected to derivatization. The halogenated esters obtained in the process increase the electron affinity of the compounds, which is an important advantage for special detection techniques such as the negative chemical ionization mode (NCI).

A mixture of heptafluorobutyric anhydride (HFBA) and 1,1,1,3,3,3-hexafluoroisopropanol (HFPIOH) was used by Segura et al.[6] to derivatize cocaine and opiate compounds. Uhl[14] changed the anhydride; he derivatized with a mixture of pentafluoropropionic anhydride (PFPA) and HFIPOH before simultaneous analysis of opiates, cocainics, amphetamine-related compounds, and methadone by GC-MS/MS. The combination of trifluoroacetic anhydride (TFAA) and HFIPOH was also applied by other authors.[33,15] In addition to the previous derivatization methods, other procedures have been proposed, such as the propionylation by propionic anhydride (PAA) in the presence of pyridine as a catalyst[9,17,18] or without any catalyst.[11]

Brewer et al.[13] compared the chromatograms obtained from a hair sample extracted by SFE and after derivatizing with BSTFA or with a mixture of PFPA and HFIPOH. After silylation, too many interference peaks were observed, presumably due to derivatization of other components, such as fatty acids. Derivatization with PFPA/HFIPOH, on the contrary, produced negligible interferences.

Segura et al.[53] also compared silylated and perfluorated derivatives when analyzing cocaine and BE, among others, in urine, but their results can be translated to hair samples. The chromatograms showed that when using cocaine as a reference, since it is not derivatized, the abundance of BE was higher when derivatizing with HFBA/HFIPOH than after derivatization with BSTFA.

More recently, mass spectrometry coupled to high-performance liquid chromatography (LC-MS) has started to be a routine instrument in toxicological laboratories, and several papers have appeared in the literature describing application of this technique. Some of them use LC-MS[34] and others LC-MS/MS.[21,22,37] The main advantage of LC-MS when compared with GC-MS is that the polar compounds can be analyzed directly, which eliminates the need for any previous derivatization procedure. This is translated into a savings of time, which is very important in routine analysis. Another advantage is the high sensitivity of the new LC-MS/MS instruments, which can detect concentrations in the range of picograms per milligram of hair.

Despite all these advantages, LC-MS is more expensive than GC-MS, and not all of the laboratories can afford it. Consequently, GC-MS continues to be the most extensively applied instrumental method in hair analysis.

4.3 QUALITY CONTROL

One of the requirements for the correct application of an analytical method in toxicological analysis is to guarantee the results. Thus quality control must be the prime objective of any analytical laboratory to eliminate systematic errors and minimize the possibility of accidental errors. "Quality assurance" is the term used to represent the practices carried out to ensure that specified quality goals are achieved. It entails both internal and external quality control.[54]

4.3.1 Internal Quality Control

Before routinely applying an analytical procedure for hair testing, several parameters have to be checked. These include: linearity, sensitivity, limit of detection, limit of quantification, recovery, precision, etc.

The problem of hair analysis compared with analysis of homogeneous body fluids is the preparation of the samples for these validation studies, since spiked control samples cannot be substituted for real hair from drug users. The ideal situation would be to obtain a sufficient quantity of real drug-user hair to prepare a homogeneous pool, where all the tests could be performed. As this, however, is very difficult, drug user hair can be substituted using soaked controls, if properly prepared. One technique, proposed by SoHT,[31] is to expose drug-free hair to aqueous solutions of drugs at high concentrations for several days and then thoroughly wash them before drying and analysis. Another possibility is to follow the protocol used at the National Institutes of Standards and Technology (NIST) to prepare the reference material. As described by Welch et al.,[55] the protocol is, briefly, as follows: known quantities of patterns of the analytes under study are placed in a beaker and dissolved in water and sonicated. Then, 0.02*M* HCl in dimethylsulfoxide is added, and the hair is allowed to soak in this solution for 16.5 days. After decanting the mother solution, the hair is rinsed several times with methanol.

Once adequate control samples are obtained, the validation tests are performed similarly to those conducted using biological body fluids.

4.3.2 External Quality Control or Interlaboratory Comparison Studies

For external quality control, the laboratory should enroll in a proficiency testing program, where authentic standard hair specimens are sent for testing.[31] The laboratory must analyze the samples in the same way as routine samples.

Several interlaboratory comparisons and proficiency tests (PT) have been and continue to be organized. In 1995, Kintz[56] performed an interlaboratory comparison by distributing one hair sample, obtained from a fatal drug overdose and containing opiates and cocainics, to 14 participant laboratories; four of them were from France, and the others were from around the world. All the French laboratories used the same method[44] consisting of extraction with 0.1*M* HCl and GC-MS analysis. The other participants applied different extraction methods, mainly acidic extraction (three labs), solvent extraction (four labs), and enzymatic digestion (three labs). Most of the participants had no difficulty identifying the target compounds. Quantitative results obtained for cocaine demonstrated that no approach consistently provided higher or more precise results.

In the 1990s, the NIST organized a series of interlaboratory comparison studies to determine how well laboratories could detect and quantify drugs of abuse in hair.[57,58] Twenty laboratories participated in one or more exercises. The first exercise consisted of powdered hair, while in the subsequent exercises only samples cut in small segments were used. The samples included hair from drug users, drug-free hair, and hair into which drugs were soaked. Results from the different studies showed that laboratories performed very well qualitatively, with low rates of false positives reported on negative challenges. Some laboratories consistently performed well on all the exercises, thus proving that accurate results are possible. Quantitative results were highly scattered, in part because different analytical procedures were applied by the participants, and because of the differences in experience, as well. Various methods were used to liberate the drugs from the hair, and the most commonly used approaches — dilute hydrochloric acid and methanol extractions and buffer-enzyme digestions — all produced comparable results. With respect to the influence of the instrumentation employed in the analyses, the results obtained with LC-MS were indistinguishable from those obtained by GC-MS.

Montagna and her colleagues[59] performed an interlaboratory comparison to evaluate the performance of an analytical procedure that they were attempting to propose as a standardized protocol. Sixteen forensic and clinical laboratories with different experience in hair testing (from none to extensive) participated in the study. Each participant received three real samples (one negative, one with low concentrations, and one with high concentrations), and they were asked to apply the same method, consisting of extraction with 0.1*M* HCl, purification by SPE, derivatization with MSTFA, and GC-MS analysis. The results showed that the proposed method improved the quality and uniformity of results when carried out by laboratories with experience in hair testing, since in these cases, the coefficients of variation were lower than those resulting from other studies where different methods were applied.[58,60,61]

Several societies in relation to toxicology and/or hair testing have implemented proficiency testing programs within their activities. The French Society of Analytical Toxicology (SFTA) has been organizing comparisons since 1992 in an effort to improve the laboratories' performance of hair analysis in forensic cases. At the beginning, four laboratories participated in three exercises, and in 1994 a consensus was reached and published for opiates and cocaine.[44] The procedure consists of decontamination with dichloromethane, extraction with 0.1*M* HCl, purification by liquid-liquid extraction, and GC-MS analysis. Currently, around ten laboratories participate in each exercise, and one or two exercises are planned per year. Each survey has been dedicated to one drug of abuse or one pharmacological family.[62] For cocaine, qualitative results were excellent — no false positives and only 1% of false negatives — and quantitative results appear to be good, with narrow ranges when compared with other international surveys.[57] This is probably due to the fact that a joint analytical procedure was used by all the participants.

One of the aims of the SoHT is the development of proficiency tests (PT) so that all labs that perform hair analysis can produce comparable results, or at least detect the same compounds. As a consequence, since the creation of the SoHT in 1995, several PTs have been organized, beginning sporadically with the first in 1995[60] and a second in 1997. However, since 2001, a PT has been organized annually.[63,64] The number of participants has been more or less similar every year, around 20 — ranging from 18 in 2001 to 25 in 2004 — three of them being reference laboratories. The positive samples were obtained from drug abusers who consumed different types of drugs, and these were sent in the form of short segments. Laboratories were asked to analyze opiates, cocainics, amphetamines, and cannabis. All of the participants analyzed opiate and cocaine compounds in all the exercises, but not all the labs analyzed amphetamines and cannabis as well. In general, qualitative results were very good and similar for all the exercises. In the case of positive samples, about 5% of false negatives were reported every year, the majority coming from the less experienced participants, while in the case of negative samples, only one false positive was reported for MAM in 4 years.

All of the participants simultaneously extracted cocaine and opiate compounds from the hair. They applied different methods of extraction, including acidic extraction, enzymatic digestion, and extractions with methanol and different types of buffer. The majority applied acidic and methanol extractions. Figure 4.2a shows the concentrations of cocaine reported by the participants performing methanol and acidic extractions in one of the samples included in the 2004 exercise. From the results presented in Figure 4.2a, it was not possible to conclude that one approach is better than the other, since both methods provided similar and very scattered recoveries. Figure 4.2b shows the results from the same sample, when taking into consideration the experience of the laboratory — fewer or more than 100 analyses per year. In this case, experienced participants reported similar and homogeneous results, independently of the applied method of extraction, while just the opposite happened with the other group, where the data were very scattered. The findings from the different exercises indicated that good laboratory technique and a high level of experience are more important for achieving good results than the particular approach chosen for extraction.

The importance of the experience in hair testing was corroborated with the results obtained in the "HAIRVEQ," a quality control in hair to evaluate performance in hair testing for drugs of abuse in the Italian laboratories.[65] There were 23 participants from the Italian Health System (20 labs) and from the Institutes of Forensic Medicine (three labs). Most of the participants had no or very little experience in these analyses. As a consequence, a big incidence of false-positive results was reported. Globally, when evaluating qualitative results, 19 laboratories of the 23 participants (around 82%) reported incorrect results (six false negatives, six false positives, and seven both false positives and false negatives).

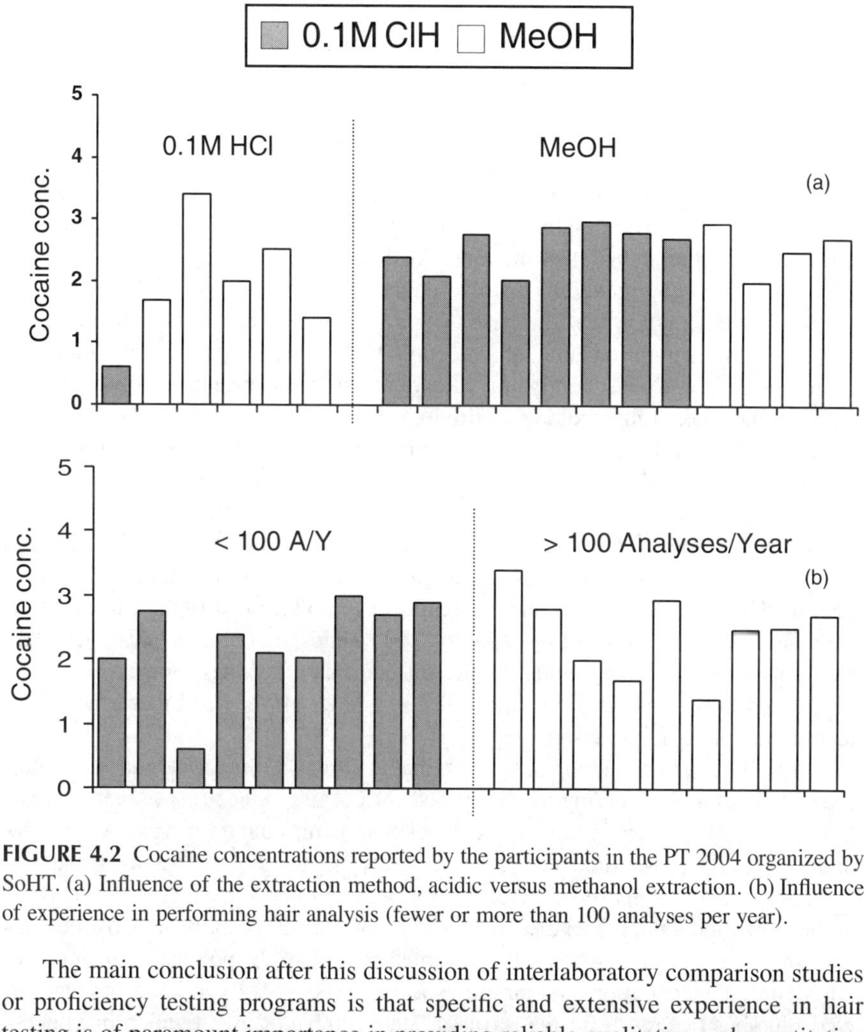

FIGURE 4.2 Cocaine concentrations reported by the participants in the PT 2004 organized by SoHT. (a) Influence of the extraction method, acidic versus methanol extraction. (b) Influence of experience in performing hair analysis (fewer or more than 100 analyses per year).

The main conclusion after this discussion of interlaboratory comparison studies or proficiency testing programs is that specific and extensive experience in hair testing is of paramount importance in providing reliable qualitative and quantitative results, independent of the analytical procedure.

4.4 INTERPRETATION OF RESULTS

One of the most critical issues in hair testing is the interpretation of the analytical results. There is no doubt that there is great variability in the outcome of assay results between persons. An unspecified and probably unknowable set of factors are likely contributors to this variance, and some of these are addressed below. In the following subsections, we discuss the need to establish adequate cutoff values for an evidentiary definition of positive results. Furthermore, and based on the literature, we consider some routinely asked questions, such as whether it is possible to establish (a) a relationship between the amount of drug consumed and concentrations found in hair or (b) the time delay between cocaine consumption and its detection in the hair. Finally, we consider the influence of the cosmetic treatments applied on the hair and seek to determine whether a possible bias can be attributed to the hair color of the individual.

4.4.1 Cutoff Values for the Analysis of Cocaine in Hair Samples

In the early days of hair testing, considerable confusion was caused by the fact that the feasibility of these analyses was largely cast in terms of the avoidance of erroneous interpretations of positive results due to environmental contamination of hair. Such exposures generally involve concentrations of drugs that are very low, but the instrumentation used in these tests has become increasingly sensitive, with some MS/MS setups capable of detection within the range of fentograms per milligram of hair. Consequently, it is of paramount importance to establish adequate cutoff values, i.e., a threshold of positivity.[66]

One of the most controversial and most extensively discussed points in hair analysis is the establishment of adequate cutoff values. Different situations lead to different questions and require different cutoffs. Such situations could be, among others, the purpose of the analysis, since a drug dealer who lives in a drug-contaminated environment is not in the same situation as a person trying to obtain a driving license. The incorporation of the different drugs into hair is different; for example, cocaine has an incorporation capacity 3600 times higher than THC-COOH.[67] Consequently, both compounds require different cutoff values. Something similar happens with the analytical method, because neither all the instruments nor all the techniques have the same sensitivity.

In 1993, during a meeting of the National Institutes of Standards and Technology (NIST), a cutoff of 1 ng/mg was proposed for cocaine. Since then, several authors have proposed different cutoff values, depending on the country, purpose of analysis, and the analytical method employed. In Italy, firstly Tagliaro et al.[68] and later Montagna et al.[4] proposed a cutoff of 0.1 ng/mg for driving licenses. The latter authors explain that the choice of such a low cutoff is motivated by the high selectivity and sensitivity of the GC/MS method and by the population under study, where drug concentrations in hair are expected to be low. The criteria for reporting a cocaine-positive result for the Bavarian State Bureau of Investigation in Munich[14] is when cocaine concentration exceeds 0.5 ng/mg of hair and BE is detectable, as well as, occasionally, EBE. Pépin and Gaillard[66] established a cutoff of 1 ng/mg based on their experience with judicial cases. Kintz and Mangin[69] suggested two cutoff values of 0.5 and 1 ng/mg, depending on the characteristics of the person under analysis. The highest cutoff, 2 ng/mg, was reported by Quintela et al.[70] when they tried to evaluate the use of cocaine, among other drugs, in Spanish university students. In the U.S., Baumgartner and Hill[71] proposed a cutoff of 0.5 ng/mg for workplace drug testing to protect against passive endogenous drug exposure, while the Hair Testing Working Group[72] established a cutoff of 1.0 ng/mg by using GC/MS for all types of samples.

In 2004, two organizations, the SoHT[31] and SAMHSA,[73] proposed cutoff values that are summarized in Table 4.2. SoHT recommends that, in the case of forensic samples, a cocaine level of 0.5 ng/mg must produce a positive result when applying

TABLE 4.2
Cutoffs Proposed for Screening and Confirmation Methods for the Analysis of Cocaine

Screening Methods (pg/mg)			Confirmation Methods (pg/mg)		
Drug	**SAMHSA**	**SoHT**	**Compound Analyzed**	**SAMHSA**	**SoHT**
Cocaine	500	500	Cocaine	500	500
—	—	—	Cocaine metabolites [a]	50	50

[a] Cocaine metabolites: benzoylecgonine, ethylbenzoylecgonine, norcocaine, or ecgonine methyl ester.

immunochemical tests, and SAMHSA proposed the same value for the screening methods in drug testing at the workplace. With respect to the confirmation techniques, by mass spectrometry, both societies agreed in their proposed cutoffs, as well: concentrations lower than or equal to 0.5 and 0.05 ng/mg for cocaine and its metabolites, respectively. In addition, SoHT recommends that, for a positive result, the chromatographic analysis should include cocaine and at least one of the following metabolites: BE, EBE, norcocaine, or EME. To report a specimen as positive for cocaine, SAMHSA states that cocaine concentration should be greater or equal to the confirmatory cutoff and, in addition, one of the following requirements must be met: the ratio BE/cocaine has to be greater than or equal to 0.05, or EBE or norcocaine must be greater than or equal to 0.05 ng/mg.

4.4.2 Dose–Concentration Relationship

When interpreting hair analysis results, one of the most frequently asked questions is whether there is a predictable relationship between the amount of drug eventually detected in the hair of the subject under study and the dose consumed. To date, the papers that have been published on this matter show major controversy between pros and cons. Relationships between hair concentration and daily dose have been published for several drugs of abuse and pharmaceuticals, but we will concentrate on cocaine, which is the drug of interest in this chapter.

Some authors do not find any relationship. Puschel et al.[74] compared the concentrations of drugs of abuse present in the hair of 13 drug abusers with self-reported consumption, but they were unable to establish any positive correlation. Henderson et al.,[75] who administered cocaine-d_5 in doses of 0.6 to 4.2 mg/kg to 25 volunteers under laboratory clinical conditions. found that when increasing the dose of cocaine, a greater amount of drug in the hair was generally present. Nevertheless, there was a poor correlation between the amount of drug incorporated into hair and the dose received by the subjects (the correlation coefficient ranged from 0.5 to 0.6), mainly because high increases in dose resulted in only small increases in the amount of cocaine incorporated into hair.

Opposite results were obtained in our laboratory[76] when studying the dose-concentration relationship in two lots of nine rats each that were administered 40 or

60 mg/kg of cocaine intraperitoneally. Our findings indicated that higher doses corresponded to higher concentration. Moreover, the correlation coefficient between the doses of cocaine administered and the concentrations found in hair was very good ($r^2 = 0.86$), thus demonstrating that cocaine incorporation into hair is dose dependent. Similarly, Ferko et al.[77] administered increasing doses of cocaine to rats over a 28-day period and observed that higher doses resulted in higher concentrations of cocaine accumulated in the hair.

Ropero-Miller et al.[78] demonstrated dose-related concentrations of cocaine and metabolites in human hair after controlled subcutaneous cocaine administration. The study was performed with eight volunteers enrolled in a 10-week inpatient clinical study. During the low-dose week, they received 75 mg/70 kg on alternative days, while for the high doses, they received 150 mg/70 kg. There was considerable intersubject variability in the maximum concentration for low doses (ranging from 1.7 to 15 ng/mg) and for high doses (ranging from 5.1 to 27 ng/mg); nevertheless, in the same person, the mean peak concentration in hair after low dosing was around half the concentration observed after high-dose administration.

In a similarly designed experiment performed with ten volunteers residing in a secure research ward, Scheidweiler et al.[79] observed a significant dose-concentration relationship in the hair samples. Maximum hair concentrations were found 1 to 3 weeks after low and high doses. Considerable intersubject variability was observed in hair concentrations; dose-concentration relationships, nevertheless, were consistent in nine of ten subjects.

These studies corroborate previous animal and human studies that reported dose-related cocaine concentrations in hair. Hubbard et al.[80] found dose-related concentrations of cocaine, EME, BE and norcocaine in rat hair collected 2 weeks after beginning daily 5-, 10-, or 20-mg/kg intraperitoneal cocaine injections on five consecutive days.

To date, a relationship between the amount of drug taken and hair levels has only been observed in prospective studies with controlled drug administration and in intramural, secure places. Obviously, this is an unrealistic situation, and it is not surprising that other studies failed to establish any relationship, especially if we consider the many factors that could affect this correlation, e.g., when the amount of drug in retrospective studies is estimated on the basis of a self-reported consumption. This choice has several disadvantages, such as establishing the purity of the street drug, which is unknown, or the doses consumed, which can be over- or underestimated, since cocaine is an illicit compound.

Some individual circumstances may also intervene more or less as biasing factors in the dose-concentration relationship, including the hair growth cycle, which is not homogeneous, the color of the hair, and cosmetic treatments. Finally, differences in sweat and sebum secretions probably exert a certain influence, since cocaine — a nonionized and lipid-soluble drug — can enter hair by way of contact with these secretions.

In conclusion, from the results obtained in hair analysis, we can deduce that, in the same person, a higher concentration of cocaine corresponds to a higher consumption, and vice versa. However, the idea of using quantitative drug measurements in hair to determine the quantity of drug consumed is not feasible.

4.4.3 Window of Detection of Cocaine in Hair Samples

Several circumstances lead to several questions. On the one hand, some persons might be interested in knowing how much time must pass from the time cocaine is first consumed until it can be detected in the hair. On the other hand, imprisoned people or those enrolled in detoxification programs would like to know how long the parent drug or its metabolites can be detected in the hair after consumption has ended. It is difficult to answer these questions because very few studies have focused on the detection window of cocaine in hair samples.

Due to ethical problems related to the administration of an illicit drug like cocaine to healthy volunteers, the majority of the experiments have been performed with animals. Thusly Ferko et al.[77] administered rats 5-, 10-, and 20-mg/kg intraperitoneal doses of cocaine during a 28-day period. Hair samples were collected until cocaine and BE were no longer detected. Both compounds, cocaine and BE, were detected in the first sampling, 4 days after initial administration, while 25 to 30 days were required to eliminate both compounds from hair after ending the highest-dose administration. Moreover, the study established that the disappearance followed first-order kinetics.

Similar results were obtained by Jurado and coworkers in experiments performed firstly with rabbits[81] and then with rats.[76] Rabbits received a single intraperitoneal dose of 5 mg/kg of cocaine, while rats were divided into two lots, and each one was administered a single dose of 40 mg/kg and 60 mg/kg of cocaine. Hair was collected daily during three weeks. In both animals, cocaine started to be detected in the first sampling, one day after administration, and continued to be detected for nine days, in the rabbits. In the experiment with rats, the detection time increased with the dose administered. In the lot receiving 40 mg/kg of cocaine, the drug was detected for 11 days, and in the rats administered 60 mg/kg, cocaine remained detectable for 14 days.

Another study in agreement with those previously described was performed by Hubbard et al.[80] They administered to Long-Evans rats intraperitoneal cocaine doses of 5, 10, and 20 mg/kg daily for 5 days. The hair was collected daily for 14 days. Cocaine was detected 1 h after a single dose administration and continued being detected for the entire 14-day period of the study.

An intramural study with human volunteers was performed by Henderson et al.[75] Subjects received 0.3, 0.6, and 1.2 mg/kg intravenous and 0.6 and 1.2 mg/kg intranasal doses of cocaine-d5. Despite the finding of a considerable intersubject variability, they were able to detect cocaine 8 h after administration (in one subject) and 1 to 3 days after dosing in four other subjects. The results corroborated previous studies, since higher doses led to a longer period of detection, even 2 to 6 months after single and multiple doses.

In conclusion, all of the studies agreed that cocaine is very quickly incorporated into the hair and that the disappearance is dose-dependent, since the larger the dose, the longer the time period cocaine can be detected in the hair.

4.4.4 Influence of Hair Color

There is some debate as to whether a hair-color bias exists when testing for drugs of abuse in hair. Melanin is the component of hair responsible for pigmentation. There are two types: eumelanin, which predominates in dark hair, and yellow-red pheomelanin. The total amount of melanin copolymers and the eumelanin/pheomelanin ratio produce variation in hair color. The highest eumelanin to pheomelanin ratio is found in black hair, followed by brown and blond hair, and finally by red hair, which contains a substantial amount of pheomelanin relative to eumelanin.[82] Nakahara et al.[67] demonstrated by *in vitro* experiments that drug incorporation rates into hair are correlated ($r^2 = 0.947$) with the melanin affinity of drugs.

Several researchers have demonstrated that melanin does bind to abused drugs. Studies with animal models and other studies using *in vitro* techniques have shown a difference in concentrations that appeared to be related to hair color. Reid et al.[83] incubated different types of hair in the presence of BE and found that the degree of incorporation was higher in black hair, followed by brown hair, and finally by blond hair. Joseph et al.[84] studied the *in vitro* incorporation of cocaine-d_3 into hair of different colors and observed that African black hair incorporated a ten-times higher quantity of cocaine-d_3 than did Caucasian blond hair.

These findings have been corroborated for several *in vivo* studies, as well. In this way, a linear relationship between total melanin content and cocaine maximal concentrations was reported by Scheidweiler et al.[79] following the administration of both low- and high-cocaine controlled doses to humans. This study was extended to cocaine metabolites and revealed that the correlation was established not only for the parent drug, but also for the metabolites (BE, EME, norcocaine, EBE). These findings are not in accordance with a previous *in vitro* study that reported that BE did not bind to melanin.[82] Borges et al.[82] performed an experiment to document the *in vitro* binding of cocaine and BE to synthetic melanin subtypes: two black eumelanin subtypes and two mixed eumelanin/pheomelanin copolymers. The results showed that cocaine bound to eumelanins and mixed copolymers to varying degrees, but not to pure pheomelanin, while BE did not bind to any type of melanin. The results revealed that basic drugs have a greater affinity for melanin than their neutral metabolites.

Removal of the melanin from hair digests prior to drug analysis may, theoretically, reduce the effects of melanin on the total drug concentration by excluding the drug bound to the pigment. Höld et al.[85] concluded that the removal of melanin from hair digests by centrifugation did not eliminate hair-color bias. They digested hair from five cocaine users with proteinase K. After centrifugation, the pellet and the supernatant obtained were analyzed separately. Only a mean of $8.8 \pm 7.0\%$ of total cocaine was left in the melanin pellet.

Some studies found no differences in drug concentration among persons with different hair pigmentation patterns. Hill and coworkers[86] did not find any evidence of a bias due to an influence of hair color in the concentrations of cocaine and its metabolite BE. The study included 5352 black hair samples and 3600 brown-blonde samples from workplace preemployment analysis. Nevertheless, they point out that the analyses were performed by using an aggressive washing protocol[20] followed by enzymatic digestion of hair. Similarly Mieczkowski and Newel[87] reviewed eight different data sets to assess a possible systematic bias in the interpretation of hair analysis due to the color of the hair, and they conclude that color plays a role in the accumulation of drugs into hair. Nevertheless it is likely to account for only a very small part of the complex process of drug accumulation, as the effect so far has been statistically undetectable.

4.4.5 Influence of Cosmetic Treatment in Drug Concentrations

An important issue of concern for drug analysis in hair is the change in drug concentrations induced by the cosmetic treatment of hair. The most popular hair treatments are bleaching, dyeing, and permanent waving. Bleaching and dyeing formulas are combinations of hydrogen peroxide with an agent that basically contains ammonium hydroxide, plus ethanol or natural pigments for bleaching or dyeing, respectively. The aim of bleaching is a partial or complete degradation of natural pigment to obtain a lighter color of hair, and it is used to prepare the hair for dyeing. The bleaching process involves two phases: the degradation of the melanin granule and the decoloration of the pigment.[88] In the case of dyeing, after decoloration, the pigments contained in the dyeing formula provide the desired color. Hair waving is accomplished in two phases: firstly a reducing step, generally with alkaline thioglycolate, and then a subsequent reoxidation using acidic solutions of hydrogen peroxide.

Because cocaine is a very labile compound, it is expected to be degraded or changed to other compounds in the presence of such strong treatments. Tanaka and coworkers[89] studied the change of chemical structure of cocaine in the presence of hydrogen peroxide (H_2O_2). They incubated a mixture of 100 μg/ml cocaine solution and 30% H_2O_2 at 39°C for 24 h and found six reaction products (EME, BE, ortho-, meta-, and para-hydroxycocaines, and dihydroxycocaine) in the analysis using LC-MS. These products were formed immediately after mixing cocaine and H_2O_2, and their areas increased over time, while the area of cocaine decreased with the time of incubation.

Reviewing the literature, the majority of the studies on the effects of cosmetic treatments on cocaine concentrations were performed *in vitro*, either with spiked hair or hair samples obtained from drug abusers and subjected to different treatments. Welch et al.[90] divided a hair sample that tested positive for cocaine and BE into eight portions, two of which were untreated to be used as reference. The other six portions underwent a 20-h treatment with one of the following: absolute ethanol, 30% hydrogen peroxide, alkaline permanent wave, dandruff shampoo, 1% aqueous sodium chloride, or hair dye. A decrease in drug concentration was observed after all of the treatments, the most drastic reduction (80 to 95%) occurring with alkaline wave solution and 30% hydrogen peroxide. The hair dye, the simulated perspiration (1% NaCl), and ethanol decreased the concentrations only slightly, while the dandruff shampoo had an intermediate effect. Because the conditions employed were very extreme — 20-h treatment is much longer than usually employed in cosmetic treatment — the same authors[90] performed a new experiment with hair soaked with cocaine under more realistic conditions, where the contact times were 0, 10, 20, and 30 min. Under these conditions, differences in treatments did not produce large differences in results. After 30 min, the hair retained 20 to 40% of the original cocaine content.

Cirimele et al.[91] were the first to report *in vivo* differences in cocaine concentrations after cosmetic treatment. They selected and analyzed separately bleached and unbleached hair from a female who had treated her hair with hydrogen peroxide. A 65% decrease in cocaine concentrations was found in bleached hair. Similarly, Jurado et al.[92] investigated the effects of cosmetic treatment *in vivo* by analyzing hair samples selected from people who had treated their hair by bleaching or dyeing before sample collection. They found high decreases in hair that had undergone cosmetic treatment, and these decreases tended to be higher in bleached hair (mean 66.2 and 61.2% for cocaine and BE, respectively) than in dyed hair (mean 43.4 and 36.6% for cocaine and BE, respectively). Comparing cocaine and BE, there was generally good agreement between the decrease of drug and metabolite. When studying the influence of the degree of hair damage, the same authors concluded that the more damaged the hair, the larger are the differences in the concentration levels of drugs.[92] The study performed by Yegles et al.[93] in hair from a fatal drug overdose revealed that *in vitro* bleaching diminished the drug content in hair. The decreases found were 34.2, 60.4, and 38.4% for cocaine, BE, and EBE, respectively.

Another problem of cosmetic treatment is the possible uptake of cocaine for cosmetically treated hair under conditions of environmental contamination (see also Chapter 2). Two studies have been concluded with opposite points of view. Kidwell and Blank[23] treated the hair by exposure to Clairol® Nice 'n Easy® hair coloring for varying lengths of time ranging from 20 to 80 min. After that, hair was exposed to a cocaine solution of 1 μg/ml. The results revealed that the longer the treatment was applied, the greater the incorporation of cocaine into the hair samples.

In contrast, Skopp et al.[94] claimed that an increased risk of false-positive results on bleached and permanent-waved hair does exist, but is not particularly severe. They prepared four sets of dark blond virgin hair. One was maintained virgin, and the others were submitted to three different treatments: permanent waving and mild and severe bleaching. Afterward, they were incubated in 2.0 g of drugs containing artificial sweat or sebum. Cocaine was incorporated at concentrations ranging from 0.33 to 0.90 ng/mg, depending on the treatment, being higher after severe bleaching. In the case of BE, it was not detected in virgin and permed hair, while it was detected in both bleached samples (1.35 and 1.15 ng/mg). In general, drug concentrations in virgin hair were slightly lower compared with cosmetically treated hair; the amounts, however, were very small and close to the cutoff values.

In conclusion, the effects of cosmetic treatment on hair have to be taken into account when interpreting drug abuse analyses in hair samples, especially in cases of severely damaged hair.

ACKNOWLEDGMENTS

The author gratefully acknowledges the collaboration of Dr. Manuel Menéndez with the bibliographic review and the assistance of Glenn Figueroa with the English style.

ABBREVIATIONS

APCI	atmospheric pressure chemical ionization
BE	benzoylecgonine
BSTFA	*N,O*-bistrimethylsilyl-trifluoroacetamide
CH_2Cl_2	dichloromethane
CO_2	carbon dioxide
DTE	dithiothreitol
EBE	ethyl benzoylecgonine or cocaethylene
EI	electronic impact
EIA	microplate enzyme immunoassay
ELISA	enzyme-linked immunosorbent assay
EME	ecgonine methyl ester
FPIA	fluorescence polarization immunoassay
GC-MS	gas chromatography-mass spectrometry
HCl	hydrochloric acid
HFBA	heptafluorobutyric anhydride
HFPIOH	1,1,1,3,3,3-hexafluoro-isopropanol
HPLC	high-performance liquid chromatography
HPLC-FL	high-performance liquid chromatography with fluorescence detector
HS-SPME	headspace–solid-phase microextraction
LC-MS	high-performance liquid chromatography-mass spectrometry
LLE	liquid-liquid extraction
MeOH	methanol
MS	mass spectrometry
MSTFA	*N*-methyl-*N*-trimethylsilyltrifluoroacetamide
MTBSTFA	*N*-methyl-*N-tert*,-butyldimethylsilyltrifluoroacetamide
NCI	negative chemical ionization
NIST	National Institute of Standards and Technology
PAA	propionic anhydride
PCI	positive chemical ionization
PFPA	pentafluoropropionic anhydride
PT	proficiency test
Py	pyridine
r.t.	room temperature
RIA	radioimmunoassay
SFE	supercritical fluid extraction
SFTA	French Society of Analytical Toxicology
SoHT	Society of Hair Testing
SPE	solid-phase extraction
SPME	solid-phase microextraction
TEA	triethylamine
TFA	trifluoroacetic acid
TFAA	trifluoroacetic anhydride

REFERENCES

1. Garside, D. and Goldberger, B.A., Determination of cocaine and opioids in hair, in *Drug Testing in Hair*, Kintz, P., Ed., CRC Press, Boca Raton, FL, 1996, chap. 6.
2. Kintz, P., *Drug Testing in Hair*, CRC Press, Boca Raton, FL, 1996.
3. Goldberger, B., Darraj, A.G., Caplan, Y.H., and Cone, E., Detection of methadone, methadone metabolites, and other illicit drugs of abuse in hair of methadone-treatment subjects, *J. Anal. Toxicol.*, 22, 526, 1998.
4. Montagna, M., Stramessi, C., Vignale, C., Groppi, A., and Polettini A., Simultaneous hair testing for opiates, cocaine and metabolites by GCMS: a survey of applicants for driving licences with a history of drug use, *Forensic Sci. Int.*, 107, 157, 2000.
5. Romolo, F.S., Rotolo, M.C., Palmi, I., Pacifici, R., and Lopez, A., Optimized conditions for simultaneous determination of opiates, cocaine and benzoylecgonine in hair samples by GC-MS, *Forensic Sci. Int.*, 138, 17, 2003.
6. Segura, J., Stramesi, C., Redon, A., Ventura, M., Sanchez, C.J., Gonzalez, G., San, L., and Montagna, M., Immunological screening of drugs of abuse and gas chromatographic-mass spectrometric confirmation of opiates and cocaine in hair, *J. Chromatogr. B*, 724, 9, 1999.
7. Pichini, S., Pacifici, R., Altieri, I., Pellegrini, M., and Zuccaro, P., Determination of opiates and cocaine in hair as trimethylsilyl derivatives using gas chromatography-tandem mass spectrometry, *J. Anal. Toxicol.*, 23, 343, 1999.
8. Paterson, S., McLachlan-Troup, N., Cordero, R., Dohnal, M., and Carman, S., Qualitative screening for drugs of abuse in hair using GC-MS, *J. Anal. Toxicol.*, 25, 203, 2001.
9. Skender, L., Karai, V., Bri, I., and Bagari, A., Quantitative determination of amphetamines, cocaine and opiates in human hair by gas chromatography/mass spectrometry, *Forensic Sci. Int.*, 125, 120, 2002.
10. De Toledo, C.P.F., Yonamine, M., Lucia de Moraes Moreau, R., and Alves Silva, O., Determination of cocaine, benzoylecgonine and cocaethylene in human hair by solid-phase microextraction and gas chromatography-mass spectrometry, *J. Chromatogr. B*, 798, 361, 2003.
11. Cingolani, M., Scavella, S., Mencarelli, R., Mirtella, D., Froldi, R., and Rodriguez, D., Simultaneous detection of morphine, 6-acetylmorphine, and cocaine in toenails: comparison with hair analysis, *J. Anal. Toxicol.*, 28, 128, 2004.
12. Gambelunghe, C., Rossi, R., Ferranti, Ch., Rossi, R., and Bacci, M., Hair analysis by GC/MS/MS to verify abuse of drugs, *J. Appl. Toxicol.*, 25, 205, 2005.
13. Brewer, W.E., Galipo, R.C., Sellers, K.W., and Morgan, S.L., Analysis of cocaine, benzoylecgonine, codeine and morphine in hair by supercritical fluid extraction with carbon dioxide modified with methanol, *Anal. Chem.*, 73, 2371, 2001.
14. Uhl, M., Tandem mass spectrometry: a helpful tool in hair analysis for the forensic expert, *Forensic Sci. Int.*, 107, 169, 2000.
15. Sporkert, F. and Pragst, F., Determination of lidocaine in hair of drug fatalities by headspace solid-phase microextraction, *J. Anal. Toxicol.*, 24, 316, 2000.
16. Gentili, S., Cornetta, M., and Macchia, T., Rapid screening procedure based on headspace solid-phase microextraction and gas chromatography-mass spectrometry for the detection of many recreational drugs in hair, *J. Chromatogr. B*, 801, 289, 2004.
17. Girod, C. and Staub, C., Analysis of drugs of abuse in hair by automated solid-phase extraction, GC/EI/MS and GC ion trap CI/MS, *Forensic Sci. Int.*, 107, 261, 2000.
18. Cognard, E., Rudaz, S., Bouchonnet, S., and Staub, C., Analysis of cocaine and three of its metabolites in hair by gas chromatography-mass spectrometry using ion-trap detection for CI/MS/MS, *J. Chromatogr. B*, 826, 17, 2005.

19. Clauwaert, K.M., Van Bocxlaer, J.F., Lambert, W.E., Van den Eckhout, E.G., Lemière, F., Esmans, E.L., and De Leenheer, A.P., Narrow-bore HPLC in combination with fluorescence and electrospray mass spectrometric detection for the analysis of cocaine and metabolites in human hair, *Anal. Chem.*, 70, 2336, 1998.
20. Baumgartner, W.A. and Hill, V.A., Sample preparation techniques, *Forensic Sci. Int.*, 63, 121, 1993.
21. Schaffer, M.I., Wang, W.L., and Irving, J., An evaluation of two wash procedures for the differentiation of external contamination versus ingestion in the analysis of human hair samples for cocaine, *J. Anal. Toxicol.*, 26, 485, 2002.
22. Kronstrand, R., Nyström, I., Strandberg, J., and Druid, H., Screening for drugs of abuse in hair with ion spray LC-MS-MS, *Forensic Sci. Int.*, 145, 183, 2004.
23. Kidwell, D.A. and Blank, D.I., Environmental exposure: the stumbling block of hair testing, in *Drug Testing in Hair*, Kintz, P., Ed., CRC Press, Boca Raton FL, 1996, chap. 2.
24. Wang, W.L. and Cone, E.J., Testing human hair for drugs of abuse, IV: environmental cocaine contamination and washing effects, *Forensic Sci. Int.*, 70, 39, 1995.
25. Blank, D.I. and Kidwell, D.A., External contamination of hair by cocaine: an issue in forensic interpretation, *Forensic Sci. Int.*, 63, 145, 1993.
26. Blank, D.L. and Kidwell, D.A., Decontamination procedures for drugs of abuse in hair: are they sufficient? *Forensic Sci. Int.*, 70, 13, 1995.
27. Paulsen, R.B., Wilkins, D.G., Slawson, M.H., Sahw, K., and Rollins, D.E., Effect of four laboratory decontamination procedures on the quantitative determination of cocaine and metabolites in hair by HPLC-MS, *J. Anal. Toxicol.*, 25, 490, 2001.
28. Morrison, J.F., Chesler, S.N., Yoo, W.I., and Selavka, C.M., Matrix and modifier effects in the supercritical fluid extraction of cocaine and benzoylecgonine from human hair, *Anal. Chem.*, 70, 163, 1998.
29. Morrison, J.F., Sniegoski, L.T., and Yoo, W.I., Evaluation of Analytical Methodologies for Non-Intrusive Drug Testing: Supercritical Fluid Extraction of Cocaine from Hair, NIJ Report 601, U.S. Department of Justice, National Institute of Justice, Dec. 1998.
30. Anon., Society of Hair Testing, Statement of the Society of Hair Testing concerning the examination of drugs in human hair, *Forensic Sci. Int.*, 84, 3, 1997.
31. Anon., Society of Hair Testing, Recommendations for hair testing in forensic cases, *Forensic Sci. Int.*, 145, 83, 2004.
32. Möller, M.R. and Eser, H.P., The analytical tools for hair testing, in *Drug Testing in Hair*, Kintz, P., Ed., CRC Press, Boca Raton, FL, 1996, chap. 4.
33. Bourland, J.A., Hayes, E.F., Kelly, R.C., Sweeney, S.A., and Hatab, M.M., Quantitation of cocaine, benzoylecgonine, cocaethylene, methylecgonine and norcocaine in human hair by positive ion chemical ionization (PICI) gas chromatography-tandem mass spectrometry, *J. Anal. Toxicol.*, 24, 489, 2000.
34. Paulsen, R.B., Wilkins, D.G., Slawson, M.H., Shaw, K., and Rollins, D.E., Quantitation of cocaine and metabolites in hair via API-ES LC-MSD, Abstract. *J. Anal. Toxicol.*, 25, 363, 2001.
35. Tagliaro, F., Valentini, R., Manetto, G., Crivillente, F., Carli, G., and Marigo, M., Hair analysis by using radioimmunoassay, high-performance liquid chromatography and capillary electrophoresis to investigate chronic exposure to heroin, cocaine and/or ecstasy in applicants for driving licenses, *Forensic Sci. Int.*, 107, 121, 2000.
36. Höld, K.M., Wilkins, D.G., Rollins, D.E., Joseph, R.E., Jr., and Cone, E. J., Simultaneous quantitation of cocaine, opiates, and their metabolites in human hair by positive ion chemical ionization gas chromatography-mass spectrometry, *J. Chromatogr. Sci.*, 36, 125, 1998.

37. Scheidweiler, K.B. and Huestis, M.A., Simultaneous quantification of opiates, cocaine and metabolites in hair by LC-APCI-MS/MS, *Anal. Chem.*, 76, 4358, 2004.
38. Nakahara, Y., Kikura, R., and Takahashi, K., Hair analysis for drugs of abuse, VIII: effective extraction and determination of 6-acetylmorphine and morphine in hair with trifluoroacetic acid-methanol for the confirmation of retrospective heroin use by gas chromatography-mass spectrometry, *J. Chromatogr. B*, 657, 93, 1994.
39. Cirimele, V., Kintz, P., and Mangin, P., Comparison of different extraction procedures for drugs in hair of drug addicts, *Biomed. Chromatogr.*, 10, 179, 1996.
40. Eser, H.P., Pötsch, L., Skopp, G., and Möller, M.R., Influence of sample preparation on analytical results: drug analysis (GC/MS) on hair snippets versus hair powder using various extraction methods, *Forensic Sci. Int.*, 84, 271, 1997.
41. Staub, C. and Edder, P., Importance of supercritical fluid extraction (SFE) in hair analysis, in *Drug Testing in Hair*, Kintz P., Ed., CRC Press, Boca Raton, FL, 1996, chap. 5.
42. Maxwell, R.J. and Morrison J.F., in *Handbook of Analytical Therapeutic Drug Monitoring and Toxicology*, Wong S. and Sunshine I., Eds., CRC Press, Boca Raton, FL, chap. 5.
43. Cirimele, V., Kintz, P., Majdalani, R., and Mangin, P., Supercritical fluid extraction of drugs in drug addict hair, *J. Chromatogr. B*, 673, 173, 1995.
44. Kintz, P., Analyses des opiaés et de la cocaine dans les cheveaux par couplage CG-MS: consensus sur l'analyse des substances organiques dans les cheveaux, *Toxicorama*, 6, 1994.
45. Strano-Rossi, S. and Chiarotti, M., Solid phase microextraction for cannabinoids analysis in hair and its possible application to other drugs, *J. Anal. Toxicol.*, 23, 7, 1999.
46. Spiehler, V., Hair analysis by immunological methods from the beginning to 2000, *Forensic Sci. Int.*, 107, 249, 2000.
47. Balabanova, S., Brunner, H., and Nowak, R., Radioimmunological determination of cocaine in human hair, *Z. Rechtsmed.*, 98, 229, 1987.
48. Baumgartner, W.A., Black, C.T., Jones, P.F., and Blahd, W.H., Radioimmunoassay of cocaine in hair: concise communication, *J. Nucl. Med.*, 23, 790, 1982.
49. Valente, D., Cassani, M., Pigliapochi, M., and Vansetti, G., Hair as the sample in assessing morphine and cocaine addiction, *Clin. Chem.*, 27, 1952, 1981.
50. Moore, C., Deitermann, D., Lewis, D., Feeley, B., and Niedbala, R.S., The detection of cocaine in hair specimens using micro-plate enzyme immunoassay, *J. Forensic Sci.*, 44, 609, 1999.
51. Tagliaro, F., Poiesi, C., Aiello, R., Dorizzi, R., Ghielmi, S., and Marigo, M., Capillary electrophoresis, a new tool for the investigation of illicit drugs in hair: determination of cocaine and morphine, *J. Chromatogr.*, 638, 303, 1993.
52. Tagliaro, F., Manetto, G., Aiello, R., Crivellente, F., Scarcella, D., and Marigo, M., Hair analysis for abused drugs by capillary-zone electrophoresis and field-amplified sample stacking, *Forensic Sci. Int.*, 92, 259, 1998.
53. Segura, J., Ventura, R., and Jurado, C., Derivatization procedures for gas chromatographic-mass spectrometric determination of xenobiotics in biological samples, with special attention to drugs of abuse and doping agents, *J. Chromatogr. B Biomed. Appl.*, 713, 61, 1998.
54. Ferrara, S.D., Importance of quality assurance in testing drugs of abuse, *Forensic Sci. Int.*, 63, 305, 1993.
55. Welch, M.J., Sniegoski, L.T., and Tai, S., Two new standard reference materials for the determination of drugs of abuse in human hair, *Anal. Bioanal. Chem.*, 376, 1205, 2003.

56. Kintz, P., Interlaboratory comparison of quantitative determinations of drugs in hair samples, *Forensic Sci. Int.*, 70, 105, 1995.
57. Welch, M.J., Sniegoski, L.T., and Allgood, C.C., Interlaboratory comparison studies on the analysis of hair for drugs of abuse, *Forensic Sci. Int.*, 63, 295, 1993.
58. Sniegoski, L.T. and Welch, M.J., Interlaboratory studies on the analysis of hair for drugs of abuse: results from the fourth exercise, *J. Anal. Toxicol.*, 20, 242, 1996.
59. Montagna, M., Polettini, A., Stramesi, C., Groppi, A., and Vignali, C., Hair analysis for opiates, cocaine and metabolites: evaluation of a method by interlaboratory comparison, *Forensic Sci. Int.*, 128, 79, 2002.
60. Sachs, H., Quality control by the society of hair testing, *Forensic Sci. Int.*, 84, 145, 1993.
61. Sachs, H. and Möller, M.R., Interlaboratory comparison of quantitative GC/MS methods for drugs in hair, Proceedings of the 30th TIAFT International Meeting, Fukuoka, Japan, Oct. 19–23, 1992, p. 33.
62. Deveaux, M., Kintz, P., Goullé, J.P., Bessard, J., Pepin, G., and Gosset, D., The hair analysis proficiency testing program of the French Society of Analytical Toxicology, *Forensic Sci. Int.*, 107, 389, 2002.
63. Anon., Proficiency test for the analysis of hair for drugs of abuse, organized by the Society of Hair Testing, *Forensic Sci. Int.*, 133, 175, 2002.
64. Jurado, C. and Sachs, H., Proficiency test for the analysis of hair for drugs of abuse: the three years experience of the Society of Hair Testing, presented at Third European Meeting on Hair Analysis, Heraklion, Crete, Oct. 6–8, 2003, p. 14.
65. Pichini, S., Ventura, M., Pujadas, M., Ventura, R., Pellegrini, M., Zuccaro, P., Pacifici, R., and de la Torre, R., HAIRVEQ: an external quality control scheme for drugs of abuse analysis in hair, *Forensic Sci. Int.*, 145, 109, 2004.
66. Pépin, G. and Gaillard, Y., Concordance between self-reported drug use and findings in hair about cocaine and heroin, *Forensic Sci. Int.*, 84, 37, 1997.
67. Nakahara, Y., Takahashi, K., and Kikura, R., Hair analysis for drugs of abuse, X: effect of physicochemical properties of drugs on the incorporation rates into hair, *Biol. Pharm. Bull.*, 18, 1223, 1995.
68. Tagliaro, F., De Battisti, Z., Lubli, G., Neri, C., Manetto, G., and Marigo, M., Integrated use of hair analysis to investigate the physical fitness to obtain the driving licence: a case work study, *Forensic Sci. Int.*, 84, 129, 1997.
69. Kintz, P. and Mangin, P., What constitutes a positive result in hair analysis: proposal for the establishment of cut-off values, *Forensic Sci. Int.*, 70, 3, 1995.
70. Quintela, O., Bermejo, A.M., Tabernero, M.J., Strano-Rossi, S., Chiarotti, M., and Lucas, A.C.S., Evaluation of cocaine, amphetamines and cannabis use in university students through hair analysis: preliminary study, *Forensic Sci. Int.*, 107, 273, 2000.
71. Baumgartner, W.A. and Hill, V.A., Hair analysis for organic analytes: methodology, reliability issues, and field studies, in *Drug Testing in Hair*, Kintz, P., Ed., CRC Press, Boca Raton, FL, 1996, chap. 10.
72. Anon., HTWG: final consensus after the third meeting of the Hair Testing Working Group in Texas, May 1999.
73. SAMHSA, Department of Health and Mental Services, Substance Abuse and Mental Health Services Administration, Proposed Revisions to Mandatory Guidelines for Federal Workplace Drug Testing Programs, *Federal Register*, 69, no. 71, 19673–19732 (13 April 2004).
74. Puschel, K., Thomasch, P., and Arnold, W., Opiate levels in hair, *Forensic Sci. Int.*, 21, 181, 1983.

75. Henderson, G.L., Harkey, M.R., Zhou, C.H., Jones, R.T., and Peyton, J., III, Incorporation of isotopically labeled cocaine and metabolites in human hair, 1: dose-response relationships, *J. Anal. Toxicol.*, 20, 1, 1996.
76. Jurado, C., El pelo como matriz biológica en el diagnóstico toxicológico, doctoral thesis, University of Sevilla, Spain, 1999.
77. Ferko, A.P., Barbieri, E.J., DiGregorio, G.J., and Ruch, E.K., The accumulation and disappearance of cocaine and benzoylecgonine in rat hair following prolonged administration of cocaine, *Life Sci.*, 51, 1823, 1992.
78. Ropero-Miller, J.D., Goldberger, B.A., Cone, E.J., and Joseph, R.E., Jr., The disposition of cocaine and opiate analytes in hair and fingernails of humans following cocaine and codeine administration, *J. Anal. Toxicol.*, 24, 496, 2000.
79. Scheidweiler, K.B., Cone, E.J., Moolchan, E.T., and Huestis, M.A., Dose-related distribution of codeine, cocaine and metabolites into human hair following controlled oral codeine and subcutaneous cocaine administration, *J. Pharmacol. Exp. Ther.*, 313, 909, 2005.
80. Hubbard, D.L., Wilkins, D.G., and Rollins, D.E., The incorporation of cocaine and metabolites into hair: effects of dose and hair pigmentation, *Drug Metab. Dispos.*, 28, 1464, 2000.
81. Jurado, C., Rodriguez-Vicente, C., Menéndez, M., and Repetto, M., Time course of cocaine in rabbit hair, *Forensic Sci. Int.*, 84, 61, 1997.
82. Borges, Ch. R., Roberts, J.C., Wilkins, D.G., and Rollins, D.E., Cocaine, benzoylecgonine, amphetamine and N-acetylamphetamine binding to melanin subtypes, *J. Anal. Toxicol.*, 27, 125, 2003.
83. Reid, R.W., O'Connor, F.L., and Crayton, J.W., The *in vitro* differential binding of benzoylecgonine to pigmented human hair samples, *J. Toxicol. Clin. Toxicol.*, 32, 405, 1994.
84. Joseph, R.E., Jr., Su, T.P., and Cone, E.J., *In vitro* binding studies of drugs to hair: influence of melanin and lipids on cocaine binding to Caucasoid and Africoid hair, *J. Anal. Toxicol.*, 20, 338, 1996.
85. Höld, K.M., Hubbard, D.L., Wilkins, D.G., and Rollins, D.E., Quantitation of cocaine in human hair: the effect of centrifugation of hair digests, *J. Anal. Toxicol.*, 22, 414, 1998.
86. Hill, V., Schaffer, M., and Cairns, T., Absence of Hair Color in Hair Analysis Results for Cocaine, Benzoylecgonine, Morphine, 6-Monoacetylmorphine, Codeine and 11-nor-9-THC in Large Workplace Populations, presented at the meeting of the Society of Hair Testing, Strasbourg, 28–30 Sept. 2005.
87. Mieczkowski, T. and Newel, R., Statistical examination of hair color as a potential biasing factor in hair analysis, *Forensic Sci. Int.*, 107, 13, 2000.
88. Wolfram, L., Hall, K., and Hui, J., The mechanism of hair bleaching, *J. Soc. Cosm. Chem.*, 21, 875, 1970.
89. Tanaka, S., Lio, R., Chinaka, S., Takayama, N., and Hayakawa, K., Analysis of reaction products of cocaine and hydrogen peroxide by high-performance liquid chromatography/mass spectrometry, *Biomed. Chromatogr.*, 16, 390, 2002.
90. Welch, M.J., Sniegoski, L.T., Allgood, Ch., and Habram, M., Hair analysis for drugs of abuse: evaluation of analytical methods, environmental issues, and development of reference materials, *J. Anal. Toxicol.*, 17, 389, 1993.
91. Cirimele, V., Kintz, P., and Mangin, P., Drug concentrations in human hair after bleaching, *J. Anal. Toxicol.*, 19, 331, 1995.
92. Jurado, C., Kintz, P., Menendez, M., and Repetto, M., Influence of the cosmetic treatment of hair on drug testing, *Int. J. Legal Med.*, 110, 159, 1997.

93. Yegles, M., Marson, Y., and Wenning, R., Influence of bleaching on stability of benzodiazepines in hair, *Forensic Sci. Int.*, 107, 87, 2000.
94. Skopp, G., Pötsch, L., and Moeller, M.R., On cosmetically treated hair: aspects and pitfalls of interpretation, *Forensic Sci. Int.*, 84, 43, 1997.

5 Determination of Cannabinoids in Human Hair

Michael Uhl

CONTENTS

5.1 INTRODUCTION

Cannabis sativa, one of the oldest cultivated plants,[1] originated in Central Asia. It was not only used as raw material for the production of ropes and fabrics, but the psychoactive and physiological effects of this herb were also very well known. The euphoric effects of cannabis have been appreciated for over 4000 years,[2,3] and medications with the drug are documented in India from 3400 years ago.[4] Even then, shamans utilized the helpful psychotropic effects of cannabis during ritual ceremonies.[4]

Botanists now generally agree that cannabis is a genus with a single species (*Cannabis sativa*) that has diversified into a great number of ecotypes (e.g., *Cannabis indica*) and cultivated races.[1]

There are three preparations of cannabis. Marijuana, a crude drug made from the dried herbaceous annual plant *Cannabis sativa*, is the form most commonly consumed in the U.S.[5] Hashish, a resinous form, predominates in Africa and Asia,[6] and in Europe both variations are common. A special feature is hash oil, a very potent variation produced from hashish by distillation.

The major psychoactive ingredient in *Cannabis sativa* is Δ^9-tetrahydrocannabinol (THC). The concentration varies considerably in different plants and preparations. In a long-term study over a period of more than 20 years,[7,8] the concentration of THC in different preparations was determined. It was reported that in 2004 the average level of THC in marijuana was 5.8%, in hashish 11.2%, and in hash oil 42%. The content of high-potency bud-type sinsemilla was 13.3%. The quality of cannabis preparations officially sold in Dutch coffee shops was examined in 1999, where the average THC content for marijuana was shown to be 7.5%, hashish 12.6%, and 20.9% for hashish derived from Dutch hemp.[9]

Many countries have laws regarding the cultivation, possession, supply, or use of cannabis. In countries where cultivation of fiber-producing plants is allowed, the cultivars are tested so that the psychoactive potency is below a certain level.[10]

Although possession of small quantities for personal use is not illegal in some countries of South America (Colombia, Uruguay) and Europe (Netherlands, Portugal),[11] cannabis is generally the most widely used illicit drug.[2,12,13]

5.2 METABOLISM, INCORPORATION OF CANNABINOIDS INTO HAIR

Cannabis is usually consumed by smoking; an alternative form is oral route of administration.[2,5] *Cannabis sativa* contains over 420 different chemical compounds, including more than 60 cannabinoids.[2,14] Three main constituents have a special importance: Δ^9-tetrahydrocannbinol (THC), the major psychoactive component of cannabis[5] has a pKa of 10.6, is very lipophilic, and is extensively protein-bound in plasma.[15–17] Cannabinol (CBN), which is formed as THC oxidizes, and cannabidiol (CBD), a biogenetic precursor of THC, are not psychoactive.

In the major metabolic pathway, hydroxylation of THC leads to primary production of the active metabolite 11-hydroxy-Δ^9-tetrahydrocannabinol[18] (11-hydroxy-THC) and the inactive metabolite 8-hydroxy-Δ^9-tetrahydrocannabinol.[19] Further oxidation produces the inactive main metabolite 11-nor-9-carboxy-^{9}-tetrahydrocannabinol (9-carboxy-THC).

The bioavailability of THC during smoking is about 18%, ranging from 12% for an occasional user to even more than 25% for a frequent user.[20,21] In the case of oral administration of cannabis, the bioavailability is lower, with an average value of 10%.[22]

Drugs like cannabinoids can be transferred to/into hair via a complex multicompartment model described by Henderson.[23] Cannabinoids are deposited from blood within the hair follicle during the formation period and later from tissue surrounding the hair follicle, such as sebaceous glands and sweat glands, into the completed hair shaft. Moreover, drugs may also be excreted with sweat, which wet or cover the hair and may diffuse into the hair matrix.[2,24] THC, but not the metabolites 11-hydroxy-THC and 9-carboxy-THC, has been detected in sweat.[3,24] The pH of keratinocytes and melanocytes is assumed to be more acidic than blood.[24] Only the nonionized part of the drug, which is not protein-bound, can penetrate the cell membrane. Since the composition of sebum is rather nonpolar it should preferentially contain lipophilic drugs, which may migrate along the cell membrane complex of keratinized hair cells.

The relatively low concentrations of cannabinoids determined in hair can be explained by the following parameters: THC is highly bound to protein in plasma,[5] THC exhibits no melanin affinity,[24,25] and a negatively charged compound like 9-carboxy-THC will be repelled by the hair matrix.[26]

5.3 ANALYTICAL TECHNIQUES FOR THE DETECTION OF CANNABINOIDS

The detection of cannabinoids in hair is a great analytical challenge, since the concentration of analytes to be detected is low.[3] Due to the weak incorporation rate of the acidic metabolite into the hair matrix, the concentration of 9-carboxy-THC is even very low.[3,13] The selection of an appropriate testing method is difficult, and different approaches to the problem have been described in literature.

Initially, a sensitive screen for cannabis detection must be found; secondly a confirmatory procedure for the identification of specific analytes is essential.

An immunoassay, gas chromatography-mass spectrometry (GC-MS), or GC-MS/MS can be employed as screening methods. Then the specific identification of cannabis ingredients or metabolites is performed by chromatographic methods combined with mass-spectrometry or tandem-mass-spectrometry.

Immunoassays are usually used as screening tests for the identification of a presumptive drug-positive result such as cannabis-positive hair samples. Among these assays, Cannabinoid Microplate EIA (enzyme immunoassay) (Orasure Technologies Inc.), Immunalysis cannabinoids RIA (radioimmunoassay), and Cozart cannabinoids microplate EIA seem to have suitable cross-reactivity with THC.[27–29]

The most common analytical technique for the detection of cannabis components in hair is still GC-MS.[30] It is mostly used in the electron impact (EI) mode. Negative chemical ionization (NCI) and procedures making use of modifications in different methodologies have been selected for special applications.[13,31–36]

The automated detection of ingredients in cannabis using headspace solid-phase microextraction (HS-SPME) followed by on-fiber derivatization and GC-MS-EI detection has been described.[37–39] According to the authors, this procedure worked particularly fast. The limit of detection (LOD) was 0.05 ng/mg for THC, 0.08 ng/mg for CBD, and 0.14 ng/mg for CBN. However, 9-carboxy-THC could not be detected.

Using GC-MS-EI, Monsanto et al.[13] showed the presence of THC, CBN, and CBD in hair samples. The determination of 9-carboxy-THC could only be realized by negative chemical ionization mode (GC-MS-NCI) after a liquid-liquid extraction. The authors reported an average concentration of 28 pg/mg hair.

Sachs and Dressler[33] obtained an LOD of 0.3 pg/mg hair for the detection of 9-carboxy-THC and a limit of quantification (LOQ) of 1.1 pg/mg hair by combining a liquid/liquid extraction (LLE), HPLC cleanup, and finally GC-MS-NCI detection.

Moore, Guzaldo, and Donahue[34] described the use of high-volume injection and GC-MS-NCI for the determination of 9-carboxy-THC. In this procedure, a ProSep injector, having a rapid capability of heating and cooling, was utilized to inject up to 25 μl of hair extract onto the GC column. The LOD reported was 0.3 pg/mg hair, the LOQ 0.4 pg/mg hair.

A new approach to determine 9-carboxy-THC is the application of two-dimensional GC in combination with MS (Agilent 6890N-5973).[35] After solid-phase extraction (SPE), the hair extract is injected into the GC. The helium gas flow is diverted from the primary column to the analytical column by the Dean's Switch System (GC/GC). Using cryogenic focusing, the analyte is cold trapped as it passes through the analytical column. Detection is performed in NCI mode using ammonia as the reagent gas. The method described uses a single quadrupole instrument to achieve an LOD of 0.05 pg/mg hair for 9-carboxy-THC.

The conventional technique to detect the low concentration of 9-carboxy-THC is GC-MS/MS instrumentation.[12,40–46] Pioneering publications by Baumgartner,[40] by Cairns,[41] and by Mieczkowski[42] demonstrated that hair samples with a positive RIA for cannabinoids should be qualified by the presence of 9-carboxy-THC using GC-MS/MS. This method is also applied to screen for the main constituents of cannabis,[12,43,45] initially followed by the separate determination of a specific metabolite. The regulatory cutoff for this assay has been experimentally determined to be 0.05 pg/mg hair.[41] An innovative approach involves searching for constituents of cannabis and more than a single metabolite by using a collective detection rather than via distinct procedures. Wicks and Tsanaclis[46] described a simultaneous extraction of THC, CBN, CBD, 9-carboxy-THC, and 11-hydroxy-THC with LODs for the metabolites of 1.0 pg/mg hair. The obtained extract was suitable for a GC-MS/MS analysis. The detection of 11-hydroxy-THC in hair was reported in this publication for the first time.

Liquid chromatography-mass spectrometry (LC-MS) or liquid chromatography-tandem mass spectrometry (LC-MS/MS) are often used as instruments for screening and target analysis of specific illicit drugs and hypnotics in hair. However, it has been shown that LC-MS/MS is a useful instrumentation setup to detect cannabinoids and their metabolites in urine samples and plasma,[47–49] but not in hair. Out of the 25 and 22 participants in the proficiency tests of the Society of Hair Testing (SoHT) in 2004 and 2005, respectively, just one laboratory per year used a methodology based on liquid chromatography.[50] The lack of publications on the subject of determination of cannabinoids in hair using LC-MS or LC-MS/MS shows that, at present, this instrumentation is not equivalent to GC-MS or GC-MS/MS.

Additional analytical instrumentations such as capillary electrophoresis[51,52] have also been used for the detection of cannabinoids, but they seem to have little popularity in this special application of hair analysis.

Table 5.1 summarizes the essential factors of some selected analytical methodologies used to identify cannabinoids in hair, including analytical instrumentation used for screening and confirmation methods, decontamination steps, extraction methods, analytes to be detected.

5.4 DECONTAMINATION PROCESSES

Baumgartner[55] started from the principle that drugs are sequestered in hair in three compartments: the accessible, the semiaccessible, and the inaccessible domain.

TABLE 5.1
Selected Analytical Methodologies

Detection	Decontamination	Extraction/ Digestion	Cleanup	Analyte (LOD/LOQ in pg)	Ref.
Screening: GC-MS-EI	sodium dodecyl sulfate, water	β-glucuronidase, arylsulfatase	LLE	THC/CBD 20; CBN 50;	13
Confirmation: GC-MS-NCI	sodium dodecyl sulfate, water	β-glucuronidase, arylsulfatase	LLE	9-carboxy-THC 500 9-carboxy-THC 5	
Confirmation: GC-MS/MS-EI	N/A	NaOH	LLE	9-carboxy-THC	44
Screening: GC-MS-EI	methylene chloride	1*M* NaOH	LLE	THC 100; CBD 20; CBN 10	32
Screening: GC-MS-EI	water, acetone, petroleum ether	methanol	—	THC 100 (LOD)	53
Confirmation: GC-MS-NCI	methylene chloride	1*M* NaOH	SPE	9-carboxy-THC 0.3	34
Confirmation: GC/GC-NCI	N/A	methanol, EtAc, NAOH	SPE	9-carboxy-THC 0.05	35, 36
Screening: GC-MS-EI	water, petroleum ether, methylene chloride	1*M* NaOH	HS-SPME	CBD 80; THC 50; CBN 140	37
Confirmation: GC-MS-NCI	N/A	2*M* NaOH	LLE, HPLC	9-carboxy-THC 0.32	33
Confirmation: GC-MS/MS-NCI	—	10*M* NaOH	SPE	9-carboxy-THC 0.05	41
Screening: GC-MS/MS-CI	n-hexane, acetone	methanol	—	THC/CBN 100	54
Confirmation: GC-MS/MS-NCI	—	methanol / 10*M* KOH	SPE	9-carboxy-THC 0.1	
Screening 1: ELISA[a]				THC/CBN 100	12
Screening 2: GC-MS	water, petroleum ether, methanol	methanol	—		
Confirmation: GC-MS/MS-NCI	—	methanol / 10*M* KOH	SPE	9-carboxy-THC 0.1	
Screening and confirmation: GC-MS/MS-NCI	N/A	N/A	SPE	CBN/CBD/THC 10 9-carboxy-THC 1.0 11-hydroxy-THC 1.0	46

[a] ELISA = enzyme-linked immunosorbent assay.

Drugs coming from the environment (via external contamination) that bind to hair are often found on the surface of hair, according to the three-compartment model, in the accessible domain. From there, they are readily removed by wash solutions. Since organic solvents like isopropanol, hexane, and methylene chloride are unable to swell hair, these solvents can only remove oily residues and particulate matter from the hair surface, but not from deeper lying structures of the hair shaft. Drug contaminants can be carried into the deeper lying hair structures by hair-swelling media such as sweat. Therefore drugs can only be removed from this domain by hair-swelling solvents (e.g., water, methanol, acids, bases).

In a study[56] published in 1995, four laboratory wash procedures were evaluated for their effect on the measured concentration of THC in hair. Drug-free hairs were soaked in a solution containing THC, 11-hydroxy-THC, and 9-carboxy-THC. This was followed by evaporation and washing (using methanol or methylene chloride or phosphate buffer or anhydrous isopropanol). It was found that the methanol, methylene chloride, and anhydrous isopropanol washing procedures were sufficient to remove the three fortified cannabinoids. However, phosphate buffer was not effective for complete removal.

Strano-Rossi and Chiarotti[57] described the effectiveness of different decontamination procedures on passively contaminated hair. In this study, negative hair samples were exposed to cannabis smoke in a smoking machine. Various decontamination techniques comprising repeated solvent washing and ultrasonication for 10 min were evaluated. The authors observed that three consecutive petroleum ether washes were adequate to completely remove a heavy external contamination.

Washing hair samples twice in 5 ml methylene chloride for 2 min was considered to be sufficient for decontamination in a rapid screening procedure for the simultaneous identification of THC, CBN, and CBD.[32]

In a subsequent washing procedure, deionized water, petroleum ether, and finally methylene chloride were applied for decontamination to exclude a contamination.[37] The washing solutions were tested by conventional GC-MS.

5.5 ISSUES TO BE CONSIDERED

5.5.1 Issue of External Contamination

Generally, the issue of passive contamination and the ability to distinguish passive exposure from active, willful ingestion is an interpretative problem in hair testing.[12] The disadvantage of an exclusive detection of cannabis constituents is that contamination can never be excluded. Smoke deposits from cannabis preparations contains THC, CBN, and CBD,[25,58] and diffusion into the hair may lead to an incorporation that cannot be distinguished from internal sources, i.e., consumption.[2,12]

An *in vitro* study was carried out to determine whether exposure to cannabis smoke could produce a hair sample positive for cannabinoids.[25] Furthermore, potential influencing factors of drug deposition on the keratin matrix, such as moisture, sebum, and bleaching or perming, were also investigated. Commonly used washing procedures were applied to determine their effectiveness in removing contamination from hair exposed to cannabis smoke.

Strands of natural hair were moistened with water, greased with sebum or sebum/sweat, or bleached or permed. Treated and untreated hair strands were exposed to cannabis smoke for 60 min. Each hair strand was either subjected to a decontamination procedure by washing with different solvents or remained unwashed. Each hair sample was tested for cannabinoids using GC-MS.

Cannabinoids from cannabis smoke were deposited on hair fibers, fewer on untreated than on pretreated hair. Concentrations were increased in damp hair and were even higher in greased hair. External contaminants were completely removed by washing with methanol or methylene chloride in untreated hair only; washing with dodecylsulfate was insufficient. Therefore, exposure to environmental marijuana smoke may produce false-positive or falsely increased test results in hair.

5.5.2 Issue of Influence of Cosmetic Treatment

Every cosmetic hair treatment may have an influence on the quantitative results of an analysis. Superficial treatments of hair interacting on or near the hair surface include products such as shampoo, conditioner, temporary hair dye, sprays, or gel. Products used for long-term effects alter hair chemistry at and within the cuticle layer and even deeper within the hair fiber.[59] These products are used for perming, bleaching, semipermanent, and permanent dyeing. Whereas the binding between a polar dye molecule and the hair occurs through weak polar and Van der Waals forces in the case of semipermanent dyeing, oxidizing agents are applied for perming, permanent coloration, and bleaching.

The potential influence of cosmetic treatment on drug testing in hair was investigated in an *in vivo* study.[60] Hair samples were collected from self-reported drug users who had previously dyed or bleached their hair. Treated hair was separated from untreated hair under the microscope, and the selected portions obtained were analyzed for illicit drugs. A drop in the concentrations of THC and 9-carboxy-THC was observed when comparing treated hair with untreated hair. For dyed or bleached strands, the decrease in concentration of THC ranged from 12.3 to 61.3%; the decrease in the case of 9-carboxy-THC ranged from 5 to 77.6%.

A particular application is the use of shampoos that eliminate unwanted impurities from within the hair shaft. The influence of a special cleansing product on the results of hair analyses was investigated.[61] After application of a cleansing shampoo, a 36% reduction in the THC concentration in hair was observed. However, it was also shown that traces of THC were not sufficiently removed from human hair by the single use of a special shampoo.

Cannabis plants may be used in shampoo preparations. A study[62] revealed the presence of three constituents in Cannabio® shampoo: THC 412 ng/ml, CBN 380 ng/ml, and CBD 4079 ng/ml. The authors concluded that the use of Cannabio shampoo during normal hygiene practice can scarcely be considered as a source of potential contamination. However, extensive and unrealistic use can cause drug-free hair to test positive for CBN and CBD but not for THC.

5.5.3 Degradation Processes by UV Light, Cause of Damage to the Hair Matrix

The influence of sunlight and humidity on the concentration of the cannabinoid content of hair was repeatedly investigated.[63,64] In an experiment, authentic hair samples from cannabis users and a drug-free sample spiked with THC, CBN, and CBD were exposed to sunlight and elevated humidity in quartz glass tubes for

8 weeks. Under all of the conditions chosen, the concentrations of cannabis components decreased. THC was the most unstable compound. At high humidity, the concentrations declined more rapidly. These findings demonstrate that a sample below the top hair should preferably be collected.

5.6 CRITERIA FOR OBTAINING A CANNABIS-POSITIVE HAIR-TEST RESULT

Cutoffs are designated points used to separate a negative from a positive sample. In a consensus initiated by the SoHT,[65] the determination of 9-carboxy-THC was recommended for a THC-positive hair test result.

In its latest Mandatory Guidelines for Federal Workplace Drug Testing Program, SAMHSA (Substance Abuse and Mental Health Services Administration) suggested 1.0 pg/mg as the initial cutoff concentration for marijuana metabolites and 0.05 pg/mg hair as the cutoff concentration for the confirmatory test.[66]

The recommendations for hair testing for cannabinoids in forensic cases published by the SoHT in 2004 are as follows:[67] using an immunochemical test a THC concentration of 0.1 ng/mg must produce a positive result. The recommended LOQ determining THC by a chromatographic test is 0.1 ng/mg and for 9-carboxy-THC 0.2 pg/mg.

According to the recommendations set forth by the GTFCh (Gesellschaft für Toxikologische und Forensische Chemie) and the SoHT, a cutoff value of 0.1 ng/mg hair is used for THC in the context of driving-ability examinations in Germany.[68]

5.7 CONTROLLED STUDIES: EMPIRICAL DATA ANALYSIS OF A LARGE SAMPLE OF HAIR SPECIMENS

The number of controlled studies on the correlation of cannabis use and the evaluation of the outcome of the hair analyses is limited. Empirical data has been published by several authors.

An article reports the outcome of GC-MS/MS confirmation for THC and 9-carboxy-THC on 93 hair samples screened for cannabis using RIA.[42] These test series have been completed by RIA screens that were also done on urine samples. For THC, the GC-MS/MS procedure yielded a range of 0.003 to 0.438 ng/mg hair, with a mean value of 0.0431 ng/mg. The concentration of 9-carboxy-THC was determined to be 0.03 to 1.53 pg/mg hair (mean value 0.322 pg/mg hair). Only regarding the outcome of the hair tests, 58 hair samples were all found to be positive by RIA, and both analytes were confirmed by GC-MS/MS. In 24 samples, THC was detected, but no 9-carboxy-THC; and in 4 samples the metabolite was identified, but no THC.

In 1996, Kauert and Röhrich[53] reported on the concentrations of THC determined in hair samples collected from six self-reported marijuana or hashish smokers. The authors assumed a correlation between self-reported use and the THC levels detected in hair, and they concluded that a rough classification into two user groups seemed to be possible. A THC concentration in the range of 0.1 ng/mg to 1.0 ng/mg was suggestive of weekly up to daily consumption. Concentrations above 1.0 ng/mg hair seemed to be linked with cannabis use multiple times daily.

Moore, Guzaldo, and Donahue[34] analyzed hair specimens collected from six self-reported marijuana smokers along with hair from three known negative donors. The authors used a bench-top GC-MS with high-volume injection for hair testing. The LOD was 0.3 pg/mg, the LOQ 0.4 pg/mg. The concentrations of 9-carboxy-THC in the case of reported daily smoking were in the range of 0.60 to 1.39 pg/mg hair. An individual who admitted to smoking once a week had the highest concentration (12.9 pg/mg hair). The nondrug users as well as the monthly user also tested negative for this metabolite.

Huestis[69] reported about a study on 53 hair specimens collected from cannabis users. Of these 53 test subjects: 17 were self-reported daily users; 21 admitted to consuming one to five joints per week; 13 were collected from participants after controlled cannabis smoking of a total of 48 mg THC; and 2 ingested 116 mg of THC over a 10-week period. GC-MS/MS instrumentation was utilized to detect the analytes. An LOQ of 1.0 pg/mg was used for THC, for 9-carboxy-THC 0.1 pg/mg. According to these criteria, no more than 64% were regarded to be positive, regardless of whether or not the hair samples were from daily or nondaily users. Both THC and 9-carboxy-THC were detected in 34% of the specimens, exclusively the metabolite in 26%, and only THC was found to be positive in 4%. A negative result was obtained in 36% of the specimens. There were no significant differences between samples taken from daily or nondaily users. As a consequence of these results, Huestis recommended a low pg/mg cutoff for 9-carboxy-THC to improve the identification of cannabis use.

A total of 2155 hair samples collected from a population mostly known as former and current drug users was screened for cannabinoids using GC-MS/MS.[46] Of these, 1272 specimens were confirmed to be positive by GC-MS/MS, and 620 (48.7%) showed the presence of one or two metabolites (9-carboxy-THC, 11-hydroxy-THC). Out of these 620 samples, 9-carboxy-THC was detected as a metabolite in 543 samples, and in 77 samples the specific metabolite exclusively ascertained was 11-hydroxy-THC. However, 652 samples (51.3%) only showed the presence of single or multiple constituents (THC, CBN, CBD). The reported LODs for each analyte were CBN 10 pg/mg, CBD 10 pg/mg, THC 10 pg/mg, 11-hydroxy-THC 1 pg/mg, and 9-carboxy-THC 1 pg/mg.

Analyses of a larger quantity of 10,300 specimens resulted in 6272 cannabis-positive samples.[70] CBN was detected in 58.3% of the samples, THC in 57.7%, and CBD in 51.0%. The presence of metabolites was confirmed in 22.2% of specimens for 9-carboxy-THC and 18.8% for 11-hydroxy-THC.

In a large-sample study, potential effects of hair color on the concentration of 9-carboxy-THC in hair were evaluated.[71] Out of more than 80,000 samples, the presence of 9-carboxy-THC was confirmed in 3678 cases by GC-MS/MS. The mean concentration of this metabolite was found to be 0.716 pg/mg hair, with the median being 0.41 pg/mg. According to the findings, there was no significant relationship between the concentration of 9-carboxy-THC and the hair color category.

In principle, a metabolite-to-parent ratio could be convenient to differentiate active use from passive exposure. However, there are cases considered to be positive

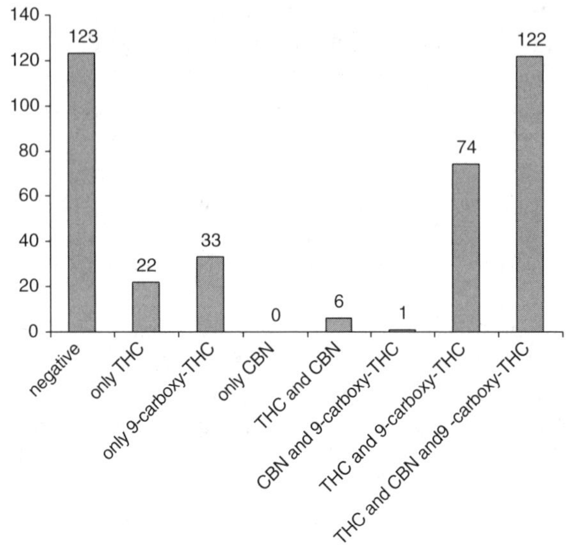

FIGURE 5.1 Outcome of 381 hair specimens from forensic cases.

for 9-carboxy-THC, but negative for THC/CBN.[12,46,71] A hair sample with detectable constituents and metabolites of cannabis as well is not a conclusive finding.

A comparative study[12] presented a three-stage combination: screening for cannabinoids using an ELISA test, followed by the determination of THC and CBN by GC-MS, and finally, confirmation of 9-carboxy-THC by GC-MS/MS. It was shown that only 26 of 66 samples that tested positive for THC/CBN using ELISA and GC-MS were confirmed for 9-carboxy-THC. However, 6 out of 66 cases with traces of THC/CBN had a negative result for the metabolite.

The outcome of 381 hair specimens from forensic cases is presented in Figure 5.1. Of 381 specimens, 122 (32.0%) were found to be positive for THC, CBN (LOQ 0.1 ng/mg), and 9-carboxy-THC (LOQ 0.1 pg/mg). Of these positive specimens, 33 (8.7%) had a negative result for cannabis constituents but were found to be positive for 9-carboxy-THC; 28 of the positive specimens (7.3%) had a positive result for THC or CBN; however, the metabolite could not be confirmed.[72]

There is a tendency of increasing concentrations of cannabis constituents from proximal to distal segments.[73] Whether or not sebum provides an essential contribution to this effect has yet to be proven. A typical segmental pattern was documented in an analysis of a long hair sample of 70 cm cut into 14 segments, each 5 cm in length. There was a gradual increase in the concentration of THC/CBN/CBD from the first proximal segment to the third segment, and except in the case of CBN, this was followed by a gradual decrease beginning at the fourth segment up to the eleventh segment.

In the majority of segmental hair analyses, the concentration of 9-carboxy-THC decreases from proximal to distal segments (Figure 5.2); the concentrations of THC and CBN, however, increase in the same direction.[72] These data were collected from 11 hair analyses in which the samples were cut into three segments.

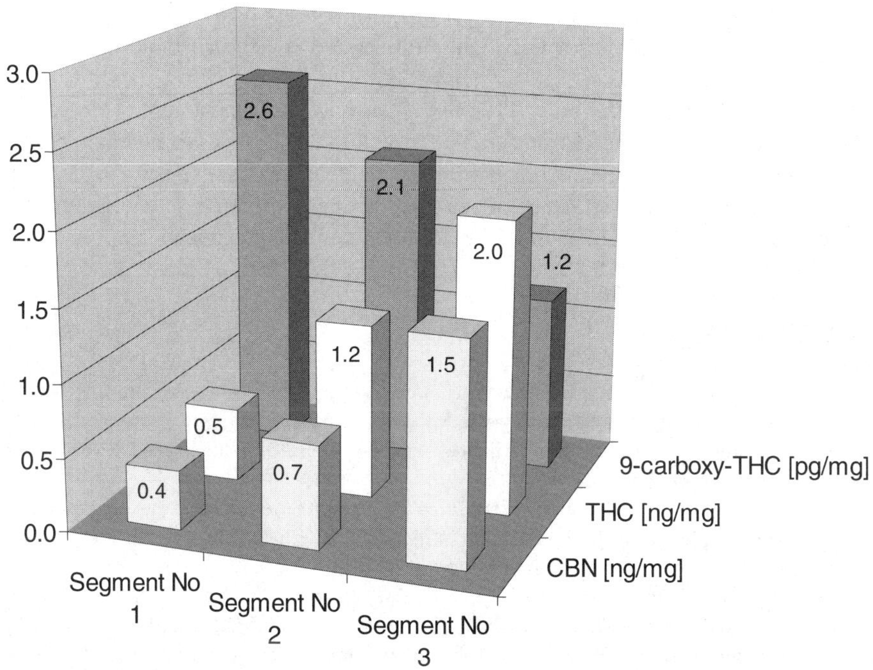

FIGURE 5.2 Median concentrations of THC/CBN and 9-carboxy-THC in segmental analyses.

5.8 REPORTED CONCENTRATIONS OF CANNABINOIDS IN HAIR

Usually , the concentrations detected in head hair range from 0.03 to 3.00 ng/mg for CBD, 0.01 to 1.07 ng/mg for CBN, and from 0.10 to 0.29 ng/mg for THC.[32] A large concentration range from 0.009 to 16.7 ng/mg for THC was even reported.[53] The median concentration determined in a large sample of hair specimens was reported to be 0.084 ng/mg THC, 0.036 ng/mg CBN, and 0.052 ng/mg CBD. The maximum concentration was determined to be 18.37 ng/mg THC, 6.42 ng/mg CBN, and 19.43 ng/mg CBD.[70]

The mean concentration of 9-carboxy-THC determined in 3886 scalp hair specimens was 0.716 pg/mg.[71] The median concentration for 9-carboxy-THC determined in 381 hair specimens (a total of 820 segments) from forensic cases was 2.3 pg/mg.[72]

Compared with head hair, higher concentrations of cannabinoids were generally found in pubic hair and lower concentrations in axillary hair.[74,75]

5.9 CONCLUSIONS

What conclusions can be drawn if a hair specimen was found to be positive for a single or additional constituent of cannabis? After all, these compounds are also present in smoke and in sweat. Detection of the main constituents provides at least a positive association with cannabis. The use of a suitable decontamination procedure with repeated washings might be helpful to avoid false-positive results. However, the presence of THC/CBN or CBD cannot be regarded as an absolute indicator of cannabis use.

The metabolites 11-hydroxy-THC and 9-carboxy-THC have never been identified in sweat and in cannabis smoke. The detection of one or even two metabolites is of crucial interest to prevent misinterpretation due to passive exposure to cannabis smoke. A positive test result for metabolites can be considered as an unequivocal finding. It can be regarded as the criterion for establishing cannabis use.

REFERENCES

1. Siniscalco, G.G., *Cannabis sativa* L.: botanical problems and molecular approaches in forensic investigations, *Forensic Sci. Rev.*, 13, 1, 2001.
2. Huestis, M.A., Cannabis (marijuana): effects on human behavior and performance, *Forensic Sci. Rev.*, 14, 15, 2002.
3. Staub, C., Chromatographic procedures for determination of cannabinoids in biological samples, with special attention to blood and alternative matrices like hair, saliva, sweat and meconium, *J. Chromatogr. B*, 733, 119, 1999.
4. Rätsch, C., *Enzyklopädie der psychoaktiven Pflanzen: Botanik, Ethnopharmakologie und Anwendung*, Wissenschaftliche Verlagsgesellschaft, Stuttgart, 1998.
5. Chiang, C.N. and Barnett, G., Marijuana pharmacokinetics and pharmacodynamics, in *Cocaine, Marijuana, Designer Drugs: Chemistry, Pharmacology and Behaviour*, Redda, K.K., Walker, C.A., and Barnett, G., Eds., CRC Press, Boca Raton, FL, 1989, pp. 113–125.
6. Schmidbauer, W. and Von Scheidt, J., *Handbuch der Rauschdrogen, 3: Cannabis: Haschisch oder Marihuana*, Herbig Verlagsbuchhandlung, München, 1997.
7. El Sohly, M.A. et al., Potency trends of Δ^9-THC and other cannabinoids in confiscated marijuana from 1980–1997, *J. Forensic Sci.*, 45, 24, 2000.
8. El Sohly, M.A. et al., Quarterly Report, Potency Monitoring Project, report 87, National Center for Natural Products Research, School of Pharmacy, University of Mississippi, Aug. 9–Nov. 8, 2004.
9. Niesink, R.J.M., THC concentrations in marihuana products sold in Dutch coffeeshops, Utrecht, Trimbos Inst.; available on-line at www.cannabislegal.de/international/nl-niesink.htm, Sep. 2000.
10. Hewavitharana, A.K. et al., Quantitative GC-MS analysis of Δ^9-tetrahydrocannabinol in fiber hemp varieties, *J. Anal. Toxicol.*, 29, 261, 2005.
11. Anon.; available on-line at www.Erowid.org, 2005.
12. Uhl, M. and Sachs, H., Cannabinoids in hair: strategy to prove marijuana/hashish consumption, *Forensic Sci. Int.*, 145, 143, 2004.
13. Monsanto, P.V. et al., Hair analysis for Δ^9-THC, Δ^9-THC-COOH, CBN and CBD by GC/MS-EI: comparison with GC/MS-NCI for Δ^9-THC-COOH, *Forensic Sci. Int.*, 128, 66, 2002.
14. Kleiber, D. and Kovar, K.-A., *Auswirkungen des Cannabiskonsums: Eine Expertise zu pharmakologischen und psychosozialen Konsequenzen*, Wissenschaftliche Verlagsgesellschaft, Stuttgart, Germany, 1998.
15. Garett, E.R. and Hunt, C.A., Physicochemical properties, solubility and protein binding of delta-9-tetrahydrocannabinol, *J. Pharm. Sci.*, 63, 1056, 1974.

16. Hunt, C.A. and Jones, R.T., Tolerance and disposition of tetrahydrocannabinol in man, *J. Pharmacol. Exp. Ther.*, 215, 35, 1980.
17. Kelly, J. and Jones, R.T., Metabolism of tetrahydrocannabinol in frequent and infrequent marijuana users, *J. Anal. Toxicol.*, 16, 264, 1992.
18. Lemberger, L., Crabtree, R.E., and Rowe, H.M., 11-hydroxy-delta-9-tetrahydrocannabinol: pharmacology, disposition, and metabolism of a major metabolite in man, *Science*, 177, 62, 1972.
19. *Clarke's Analysis of Drugs and Poisons*, 3rd ed., Moffat, A.C., Osselton, M.D., and Widdop, B., Eds., Pharmaceutical Press, London, 2004, p. 740.
20. Busto, U., Bendayan, R., and Sellers, E.M., Clinical pharmacokinetics of non-opiate abused drugs, *Clinical Pharmacokinetics*, 16, 1, 1989.
21. Ohlson, A. et al., Single dose kinetics of deuterium labelled delta-1-tetrahydrocannabinol in heavy and light cannabis users, *Biomed. Environ. Mass. Spectrom.*, 9, 6, 1982.
22. Ohlson, A. et. al., Plasma Δ-9-tetrahydrocannabinol concentrations and clinical effects after oral and intravenous administration and smoking, *Clinical Pharmacol. Therapeutics*, 28, 409, 1980.
23. Henderson, G.L., Mechanisms of drug incorporation into hair, *Forensic Sci. Int.*, 63, 19, 1993.
24. Pragst, F. et al., Illegal and therapeutic drug concentrations in hair segments: a timetable of drug exposure? *Forensic Sci. Ref.*, 10, 81, 1998.
25. Thorspecken, J., Skopp, G., and Pötsch, L., *In vitro* contamination of hair by marijuana smoke, *Clin. Chem.*, 50, 596, 2004.
26. Kidwell, D.A. and Blank, D.L., Environmental exposure: the stumbling block of hair testing, in *Drug Testing in Hair*, Kintz, P., Ed., CRC Press, Boca Raton, FL, 1996.
27. Spiehler, V., Hair analysis by immunological methods from the beginning to 2000, *Forensic Sci. Int.*, 107, 249, 2000.
28. Quintela, O. et al., Evaluation of cocaine, amphetamines and cannabis use in university students through hair analysis: preliminary results, *Forensic Sci. Int.*, 107, 273, 2000.
29. Kintz, P., Cirimele, V., and Mangin, P., Detection of drugs in human hair using Abbott ADx, with confirmation by gas chromatography/mass-spectrometry (GC/MS), *J. Forensic Sci.*, 37, 328, 1992.
30. Sachs, H. and Kintz, P., Testing for drugs in hair: critical review of chromatographic procedures since 1992, *J. Chromatogr. B.*, 713, 147, 1998.
31. Kintz, P., Cirimele, V., and Mangin, P., Testing human hair for cannabis, II: identification of THC-COOH by GC-MS-NCI as a unique proof, *J. Forensic Sci.*, 40, 619, 1995.
32. Cirimele, V. et al., Testing human hair for cannabis, III: rapid screening procedure for the simultaneous identification of Δ^9-tetrahydrocannabinol, cannabinol, and cannabidiol, *J. Anal. Toxicol.*, 20, 13, 1996.
33. Sachs, H. and Dressler, U., Detection of THC-COOH in hair by MSD-NCI after HPLC clean-up, *Forensic Sci. Int.*, 107, 239, 2000.
34. Moore, C., Guzaldo, F., and Donahue, T., The determination of 11-nor-9-tetrahydrocannabinol-9-carboxylic acid (THC-COOH) in hair using negative ion gas chromatography-mass spectrometry and high-volume injection., *J. Anal. Toxicol.*, 25, 555 , 2001.
35. Feyerherm, F., Improvements in the Determination of THC in Hair by 2D GC with Single Quadrupole MS Detection, presented at Annual Conference Mid-West Association of Toxicology and Therapeutic Drug Monitoring and the Society of Hair Testing, Chicago, May 2004.

36. Moore, C. et al., The Determination of THC-COOH (THCA) in Hair Using GC-GC-MS, presented at the meeting of California Association of Toxicologists, Las Vegas, Fall 2005.
37. Musshoff, F. et al., Fully automated determination of cannabinoids in hair samples using headspace solid-phase microextraction and gas chromatography-mass spectrometry, *J. Anal. Toxicol.*, 26, 554, 2002.
38. Sporkert, F. and Pragst, F., Use of headspace solid-phase microextraction (HS-SPME) in hair analysis for organic compounds, *Forensic Sci. Int.*, 107, 129, 2000.
39. Musshoff, F. et al., Automated headspace solid-phase dynamic extraction for the determination of cannabinoids in hair samples, *Forensic Sci. Int.*, 133, 32, 2003.
40. Baumgartner, W.A. and Hill, V.A., Sample preparation techniques, *Forensic Sci. Int.*, 63, 121, 1993.
41. Cairns, T. et al., Determination of carboxy-THC in hair by mass spectrometry/mass spectrometry, in *Proceedings of the 1995 International Conference and Workshop for Hair Analysis in Forensic Toxicology*, de Zeeuw, R.A. et. al., Eds., Abu Dhabi, Nov. 1995, p. 185.
42. Mieczkowski, T., A research note: the outcome of GC/MS/MS confirmation of hair assays on 93 cannabinoid (+) cases, *Forensic Sci. Int.*, 70, 83, 1995.
43. Uhl, M., Determination of drugs in hair using GC/MS/MS, *Forensic Sci. Int.*, 84, 281, 1997.
44. Chiarotti, M. and Costamagna L., Analysis of 11-nor-9-carboxy-Δ^9-tetrahydrocannabinol in biological samples by gas chromatography tandem mass spectrometry (GC/MS-MS), *Forensic Sci. Int.*, 114, 1, 2000.
45. Uhl, M., Tandem mass spectrometry: a helpful tool in hair analysis for the forensic expert, *Forensic Sci. Int.*, 107, 169, 2000.
46. Wicks, J. and Tsanaclis, L.M.T., Hair analysis for assessing cannabis use: where is the cut-off? *Ann. Toxicol. Anal.*, 17, 120, 2005.
47. Weinmann, W. et al., Simultaneous determination of THC-COOH and THC-COOH-glucuronide in urine samples by LC/MS/MS, *Forensic Sci. Int.*, 113, 381, 2000.
48. Weinmann, W. et al., Fast confirmation of 11-nor-9-carboxy-Δ^9-tetrahydrocannabinol (THC-COOH) in urine by LC/MS/MS using negative atmospheric-pressure chemical ionisation (APCI), *Forensic Sci. Int.*, 121, 103, 2001.
49. Maralikova, B. and Weinmann, W., Simultaneous determination of Δ^9-tetrahydrocannabinol, 11-hydroxy-Δ^9-tetrahydrocannabinol and 11-nor-9-carboxy-Δ^9-tetrahydrocannabinol in human plasma by high-performance liquid chromatography/tandem mass spectrometry, *J. Mass Spectrom.*, 39, 526–531, 2004.
50. Jurado, C., personal communication, Nov. 2005.
51. Tagliaro, F., Deyl, Z., and Marigo, M., Capillary electrophoresis: a novel tool for toxicological investigation: its potential in the analysis of body fluids and hair, in *Hair Testing for Drugs of Abuse: International Research on Standards and Technology*, Cone, E.J., Welch, M.J., and Grigson-Babecki, M.B., Eds., NIH Publication 95-3727, National Institute for Drug Abuse, Rockville, MD, 1995, p. 225.
52. Backofen, U., Hoffmann, W., and Matysik, F.M., Determination of cannabinoids by capillary liquid chromatography with electrochemical detection, *Biomed. Chromatogr.*, 14, 49, 2000.
53. Kauert, G. and Röhrich, J., Concentrations of Δ^9-tetrahydrocannabinol, cocaine and 6-monoacetylmorphine in hair of drug abusers, *Int. J. Legal Med.*, 108, 294, 1996.
54. Uhl, M. and Scheufler, F., unpublished data, 2005.
55. Baumgartner, W. and Hill, V., Hair analysis for organic analytes: methodology, reliability issues, and field studies, in *Drug Testing in Hair*, Kintz, P., Ed., CRC Press, Boca Raton, FL, 1996.

56. Wilkins, D. et al., Quantitative analysis of THC, 11-OH-THC, and THC-COOH in human hair by negative ion chemical ionization mass spectrometry, *J. Anal. Toxicol.*, 19, 483, 1995.
57. Strano-Rossi, S. and Chiarotti, M., Solid-phase microextraction for cannabinoids analysis in hair and its possible application to other drugs, *J. Anal. Toxicol.*, 23, 7, 1999.
58. Tjerdeema, R.S., The pyrolysis of cannabinoids, *Rev. Environ. Contam. Toxicol.*, 99, 61, 1987.
59. Nelson, D. and De Forest, P., Forensic examination of hairs for cosmetic treatment, in *Forensic Examination of Hair*, Robertson, J., Ed., Taylor & Francis, London, 1999, p. 229.
60. Jurado, C. et al., Influence of the cosmetic treatment of hair on drug testing, *Int. J. Legal Med.*, 110, 159, 1997.
61. Röhrich, J. et. al., Effect of the shampoo Ultra Clean on drug concentrations in human hair, *Int. J. Legal Med.*, 113, 102, 2000.
62. Cirimele, V., Are cannabinoids detected in hair after washing with Cannabio® shampoo? *J. Anal. Toxicol.*, 23, 349, 1999.
63. Skopp, G., Pötsch L., and Mauden, M., Stability of cannabinoids in hair samples exposed to sunlight, *Clin. Chem.*, 46, 1846, 2000.
64. Kury, M., Skopp, G., and Mattern, R., Untersuchungen zu witterungsbedingten Einflüssen auf den Cannabinoidgehalt im Haar, *Arch. f. Krim.*, 211, 9, 2003.
65. Anon., Statement of the Society of Hair Testing concerning the examination of drugs in human hair, *Forensic Sci. Int.*, 84, 3, 1997.
66. Anon.; available on-line at www.workplace.samshsa.gov/DrugTesting/Specimen-Collection/guidelinesdraft2.pdf, Dec. 2005.
67. Anon., Society of Hair Testing, Recommendations for hair testing in forensic cases, *Forensic Sci. Int.*, 145, 83, 2004.
68. Pragst, F. and Nadulski, T., Cut-off for THC in hair in context of driving ability, *Ann. Toxicol. Anal.*, 17, 120, 2005.
69. Huestis, M.A., Δ-9-Tetrahydrocannabinol and 11-nor-9-Carboxy-THC in Hair Prior to and following Controlled Cannabinoid Administration, presented at the meeting of the Mid West Association for Toxicology and Therapeutic Drug Monitoring/Society of Hair Testing, Chicago, May 2004.
70. Tsanaclis, L.M.T., personal communication, Sept. 2005.
71. Mieczkowski T., Assessing the potential of a "color effect" for hair analysis of 11-nor-9-carboxy-Δ^9-tetrahydrocannabinol: analysis of a large sample of hair specimens, *Life Sci.*, 74, 463, 2003.
72. Uhl, M. and Scheufler, F., unpublished results, 2005.
73. Pragst, F., Pitfalls in hair analysis resulting from variability of human hair growth and from alternative drug incorporation mechanisms, *Ann. Toxicol. Anal.*, 17, 128, 2005.
74. Cirimele, V., Kintz, P., and Mangin, P., Testing human hair for cannabis, *Forensic Sci. Int.*, 70, 175, 1995.
75. Cirimele, V., Cannabis and amphetamine determination in human hair, in *Drug Testing in Hair*, Kintz, P., Ed., CRC Press, Boca Raton, FL, 1996.

6 Amphetamine Determination in Hair

Vincent Cirimele

CONTENTS

6.1 INTRODUCTION

Amphetamines are CNS (central nervous system) stimulants used in therapy for the treatment of obesity, narcolepsy, and hypotension, but also misused by drug addicts and athletes or students to enhance their performances. Consumption of stimulants has been recognized as one of the most significant trends in drug abuse. Abuse of the powerful psychostimulants amphetamine and methamphetamine is prevalent in some geographical regions (U.S., Far East, Japan), with increasing consumption of entactogenic methylenedioxy- and methoxy-substituted amphetamines being observed in European countries.

Amphetamines and related designer drugs are weak bases with a relatively low molecular weight, allowing them to easily diffuse across the membranes before incorporation in nonconventional biological matrices such as hair or nail. If measurements of drug in blood or urine only reflect exposure over several hours or days before sampling, it is well established now that hair analysis allows verification of an individual's past history of medication, compliance, or drug abuse. For example, hair analysis is routinely used in laboratories as a tool for the identification of drug exposure in forensic cases.

While a final and definitive consensus on the use of hair specimens for drugs analysis is still in discussion, only general recommendations for hair testing in forensic cases have been proposed by the Society of Hair Testing. If gas chromatography-mass spectrometry (GC-MS) remains the most common analytical technique for the detection of amphetamines in hair, a great variety of preparation procedures have been published.

The aim of this paper is to review the different methodologies reported in the international literature for the detection of amphetamine derivatives in hair samples, with a special focus on basic aspects such as washing procedures, extraction or purification methods, and analytical characteristics.

6.2 PREAMBLE

Collection procedures have not been standardized, but the recommendation of the Society of Hair Testing is to cut the sample from the posterior vertex region of the head, as close as possible to the scalp, since it is the region with the least variation in growth rate (approximately 1.0 cm/month), the number of hairs in the growing phase is more constant, and the hair is less subject to age- and sex-related influences. Head hair is the preferred specimen, but occasionally, alternative hairs such as axillary or pubic hair have been tested. The sample size varied considerably among laboratories and ranged from one single hair to 250 mg. For example, Suzuki et al. [1] have published a method for the detection of methamphetamine and amphetamine in a single human hair by mass spectrometry. A rather large amount of hair (250 mg) from stimulant abusers was used by Aoki and Kuroiwa [2] for the detection of methamphetamine by enzyme immunoassay.

In most cases, laboratories include a washing step before the extraction using 0.01*M* HCl, methylene chloride, 50% aqueous methanol with ultrasonic bath, 0.1% sodium dodecyl sulfate (SDS)/water, ethanol at 37°C, methanol/water, or acetone/water. However, there is no consensus or uniformity in the procedures. The most crucial issue facing hair analysis is to avoid false positives caused by passive exposure to smoked drugs. Therefore, the washing step of hair samples has been well investigated, mostly for the analysis of smoked drugs such as cocaine. In the case of amphetamines, the essential aim of the washing step is to remove unnecessary dirt or grease from the surface of the hair.

When comparing four different procedures (methanolic sonication and acid, alkaline, and enzymatic hydrolyses) for amphetamine, MDA (3,4-methylenedioxyamphetamine), and MDMA (3,4-methylenedioxymethamphetamine), Kintz and Cirimele [3] concluded that the best recoveries were observed after alkaline hydrolysis.

6.3 AMPHETAMINE DETERMINATION

6.3.1 Nonchromatographic Methods

Several major studies have reported the determination of amphetamines by immunological tests.

An enzyme immunoassay for methamphetamine with alkaline phosphatase-labeled methamphetamine, Sepharose antibody, and p-nitrophenylphosphate as substrate was developed by Aoki and Kuroiwa [2]. The antimethamphetamine antisera produced in rabbits by immunization with N-(4-aminobutyl) methamphetamine-BSA conjugate were specific for methamphetamine and showed low cross reactivities with metabolites of methamphetamine, p-OH methamphetamine, and amphetamine. The range of methamphetamine measurable by the enzyme immunoassay was 1 to 300 ng/tube, which makes it possible to detect methamphetamine in hair extract.

An enzyme-linked immunosorbent assay (ELISA) was developed by Sweeney et al. [4]. After decontamination with methanol to remove external contamination, drugs were recovered from hair samples using hot methanol for 2 h. The extracts were evaporated to dryness, reconstituted in buffer, and analyzed using an ELISA technique adapted for the detection of amphetamines in hair. GC-MS was used as the reference technique. Cross-reactivity (ligand concentration resulting in 50% of inhibition and expressed as percentage of d-methamphetamine response) values were 30.8% for d-amphetamine, 7.4% for I-methamphetamine, 4.3% for phentermine, 2.9% for I-amphetamine, and <1% for ephedrine, MDA, and MDMA. Cross reactivity of unrelated compounds was found to be nonexistent. The optimum cutoff concentration was determined to be 300 pg/mg, and the observed limit of detection was 60 pg/mg. The sensitivity and specificity of the method were 83 and 92%, respectively.

Radioimmunoassay (RIA) technology was used to screen for amphetamines, cocaine, marijuana, opiates, and phencyclidine (PCP) in hair of patients with serious mental illness [5]. Of the 203 participants, only 33 (16.3%) self-reported illicit substance use, and only 25 (12.4%) had a positive urine test, but 63 (31.0%) had a positive hair assay. These results confirmed that hair analysis is able to detect more positive cases than urine tests.

To eliminate unnecessary analyses on GC-MS, Miki et al. [6] proposed a rapid, simple, and fairly sensitive screening method for methamphetamine, MDMA, and MDEA (3,4-methylenedioxyethylamphetamine) incorporated in hair by the use of a one-step immunoassay drug test for oral fluid. These drugs, in a 10-mg portion of hair, were extracted into 5*M* HCl/methanol (1:20, v/v), and the extract reconstituted in 100 μl water, which was assayed with the saliva drug test ORAL.screen™. The optimal cutoff concentration of methamphetamine in hair was found to be 1.0 ng/mg hair, and the detection limits were calculated to be 0.5 ng/mg hair for d-methamphetamine, 0.8 ng/mg for dl-MDMA, and 1.0 ng/mg for dl-MDEA. The semiquantitative screening was possible over the concentration range from 1.0 to 200 ng/mg, and the results were in good agreement with those by GC-MS determination. This screening method combined a simple preparation technique and did not require any instrumentation.

Finally, a simple and highly sensitive time-resolved fluoroimmunoassay of methamphetamine using a new fluorescent europium chelate (BHHCT-Eu^{3+}) as a label was published by Kimura et al. in 1999 [7]. Two variations of competitive immunoassay were attempted. In the first (one-step) assay, microtiter plates coated with anti-methamphetamine were used, and the new label was bound to a conjugate of bovine serum albumin (BSA) and N-(4-aminobutyl)-methamphetamine (MA-BSA). In the second (two-step) assay, instead of the labeled MA-BSA, biotinylated MA-BSA and BHHCT-Eu^{3+}-labeled streptavidin-BSA were used. The lowest measurable concentrations of methamphetamine for the one-step and the two-step methods were 1 ng/ml (25 pg/assay) and 1 pg/ml (25 fg/assay), respectively. These were 10 to 1000 times superior to the detection limits of methamphetamine in any other immunoassay. The high detectability of the present assay also enabled segmental hair analysis with a few centimeters of a hair.

However, the specificity of most immunoassays is directed to a group of amphetamine derivatives rather than a single substance due to the cross reactivity of the antibodies used. So quantification by immunoassay is not accurate. Additionally, positive hair results must be confirmed by a more specific method, preferably by GC-MS, particularly in forensic investigations. This is why chromatography methods represent the majority of the published papers for amphetamine determination in hair samples.

6.3.2 Chromatographic Methods

6.3.2.1 Gas Chromatography

Methamphetamine has been abused in Japan since the end of World War II. As a result, since the early 1980s, the major papers dealing with stimulant detection in hair have come from Japanese researchers.

In 1984, Takahashi [8] and Nagai et al. [9] reported the detection of methamphetamine and amphetamine in hairs. The authors used N-ethylbenzylamine as the internal standard, packed columns (OV-101, 5% PEG 6000), and trifluoroacetic anhydride as derivatization agent. The same year, a detailed procedure of an extremely sensitive method for quantitation of methamphetamine and amphetamine in human hair by GC-MS-CI (chemical ionization) was proposed [1]. N-methylbenzylamine was used as an internal standard. The samples, after extraction with an organic solvent, were derivatized with trifluoroacetic anhydride before the GC-MS analysis. Quantitation was made with quasimolecular ions of the derivatives by selected-ion monitoring in the CI mode. The detection limit was about 10 pg in an injected volume. The high sensitivity enabled them to measure both stimulants in a single human hair. At the end of the 1980s, original papers from Japanese researchers began to emerge about chiral separation of amphetamines (see discussion below).

In 1997, Cirimele et al. [10] included MDMA, BDB (3,4-methylenedioxyphenyl)-2-butanaminedesmethylated metabolite of MBDB), and MBDB (*N*-methyl-1-(3,4-methylenedioxyphenyl)-2=butanamine) and changed the derivatization step of their previously described procedure to enable a complete screening for amphetamine, methamphetamine, MDA, MDMA, MDEA, BDB, and MBDB in human hair. Briefly, after decontamination with methylene chloride, a 50-mg hair sample was dissolved in 1*M* NaOH in presence of the corresponding penta-deuterated internal standards.

After extraction with ethyl acetate and evaporation of the organic phase in presence of 2-propanol-concentrated HCl (99:1, v/v), the dry extract was derivatized using heptafluorobutyric anhydride (HFBA). Chromatographic separation was achieved on a 25-m-long capillary column, and acquisition was obtained in full scan mode after electronic impact (EI) ionization. Limits of detection were in the range 0.02 to 0.05 ng/mg, with recoveries in the range 82 to 91%.

GC-MS detection of amphetamine and its methylenedioxy-derivatives (MDA, MDMA, and MDEA) in hair was done after applying a direct methanolic sonication extraction technique [11]. The extracted drugs were derivatized either with propionic acid anhydride (PSA) or trifluoroacetic acid anhydride (TFAA). According to the authors, the derivatization with TFAA induces more-specific mass spectrometric information, but TFAA derivatives are less stable than those obtained with PSA. The detection limit for all compounds was in a range of about 0.01 ng/mg if at least 50 to 100 mg of hair were analyzed, independent of the derivatization used. A total of 303 hair samples were tested, and 28 (9.2%) contained amphetamine derivatives in the range of 0.02 to 6.52 ng/mg.

Laznickova et al. [12] present a procedure of concurrent identification and quantification of amphetamine and methamphetamine in human hair. The method involves rinsing of the hair (distilled water, 55°C, 0.1*M* hydrochloric acid; distilled water to neutral reaction; methanol), homogenization by cutting, and warm (55°C) and alkaline hydrolysis in 1*M* NaOH for 120 min. After neutralization, extracting benzoylation with 2,3,4,5,6-pentafluorobenzoyl chloride was performed, and 2 ml of the cyclohexane layer was evaporated. The derivatized extract was analyzed by the GC-MS. The procedure was used for segmentation analysis of hair of two subjects abusing methamphetamine for prolonged periods. The revealed concentrations varied within the range of 0.99 to 5.25 ng/mg hair for methamphetamine and 0.13 to 0.73 ng/mg hair for amphetamine.

Another procedure based on GC-MS is described by Pujadas et al. [13] for the determination of amphetamine, methamphetamine, MDA, MDMA, MDEA, and MBDB in hair. Hair samples were digested with 1*M* sodium sulfide at 37°C by shaking for 3 h, then kept at room temperature overnight, and extracted with two sequential extraction procedures: liquid-liquid extraction with tert-butyl methyl ether and solid-phase extraction with Bond-Elut Certify columns. Extracted analytes were derivatized with N-methyl-bis(trifluoroacetamide), separated by a 5% phenylmethylsilicone column, and determined by a mass spectrometer detector in selected-ion monitoring mode.

A new analytical approach, based on derivatization with 2,2,2-trichloroethyl chloroformate and GC-MS, was investigated by Frison et al. [14] for qualitative and quantitative analyses of a large range of amphetamine-related drugs and ephedrines in hair samples. Sample preparation involved alkaline extraction of analytes using Extrelut columns, after addition of the internal standard 3,4-methylenedioxypropylamphetamine and subsequent derivatization, to produce 2,2,2-trichloroethylcarbamates. GC-MS analyses, using a slightly polar 30-m capillary column, were performed with quadrupole or ion-trap instruments. MS acquisition modes were electron ionization (EI) in full-scan or selected-ion monitoring (SIM) modes (quadrupole), and full-scan MS or tandem MS/MS modes with chemical ionization (CI) conditions (ion trap). Quantitative studies using EI SIM conditions gave recoveries in the range 74 to 89%, with corresponding limits of detection in the range of 0.1 to 0.2 ng/mg.

Finally, a new GC-MS method for the simultaneous identification and quantitation of amphetamine, methamphetamine, MDA, MDMA, and MDEA in hair was proposed by Villamor et al. [15]. Hair was hydrolyzed in 1*M* NaOH at 40°C, subjected to extraction with 4:1 (v/v) methylene chloride/isopropanol, and derivatized with pentafluoropropionic anhydride (PFPA) and ethyl acetate. The limits of detection and quantitation obtained were, respectively, 0.045 and 0.151 ng/mg for amphetamine, 0.014 and 0.048 ng/mg for methamphetamine, 0.013 and 0.043 ng/mg for MDA, 0.017 and 0.057 ng/mg for MDMA, and 0.007 and 0.023 ng/mg for MDEA. Overall, 24 hair specimens tested positive for one or more amphetamines, with average concentrations of 0.88 ng/mg for amphetamine, 10.14 ng/mg for methamphetamine, 1.30 ng/mg for MDA, and 8.87 ng/mg for MDMA. Only one specimen tested positive for MDEA, with a concentration of 0.84 ng/mg.

In fact, gas chromatographic procedures are more common for the analysis of amphetamines in hair. The enormous number of possible exogenous and endogenous compounds that can be found in hair makes the interpretation of chromatograms with flame ionization detection or even nitrogen-phosphorus flame ionization detection very difficult. With the development of the mass fragmentography technology, deuterated internal standards have been preferentially used for the identification and quantification of amphetamines. Presently, GC-MS represents the gold standard, but during last decade, more and more analytical methods referred to high-performance liquid chromatography (HPLC) technology coupled to various detectors.

6.3.2.2 Liquid Chromatography

In 1997, Takayama et al. [16] developed an original HPLC method with chemiluminescence detection of trace levels of methamphetamine and its major metabolite, amphetamine, in hair samples. After washing the hair sample with water and methanol, it was cut into pieces, extracted with a mixed solution of methanol and hydrochloric acid for 1 h under ultrasonication, and allowed to stand at room temperature overnight. After evaporation of the organic phase, the residue was dissolved in carbonate buffer and heated at 45°C for 1 h in presence of dansyl chloride solution. The method was very sensitive (detection limit about 2 pg injected) and allowed the detection of the chemiluminogenically dansyl derivatives of methamphetamine and amphetamine starting from a single hair.

A second sensitive HPLC method with fluorescence detection for determining methamphetamine and its major metabolite in abusers' hair segments was developed by Al-Dirbashi et al. [17]. Methamphetamine and amphetamine in hair samples collected from addicts were extracted into acidified methanol, derivatized with 4-(4,5-diphenyl-1H-imidazol-2-yl)benzoyl chloride, separated isocratically on an octadecyl-silane (ODS) column using 0.1*M* TRIS-HCl buffer (pH 7.0) methanol (30/70, v/v) mobile phase. The derivatized analytes were detected fluorimetrically at 440 nm (lambda excitation 330 nm). The detection limits (51.4 and 74.6 pg/mg hair for amphetamine and methamphetamine, respectively) were found accurate for the detection and quantification of methamphetamine in abusers' hair samples.

A simple, but sensitive, and specific HPLC assay for the simultaneous determination of MDMA and MDA with direct fluorimetric detection is described in a paper by Tagliaro et al. [18]. Hair samples were incubated overnight in 0.25*M* HCl at 45°C and extracted with a commercial liquid-liquid method. The dried residue reconstituted with 0.05*M* NaH_2PO_4, pH 5.2, was injected onto a 250 × 4.6-mm i.d. packed column with spherical 5-μm poly(styrene-divinylbenzene). The excitation and emission wavelengths were set to 285 and 320 nm, respectively. The limit of detection was lower than 1 ng/ml for each compound in solution, allowing a cutoff of 0.1 ng/mg in the hair matrix to be established. Interferences from as many as 92 therapeutic or abused drugs currently in use in the population were excluded, including *N*-methyl-1-(3,4-methylenedioxyphenyl)-2 butanamine (MBDB).

A highly sensitive HPLC method for the determination of amphetamine and methamphetamine in hair samples was proposed by Nakashima et al. [19]. After derivatization with DIB-Cl=4-(4,5-diphenyl-1H-imidazol-2-yl) benzoyl chloride (DIB-Cl), a fluorescent reagent, extracts were separated on an ODS column with isocratic mobile phases composed of acetonitrile-methanol-citrate buffer (45:20:37.5, v/v/v) and analyzed by HPLC with fluorescence detection at excitation and emission wavelengths of 325 and 430 nm for amphetamine and methamphetamine, respectively. The limits of detection were less than 0.12 ng/mg in hair samples for both amphetamine and methamphetamine.

An original automated column-switching liquid chromatographic-electrospray ionization-mass spectrometric (LC-ESI-MS) method has been established by Miki et al. [20] for the determination of methamphetamine, amphetamine, and p-hydroxymethamphetamine in hair. The combination of an N-vinylacetamide-containing hydrophilic polymer online extraction column, an SCX semimicro LC column, and an electrospray ionization interface provided the successful concentration, separations, and highly sensitive MS determinations of these analytes in a hair extract without tedious sample pretreatments. The limits of detection of these analytes were 0.02 ng/mg and 0.1 to 0.2 ng/mg in the selected-ion monitoring (SIM) and full-scan modes, respectively, when using a 100-μl hair extract sample that corresponded to a 2.5-mg sample of hair. The p-hydroxymethamphetamine was detectable in all the tested hair specimens from which 1 ng or more of methamphetamine was detected per milligram of hair. The detection of amphetamine and p-hydroxymethamphetamine, in addition to the parent drug methamphetamine with reasonable ratios, was found to be a useful indicator for distinguishing internal methamphetamine incorporation from external contamination.

The paper published by Kaddoumi et al. [21] presents a highly sensitive HPLC method for the simultaneous determination of MDMA, MDA, amphetamine, and methamphetamine in human hair samples. The method was different from the one published by Nakashima et al. [19] by the addition of MDA and MDMA to the list of detected drugs and a new mobile-phase composition. The amphetamines investigated were derivatized with the fluorescent reagent, DIB-Cl to yield highly fluorescent DIB derivatives, which were then analyzed by HPLC with fluorescence detection at excitation and emission wavelengths of 325 and 430 nm, respectively. The separation was achieved on an ODS column with an isocratic mobile phase composed of acetonitrile-methanol-water (30:40:30, v/v/v). The limits of detection for the four compounds obtained by the proposed method ranged from 11 to 200 pg/mg. The method was successfully applied to the determination of MDMA and MDA in hair samples obtained from an MDMA abuser.

In 2004, Stanaszek and Piekoszewski [22] developed an analytical procedure to determine a group of eight amphetamines — amphetamine, ephedrine, methcathinone, paramethoxyamphetamine, methamphetamine, MDA, MDMA, and MDEA — in hair. The target substances were extracted with 1-chlorobutane after alkaline (1*M* NaOH) digestion and analyzed underivatized with high-performance liquid chromatography-atmospheric pressure chemical ionization-mass spectrometry (LC-APCI-MS). Quantitation was performed using selected ion monitoring of protonated molecular ions of the studied drugs, and their deuterated analogs were used as internal standards. The limits of detection were 0.05 ng/mg for methamphetamine, MDA, MDMA, and MDEA; 0.10 ng/mg for ephedrine and amphetamine; and 0.20 ng/mg for methcathinone and paramethoxyamphetamine. The method was applied to the determination of amphetamines in 93 authentic hair samples obtained from detoxification and methadone treatment patients.

6.3.2.3 Other Chromatographic Methods

6.3.2.3.1 HS-SPME/SPDE

A simple and rapid method for the determination of amphetamine and methamphetamine in human hair was developed by headspace solid-phase microextraction (SPME) and gas chromatography with nitrogen-phosphorus detection [23]. For this, 1 mg of hair was dissolved in 5*M* NaOH solution in a tightly sealed vial by shaking at 75°C for about 5 min. The polydimethylsiloxane fiber was exposed to the headspace of the vial and warmed at 55°C for 20 min to adsorb the target analytes. Finally, the fiber was removed from the vial and inserted into the injection port of the analyzer using a CBJ-17 capillary column to release the compounds by heating at 220°C for 30 s. The percentages of amphetamine and methamphetamine extracted from human hair were 48 and 62% with detection limits of 0.1 and 0.4 ng/mg hair, respectively.

A simple method for hair analysis of methamphetamine and amphetamine by GC-MS was developed by Liu et al. [24] using simultaneous headspace solid-phase microextraction (HS-SPME) with derivatization. After alkaline digestion of hair, the analytes derivatized with heptafluoro-n-butyryl chloride were adsorbed on a polydimethylsiloxane-coated fiber by HS-SPME and analyzed by GC-MS. The applicability of this method was demonstrated in some case studies.

A headspace solid-phase microextraction and GC-MS (HS-SPME-GC-MS) procedure for the simultaneous detection of MDA, MDMA, MDE, and MBDB in hair has been developed by Gentili et al. [25]. This method was suitable for the separation of primary and secondary amines, was reproducible, was not time consuming, required small quantities of sample, and did not require any derivatization. It provides sufficient sensitivity and specificity, with limits of detection and limits of quantitation for each substance of <0.7 and 1.90 ng/mg, respectively. This method was found to be suitable for routine clinical, epidemiological, and forensic purposes and was proposed to be used for the preliminary screening of many other substances such as amphetamine, methamphetamine, ketamine, ephedrine, nicotine, phencyclidine, and methadone in hair.

Headspace solid-phase dynamic extraction (SPDE) is a novel method for the solventless extraction of organic compounds in aqueous samples. In a so-called inside-needle capillary-absorption trap, a hollow needle with an internal coating of polydimethylsiloxane is used as an extraction and preconcentration medium. This technology was proposed by Musshoff et al. [26, 27] for the determination of amphetamines, methamphetamine, MDA, MDMA, MDEA, BDB, and MBDB in hair samples. For this, 10 mg of hair were washed with deionized water, petroleum ether, and dichloromethane. After the addition of deuterated internal standards, the sample was hydrolyzed with NaOH and directly submitted to headspace solid-phase microextraction or headspace solid-phase dynamic extraction. Sampling was performed on the solution headspace by passing the gas through the device actively by a syringe. After the absorption of analytes present in the sample onto the deposited stationary phase, on-fiber derivatization was accomplished by placing the fiber directly into the headspace of a second vial containing N-methyl-bis(trifluoroacetamide). In comparison with conventional methods of hair analysis, this fully automated HS-SPDE-GC-MS procedure was found to be substantially faster and easier to perform without using solvents, but with the same degree of sensitivity and reproducibility. Compared with solid-phase microextraction, SPDE was found to have a higher extraction rate coupled with a faster automated operation.

6.3.2.3.2 SFE

An original technology, supercritical fluid extraction (SFE), followed by GC-MS analysis was applied to extract MDA and MDMA from hair using mephentermine used as internal standard [28]. Hair specimens were degreased twice for 15 min under sonication with SDS, methylene chloride, methanol, and finally with water. Hairs were finely cut, and 50 mg were placed in the extraction cell. Extraction was conducted in static (30 min) and dynamic mode using 10% modifier (chloroform/isopropyl alcohol, 90:10, v/v) under 3800 psi of CO_2. Derivatization was carried out using PFPA/ethylacetate (1:1, v/v) before analysis by GC-MS. Detection limits were 0.02 ng/mg for MDA and 0.1 ng/mg for MDMA and MDEA, with relative extraction recoveries of 84% for MDA and 71 and 77% for MDMA and MDEA, respectively. Despite a relatively reproducible extraction procedure, results of this study show that amphetamine use can be detected in authentic human hair after this alternative extraction technique.

6.3.2.4 Other Technologies

6.3.2.4.1 Laser Microscopy

An original paper on the detection of methamphetamine by laser microscopy and immunohistochemical staining, which uses antimethamphetamine labeled with colloidal gold, was presented by Kimura et al. [29]. The intensity of reflection of colloidal gold at a 488- and 514-nm line of Ar laser was measured with a laser microscope equipped with a computerized image-processing system. Microtomed hair samples from five drug users who died from methamphetamine intoxication were used. The drug distribution in the hair was quite different in these five cases, but the levels of drug concentration in two different hair samples from the same abuser were correlated. The results from two hair samples with roots showed a correlation between drug concentration in hair roots and plasma samples. The proposed method was found sensitive enough to estimate the drug concentration using only a segment of hair.

6.3.2.4.2 IMS

Using ion mobility spectrometry (IMS), a simple, sensitive, and rapid screening for methamphetamine incorporated in user's hair has been developed by Miki et al. [30]. To completely unbind methamphetamine from hair matrix and to achieve its effective vaporization for the IMS detection, the hair sample was digested in 5*M* NaOH (methanol-water, 4:1, v/v) solution prior to IMS measurement. The method was found to be sensitive, with a limit of detection of 0.5 ng/mg, and was able to detect methamphetamine in a limited amount of hair (minimum amount required is 2 mg). The results obtained by IMS were in good agreement with their GC-MS determination.

6.3.3 Isomer Separation

At the end of the 1980s, Japanese researchers presented several original papers discussing the chiral separation of amphetamines [31–33]. Several papers on a rapid and sensitive HPLC method for the determination of low concentrations of the stereoisomers (d and l form) of methamphetamine and the demethylated metabolite, amphetamine, have been published by Nagai et al. [31–33]. The acetyl derivatives of the stereoisomers of methamphetamine and amphetamine extracted from hair specimens of drug addicts were clearly separated on two stereoisomer-analytical columns (Chiralcel OB and OJ) connected in series at 50°C. The mobile phase was a mixture of *n*-hexane and isopropanol (9:1, v/v), and the UV detector was set at 220 nm. The practical limit of sensitivity for the analysis, with a good reproducibility, was 62.5 ng of the stereoisomers of methamphetamine and amphetamine. The analysis of real hair specimens led the authors to observe the unique presence of d-methamphetamine and d-amphetamine in the hair of stimulant abusers.

Because of the forensic importance of the chiral analysis of amphetamine and other phenethylamines for investigating their synthetic pathways and the metabolic patterns of these compounds, a capillary electrophoresis method has been developed by Scarcella et al. [34] based on the chiral selectivity of beta-cyclodextrin. Under optimized analytical conditions, amphetamine, methamphetamine, and ephedrine have been easily separated, with baseline resolution of the respective enantiomers. The preliminary analysis of amphetamine in human hair samples, subjected to a simple workup procedure based on liquid-liquid extraction, showed clean blank electropherograms, excellent chiral resolution, and sensitivity suitable for the analysis of real samples from amphetamine users.

In a latter work of the same authors [35], the simultaneous chiral analysis of ephedrine, amphetamine, methamphetamine, MDMA, MDA, and MDEA is reported, by using capillary electrophoresis with native beta-cyclodextrin (15m*M*) as the chiral selector. At this time, detection was either by fixed wavelength (200 nm) or multiwavelength (190 to 400 nm) UV absorbance. For hair samples, sensitivity was increased by applying a field-amplified sample stacking procedure, which allowed the chiral determination of MDA, MDMA, and MDEA at concentrations occurring in real samples from ecstasy users, with the possibility of recording UV spectra of the peaks.

In 1999, Al-Dirbashi et al. [36] proposed an enantiomer-specific HPLC with fluorescence detection using 4-(4,5-diphenyl-1H-imidazol-2-yl)-benzoyl chloride as a fluorescence labeling reagent. Its application to four hair samples of abusers showed that only the S(+)-enantiomers of methamphetamine and its N-demethylated metabolite, S(+)-amphetamine, were detected. Satisfactory correlation (r = 0.901) between the results of HPLC-fluorescence and those of GC-nitrogen phosphorous detection was obtained.

Achiral and chiral semimicro column HPLC methods with fluorescence detection to determine methamphetamine and amphetamine in human hair was described by the same authors in 2000 [37]. These compounds were extracted into 5% trifluoroacetic acid (TFA) in methanol, derivatized with 4-(4,5-diphenyl-1H-imidazol-2-yl)-benzoyl chloride and separated either on a 250 × 1.5-mm i.d. octadecyl-silane (ODS) or a 150 × 2-mm i.d. OD-RH column. The limits of detection at a signal-to-noise ratio of 3 obtained by both the methods were in the range of 1.0 to 4.7 fmol/5 μl injection, with the achiral method being more sensitive. Abusers' hair samples were analyzed by the two methods, and only the S(+)-enantiomers were found in eight Japanese abusers' hair samples. The achiral method was sensitive enough to study the concentrations of these compounds in single black and white hair strands of abusers.

The incorporation of unlabeled and tritiated enantiomers of methamphetamine (MA) and a more lipophilic analog N-(n-butyl)-amphetamine (BA) into the hair of pigmented (C57) and nonpigmented (Balb/C) mice after systemic administration was examined by Stout et al. [38]. R(−)-MA, S(+)-MA, [(3)H]R(−)-MA, [(3)H]S(+)-MA, R(−)-BA, S(+)-BA, [(3)H]R-(−)-BA, and [(3)H]S-(+)-BA were each administered to C57 and Balb/C mice (23 days of age) by i.p. injection at 8.8 mg/kg daily for 3 days. At 44 days of age, hair samples from the animals were treated with a brief methanol wash, a 24-h extraction with pH 6 phosphate buffer, and a final digestion in 1*N* NaOH to free residual drugs from the hair. Labeled drugs in the extracts were quantitated by liquid scintillation counting and unlabeled drugs by gas chromatography/mass spectrometry (GC-MS). The authors observed that hair concentrations of S(+)-MA were greater than those of R(−)-MA in both mouse strains, paralleling blood concentrations, and no enantiomeric differences existed with BA hair accumulation in either strain of mouse. As it is generally observed for other drugs in hair, significantly more MA and BA enantiomers were deposited in pigmented than in nonpigmented hair. Using labeled and unlabeled compounds, they proved that approximately 30% of S(+)-MA and 60% of R(−)-MA in pigmented hair could be removed by a phosphate extraction, and greater amounts of drug could be extracted from nonpigmented hair than pigmented. The results of this study demonstrated that hair pigmentation is an important determinant in MA and BA deposition, that MA and BA deposition is not enantioselective, and that a significant amount of MA and BA stored in pigmented hair is structurally different from parent MA and BA, perhaps associated with melanin components of hair.

Recently, an original enantioselective quantification of amphetamine, methamphetamine, MDA, MDMA, and MDEA enantiomers in hair using GC-MS has been described by Martins et al. [39]. Hair specimens were digested with 1*M* NaOH at 100°C for 30 min and extracted by a solid-phase procedure using Cleanscreen ZSDAU020. Extracted analytes were derivatized with (S)-heptafluorobutyrylprolyl chloride, and the resulting diastereoisomers were quantified by GC-MS operating in the negative chemical ionization mode. Extraction yields were between 73.0 and 97.9%, and limits of detection varied in the range of 2.1 to 45.9 pg/mg hair, whereas the lowest limits of quantification varied between 4.3 and 91.8 pg/mg hair. Only methamphetamine and amphetamine enantiomers were detectable in hair from suspected amphetamine abusers, and the quantification data showed in most cases higher concentrations of (R)-methamphetamine and (R)-amphetamine than those of the corresponding (S)-enantiomers.

6.3.4 Screening Methods

Since 1983, ten major papers have described screening procedures for amphetamines in hair containing one or more drugs of abuse or pharmaceuticals.

In 1983, Ishiyama et al. [40] proposed a procedure for the detection of basic drugs, methamphetamine, antidepressants, and nicotine from human hair. Hair was dissolved by treatment with NaOH and then HCl, extracted with chloroform, trifluoroacetylated, and analyzed on an OV-17 column. Methamphetamine and amphetamine were found in the hair of drug addicts.

Amphetamine was analyzed from hair with other drugs of abuse in one procedure presented by Moeller et al. [41]. The hair was washed with warm water and acetone, pulverized, and incubated with diluted NaOH (2%) for 30 min in presence of levalorphan used as internal standard. After addition of 2% HCl, the solution was incubated overnight at room temperature. The solution was separated and the residue of the hair dissolved in NaOH. Both solutions were buffered to pH 8, extracted on a solid phase (Backerbond Octadecyl) with dichloromethane-acetone, derivatized with PFPA-PFPOH, and analyzed by GC-MS. The chromatography was carried out on an HP-1 capillary column, and detection was achieved using EI-SIM technique. In an improved procedure, the same authors incorporated deuterated analogs of the drug and preincubated the hair with glucuronidase-arylsulfatase [42].

In 1993, Kintz and Mangin [43] described a method where they analyzed amphetamine, other drugs of abuse, benzodiazepines, and nicotine in the hair of neonates.

The paper of Tagliaro et al. [44] describes the methodological optimization and validation of a capillary zone electrophoresis method for the determination of morphine, cocaine, and MDMA in hair, with injection based on field-amplified sample stacking. Diode-array UV absorption detection was used to improve analytical selectivity and identification power. Detection was achieved by UV absorption at the fixed wavelength of 200 nm or by recording the full spectrum between 190 and 400 nm. Under the described conditions, the limit of detection was 2 ng/ml for MDMA, 8 ng/ml for cocaine, and 6 ng/ml for morphine (with a signal-to-noise ratio of 5). The lowest concentration suitable for recording interpretable spectra was about 10 to 20 times the limit of detection of each analyte.

In 2001, Paterson et al. [45] modified a previously described method for opiates analysis in hair to include amphetamines, benzodiazepines, cocaine, methadone, and phencyclidine. Hair samples were washed twice with methylene chloride and cut into 1-mm segments prior to extraction with methanol at 45°C for 18 h. The extracts were split into two parts; both were evaporated to dryness. One half of the extract was derivatized using MBTFA (N-Methyl-bis-trifluoroacetamide) for analysis of amphetamines, and the other half was derivatized using MTBSTFA (*N*-methyl-*N*-*tert*,-butyldimethylsilyltrifluoroacetamide) for analysis of the remaining drugs. The extracts were analyzed using electron-impact GC-MS operating in selected-ion monitoring mode. In total, 20 hair samples obtained from patients attending a methadone-maintenance clinic were screened by this method, where 18 drugs of abuse/metabolites could be detected.

In 2002, Skender et al. [46] proposed two methods for the simultaneous analysis of morphine, codeine, heroin, 6-acetylmorphine, cocaine, methadone, amphetamine, methamphetamine, MDA, MDMA, and MDEA in hair. The procedure included incubation in methanol, solid-phase extraction, derivatization by the mixture of propionic acid anhydride and pyridine, and GC-MS. For amphetamine, methamphetamine, MDA, MDMA, and MDEA analysis, hair samples were incubated in 1*M* NaOH, extracted with ethyl acetate, derivatized with heptafluorobutyric acid anhydride (HFBA), and assayed by GC-MS. Hair specimens of 36 young subjects suspected of drug abuse were analyzed by the screening procedures and confirmed consumption of heroin in 18 subjects based on positive 6-acetylmorphine. Among these 18 heroin consumers, methadone was found in four, MDMA in two, and cocaine in two subjects. Cocaine only was present in two, methadone only in two, methamphetamine only in two, and MDMA only in seven of the 36 subjects tested.

A new method combination, headspace solid-phase dynamic extraction coupled with gas chromatography-tandem mass spectrometry (HS-SPDE-GC-MS/MS), was introduced by Lachenmeier et al. [47] to determine drugs of abuse in hair samples. This highly automated procedure utilizes SPDE for preconcentration and on-coating derivatization as well as GC and triple quadrupole MS/MS for selective and sensitive detection. The analytes are absorbed from the sample headspace directly into a hollow needle with an internal coating of polydimethylsiloxane by repeated aspirate/dispense cycles. The HS-SPDE-GC-MS/MS procedure was applied to the analysis of methadone, the trimethylsilyl derivatives of cannabinoids, and the trifluoroacetyl derivatives of amphetamines and designer drugs. The method was shown to be sensitive, with detection limits between 6 and 52 pg/mg hair matrix. Compared with conventional methods of hair analysis, HS-SPDE-GC-MS/MS appeared easier to use and was substantially faster.

Recently, a rapid screening method has been proposed by Kronstrand et al. [48] using an LC-MS/MS method for the simultaneous analysis of several drugs of abuse in human hair as an alternative to immunological screening tests. The method included nicotine, cotinine, morphine, codeine, 6-acetylmorphine, ethylmorphine, amphetamine, methamphetamine, MDA, MDMA, benzoylecgonine, cocaine, 7-aminoflunitrazepam, and diazepam. The LC-MS/MS instrumentation was equipped with an electrospray interface. To 20 to 50 mg of hair, 0.5 ml of mobile phase A (acetonitril:methanol:20m*M* formate buffer, pH 3.0, 10:10:80) and 25 μl of internal standard were added, and the sample was incubated in a water bath at 37°C for 18 h. In 75 randomly selected autopsy cases, hair was analyzed in addition to the usual specimens of blood and urine. Using a threshold of 20 ng/sample, equivalent to 1 ng/mg if 20 mg hair is used, 26 positive results were found in 16 cases. Three of the 26 positive detections could not be confirmed by GC-MS. Two of the cases were not previously known as drug users. Of the 59 negative cases, only one case had a positive blood sample for 6-acetylmorphine and morphine. The authors concluded that the proposed LC-MS/MS method showed high sensitivity, was very easy to perform, and seemed appropriate for screening purposes.

Finally, Gentili et al. [49] performed a new headspace solid-phase microextraction and gas chromatography-mass spectrometry (HS-SPME-GC-MS) procedure for the simultaneous detection of cocaine, amphetamine, methamphetamine, MDA, MDMA, MDEA, MBDB, ketamine, and methadone in human hair. Hair samples were washed with water and acetone in an ultrasonic bath and extracted with 1*M* hydrochloric acid. The fiber was exposed to a 5-min absorption at 90°C and thermal desorption was performed at 250°C for 3 min. The procedure was simple, rapid, required small quantities of sample, and was sufficiently sensitive. Detection limits were lower than 1 ng/mg of hair for the majority of substances.

6.3.5 Head Hair versus Other Hair and Nails

In 1984, Suzuki et al. [50] published a sensitive gas chromatography/chemical ionization mass spectrometry method for the detection of methamphetamine and amphetamine in nail clippings obtained from methamphetamine users. The major findings were that the methamphetamine levels in fingernails were comparable with those found in hair and that both stimulants were more concentrated in toenails than in fingernails.

A method for the detection and quantitation of methamphetamine and its major metabolite in hair, nails, sweat, and saliva from habitual users of methamphetamine by mass fragmentography has been developed by Suzuki et al. [51]. Hair and nail samples were washed with water and methanol to remove the external contamination, processed with 0.6*M* HCl, alkalinized, and extracted with $CHCl_3$/isopropanol (3:1 v/v). Sweat and saliva samples were extracted with methanol. After trifluoroacetyl derivatization, the samples were analyzed by mass fragmentography. Methamphetamine and its major metabolite, amphetamine, were detected in hair, nail, and sweat samples, but methamphetamine alone was detected in saliva samples.

A paper published by Cirimele et al. [52] related a forensic case of a 22-year-old male known to be a drug abuser. Hair and fingernails were collected, decontaminated in methylene chloride, and pulverized in a ball mill. After complete dissolution in NaOH in presence of deuterated internal standards and extraction with ethyl acetate, the organic phase was evaporated in presence of methanol/concentrated HCl (99:1, v/v) to ensure nonvolatility of the analytes. After derivatization using PFPA, analyses were performed by GC-MS. The authors observed that fingernail concentrations were slightly higher (12.0, 9.7, and 60.2 ng/mg for amphetamine, MDA, and MDMA, respectively) than those obtained with head hair (10.2, 8.0, and 53.4 ng/mg for amphetamine, MDA, and MDMA, respectively).

In 2004, Lin et al. [53] analyzed fingernail clippings for the presence of methamphetamine and amphetamine collected from 97 consenting females, who admitted amphetamine or opiate use, or both. Sixty-two subjects were found positive for methamphetamine/amphetamine. Paired nail-hair specimens were collected from six of these subjects for a 12-week period. The authors observed that methamphetamine and amphetamine were found in the nails of 62 subjects collected at the initial stage of the study (0.46 to 61.50 ng/mg, mean 9.96 ng/mg for methamphetamine, and <0.20 to 5.42 ng/mg, mean 0.93 ng/mg for amphetamine) and that the concentrations of methamphetamine and amphetamine in nail clippings were generally lower than those observed in the first 1.5-cm section of hair samples collected at the same time from the same individual. They also observed that amphetamine/methamphetamine concentration ratios in nail clippings and hair samples were found comparable, and methamphetamine concentration in the nail clippings collected at weeks 0, 4, 8, and 12 decreased in a pattern similar to that exhibited by the first 1.5-cm sections of the hair samples collected at the same time.

Finally, Han et al. [54] conducted a study to compare the qualitative results and concentrations of methamphetamine and its metabolite amphetamine in head hair and hair collected from different parts of the body (axillae and pubis). Hair from 14 subjects who were suspected methamphetamine users was simultaneously collected. Hair preparation involved a washing step, fine cutting, overnight extraction, derivatization by trifluoroacetic anhydride, and GC-MS using selective-ion monitoring. The authors found a good correlation of the qualitative results for methamphetamine between head hair and hair on other parts of the body, but the concentrations of methamphetamine and amphetamine were higher in axillary and pubic hair than in head hair.

6.3.6 Effects of Cosmetic Treatments

In 1999, Takayama et al. [55] collected black hairs from a methamphetamine addict to treat them with permanent wave, dye, or decolorant liquids. Quantitation of methamphetamine and amphetamine by HPLC-chemiluminescence detection method showed that methamphetamine and amphetamine concentrations in the hair decreased significantly in all cases of cosmetic treatments. Analytes were found stable in the permanent-wave treatments, but not stable in the dye or decolorant treatments. As possible reasons for the decrease, the authors considered the elution of methamphetamine and amphetamine from hair in the permanent-wave treatment, and the degradation of methamphetamine and amphetamine in the dye or decolorant treatments. Their results suggested that treatments of hair with permanent wave, dye, or decolorant liquids interfered with determination of methamphetamine and amphetamine in hair.

6.4 CONCLUSION

The concentrations of amphetamines in hair are generally in the nanogram to milligram range, at least in cases of chronic abuse. There is no available information on the minimum dose of drug intake that can be detected by hair analysis. However, hair analysis for amphetamines gives a way to uncover chronic use when blood and urine analyses fail.

Depending on the amount of specimen used, immunoassays are a good method of preanalyzing hair samples. Obviously, positive results must be confirmed by a more specific method, particularly in forensic situations.

Up to now, GC-MS methods exceed by far all other chromatographic methods used. They represent the gold standard, including the ones coupled with headspace solid-phase microextraction and headspace solid-phase dynamic extraction as preparation and introduction techniques. However, the increasing number of HPLC methods published recently confirm the growing interest in technologies that are more universal and less tedious.

REFERENCES

1. Suzuki, O. et al., Detection of methamphetamine and amphetamine in a single human hair by gas chromatography/chemical ionization mass spectrometry, *J. Forensic Sci.*, 29, 611, 1984.
2. Aoki, K. and Kuroiwa, Y., Enzyme immunoassay for methamphetamine, *J. Pharm. Dyn.*, 6, 33, 1983.
3. Kintz, P. and Cirimele, V., Interlaboratory comparison of quantitative determination of amphetamine and related compounds in hair samples, *Forensic Sci. Int.*, 84, 151, 1997.
4. Sweeney, S.A. et al., Amphetamines in hair by enzyme-linked immunosorbent assay, *J. Anal. Toxicol.*, 22, 418, 1998.
5. Swartz, M.S. et al., Detection of illicit substance use among persons with schizophrenia by radioimmunoassay of hair, *Psychiatr. Serv.*, 54, 891, 2003.
6. Miki, A. et al., Application of ORAL.screen saliva drug test for the screening of methamphetamine, MDMA, and MDEA incorporated in hair, *J. Anal. Toxicol.*, 28, 132, 2004.
7. Kimura, H. et al., Highly sensitive quantitation of methamphetamine by time-resolved fluoroimmunoassay using a new europium chelate as a label, *J. Anal. Toxicol.*, 23, 11, 1999.
8. Takahashi, K., Determination of methamphetamine and amphetamine in biological fluids and hair by gas chromatography, *Nippon Hoigaku Zasshi*, 38, 319, 1984.
9. Nagai, T. et al., Detection of methamphetamine and amphetamine from hair, bone and teeth, in *TIAFT Proceedings of the 21st International Meeting,* Dunnett, N. and Kimber, K.J., Eds., New York, 1984, p. 89.
10. Cirimele, V. et al., Dosage de la méthylènedioxyéthylamphétamine (MDEA) et de son métabolite, la méthylènedioxyamphétamine (MDA) dans les cheveux par CPG/SM, *Toxicorama*, 2, 87, 1997.
11. Rohrich, J. and Kauert, G., Determination of amphetamine and methylenedioxy-amphetamine-derivatives in hair, *Forensic Sci. Int.*, 84, 179, 1997.
12. Laznickova, J. et al., Determination of amphetamine and methamphetamine in human hair using gas chromatography/mass spectrometry, *Soud. Lek.*, 45, 26, 2000.
13. Pujadas, M. et al., Development and validation of a gas chromatography-mass spectrometry assay for hair analysis of amphetamine, methamphetamine and methylenedioxy derivatives, *J. Chromatogr. B Anal. Technol. Biomed. Life Sci.*, 798, 249, 2003.

14. Frison, G. et al., Gas chromatography/mass spectrometry determination of amphetamine-related drugs and ephedrines in plasma, urine and hair samples after derivatization with 2,2,2-trichloroethyl chloroformate, *Rapid Commun. Mass. Spectrom.*, 19, 919, 2005.
15. Villamor, J.L. et al., A new GC-MS method for the determination of five amphetamines in human hair, *J. Anal. Toxicol.*, 29, 135, 2005.
16. Takayama, N. et al., Determination of stimulants in a single human hair sample by high-performance liquid chromatographic method with chemiluminescence detection, *Biomed. Chromatogr.*, 11, 25, 1997.
17. Al-Dirbashi, O. et al., HPLC with fluorescence detection of methamphetamine and amphetamine in segmentally analyzed human hair, *Analyst*, 124, 493, 1999.
18. Tagliaro, F. et al., High sensitivity simultaneous determination in hair of the major constituents of ecstasy (3,4-methylenedioxymethamphetamine, 3,4-methylenedioxyamphetamine and 3,4-methylene-dioxyethylamphetamine) by high-performance liquid chromatography with direct fluorescence detection, *J. Chromatogr. B Biomed. Sci. Appl.*, 723, 195, 1999.
19. Nakashima, K. et al., Determination of methamphetamine and amphetamine in abusers' plasma and hair samples with HPLC-FL, *Biomed. Chromatogr.*, 17, 471, 2003.
20. Miki, A. et al., Determination of methamphetamine and its metabolites incorporated in hair by column-switching liquid chromatography-mass spectrometry, *J. Anal. Toxicol.*, 27, 95, 2003.
21. Kaddoumi, A. et al., High-performance liquid chromatography with fluorescence detection for the simultaneous determination of 3,4-methylenedioxymethamphetamine, methamphetamine and their metabolites in human hair using DIB-Cl as a label, *Biomed. Chromatogr.*, 18, 202, 2004.
22. Stanaszek, R. and Piekoszewski, W., Simultaneous determination of eight underivatized amphetamines in hair by high-performance liquid chromatography-atmospheric pressure chemical ionization mass spectrometry (HPLC-APCI-MS), *J. Anal. Toxicol.*, 28, 77, 2004.
23. Koide, I. et al., Determination of amphetamine and methamphetamine in human hair by headspace solid-phase microextraction and gas chromatography with nitrogen-phosphorus detection, *J. Chromatogr. B Biomed. Sci. Appl.*, 707, 99, 1998.
24. Liu, J. et al., New method of derivatization and headspace solid-phase microextraction for gas chromatographic-mass spectrometric analysis of amphetamines in hair, *J. Chromatogr. B Biomed. Sci. Appl.*, 758, 95, 2001.
25. Gentili, S. et al., Simultaneous detection of amphetamine-like drugs with headspace solid-phase microextraction and gas chromatography-mass spectrometry, *J. Chromatogr. B Anal. Technol. Biomed. Life Sci.*, 780, 183, 2002.
26. Musshoff, F. et al., Fully automated determination of amphetamines and synthetic designer drugs in hair samples using headspace solid-phase microextraction and gas chromatography-mass spectrometry, *J. Chromatogr. Sci.*, 40, 359, 2002.
27. Musshoff, F. et al., Automated headspace solid-phase dynamic extraction for the determination of amphetamines and synthetic designer drugs in hair samples, *J. Chromatogr. A*, 958, 231, 2002.
28. Allen, D.L. and Oliver, J.S., The use of supercritical fluid extraction for the determination of amphetamines in hair, *Forensic Sci. Int.*, 107, 191, 2000.
29. Kimura, H. et al., Detection of stimulants in hair by laser microscopy, *J. Anal. Toxicol.*, 23, 577, 1999.
30. Miki, A. et al., Application of ion mobility spectrometry to the rapid screening of methamphetamine incorporated in hair, *J. Chromatogr. B Biomed. Sci. Appl.*, 692, 319, 1997.

31. Nagai, T. et al., A new analytical method for methamphetamine optical isomers and its habitual users' hair by HPLC, *Igaku to Seibutsugaku*, 115, 147, 1987.
32. Nagai, T. et al., Forensic toxicologic analysis of methamphetamine optical isomers by high-performance liquid chromatography, *Z. Rechtsmed.*, 101, 151, 1988.
33. Nagai, T. et al., A new analytical method for stereoisomers of methamphetamine and amphetamine and its application to forensic toxicology, *Clin. Biochem.*, 22, 439, 1989.
34. Scarcella, D. et al., Optimization of a simple method for the chiral separation of phenethylamines of forensic interest based on cyclodextrin complexation capillary electrophoresis and its preliminary application to the analysis of human urine and hair, *Forensic Sci. Int.*, 89, 33, 1997.
35. Tagliaro, F. et al., Simultaneous chiral separation of 3,4-methylenedioxymethamphetamine, 3-4-methylenedioxyamphetamine, 3,4-methylenedioxyethylamphetamine, ephedrine, amphetamine and methamphetamine by capillary electrophoresis in uncoated and coated capillaries with native beta-cyclodextrin as the chiral selector: preliminary application to the analysis of urine and hair, *Electrophoresis*, 19, 42, 1998.
36. Al-Dirbashi, O. et al., Enantiomer-specific high-performance liquid chromatography with fluorescence detection of methamphetamines in abusers' hair and urine, *Biomed. Chromatogr.*, 13, 543, 1999.
37. Al-Dirbashi, O. et al., Quantification of methamphetamine, amphetamine and enantiomers by semi-micro column HPLC with fluorescence detection; applications on abusers' single hair analyses, *Biomed. Chromatogr.*, 14, 293, 2000.
38. Stout, P.R. et al., Incorporation and retention of radiolabeled S-(+)- and R-(−)-methamphetamine and S(+)- and R(−)-N-(n-butyl)-amphetamine in mouse hair after systemic administration, *Drug. Metab. Dispos.*, 28, 286, 2000.
39. Martins, L. et al., Simultaneous enantioselective determination of amphetamine and congeners in hair specimens by negative chemical ionization gas chromatography-mass spectrometry, *J. Chromatogr. B Anal. Technol. Biomed. Life Sci.*, 825, 57, 2005.
40. Ishiyama, I. et al., Detection of basic drugs (methamphetamine, antidepressants and nicotine) from human hair, *J. Forensic Sci.*, 28, 380, 1983.
41. Moeller, M.R. et al., Drug Analysis in Hair by GC/MS, presented at SOFT Conference on Hair Analysis for Drugs of Abuse, Washington, DC, May 27–29, NIDA Research Monograph Series, 1990.
42. Moeller, M.R. and Fey P., Screening Procedure for Drugs in Hair, presented at 43rd meeting of the American Academy of Forensic Sciences, Anaheim, CA, Feb. 18–23, Abstract, K45 182, 1991.
43. Kintz, P. and Mangin P., Determination of gestational opiate, nicotine, benzodiazepine, cocaine and amphetamine exposure by hair analysis, *J. Forensic Sci.*, 63, 139, 1993.
44. Tagliaro, F. et al., Hair analysis for abused drugs by capillary zone electrophoresis with field-amplified sample stacking, *Forensic Sci. Int.*, 92, 201, 1998.
45. Paterson, S. et al., Qualitative screening for drugs of abuse in hair using GC-MS, *J. Anal. Toxicol.*, 25, 203, 2001.
46. Skender, L. et al., Quantitative determination of amphetamines, cocaine, and opiates in human hair by gas chromatography/mass spectrometry, *Forensic Sci. Int.*, 125, 120, 2002.
47. Lachenmeier, D.W. et al., Application of tandem mass spectrometry combined with gas chromatography and headspace solid-phase dynamic extraction for the determination of drugs of abuse in hair samples, *Rapid Commun. Mass Spectrom.*, 17, 472, 2003.
48. Kronstrand, R. et al., Screening for drugs of abuse in hair with ion spray LC-MS-MS, *Forensic Sci. Int.*, 145, 183, 2004.

49. Gentili, S. et al., Rapid screening procedure based on headspace solid-phase microextraction and gas chromatography-mass spectrometry for the detection of many recreational drugs in hair, *J. Chromatogr. B Anal. Technol. Biomed. Life Sci.*, 801, 289, 2004.
50. Suzuki, O. et al., Nails as useful materials for detection of methamphetamine or amphetamine abuse, *Forensic Sci. Int.*, 24, 9, 1984.
51. Suzuki, S. et al., Analysis of methamphetamine in hair, nail, sweat, and saliva by mass fragmentography, *J. Anal. Toxicol.*, 13, 176, 1989.
52. Cirimele, V. et al., Detection of amphetamines in fingernails: an alternative to hair analysis, *Arch. Toxicol.*, 70, 68, 1995.
53. Lin, D.L. et al., Deposition characteristics of methamphetamine and amphetamine in fingernail clippings and hair sections, *J. Anal. Toxicol.*, 28, 411, 2004.
54. Han, E. et al., Correlation of methamphetamine results and concentrations between head, axillary, and pubic hair, *Forensic Sci. Int.*, 147, 21, 2005.
55. Takayama, N. et al., High-performance liquid chromatography study on effects of permanent wave, dye and decolorant treatments on methamphetamine and amphetamine in hair, *Biomed. Chromatogr.*, 13, 257, 1999.

7 Pharmaceuticals in Hair

Marjorie Chèze, Marc Deveaux, Gaëlle Duffort, Francis Billault, and Gilbert Pépin

CONTENTS

7.1 INTRODUCTION

The aim of this chapter is to review the articles (case reports and reviews) dealing with the detection of the most frequent pharmaceuticals in hair (except those presented in other chapters). They have been categorized as follows:

1. Antiepileptic drugs
2. Psychotropic drugs
   - 2.1 Antipsychotics (major tranquilizers)
     - 2.1.1 Typical antipsychotics
     - 2.1.2 Atypical antipsychotics
   - 2.2 Anxiolytic sedatives (minor tranquilizers)
   - 2.3 Sedative antihistamines
   - 2.4 Antidepressants
3. Anesthetic drugs
4. Cardiovascular drugs
   - 4.1 Beta-blockers (Class II and III antiarrhythmics)
   - 4.2 Cardiac glycosides
   - 4.3 Class Ic antiarrhythmics
   - 4.4 Centrally active antihypertensives

It is well known that most pharmaceuticals — in the same way as illicit drugs, metals, or metabolites like ethylglucuronide — are likely to bind to hair cuticle and cortex. Incorporation is achieved by blood capillaries at the hair root, sweat, or sebum. Even if deposition of pharmaceutical drugs from the external environment is not obvious — unlike many illicit drugs — the effects of pollution, cosmetic treatments, and sebum must be eliminated, and this is accomplished using appropriate washing procedures. Decontamination steps typically involve the use of small volumes (5 to 10 ml) of common solvents — methanol, acetone, water, or dichloromethane — for only a few minutes at room temperature. Hair samples are then dried, pulverized, or cut in very small pieces with scissors and weighed.

Pretreatment is needed to extract drugs from the hair cortex. Incubation overnight in buffers is generally preferred to ultrasonic bath in solvents, which tend to give dirty extracts. Basic or acidic digestion is also used, depending on molecular properties and stability. Liquid-liquid and solid-phase extractions are the preferred extraction methods, while solid-phase microextraction is not widely used because of its poor accuracy for quantification.

Gas chromatography, and to a lesser extent liquid chromatography with ultraviolet or photodiode array detection, is widely used for the determination of most pharmaceuticals in hair, especially for clinical treatments or chronic abuse. However, the use of liquid chromatography with tandem mass spectrometry for detection has recently become more common. This analytical technique has gained in popularity because it can detect a wide range of concentrations, including trace amounts, which facilitates the use of smaller samples, with shorter extraction steps and no derivatization. Capillary electrophoresis is being used less and less.

Studies for pharmaceuticals in hair have been conducted mainly on patients in clinical or hospital treatment because of the long-term information available that allows verification of any correlation between doses and concentrations. However, cases of overdoses, suicides, and drug addiction with anesthetics (e.g., fentanyl) are also presented in this chapter. Regarding the increasing number of drug-facilitated sexual assault cases reported, Chapter 12 deals specifically with this matter, so no information about this topic is presented here.

Drugs are mainly bound to melanin. Consequently, basic or amphoteric drugs are most likely to be found in hair. On the other hand, acidic drugs usually have higher blood concentrations. As a result, concentrations of most drugs in hair are approximately of the same magnitude. Measured concentrations are typically in the range of one to hundreds of nanograms per milligram of hair for clinical treatments. Lower concentrations of a few picograms per milligram of hair are observed for flupentixol, penfluridol, anesthetics with very short half-lives, and ß-adrenergic compounds. Detection of such low levels in hair requires tandem mass spectrometry.

Pretreatment, extraction procedures, and techniques of analysis are summarized in Table 7.1, as well as drug levels in hair found in real cases and information about the population studied.

7.2 DISCUSSION

Since the publication of the first edition of this book in 1996, a few additional pharmaceutical drugs have been tested in hair and results published, even after the 1999 review by Gaillard and Pépin.[52] These newly tested molecules are: oxcarbazepine, levomepromazine, pipamperone, carisoprodol, alfentanyl, GHB, lidocaine, propofol, acebutolol, and flecainide. However, screening procedures for classes of drugs are increasingly being described, and liquid chromatography coupled with tandem mass spectrometry is widely used for this purpose.[10,13,15,16,28] Tandem mass spectrometry appears to be a prerequisite for detection at very low concentrations in hair or to reduce sample amounts.

TABLE 7.1
Pharmaceuticals in Hair

Compound	Procedure: Pretreatment	Procedure: Extraction	Procedure: Analysis	Drug Levels	Comments	Ref.
1. Antiepileptic drugs						
Carbamazepine	0.1*M* NaOH, 80°C, 30 min, adjusted at pH = 9.5–10 with HCl	LLE: ether	GC-MS column: DB-5	2.8–22.5 ng/mg (200 to 400 mg/day) ($n = 6$)	Study on 35 psychiatric patients	1
	0.1*M* NaOH, overnight at 40°C, then neutralized with 1.5*M* HCl	LLE: pH = 7.6, methyl-tert-butyl ether	LC-UV: lambda wavelength = 214 nm column: C_{18}	20.4–200.1 ng/mg ($n = 135$ in 23 patients)	23 epileptic patients monitored for 6 months	2
	2m*M* NaOH, 80°C, 15 min, then 37% HCl for 20 min at 80°C	SPE: C_{18} cartridges, pH = 9	FPIA (TDx) and GC-FID column: methyl phenyl silicone	15.4–69.2 ng/mg by FPIA 13.9–66.3 ng/mg by GC ($n = 17$ in both cases)	Study on 17 patients under carbamazepine treatment	3
	1.5*M* NaOH, overnight at 37°C, then neutralized with 1.5*M* HCl	LLE: pH = 7.6, methyl-tert-butyl ether	LC-UV: lambda wavelength = 214 nm column: C_{18}	0.6–63.7 ng/mg ($n = 14$)	Study on patients with epilepsy	4
	Phosphate buffer, pH = 5.5, arylsulfatase, β-glucuronidase	LLE: pH = 5.5, hexane-diethylether-propanol	GC-MS column: HP-5	1.2–57.4 ng/mg ($n = 30$)	Study on epileptic patients	5

TABLE 7.1 (continued)
Pharmaceuticals in Hair

Compound	Procedure: Pretreatment	Procedure: Extraction	Procedure: Analysis	Drug Levels	Comments	Ref.
Oxcarbazepine	0.1*M* HCl at 57°C for 24 h, pH = 9.3	SPE, pH = 9.3	LC-APCI/MS column: LiChroCART	three segments of the same case: 3.9, 10.4, and 13.0 ng/mg	Suicide case (levomepromazine) of an epileptic patient treated with oxcarbazepine	6
Phenobarbital	MeOH/acetone/ NH_4OH (10:10:1), 1 h US, stored at room temperature overnight	LLE: pH = 6 CH_2Cl_2/isopropanol	GC-MS derivatization: TMAH column: methylsilicone TC1	16.2 and 14.7 ng/mg ($n = 2$)	Overdoses of phenobarbital (2 patients)	7
	Water, 56°C overnight	SPE: C_{18} cartridges, pH = 2	GC-MS column: CP-Sil-8CB	1.2 and 1.5 ng/mg ($n = 2$)	Young brothers found dead by their parents (suffocated by vapors from toys that had burns)	8
	Acidic buffer, pH = 2, 10 min	SPE: Extrelut and chloroform/isopropanol/ heptane, pH = 2	GC-MS capillary column	1.5–194.0 ng/mg ($n = 40$)	Hair samples obtained from ambulant and hospitalized patients	9
Phenytoin	MeOH/acetone/ NH_4OH (10:10:1), 1 h US, stored at room temperature overnight	LLE: pH = 6 CH_2Cl_2/isopropanol	GC-MS derivatization: TMAH column: methylsilicone TC1	3.3 and 0.1 ng/mg (100 mg/day) ($n = 2$)	Two volunteers who took phenytoin during 5 days	7
	1.5*M* NaOH, overnight at 37°C	LLE: pH = 7.6 methyl-tert-butyl ether	LC-UV: lambda wavelength = 214 nm column: C_{18}	6.0–157.8 ng/mg ($n = 14$)	Study on epileptic patients	4

2. Psychotropic drugs						
2.1. Antipsychotics (major tranquilizers)						
2.1.1. Typical antipsychotics						
Chlorpromazine	0.1*M* NaOH, 80°C, 30 min, pH = 9.5–10 with HCl	LLE: ether	GC/MS column: DB-5	2.9–68.2 ng/mg ($n = 16$)	Study on 35 psychiatric patients	1
	NaOH, 80°C, 30 min, pH = 8–10 with HCl	LLE: hexane	LC-MS/MS column: C_{18}	1.2 ng/mg ($n = 1$)	One patient under clinical treatment for schizophrenia	10
	NaOH, incubated in a shaking water bath at 70°C, 30 min HCl until pH = 9.5–10	for GC: tris buffer, butyl chloride, back extraction with HCl twice for LC: butyl chloride, back extraction in orthophosphoric acid	GC-MS column: Ultra-2 LC-UV column: NR	1.3 and 29.0 ng/mg ($n = 2$)	Postmortem cases	11
	2*M* NaOH, 80°C, 30 min	LLE: hexane-isoamylalcohol	LC with coulometric detector column: C_{18}	1.6–27.5 ng/mg ($n = 23$) (oral dosage of 30–300 mg/day)	Study on 23 psychiatric patients	12
Chlorprothixene	0.1*M* NaOH, 80°C, 30 min, pH = 9.5–10 with HCl	LLE: ether	GC-MS column: DB-5	30.0 ng/mg ($n = 1$)	Study on 35 psychiatric patients	1
Cyamemazine	0.1*M* HCl, 56°C, overnight	SPE: C_{18} cartridges, pH = 8.6	GC-MS column: CP-Sil-8CB	11.2 ng/mg ($n = 1$)	A woman found dead in her bath (acute poisoning)	8

TABLE 7.1 (continued)
Pharmaceuticals in Hair

Compound	Procedure: Pretreatment	Procedure: Extraction	Procedure: Analysis	Drug Levels	Comments	Ref.
Flupentixol	NaOH, 80°C, 30 min	LLE: hexane, pH = 8–10	LC-MS/MS column: C_{18}	0.22 ng/mg	One patient under clinical treatment for schizophrenia	10
Haloperidol	0.1*M* NaOH 80°C, 30 min, pH = 9.5–10 with HCl	LLE: ether	GC-MS column: DB-5	20.1 ng/mg (n = 1)	Study on 35 psychiatric patients	1
	US with MeOH, 2 h, phosphate buffer	SPE: Chromabond, pH = 6	LC-MS/MS column: RP-C8-select B	12.2 ng/mg (n = 1)	Study on 6 psychiatric patients	13
	0.1*N* HCl, overnight	LLE: pH = 7 (solvents NR)	GC-MS column: NR	50 hairs sampled of the same case: 0.12–0.68 ng/mg (n = 1)	Study on 1 paranoid patient treated with haloperidol	14
	NaOH and incubated in a shaking water bath at 70°C for 30 min, HCl until pH = 9.5–10	for GC: tris buffer, butyl chloride, back extraction with HCl twice for LC: butyl chloride, back extraction in orthophosphoric acid	GC-MS column: Ultra-2 LC-UV column: NR	17.0 and 242.0 ng/mg (n = 2)	Postmortem cases	11

Levomepromazine	0.1*M* HCl 0.1*M* NaOH	MLE	HPTLC	3.0–7.0 ng/mg	Screening of psychotropic drugs in patients' hair	15
Penfluridol	US with MeOH, 2 h, phosphate buffer	SPE: Chromabond, pH = 6	LC-MS/MS column: RP-C8-select B	ND and 0.08 ng/mg ($n = 2$)	Study on 6 psychiatric patients	13
Pipamperone	US with MeOH, 2 h, phosphate buffer	SPE: Chromabond and automated SPE device	LC-ESI-CID/MS LC-MS/MS column: RP-C8-select B	two segments: 0.9 and 1.0 ng/mg ($n = 1$)	Suicide case	16
Thioridazine	US with MeOH, 2 h, phosphate buffer	SPE: Chromabond, pH = 6	LC-MS/MS column: RP-C8-select B	ND, 5.6, 0.3, and 9.9 ng/mg ($n = 4$)	Study on 6 psychiatric patients	13
	NaOH and incubated in a shaking water bath at 70°C, 30 min, HCl until pH = 9.5–10	for GC: tris buffer, butyl chloride, back extraction with HCl twice for LC: butyl chloride, back extraction in orthophosphoric acid	GC-MS column: Ultra-2 LC-UV column: NR	4.5–71.0 ng/mg (mean = 28 ng/mg) ($n = 3$)	Postmortem cases	11
Trifluoperazine	0.1*M* NaOH 80°C, 30 min, pH = 9.5–10 with HCl	LLE: ether	GC-MS column: DB-5	368.0 ng/mg ($n = 1$)	Study on 35 psychiatric patients	1
	NaOH at 80°C, 30 min, pH = 8–10 with HCl	hexane extraction	LC-MS/MS column: C_{18}	18.9 ng/mg ($n = 1$)	One patient under clinical treatment for schizophrenia	10

TABLE 7.1 (continued)
Pharmaceuticals in Hair

Compound	Procedure: Pretreatment	Procedure: Extraction	Procedure: Analysis	Drug Levels	Comments	Ref.
2.1.2. Atypical antipsychotics						
Clozapine	US with MeOH, 2 h, phosphate buffer	SPE: Chromabond, pH = 6	LC-MS/MS column: RP-C8-select B	0.92, 0.47, and 0.62 ng/mg ($n = 3$)	Study on 6 psychiatric patients	13
	0.1*M* NaOH, 80°C, 30 min, pH = 9.5–10 with HCl	LLE: ether	GC-MS column: DB-5	16.7–59.2 ng/mg ($n = 16$)	Study on 35 psychiatric patients	1
	MeOH, overnight at 45°C	—	GC-MS column: HP-5	0.2–34.2 ng/mg ($n = 23$)	Study on 36 patients treated with clozapine	17
Tiapride	0.1*M* HCl, overnight at 56°C	SPE: C_{18} cartridges, pH = 8.6	GC-MS column: CP-Sil-8CB	8.9 ng/mg ($n = 1$)	A 29-year-old female medical doctor drug abuser	8
2.2. Anxiolytic sedatives (minor tranquilizers)						
Benzodiazepines (cf. applications of hair in drug-facilitated crimes, Chapter 12)						
Carisoprodol Meprobamate	1*M* HCl, overnight at 50°C	SPE: pH = 6.5	GC-MS derivatization: BSTFA-TMCS	Linearity: 0.5–10.0 ng/mg ($n = 1$)	Hair sample from an actual abuser	18
Meprobamate	1*M* HCl, overnight at 60°C	LLE: pH = 5.5, phosphate buffer/$CHCl_3$	GC-MS derivatization: (m-trifluoromethylphenyl) trimethylammonium hydroxide column: HP-1	4.3–17.6 ng/mg (during 21 days) ($n = 16$)	Study on the beard hair from 16 subjects after oral administration	19

	1*M* HCl, overnight at 60°C	LLE: pH = 5.5, phosphate buffer/$CHCl_3$	GC-MS derivatization: TMAH column: HP-1	3.3 and 4.2 ng/mg (200 mg/day) (*n* = 2)	Two patients receiving a daily dose of meprobamate	20
2.3. Sedative antihistamines						
Alimemazine	0.1*M* HCl, overnight at 56°C	SPE: C_{18} cartridges, pH = 8.6	GC-MS column: CP-Sil-8CB	2.0 ng/mg (*n* = 1)	A psychiatric patient found dead in a wood	8
Hydroxyzine	0.1*M* HCl, overnight at 56°C	SPE: C_{18} cartridges, pH = 8.6	GC-MS column: CP-Sil-8CB	8.3 ng/mg (*n* = 1)	A woman died following Sturg-Stauss illness; hydroxyzine was given by her husband	21
2.4. Antidepressants						
Amitriptyline	0.1*M* NaOH, 80°C, 30 min, pH = 9.5–10 with HCl	LLE: ether	GC-MS column: DB-5	2.5–57.7 ng/mg (*n* = 3)	Study on 35 psychiatric patients	1
	0.5*M* NaOH, US, 30 min	MLE with hexane (100 µl)	HPTLC	3.0–7.0 ng/mg (*n* = NR)	Screening of psychotropic drugs in patients hair	15
	1*M* NaOH, 100°C, 30 min	LLE: heptane-isoamylalcohol, pH = 8.5	GC-MS column: BP-5	ND–17.2 ng/mg (mean = 4.06 ± 4.7) (*n* = 30)	Study on 60 psychiatric patients	22
Amitriptyline	1*M* NaOH, 80°C, 30 min	SPE: Extrelut, ethyl acetate/ether	GC-MS column: HP-1 derivatization: PFPA	Amitriptyline: 0.6–11.0 ng/mg (*n* = 25) Nortriptyline: 0.5–7.9 ng/mg (*n* = 25)	Hair samples of 56 patients' under permanent treatment with TCA	23

TABLE 7.1 (continued)
Pharmaceuticals in Hair

Compound	Procedure: Pretreatment	Procedure: Extraction	Procedure: Analysis	Drug Levels	Comments	Ref.
Amitriptyline	NaOH and incubated in a shaking water bath at 70°C, 30 min, pH = 9.5–10 with HCl	for GC: tris buffer, butyl chloride, back extraction with HCl twice for LC: butyl chloride, back extraction in orthophosphoric acid	GC-MS (identification) column: Ultra-2 LC-UV (quantification) column: NR	Amitriptyline: 3.5–34.0 ng/mg (mean concentration 18 ± 10) (n = 6) Nortriptyline: 3.8–9.2 ng/mg (mean 6.5 ± 2.3) (n = 5)	Postmortem cases known to have taken antidepressant	11
Citalopram	US with MeOH, 2 h, phosphate buffer	SPE: Chromabond and automated SPE device	LC-ESI-CID/MS LC-MS/MS column: RP-C8-select B	two segments: 1107 and 557 ng/mg (n = 1)	One patient treated with citalopram	16
Clomipramine	0.1*M* HCl 57°C, 24 h, neutralized with 0.1*M* NaOH and treated with ammonium carbonate buffer to pH = 9.3	SPE: RP-18	LC-APCI/MS column: LiChroCART	three segments: Clomipramine: 7.6, 4.9, and 1.9 ng/mg Norclomipramine: 5.71, 9.71, and 4.13 ng/mg (n = 1)	Fatal poisoning with suicidal intent	24
	1*M* NaOH, 80°C, 30 min	SPE: Extrelut with ethyl acetate/ether	GC-MS derivatization: PFPA column: HP-1	Clomipramine: 0.4–3.9 ng/mg (n = 7) Norclomipramine: ND–1.5 ng/mg (n = 7)	Hair samples of 56 patients under permanent treatment with TCA	23

Dothiepin (dosulepin)	1*N* NaOH, 95°C, 10 min	LLE: Na_2CO_3 buffer, heptane/isoamyl alcohol (99:1)	GC-MS column: HPS-5MS	1.9 ng/mg ($n = 1$)	Fatal dothiepin overdose	25
	NaOH and incubated in a shaking water bath at 70°C for 30 min, pH = 9.5–10 with HCl	for GC: tris buffer, butyl chloride, back extraction with HCl twice for LC: butyl chloride, back extraction in orthophosphoric acid	GC-MS column: Ultra-2 LC-UV column: NR	Dothiepin: 6.7–137.0 ng/mg (mean: 66 ± 55 ng/mg) Northiaden: (desmethyldosulepin) detected ($n = 6$)	Postmortem cases	11
Doxepin	0.1*M* NaOH, 80°C, 30 min, pH = 9.5–10 with HCl	LLE: ether	GC-MS column: DB-5	55.6–183.3 ng/mg ($n = 5$)	Study on 35 psychiatric patients	1
	NaOH and incubated in a shaking water bath at 70°C for 30 min, pH = 9.5–10 with HCl	for GC: tris buffer, butyl chloride, back extraction with HCl twice for LC: butyl chloride, back extraction in orthophosphoric acid	GC-MS column: Ultra-2 LC-UV column: NR	7.7 and 87.0 ng/mg ($n = 2$)	Postmortem cases	11
Doxepin	0.1*M* HCl, 50°C, overnight (18–24 h)	SPE: HCX Isolute columns	GC-MS derivatization: : BSTFA-1% TMCS column: HP-5	Doxepin: 0.09–0.59 ng/mg (5 hair collections every 2 months) Desmethyldoxepin: 0.04–0.4 ng/mg	Hair samples collected from a patient daily treated with doxepin for 4 months	26

TABLE 7.1 (continued)
Pharmaceuticals in Hair

Compound	Procedure: Pretreatment	Procedure: Extraction	Procedure: Analysis	Drug Levels	Comments	Ref.
Doxepin	1*M* NaOH, 80°C, 30 min	SPE: Extrelut, ethyl acetate ether	GC-MS derivatization: PFPA column: HP-1	Doxepin: 1.0–3.0 ng/mg ($n = 6$) Nordoxepin: 0.5–2.1 ng/mg ($n = 6$)	Hair samples of 56 patients under permanent treatment with TCA	23
Imipramine	1*M* NaOH, 80°C, 30 min	SPE: Extrelut, ethyl acetate/ether	GC-MS derivatization: PFPA column: HP-1	Imipramine: 0.9–9.5 ng/mg ($n = 5$) Desipramine: 0.6–5.3 ng/mg ($n = 5$)	Hair samples of 56 patients under permanent treatment with TCA	23
	NaOH and incubated in a shaking water bath at 70°C for 30 min, pH = 9.5–10 with HCl	for GC: tris buffer, butyl chloride, back extraction with HCl twice for LC: butyl chloride, back extraction in orthophosphoric acid	GC-MS column: Ultra-2 LC column: NR	Imipramine: 104.0 ng/mg Desipramine: 88.0 ng/mg ($n = 1$)	Postmortem cases	11
Maprotiline	US with MeOH for 2 h, phosphate buffer	SPE: Chromabond and automated SPE device	LC-ESI-CID/MS LC-MS/MS column: RP-C8-select B	3.1 ng/mg ($n = 1$)	Suicide case	16
	1*M* NaOH, 80°C, 30 min	SPE: Extrelut with ethyl acetate/ether	GC-MS derivatization: PFPA column: HP-1	1.4–40.0 ng/mg ($n = 13$)	Hair samples of 56 patients under permanent treatment with TCA	23

Mianserin	NaOH and incubated in a shaking water bath at 70°C for 30 min, pH = 9.5–10 with HCl	for GC: tris buffer, butyl chloride, back extraction with HCl twice; for LC: butyl chloride, back extraction in orthophosphoric acid	GC-MS column: Ultra-2; LC-UV column: NR	9.2 ng/mg ($n = 1$)	Postmortem cases	11
Trimipramine, Desmethyl-trimipramine	NaOH and incubated in a shaking water bath at 70°C for 30 min, pH = 9.5–10 with HCl	for GC: tris buffer, butyl chloride, back extraction with HCl twice; for LC: butyl chloride, back extraction in orthophosphoric acid	GC-MS column: Ultra-2; LC-UV column: NR	detected	Postmortem cases	11
3. Anesthetic drugs						
Fentanyl, Sufentanyl, Alfentanyl	Phosphate buffer, pH = 8.4, overnight	LLE: CH_2Cl_2/isopropanol/n-heptane (50/17/33)	GC-MS/MS TSQ column: HP5	Fentanyl: 101, 644, and 8 pg/mg ($n = 3$) Sufentanyl: 2 pg/mg Alfentanyl: 2 and 30 pg/mg ($n = 2$)	Addiction of anesthesiologist	27
	0.25m*M* HCl, overnight at 45°C	SPE: Oasis MCX LP	capillary electrophoresis	—	Screening with opiates; results only for morphine	28
Fentanyl, Sufentanyl	Sorensen buffer, pH = 7.6, 40°C, 2 h	SPE: Chromabond 18, pH = 7.6	GC-MS/MS TSQ PCI (CH_4) column: DB5	Fentanyl: 100 pg/mg ($n = 1$) Sufentanyl: 5–10 pg/mg ($n = 1$)	Overall intake: Fentanyl: 15 mg percutaneously Sufentanyl: 7.75 mg intravenously	29

TABLE 7.1 (continued)
Pharmaceuticals in Hair

Compound	Procedure: Pretreatment	Procedure: Extraction	Procedure: Analysis	Drug Levels	Comments	Ref.
Fentanyl	—	warm MeOH, 40°C, 18 h; filtration 0.2 μm	LC-MS/MS TSQ column: Altima C_{18}	20–93 pg/mg ($n = 1$)	Nurse, chronic abuse	30
	Dilute HCl, overnight at 56°C	T-LLE: acidic back extraction with CH_2Cl_2	GC-MS for identification; GC-NPD for quantification derivatization: BSTFA column: NR	20–93 pg/mg ($n = 1$)	Chronic abuse (patches)	31
	—	MeOH, 40°C, overnight, reconstituted in citrate buffer, pH = 6.0	RIA	background: 0–8 pg/mg ($n = 19$) patients: 13–48 pg/mg ($n = 8$)	Surgery patients	32
GHB Gamma-Hydroxybutyrate	0.01*N* NaOH	acidic with ethyl acetate, MTBSTFA	GC-MS/MS column: HP5	pubic hair: 19.4–25.0 ng/mg	Overdosage	33
Ketamine	0.5*M* HCl, overnight at 45°C	SPE: C_{18} Bond Elut, pH = 8.0	GC-MS column: HP5 SIM mode	Ketamine: 0.6–489.0 ng/mg (mean = 49.0 ng/mg) ($n = 51$) Norketamine: 0.8–196.3 ng/mg (mean = 12.1 ng/mg) ($n = 51$)	Ketamine abuse in Singapore population	34

	—	HS: HCl 1*M*, 60°C, 1 h, addition of K_2CO_3 SPME: 100 μm PDMS fiber	GC-MS column: HP5	Ketamine 0.6 ng/mg (n = 17 among 183 tested)	Study on 183 young people in the Rome area at recreational settings	35
	Water, overnight at 56°C	SPE: C_{18} cartridges, pH = 2	LC-DAD column: C_{18}	Ketamine: 8.17–17.26 ng/mg Norketamine: 0.33–2.07 ng/mg (n = 1)	Polydrug use	36
Lidocaine	—	HS: 0.5 g Na_2SO_4 and 4% NaOH, 70°C, 30 min SPME: 65 μm CW/DVB fiber	GC-MS column: Supelcowax10	0.4–675 ng/mg (mean = 65 ng/mg) (n = 31 among 49 tested)	Illicit drug fatalities (cocaine, amphetamine, and heroin)	37
Propofol	Sorensen buffer, overnight at 40°C	HS: 80°C, 15 min	GC-MS column: HP-Wax SIM mode	1.5–3.5 ng/mg	Chronic abuse	38
	Sorensen buffer, overnight at 40°C	HS: 80°C, 15 min	GC-MS column: HP-Wax SIM mode	head hair: 0.89–1.39 ng/mg pubic hair: 19.68 ng/mg (n = 1)	44-year-old female nurse in anesthesiology; dead at home	39
	—	MeOH, US 4 h, twice, plus EtOH and NaOH	GC-MS column: HP5	1.05–3.5 ng/mg (n = 1)	26-year-old nurse; chronic abuse	40
Thiopental	0.1 $NaHCO_3$, overnight at 30°C	HS: phosphate buffer, pH = 5.5 SPME: 10 μm CW/TPR fiber	GC-MS/MS-IT PCI (C_3H_6O) column: CP-Sil-8CB	Thiopental: 0.15–0.3 ng/mg Pentobarbital: 0.2–0.4 ng/mg in proximal segments (n = 1)	DFSA	41
	Water, overnight at 56°C	SPE: C_{18} cartridges, pH = 2	LC-DAD column: C_{18}	Thiopental: 4.85–7.74 ng/mg Pentobarbital: 5.68–17.06 ng/mg (n = 1)	Polydrug user	36

TABLE 7.1 (continued)
Pharmaceuticals in Hair

Compound	Procedure: Pretreatment	Procedure: Extraction	Procedure: Analysis	Drug Levels	Comments	Ref.
4. Cardiovascular drugs						
4.1. Beta-blockers (Class II and III antiarrhythmics)						
Acebutolol	0.1*M* HCl, overnight at 56°C, then neutralized with 0.1*M* NaOH	SPE: Isolute C18, pH = 8.6	GC-MS derivatization: TMBEA column: HP5-MS	LOD: 10 pg/mg	Screening for β-blocking agents; in doping control	42
Atenolol	0.1*M* HCl, overnight at 56°C, then neutralized with 0.1*M* NaOH	SPE: Isolute C18, pH = 8.6	GC-MS derivatization: TMBEA column: HP5-MS	LOD: 4 pg/mg	Screening for β-blocking agents; in doping control	42
	1*M* NaOH, 100°C, 10 min	LLE: diethylether-dichloromethane	HPLC-UV = 265 nm column: RSil-CN	0.9 ng/mg ($n = 1$)	Chronic intake of β-blocking agents in hypertensive patients (compliance)	43
Betaxolol	1*M* NaOH, 100°C, 10 min	LLE: diethylether-dichloromethane	HPLC-UV = 265 nm column: RSil-CN	1.2–2.7 ng/mg ($n = 3$)	Compliance study, cross-sectional analysis on 1-cm segments	43
	1*M* NaOH, 100°C, 10 min	LLE: diethylether-dichloromethane	HPLC-UV = 265 nm column: RSil-CN	0.6–2.8 ng/mg ($n = 8$)	Compliance studies	44, 45
Bisoprolol	0.1*M* HCl, overnight at 56°C, then neutralized with 0.1*M* NaOH	SPE: Isolute C18, pH = 8.6	GC-MS derivatization: TMBEA column: HP5-MS	LOD: 8 pg/mg	Screening for β-blocking agents; in doping control	42

Labetalol	0.1*M* HCl overnight at 56°C, then neutralized with 0.1*M* NaOH	SPE: Isolute C18, pH = 8.6	GC-MS derivatization: TMBEA column: HP5-MS	LOD: 8 pg/mg	Screening for β-blocking agents; in doping control	42
Metoprolol	0.1*M* HCl overnight at 56°C, then neutralized with 0.1*M* NaOH	SPE: Isolute C18, pH = 8.6	GC-MS derivatization: TMBEA column: HP5-MS	8.41 pg/mg ($n = 1$) LOD: 4 pg/mg	Doping control; chronic use	42
Oxprenolol	0.1*M* HCl overnight at 56°C, then neutralized with 0.1*M* NaOH	SPE: Isolute C18, pH = 8.6	GC-MS derivatization: TMBEA column: HP5-MS	LOD: 8 pg/mg	Screening for β-blocking agents; in doping control	42
Pindolol	0.1*M* HCl overnight at 56°C	SPE: Isolute C18, pH 8.6	GC-MS derivatization: TMBEA column: HP5-MS	LOD: 10 pg/mg	Screening for β-blocking agents; in doping control	42
Propranolol	0.1*M* HCl overnight at 56°C, then neutralized with 0.1*M* NaOH	SPE: Isolute C18, pH = 8.6	GC-MS derivatization: TMBEA column: HP5-MS	LOD: 8 pg/mg	Screening for β-blocking agents; in doping control	42
	1*M* NaOH, 100°C, 10 min	LLE: diethylether-dichloromethane	HPLC-UV = 265 nm column: RSil-CN	1.6–2.4 ng/mg ($n = 2$)	Chronic intake of β-blocking agents in hypertensive patients (compliance)	43
Sotalol	0.1*M* HCl overnight at 56°C, then neutralized with 0.1*M* NaOH	SPE: Isolute C18, pH = 8.6	GC-MS derivatization: TMBEA column: HP5-MS	261 pg/mg ($n = 1$) LOD: 4 pg/mg	Doping control	42
	1*M* NaOH, 100°C, 10 min	LLE: diethylether-dichloromethane	HPLC-UV = 265 nm column: RSil-CN	4.4–5.3 ng/mg ($n = 2$)	Chronic intake of β-blocking agents in hypertensive patients (compliance)	43

TABLE 7.1 (continued)
Pharmaceuticals in Hair

Compound	Procedure: Pretreatment	Procedure: Extraction	Procedure: Analysis	Drug Levels	Comments	Ref.
Tertatolol	0.1*M* HCl overnight at 56°C, then neutralized with 0.1*M* NaOH	SPE: Isolute C18, pH = 8.6	GC-MS derivatization: TMBEA column: HP5-MS	LOD: 4 pg/mg	Screening for β-blocking agents; in doping control	42
Timolol	0.1*M* HCl overnight at 56°C, then neutralized with 0.1*M* NaOH	SPE: Isolute C18, pH = 8.6	GC-MS derivatization: TMBEA column: HP5-MS	LOD: 4 pg/mg	Screening for β-blocking agents; in doping control	42
4.2. Cardiac glycosides						
Digoxin	—	solvent extraction	RIA	2–6 pg/mg	—	46, 47
	Enzymatic digestion, pH = 7.2, overnight at 40°C	—	MEIA	3.6–11.4 pg/mg (mean = 5.9) (n = 35)	Chronic intake of digoxin in elderly patients; no correlation between hair and blood digoxin	48
	Enzymatic digestion, pH 7.2, overnight at 40°C	—	MEIA	5 pg/mg (n = 1)	Forensic case, one 4-cm segment	48

4.3. Class Ic antiarrythmics						
Flecainide	1*M* NaOH, 70°C, 20 min	LLE: ethylacetate, pH = 7.4	HPLC-fluorescence detector	—	Animal study; good correlation between flecainide concentrations in hair and plasma; determinant effects of hair pigmentation	49
	1*M* NaOH, 70°C, 20 min	LLE: ethylacetate, pH = 7.4	HPLC-fluorescence detector	38–412 ng/mg ($n = 15$) (daily dose 100–150 mg)	Individual drug-taking behavior; cross-sectional analysis on 1-cm segments; good correlation between flecainide concentrations in hair and plasma; determinant effect of hair pigmentation	50
4.4. Centrally active antihypertensives						
Methyldopa	—	—	—	—	Animal study	51

Note: See Table 7.2 for a list of abbreviations used in this table.

TABLE 7.2
List of Abbreviations Used in Table 7.1

APCI	atmospheric-pressure chemical ionization
BSTFA	bis(trimethylsilyl)trifluoroacetamide
CID	in-source collision-induced dissociation
DAD	diode array detector
DFSA	drug-facilitated sexual assault
ESI	electrospray ionization
FID	flame ionization detection
FPIA	fluorescence polarization immunoassay
GC	gas chromatography
GHB	gamma-hydroxybutyrate
HPTLC	high-performance thin-layer chromatography
HS	headspace
IT	ion trap
LC	liquid chromatography
LLE	liquid-liquid extraction
LOD	limit of detection
MEIA	microparticulate enzyme immunoassay
MeOH	methanol
MLE	microliquid extraction
MS	mass spectrometry
MS/MS	tandem mass spectrometry
MTBSTFA	*n*-methyl-*N*-*tert*-butyldimethylsilyltrifluoroacetamide
n	number of cases
ND	not detected
NPD	nitrogen-phosphorus detector
NR	not reported
PCI	positive chemical ionization
PFPA	pentafluoropropionic anhydride
RIA	radioimmunoassay
SPE	solid-phase extraction
SPME	solid-phase microextraction
TCA	tricyclic antidepressant
T-LLE	liquid-liquid triple extraction
TMAH	tetramethylammonium hydroxide
TMBEA	trimethylboroxine ethyl acetate
TMCS	trimethylchlorosilane
TSQ	triple-stage quadrupole
US	ultrasonication bath
UV	ultraviolet

7.3 CONCLUSION

Hair analysis for pharmaceuticals is mainly used for clinical survey, but it also provides useful information in forensic toxicology about personal drug history when the usual matrices (blood, urine) are not available. It is also of great interest in cases of drug-facilitated crimes, a topic that is discussed in greater detail in Chapter 12. Nevertheless, pitfalls in hair analysis must be kept in mind, and the results should be interpreted cautiously. These are compelling reasons for focusing future investigations on standardized extraction procedures for validation of analytical methods in hair analysis.

REFERENCES

1. Shen, M. et al., Detection of antidepressant and antipsychotic drugs in human hair, *Forensic Sci. Int.*, 126, 153, 2002.
2. Williams, J., Patsalos, P.N., and Wilson, J.F., Hair analysis as a potential index of therapeutic compliance in the treatment of epilepsy, *Forensic Sci. Int.*, 84, 113, 1997.
3. Tsatsakis, A.M. et al., Carbamazepine levels in the hair of patients under long-term treatment: a preliminary study, *Clin. Chim. Acta*, 263, 187, 1997.
4. Mei, Z. and Williams, J., Simultaneous determination of phenytoine and carbamazepine in human hair by high-performance liquid chromatography, *Ther. Drug Monitor.*, 19, 92, 1997.
5. Kintz, P., Marescaux, C., and Mangin, P., Testing human hair for carbamazepine in epileptic patients: is hair investigation suitable for drug monitoring? *Hum. Exp. Toxicol.*, 14, 812, 1995.
6. Klys, M., Rojek, S., and Bolechala, F., Determination of oxcarbazepine and its metabolites in postmortem blood and hair by means of liquid chromatography with mass detection (HPLC/APCI/MS), *J. Chromatogr. B*, 825, 38, 2005.
7. Saisho, K., Tanaka, E., and Nakahara, Y., Hair analysis for pharmaceutical drugs, I: effective extraction and determination of phenobarbital, phenytoine and their major metabolites in rat and human hair, *Biol. Pharm. Bull.*, 24, 59, 2001.
8. Gaillard, Y. and Pépin, G., Screening and identification of drugs in human hair by high-performance liquid chromatography-photodiode-array UV detection and gas chromatography-mass spectrometry after solid-phase extraction: a powerful tool in forensic medicine, *J. Chromatogr. A*, 762, 251, 1997.
9. Goullé, J.P. et al., Phenobarbital in hair and drug monitoring, *Forensic Sci. Int.*, 70, 191, 1995.
10. McClean, S., O'Kane, E.J., and Smyth, W.F., Electrospray ionisation-mass spectrometric characterisation of selected anti-psychotic drugs and their detection and determination in human hair samples by liquid chromatography-tandem mass spectrometry, *J. Chromatogr. B*, 740, 141, 2000.
11. Couper, F.J., McIntyre, I.M., and Drummer, O.H., Detection of antidepressant and antipsychotic drugs in postmortem human scalp hair, *J. Forensic Sci.*, 40, 87, 1995.
12. Sato, H. et al., Chlorpromazine in human scalp hair as an index of dosage history: comparison with simultaneously measured haloperidol, *Eur. J. Pharmacol.*, 44, 439, 1993.
13. Weinmann, W. et al., LC-MS-MS analysis of the neuroleptics clozapine, flupentixol, haloperidol, penfluridol, thioridazine, zuclopenthixol in hair obtained from psychiatric patients, *J. Anal. Toxicol.*, 26, 303, 2002.
14. Lipman, J.J., Multiple homicides occurring during a time of abnormally low drug concentration in the hair of a treated paranoid schizophrenic, *Forensic Examiner*, 2, 9, 1996.
15. Polenova, T.V. et al., Screening of psychotropic drugs in human hair based on high-performance thin-layer chromatography and microliquid extraction, *J. Chromatogr. Sci.*, 39, 293, 2001.

16. Müller, C. et al., Identification of selected psychopharmaceuticals and their metabolites in hair by LC/ESI-CID/MS and LC/MS/MS, *Forensic Sci. Int.*, 113, 415, 2000.
17. Cirimele, V. et al., Clozapine dose-concentration relationships in plasma, hair and sweat specimens of schizophrenic patients, *Forensic Sci. Int.*, 107, 289, 2000.
18. Kim, J.Y. et al., Simultaneous determination of carisoprodol and meprobamate in human hair using solid-phase extraction and gas chromatography/mass spectrometry of trimethylsilyl derivatives, *Rapid Commun. Mass Spectrom.*, 19, 3056, 2005.
19. Kintz, P., Tracqui, A., and Mangin, P., Pharmacological studies on meprobamate incorporation in human beard hair, *Int. J. Leg. Med.*, 105, 283, 1993.
20. Kintz, P. and Mangin, P., Determination of meprobamate in human plasma, urine and hair by gas chromatography and electron impact mass spectrometry, *J. Anal. Toxicol.*, 17, 408, 1993.
21. Gaillard, Y. and Pépin, G., Hair testing for pharmaceuticals and drugs of abuse: forensic and clinical applications, *Am. Clin. Lab.*, 18, 1997.
22. Tracqui, A. et al., Determination of amitriptyline in the hair of psychiatric patients, *Hum. Exp. Toxicol.*, 11, 363, 1992.
23. Pragst, F. et al., Structural and concentration effects on the deposition of tricyclic antidepressants in human hair, *Forensic Sci. Int.*, 84, 225, 1997.
24. Klys, M. et al., A fatal clomipramine intoxication case of a chronic alcoholic patient: application of postmortem hair analysis method of clomipramine and ethyl glucuronide using LC/APCI/MS, *Leg. Med.*, 7, 319, 2005.
25. Cirimele V. et al., A fatal dothiepin overdose, *Forensic Sci. Int.*, 76, 205, 1995.
26. Negrusz, A., Moore, C.M., and Perry, J.L., Detection of doxepin and its major metabolite desmethyldoxepin in hair following drug therapy, *J. Anal. Toxicol.*, 22, 531, 1998.
27. Kintz, P. et al., Evidence of addiction by anesthesiologists as documented by hair analysis, *Forensic Sci. Int.*, 153, 81, 2005.
28. de Lima, E.C. et al., Critical comparison of extraction procedures for the capillary electrophoresis analysis of opiates in hair, *J. Capillary Electrophor.*, 8, 111, 2003.
29. Sachs, H. et al., Analysis of fentanyl and sufentanyl in hair by GC/MS/MS, *Int. J. Leg. Med.*, 109, 213, 1996.
30. LeBeau, M.A. et al., Fentanyl in human hair by liquid chromatography-tandem mass spectrometry, *Ann. Toxicol. Anal.*, 14, 218, 2002.
31. Selavka, C.M. et al., Determination of fentanyl in hair: the case of the crooked criminalist, *J. Forensic Sci.*, 40, 681, 1995.
32. Wang, W.L., Cone, E.J., and Zacny, J., Immunoassay evidence for fentanyl in hair of surgery patients, *Forensic Sci. Int.*, 61, 65, 1993.
33. Kintz, P. et al., Unusually high concentrations in a fatal GHB case, *J. Anal. Toxicol.*, 29, 582, 2005.
34. Leong, H.S., Tan, N.L., and Lee, T.K., Evaluation of ketamine abuse using hair analysis: concentration trends in a Singapore population, *J. Anal. Toxicol.*, 29, 314, 2005.
35. Gentili, S., Cornetta, M., and Macchia, T., Rapid screening procedure based on headspace solid phase microextraction and gas chromatography-mass spectrometry for the detection of many recreational drugs in hair, *J. Chromatogr. B*, 801, 289, 2004.
36. Gaillard, Y. and Pépin, G., Evidence of polydrug use using hair analysis: a fatal case involving heroin, cocaine, cannabis, chloroform, thiopental and ketamine, *J. Forensic Sci.*, 43, 435, 1998.
37. Sporkert, F. and Pragst, F., Determination of lidocaine in hair of drug fatalities by headspace solid-phase microextraction, *J. Anal. Toxicol.*, 24, 316, 2000.

38. Cirimele, V., Kintz, P., and Ludes, B., Rapid determination of propofol in biological specimens and human hair by HS-GC/MS, *Acta Clin. Belg.*, 1, 47, 2002.
39. Cirimele, V. et al., Determination of chronic abuse of the anaesthetic agents midazolam and propofol as demonstrated by hair analysis, *Int. J. Leg. Med.*, 116, 54, 2002.
40. Iwersen-Bergmann, S. et al., Death after excessive propofol abuse, *Int. J. Leg. Med.*, 114, 248, 2001.
41. Frison, G. et al., Detection of thiopental and pentobarbital in head and pubic hair in case of drug-facilitated sexual assault, *Forensic Sci. Int.*, 133, 171, 2003.
42. Kintz, P. et al., Doping control for β-adrenergic compounds through hair analysis, *J. Forensic Sci.*, 45, 170, 2000.
43. Kintz, P. and Mangin, P., Hair analysis for detection of beta-blockers in hypertensive patients, *Eur. J. Clin. Pharmacol.*, 42, 351, 1992.
44. Kintz, P. and Mangin, P., L'analyse des médicaments et des stupéfiants dans les cheveux: Intérêt et limites pour le diagnostic clinique te la toxicologie médicolégale, *J. Méd. Strasbourg*, 22, 518, 1991.
45. Kintz, P., Tracqui, A., and Mangin, P., Detection of drugs in human hair for clinical and forensic applications, *Int. J. Leg. Med.*, 105, 1, 1992.
46. Baumgartner, W.A. et al., Detection of drug use by analysis of hair, *J. Nucl. Med.*, 5, 980, 1988.
47. Baumgartner, W.A., Hill, V.A., and Blahd, W.H., Hair analysis for drugs of abuse, *J. Forensic Sci.*, 34, 1433, 1989.
48. Deveaux, M. et al., Immunoassay of digoxin in hair, *Forensic Sci. Int.*, 84, 219, 1997.
49. Takiguchi, Y. et al., Measurement of flecainide in hair as an index of drug exposure, *J. Pharm. Sci.*, 90, 1891, 2001.
50. Takiguchi, Y. et al., Hair analysis of flecainide for assessing the individual drug-taking behaviour, *Eur. J. Clin. Pharmacol.*, 58, 99, 2002.
51. Harrison, W.H., Gray, R.H., and Salomon, L.M., Incorporation of L-dopa, L-alpha-methyl-dopa and DL-isoproterenol into guinea-pig hair, *Acta Derm. Venerol.*, 54, 249, 1974.
52. Gaillard, Y. and Pépin, G., Review: testing hair for pharmaceuticals, *J. Chromatogr. B*, 733, 231, 1999.

8 Screening Strategies in Hair Analysis on Drugs

Hans Sachs

CONTENTS

8.1 INTRODUCTION

Analytical strategies in forensic toxicology, as well as adjacent disciplines like veterinary drug residue analysis or doping control, include a variety of procedures, from general unknown analysis via screening procedures for well-defined subgroups (e.g., drugs of abuse) to the specific confirmation and quantitation of individual compounds. This implies the necessity to find appropriate analytical approaches representing a problem-related specificity–comprehensiveness trade-off.

The number of analytes to be considered is always restricted. Even the most comprehensive "general unknown" screening strategies are determined by the choice of the sample material, sample preprocessing, substance properties, and analytical parameters. Only substances that are excreted in the respective sample material can be hydrolyzed (if necessary), extracted, derivatized, and potentially detected by the relevant analytical principle can be positively analyzed, which hugely diminishes the number of *all* toxicologically relevant substances. On the other hand, specific confirmation procedures are barely restricted to a single analytical signal, since qualifier properties, metabolites, and internal standards need to be included.

The strategy for general unknown screenings in forensic cases is similar in institutes of legal medicine and depend on the problem to be solved and the available material (Table 8.1).

TABLE 8.1
"General Unknown" Procedures in Forensic Toxicology in Postmortem Cases to Detect Drug-Impaired or Drug-Dependent Drivers

Matrix	Test
Urine/Blood	Immunochemical screening
	Confirmation:
	GC-MS
	HPLC-DAD
	HPLC fluorescence
	LC-MS/MS
	Extended screening:
	GC-MS
	HPLC-DAD
Hair	"General unknown" not available
	Screen for opiates, cocaine, amphetamines, cannabinoids, methadone, benzodiazepines:
	GC-MS
	ELISA
	Special tests:
	GC-NCI-MS
	LC-MS/MS

In cases of driving under the influence of drugs in Germany and some other countries, only blood samples are relevant for the evaluation of the driver's fitness. In cases where the license to drive is withdrawn, the driver typically has to prove a one-year abstinence from all psychotropic substances by several urine tests or by a hair analysis on all relevant drugs before the driver's license is reissued [1].

In recent years narcotic, neuroleptic, and new antidepressive drugs were developed that are not detected by routine screening methods after therapeutic dosages (e.g., sulpiride, amisulpride, zopiclon, paroxetine). Even the benzodiazepines triazolam, brotizolam, and lormetazepam are not always identified in general unknown, even more unlikely in hair, although they are taken in dosages that can impair a driver. In postmortem cases, a variety of substances can be identified by screening urine or stomach contents with gas chromatography-mass spectrometry (GC-MS) and high-performance liquid chromatography diode array detection (HPLC-DAD) using the computer-based libraries like the one of Pfleger-Maurer-Weber [2] for GC-MS or Pragst [3] for detection using a diode array.

In hair analysis, true "general unknown" screening does not exist. Only a restricted screening for several substance groups is available. Examinations for substances beyond these groups can only be performed by special procedures. Contrary to urine, in hair analysis the possible number of examinations is limited because of the lack of material. Similarly, the reproducibility of quantitative analysis of hair sample is limited by the amount of sample material and unknown recovery of the extraction. Therefore, estimations of a semiquantitative results, based on single injections, are more characteristic than establishing validated, high-throughput assays.

However, since the review of hair analysis by Sachs and Kintz in 1998 [4], major progress has been made, in particular by the introduction of liquid chromatography combined with tandem mass-spectrometry (LC-MS/MS). Recently, libraries have been built up for screening in overdose cases, and some methods have been published to screen for a total group like amphetamines with single MS [5]. But most of them reported confirmation data of substances that cannot be detected with GC-MS or only with minor sensitivity, or only after time-consuming preparation. For screening purposes, especially in hair analysis, selective and sensitive methods had to be developed to cover larger groups of substances, with the awareness that a real "general unknown" screening of thousands of substances will not be available with the required sensitivity.

8.2 IMMUNOCHEMICAL SCREENING IN HAIR ANALYSIS

In forensic toxicological analyses for urine or blood, the procedure starts typically with an immunological screening. Commonly, only positive results are confirmed by identifying the single substances. Negative results (below cutoff) are reported without confirmation. This strategy requires immunochemical techniques that are surely more sensitive than the confirmation method. This is mostly true for urine, as the assays are validated for the detection of relevant metabolites. Hair contains very often the parent drug in higher concentrations than the metabolites, which are, if at all, mostly detectable only in the low pg/mg region. That is the reason why only kits with a relatively high cross reaction of the parent drug can be validated for hair analysis. Kintz [6] used Abbott ADx for hair screening on drugs of abuse, and Spiehler [7] reported on experiences with coated-tube radio-immunoassays (RIA) from DPC and coated-plate enzyme-linked immunosorbent assay (ELISA) tests from STC and Cozard for screening opiates, cocaine, cannabinoids, amphetamines, barbiturates, and benzodiazepines. Because of strict safety regulations, RIA can only be cost effective in large series. But the costs of ELISA tests also exceed the costs of direct GC-MS or LC-MS/MS determination until several hundred samples have to be determined per month. The required sensitivities of immunological tests is described in the recommendations of the Society of Hair Testing [8]. The following concentrations must lead to positive results:

0.2 ng/mg of morphine or 6-acetylmorphine
0.5 ng/mg of cocaine
0.2 ng/mg of MDMA, methamphetamine, amphetamine, MDE, or MDA
0.1 ng/mg of THC

Based on our own experiences, the MTP kits Diagnostix Single Step® for cocaine, the OraSure MTP-EIA kits for opiates and amphetamine, as well as the Intercept Oral Fluid Tests for cocaine, cannabinoids, and methadone fulfill these demands, of which the validations of the opiate and the cocaine kits were published by Lachenmeier et al. [9].

Although reliable hair analysis on drugs started in 1979 with a radio-immunological method for opiates [10], immunological screening is restricted to common drugs like cocaine, cannabinoids, methadone, and opiates. Unusual designer drugs of the amphetamine type are not always detected if the validated cutoff for amphetamine or methamphetamine is used. Benzodiazepine kits normally have good cross reactivity with nordazepam-type substances or sometimes high cross reactivity with alprazolam, but these are often not sensitive enough for lorazepam, triazolam, or brotizolam. This means that for general screening, immunoassays can lead the procedure in a certain direction but cannot substitute for a chromatographic analysis.

8.3 SCREENING AND CONFIRMATION BY GC-MS/MS

In the early 1990s, methods for screening drugs in hair by GC-MS were already developed [14, 15], but always only with a small number of compounds, far away from a general unknown screening. Some examples are given in Table 8.2 to demonstrate the limits.

The examination of Paterson et al. [12] includes a relatively high number of analytes, but concerning the detection limits, all published screening procedures would not fulfill the requirements for abstinence control for the relevant drugs. Detection limits for morphine of 0.4 ng/mg or nordazepam of 0.21 ng/mg would not be accepted in probation control or by psycho-medical examiners. Even after not intensive but regular use of benzodiazepines, the concentration of benzodiazepines lies in a range below 0.1 ng/mg.

The article "Analytical developments in toxicological investigation of drug-facilitated sexual assault" by Negrusz [18] makes clear that a comprehensive screening requires a variety of GC-MS procedures like EI (electron impact), PCI (positive chemical ionization), or NCI (negative chemical ionization). GC-MS/MS is needed to have a chance to differentiate between endogenous and administered -hydroxybutyrate and -butyrolactone [19].

8.4 MULTIANALYTE SCREENING USING LC-MS/MS

8.4.1 Multianalyte Procedures for Urine and Blood

The literature concerning urine and blood is mentioned here because there are only a few articles about LC-MS in hair analysis, and if we are asked to examine hair on rarely administered or just recently offered drugs, we refer to the literature concerning their blood analysis. A comprehensive review was published by Maurer [22] about multianalyte screening of drugs in blood by LC-MS/MS. Smink et al. [26] published a list of 33 benzodiazepines in blood, giving the precursor and product ions and collision energies. The limits of detection ranged from 0.1 ng/ml for triazolam to 12.6 ng/ml for norchlordiazepoxide.

8.4.2 Multianalyte Procedures in Hair Analysis

There have been only a few attempts to perform screenings using HPLC and DAD. El-Mahjoub and Staub [21] detected clonazepam, diazepam, flunitrazepam, midazolam, and oxazepam at the same time. The breakthrough did not come before the application of LC-MS/MS in hair analysis. Some examples are given in Table 8.3.

TABLE 8.2
Examples for Multianalyte Screening Using GC-MS/MS

Reference	Analytes	Limit of Detection (pg/mg)
Cirimele et al. [11]	diazepam	<10
	nordazepam	
	oxazepam	
	bromazepam	
	flunitrazepam	
	lorazepam	
	triazolam	
	alprazolam	
Paterson et al. [12]	amphetamine	20
	methamphetamine	30
	MDA	60
	MDMA	70
	(each as a TFA derivative)	
	ecgoninmethylester	70
	benzoylecgonine	90
	6-acetylmorphine	60
	morphine	400
	nordazepam	210
	oxazepam	110
	temazepam	300
	(each as TBDMS together with underivatized):	
	dihydrocodeine	250
	cocaine	120
	cocaethylene	160
	methadone	150
	EDDP	270
	diazepam	110
	phencyclidine	170
Gentili et al. [13]	amphetamine	1290
	methamphetamine	370
	MDA	1610
	MDMA	760
	MDE	660
	MBDB (*N*-methyl-1-(3,4-methylenedioxyphenyl)-	600
	2-butanamine)	590
	ketamine	350
	methadone	350
	cocaine	

TABLE 8.3
Examples for Multianalyte Screening Using LC-MS/MS

Reference	Analytes	Limit of Detection (pg/mg)
Kronstrand et al. [20]	nicotine	24
	cotinine	25
	amphetamine	33
	methamphetamine	6
	MDA	12
	MDMA	4
	cocaine	3
	benzoylecgonine	5
	morphine	9
	6-acetylmorphine	15
	codeine	25
	ethylmorphine	4
	diazepam	70
	7-aminoflunitrazepam	17
Chèze et al. [23]	alprazolam	0.5
	bromazepam	1–2
	clobazam	1
	clonazepam	0.5
	7-aminoclonazepam	1
	diazepam	1
	estazolam	0.5
	flunitrazepam	1
	7-aminoflunitrazepam	0.5
	lorazepam	2
	loprazolam	2
	lormetazepam	1
	midazolam	1
	nitrazepam	2
	7-aminonitrazepam	5
	nordazepam	1
	oxazepam	1
	prazepam	2
	temazepam	1
	tetrazepam	10
	triazolam	0.5
	zolpidem	1
	zopiclone	1

TABLE 8.3 (continued)
Examples for Multianalyte Screening Using LC-MS/MS

Reference	Analytes	Limit of Quantification (pg/mg)
Villain et al. [24]	alprazolam	1
	bromazepam	5
	clobazam	2
	7-aminoclonazepam	2
	diazepam	2
	7-aminoflunitrazepam	1
	lorazepam	5
	lormetazepam	2
	midazolam	0.5
	nordazepam	2
	oxazepam	1
	temazepam	1
	tetrazepam	5
	triazolam	0.5
	zaleplon	1
	zolpidem	0.5

The progress in sensitivity is also demonstrated by the fact that concentrations are now usually given in pg/mg. Chèze et al. [23] and Villain et al. [24] described independently the examinations of selected compounds in hair, which is very interesting in cases of drug-facilitated crime (DFC) like sexual assault. The progress in this field was even accelerated when data systems where offered supporting the screening on more than 100 targets in one run. Thieme and Sachs [25] reported on a system where hair can be screened at the same time on neuroleptics, antidepressants, opioids, narcotics, stimulants, hallucinogens, and benzodiazepines. As examples, the lists for neuroleptics/antidepressants and opioids are shown in Table 8.4.

An example for a screening is shortly described in the following six to eight steps:

1. 50 mg hair cut to pieces of 1-mm length
2. 2 ml methanol, 4-h sonication
3. 1 ml methanol phase dried
4. Reconstituted in 50-μl mobile phase
5. Installation of modules depending on the question (e.g., neuroleptics/antidepressants/opioids for DFC cases)
6. Injection 10 μl, screening over all substances
7. Additional injection, confirmation with qualifier
8. (optional) Segmental analysis

Table 8.4
Target Ions of Three Modules Typically Chosen for Screening Cases of Drug-Facilitated Crime

Antidepressants/Neuroleptics	Benzodiazepines	Opioids
amisulprid	alprazolam	heroin
amitriptylin		6-acetylmorphine
benperidol	bromazepam	morphine
citalopram	hydroxy-bromazepam	buprenorphine
clozapine		codeine
chlorpromazin	clobazam	dihydrocodeine
chlorprotrixen	norclobazam	
clomipramin		methadone
clotiapin	flurazepam	EDDP
desipramin	2-hydroxyethylflurazepam	
dibenzepin	desalkylflurazepam	fentanyl
dothiepine		alfentanil
doxepin	nordazepam	remifentanil
fluoxetine	diazepam	sufentanil
flupirtin	oxazepam	
fluvoxamin	temazepam	tilidine
haloperidol		nortilidine
hydroxyzin	nitrazepam	
imipramin		pentazocine
levomepromazin	flunitrazepam	pethidine
maprotilin	7-amino-flunitrazepam	phenazocine
mirtazapin	acetamido-flunitrazepam	pipamperone
melperon		piritramide
moclobemid	clonazepam	propoxyphene
nordoxepin	7-amino-clonazepam	
nortriptyline		
olanzapin	tetrazepam	
opipramol		
paroxetin	midazolam	
perazin	triazolam	
promazin	lorazepam	
promethazin	lormetazepam	
prothipendyl		
quetiapin		
reboxetin		
risperidon		
sertralin		
sulpirid		
thioridazin		
tiaprid		
trazodon		
trimipramin		
venlafaxin		

Table 8.4 (continued)
Target Ions of Three Modules Typically Chosen for Screening Cases of Drug-Facilitated Crime

Antidepressants/Neuroleptics	Benzodiazepines	Opioids
zaleplon		
ziprasidon		
zolpidem		
zopiclon		
zotepin		
zuclopenthixol		

The actual screening reaches to step 6. It may end in a result shown in Figure 8.1. In the chosen example, the screening of the hair proved an abuse of piritramide by a male nurse working in an intensive-care unit. Particularly, the screening of opioids including piritramide and fentanyl derivatives has been successful in cases where medical doctors and clinical staff had to be examined because drugs had been stolen in the unit. In the case of positive findings, a second injection is needed, where the transitions of the alleged analytes are recorded together with one or two qualifier transitions (step 7). The injection amount allows sufficient confirmations without additional extractions of hair.

In many cases of rape or other sexual assault, a positive result leads to further examinations (step 8), which may end in a one-hair segmental analysis, as described in Chapter 5.

8.5 CRIME CASES SOLVED BY SCREENING HAIR USING LC-MS/MS

Our most spectacular case solved by hair screening took place in 2005, when a professional child minder was suspected of giving drugs to calm children down. Some parents observed that their children were sleepy or sometimes drowsy when they came from the child minder and recovered during the day without going to sleep. It took a while before one of the consulted doctors asked for a hair analysis because he could not explain the symptoms. Surprisingly, high concentrations of amitriptyline and nortriptyline were found in the hair of the first child (Figure 8.2), accompanied by small concentrations of diphenhydramine and promethazine.

Later in the proceedings of this case, it was reported that the child had also been administered alimemazine, which was not detected. This demonstrates the difference between general unknown screening with full-scan spectra and a target screening, where only chosen transitions are recorded. In the case of a full-scan screening, an unknown peak could at least have signaled the presence of alimemazine. Target screenings only record the transitions in the lists of the modules. Alimemazine was not in the module of neuroleptics/antidepressants because it is no longer sold as a narcotic drug for children in Germany, but it is in France. When it became known that alimemazine had been administered to the children, it was also found in their hair (Figure 8.3).

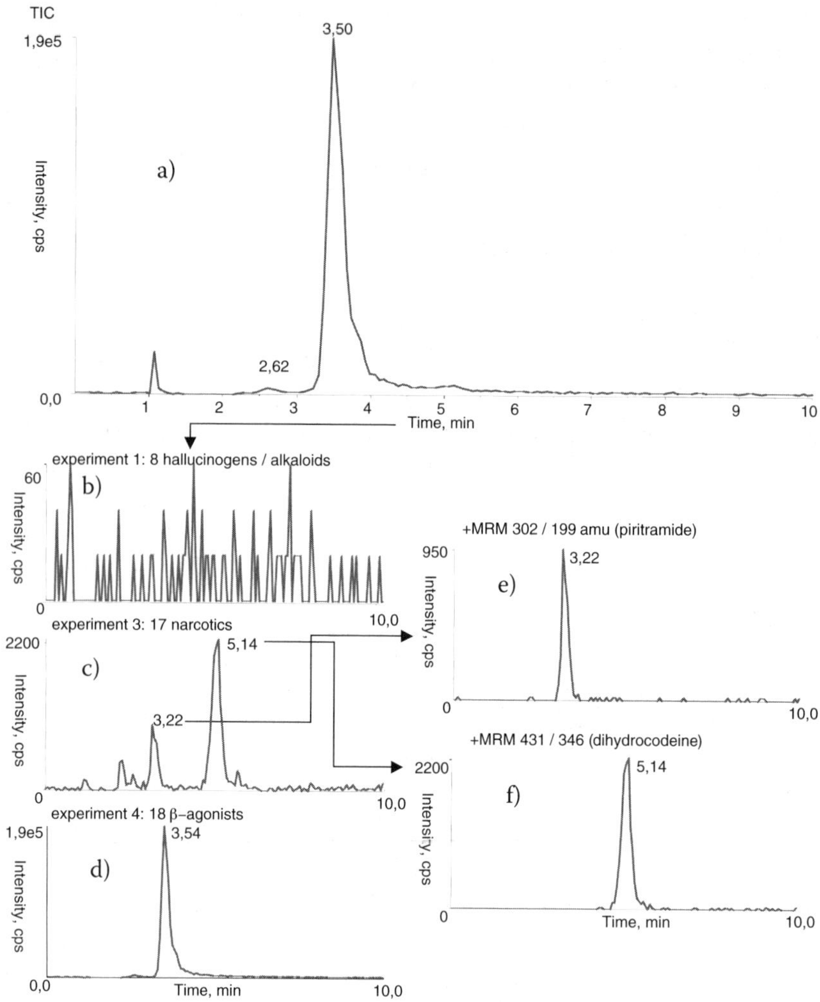

FIGURE 8.1 Example for a target screen with hallucinogens, narcotics, and β-agonists as chosen modules (lists of target analytes).

When the parents of the other children were alerted to the results, they also asked for a hair analysis. The hair of 29 out of 41 children was positive on amitriptyline and nortriptyline. The concentrations differed from the low pg/mg range to 20 ng/mg, depending on the duration of the child's stay with the child minder. Additionally, Z- and E-isomers of OH-amitriptyline and OH-nortriptyline could be detected at amitriptyline concentrations higher 30 pg/mg. This case demonstrates very well how the high sensitivity of the technique leads from the general screening to a detailed target analysis, where the sensitivity can be used for metabolite examinations or to estimate the number of drug administrations. Figure 8.4 shows quite well that the administration was not permanent but at least five times, with breaks in between.

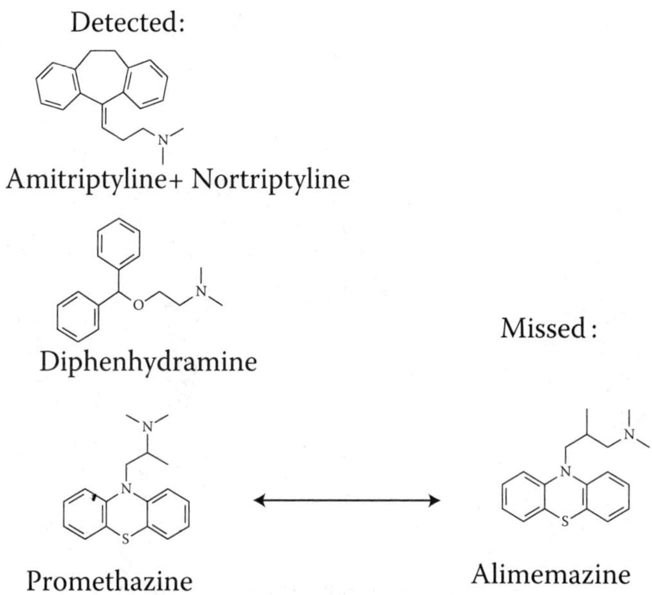

FIGURE 8.2 Detected and undetected substances in a child's hair after administration by a child minder.

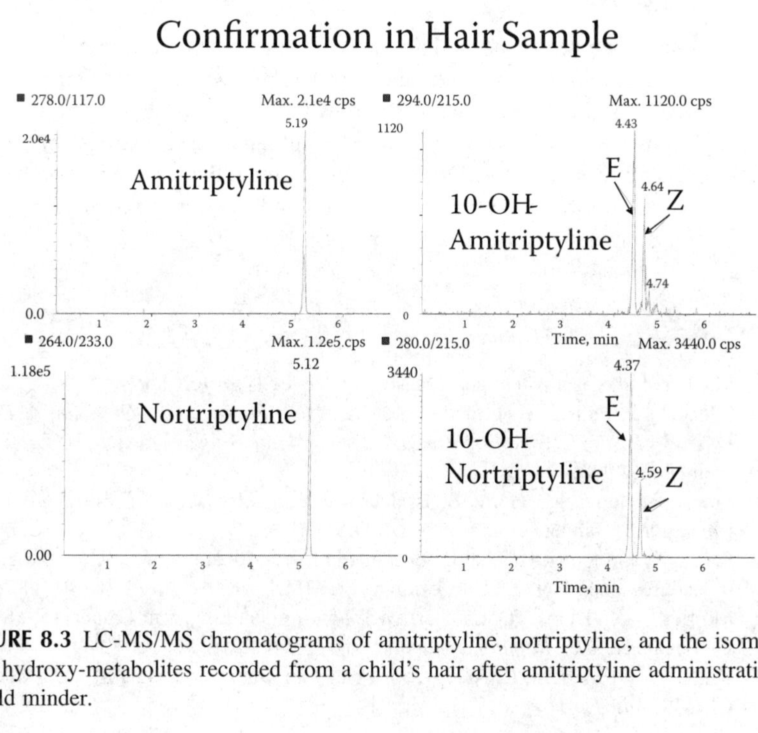

FIGURE 8.3 LC-MS/MS chromatograms of amitriptyline, nortriptyline, and the isomers of their hydroxy-metabolites recorded from a child's hair after amitriptyline administration by a child minder.

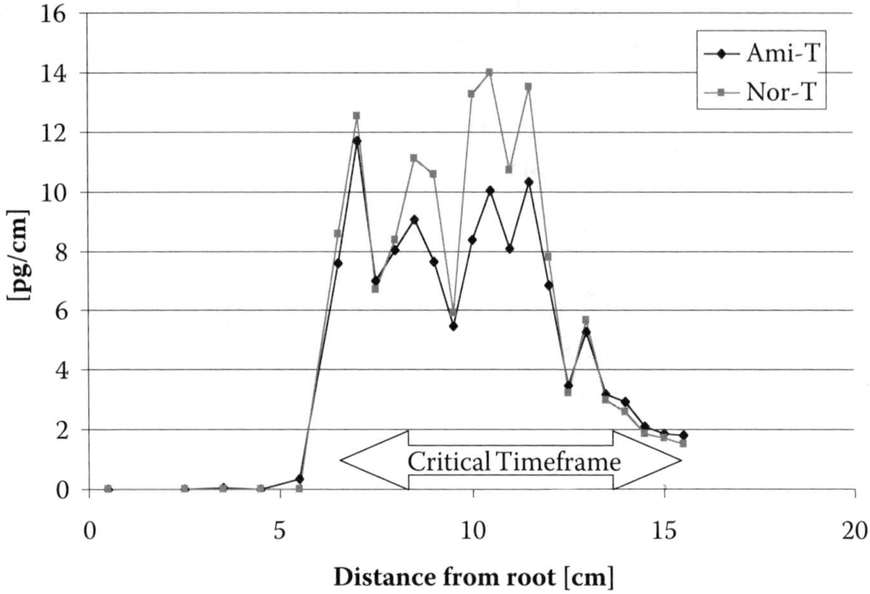

FIGURE 8.4 Amitriptyline and nortriptyline concentration in a single hair, examined in sections of 2.5-mm length, related to the alleged time of administration of amitriptyline.

8.6 CONCLUSIONS

The general unknown screening on hair analysis can only be performed as a target screening. Using immunochemical methods or GC-MS/MS, the number of targets is limited because of the decreasing sensitivity with the increasing number of targets. But the high sensitivity of LC-MS/MS allows a multianalyte screening of more than 100 substances at the same time. Once a target is found, the sensitivity can be used to obtain detailed information about the duration and intensity of administration as well as about the metabolism of the parent drug.

REFERENCES

1. Moeller, M.R., Sachs, H., and Pragst, F., Chapter 13 of this book.
2. Pfleger, K., Maurer, H.H., and Weber, A., *Mass Spectral and GC Data of Drugs, Poisons, Pesticides, Pollutants, and Their Metabolites*, Wiley-VCH Publishers, Weinheim, 2000.
3. Pragst, F., Herler, M., Herre, S., Erxleben, B.T., and Rothe, M., *UV-Spectra of Toxic Compounds*, Happenheim: Verlag, Dr. Dieter Helm, 2001.
4. Sachs, H. and Kintz, P., Testing for drugs in hair: critical review of chromatographic procedures since 1992, *J. Chromatogr. B*, 173, 147, 1998.
5. Mortier, K.A., Dams, R., Lambert, W.E., De Letter, E.A., Van Calenbergh, S., and De Leenheer, A.P., *Rapid Commun. Mass Spectrom.*, 16, 865, 2002.
6. Kintz, P. and Mangin, P., Analysis of opiates in human hair with FPIA, EMIT, and GC/MS, *Adli Tip Dergisi*, 7, 129, 1991.

7. Spiehler, V., Hair analysis by immunological methods from the beginning to 2000, *Forensic Sci. Int.*, 107, 249, 2000.
8. Anon., Statement of the Society of Hair Testing concerning the examination of drugs in human hair, *Forensic Sci. Int.*, 84, 3, 1997.
9. Lachenmeier, K., Musshoff, F., and Madea, B., Determination of opiates and cocaine in hair using automated enzyme immunoassay screening methodologies followed by gas chromatographic-mass spectrometric (GC-MS) confirmation, *Forensic Sci. Int.*, 159, 189, 2006.
10. Baumgartner, A.M., Jones, P.F., Baumgartner, W.A., and Black, C.T., Radioimmunoassay of hair for determining opiate-abuse histories, *J. Nucl. Med.*, 20, 748, 1979.
11. Cirimele, V., Kintz, P., and Ludes, B., Screening for forensically relevant benzodiazepines in human hair by GC/MS-neg. ion-CI, *J. Chromatogr. B*, 700, 119, 1997.
12. Paterson, S., McLachlan-Troup, N., Cordero, R., Dohnal, M., and Carman, S., Qualitative screening for drugs of abuse using GC/MS, *J. Anal. Toxicol.*, 25, 203, 2001.
13. Gentili, S., Cornetta, M., and Macchia, T., Rapid screening procedure based on headspace solid-phase microextraction and gas chromatography-mass spectrometry for the detection of many recreational drugs in hair, *J. Chromatogr. B*, 801, 289, 2004.
14. Kintz, P., Tracqui, A., and Mangin, P., Detection of drugs in human hair for clinical and forensic applications, *Int. J. Leg. Med.*, 105, 1, 1992.
15. Moeller, M.R., Drug detection in hair by chromatographic procedures, *J. Chromatogr. B*, 580, 125, 1992.
16. Musshoff, F., Lachenmeier, D.W., Kroener, L., and Madea, B., Automated headspace solid-phase dynamic extraction for the determination of amphetamines and synthetic designer drugs in hair samples, *J. Chromatogr. A*, 958, 231, 2002.
17. Uhl, M., Determination of drugs in hair using GC/MS/MS, *Forensic Sci. Int.*, 84, 281, 1997.
18. Negrusz, A. and Gaensslen, R.E., Analytical developments in toxicological investigation of drug-facilitated sexual assault, *Anal. Bioanal. Chem.*, 376, 1192, 2003.
19. Kintz, P., Cirimele, V., Jamey, C., and Ludes, B., Testing for GHB in hair by GC/MS/MS after a single exposure, *J. Forensic Sci.*, 48, 1, 2003.
20. Kronstrand, R., Nyström, I., Strandberg, J., and Druid, H., Screening for drugs of abuse in hair with ion spray LC-MS-MS, *Forensic Sci. Int.*, 145, 183, 2004.
21. El-Mahjoub, A. and Staub, C., Determination of benzodiazepines in human hair by on-line high-performance liquid chromatography using a restricted access extraction column, *Forensic Sci. Int.*, 123, 17, 2001.
22. Maurer, H.H., Multi-analyte procedures for screening and quantification of drugs in blood, plasma, or serum by liquid chromatography: single stage or tandem mass spectrometry (LC-MS or LC-MS-MS) relevant to clinical and forensic toxicology, *Clin. Biochem.*, 38, 310, 2005.
23. Chèze, M., Duffort, G., Deveaux, M., and Pépin, G., Hair analysis by liquid chromatography-tandem mass spectrometry in toxicological investigation of drug-facilitated crimes, *Forensic Sci. Int.*, 153, 3, 2005.
24. Villain, M., Concheiro, M., Cirimele, V., and Kintz, P., Screening method for benzodiazepines and hypnotics in hair at pg/mg level by LC-MS-MS, *J. Chromatogr. B*, 825, 72, 2005.
25. Thieme, D. and Sachs, H., Improved screening capabilities in forensic toxicology by application of liquid chromatography–tandem mass spectrometry, *Anal. Chim. Acta*, 483, 171, 2003.

26. Smink, B.E., Brandsma, J.E., Dijkhuizen, A., Lusthof, K.J., de Gier, J.J., Egberts, A.C.G., and Uges, D.R.A., Quantitative analysis of 33 benzodiazepines, metabolites and benzodiazepine-like substances in whole blood by liquid chromatography–(tandem) mass spectrometry, *J. Chromatogr. B*, 811, 13, 2004.

9 Clinical Applications of Hair Analysis

Simona Pichini, Óscar García-Algar, and Rafael de la Torre

CONTENTS

9.1 INTRODUCTION

Up to the 1980s, the presence and the disposition of a drug in the human body, and its eventual association with clinical effects, was typically obtained by plasma and urine testing, since it was not always possible or desirable (too difficult or invasive) to sample other biological matrices and fluids. However, in the last two decades, the measurement of drug concentration in fluids and matrices other than blood and urine (the so-called nonconventional fluids and matrices) has gained increasing importance.[1] On the one hand, improved technology (noninvasive dedicated devices for sample collection, different possibilities of extraction procedures, and new analytical methods) has made possible the measurement of minute quantities of substances extracted from complex biological matrices. On the other hand, it appeared that the determination of drug and metabolite concentrations in nonconventional human body materials might be useful for two principal applications: firstly, the possibility of determining pharmacokinetic parameters at the target organ and target concentration intervention; secondly, and most importantly, the application of the information obtained by drug testing in nonconventional fluids and matrices not only in forensic toxicology, but also in clinical settings.

In particular, clinical applications of hair analysis have received enormous attention, largely because of several advantages over testing methodologies employing body fluids such as urine or serum:

1. Drugs and metabolites remain sequestered in the hair shaft with no observed time degradation, providing a window of detection that is much wider (on the order of weeks to several months) than that of serum or urine, in which drug levels decrease rapidly over a relatively short period of time (hours to days).
2. Hair collection is simple, noninvasive, and replicable for eventual confirmation of the original results.
3. There is low potential for evasion or manipulation of results from hair testing.
4. There is a low risk of disease transmission in the handling of samples.
5. Hair samples are stable indefinitely and very difficult to manipulate to alter their drug content.
6. Results from a hair analysis can allow a distinction between low, moderate, and heavy consumers of a specified substance.

Furthermore, since hair grows at an average rate of 1.0 to 1.3 cm/month, it is theoretically possible to extrapolate a record of eventual drug usage by segmental hair analysis.[2] Since the major application of drug testing in hair has traditionally been the detection of past or chronic consumption of drugs of abuse, a crucial problem has been the differentiation of passive exposure from consumption, especially in the case of smoked drugs.[3] However, at present the problem of external drug contamination appears to have been successfully overcome.[4–6] Another controversial issue in hair analysis is the interpretation of dose and time relationships. Whereas some authors presented data indicating a linear relationship between drug dose and amount of parent drug and metabolites found in hair,[7,8] some others showed the lack of dose-concentration association, advocating intersubject variability of drug incorporation in hair, drug diffusion along the hair shaft with time, and finally incorporation of drug into hair by multiple mechanisms (i.e., through sweat or sebum).[9,10] Nonetheless, it seems apparent that hair analysis can distinguish categorized patterns of drug consumption.[11]

Different clinical applications of hair analysis published in the last decade are presented and discussed in the following sections.

9.2 HAIR ANALYSIS IN PSYCHIATRIC PATIENTS

Substance abuse within the mentally ill population is common, and at the same time, psychiatric symptoms are frequently seen in drug-dependent individuals.[12] Drug testing can document substance abuse, generally denied or misreported, and help the clinician to achieve a more accurate diagnosis when all other sources of information are negative. A screening test, which can cover the larger possible time window, may be useful at the time of first psychiatric exploration and later in treatment. Shearer et al.[13] proposed, among other possibilities, hair testing for abused drugs in psychiatric patients as an alternative matrix with a wide surveillance window.

Hair analysis for amphetamines, cocaine, cannabis, opiates, and phencyclidine was performed in individuals with schizophrenia to verify self-reported substance abuse.[14] A 3-cm hair segment proximal to the scalp was examined by radioimmunoassay to investigate drug use in the preceding 3 months. Of 203 participants, only 16.3% self-reported illicit substance abuse, 12.5% had a positive urine drug test, while a 31% had a positive hair analysis. Although hair testing is not a good biomarker of very recent substance use, in this study a roughly doubled detection of substance use was observed in comparison with urinalysis. Importantly, the majority of these mentally ill individuals found hair sampling as an acceptable and nonintrusive procedure, which made easier procurement of a biological matrix in these particular individuals.

In schizophrenics, an analysis of factors associated with medication noncompliance revealed that comorbid substance abuse is among the most important ones and that the combination of medication noncompliance and illicit drug use was significantly associated with the likelihood of committing violent acts.[15] Hair testing for opiates, cocaine, methamphetamine, and phencyclidine in the proximal 1.2-cm segment has been used to examine association between drug abuse in the previous month and antipsychotic medication adherence (tested by urinalysis) in predicting criminal recidivism among mentally ill parolees (about 74% of initial participants).[16] Since the majority of hair samples tested positive for cocaine (55% versus 8.1% for opiates, 2% for methamphetamine, and 2% phencyclidine), subsequent analyses focused on this drug specifically. A significant relationship was shown between cocaine use (hair positive to cocaine) and the likelihood of being returned to custody during a one-year follow-up period. Among cocaine users, antipsychotic medication adherence significantly reduced the risk of recidivism by 26%.

Similarly, it has been proposed that testing for the presence of cannabinoids and amphetamines in hair samples from individuals with psychotic disorders, as their consumption may contribute to the etiology of the disease. Preliminary results in a small population did not allow the researchers to draw definitive conclusions on this possible application.[17]

9.3 HAIR ANALYSIS IN EPILEPTIC MANAGEMENT

Hair analysis of antiepileptic drugs (AEDs) offers the possibility of verifying drug-taking behavior in epileptic patients retrospectively over the preceding weeks or months. This has stimulated the investigation of hair analysis of AEDs to assess therapeutic compliance in treated individuals. Early data on drugs such as phenobarbital and carbamazepine have stimulated further investigation in recent years.[18]

Carbamazepine and phenytoin were detected in the respective ranges of 0.6 to 63.7 ng/mg and 6.0 to 157.8 ng/mg in hair of 14 outpatients receiving either drug. However, different drug dosages, the lack of segmental hair analysis, and concomitant plasma concentration allowed proof of intake, but excluded the possibility of assessing continued compliance.[19] Nevertheless, in a highly supervised inpatient population receiving an unchanged dosage of carbamazepine, Williams et al.[20] demonstrated that the intrapatient variability in drug concentration from different hair segments was quite small ($15.0 \pm 5.2\%$) and independent of administered daily dosage. Such a relatively small variability induced the authors to suggest using hair analysis as a noninvasive tool to assess drug-taking behavior, although the ability of predicting drug dosage from a hair concentration was quite poor.

The good relation between the prescribed dose and individual hair concentration for carbamazepine prompted Williams et al.[21] to assess AED-taking behavior in pregnant women compared with nonpregnant female controls by hair analysis of carbamazepine and lamotrigine in 1-cm hair consecutive segments. Within-subject variance in hair concentration was higher in pregnant women than in controls (variance ratio for pregnant to nonpregnant women: 1.59, $p < 0.01$). Of the pregnant women, 15% showed a decline in drug concentration in the more proximal segments, suggesting reduction or discontinuation of medication for concerns over teratogenicity of AEDs.

9.4 HAIR ANALYSIS AS EVIDENCE OF PRENATAL AND POSTNATAL EXPOSURE TO DRUGS AND TOBACCO

Monitoring exposure to illicit and therapeutic drugs in a pediatric population is more difficult to perform than in adults because of the need for noninvasive or less invasive, yet highly sensitive, analytical methods to assess prenatal and postnatal exposure to drugs. This fact has stimulated the application of hair analysis in pediatrics in the last decade.[22]

Neonatal hair is a sensitive biological marker that can define cumulative exposure to drugs during the last months of intrauterine life.[23,24] Indeed, hair starts growing during the last three to four months of gestation, reflecting exposure for the last part of gestation. Although the detection window of prenatal exposure is smaller than for meconium, hair has the advantage of being available for as long as 4 to 5 months of postnatal life.[25] Nonetheless, hair samples, which can be obtained in newborns, are often a sparse amount, and collection in this particular case can be still considered "almost" invasive. Newborn hair samples are externally contaminated by the amniotic fluid, which not only reaches hair but also the fetus via the transdermal route.[22] Nevertheless this contamination should not be considered as external in the context of a diagnostic of intrauterine drug/tobacco exposure.

Cases of hair testing for confirmation of gestational exposures to different drugs of abuse and eventual association with birth outcomes have been recently reported by Vinner et al.[26] In a small group of neonates exposed to principal drugs of abuse, positivity to cannabinoids was detected in two exposed newborns, in one case with analytes under the limit of quantification and in the other with cannabinol at 0.5 ng/mg. In two other newborns, cocaine and ecgonine methylester (EME) were detected, in the first case with analytes under the limit of quantification and in the other with cocaine at 17.9 ng/mg and EME < 2 ng/mg. In 11 newborns from opiates-addicted mothers, 6-monoacetylmorphine (6-MAM) concentrations in hair ranged from 2 to 29 ng/mg, morphine from <2 to 3.1 ng/mg, and codeine from <2 to 3.47 ng/mg. These data on chronic fetal exposure to opiates contributed in estimating the occurrence of neonatal withdrawal syndrome.[27] Such occurrence seemed to appear more frequently after fetal exposure to an association of heroin and opiates used in therapeutics of drug addicts (i.e., methadone and buprenorphine).

The Canadian group of Gideon Koren and Julia Klein[28] has been working extensively in hair testing of cocaine in combination with nicotine and cotinine and fatty acid esters (as biomarkers of alcohol consumption) in newborns. This was justified by the dramatic increase in the misuse of cocaine in the general population, including women at reproductive age, and the coexistence of a high prevalence of cigarette and alcohol consumption besides cocaine abuse.[29] Using neonatal hair testing for cocaine (amount in the range from tenth to tens ng/mg hair), these authors could find in Toronto a prevalence rate of 6.2% fetal exposure to cocaine in the years 1990–1991 that rose to 27.4% in the year 2000.[29,30] In the last survey, the authors could also detect through hair testing rates a positivity of 14.1% for opiates, 15.9% for cannabis, 9% for amphetamine, 14.3% for methamphetamine, and finally 10% for barbiturates.

Interestingly, in agreement with other studies that evidenced a concentration-response relationship between hair cocaine concentrations and microcephaly or impaired neonatal neurologic function,[31,32] infants exposed to cocaine *in utero*, ascertained by hair testing, were of significantly lower birth weight and birth length.[29]

Whereas adverse fetal effects of cocaine are well recognized, there is wide variability in the health outcomes of exposed infants that should be explored and included in models of developmental outcomes along with drug exposure. Among the issues to be explored are medical complications, social/environmental risks, and drug bioavailability in fetus.[33]

In this context, different concentrations of cocaine and cannabinoids in hair of dizygotic pairs of newborn twins suggested that placenta may have a major role in modulating the amounts of drug reaching the fetus. Thus, the rate and the extent of placental transport of cocaine are important determinants of fetal protection and the outcomes following birth.[34] The importance of the placental role for cocaine transfer to the fetus and consequent relation to neonatal somatometry was evident also in a cohort of 251 predominantly African-American newborns from addicted mothers. Subjects were categorized for hair concentrations of benzoylecgonine (BZE), either coming from maternal cocaine (hydrolyzed to BZE during sample preparation) or native BZE arising from cocaine metabolism, deposited in the fetal hair follicle. The range of BZE concentrations was 0.099 to 23.3 ng/mg of hair, with 79% of samples displaying BZE concentrations lower than 5 ng/mg of hair. In 18 mother/infant pairs tested, the hair BZE ratio (maternal to neonatal) varied from 0.5 to 8.9 in 13 pairs, but in 5 newborns there was no evidence of hair BZE despite high BZE concentrations in maternal hair, stressing the role of transplacental passage. After controlling for gestational age, higher BZE concentrations significantly correlated with smaller head circumference ($p < 0.03$) and birth weight ($p < 0.01$).[35]

Another confounder in adverse outcomes due to intrauterine exposure to cocaine is cigarette smoke. Indeed, stratification of newborns exposed to cocaine by maternal cigarette smoking suggested that tobacco smoking accounted for most of the variability in somatometric measures.[29]

The assessment of chronic exposure to maternal active and passive cigarette smoke and birth outcomes has been the most frequent clinical application of neonatal hair testing for nicotine and cotinine in the last decade.[28,30] Well-established intervals have been reported for neonatal hair nicotine and cotinine to distinguish newborns from smoking mothers, from passive smokers, and from nonexposed nonsmokers (Table 9.1).[36,37] A higher incidence of premature delivery and decreased infant somatometry was observed in relation to prenatal exposure to smoke, assessed by nicotine and cotinine content in keratin matrix.[36,38,39]

Hair cotinine was shown to be the best biomarker when compared with hair nicotine to differentiate the three groups of newborns, and the results were directly associated with maternal cigarette consumption.[40] This is because hair nicotine concentration could only discriminate active maternal smoking.[39] Similar to tobacco, prenatal exposure to alcohol can result in a series of adverse fetal outcomes known as fetal alcohol spectrum disorders, including craniofacial dysmorphology, growth retardation, and neurodevelopmental deficits.[41] Analysis of fatty acid ethyl esters (FAEE), biomarkers of repeated exposure to ethanol, to identify *in utero*-exposed infants has been well established in meconium.[28] However, meconium exists only during the first two postnatal days. Chan et al.[28] postulated that by extending the use of FAEE analysis into neonatal hair, it might have been possible to increase the window of opportunity to confirm this suspicion in the immediate months after birth (when neonatal hair is still available). Up to now, the only attempt to use neonatal hair analysis of FAEE was that of Klein et al.,[42] who detected four fatty acid ethyl esters — ethyl myristate, ethyl palmitate, ethyl oleate, and ethyl stearate — for a total of 0.4 pmol/mg in a hair sample of a newborn girl from a social drinker, whose hair contained 2.6 pmol/mg.

In recent years, there has been a growing interest in using hair testing also during childhood to assess chronic postnatal exposure to illicit drugs and environmental tobacco smoke (ETS). One of the main contexts of this application is in child-custody cases, where one parent (or caregiver) may be accused of exposing the child passively or actively to any drug. In this application, the determination of drug exposure is required, not necessarily drug use, and thus, as in the case of newborns, the problem of environmental drug contamination is of minor importance. Indeed, just the simple passive exposure to drugs of abuse is of use in removing children from dangerous households or to alert social services.

Indeed, examining 37 hair samples of children from child protective services, Lewis et al.[43] found 15 samples positive to cocaine and benzoylecgonine that could be attributable to both active or passive exposure. In this context, Smith and Kidwell,[44] examining hair from cocaine users' children (found cocaine concentration range: 0.2 to 14.4 ng/mg), asserted that, even in presence of high cocaine concentration in hair from young and small children, ingestion may not be the reason for that concentration, but more likely is the result of hand-to-mouth activity and frequent handling by parents. The authors did not exclude intentional cocaine use among older children, while they discarded intrauterine exposure, since all the examined children were one year or older. In contrast with this last affirmation (previous authors did not declare how many centimeters from infants were examined to discard prenatal exposure), both prenatal and postnatal chronic exposure to cocaine were advocated in a 15-month-old child, admitted to the emergency department unconscious and with apparent generalized seizures, whose urine was found positive to cocaine. Values of 10.5 and 57.5 ng cocaine/mg hair were found in the proximal 2-cm and in the distal 5-cm segments (with benzoylecgonine concentration of 2.2 and

TABLE 9.1
Concentration of Hair Nicotine and Cotinine (ng/mg hair) in Newborns, Children, and Mothers According to Reported Smoking Habit and Exposure

Population	Nonexposure	Exposure to ETS	Exposure to Parental Smoke	References
		Newborns		
Hair nicotine	0.41 ± 0.47	0.29 ± 0.25	2.41 ± 5.35	36, 37, 60
Hair cotinine	0.26 ± 0.24	0.62 ± 0.72	2.81 ± 4.74	36, 37, 60
		Infants and Children		
Hair nicotine	1.3 ± 1.7	6.8 ± 2.1	15.4 ± 6.7	50
Hair cotinine	0.12 (0.06–0.48) [a]		0.69 ± 0.74 asthmatic children	37
			0.40 ± 0.38 nonasthmatic children	
			1.33 (0.61–2.39) [a]	49
		0.07 white children		51
		0.25 Afro-American children		
Mothers	**Nonexposure**	**Exposure to ETS**	**Active Smoker**	
Hair nicotine			13.32 (3.95) [b]	59
	1.2 (0.4) [b]	3.2 (0.8) [b]	19.2 (4.9) [b]	37, 60
	2.80 (0–2.5-cm segment) [c]	4.30 (0–2.5-cm segment) [c]	2.80 (0–2.5-cm segment) [c]	
	3.84 (2.5–5-cm segment) [c]	6.06 (2.5–5-cm segment) [c]	11.08 (2.5–5-cm segment) [c]	
			14.40 (2.5–5-cm segment) [c]	
Hair cotinine	0.3 (0.06) [a]	0.9 (0.3) [a]	1.18 (0.28) [a]	59
			6.3 (4.0) [a]	60

[a] Median (25th, 75th percentile).
[b] Scanning electron microscope.
[c] Geometric mean.

7.7 ng/mg), respectively, with the most distal segment containing 55.9 ng/mg cocaine and 7.0 ng/mg benzoylecgonine.[45] Confronted with these results, the child's mother admitted to cocaine consumption even during pregnancy and to the continuous presence of cocaine in the household, since her other 4-year-old child was also found positive to cocaine in hair (1 and 5.4 ng/mg in the proximal and distal segments, respectively).

Passive environmental exposure to cocaine leading to positive hair testing of 16 ng/mg cocaine and 0.6 ng/mg benzoylecgonine in a 6-year-old child has been also reported by De Giorgio et al.[46] Concerns regarding eventual health effects of chronic exposure to cocaine during childhood and the general increase in cocaine abuse in recent years prompted some Spanish investigators to introduce hair testing for cocaine and other drugs of abuse to all children attending the emergency care in cases where the physician perceives a high index of suspicion.[45,47] A first application of this protocol was the previous case of the 15-month-old child, and a second concerned a chronic exposure to cocaine (1.3 ng/mg cocaine and 0.4 benzoylecgonine in 4-cm proximal hair segment and 4.6 ng/mg cocaine and 0.5 benzoylecgonine in 4-cm distal hair segment) evidenced in an 11-month-old child admitted to the emergency department for acute MDMA (3,4-methylenedioxymethamphetamine) intoxication.[45] A similar approach of submitting children from compromised environments to hair testing for drugs of abuse was proposed by Canadian investigators.[24] They detected several cases of children's exposure in the household by hair testing, such as that of a 5-year-old boy acutely intoxicated by methylphenidate, whose hair was highly positive to cocaine, resembling the above-reported case of MDMA intoxication in an infant chronically exposed to cocaine.

Exposure to environmental tobacco smoke (ETS) is a major cause of morbidity among children.[48] During the last decade, hair testing for nicotine and cotinine has been used as a complement to serum and urinary cotinine for detecting exposure to cigarette smoke with a longer time-window. The promise was that of rendering assessment more objective, since hair testing accounts for a mean repeated exposure, whereas serum and urine provide information on punctual exposure in the days immediately previous to analysis. As a matter of fact, Klein and Koren[37] interestingly demonstrated that, in children and adolescents (2 to 18 years of age), similar exposure to cigarette smoke resulted in twofold higher accumulation of cotinine in the hair of asthmatic subjects as compared with nonasthmatics, with similar urinary cotinine concentrations when standardized per milligram of creatinine (Table 9.1). The authors postulated a lower clearance rate of body dose of nicotine, and therefore a higher systemic exposure to ETS, in the asthmatics. Determination of hair cotinine in 291 children (birth to 3 years of age) proved useful in deriving a simple and specific three-question model that can be used in pediatric offices to identify children at risk of ETS. Indeed the three questions — "Does the mother smoke?" "Do others smoke?" "Do others smoke inside?" — proved to be good predictors of hair cotinine in children from both smoking and nonsmoking mothers.[49]

In the same way, hair nicotine could statistically discriminate nursery-school infants not exposed, occasionally exposed, and regularly exposed to parental smoke.[50] Racial differences in exposure to ETS were found by hair cotinine: 0.25 ng/mg in African-American children as compared with 0.07 ng/mg in white children and associated with tobacco-related illnesses, despite the fact that African-American children showed a lower reported exposure.[51] This last evidence enlightens the well-known unreliability of self-reported questionnaires, where parents tend to underreport their children's exposure to any drugs.[52] Conversely, accurate assessment of both acute and chronic exposure of young children to drugs of abuse and tobacco smoke through the objective measure of a biomarker is of major importance, since it provides the basis for appropriate immediate treatment, adequate medical follow-up, and social intervention for child care.

9.5 HAIR NICOTINE AS A MARKER OF ACTIVE AND PASSIVE EXPOSURE TO TOBACCO

It has been extensively demonstrated that hair concentration of nicotine is a reliable marker to assess smoking status, and smoking behavior history can be verified by analyzing axial distribution of this substance along the length of scalp hair. Several investigations have been carried out by the Japanese group of Uematsu, Mizuno, and coworkers. These scientists were the first to demonstrate that nicotine concentration in subsequent segments of the hair shaft positively correlated with self-reported smoking behavior,[53] and on the basis of their experience, a baseline value of 5 ng/mg hair nicotine (less conservative than that of 2 ng/mg proposed in 1992 by Kintz et al.[54]) was set to distinguish active smokers from nonsmokers. Fair results were obtained by the same authors when measurement of hair nicotine was applied to verify clinical outcomes of smoking-cessation trials including the aid of nicotine chewing gum.[55] Indeed, the concentration of nicotine decreased along the 1-cm hair segments in agreement with daily reported number of smoked cigarettes and consumed chewing gum. However, even when participants succeeded in smoking cessation (as measured by plasma concentration of thiocyanate), nicotine concentration in hair segment proximal to the scalp significantly overcame the established cutoff of 5 ng/mg. In the authors' opinion, this can be due to nicotine's slow dissociation from hair follicle cells. In reality, it must be emphasized that uncertainties regarding the stage of hair growth, the hair tuft that has grown since the last drug consumption, and cosmetic hair treatment must be taken into account.[56]

Hair nicotine was measured in workers exposed to environmental tobacco smoke (ETS) to define different levels of occupational exposure and the effectiveness of recent smoking policies toward banning smoking in the workplace.[57] Indeed, hair nicotine in hospitality workers significantly varied according to the smoke-free policy at the workplace.[58] Concerned by the fact that the presence of nicotine in hair could have been the result not only of both passive and active exposure to tobacco, but also of external deposition of the substance from the environment, Canadian researchers[59] proposed hair cotinine as a more effective long-term biomarker of smoking history. They applied the evaluation of hair cotinine not only in newborns and children (as reported above), but also in adults. A significant correlation ($r = 0.57$, $p < 0.05$) was found between nicotine daily intake and hair concentration of cotinine in healthy smokers with a constant smoking habit in the previous years. However, the same group of authors[60] admitted that this correlation could not be found in smoking pregnant women, and they attributed this result to changes and misreporting in smoking habits during pregnancy. In the attempt to solve this lack of correlation, the same group of authors[28] recently used segmental hair analysis of nicotine and cotinine in hair from pregnant women and observed a trend toward decreasing hair nicotine values during pregnancy without any reduction in smoking and in hair cotinine. An increased nicotine metabolism was supposed, in accordance with other works. Significantly decreased nicotine concentration in two subsequent hair segments were also found by Pichini et al.[39] when examining nonsmoking and smoking pregnant women (Table 9.1). As a final consideration, it has to be said that even if both nicotine and cotinine in hair have been shown to be good biomarkers of tobacco exposure, the amounts of cotinine in keratin matrix can be more than 10 times less than those of nicotine.[59,60] The need for more-sensitive and specific techniques for cotinine determination in this complex matrix, especially in the case of assessment of passive exposure to smoke, oriented the choice of investigators toward hair nicotine as reliable biomarker of long-term smoking history.[61]

9.6 DRUG ADDICTION AND OPIATE-MAINTENANCE PROGRAMS

Given the unreliability of self-reports of drug use, testing for illicit drugs is important in all situations where addiction has to be verified and for most treatment programs, i.e., when monitoring the progress of the patient and when assessing the effectiveness of particular interventions in controlled clinical trials.[62]

Pépin and Gaillard[11] first established a concordance between self-reported drug use and hair concentration of cocaine metabolites and heroin metabolites detected by gas chromatography-mass spectrometry (GC-MS). They found a good proportionality between the quantities of consumed drugs and hair concentration of 6-MAM for heroin intake and cocaine for its intake in the 2-cm hair segments of users. From all the gathered data, the authors could propose three different levels of consumption: low, medium, and high. In the case of heroin use, this corresponded to hair levels of 6-MAM corresponding to: lower than 2 ng/mg, between 2 and 10 ng/mg, and higher than 10 ng/mg, respectively. In the case of cocaine, low, medium, and high consumption corresponded to concentrations lower than 4, between 4 and 20, and higher than 20 ng/mg, respectively. In the years following this first proposal, hair analysis was tested for its usefulness in monitoring drug addiction, and contradictory results regarding association between analytical findings in hair and self-reported declarations were found in the international literature.

Generally speaking, when examining patients on substitution maintenance, the major advantage of hair versus urine is that multisectional analysis can be performed to verify both the previous drug history of patients before their admission to rehabilitation centers and the subsequent enforced abstinence. An early application of segmental hair analysis in drug abusers participating in a maintenance program was that of Strano-Rossi et al.[63] Examining hair samples cut into 2-cm length for their content of cocaine and morphine equivalents by radioimmunoassay, the history of drug addiction and progressive abstinence was obtained in 18 individuals. Cocaine equivalents ranged from thousands of ng/mg hair to hundreds or tens ng/mg; morphine equivalents varied from around 10 ng/mg to less than 1 ng/mg. In the majority of cases, a decrease in the concentration of both drugs from the distal to the proximal ends of the hair matched with the attempts of detoxifications of the subjects, with some cases of relapse evidenced by an increase in drug value in any of the central hair segments. In agreement with these preliminary data, in a group of eight subjects receiving buprenorphine maintenance, concentrations of 6-MAM, a marker of heroin consumption, ranged between 0.9 and 24.3 ng/mg hair before admission to treatment, while 6 months later concentration of 6-MAM varied between 0.0 and 4.8 ng/mg and that of buprenorphine between 0.12 and 0.53 ng/mg.[62]

In contrast with these results, segmental hair analysis of ten individuals entering in an intensive treatment with buprenorphine for opiate addiction did not succeed in accurately verifying discontinuation of opiate use.[64] Whereas hair data suggested that six out of ten subjects discontinued opiate use by the end of the study and three individuals reduced their use, weekly urinalysis demonstrated that only four subjects significantly reduced use, while others continued abuse at least on an intermittent basis. However, a criticism to this study is that the weekly time window used to compare findings from last-centimeter hair and those from urine was a short time interval for hair retesting due to slow hair growth during this period. In fact, as demonstrated by Sachs[56] in 1995, hair growth even from the shaved skin after a single dose of a certain drug cannot possibly contain the same concentration as hair after the same dose that has not been cut over a long period. Concentrations can even change during the hair growth in cases where the hair had been cut a couple of months before the hair sample was taken. This may lead to misinterpretations at low concentrations. Hence, when considering short time periods, urine is certainly a better indicator, while hair concentration expresses a mean value in "past period time" which should be at least 1 month.

Hair testing for buprenorphine was used not only to verify the compliance to its administration in detoxification centers, but also its abuse and following abstinence when passing to a methadone treatment. A 1-cm segmental hair analysis of an 11-cm hair lock from an addict receiving 16 mg buprenorphine/day for 3 years showed a constant concentration of buprenorphine (around 0.15 to 0.2 ng/mg) and norbuprenorphine (0.6 to 0.9 ng/mg), with a parent drug metabolite ratio close to 0.2. Then, the withdrawal treatment induced a decrease in hair concentration until the levels were undetectable.[65]

Apart from buprenorphine, maintenance programs are usually based on methadone treatment. Methadone assay of hair segments was shown to provide long-term histories of methadone intake under both controlled and noncontrolled conditions. Evidence that a dose relationship between hair drug levels and intake could exist was presented by Marsh et al.[66] Results of hair analysis by radioimmunoassay, expressed as ng methadone/mg hair, from drug users (range 0.20 to 10.63 ng/mg hair) were different when compared with a predetermined cutoff of 0.1 ng methadone/mg hair, obtained from the analysis of a known drug-free population (n = 23). Subsequently, when a GC-MS methodology was available for the detection of methadone and its metabolites, D,L-2-ethyl-1,5-dimethyl-3, 3-diphenylpyrrolinium (EDDP) and D,L-2-ethyl-5-methyl-3,3-diphenyl-1-pyrroline (EMDP), it was shown that in two subjects receiving 60 and 80 mg of methadone daily for at least last 6 months, hair concentrations of methadone were 10.1 ng/mg and 21.0 ng/mg, respectively. Those of EDDP were 0.5 ng/mg and 2.6 ng/mg, respectively, and EMDP was not detected.[67] In all nine specimens obtained from subjects under racemic methadone treatment in a detoxification center, *R*- and *S*-enantiomers of methadone and EDDP were identified with the following concentrations: 2.58 to 10.22, 1.89 to 9.53, 0.42 to 1.73, and 0.40 to 2.10 ng/mg for *R*-methadone, *S*-methadone, *R*-EDDP, and *S*-EDDP, respectively, suggesting a predominance of the *R* enantiomer of methadone in human hair.[68] Finally, Goldberger et al.[69] found concentrations of methadone in the range of 0 to 15 ng/mg and traces of EDDP in 18 outpatients from a detoxification center.

Notwithstanding all this positive evidence of the presence of methadone in hair of treated subjects, in 2001 Girod and Staub[70] demonstrated in 26 different individuals that there was no relationship between the administered dose and methadone and EDDP concentrations in hair, while there was a relationship for blood concentration. The study of Paterson et al.[71] on 60 subjects in methadone therapy supported the finding of Girod and Staub.[70] Also, in this case, no correlation was found irrespective of whether the methadone was administered orally or by the intravenous route. These last reports seriously questioned the potential usefulness of hair testing in assessing the compliance toward maintenance treatment.

Hair testing for drugs of abuse has been used to validate surveys of self-reported use in epidemiological studies looking for different characteristics of the population under analysis. As demonstrated in the below-reported studies, the use of hair drug value as an objective biomarker served to render more reliable the conclusions of different investigations and disclose hidden consumption.

In a study that examined whether neighborhood racial characteristics were associated with the underreporting of lifetime cocaine and crack use, hair testing was applied to objectively assay for cocaine use. A 3-cm proximal segment was analyzed to assess approximately the last 3 months of consumption. Of the individuals who tested positive for hair cocaine (n = 111 out of 322), only 18% reported past-month use, about 19% reported past-year use, and 27% reported lifetime use. When crossing these data with sociodemographic characteristics, responders from more segregated neighborhoods were more likely than those from diverse neighborhood to underreport drug use.[72] The problem of validity of declared drug use was also reported in a paper describing the comparison of household survey responses of cocaine and heroin use with hair tests in Puerto Rico.[73] Using hair results with a cutoff of 0.2 ng substance or metabolites per milligram hair as a gold standard, specificity of self-reports was higher than 98% for both drugs. However, the estimates of recent cocaine and heroin use based on 3-cm-segment hair tests were 13.7 and 2.9 times the rates generated from the interview reports. With the hair test results as the gold standard, the same authors[74] reported a better sensitivity of self-reported drug use (69.6 and 78.6% for reports of recent cocaine and heroin use, respectively) when switching from household residents to hard-core drug users in Puerto Rico. The conclusion was that infrequent drug users might be less prone to disclose their use of drugs than regular and heavy users. As a confirmation of this hypothesis, among 336 heroin users who tested positive for cocaine in hair, 34.2% did not report their recent cocaine use.[75] Disclosers had a mean value of 47.1 ng/mg hair cocaine, significantly greater than the mean level of 10.9 ng/mg for nondisclosers. Similarly, in a group of 179 homeless and transient adults in New York state, only 26% of 115 subjects whose proximal 1.5-cm hair segment tested positive for cocaine (at a cutoff of 0.2 ng/mg hair) admitted drug use in the previous month.[76] Once again, dependent subjects, eligible for treatment, were about four times as likely to admit drug consumption than those who were not dependent. Gathered together, all these data demonstrate that individuals with more severe drug problems were shown as more willing to report drug use.

Hair testing for cocaine was also successfully applied in a 5-year follow-up of treatment outcomes for cocaine dependence. A total of 546 hair specimens were collected and segmental analysis was performed for past drug history use. Self-reported drug use, which showed an overall agreement with hair analysis (80%), demonstrated that poorer long-term outcomes were related to the higher severity of the user's drug problem at treatment admission and to low treatment exposure.[77]

Likewise, the success of a treatment in 770 heroin and cocaine abusers was monitored by segmental hair analysis comparing hair concentration of cocaine and opiates in 403 subjects undergoing brief motivational intervention and 375 subjects who received basic information of treatment options. At the six-month follow-up, cocaine levels in hair were reduced by 29% (from a mean of 6.2 to 4.4 ng/mg) for the intervention group and only 4% (from 48.5 to 46.4 ng/mg) in the control group. Reductions in opiate concentration were similar for both groups: 29% (from a mean of 2.6 to 1.9 ng/mg) versus 25% (from 3.1 to 2.3 ng/mg).[78]

Self-reported illicit drug use compared with quantitative hair test results in 95 community-recruited young drug users in Amsterdam revealed a good agreement between reported amounts of cocaine, heroin, or methadone used and concentrations of these drugs or their metabolites in hair, with correlation coefficients ranging from 0.45 to 0.59 in the unadjusted analyses and from 0.63 to 0.87 when adjusting for hair color, ethnicity, and sex.[8] In the opinion of the authors, the different adjustments and the number of the recruited subjects led to better results than those obtained by Kintz et al.[9] when investigating the drug dose-response relationship in the hair of 20 subjects from a controlled heroin-maintenance program. With heroin doses ranging from 30 to 800 mg/day, hair concentration of heroin, 6-MAM, and morphine varied from 0 to 4.43, 0.38 to 10.11, and 0.71 to 5.20 ng/mg hair, respectively. No correlation between doses of administered drug and the total hair concentration of opiates was observed ($r = 0.346$). The importance of considering hair pigmentation when confirming drug use by hair analysis was reinforced by Ursitti et al.,[79] who sought to verify sensitivity of cocaine hair test in admitted users. Hair test was positive in 97% (37 out of 38 subjects) of the cases of people who refrained from drug consumption in the few days or months before test and had a negative urine analysis. Interestingly, the authors noted that although the individuals with black hair color had the lowest reported use (6.1 g cocaine/month), mean hair cocaine and benzoylecgonine concentrations were 183 and 8.9 ng/mg, respectively. Blond and brown hair color groups with similar reported use (16 g/month) presented hair cocaine concentrations of 7.3 and 36.2, respectively, while benzoylecgonine was 1.1 and 3.6 ng/mg, respectively.

As reported above, hair testing for cocaine and other drugs of abuse is mainly performed in populations with a certain degree of suspicion of drug consumption, which is identified by looking at an objective biomarker of drug misuse. However, hair testing has also been applied for screening in general populations, such as that of university students. A first study by Kidwell et al.[80] on a group of 158 college students from Alabama found a 6% cocaine use rate by hair analysis (cutoff: 0.05 ng/mg hair), greater than the 2% expected in this type of population when considering general interview surveys. However, since matched sweat analysis detected two times more use than did hair (12% with a cutoff of 1 ng/swab), this matrix could be considered of more use. However, since the author admitted that, for both matrices, the problem of external contamination could overestimate the real use and that in low-dose populations a selection bias towards black individuals (which are known to accumulate more drug due to higher melanin hair content) is likely to exist, a definitive conclusion on the effectiveness of this application was not presented. In the report from Quintela et al.,[81] where a cutoff 40 times higher than that of Kidwell et al. (2 ng/mg), 19.5% positive hair cocaine was found in a population of 200 Spanish university students. In this case, too, hair testing identified around ten times more users than those reported in the annual Spanish National Survey on Drug Abuse with a cutoff that was more likely to detect real consumption while excluding possible cases of environmental contamination.

From all the presented data, it can be observed that, during the last decade, clinical applications of hair analysis in drug addiction mainly concern heroin and cocaine abuse. Few reports are available regarding hair testing and self-reported abuse history of amphetamine and related compounds.

As a means of checking the veracity of self-reported drug use, hair samples of 20 German volunteers of the techno music scene, who declared sporadic and regular consumption of ecstasy tablets (3,4-methylenedioxymethamphetamine, MDMA) and speed (methamphetamine or amphetamine) were segmentally analyzed.[82] Furthermore, since the real content of these illicit preparations is usually unknown, substances other than MDMA, methamphetamine, and amphetamine were also investigated. Therefore, subsequent 3-cm hair segments from volunteers were examined for the content of amphetamine, methamphetamine (MA), MDMA, 3,4-methylenedioxyamphetamine (MDA), 3,4-methylenedioxyethylamphetamine (MDE), and *N*-methyl-1-(3,4-methylenedioxyphenyl)-2-butanamine (MBDB). In no case was MA found, while amphetamine concentrations ranged from 0.1 to 4.8 ng/mg, MDA from 0.05 to 0.89 ng/mg, MDMA from 0.1 to 8.3 ng/mg, and MDE from 0.12 to 15 ng/mg. MBDB was found only in two cases in a range of concentrations between 0.21 and 1.3 ng/mg. All of the substances were also sensitively detected in the cases of declared low consumption. In cases of ecstasy abuse, the intake of even one tablet could be disclosed by hair concentration on the order of 1 ng/mg hair. In general, hair concentrations increased with increased self-declared consumption, although large interindividual differences were observed. High concentrations found in segments proximal to the scalp were attributed to deposition from sweat.

Slightly higher values were obtained in 17 Spanish consumers of ecstasy and speed by Pujadas et al.[83] In the proximal 1-cm hair segment of users with different patterns of consumption, MA content varied from 0.22 to 2.18 ng/mg, that of MDA from 0.22 to 0.89 ng/mg, and that of MDMA from 1.2 to 12.60 ng/mg. MDE was detected in only one case at a concentration of 0.7 ng/mg, as was amphetamine at 0.74 ng/mg. The suitability of segmental hair analysis of MDMA to monitor past chronic exposure to the drug was investigated in a follow-up study of 13 ecstasy consumers with naturally colored hair that, among other goals, aimed to look for an objective biomarker of the history of drug consumption.[84] Concordance between the self-reported data on last month's ecstasy use and MDMA hair concentration in proximal 1-cm segment was quite good ($r^2 = 0.92$) in all the examined subjects, excluding the two individuals who declared a high consumption of the drug (12 tablets in the last month). When comparing self-declaration of monthly consumed tablets within the last 6 months, concordance with 6-cm segment hair MDMA values decreased, and no correlation seemed to exist between the number of mean consumed tablets in the last 12 months and MDMA in 9-cm hair. However, when grouping subjects with similar declared drug use (independently if in the last month, last 6 months, and last 12 months) and comparing that value with the mean of MDMA concentrations found in the corresponding hair segments, an excellent concordance was found in groups of subjects consuming fewer than five tablets of MDMA per month ($r^2 = 0.93$). The authors concluded that a cutoff of 0.5 ng MDMA per mg hair seemed reasonable to assess drug consumption, unless once in a month or in the last 12 months. Doubling the monthly consumption increases hair MDMA by around 1 ng/mg hair up to four consumed tablets a month. When higher concentrations are encountered in hair samples, definitive conclusions seem not to be drawn. As it was shown in the case of opiates, melanin content influences amphetamine incorporation in hair, and association with consumption improves when taking this factor into account.[85] This was demonstrated by a single oral administration of 15 mg of selegiline in ten volunteers with different hair color.[86] Content of its two metabolites, methamphetamine and amphetamine in proximal 2-cm hair segments collected from 1 to 4 weeks after intake, was exponentially related to melanin content in hair. In addition, the individual hair sample results over the 4 weeks were similar, indicating that, once incorporated, methamphetamine and amphetamine are stable in the hair matrix.

A particular application of hair testing for drugs of abuse is that of Mahl et al.,[87] which tested opiates, cocaine, cannabinoids, and amphetamines in hair samples of 100 potential blood donors, who denied having ever consumed any drug. Seven individuals out of 100 showed a total of nine positive results (one for morphine, one for cannabinoids, two for dihydrocodeine, and finally three for benzoylecgonine, two of which also contained cannabinoids and dihydrocodeine). This finding confirmed that some persons willing to donate blood use illicit drugs, with a possible consequent increase in the risk of transmission of viral infections, often associated with drug abuse. Although inapplicable on a routine scale, due to the high cost of analysis, authors supported randomized hair testing for identifying risk-bearing blood donors.

Estimates of prevalence of illicit drug use among pregnant women and adherence to maintenance programs, based on self-reported questionnaires, are known to be unreliable for feelings of guilt and fear of legal consequences. The need for an objective biomarker of drug addiction during pregnancy lies on possible adverse birth outcomes. Since urine testing can be negative, because of the short time window after drug exposure, hair testing is currently applied in these kinds of studies.[88] In a cohort study of 789 pregnant women from Philadelphia (91% African American and 55.3% receiving public assistance), 24% of the population was identified as cocaine users by hair analysis. In comparison with urinalysis, hair analysis identified four times as many women with cocaine exposure among self-reported never users (3.6 versus 19.7%) and twice as many exposed among past users (22.7 versus 51.5%). From a total of 206 women with biologic evidence of cocaine use (by urine or hair), only 7.8% ($n = 16$) were detected by urinalysis but not by hair analysis.[89] A significantly lower percentage of positive cases (1.9%) was found by examining pubic hair (collected within the trichotomies routinely performed at delivery) in 615 pregnant Italian women. Interestingly, when considering normal deliveries (n = 549) and spontaneous abortions (n = 66), 1.4% positive cases were observed in the full-term delivery group and 6.0% in women undergoing spontaneous abortion. This result was interpreted as a clear confirmation of established adverse effects of cocaine consumption during pregnancy.[90] Indeed, in a cohort of 345 pregnant women from a New York City hospital, intentionally designed to overrepresent cocaine users, cocaine concentrations in hair (identified in 168 cases, 48.7%) had a significant dose-response negative relationship with birth weight (a 27-g decrease with each log-unit increase in cocaine concentration).[91]

Alcohol abuse remains one of the principal problems of addiction for modern developed countries, due to the fact that, similarly to tobacco, alcohol is freely available. During the last decade, two biomarkers of ethanol intake in keratin matrix — hair fatty acid ethyl esters (FAEE: ethyl myristate, palmitate, oleate, and stearate) and hair ethyl-glucuronide — have attracted attention.[92–94] Recent investigations showed that teetotalers and social drinkers present hair concentrations of ethyl glucuronide <0.002 ng/mg and FAEE from 0.37 and 0.50 ng/mg, respectively, while alcoholic individuals had hair ethyl glucuronide ranging from 0.030 to 0.425 ng/mg and FAEE varying between 0.65 and 20.50 ng/mg.[95] These concentration intervals confirmed the established cutoff above 1.0 ng/mg and 0.03 ng/mg for hair FAEE and ethyl glucuronide, respectively, to define and verify chronic alcohol consumption.[94,96] However, when applying segmental hair analysis to look for concentration homogeneity along the hair shaft, FAEE concentrations in hair calculated for the proximal 0- to 6-cm segment were 0.92 to 11.6 ng/mg (mean, 4.0 ng/mg) for 17 alcoholics in treatment, 0.20 to 0.85 ng/mg (mean, 0.41 ng/mg) for 13 moderate social drinkers, and 0.06 to 0.37 ng/mg (mean, 0.16 ng/mg) for 5 teetotalers. In almost all cases, the segmental concentrations increased from proximal to distal with no agreement between the self-reported drinking histories of the participants and the FAEE concentrations along the hair length. These further data support that, at the moment, due to large individual differences, FAEE hair concentrations can be used with relatively high accuracy only as markers for excessive alcohol consumption.[97]

9.7 THERAPEUTIC DRUG MONITORING

Hair has been suggested as a long proof record of drug intake, since it can reflect consumption over a time window wider than that of urine and blood.[1] Opposite points of view regarding eventual application of hair testing for therapeutic drug monitoring (TDM) expressed in early reviews are still apparent in the literature.[98,99] As discussed in the first edition of this book,[18] there are contradictory findings concerning the association between administered doses of therapeutic agents and hair concentrations. Many intervening events could in fact screen, weaken, or eliminate potential dose-hair concentration relationship. Among these factors, methodological bias (e.g., collection of data on drug intake), the uncertainty regarding hair-growth stage, and hygienic and cosmetic hair treatments are often cited.[100]

Some examples of hair analysis to verify drug compliance were illustrated in 1999 by Nakahara,[101] who presented data from other authors on haloperidol, carbamazepine, and tricyclic antidepressants. In reality, the obtained results were used to assess drug compliance intended as the mere consumption of a certain drug detected in hair.[101] As a confirmation of this simplified application, Pragst et al.[102] detected amitriptyline, clomipramine, doxepine, impramine, and maprotiline in hair from a treated patient, but no correlation was found between hair concentration and the daily administered drug dosage. In any case, even when a significant dose-concentration relationship was observed, as it was for clozapine in 23 treated patients (hair concentration range from 0.17 to 34.24 ng/mg, $r^2 = 0.54$), interindividual variations in hair concentration for the same drug dosage prevented its use in compliance monitoring.[103]

Different authors tried to better understand why, for some drugs, a correlation exists between hair concentration and administered drug over time, while for others this relationship is lacking. An important advance in understanding the mechanism of drug incorporation into hair came from a paper by Kronstrand et al.[85] These authors studied the hair content of codeine after a single-dose drug administration in relation to hair content of total melanin and eumelanin. An exponential relationship between hair codeine concentration and total melanin ($r^2 = 0.95$) and eumelanin ($r^2 = 0.83$) was found and confirmed when results were normalized by the area under the curve for codeine in plasma as a measurement of total absorbed drug. As a consequence of this finding, the authors postulated that drug concentration in hair may be worthwhile in therapeutic drug monitoring if results are normalized for hair melanin content.

Beumer et al.[2] reviewed the correlation between hair concentrations, plasma levels, dosage, and clinical effects of various drugs in studying the potential of hair as a biological specimen in TDM. From reviewed data, they concluded that when a correlation exists between plasma and hair concentration for administered drugs such as the case of carbamazepine, phenobarbital, amitriptyline, chlorpromazine, haloperidol, and betaxolol, segmental hair analysis of these drugs is useful in establishing drug compliance. Furthermore, in the case of meprobamate and ofloxacin, hair concentrations correlated with administered dosage. The authors suggested the inclusion of hair analysis in clinical trials preceding the registration of new drugs.

REFERENCES

1. Pichini, S. et al., Drug monitoring in non-conventional biological fluids and matrices, *Clin. Pharmacokinet.*, 30, 211, 1996.
2. Beumer, J.H., Bosman, I.J., and Maes, R.A., Hair as a biological specimen for therapeutic drug monitoring, *Int. J. Clin. Pract.*, 55, 353, 2001.

3. Wang, W.L. and Cone, E.J., Testing human hair for drugs of abuse, IV: environmental cocaine contamination and washing effects, *Forensic Sci. Int.*, 70, 39, 1995.
4. Schaffer, M.I., Wang, W.L., and Irving, J. An evaluation of two wash procedures for the differentiation of external contamination versus ingestion in the analysis of human hair samples for cocaine, *J. Anal. Toxicol.*, 26, 485, 2002.
5. Cairns, T., Hill, V., Schaffer, M., and Thistle, W., Levels of cocaine and its metabolites in washed hair of demonstrated cocaine users and workplace subjects, *Forensic Sci. Int.*, 145, 175, 2004.
6. Cairns, T. et al., Amphetamines in washed hair of demonstrated users and workplace subjects, *Forensic Sci. Int.*, 29, 137, 2004.
7. Mizuno, A. et al., Analysis of nicotine content of hair for assessing individual cigarette smoking behaviour, *Ther. Drug Monit.*, 15, 99, 1993.
8. Welp, E.A. et al., Amount of self-reported illicit drug use compared to quantitative hair test results in community-recruited young drug users in Amsterdam, *Addiction*, 98, 987, 2003.
9. Kintz, P., Bundeli, P., Brenneisen, R., and Ludes, B., Dose-concentration relationships in hair from subjects in a controlled heroin-maintenance program, *J. Anal. Toxicol.*, 22, 231, 1998.
10. Wennig, R., Potential problems with the interpretation of hair analysis results, *Forensic Sci. Int.*, 10, 5, 2000.
11. Pépin, G. and Gaillard, Y., Concordance between self-reported drug use and findings in hair about cocaine and heroin, *Forensic Sci. Int.*, 17, 37, 1997.
12. Warner, R. et al., Substance use among mentally ill: prevalence, reasons for use, and effects on illness, *Am. J. Orthopsychiatry*, 64, 30, 1994.
13. Shearer, D.S., Baciewicz, G.J., and Kwong, T.C., Drugs of abuse testing in a psychiatric outpatient service, *Clin. Lab. Med.*, 18, 713, 1998.
14. Swartz, M.S., Swanson, J.W., and Hannon, M.J., Detection of illicit substance use among persons with schizophrenia by radioimmunoassay of hair, *Psychiatr. Serv.*, 54, 891, 2003.
15. Swartz, M.S. et al., Violence and severe mental illness: the effects of substance abuse and nonadherence to medication, *Am. J. Psychiatry*, 155, 226, 1998.
16. Farabee, D. and Shen, H., Antipsychotic medication adherence, cocaine use, and recidivism among a parolee sample, *Behav. Sci. Law*, 22, 467, 2004.
17. Selten, J.P. et al., Hair analysis for cannabinoids and amphetamines in a psychosis incidence study, *Eur. Neuropsychopharmacol.*, 12, 27, 2002.
18. Kintz, P., Clinical application of hair analysis, in *Drug Testing in Hair*, Kintz, P., Ed., CRC Press, Boca Raton, FL, 1996, p. 269.
19. Mei, Z. and Williams, J., Simultaneous determination of phenytoin and carbamazepine in human hair by high-performance liquid chromatography, *Ther. Drug. Monit.*, 19, 92, 1997.
20. Williams, J. et al., Relation between dosage of carbamazepine and concentration in hair and plasma samples from a compliant inpatient epileptic population, *Ther. Drug Monit.*, 23, 15, 2001.
21. Williams, J. et al., Self-discontinuation of antiepileptic medication in pregnancy: detection by hair analysis, *Epilepsia*, 43, 824, 2002.
22. Bailey, B., Klein, J., and Koren, G., Noninvasive methods for drug measurement in pediatrics, *Pediatr. Clin. North Am.*, 44, 15, 1997.
23. Ostrea, E.M., Jr., Testing for exposure to illicit drugs and other agents in the neonate: a review of laboratory methods and the role of meconium analysis, *Curr. Probl. Pediatr.*, 29, 37, 1999.

24. Klein, J., Karaskov, T., and Koren, G., Clinical applications of hair testing for drugs of abuse: the Canadian experience, *Forensic Sci. Int.*, 10, 281, 2000.
25. Bar-oz, B., Klein, J., Karaskov, T., and Koren, G., Comparison of meconium and neonatal hair analysis for detection of gestational exposure to drugs of abuse, *Arch. Dis. Child. Fetal Neonatal Ed.*, 88, F98, 2003.
26. Vinner, E. et al., Neonatal hair analysis contribution to establishing a gestational drug exposure profile and predicting a withdrawal syndrome, *Ther. Drug. Monit.*, 25, 421, 2003.
27. Vinner, E. et al., Hair analysis of opiates in mothers and newborns for evaluating opiate exposure during pregnancy, *Forensic Sci. Int.*, 231, 57, 2003.
28. Chan, D. et al., Recent developments in meconium and hair testing methods for the confirmation of gestational exposures to alcohol and tobacco smoke, *Clin. Biochem.*, 37, 429, 2004.
29. Koren, G., Measurement of drugs in neonatal hair: a window to fetal exposure, *Forensic Sci. Int.*, 5, 77, 1995.
30. Koren, G. et al., Estimation of fetal exposure to drugs of abuse, environmental tobacco smoke, and ethanol, *Ther. Drug Monit.*, 24, 23, 2002.
31. Chiriboga, C.A. et al., Dose response effect of fetal cocaine exposure on newborn neurologic function, *Pediatrics*, 103, 79, 1999.
32. Bateman, D.A. and Chiriboga, C.A., Dose-response effect of cocaine on newborn head circumference, *Pediatrics*, 106, E33, 2000.
33. LaGasse, L.L., Seifer, R., and Lester, B.M., Interpreting research on prenatal substance exposure in the context of multiple confounding factors, *Clin. Perinatol.*, 26, 39, 1999.
34. Boskovic, R. et al., The role of the placenta in variability of fetal exposure to cocaine and cannabinoids: a twin study, *Can. J. Physiol. Pharmacol.*, 79, 942, 2001.
35. Katikaneni, L.D., Salle, F.R., and Hulsey, T.C., Neonatal hair analysis for benzoylecgonine: a sensitive and semiquantitative biological marker for chronic gestational cocaine exposure, *Biol. Neonate*, 81, 29, 2002.
36. Eliopoulos, C., Nicotine and cotinine in maternal and neonatal hair as markers of gestational smoking, *Clin. Invest. Med.*, 19, 231, 1996.
37. Klein, J. and Koren, G., Hair analysis: a biological marker for passive smoking in pregnancy and childhood, *Hum. Exp. Toxicol.*, 18, 279, 1999.
38. Jaakkola, J.J., Jaakkola, N., and Zahlsen, K., Fetal growth and length of gestation in relation to prenatal exposure to environmental tobacco smoke assessed by hair nicotine concentration, *Environ. Health Perspect.*, 109, 557, 2001.
39. Pichini, S. et al., Assessment of chronic exposure to cigarette smoke and its change during pregnancy by segmental analysis of maternal hair nicotine, *J. Expo. Anal. Environ. Epidemiol.*, 13, 144, 2003.
40. Jacqz-Aigrain, E. et al., Maternal smoking during pregnancy and nicotine and cotinine concentrations in maternal and neonatal hair. *B.J.O.G.*, 109, 909, 2002.
41. Barr, H.M. and Streissguth, A.P., Identifying maternal self-reported alcohol use associated with fetal alcohol spectrum disorders, *Alcohol Clin. Exp. Res.*, 25, 283, 2001.
42. Klein, J., Chan, D., and Koren, G., Neonatal hair analysis as a biomarker for *in utero* alcohol exposure. *N. Engl. J. Med.*, 347, 2086, 2002.
43. Lewis, D. et al., Determination of drug exposure using hair: application to child protective cases, *Forensic Sci. Int.*, 17, 123, 1997.
44. Smith, F.P. and Kidwell, D.A., Cocaine in hair, saliva skin swabs and urine of cocaine users' children, *Forensic Sci. Int.*, 83, 179, 1996.

45. Garcia-Algar, O., Intoxicación aguda y exposición crónica a cocaína en un niño, *Med. Clin. (Barc.)*, in press, 2005.
46. De Giorgio, F. et al., Cocaine found in a child's hair due to environmental exposure? *Int. J. Leg. Med.*, 118, 310, 2004.
47. Garcia-Algar, O. et al., MDMA (3,4-methylenedioxymethamphetamine) intoxication in an infant chronically exposed to cocaine, *Ther. Drug Monit.*, 27, 409, 2005.
48. Tutka, P., Wielosz, M., and Zatonski, W., Exposure to environmental tobacco smoke and children health, *Int. J. Occup. Med. Environ. Health*, 15, 325, 2002.
49. Groner, J.A. et al., Screening for children's exposure to environmental tobacco smoke in a pediatric primary care setting, *Arch. Pediatr. Adolesc. Med.*, 159, 450, 2005.
50. Pichini, S., The analysis of nicotine in infants' hair for measuring exposure to environmental tobacco smoke, *Forensic Sci. Int.*, 17, 253, 1997.
51. Wilson, S.E. et al., Racial differences in exposure to environmental tobacco smoke among children, *Environ. Health Perspect.*, 113, 362, 2005.
52. Pichini, S. et al., Cord serum cotinine as a biomarker of foetal exposure to cigarette smoke at the end of pregnancy, *Environ. Health Perspect.*, 1080, 1079, 2000.
53. Uematsu, T. et al., The axial distribution of nicotine content along hair shaft as an indicator of changes in smoking behaviour: evaluation in a smoking-cessation programme with or without the aid of nicotine chewing gum, *Br. J. Clin. Pharmacol.*, 39, 665, 1995.
54. Kintz, P., Ludes, B., and Mangin, P., Evaluation of nicotine and cotinine in human hair, *J. Forensic Sci.*, 37, 72, 1992.
55. Mizuno, A. et al., Clinical outcome of smoking-cessation trial of nicotine chewing gum evaluated by analysis of nicotine in hair, *Ther. Drug Monit.*, 19, 407, 1997.
56. Sachs, H., Theoretical limits of the evaluation of drug concentration in hair due to irregular hair growth, *Forensic Sci. Int.*, 70, 53, 1995.
57. Dimich-Ward, H. et al., Impact of smoking policy on the respiratory health of food and beverage servers, *Scand. J. Work. Environ. Health*, 31, 75, 2005.
58. Al-Delaimy, W., Fraser, T., and Woodward, A., Nicotine in hair of bar and restaurant workers, *N. Z. Med. J.*, 114, 80, 2001.
59. Eliopoulos, C., Klein, J., and Koren, G., Validation of self-reported smoking by analysis of hair for nicotine and cotinine, *Ther. Drug Monit.*, 18, 532, 1996.
60. Eliopoulos, C. et. al., Hair concentration of nicotine and cotinine in women and their newborn infants, *JAMA*, 271, 621, 1994.
61. Al-Delaimy, W., Hair as a biomarker for exposure to tobacco smoke, *Tob. Control*, 11, 176, 2002.
62. Kintz, P., Drug testing in addicts: a comparison between urine, sweat, and hair, *Ther. Drug Monit.*, 18, 450, 1996.
63. Strano-Rossi, S., Bermejo-Barrera, A., and Chiarotti, M., Segmental hair analysis for cocaine and heroin abuse determination, *Forensic Sci. Int.*, 5, 211, 1995.
64. Charles, B.K. et al., Opiate recidivism in a drug-treatment program: comparison of hair and urine data, *J. Anal. Toxicol.*, 27, 412, 2003.
65. Vincent, F. et al., Determination of buprenorphine and norbuprenorphine in urine and hair by gas chromatography-mass spectrometry, *J. Anal. Toxicol.*, 23, 270, 1999.
66. Marsh, A., Evans, M.B., and Strang, J., Radioimmunoassay of drugs of abuse in hair, Part 2: the determination of methadone in the hair of known drug users, *J. Pharm. Biomed. Anal.*, 13, 829, 1995.
67. Wilkins, D.G., Quantitative analysis of methadone and two major metabolites in hair by positive chemical ionization ion trap mass spectrometry, *J. Anal. Toxicol.*, 20, 355, 1996.

68. Kintz, P. et al., Enantioselective separation of methadone and its main metabolite in human hair by liquid chromatography/ion spray-mass spectrometry, *J. Forensic Sci.*, 42, 291, 1997.
69. Goldberger, B.A. et al., Detection of methadone, methadone metabolites, and other illicit drugs of abuse in hair of methadone-treatment subjects, *J. Anal. Toxicol.*, 22, 526, 1998.
70. Girod, C. and Staub, C., Methadone and EDDP in hair from human subjects following a maintenance program: results of a pilot study, *Forensic Sci. Int.*, 1, 175, 2001.
71. Paterson, S. et al., Interindividual dose/concentration relationship for methadone in hair, *J. Anal. Toxicol.*, 27, 20, 2003.
72. Richardson, J., Fendrich, M., and Johnson, T.P., Neighbourhood effects on drug reporting, *Addiction,* 98, 1705, 2003.
73. Colon, H.M., Robles, R.R., and Sahai, H., The validity of drug use responses in a household survey in Puerto Rico: comparison of survey responses of cocaine and heroin use with hair tests, *Int. J. Epidemiol.*, 30, 1042, 2001.
74. Colon, H.M., Robles, R.R., and Sahai, H., The validity of drug use self-reports among hard core drug users in a household survey in Puerto Rico: comparison of survey responses of cocaine and heroin use with hair tests, *Drug. Alcohol Depend.*, 67, 269, 2002.
75. Tassiopoulos, K. et al., Hair testing and self-report of cocaine use by heroin users, *Addiction*, 99, 590, 2004.
76. Appel, P.W. et al., Comparison of self-report and hair analysis in detecting cocaine use in a homeless/transient sample, *J. Psychoactive Drugs*, 33, 47, 2001.
77. Simpson, D.D., Joe, G.W., and Broome, K.M., A national 5-year follow-up of treatment outcomes for cocaine dependence, *Arch. Gen. Psychiatry*, 59, 538, 2002.
78. Bernstein, J. et al., Brief motivational intervention at a clinic visit reduces cocaine and heroin use, *Drug Alcohol Depend.*, 7, 49, 2005.
79. Ursitti, F. et al., Use of hair analysis for confirmation of self-reported cocaine use in users with negative urine tests, *J. Toxicol. Clin. Toxicol.*, 39, 361, 2001.
80. Kidwell, D.A., Blanco, M.A., and Smith, F.P., Cocaine detection in a university population by hair analysis and skin swab testing, *Forensic Sci. Int.*, 17, 75, 1997.
81. Quintela, O. et al., Evaluation of cocaine, amphetamines and cannabis use in university students through hair analysis: preliminary results, *Forensic Sci. Int.*, 10, 273, 2000.
82. Rothe, M. et al., Hair concentrations and self-reported abuse history of 20 amphetamine and ecstasy users, *Forensic Sci. Int.*, 19, 111, 1997.
83. Pujadas, M. et al., Development and validation of a gas chromatography-mass spectrometry assay for hair analysis of amphetamine, methamphetamine and methylenedioxy derivatives, *J. Chromatogr. B Anal. Technol. Biomed. Life Sci.*, 25, 249, 2003.
84. Pichini, S. et al., Assessment of chronic exposure to MDMA in a group of consumers by segmental hair analysis, *Ther. Drug Monit.*, 27, 409, 2005.
85. Kronstrand, R. et al., Codeine concentration in hair after oral administration is dependent on melanin content, *Clin. Chem.*, 45, 1485, 1999.
86. Kronstrand, R. et al., Incorporation of selegiline metabolites into hair after oral selegiline intake, *J. Anal. Toxicol.*, 25, 594, 2001.
87. Mahl, M.A., Hirsch, M., and Sugg, U., Verification of the drug history given by potential blood donors: results of drug screening that combines hair and urine analysis, *Transfusion*, 40, 637, 2000.
88. Kwong, T.C. and Shearer, D., Detection of drug use during pregnancy, *Obstet. Gynecol. Clin. North Am.*, 25, 43, 1998.

89. Markovic, N. et al., Substance use measures among women in early pregnancy, *Am. J Obstet. Gynecol.*, 183, 627, 2000.
90. Chiarotti, M. et al,. Evaluation of cocaine use during pregnancy through toxicological analysis of hair, *J. Anal. Toxicol.*, 20,555, 1996.
91. Kuhn, L., Cocaine use during pregnancy and intrauterine growth retardation: new insights based on maternal hair tests, *Am. J. Epidemiol.*, 15, 112, 2000.
92. Pragst, F. et al., Are there possibilities for the detection of chronically elevated alcohol consumption by hair analysis? A report about the state of investigation, *Forensic Sci. Int.*, 10, 201, 2000.
93. Hartwig, S., Auwarter, V., Pragst, F., Fatty Acid ethyl esters in scalp, pubic, axillary, beard and body hair as markers for alcohol misuse, *Alcohol Alcohol.*, 163, 2003.
94. Jurado, C. et al., Diagnosis of chronic alcohol consumption. Hair analysis for ethyl-glucuronide, *Forensic Sci. Int.*, 145,161, 2004.
95. Yegles, M. et al., Comparison of ethyl glucuronide and fatty acid ethyl ester concentrations in hair of alcoholics, social drinkers and teetotalers, *Forensic Sci. Int.*, 145, 167, 2004.
96. Hartwig, S., Auwarter, V., and Pragst, F., Effect of hair care and hair cosmetics on the concentrations of fatty acid ethyl esters in hair as markers of chronically elevated alcohol consumption, *Forensic Sci. Int.*, 28, 90, 2003.
97. Auwarter, V., Fatty acid ethyl esters in hair as markers of alcohol consumption: segmental hair analysis of alcoholics, social drinkers, and teetotalers, *Clin. Chem.*, 47, 2114, 2001.
98. Uematsu, T., Therapeutic drug monitoring in hair samples: principles and practice, *Clin. Pharmacokin.*, 25, 83, 1993.
99. Tracqui, A., Kintz, P., and Mangin, P., Hair analysis: a worthless tool for therapeutic compliance monitoring, *Forensic Sci. Int.*, 70, 183, 1995.
100. Villain, M., Cirimele, V., and Kintz, P., Hair analysis in toxicology, *Clin. Chem. Lab. Med.*, 42, 1265, 2004.
101. Nakahara, Y., Hair analysis for abused and therapeutic drugs, *J. Chromatogr. B Biomed. Sci. Appl.*, 15, 161, 1999.
102. Pragst, F. et al., Structural and concentration effects on the deposition of tricyclic antidepressants in human hair, *Forensic Sci. Int.*, 84, 225, 1997.
103. Cirimele, V. et al., Clozapine dose-concentration relationships in plasma, hair and sweat specimens of schizophrenic patients, *Forensic Sci. Int.*, 10, 289, 2000.

10 Hair in Postmortem Toxicology

Robert Kronstrand and Henrik Druid

CONTENTS

10.1 INTRODUCTION

In postmortem toxicology, many matrices can be obtained to shed light over what happened to the deceased. In recent years, drug analysis in keratinized matrices, such as hair and nails, has received considerable attention because of several advantages over drug-testing methodologies employing body fluids, such as urine or serum. One advantage that should be emphasized is the stability of drugs in hair and nails, which means that such samples can be stored at room temperature for very long periods without major degradation of incorporated drugs. Drugs are incorporated into nails via both the root of the growing nail and the nail bed [1]. This implies that drugs follow the movement of the keratinized matrix during the growth of the nail, both upward and forward. In addition, the growth of nails is variable and generally slow. Hence, a temporal mapping of previous drug intake using analysis of nails is not possible. In contrast, hair provides a unique possibility to look back into the drug use history as a complement to the snapshot provided by blood.

A common opinion in drug-overdose cases is that the death is caused by lack of tolerance after a period of abstinence. Although this notion seems reasonable, there is limited evidence for this hypothesis. An objective way to evaluate past drug use or abstinence is the analysis of hair from the deceased. As the period of abstinence need not be long, segmental analysis is of paramount importance.

The analysis of drugs in hair usually involves several measures to ensure reliable and valid results. Besides variations in washing procedures, the extraction or digestion procedures come in such a variety that the comparison of results is very difficult. Several papers have evaluated different procedures for removing drugs such as cocaine and heroin metabolites from the hair matrix [2–14]. The methods used involved enzymatic digestion, digestion by strong acid or base at elevated temperatures, or solvent extraction of cut or pulverized hair. Basic conditions degraded unstable drugs such as heroin, cocaine, and benzodiazepines, whereas the softer enzymatic digestions and the solvent extractions showed no or little degradation of the analytes. In general though, the complete dissolution of the hair matrix produced the best recoveries, whereas direct extraction of hair with organic solvents seemed to give lower recoveries. Baumgartner and Hill [14] have proposed enzymatic digestion at neutral pH as a universal extraction procedure for any substances. After the drugs have been liberated from the hair matrix, extraction and detection procedures are very similar to the ones used for the extraction of drugs from blood, plasma, or urine.

Prior to these cumbersome analyses, a rapid screening for drugs commonly encountered in overdose cases, such as cocaine, opiates, amphetamines, and benzodiazepines, is helpful. In workplace drug testing, analysis is usually performed with an initial screening by immunoassay followed by confirmation of positive results by mass spectrometry [15–17]. Hair analysis has also been used in forensic casework in various contexts. Many papers are available where hair-drug concentrations from living drug addicts or suspects as well as fatal overdoses are reported [18–30].

Nakahara and Kikura [31] described the use of hair and hair root analysis in acute poisonings of MDMA (3,4-methylenedioxymethamphetamine), and Tagliaro et al. [28], Kronstrand et al. [22], and Darke et al. [29] evaluated heroin metabolite concentrations in hair from fatal overdoses. All came to the conclusion that the low concentrations found in the hair of the deceased suggested abstinence from heroin and possibly lowered tolerance, resulting in the overdose death. This chapter focuses on how analysis of hair can contribute to the interpretation of overdose cases, but included are also some practical and technical suggestions for toxicologists performing hair analyses.

10.2 METHODOLOGICAL ASPECTS

10.2.1 Hair Sampling

Different estimates of the growth rate of human scalp hair have been reported. Harkey [32] found an average growth rate of 0.44 mm/day. Pötsch et al. [33] found a variation between 0.07 and 0.78 mm/day, with 82% of the examined population between 0.32 and 0.46 mm/day. The hair growth cycle consists of periods of growth and dormancy where, in humans, each hair follicle has its own cycle independent of its neighbors. The growing phase usually continues between 7 to 94 weeks, but it may

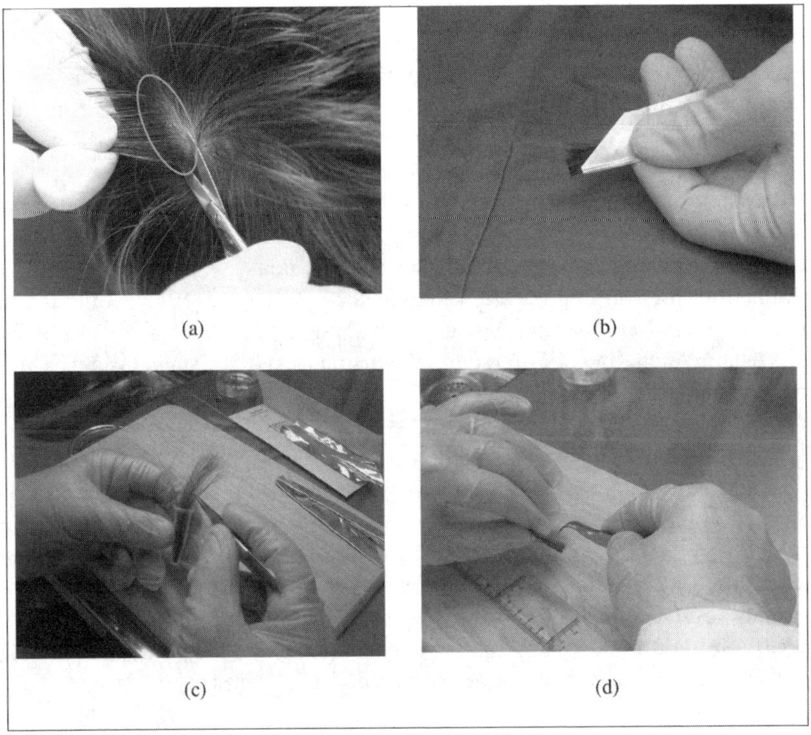

FIGURE 10.1 Recommended procedure for collection and handling of hair for segmental analysis.

last several years [34]. At the posterior vertex, the percentage of growing hair is rather constant, at approximately 85%. Therefore, it has been suggested as the best collection site. Since there is a high chance that several segments of hair will be analyzed, it is of paramount importance to obtain a sample that is well aligned and fixed. Figure 10.1(a–d) shows the collection of hair from the posterior vertex.

Due to androgenic hair loss, collection of hair from the posterior vertex may prove unrewarding in thin-haired or bald subjects. Preferably, the samples should then be collected somewhat further down at the back of the head. To access the posterior vertex or the back of the head, the body can be turned over, or at least turned on the side. Such a maneuver improves the illumination of the area and improves the conditions for accurate sampling, which is necessary for a correct interpretation. Further, it is advantageous to collect hair samples before the autopsy has started, because the hair will then typically get wet, or contaminated with blood. If the hair already is soaked with blood before the autopsy, the hair could be washed with water and then dried with a hair-dryer before collection. It is wise to make a note that such contamination has occurred if it turns out that the blood contains high levels of drugs.

If segmental hair analysis should be conducted, a hair sample from a 2 × 1-cm area is usually sufficient to allow for analysis of 0.5-cm-long segments, provided that the method is based on 10 to 20 mg of hair. If several analyses with different extraction techniques are desired, additional samples have to be collected, and depending on the sensitivity of the analytical method, the amount of hair can be adjusted accordingly. If segmental analysis is to be carried out, the cutting of the hair strands accurately as close to the scalp as possible is vital. Curly hair is more difficult to collect and handle appropriately. If segmental analysis is needed in such cases, it might be necessary to pluck hair and cut every hair strand separately at defined intervals from the root. Plucked hair may also be preferred in suspected fatal poisonings resulting in a somewhat delayed death. A period of 1 to 3 days of coma after an acute intoxication may hence result in negative results in blood and urine due to elimination, but even cut hair may test negative. Analysis of plucked hair, including the intradermal portion, might in such instances reveal traces of the drug.

Once collected, hair samples should be wrapped in, for example, aluminum foil (Figure 10.1b) to preserve the alignment, and the scalp end should be clearly indicated. Such wrapped-in samples are then put into an envelope that is labeled similarly to other samples from the same subjects. Tape should be avoided because it can be very laborious to remove the hair strands from the tape. Further, putting plucked hair onto regular sheets of paper that are subsequently folded will almost invariably result in a loss of hair roots when the hair strands are removed from the paper. Typically, the sticky hair roots will become fixed to the porous surface of the paper, and the strands will break at variable distance from the root.

10.2.2 Segmentation and Preparation

There are two main situations when analysis of separate hair segments may be important. First, in date-rape cases and other alleged criminal poisonings, a detection of a particular drug in a segment corresponding to the time when the intake should have occurred may give strong support to the police investigation. Second, segmental hair analysis can provide detailed temporal mapping of the drug abuse pattern, which can be compared with the blood levels of the drugs. In particular, indications of recent discontinuation of drug use may suggest that a deceased subject had a reduced tolerance to that particular drug and other drugs that might confer cross tolerance. This is further discussed in some detail below.

Segmental hair analysis is meaningless if the collection and handling of the hair sampling is inappropriate. Thus, the hair should be carefully aligned as shown in Figure 10.2a. If this is not the case, each segment will contain different portions of the hair strands and thus represent longer and overlapping time periods, as shown in Figure 10.2b. For straight hair, the segmentation may be accomplished by keeping the (aligned) hair fixed in aluminum foil and cutting the segments with a pair of scissors. If shorter segments are desired, it is usually more precise to put the sample on a cutting board along a ruler and cut the hair with a scalpel. A practical advice is to make sure that the environment has sufficient moisture, as dry air will cause static electricity and make the small pieces of hair play around uncontrollably. It is suggested that each segment be directly put away for weighing and subsequently into a beaker or test tube once it has been cut before the next segment is cut to avoid

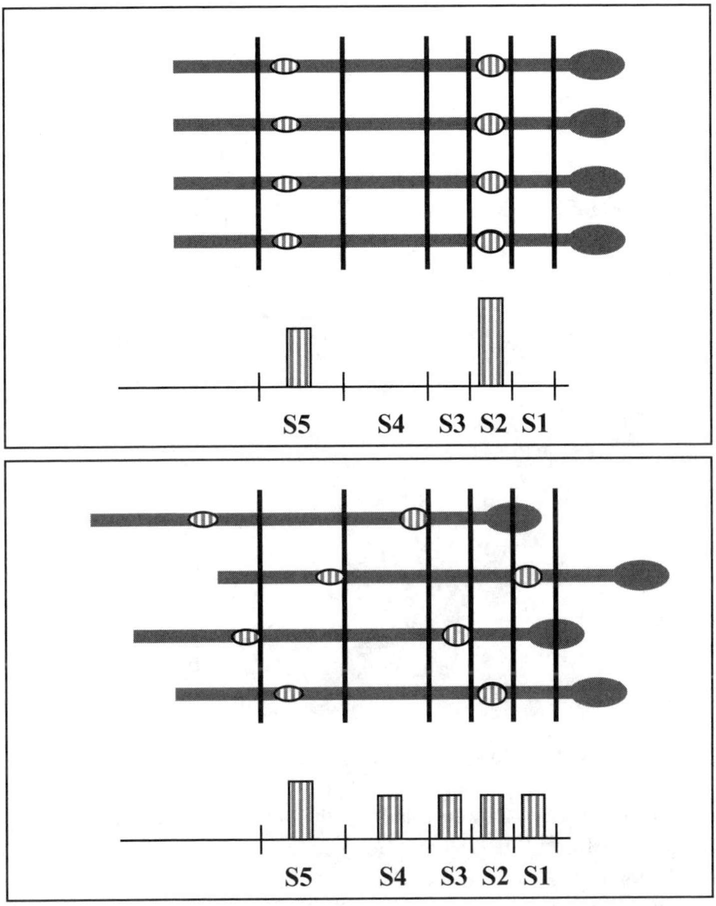

FIGURE 10.2.2 The effect of disarray of hair strands on the analytical results. Striped bars represent drug concentrations in segments containing a drug (circular areas in the hair).

intermixing. The cutting board and the instruments should, of course, be carefully cleaned before a new sample is to be processed. Brushing off the instruments and the cutting board, followed by cleaning with isopropanol will effectively prevent carryover (unpublished data).

The number and length of the hair segments can vary, depending on the purpose of the analysis. In date-rape cases, the task is typically to look for the possible presence of a substance that allegedly had been used at a specific time point before sampling. The portions of the hair to be analyzed are then selected so as to roughly correspond to that time point (and preferably other time periods for comparison). If the purpose instead is to evaluate the possible tolerance or possible nontolerance to certain drugs or groups of drugs, the more recent hair segments are most relevant to analyze.

For opioid drugs, tolerance development is significant but occurs gradually, and that is also true for the loss of tolerance. The time frame for this process is poorly

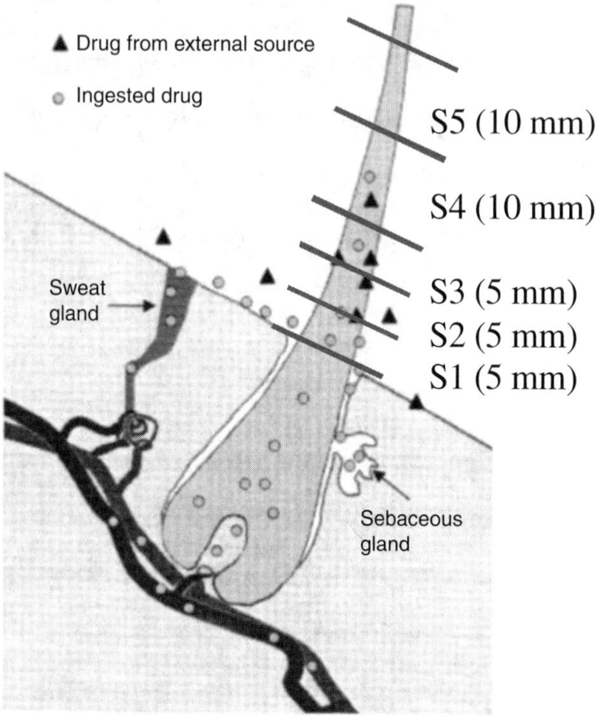

FIGURE 10.3 Proposed segmentation of hair in suspected opioid overdose cases.

characterized, and is also complicated by the fact that tolerance to the euphoric effects may be different from the tolerance to the respiratory depression [35]. A period of abstinence of 7 to 14 days is, however, likely to result in a marked reduction in tolerance to opioid drugs, implying that hair segments should be rather short to capture this time period accurately. Positive detections in hair segments of 1 cm or longer may not discriminate between an intake that occurred during the few days before the demise from exposure(s) about 4 weeks back. A segmentation into 5-mm-long segments for the most recent three segments seems to be relevant in opioid overdose cases to separate cases with a recent abstinence from cases with continuous use (Figure 10.3).

10.2.3 Washing

As hair grows, it is exposed to the environment and thus to potential contamination by drugs present in the surroundings. Indeed, the incorporation of drugs from sweat or other secretions may be characterized as contamination, even though it is not strictly external. When the mature hair shaft is "bathed" in sweat, the distinct bands of incorporated drug originating from the bloodstream might be broadened. A consequence of this is that a segmental analysis, however carefully performed, will be precluded by the presence of drugs from sweat. Therefore, washing is needed to enable correct interpretation. Over the years, Baumgartner and his colleagues at

Psychemedics have made headway in this area [17, 36–38]. The possible contribution of contamination of drugs in sweat is of larger concern when curly hair, e.g., from black subjects, is examined. Curly hair may lie close to the scalp for longer periods of time and be more exposed to sweat than straight hair.

The cutoff levels for possible contamination that are recommended for living subjects may not be applicable to hair results from postmortem hair samples. For example, in 40 autopsy cases where amphetamine was found in a distal segment (not including the root), the mean ratio between the concentration in hair and the last wash was 19.6, whereas the median was only 6.7 (unpublished data) compared with the recommended ratio of 10 for living subjects. However, our experience is that external contamination is not a major problem in postmortem cases and that the contribution from drugs in sweat is washed out efficiently. Of course, there is an important difference in the social and legal aspects between analytical results that are used for workplace testing and results that are used as an ancillary tool in postmortem casework.

10.2.4 Further Preparation

For certain analyses, organic extraction may be desirable to prevent degradation of labile compounds. Such extraction procedures require sufficient contact between the drugs within different compartments of the hair and the solvent. Mechanical treatment of the hair to increase the contact area can then be applied. We compared the impact of different mechanical procedures on the recovery of 6-acteylmorphine, morphine, and codeine in seven genuinely positive samples and of cocaine and benzoylecgonine in an additional sample. Each hair sample was divided into three portions: 1-cm-long pieces, 1-mm-long pieces, and pulverized fragments, produced after mincing in a ball mill. Pulverized hair generally contained higher concentrations of the analytes, whereas only small differences were observed between 1-mm-long or 1-cm-long hair pieces. The advantage of mincing was somewhat reduced by a larger loss of hair fragments retained in the ball mill. Since the differences were not very large, we believe that a fast cutting procedure with a razor, scalpel, or scissors is suitable for preparing postmortem hair segments for organic solvent extraction.

10.2.5 Screening

The purpose of screening methods differs depending on the context. Today, screening tests are used primarily to rapidly and with low cost dismiss numerous negative samples in a vast amount of samples. This is achieved with immunological tests such as radioimmunoassay (RIA) [14, 17] and enzyme-linked immunosorbent assay (ELISA) [15]. The main goal is to save time and money. Another purpose of screening tests originates from the valuable forensic concept of using two independent methods to confirm a positive result. The main goal, then, is to add quality to the results. The use of an LC-MS (liquid chromatography-mass spectrometry) method for screening does not fulfill the former criteria, but instead it is an excellent choice for the latter. Another advantage with chromatography is that one can design the screening method to cover all of the analytes that are included in the confirmation methods. Immunological tests suffer from cross reactivity, making both qualitative and quantitative data difficult to extrapolate to specific confirmation results. In contrast, LC-MS provides the analyst with comparable results. Kronstrand et al. [39] described a screening method using LC-MS/MS on a SCIEX API 2000 MS/MS instrument run in multiple reaction mode. To 10 to 50 mg of hair was added 0.5 ml of mobile phase A and 25 µl of internal standard, and the sample was incubated in a water bath (with orbital shaking) at 37°C for 18 h. A 150-ml aliquot was transferred to an autosampler vial and 10 ml were injected onto the chromatographic system.

10.2.6 Confirmation

The first prerequisite in confirmative analysis is to use a different analytical technique than that used for screening. Confirmation of a positive hair test has almost exclusively been performed by mass spectrometry because of a lack of sensitivity for other techniques. Even though gas chromatography-mass spectrometry (GC-MS) has dominated over the past 15 years, LC-MS/MS is now emerging as a valid confirmation technique. Confirmation, or so-called target analysis, is covered in depth in other chapters of this book.

10.3 STRATEGIES IN POSTMORTEM WORK

10.3.1 Investigation of Overdose Cases

The diagnosis of fatal intoxication remains a challenge to the forensic pathologist and toxicologist, and requires that the circumstances surrounding death, the autopsy findings, and the toxicological results be carefully evaluated. For many drugs, postmortem reference values in certified poisonings and nonpoisonings may assist in the interpretation [40], but there are several pitfalls that need to be considered. In addition to postmortem redistribution, drug interactions, genetic differences in metabolism, or receptor functions, the sensitivity to various drugs may differ between individuals. After a period of continuous use of a drug, tolerance is often developed, implying a need for higher doses to achieve the desired pharmacological effects. This tolerance is for most drugs an effect of pharmacokinetic changes, i.e., depending on an increased metabolism by enzymatic induction. Such changes will typically not affect the interpretation of toxic or fatal levels. For some drugs, however, the tolerance is more dependent on pharmacodynamic adaptations. This means that a blood concentration that caused a fatal overdose in a naïve person could be pharmacologically insignificant in a regular user. The phenomenon is true for several illicit drugs, particularly opioid drugs.

In heroin overdose cases where low blood morphine levels are found, it is often assumed that the victim either was a naïve user or had had a drug-free period prior to the final dose. In the absence of a reliable biomarker of opioid tolerance, information about previous use, for example from medical records and relatives, have been used to estimate the degree of tolerance. However, information from relatives and friends, from medical charts, and documents from prisons may not give a correct picture of the abuse pattern for various reasons. A more reliable alternative is to perform hair analysis for opioids. This approach has revealed abstinence in a

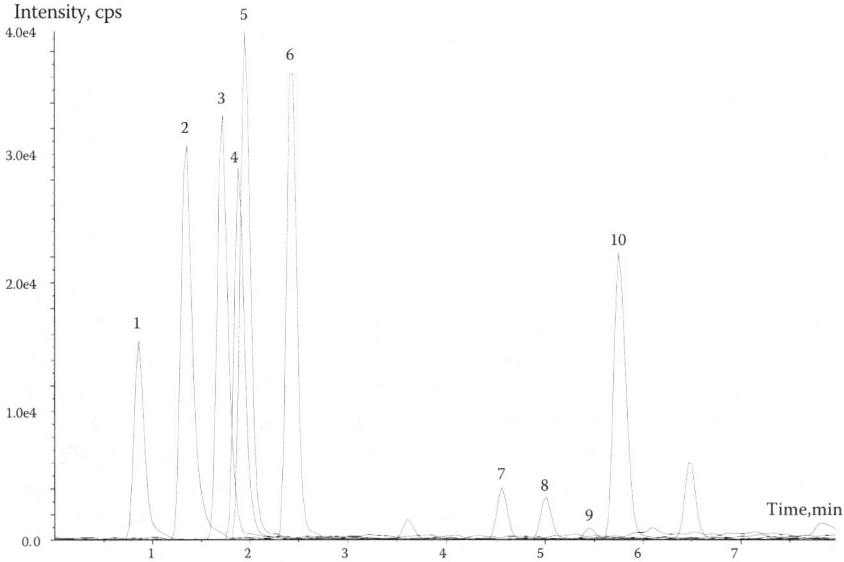

1) Morphine
2) Codeine
3) Acetylmorphine
4) Ketobemidone
5) Ethylmorphine
6) Tramadol
7) Fentanyl
8) Buprenorphine
9) Dextropropoxyphene
10) Methadone

FIGURE 10.4 Selected chromatograms from the analysis of μ-agonists in hair. Control sample at 30 ng/sample for all analytes except fentanyl and buprenorphine (3 ng/sample).

subgroup of overdose victims [22]. Tagliaro et al. [28] further reported that morphine levels were lower in hair from heroin overdose victims than in hair from active heroin addicts. Similar results, supporting the hypothesis that heroin deaths may be explained by reduced tolerance, were reported by Darke et al. [29]. Recently, another study compared hair concentrations in subjects in a heroin program and in fatal heroin overdose victims, and did not find obvious differences in concentrations [41]. To more closely address the question of the importance of abstinence, we carried out the following study.

Sixty deceased drug abusers were examined during 2003–2004 at the Department of Forensic Medicine in Stockholm, Sweden. In all cases, a full autopsy, extensive toxicological testing, and microscopic examination were performed. Information about the circumstances and history of the deceased was compiled from the police investigation and medical records. Three portions of hair were collected from the posterior vertex. One portion was subjected to a drug screen with a sensitive LC-MS/MS method [39], modified to also include the μ-opioid receptor agonists fentanyl, buprenorphine, methadone, propoxyphene, tramadol, and ketobemidone (see Figure 10.4). Positive results were confirmed and quantified with a second analysis [22] preceded by segmentation and a standardized washing procedure to minimize possible contribution from external contamination of drugs. To this end, the hair strands were carefully aligned and sectioned into short segments; 5 mm long for the most recent segments (S1 to S3), and 10 mm long for the outer segments (S4, S5). Assuming a hair growth of 0.44 mm/day [32], a positive detection in S1 should imply exposure within approximately 10 to 15 days before death, considering differences in hair growth. Negative results of opioids in S1 should indicate reduced tolerance, although keeping in mind that loss of tolerance is a gradual process. Using this protocol, the μ-opioid receptor agonists, as well as other drugs such as cocaine, amphetamine, methamphetamine, MDMA (ecstasy), benzodiazepines, and their main metabolites could be detected and quantified in hair as well as in postmortem femoral blood.

In 28 cases, the circumstances and medicolegal findings strongly indicated a heroin overdose. Almost invariably, they presented with froth in the airways and prominent lung edema. The presence of opioids in the hair samples from the 28 overdose subjects is illustrated in Table 10.1. This table also shows the femoral blood concentration of free morphine, the presence of other drugs in blood and hair, age, sex, contributing pathologies, manner of death, and whether death was delayed or not. In 18 cases, opioids were absent in the most recent hair segment (S1), suggesting that these individuals had a reduced tolerance to opioids. The mean and median femoral blood morphine concentrations were 0.38 and 0.16 μg/g, respectively. These levels conform to those reported in many postmortem studies. Surprisingly, the corresponding concentrations for the 10 subjects that showed a continuous use of opioids were almost identical (0.37 and 0.15 μg/g blood). In some cases, there was circumstantial evidence of a delayed death (i.e., after several hours to parts of a day), and this could have caused a drop in the blood morphine levels. However, if these cases are excluded, the abstinent subjects actually show a higher mean and median blood concentration of morphine than the subjects with a continuous use. This finding should not be considered to rule out the hypothesis of abstinence as a risk factor. Indeed, the careful preparation of short segments, allowed for the detection of recently abstinent subjects, and this group was even larger than the group with continuous use, lending support to the notion that abstinent users are at risk for overdosing. The lack of difference in blood morphine concentrations is rather more likely explained by the presence of a large number of drugs in both hair and blood, providing opportunities for several pharmacodynamic interactions.

We believe that segmental hair analysis results will come out differently when blood levels in pure heroin overdose fatalities are evaluated. Still, given the extensive polydrug use, the analysis of multiple drugs in blood and hair may eventually prove beneficial in the effort to identify particularly hazardous drug combinations.

Recent research has provided evidence of extensive cross talk between different transmitter systems that directly or indirectly affect the respiratory centers in the medulla. Hence, the discovery of pharmacodynamic links between the opioid and both the serotonergic [42] and the dopaminergic [43] systems in the respiratory centers of the rat may imply that drugs and psychiatric states that affect other transmitter systems influence the susceptibility to opioid toxicity. Further, in rats, flunitrazepam has been demonstrated to quite variably influence the median lethal dose for morphine, methadone, and buprenorphine [44].

These findings motivate toxicological testing that includes several nonopioid drugs. To pinpoint potentially dangerous drug use patterns, studies of a much larger material than that reported here are required, and the application of the proposed approach by other investigators is therefore encouraged.

10.3.2 Medications

Given the limited evaluation of hair detections of illicit drugs in opioid overdose cases, the use of hair to confirm or exclude abstinence from other groups of drugs is even less explored. A number of reports, for example [45–48], have included side information about hair levels of certain drugs in case reports on poisonings. It seems likely that such analyses may be helpful to identify abstinent/naïve users with possible low tolerance to certain groups of pharmaceutical drugs. In addition to the problems of making the diagnosis intoxication, another issue is the manner of death, which in many instances may be just as important to the forensic pathologist. The finding of a substance considered to have caused death also in several hair segments can indicate that the concentrations found in blood emanate from a chronic use, and thus are not related to an acute intake (although an acute-upon-chronic sometimes may be difficult to exclude). Evaluation of segmental hair analysis in combination with evaluation of the levels of parent drug and metabolite in peripheral postmortem blood [49], and perhaps in additional body fluids, should most likely improve the interpretation of both cause and manner of death.

Finally, in addition to the possible assistance of hair analysis for determination of cause and manner of death, drug detections in hair can also be of importance for identification purposes, e.g., in cases of severely decomposed bodies, or even skeletonized bodies, as long as hair is still available. Detection of 6-acetylmorphine, cocaine, or amphetamine in hair is a strong indication that the deceased was a drug addict, and hence limit the search for possible matches among reported missing persons.

10.4 CONCLUSIONS AND TAKE-HOME MESSAGE

Screening for drugs with LC-MS/MS without a washing procedure is a convenient procedure to identify cases where more detailed analysis is warranted. Analysis for drugs of abuse in short hair segments can provide detailed information of the recent and past drug abuse pattern and may improve the diagnostic accuracy of fatal poisonings.

TABLE 10.1
Drug Detections in Hair and Femoral Blood, Manner of Death, evidence of Delayed Death, and Contributing Pathology in Heroin-Overdose Deaths

Case No.	Drugs in Hair (S5, S4, S3, S2, and/or S1)	Opiates in Hair S5	S4	S3	S2	S1	MO in Blood (μg/g)	Other Drugs in Blood	Age (Sex)	MoD/DD	Contributing Pathology
								Abstinent			
1	FLU, 7-a-FLU, DIA	na	na	na	–	–	0.30	7-a-FLU, DIA, dmDIA, THC	20 (M)	A / No	—
2	AMPH	na	na	na	na	–	0.16	AMPH, THC	25 (M)	A / Yes	pneumonia, myocard ischemia
3	6-MAM	+	–	–	–	–	0.33	COD, 7-a-FLU	27 (M)	A / No	—
4	AMPH, DIA	–	–	–	–	–	0.24	6-MAM, COD, AMPH, DIA, dmDIA, LEV, dmLEV, CIT, dmCIT	38 (M)	A / No	—
5	AMPH	–	–	–	–	–	0.11	6-MAM, COD, EtOH, CMZ, ALP, FLX	43 (M)	A / No	—
6	AMPH	na	–	–	–	–	0.02	AMPH, THC	48 (M)	A / Yes	acute bronchitis, duodenal ulcer
7	AMPH	–	–	–	–	–	0.10	6-MAM, COD, EtOH, THC	40 (M)	A / No	fatty liver
8	—	–	–	–	–	–	0.11	6-MAM, COD, EtOH, THC	39 (M)	A / No	—
9	MO, 6-MAM, COD, TRAM	+	+	+	–	–	0.15	COD, FENT, TRAM, OdmTRAM	35 (M)	A / No	—
10	COC, BE	–	–	–	–	–	0.04	EtOH, BE	39 (M)	A / Yes	—
11	6-MAM, COC	+	–	–	–	–	0.69	6-MAM, COD, DIA, dmDIA, ALI, COC, BE	25 (M)	A / No	pneumonia
12	6-MAM, COD, AMPH	na	+	–	–	–	0.26	6-MAM, COD, AMPH, 7-a-FLU	29 (M)	A / No	hepatitis, cardiomegaly
13	6-MAM, AMPH, MA, TRAM	+	–	–	–	–	3.30	EtOH, AMPH, MA, DIA, dmDIA, DPROP, dmSERT, PARA	46 (F)	S / No	—
14	AMPH	–	–	–	–	–	0.04	COD, AMPH, DIA, dmDIA, THC	43 (M)	A / Yes	pneumonia
15	—	na	na	na	na	–	0.16	COD, EtOH	42 (M)	A / No	myocarditis, hepatitis

16	AMPH, MA	–	–	–	–	–	0.28	6-MAM, COD, CIT, dmCIT, dmDIA, THC	66 (M)	U / U	pneumonia, asthma, hepatitis
17	COC	na	na	na	na	–	0.08	COD, DIA, dmDIA, COC, BE	23 (M)	U / U	asthma
18	—	na	na	na	na	–	0.39	6-MAM, COD, EtOH	28 (M)	U / No	hepatitis
Mean ± SD							0.38 ± 0.75		37 ± 11		
Median							0.16		39		
								Tolerant			
19	MO	na	na	+	+	+	0.27	EtOH	40 (M)	S / No	fatty liver
20	MO, 6-MAM, COD, FENT	+	+	+	+	+	0.07	EtOH, 7-a-FLU, dmDIA, FENT	38 (M)	A / No	hepatitis
21	MO, 6-MAM, COD, FENT, AMPH	+	+	+	+	+	0.11	FENT, AMPH, DIA, dmDIA	31 (M)	A / Yes	acute bronchitis
22	MO, 6-MAM, COD, 7-a-CLO	na	na	+	+	+	0.30	COD, 7-a-CLO	22 (M)	A / No	—
23	6-MAM, COC, BE	na	na	+	+	+	0.02	DIA, THC	31 (M)	A / Yes	pneumonia, pericarditis
24	6-MAM, COC, BE	na	na	na	na	+	0.09	COD	34 (M)	A / No	—
25	MO, 6-MAM, COD, FLU, 7-a-FLU	+	+	+	+	+	1.80	6-MAM, COD, 7-a-FLU	41 (M)	S / No	—
26	MO, 6-MAM, COD	+	+	+	+	+	0.18	COD, PARA	65 (M)	A / U	cardiomegaly
27	MO, 6-MAM, COD, FENT, MDN, FLU, 7-a-FLU	+	+	+	+	+	0.80	COD, FENT, 7-a-FLU, CHLORO, THC	46 (M)	S / Yes	—
28	MO, 6-MAM, COD, FENT, TRAM, KETO, NZ, FLU, 7-a-FLU, CLON, 7-a-CLO, DIA, dmDIA, ALP	+	+	+	+	+	0.08	COD, FENT, BUP, NBUP, DIA, dmDIA, 7-a-FLU, CHLORO	40 (F)	A / No	acute bronchitis, hepatitis
Mean ± SD							0.37 ± 0.55		39 ± 11		
Median							0.15		39		

TABLE 10.1 (continued)

Abbreviations: S1-S5 = Segment 1–5; where Segment 1 is the most recent; na = not available; + = opiates detected (MO; 6-MAM; COD; MDN; BUP; NBUP; KETO; TRAM or FENT); – = opiates not detected; M = Male; F = Female; MoD = Manner of Death; DD = Delayed Death; A = Accident; S = Suicide; U = Uncertain; *Drugs:* 6-MAM = 6-Monoacetylmorphine; 7-a-CLO = 7-amino-Clonazepam; 7-a-NZ = 7-amino-Nitrazepam; 7-a-FLU = 7-amino-Flunitrazepam; ALI = Alimemazine; ALP = Alprazolam; AMPH = Amphetamine; BE = Benzoylecgonine; BUP = Buprenorphine; CHLORO = Chloroquine; CLON = Clonazepam; CMZ = Carbamazepine; COC = Cocaine; COD = Codeine; CIT = Citalopram; dmCIT = Desmethylcitalopram; dmLEV = Desmethyllevomepromazine; DPROP = Dihydropropiomazine; dmSERT = Desmethylsertraline; DIA = Diazepam; EtOH = Ethanol; FENT = Fentanyl; FLU = Flunitrazepam; FLX = Fluoxetine; KETO = Ketobemidone; LEV = Levomepromazine; MA = Methamphetamine; MDN = Methadone; MO = Morphine; NZ = Nitrazepam; NBUP = Norbuprenorphine; dmDIA = Nordazepam; OdmTRAM = O-desmethyltramadol; PARA = Paracetamol (Acetaminophen); THC = tetrahydrocannabinol; TRAM = Tramadol.

REFERENCES

1. Palmeri, A., Pichini, S., Pacifici, R., Zuccaro, P., and Lopez, A., Drugs in nails: physiology, pharmacokinetics and forensic toxicology, *Clin. Pharmacokinet.*, 38, 95–110, 2000.
2. Welch, M.J., Sniegoski, L.T., Allgood, C.C., and Habram, M., Hair analysis for drugs of abuse: evaluation of analytical methods, environmental issues, and development of reference materials, *J. Anal. Toxicol.*, 17, 389–398, 1993.
3. Couper, F.J., McIntyre, I.M., and Drummer, O.H., Detection of antidepressant and antipsychotic drugs in postmortem human scalp hair, *J. Forensic Sci.*, 40, 87–90, 1995.
4. Kintz, P. and Cirimele, V., Interlaboratory comparison of quantitative determination of amphetamine and related compounds in hair samples, *Forensic Sci. Int.*, 84, 151–156, 1997.
5. Sachs, H. and Raff, I., Comparison of quantitative results of drugs in human hair by GC/MS, *Forensic Sci. Int.*, 63, 207–216, 1993.
6. Offidani, C., Strano-Rossi, S., and Chiarotti, M., Improved enzymatic hydrolysis of hair, *Forensic Sci. Int.*, 63, 171–174, 1993.
7. Offidani, C., Carnevale, A., and Chiarotti, M., Drugs in hair: a new extraction procedure, *Forensic Sci. Int.*, 41, 35–39, 1989.
8. Nakahara, Y., Kikura, R., and Takahashi, K., Hair analysis for drugs of abuse, VIII: effective extraction and determination of 6-acetylmorphine and morphine in hair with trifluoroacetic acid-methanol for the confirmation of retrospective heroin use by gas chromatography-mass spectrometry, *J. Chromatogr. B Biomed. Appl.*, 657, 93–101, 1994.
9. Edder, P., Staub, C., Veuthey, J.L., Pierroz, I., and Haerdi, W., Subcritical fluid extraction of opiates in hair of drug addicts, *J. Chromatogr. B Biomed. Appl.*, 658, 75–86, 1994.
10. Pichini, S., Altieri, I., Pellegrini, M., Pacifici, R., and Zuccaro, P., Hair analysis for nicotine and cotinine: evaluation of extraction procedures, hair treatments, and development of reference material, *Forensic Sci. Int.*, 84, 243–252, 1997.
11. Polettini, A., Stramesi, C., Vignali, C., and Montagna, M., Determination of opiates in hair: effects of extraction methods on recovery and on stability of analytes, *Forensic Sci. Int.*, 84, 259–269, 1997.
12. Eser, H.P., Pötsch, L., Skopp, G., and Moeller, M.R., Influence of sample preparation on analytical results: drug analysis (GC/MS) on hair snippets versus hair powder using various extraction methods, *Forensic Sci. Int.*, 84, 271–279, 1997.
13. Claffey, D.J, Stout, P.R., and Ruth, J.A., A comparison of sodium hydroxide and sodium sulfide digestion of mouse hair in the recovery of radioactivity following systemic administration of [3H]-nicotine and [3H]-flunitrazepam, *J. Anal. Toxicol.*, 24, 54–58, 2000.
14. Baumgartner, W.A. and Hill, V.A., Hair analysis for organic analytes: methodology, reliability issues, and field studies, in *Drug Testing in Hair*, Kintz, P., Ed., CRC Press, Boca Raton, FL, 1996, pp. 223–266.
15. Negrusz, A. et al., Highly sensitive micro-plate enzyme immunoassay screening and NCI-GC-MS confirmation of flunitrazepam and its major metabolite 7-amino-flunitrazepam in hair, *J. Anal. Toxicol.*, 23, 429–435, 1999.
16. Moore, C., Deitermann, D., Lewis, D., Feeley, B., and Niedbala, R.S., The detection of cocaine in hair specimens using micro-plate enzyme immunoassay, *J. Forensic Sci.*, 44, 609–612, 1999.
17. Baumgartner, W.A. and Hill, V.A., Sample preparation techniques, *Forensic Sci. Int.*, 63, 121–135, 1993.

18. Martz, R., Donnelly, B., Fetterolf, D., Lasswell, L., Hime, G.W., and Hearn, W.L., The use of hair analysis to document a cocaine overdose following a sustained survival period before death, *J. Anal. Toxicol.*, 15, 279–281, 1991.
19. Gaillard, Y. and Pepin, G., Evidence of polydrug use using hair analysis: a fatal case involving heroin, cocaine, cannabis, chloroform, thiopental and ketamine, *J. Forensic Sci.*, 43, 435–438, 1998.
20. Selavka, C.M., Mason, A.P., Riker, C.D., and Crookham, S., Determination of fentanyl in hair: the case of the crooked criminalist, *J. Forensic Sci.*, 40, 681–685, 1995.
21. Kintz, P., Cirimele, V., Sachs, H., Jeanneau, T., and Ludes, B., Testing for anabolic steroids in hair from two bodybuilders, *Forensic Sci. Int.*, 101, 209–216, 1999.
22. Kronstrand, R., Grundin, R., and Jonsson, J., Incidence of opiates, amphetamines, and cocaine in hair and blood in fatal cases of heroin overdose, *Forensic Sci. Int.*, 92, 29–38, 1998.
23. Cirimele, V., Kintz, P., and Mangin, P., Detection and quantification of lorazepam in human hair by GC-MS/NCI in a case of traffic accident, *Int. J. Legal Med.*, 108, 265–267, 1996.
24. Kintz, P., Cirimele, V., Edel, Y., Tracqui, A., and Mangin, P., Characterization of dextromoramide (Palfium) abuse by hair analysis in a denied case, *Int. J. Legal Med.*, 107, 269–272, 1995.
25. Kintz, P. and Mangin, P., Toxicological findings after fatal fenfluramine self-poisoning, *Hum. Exp. Toxicol.*, 11, 51–52, 1992.
26. Tracqui, A., Kintz, P., and Mangin, P., Fatal poisoning involving amitriptyline: toxicologic data, *J. Toxicol. Clin. Exp.*, 12, 3–9, 1992.
27. Marsh, A. and Evans, M.B., Challenging declarations of abstinence by the determination of morphine in hair by radioimmunoassay, *J. Pharm. Biomed. Anal.*, 11, 693–698, 1993.
28. Tagliaro, F., De Battisti, Z., Smith, F.P., and Marigo, M., Death from heroin overdose: findings from hair analysis, *Lancet*, 351, 1923–1925, 1998.
29. Darke, S., Hall, W., Kaye, S., Ross, J., and Duflou, J., Hair morphine concentrations of fatal heroin overdose cases and living heroin users, *Addiction*, 97, 977–984, 2002.
30. Clauwaert, K.M., Van Bocxlaer, J.F., Lambert, W.E., and De Leenheer, A.P., Segmental analysis for cocaine and metabolites by HPLC in hair of suspected drug overdose cases, *Forensic Sci. Int.*, 110, 157–166, 2000.
31. Nakahara, Y. and Kikura, R., Hair analysis for drugs of abuse, XVIII: 3,4-methylenedioxymethamphetamine (MDMA) disposition in hair roots and use in identification of acute MDMA poisoning, *Biol. Pharm. Bull.*, 20, 969–972, 1997.
32. Harkey, M.R., Anatomy and physiology of hair, *Forensic Sci. Int.*, 63, 9–18, 1993.
33. Pötsch, L., A discourse on human hair fibers and reflections on the conservation of drug molecules, *Int. J. Legal Med.*, 108, 285–293, 1996.
34. Castanet, J. and Ortonne, J.P., Hair melanin and hair color, *EXS*, 78, 209–225, 1997.
35. White, J.M. and Irvine, R.J., Mechanisms of fatal opioid overdose, *Addiction*, 94, 961–972, 1999.
36. Cairns, T., Hill, V., Schaffer, M., and Thistle, W., Removing and identifying drug contamination in the analysis of human hair, *Forensic Sci. Int.*, 145, 97–108, 2004.
37. Schaffer, M., Hill, V., and Cairns, T., Hair analysis for cocaine: the requirement for effective wash procedures and effects of drug concentration and hair porosity in contamination and decontamination, *J. Anal. Toxicol.*, 29, 319–326, 2005.
38. Schaffer, M.I., Wang, W.L., and Irving, J., An evaluation of two wash procedures for the differentiation of external contamination versus ingestion in the analysis of human hair samples for cocaine, *J. Anal. Toxicol.*, 26, 485–488, 2002.

39. Kronstrand, R., Nystrom, I., Strandberg, J., and Druid, H., Screening for drugs of abuse in hair with ion spray LC-MS-MS, *Forensic Sci. Int.*, 145, 183–190, 2004.
40. Druid, H. and Holmgren, P., A compilation of fatal and control concentrations of drugs in postmortem femoral blood, *J. Forensic Sci.*, 42, 79–87. 1997.
41. Musshoff, F., Lachenmeier, K., Wollersen, H., Lichtermann, D., and Madea, B., Opiate concentrations in hair from subjects in a controlled heroin-maintenance program and from opiate-associated fatalities, *J. Anal. Toxicol.*, 29, 345–352, 2005.
42. Manzke, T. et al., 5-HT4(a) receptors avert opioid-induced breathing depression without loss of analgesia, *Science*, 301, 226–229, 2003.
43. Lalley, P.M., D1-dopamine receptor agonists prevent and reverse opiate depression of breathing but not antinociception in the cat, *Am. J. Physiol. Regulatory, Integrative Comparative Physiol.*, 289, R45–R51, 2005.
44. Borron, S.W., Monier, C., Risède, P., and Baud, F.J., Flunitrazepam variably alters morphine, buprenorphine, and methadone lethality in the rat, *Hum. Exp. Toxicol.*, 21, 599–605, 2002.
45. Cirimele, V., Kintz, P., Tracqui, A., and Mangin, P., A fatal dothiepin overdose, *Forensic Sci. Int.*, 76, 205–209, 1995.
46. Kintz, P., Cirimele, V., Tracqui, A., and Mangin, P., Fatal zipeprol intoxication, *Int. J. Legal Med.*, 107, 267–268, 1995.
47. Mantzouranis, E.C., Bertsias, G.K., Pallis, E.G., and Tsatsakis, A.M., Hair analysis differentiates chronic from acute carbamazepine intoxication, *Pediatr. Neurol.*, 31, 73–75, 2004.
48. Poklis, A. and Saady, J.J., Arsenic poisoning: acute or chronic? Suicide or murder? *Am. J. Forensic Med. Pathol.*, 11, 226–232, 1990.
49. Apple, F.S., Postmortem tricyclic antidepressant concentrations: assessing cause of death using parent drug to metabolite ratio, *J. Anal. Toxicol.*, 13, 197–198, 1989.

11 Detection of Doping Agents in Human Hair

Pascal Kintz

CONTENTS

11.1 INTRODUCTION

The use of stimulants (amphetamine, ephedrine, strychnine) in sport to improve performances was reported in the early 1900s. The Medical Commission of the International Olympic Committee (IOC) established in 1967 the first list of prohibited substances and methods and adopted a medical code to protect the health of athletes and to ensure respect for the ethical concepts implicit in fair play, the Olympic spirit, and medical practice. More recently, and after the Tour de France in 1998, the concerns about doping resulted in the formation of the World Anti-Doping Agency (WADA).

The current rules governing doping in sport have as their core that a doping violation is deemed to occur upon finding in a body fluid a prohibited substance, a metabolite of a prohibited substance, or a compound chemically or pharmacologically related to a prohibited substance. In most cases, urine is the specimen of choice, but recombinant human erythropoietin and related compounds or hormones can be detected in blood (1). To date, hair is not accepted in doping control, although France passed in 2001 a law allowing biologists to use this matrix to document doping (décret n° 2001-35 from 11 January 2001).

The major practical advantage of hair testing compared with urine or blood testing for drugs is that it has a larger surveillance window (weeks to months, depending on the length of the hair shaft, against 2 to 4 days for most xenobiotics).

TABLE 11.1
Comparison between Urine and Hair for Testing Doping Agents in Sport

Parameters	Urine	Hair
Drugs	all, except some peptidic hormones	all, except hormones
Major compound	metabolites	parent drug
Detection period	2–5 days, except anabolic steroids	weeks, months
Type of measure	incremental	cumulative
Screening	yes	no
Invasiveness	high	low
Storage	–20°C	ambient temperature
Risk of false negative	high	low
Risk of false positive	low	undetermined
Risk of adulteration	high	low
Control material	yes	needed

For practical purposes, the two tests complement each other. Urinalysis and blood analysis provide short-term information of an individual's drug use, whereas long-term histories are accessible through hair analysis. While analysis of urine and blood specimens cannot distinguish between chronic use or single exposure, hair analysis can offer the distinction. Table 11.1 summarizes major characteristics of each specimen in regard to its place in doping control.

At this time, a possible inequity in doping control, linked to racial bias, has been pointed out by those who are against hair in such a situation. Drugs appear to be incorporated into the hair during at least three stages: from the blood during hair formation, from sweat and sebum, and from external environment. From various studies, it has been demonstrated that after the same dosage, black hair incorporates much more drugs than blond hair (2, 3). This has resulted in discussions about a possible racial bias of hair analysis and is still under evaluation.

The possibility of racial bias due to differences in melanin concentrations or in hair porosity is still in discussion. Melanins are responsible for the color of hair. Two types of melanin are present, eumelanin (with low sulfur content) and pheomelanin (with high sulfur content). Black and brown hair contain more eumelanin than red and blond hair. It appears that it is not simply the concentration of drugs in blood that determines the concentration in hair. Numerous factors may influence the incorporation of drugs into hair, such as the nature of the compounds (pKa, lipid solubility, metabolism pattern) and variation in hair growth cycles. Until these mechanisms are elucidated, the quantitative results and extrapolation to the amount of drug intake of such a hair analysis should be considered with extreme caution (4).

11.2 PROCEDURES

11.2.1 Specimen Collection

Collection procedures for hair analysis for drugs have not been standardized. Hair is best collected from the area at the back of the head, called the *vertex posterior*.

Compared with other areas of the head, this area has less variability in the hair growth rate, the number of hairs in the growing phase is more constant, and the hair is less subject to age- and sex-related influences. Hair strands are cut as close as possible from the scalp, and the identification root and tip must be mentioned. Samples can be stored at ambient temperature in aluminum foil, an envelope, or a plastic tube. The sample size varies considerably among laboratories and depends on the drug to be analyzed and the test methodology. For example, when nandrolone or betamethasone are investigated, a 100-mg sample is recommended. However, cocaine or amphetamine can be investigated on a 10-mg sample. Sample sizes reported in the literature range from a single hair to 200 mg, cut as close to the scalp as possible. When sectional analysis is performed, the hair is cut into segments of about 1, 2, or 3 cm, which corresponds to about 1, 2, or 3 months' growth.

11.2.2 Decontamination Procedures

Contaminants of hair would be a problem if they were drugs of abuse or their metabolites or if they interfered with the analysis and interpretation of the test results. It is unlikely that anyone would intentionally or accidentally apply anything to their hair that would contain testosterone or any anabolic. The most crucial issue facing hair analysis is the avoidance of technical and evidentiary false positives. Technical false positives are caused by errors in the collection, processing, and analysis of specimens, while evidentiary false positives are caused by passive exposure to the drug. Various approaches for preventing evidentiary false positives due to external contamination of the hair specimens have been described.

Most but not all laboratories use a wash step; however, there is no consensus or uniformity in the washing procedures. Among the agents used in washing are detergents such as Prell shampoo, surgical scrubbing solutions, surfactants such as 0.1% sodium dodecylsulfate, phosphate buffer, or organic solvents such as acetone, diethyl ether, methanol, ethanol, dichloromethane, hexane, or pentane of various volumes for various contact times. Generally, a single washing step is used; sometimes a second identical wash is performed. In contrast to testing for crack, cannabis, or smoked heroin, decontamination when testing for doping agents does not appear as a critical step.

11.3 DETECTION OF DOPING AGENTS

11.3.1 Detection of Anabolic Steroids

Athletes use both endogenous (testosterone, dehydroepiandrosterone (DHEA)) or exogenous (nandrolone, stanozolol, mesterolone) anabolic steroids because it has been claimed that they increase lean body mass, increase strength, increase aggressiveness, and lead to a shorter recovery time between workouts.

The first data available for endogenous steroids in hair were given late in 1995 by the German group of Scherer and Reinhardt (5), who used GC-MS (gas chromatography-mass spectrometry) to detect androstenediol (9 to 19 pg/mg), testosterone (13 to 24 pg/mg), androstenedione (5 to 15 pg/mg), DHEA (21 to 56 pg/mg), dihydrotestosterone (2 to 8 pg/mg), and 17alpha-hydroxy-progesterone (1 to 7 pg/mg). Some years later, Kintz et al. (6, 7) established the physiological concentrations of both testosterone and DHEA with a distinction between hair of male and female subjects. After decontamination with dichloromethane, 100 mg of hair was incubated in 1*M* NaOH in the presence of testosterone-d_3. After neutralization, the extract was purified using solid-phase extraction with Isolute C18 columns followed by liquid-liquid extraction with pentane. After silylation, the drugs were analyzed by GC-MS. Concentrations for DHEA were in the range of 1 to 7 pg/mg (mean 4 pg/mg) and 0.5 to 11 pg/mg (mean 5 pg/mg) for the males ($n = 15$) and females ($n = 12$), respectively. Concentrations for testosterone were in the range 0.5 to 12 pg/mg (mean 4 pg/mg) and not detected to 2 pg/mg for the males ($n = 41$) and females ($n = 12$), respectively.

Unlike testosterone in urine, the interpretation of concentration findings in hair can be difficult and critical. The range between physiological concentrations of testosterone and those found in abusers seems to be rather small. Therefore, in complement of testosterone determination, the identification of unique testosterone esters in hair enables an unambiguous charge for doping because the esters are certainly exogenous substances. This approach was largely developed by Thieme et al. (8) and Gaillard et al. (9), and Rivier (10) recently claimed that although hair analysis alone cannot be useful for screening purposes, it could become a useful technique for obtaining additional information on long-term testosterone abuse.

Thieme et al. (8) published in 2000 a complete analytical strategy for detecting anabolics in hair. The preparation of the sample was carried out by a methanol extraction step with sonication for all the anabolics, except for stanozolol, which was incubated in NaOH. Extensive cleanup procedures were employed, such as HPLC (high-performance liquid chromatography) and solid-phase extraction, followed by derivatization to form the enol-TMS derivatives. Drugs were identified either by GLC-MS/MS or GC-HRMS (GC-high-resolution mass spectrometry). Metandienone and its metabolite 6β-hydroxymetandienone, stanozolol and its metabolite 3′-hydroxy-stanozolol, mesterolone, metenolone enantate, nandrolone decanoate, and several testosterone esters, such as propionate, isocaproate, decanoate, and phenylpropionate, were identified in hair of several bodybuilders.

Gaillard et al. (9) developed a method for testing both the anabolic steroids and their esters. A 100-mg amount of powdered hair was first treated with methanol for extraction of esters, then alkaline digested with 1*M* NaOH for the recovery of the other drugs. These preparations were extracted with ethyl acetate, pooled, then finally highly purified using a twin solid-phase extraction on amino and silica cartridges. After silylation, drugs were detected by GC-MS/MS. Nandrolone and testosterone undecanoate were identified in hair of two athletes at 5.1 and 15.2 pg/mg.

A sensitive, specific, and reproducible method for the quantitative determination of stanozolol in human hair was developed by Cirimele et al. (11). The sample preparation involved a decontamination step of the hair with methylene chloride and the sonication in methanol of 100 mg of powdered hair for 2 h. After elimination of the solvent, the hair sample was solubilized in 1 ml 1*N* NaOH, 15 min at 95°C, in the presence of 10 ng stanozolol-d_3 used as internal standard. The homogenate was neutralized and extracted using consecutively a solid phase (Isolute C18) and a liquid-liquid (pentane) extraction. After evaporation of the final organic phase, the dry extract was derivatized using 40 μl N-methyl-N-trimethylsilyl-heptafluorobutyramide/trimethylsilylimizadole (MBHFA/TMSI) (1000:20, v/v), incubated for 5 min at 80°C, followed by 10 μl of N-methyl-N-trimethylsilyl-heptafluorobutyramide (MBHFBA), incubated for 30 min at 80°C. The derivatized extract was analyzed by a Hewlett-Packard GC-MS system with a 5989 B Engine operating in negative chemical ionization mode of detection. The assay was capable of detecting 2 pg of stanozolol per milligram of hair when approximately 100 mg hair material was processed. The analysis of a 3-cm-long hair strand, obtained from a young bodybuilder (27 years old) declaring to be a regular user of Winstrol® (stanozolol, 2 mg), revealed the presence of stanozolol at the concentration of 15 pg/mg.

More recently, Kintz et al. (12) published a method for the quantitative determination of methenolone in human hair. The sample preparation involved a decontamination step of the hair with methylene chloride. The hair sample (about 100 mg) was solubilized in 1 ml 1*N* NaOH, 15 min at 95°C, in the presence of 1 ng testosterone-d_3 used as internal standard. The homogenate was neutralized and extracted using consecutively a solid-phase (Isolute C18 eluted with methanol) and a liquid-liquid (pentane) extraction. The residue was derivatized by adding 50 μl N-methyl-N-trimethylsilyltrifluoroacetamide/ammonium iodide (MSTFA/NH_4I)/2-mercaptoethanol (1000:2:5, v/v/v), then incubated for 20 min at 60°C. A 1.5-μl aliquot of the derivatized extract was injected into the column (HP5-MS capillary column, 5% phenyl-95 % methylsiloxane, 30 m × 0.25 mm i.d., 0.25 mm film thickness) of a Hewlett-Packard (Palo Alto, CA) gas chromatograph (6890 Series). Methenolone was detected by its parent ion at m/z 446 and daughter ions at m/z 208 and 195 through a Finnigan TSQ 700 MS/MS system. The assay was capable of detecting 1 pg/mg of methenolone when approximately 100 mg hair material was used. The analysis of a strand of hair obtained from two bodybuilders revealed the presence of methenolone at concentrations of 7.3 and 8.8 pg/mg.

Using quite the same method (except for the internal standard, where nandrolone-d_3 was used), the same group developed a procedure to test for nandrolone, the most abused anabolic agent (13). The limit of detection of the assay was 0.5 pg/mg. Nandrolone tested positive in the hair of three athletes at the concentration of 1.0, 3.5, and 7.5 pg/mg.

Nandrolone is metabolized to norandrosterone and noretiocholanolone. Other 19-norsteroids, such as norandrostenedione or norandrostenediol, classified as anabolic androgenic steroids by the IOC, are available over the counter or through the Internet and have the same metabolites as nandrolone. Although norandrostenediol and norandrostenedione are banned by the IOC, there is a great need in forensic science and for the survey of athletes, to discriminate nandrolone from other 19-norsteroids. This is obviously not possible in urine, as the metabolites are common. Hair can identify the exact nature of the parent compound (e.g., nandrolone, norandrostenediol, or norandrostenedione, in the case of positive urine for norandrosterone), as it has been accepted by the scientific community that the parent compound is the major analyte that is incorporated in hair. Thus, hair analysis would discriminate nandrolone abuse from over-the-counter preparations containing 19-norsteroids. Recently, our laboratory was requested by an attorney to evaluate potential doping practices of an athlete. The 30-year-old subject tested positive for norandrosterone in urine at 230 ng/ml. The analysis was done in an accredited laboratory, but the athlete denied the result. The analysis of a strand of hair obtained from the athlete

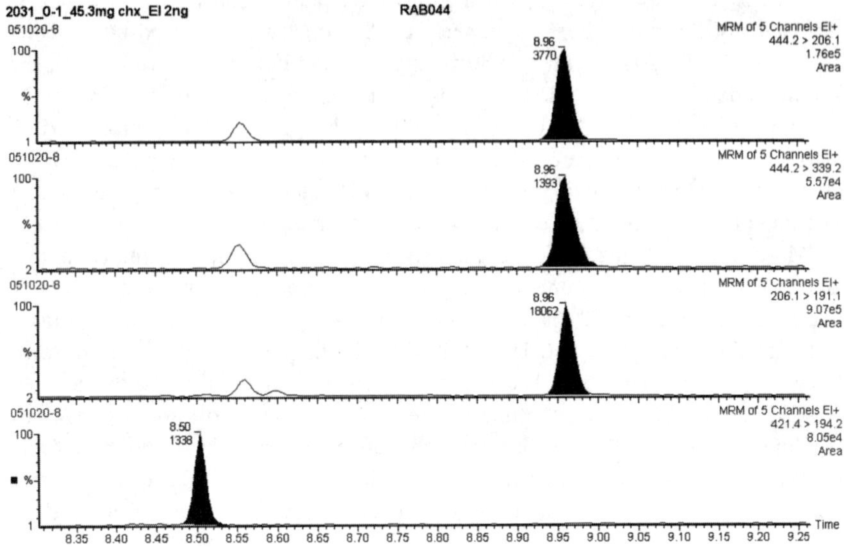

FIGURE 11.1 Chromatogram obtained after extraction by the established procedure of a 45.3-mg hair of an athlete. Metandienone was quantified at the concentration of 79.1 pg/mg. Top: quantification transition for metandienone. Middle: two qualifying transitions of metandienone. Bottom: nandrolone-d_3 with its daughter ion at m/z 194.2.

revealed the presence of 19-norandrostenedione at the concentration of 7 pg/mg (14), making a unique distinction from nandrolone doping.

In 1999 (15), two male bodybuilders were arrested by the French customs in possession of 2050 tablets and 251 ampules of various anabolic steroids. It was claimed that the steroids were for personal use and not for trafficking, as suggested by the police. Hair from both males were positive for nandrolone (196 and 260 pg/mg), testosterone (46 and 71 pg/mg), and stanozolol (135 and 156 pg/mg), clearly indicating steroid abuse.

In a series of seven steroid abusers, Deng et al. (16) identified nandrolone (20 pg/mg) and methyltestosterone (170 pg/mg). More recently, Dumestre-Toulet et al. (17), in a case of trafficking of doping agents, used GC-MS to identify nandrolone (1 to 7.5 pg/mg, $n = 3$), stanozolol (2 to 84 ng/mg, $n = 4$), methenolone (17 and 34 pg/mg), testosterone enanthate (0.6 to 18.8 ng/mg, $n = 5$), and testosterone cypionate (3.3 and 4.8 ng/mg) in the hair of bodybuilders.

This laboratory identified metandienone in the hair of an athlete who denied the use of the drug that had been identified by a WADA-accredited laboratory during a control. The analysis of a 5-cm strand of hair obtained from the athlete revealed the presence of metandienone at the concentrations of 78 pg/mg for the segment of 0 to 1 cm, 7 pg/mg for the segment of 1 to 2 cm, 10 pg/mg, for the segment of 2 to 3 cm, and 108 pg/mg for the last segment (3 cm to the end of the strand). The transition m/z 444 to 206 has been used to determine the concentrations of metandienone in the different segments. Figure 11.1 is the chromatogram obtained for the first segment (0 to 1 cm) of the athlete's hair.

TABLE 11.2
Compendium of Results for Endogenous Anabolics in Hair

Compounds	Mean (pg/mg)	Mini (pg/mg)	Maxi (pg/mg)
Testosterone	8.4	1.5	64.2
Epitestosterone	2.4	0.5	17.6
DHEA	16.9	0.8	94.2
Dehydrotestosterone	1.8	0.5	4.2

As a full example, our procedure to test for anabolics is described in detail. The hair was decontaminated twice using 5 ml of methylene chloride, for 2 min at room temperature, and then pulverized in a ball mill. Then 100 mg of decontaminated hair was incubated in 1 ml 1*N* NaOH, 15 min at 95°C, in the presence of 1 ng of testosterone-d_3 used as internal standard (IS). After cooling, the homogenate was neutralized with 1 ml 1*M* HCl, and 2 ml of 0.2*M* phosphate buffer (pH 7.0) were added.

The Isolute C18 columns were conditioned with 3 ml of methanol, followed by 3 ml of deionized water. After sample addition, the columns were washed twice with 1 ml of deionized water. After column drying, analyte elution occurred with the addition of 3 aliquots of 0.5 ml of methanol. The eluant was evaporated to dryness under nitrogen flow, and the residue reconstituted in 1 ml of 0.2*M* phosphate buffer (pH 7.0). A further purification step was achieved by addition of 100 mg of $Na_2CO_3/NaHCO_3$ (1:10, w/w) and 2 ml of pentane. After agitation and centrifugation, the organic phase was removed and evaporated to dryness. The residue was derivatized by adding 5 µl MSTFA-NH_4I-2-mercaptoethanol (250 µl, 5 mg, 15 µl, respectively) and 45 µl MSTFA, then incubated for 20 min at 60°C.

A 1-µl aliquot of derivatized extract was injected into the column of a Hewlett-Packard (Palo Alto, CA) gas chromatograph (6890 Series). The flow of carrier gas (helium, purity grade 99.9996%) through the column (HP5-MS capillary column, 5% phenyl-95% methylsiloxane, 30 m × 0.32 mm i.d, 0.25 µm film thickness) was 1.5 ml/min.

The injector temperature was 270°C, and splitless injection was employed with a split-valve off time of 1.0 min. The column oven temperature was programmed to rise from an initial temperature of 60°C to 295°C at 30°C/min and maintained at 295°C for the final 10 min.

The detector was a Waters Quattro Micro operated in the electron-impact and in selected-reaction monitoring mode. The parent ions are selected in the first quadrupole. The corresponding daughter ions are selected in the third quadrupole after collision with argon at a cell pressure of 1.00×10^{-4} Pa. The electron multiplier was operated at 650 V.

Results from about 100 hair samples are presented in Table 11.2.

11.3.2 Detection of Corticosteroids

Cortisone and hydrocortisone, naturally occurring hormones, influence metabolism, inflammation, and electrolyte and water balance. Their synthetic derivatives are used

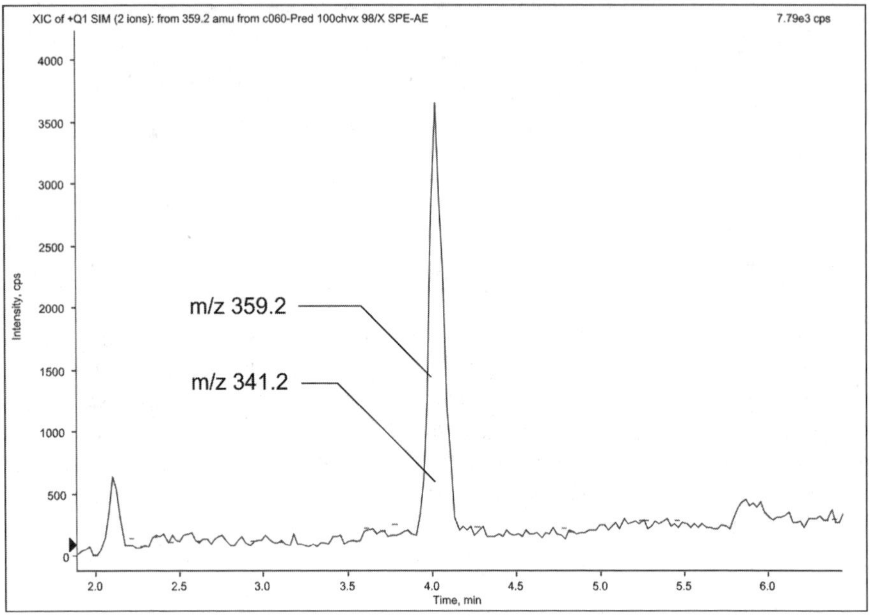

FIGURE 11.2 Typical LC-MS chromatogram of a subject under prednisone treatment. Concentration was 130 pg/mg (quantitation ion: m/z 359.2, corresponding to the M+1).

in therapeutic programs for their anti-inflammatory and immunosuppressive actions. They are also used in certain sports to improve the performances of the athletes (euphoria, motor activity).

Cirimele et al. (18) published in 1999 the first identification of such a drug, in this case prednisone, in the hair of a subject treated for years. A 50-mg hair specimen was incubated overnight in Sorensen buffer, then extracted by solid-phase extraction using an Isolute C18 column. Prednisone was detected by LC-MS at 1280 pg/mg. Using the same preparation technique, and cortisol-d_3 as an internal standard, the same group published (19) several months later a screening procedure for ten corticosteroids, with detection limits in the range 30 to 170 pg/mg. Two applications were documented for prednisone and beclomethasone, identified in hair at 140 and 230 pg/mg, respectively.

Using a 2.0-mm i.d. column, Cirimele et al. (20) demonstrated in ten patients treated with prednisone a low but not insignificant correlation ($r^2 = 0.578, p < 0.03$) between the total amount of ingested drug and the measured concentrations in hair. The procedure was sensitive enough to detect prednisone in the hair of patients treated with a low 5-mg/day dose. A typical chromatogram of one of the patient is given in Figure 11.2.

Repetitive abuse of corticosteroids by athletes can be demonstrated by segmental analysis along the hair shaft, in contrast to punctual urinalysis. A single treatment of about 1 week will show positive in a single 1-cm segment, while long-term abuse will lead to the identification of the corticoid(s) in several segments. For such an application, particularly in the case of a longitudinal survey of athletes, hair analysis appears as the solution of choice to document doping practices. Raul et al. (21) demonstrated that a single oral therapeutic treatment with 4-mg/day betamethasone for nine consecutive days is detectable through hair analysis. The drug tested positive at a concentration of 4.7 pg/mg in the corresponding hair segment, whereas no betamethasone could be identified in the distal hair strand. Extraction of the drug was classic from this group; however, to enhance sensitivity, a MIC 15 CP Nucleosil C18 column (150 × 1.0-mm i.d.) was used.

Bévalot et al. (22) published a confirmatory method for the quantitative determination in hair of the most common corticosteroids used as doping agents by athletes. They extracted drugs from 50 mg of powdered hair by methanolic extraction followed by a solid-phase extraction on a C18 column. Detection was performed with an electrospray ionization mass spectrometer in negative ion mode. The limits of sensitivity were about 100 pg/mg. Hair from athletes revealed the presence of hydrocortisone acetate, methylprednisolone, triamcinolone acetonide, and dexa/betametasone at 430, 1350, 280, and 1310 pg/mg, respectively. According to the authors, who tested in parallel the corresponding urine specimens, the comparison of the results demonstrated once again the dramatic complementary of urinalysis and hair analysis (23).

It has been advocated that high doses or repeated intake of synthetic corticoids leads to a lowering of endogenous cortisol synthesis. Raul et al. (24) postulated that a chronic use of corticoids could influence the physiological concentrations of cortisol and cortisone in hair. Using LC-MS, they established these concentrations at 5 to 91 pg/mg (mean 18 pg/mg) for cortisol and at 12 to 163 pg/mg (mean 70 pg/mg) for cortisone in a population of 17 males and 27 females, aged from 2 to 90 years. The authors did not observe influence of hair color or sex, but the did observe significantly higher cortisone concentrations before the age of 20.

11.3.3 Detection of b-Adrenergic Compounds

β2-agonists are banned because of their sympatomimetic properties (stimulant effects) and their activity as anabolic agents at higher dosages. However, salbutamol is permitted by inhalers only and must be declared in writing prior to the competition.

To date, only three papers are available in the literature for these drugs in human hair, two for clenbuterol and one for salbutamol. In their paper, Gleixner et al. (25) identified clenbuterol after incubation in 1,4-dithiothreitol, NaOH, and tertiary butylmethyl ether by enzyme immunoassay (EIA) and confirmation by HPLC-EIA. Clenbuterol accumulated in hair after 10 μg/day for 25 days at concentrations ranging from 23 to 161 pg/mg, with relatively high concentrations in dark hair. The drug was also found in the hair from two bodybuilders at 50 and 92 pg/mg.

In 1999, Machnik et al. (26) tested clenbuterol in the hair of four females who had therapeutically taken the drug as a tocolyticum. Hair was incubated in 1*M* KOH, and the drug was extracted with tertiary butylmethyl ether, followed in some cases by immunoaffinity chromatography, then derivatized with MSTFA-ammonium iodide-TMS ethanethiol. High-resolution mass spectrometry was used to identify clenbuterol. Limit of detection was about 0.8 pg/mg. The levels of clenbuterol determined in hair ranged from 2 to 236 pg/mg.

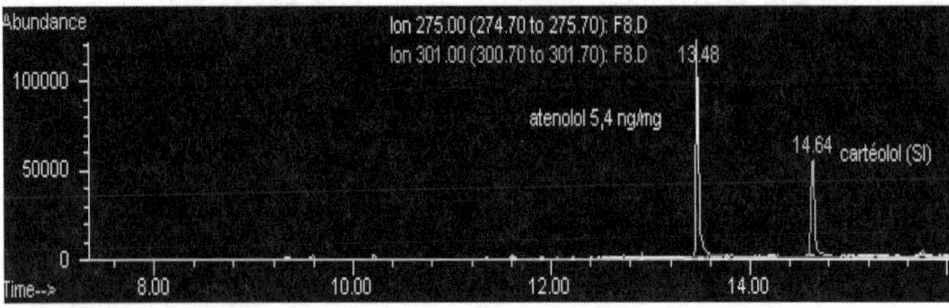

FIGURE 11.3 Typical GC-MS single ion monitoring (SIM) chromatogram of a subject under atenolol treatment. Concentration was 5.4 ng/mg.

More recently (27), Kintz et al. developed a screening procedure for the simultaneous identification of β2-agonists and β-blockers. The procedure involved overnight incubation in 0.1*M* HCl followed by neutralization, solid-phase extraction with an Isolute C18 column, derivatization with trimethylboroxine/ethyl acetate, and GC-MS detection. Limits of detection were 2 pg/mg for both salbutamol and clenbuterol. In nine asthmatic patients, the salbutamol concentrations in hair were in the range 27 to 192 pg/mg. In two asthma deaths, salbutamol concentrations in hair were 210 and 87 pg/mg. Finally, the laboratory identified salbutamol in the hair of a swimmer positive in urine at 71 pg/mg.

Most of the positive specimens are reported for salbutamol (46% of the total urines in 1999 for the IOC laboratory in France). However, as this drug is permitted for specific therapeutic purposes, together with a medical prescription, it appears very easy to evade the test, and almost all cases are considered as justified, even if it is known that the drug can be used to enhance performance. By comparison with concentrations measured in asthmatic patients, segmental analysis (repetitive positive segments) of hair would document unambiguously a doping attitude on the part of the athlete. Salbutamol (15 to 31 pg/mg, $n = 3$) and clenbuterol (15 to 122 pg/mg, $n = 6$) were identified in the hair of bodybuilders arrested for trafficking of a number of doping agents (17).

In addition to their medical use in the treatment of cardiac arrhythmias and hypertension, β-blockers have found a place in some athletic events, particularly disciplines in which good psychomotor coordination is required. In those sports, athletes can benefit from the peripheral blockade of several symptoms associated with anxiety. β-blockers are listed in the classes of drugs subject to certain restrictions, and tests will be conducted in some sports, at the discretion of the responsible authorities. A typical GC-MS chromatogram of a subject under atenolol treatment is given Figure 11.3.

11.4 DISCUSSION

There are essentially three types of problems with urinalysis drug testing: false positives when not confirmed with GC-MS, degradation of observed urine collection, and evasive maneuvers, including adulteration. These problems can be greatly mitigated or eliminated through hair analysis. It is always possible to obtain a fresh, identical hair sample if there is any claim of a specimen mix-up or breach in the chain of custody. This makes hair analysis essentially fail-safe, in contrast to urinalysis, since an identical urine specimen cannot be obtained at a later date.

Another potential use of hair analysis is to verify accidental or unintentional ingestion of drinks or food that have been laced with drugs. In the case of a single use, the hair will not test positive, particularly for anabolics or corticosteroids, that are poorly incorporated in hair. Its greatest use, however, may be in identifying false negatives, since neither abstaining from a drug for a few days or nor trying to "beat the test" by diluting urine will alter the concentration in hair. Urine does not indicate the frequency of drug intake in subjects who might deliberately abstain for several days before biomedical screenings. While analysis of urine specimens cannot distinguish between chronic use or single exposure, hair analysis can make this distinction.

Although hair is not yet a valid specimen for the International Olympic Committee or the World Anti-Doping Agency, it is accepted in most courts of justice. A key issue is that some conflicting results are observed, all involving athletes that tested positive in urine in accredited WADA laboratories and negative in hair in certified forensic laboratories.

A lot of experience has been acquired in the detection of opiates, cocaine, and more recently benzodiazepines or hypnotics in hair. In contrast, there is a serious lack of suitable references to interpret the analytical findings for doping agents. In hair, doping agents concentrations, such as anabolic steroids, corticosteroids, or β2-agonists, are in the range of picograms per milligram, whereas cocaine, amphetamines, or opiates are generally found in the range of several nanograms per milligram. Therefore, the Society of Hair Testing (SOHT) sought to obtain a consensus on hair testing for doping agents (28).

This consensus is as follows :

1. Hair analysis can essentially contribute to doping analysis in special cases, in addition to urine.
2. Hair specimens are not suitable for general routine control.
3. In the case of positive urine results, the negative hair result cannot exclude the administration of the detected drug and cannot overrule the positive urine result.
4. In the case of negative urine results, the positive hair result demonstrates drug exposure during the period prior to sample collection.
5. Before using hair analysis for doping control, sample collection and analytical methods have to be harmonized with respect to the sophisticated requirements already valid for urine.
6. The SOH feels responsible to support efforts that lead to this harmonization.

This statement was adopted on June 16, 1999, by the Society of Hair Testing.

It is clear that there is a great deal of research to be performed before the scientific questions and curiosity surrounding hair drug testing is satisfied. Some of this is due to a lack of consensus among the active investigators on how to interpret the results of an analysis of hair. Among the unanswered questions, five are of critical importance:

1. What is the minimal amount of drug detectable in hair after administration?
2. What is the relationship between the amount of the drug used and the concentration of the drug or its metabolites in hair?
3. What is the influence of hair color?
4. Is there any racial bias in hair testing?
5. What is the influence of cosmetic treatments?

Several answers were recently addressed by Kintz et al. (29) on these specific topics.

Point 5 of this discussion can be resolved by using alternative sources of hair, and it has been recommended that pubic hair be collected in the case of bleached or colored head hair. However, care should be taken when sampling hair from other anatomic regions, as the concentrations can be highly variable according to the specimens. When comparing the physiological concentrations of DHEA and testosterone in hair collected from the head, pubis, and axillae, we were surprised to find an unusually high amount of DHEA sequestered in axillary hair (29).

Unfortunately, according to the WADA, basic scientific knowledge in hair biology is still lacking to make scalp hair analysis a valid tool in the field of doping control, and the following points will have to be resolved before applications:

1. Analytical methods are missing for several doping compounds, such as diuretics.
2. Peptide hormones are not incorporated in hair.
3. Hair washing, discoloring, tinting, and hair color (resulting in potential ethnic discrimination) appear to influence the concentration of drug measured in hair.
4. Drug incorporation within the hair longitudinal axis and over time is not proved to be regular in all occasions.

11.5 CONCLUSIONS

It appears that the value of hair analysis for the identification of drug users is steadily gaining recognition. This can be seen from its growing use in preemployment screening, in forensic sciences, and in clinical applications. Hair analysis may also be a useful adjunct to conventional drug testing in doping control. Specimens can be more easily obtained with less embarrassment, and hair can provide a more accurate history of drug use. However, there are still controversies on how to interpret the results, particularly concerning external contamination, cosmetic treatments, ethnic bias, or drug incorporation. Pure analytical work in hair analysis has reached a sort of plateau, with almost all of the analytical problems having been solved.

Although GC-MS is the method of choice in practice, GC-MS/MS (30) or LC-MS/MS are today used in several laboratories, even for routine cases, particularly to target low-dosage compounds such as anabolics or corticoids. In the case of doping control, drugs are screened in urine specimens according to validated standard operating procedures in accredited laboratories. Because forensic laboratories can also be involved in testimony dealing with doping agents, the idea of using hair for doping control has emerged, as hair analysis has been accepted in court in other cases. Courts can request additional information on patterns of the use of doping substances, such as during the 1998 Tour de France cycling competition, when blood, urine, and hair were simultaneously collected. Hair can both confirm repetitive abuse and identify the exact nature of the parent compound (e.g., nandrolone, norandrostenediol, or norandrostenedione in the case of a positive result for norandrosterone in urine). Moreover, long-term use (over several months) of restricted compounds (only authorized under specific conditions and for a short period), such as salbutamol or corticoids, can be documented through hair analysis. The determination of testosterone esters in hair should allow a definitive, unambiguous confirmation of the administration of exogenous testosterone.

However, some issues remain to be resolved before hair can be considered as a valid specimen by the IOC and the international sport federations. The relationship between urine and hair results is not yet established, and a negative hair result does not mean "no doping." The potential for ethnic discrimination must also be evaluated to avoid inequality during doping control. On the other hand, external contamination of hair samples does not constitute a major problem when testing for doping agents, in contrast to the problems associated with cosmetic treatments or the absence of specimen (bald or fully shaved subject).

REFERENCES

1. Bowers, L.D., Abuse of performance-enhancing drugs in sport, *Ther. Drug Monit.*, 24, 178, 2004.
2. Borges, C.R., Wilkins, D.G., and Rollins, D.E., Amphetamine and N-acetylamphetamine incorporation into hair: an investigation of the potential role of drug basicity in hair color bias, *J. Anal. Toxicol.*, 25, 221, 2001.
3. Henderson, G.L., Harkey, M.R., and Zhou, C., Incorporation of isotopically labeled cocaine into human hair: race as a factor, *J. Anal. Toxicol.*, 22, 156, 1998.
4. Nakahara, Y. et al., Hair analysis for drug abuse, III: movement and stability of methoxyphenamine (as a model compound of methamphetamine) along hair shaft with hair growth, *J. Anal. Toxicol.*, 16, 253, 1992.
5. Scherer, C.R. and Reinhardt, G., Nachweis sechs endogener Steroide in menschlichen Haaren mit GC/MS und Isotopenverdünnungsanalyse, in *Abstract from 74*, Althoff, H., Ed., Jahrestagung der Deutschen Gesellschaft für Rechtsmedizin, Aachen, 1995, p. 55.
6. Kintz, P. et al., Identification of testosterone and testosterone esters in human hair, *J. Anal. Toxicol.*, 23, 352, 1999.
7. Kintz, P., Cirimele, V., and Ludes, B., Physiological concentrations of DHEA in human hair, *J. Anal. Toxicol.*, 23, 424, 1999.
8. Thieme, D. et al., Analytical strategy for detecting doping agents in hair, *Forensic Sci. Int.*, 107, 335, 2000.
9. Gaillard, Y. et al., Gas chromatographic-tandem mass spectrometric determination of anabolic steroids and their esters in hair: application in doping control and meat quality control, *J. Chromatogr. B*, 735, 189, 1999.
10. Rivier, L., New trends in doping analysis, *Chimia*, 56, 84, 2002.

11. Cirimele, V., Kintz, P., and Ludes, B., Testing of the anabolic stanozolol in human hair by gas chromatography-negative ion chemical ionization mass spectrometry, *J. Chromatogr. B*, 740, 265, 2000.
12. Kintz, P. et al., Doping control for methenolone using hair analysis by gas chromatography-tandem mass spectrometry, *J. Chromatogr. B*, 766, 161, 2002.
13. Kintz, P. et al., Doping control for nandrolone using hair analysis, *J. Pharm. Biomed. Anal.*, 24, 1125, 2001.
14. Kintz, P., Cirimele, V., and Ludes, B., Discrimination of the nature of doping with 19-norsteroids through hair analysis, *Clin. Chem.*, 46, 2020, 2000.
15. Kintz, P. et al., Testing for anabolic steroids in hair from two bodybuilders, *Forensic Sci. Int.*, 101, 209, 1999.
16. Deng, X.S., Kurosu, A., and Pounder, D.J., Detection of anabolic steroids in head hair, *J. Forensic Sci.*, 44, 343, 1999.
17. Dumestre-Toulet, V. et al. Hair analysis of seven bodybuilders for anabolic steroids, ephedrine and clenbuterol, *J. Forensic Sci.*, 47, 211, 2002.
18. Cirimele, V. et al., First identification of prednisone in human hair by liquid chromatography-ionspray mass spectrometry, *J. Anal. Toxicol.*, 23, 225, 1999.
19. Cirimele, V. et al., Identification of ten corticosteroids in human hair by liquid chromatography-ionspray mass spectrometry, *Forensic Sci. Int.*, 107, 381, 2000.
20. Cirimele, V. et al., Prednisone concentrations in human hair, *J. Anal. Toxicol.*, 26, 110, 2002.
21. Raul, J.S. et al., A single therapeutic treatment with betamethasone is detectable in hair, *J. Anal. Toxicol.*, 26, 582, 2002.
22. Bévalot, F. et al., Analysis of corticosteroids in hair by liquid chromatography-electrospray ionization mass spectrometry, *J. Chromatogr. B*, 740, 227, 2000.
23. Gaillard, Y., Vaysette, F., and Pépin, G., Compared interest between hair analysis and urinalysis in doping controls: results for amphetamines, corticosteroids and anabolic steroids in racing cyclists, *Forensic Sci. Int.*, 107, 361, 2000.
24. Raul, J.S., Cirimele, V., Ludes, B., and Kintz, P., Detection of physiological concentrations of cortisol and cortisone in human hair, *Clin. Biochem.*, 37, 1105, 2004.
25. Gleixner, A., Sauerwein, H., and Meyer, H.H.D., Detection of the anabolic β2-adrenoceptor agonist clenbuterol in human scalp hair by HPLC/EIA, *Clin. Chem.*, 42, 1869, 1996.
26. Machnik, M. et al., Long-term detection of clenbuterol in human scalp hair by gas chromatography-high resolution mass spectrometry, *J. Chromatogr. B*, 723, 147, 1999.
27. Kintz, P. et al., Doping control for β-adrenergic compounds through hair analysis, *J. Forensic Sci.*, 45, 170, 2000.
28. Sachs, H. and Kintz, P., Consensus of the Society of Hair Testing on hair testing for doping agents, *Forensic Sci. Int.*, 107, 3, 2000.
29. Kintz, P., Cirimele, V., and Ludes, B., Pharmacological criteria that can affect the detection of doping agents in hair, *Forensic Sci. Int.*, 107, 325, 2000.
30. Gambelunghe, C., Rossi, R., Ferranti, C., Rossi, R., and Bacci, M., Hair analysis by GC/MS/MS to verify abuse of drugs, *J. Appl. Toxicol.*, 25, 205, 2005.

12 Applications of Hair in Drug-Facilitated Crime Evidence

Marion Villain

CONTENTS

12.1 INTRODUCTION

The use of a drug to modify a person's behavior for criminal gain is not a recent phenomenon. However, the sudden increase in reports of drug-facilitated crimes (sexual assaults, robbery, etc.) has caused alarm in the general public. The drugs involved can be pharmaceuticals, such as benzodiazepines (flunitrazepam, lorazepam, etc.), hypnotics (zopiclone, zolpidem), sedatives (neuroleptics, some histamine H1-antagonists), anesthetics (gamma hydroxybutyrate [GHB], ketamine), drugs of abuse (cannabis, methadone, ecstasy, LSD), or, more often, ethanol. Most of these substances possess amnesic properties, and therefore the victims are less able to accurately recall the circumstances under which the offense occurred. As they are generally short acting, they impair an individual rapidly. Due to their low dosage, excepted for GHB, a surreptitious administration into beverages such as coffee, soft drinks (cola), or, even better, alcoholic cocktails is relatively simple (1).

To perform successful toxicological examinations, the analyst must follow some important rules:

1. Obtain in appropriate time the corresponding biological specimens (blood, urine and hair)
2. Use sophisticated analytical techniques (LC-MS [liquid chromatography-mass spectrometry], headspace/GC-MS [gas chromatography-mass spectrometry], MS/MS [tandem mass spectrometry])
3. Take care in interpreting the findings

To address this problem, guidelines for toxicological investigations have been published in both the U.S. (2) and France (3).

Urinalysis of drug use in cases of alleged sexual assault demonstrated in 3303 urine samples that ethanol, either alone or in combination with other drugs, was the most common substance found, followed by cannabis and benzodiazepines (4). In Paris, the largest study (5) conducted in France revealed that the most frequently used drugs were benzodiazepines and related hypnotics. GHB was very seldom found. In our series at Strasbourg (3), zolpidem appears as the commonest substance, followed by bromazepam.

The narrow window of detection of GHB, 6 and 10 h in blood and urine, respectively, is an example of the current limitation of these specimens to demonstrate exposure after late sampling (6). For all compounds involved in drug-facilitated crime (DFC), the detection times in blood and urine depend mainly on the dose and sensitivity of the method used. Prohibiting immunoassays and using only "hyphenated" techniques (GC-MS, LC-MS), substances can be found in blood for 6 h to 2 days and in urine for 12 h to 5 days (7). Sampling blood or urine has low interest 48 h after the offense occurred.

To address a response to this important caveat, hair was suggested as a valuable specimen. While there are a lot of papers focused on the identification of drugs (mainly drugs of abuse) in hair following chronic use, those dealing with a controlled single dose are very scarce. Data are available for codeine (8), cocaine (9), flunitrazepam (10), clonazepam (11, 12), GHB (13), zolpidem (14), zopiclone (15), and bromazepam (16). All of these authors were able to target the drug in hair after a dose corresponding to a therapeutic dosage.

This chapter presents analytical strategies for investigating drug-facilitated crimes and several forensic cases in which findings from hair clarified the use of drugs to sedate the victim quickly and commit a crime or an offense.

12.2 ANALYTICAL STRATEGY

12.2.1 Specimen Collection

Hair is best collected from the area at the back of the head, called the *vertex posterior*. Compared with other areas of the head, this area has less variability in the hair growth rate, the number of hairs in the growing phase is more constant, and the hair is less subject to age- and sex-related influences. Hair strands are cut as closely as possible from the scalp, and the location of the root-tip must be mentioned. Storage is achieved at ambient temperature in an aluminum foil, an envelope, or a plastic tube.

The sample size of material to be extracted varies considerably among laboratories and depends on the drug to be analyzed and the test methodology. For example, when GHB or benzodiazepines are investigated, a minimal weight of 5 or 20 mg per segment, respectively, is recommended.

Because GHB is present in the hair of the general population under physiological concentrations, toxicologists must be able to discriminate between endogenous levels and a concentration resulting from exposure. The implementation of a cutoff concentration must be done cautiously, due to the wide distribution of endogenous concentrations, from 0.5 to 12.0 ng/mg. The solution is to use each subject as his or her own control. From the demonstration that physiological concentrations are stable along the hair shaft, except at the root, one can suppose that exposure will lead to a peak concentration that can be detected. The use of tandem mass spectrometry (MS/MS) is mandatory because of the low amount of hair that needs to be tested as a consequence of the short 3-mm segments that need to be analyzed. To avoid difficulties in interpretation due to potential contamination by sweat, it is necessary to wait for 4 to 5 weeks before hair collection. This will permit the migration of the GHB spot along the length of the hair shaft (13, 17).

For other drugs, our laboratory also recommends waiting for 4 to 5 weeks after the offense and then collecting four strands of about 100 hairs. One strand will be used to test for drugs of abuse (mostly for cannabis, but sometimes for ecstasy-related compounds and cocaine), one for GHB, and another one for a screening of hypnotics. The last strand is collected for a potential counteranalysis. Assuming normal hair growth rate (range from 0.7 to 1.4 cm/month, with a mean of about 1 cm/month accepted by the scientific community), the authors recommend cutting the strand into three segments of 2 cm to document any drug-facilitated sexual assault (DFSA) case. Administration of a single dose would be confirmed by the presence of the drug in the proximal segment (root) while not being detected in the other segments.

A typical hair-collection procedure is presented in Figure 12.1.

12.2.2 GHB Analysis by GC-MS/MS

Kintz et al. (17) described this procedure. The hair was decontaminated twice using 5 ml of methylene chloride for 2 min at room temperature, and then cut into 3-mm segments over a length of 3 cm (ten segments). A longer decontamination time will reduce the concentration of GHB in the hair.

About 5 to 10 mg of decontaminated hair are incubated in 0.5 ml 0.01*N* NaOH, 16 h at 56°C, in presence of 10 ng of GHB-d_6 used as internal standard (IS). After cooling, the homogenate is neutralized with 0.5 ml 0.01*N* HCl, and 3 ml ethyl acetate is added together with 0.1 ml of 0.01*M* H_2SO_4.

After agitation and centrifugation, the organic phase is evaporated to dryness under nitrogen flow. The residue is derivatized by adding 20 μl BSTFA (bis(trimethylsilyl)trifluoroacetamide) + 1% TMCS and 20 μl ethyl acetate, then incubated for 20 min at 60°C.

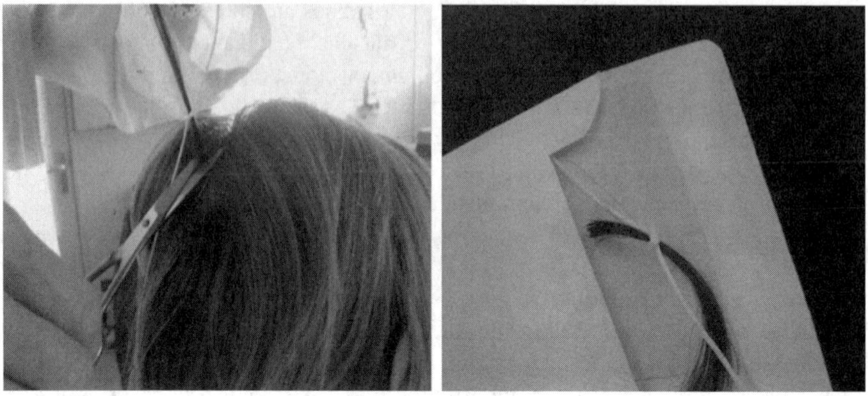

FIGURE 12.1 Hair collection procedure in case of drug-facilitated crime: Using scissors, collect 4 bunches of hair of about 100 hairs each from as close as possible to the scalp, about 4 to 5 weeks after the alleged event. Hair should be collected from the vertex posterior. Be careful not to pull out the hair or use adhesive, and store the cut hairs in an envelope at ambient temperature. Root and tip ends must be distinguished, using a string 1 cm from the root. The victim should be queried about the use and identification of pharmaceuticals and cosmetic treatments (bleaching, coloring) before and after the alleged event.

A 1-μl aliquot of the derivatized extract is injected into the column of a Hewlett-Packard (Palo Alto, CA) gas chromatograph (6890 Series). The flow of carrier gas (helium, purity grade N55) through the column (HP5-MS capillary column, 5% phenyl-95% methylsiloxane, 30 m × 0.25-mm i.d. × 0.25-mm film thickness) is 1.0 ml/min. The injector temperature is 270°C, and splitless injection is employed with a split valve off-time of 1.0 min. The column oven temperature is programmed to rise from an initial temperature of 100°C, maintained for 1 min, to 295°C at 30°C/min and maintained at 295°C for the final 5 min.

The detector is a Finnigan TSQ 700 operated in the electron ionization mode and in selected reaction monitoring. The precursor ions, m/z 233 and 239 for GHB and the IS, respectively, are selected in the first quadrupole. The common product ions, m/z 147 and 148, are selected in the third quadrupole after collision with argon at a cell pressure at 0.62 mtorr. The collision offset voltage is –8 V. The electron multiplier is operated at 1900 V.

Physiological concentrations ($n = 24$) are in the range 0.5 to 12.0 ng/mg of hair, with no influence due to hair color. No variation of concentrations is observed along the hair shaft in controlled subjects, except for the proximal segment, due to an incorporation through sweat. This demonstrates that endogenous levels, for each single subject, are constant during hair growth.

12.2.3 Hypnotics Analysis by LC-MS/MS

Villain et al. (18) screened such drugs as alprazolam, 7-aminoclonazepam, 7-aminoflunitrazepam, bromazepam, clobazam, diazepam, lorazepam, lormetazepam, midazolam, nordiazepam, oxazepam, temazepam, tetrazepam, triazolam, zaleplon, and zolpidem.

After decontamination of the hair strand with methylene chloride (2 × 5 ml for 2 min), hair is segmented, if necessary, and cut into small pieces. About 20 mg are incubated overnight in 1 ml of phosphate buffer, pH 8.4, in the presence of 1 ng of diazepam-d_5 used as internal standard (IS) and extracted by 5 ml methylene chloride/diethylether (90/10, v/v). After horizontal agitation (15 min) and centrifugation (10,000 *g* for 15 min), the organic phase is collected and evaporated to dryness using a SpeedVac®. The residue is reconstituted by adding 50 µl of methanol.

A 10-µl aliquot of the extract is injected onto the column (XTerra MS C18 3.5 µm, 100 × 2.1-mm i.d.), protected by a 1-mm C18 frit. Each 20-min chromatographic run is carried out with a gradient (5% acetonitrile-95% formic acid 0.1% to a ratio of 4:1 at 10 min) at a flow rate of 200 µl/min. The HPLC (high-performance liquid chromatography) system is a Waters Alliance 2695.

Detection is carried out by a Micromass Quattro Micro tandem mass spectrometer equipped with an ionspray atmospheric-pressure interface. The instrument is operated in the positive ionization mode. Best results are obtained with a capillary voltage of 1 kV, source block temperature of 120°C and desolvation gas (nitrogen) heated to 350°C and delivered at 550 l/h. Collision cell pressure is 3 mbar of argon.

Data are recorded in the multiple reaction monitoring (MRM) mode. Parent ions, the corresponding daughter ions, retention time, cone voltage, and collision energy optimized for the 16 benzodiazepines and IS are presented in Table 12.1.

Under the chromatographic conditions used, there was no interference with the analytes by any extractable endogenous materials present in hair.

The chromatogram of a blank hair spiked with the 16 benzodiazepines and hypnotics at 10 pg/mg is shown in Figure 12.2(a, b). The method provides good resolution of the different drugs.

The limit of quantification (LOQ) for all benzodiazepines and hypnotics ranges from 0.5 to 5 pg/mg using a 20-mg hair sample. The method is linear in hair for each compound, from the LOQ to 200 pg/mg ($r^2 > 0.99$). Precisions and accuracies, at 10 and 50 pg/mg, are <20% in all cases but one. Extraction recovery, measured at the same two concentrations, ranges from 32 to 76%, which is suitable for a screening procedure.

In the case of nitro-benzodiazepines, the target compound is the 7-amino-metabolite. Due to their stability in alkaline medium, in contrast with other benzodiazepines, it is possible to lower their LOQ about five times with a specific extraction after sodium hydroxide hydrolysis (12).

To demonstrate the applicability of this procedure, Figure 12.3 and Figure 12.4 represent the chromatograms obtained after analysis of the root segment from volunteers who were administered a single dose of 10 mg of zolpidem (women, 28 years old, 60 kg) or 6 mg of bromazepam (women, 26 years old, 50 kg) one month before. These findings demonstrate that it is possible to track a single drug exposure using an ultrasensitive procedure.

12.3 CASE REPORTS

In most cases, benzodiazepines are identified in drug-facilitated crimes. However, some unusual compounds can be observed. The following cases are from a series observed at our laboratory.

TABLE 12.1
MRM Transitions for the Detection of 16 Benzodiazepines and Hypnotics and IS by LC-MS/MS

Compound	Retention Time (min)	Parent Ion (m/z)	Daughter Ions (m/z)	Cone (V)	Collision Energy (eV)
Alprazolam	10.9	309.1	205.2	45	40
			274.2	45	26
7-Aminoclonazepam	7.5	286.1	222.2	40	25
			250.2	40	20
7-Aminoflunitrazepam	8.2	284.2	135.1	40	28
			227.2	40	25
Bromazepam	9.6	316.0	182.3	35	30
			209.3	35	25
Clobazam	11.7	301.1	224.2	30	33
			259.1	30	20
Diazepam	12.0	285.2	154.2	40	25
			193.3	40	30
Lorazepam	11.0	321.1	229.1	30	27
			275.1	30	22
Lormetazepam	11.7	335.1	177.1	28	40
			289.1	28	20
Midazolam	9.3	326.1	244.1	44	25
			291.2	44	28
Nordiazepam	11.1	271.2	140.1	40	25
			165.1	40	28
Oxazepam	10.8	269.1	163.1	45	32
			241.2	45	20
Temazepam	11.5	301.1	283.1	30	40
			255.2	30	20
Tetrazepam	11.1	289.2	225.2	40	26
			253.2	40	22
Triazolam	11.0	343.1	308.1	45	26
			315.1	45	27
Zaleplon	10.4	306.2	236.2	40	28
			264.2	40	20
Zolpidem	8.4	308.2	235.3	40	35
			263.2	40	26
Diazepam-d_5	12.0	290.2	<u>154.1</u>	40	30
			198.3	40	30

Note: The transition for quantification is underlined.

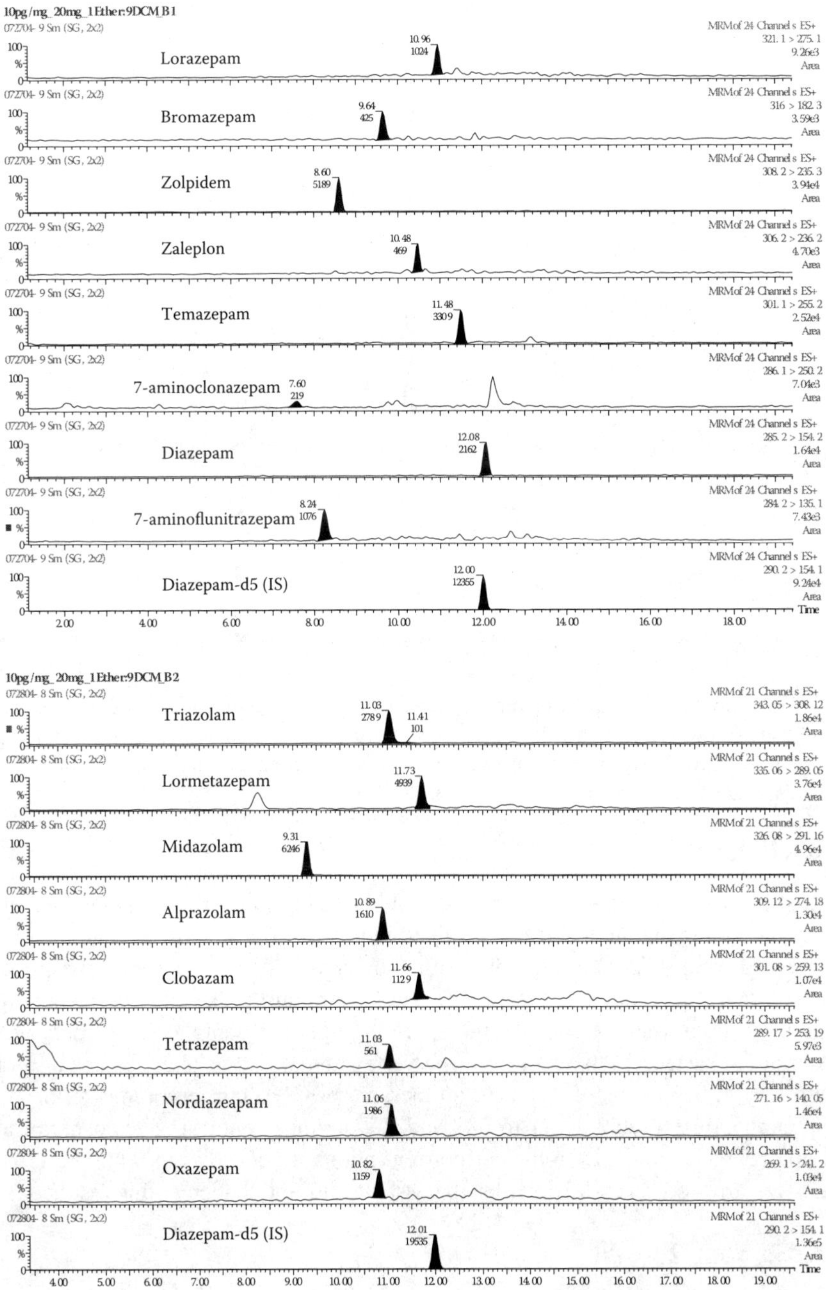

FIGURE 12.2 Chromatogram of a blank hair (20 mg) spiked at a final concentration of 10 pg/mg with, from the top to the bottom, the quantification ions of (a): lorazepam, bromazepam, zolpidem, zaleplon, temazepam, 7-amino-clonazepam, diazepam, 7-amino-flunitrazepam, and the IS (50 pg/mg) and (b): triazolam, lormetazepam, midazolam, alprazolam, clobazam, tetrazepam, nordiazepam, oxazepam, and the IS (50 pg/mg).

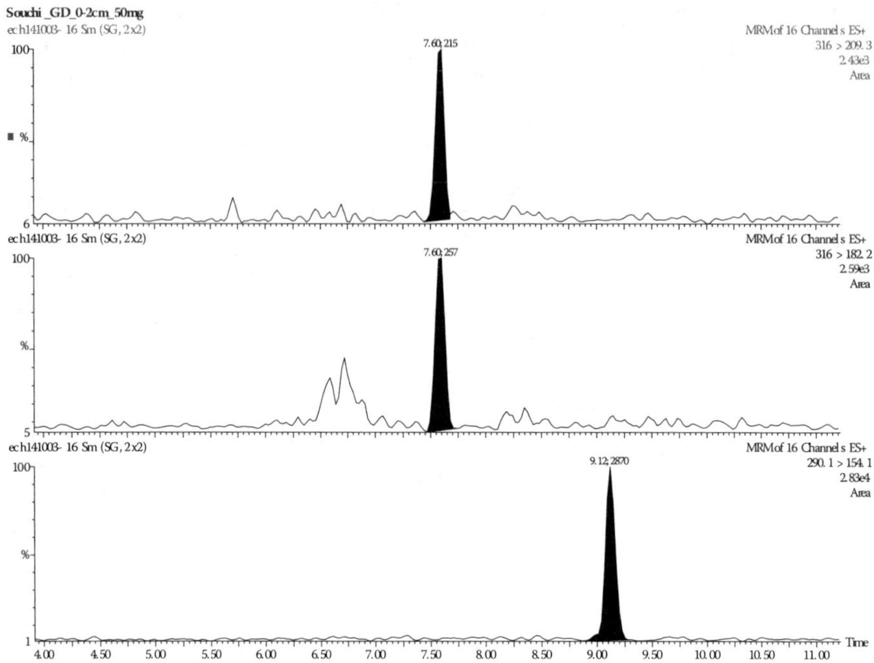

FIGURE 12.3 Chromatogram obtained after analysis of the root segment of the hair of a volunteer who was administered a single dose of 10 mg of zolpidem one month before. On the top, the two daughter ions of zolpidem; on the bottom, the daughter ion of the IS. Concentration was 1.8 pg/mg.

12.3.1 Case 1

Hair strands were obtained from a 19-year-old girl who claimed to have been sexually assaulted after drinking a soft drink spiked with a drug. She had no memory of the crime and went to the police 5 days after the rape. After contact with the police, our laboratory recommended to wait for about 1 month to have the corresponding growing hair between the root and the tip. Full-length hair samples (8 cm long) were taken at the surface of the skin from the vertex and stored in plastic tubes at room temperature. Segmentation revealed an increase of GHB concentrations at the corresponding time (Table 12.2) to 2.4 and 2.7 ng/mg, confirming exposure when compared with basal physiological concentrations around 0.7 ng/mg. The rapist, who was arrested several days after the assault, did not challenge this result.

12.3.2 Case 2

A 21-year-old woman was hospitalized for gastric disorders. One night, she was offered by a male nurse a coffee that made her unconscious. Upon recovering, she noticed an assault, but being afraid of the consequences, she did not report immediately to the police. This was done only after she went back from the hospital,

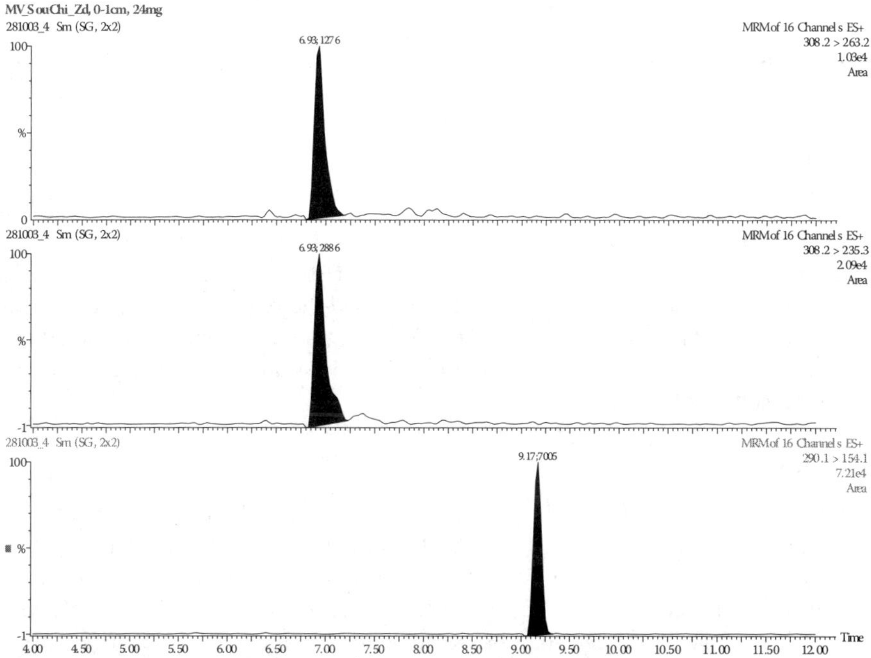

FIGURE 12.4 Chromatogram obtained after analysis of the root segment of the hair of a volunteer who was administered a single dose of 6 mg of bromazepam one month before. On the top, the two daughter ions of bromazepam; on the bottom, the daughter ion of the IS. Concentration was 4.7 pg/mg.

TABLE 12.2
GHB in Hair after Segmentation in a Case of DFSA

Segment	GHB (ng/mg)
0 (root)–0.3 cm	1.3
0.3–0.6 cm	0.6
0.6–0.9 cm	0.8
0.9–1.2 cm	2.4
1.2–1.5 cm	2.7
1.5–1.8 cm	0.7
1.8–2.1 cm	0.8
2.1–2.4 cm	0.7
2.4–2.7 cm	0.8
2.7–3.0 cm	0.7

6 days later. As blood or urine collection was without interest, we were requested to analyze the victim's hair, sampled 15 days after the alleged offense. Zolpidem was identified in the proximal segment (root to 2 cm) at 4.4 pg/mg, while the distal segment (2 to 4.5 cm) remained negative.

12.3.3 Case 3

Blood analysis (collected 9 h after the crime) from a sexually assaulted woman was positive for zolpidem at 390 ng/ml. As the claims of the victim to the police were confused, we received 4 weeks later an 8-cm hair strand to test for zolpidem. The analysis of four hair segments (4 × 2 cm) revealed the presence of zolpidem at the concentrations of 22, 47, 67, and 9 pg/mg from the root to the tip. This demonstrates repetitive exposure to zolpidem before the alleged assault and therefore makes the blood result inconclusive.

12.3.4 Case 4

During a party, a 42-year-old man was offered an alcoholic drink. Soon after, he lost all recollection of events and awoke 4 h later in a bed with a woman. Terrified, as he was married, he privately requested us to perform some analyses in an attempt to identify the sedative drug. Hair was collected at the laboratory 21 days after the event. 7-Amino-flunitrazepam was identified in the proximal (root to 2 cm) at 5.2 pg/mg, while the proximal segment (2 to 4 cm) remained negative. No flunitrazepam was detected.

12.3.5 Case 5

A 23-year-old woman told the emergency unit of a university hospital that she was intoxicated during the evening and had been unconscious for about 3 h. Lorazepam was found in her blood at 32 ng/ml. As the victim was suffering from anxiety, to exclude a possible treatment with lorazepam, hair was collected 1 month after the offense. Lorazepam was identified in the proximal segment (root to 2 cm) at 8 pg/mg, while the distal segments (2 to 4 and 4 to 6 cm) remained negative.

12.3.6 Case 6

A 19-year-old went to the police to declare a rape after having a drink that had been laced with ecstasy (MDMA). At the medicolegal unit of the hospital, a urine sample was collected (about 10 h after the rape) that revealed the presence of MDMA and its metabolite MDA at 1852 and 241 ng/ml, respectively, confirming her previous declarations. To the judge in charge of the case, she claimed that she never took ecstasy and directly gave the name of the rapist, who was rapidly arrested and sent to jail. As the circumstances were unclear, the judge requested a hair analysis that demonstrated the simultaneous presence of various stimulants, with the following concentrations: 21.3, 31.6, and 6.7 ng/mg for MDMA, MDEA, and MDA, respectively. These results were inconsistent with the claim of being drug-free. During a later confrontation with the judge, she admitted that it was a false notification, that no rape had occurred, and that it was a revenge on the alleged rapist.

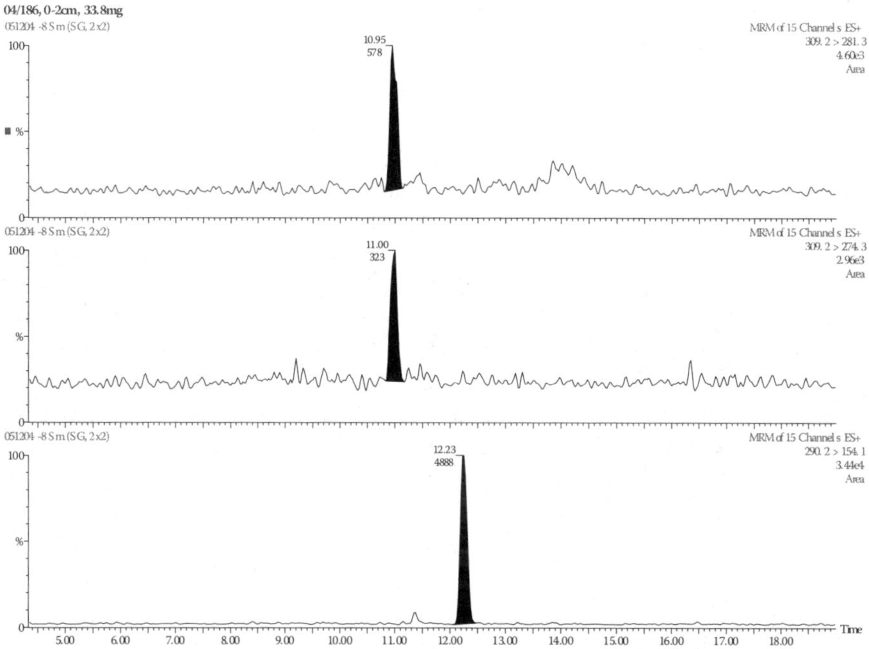

FIGURE 12.5 Chromatogram obtained after the analysis of the hair of a girl sexually abused by her father under the influence of alprazolam. Alprazolam tested positive at 4.9 pg/mg.

12.3.7 Case 7

A 12-year-old girl claimed to have been repetitively assaulted (once per week) since she was six by her father and obliged to have oral sex. During the last months, she was sometimes administered half of a white tablet of Xanax (0.5 mg) to be more willing. To the police, her father claimed that he had offered the drug on only three to four occasions during the 3 last months. We were requested to analyze the victim's hair to document alprazolam exposure.

Benzodiazepines and hypnotics were tested by LC-MS/MS, and the first 2-cm segment was positive for alprazolam at a concentration of 4.9 pg/mg, the second (2 to 4 cm) positive at 2.4 pg/mg, whereas the last segment (4 to 6 cm) was alprazolam-free. This appears to be consistent with few recent exposures to the drug. Figure 12.5 represents the chromatogram that was obtained in the proximal segment.

12.3.8 Case 8

A 39-year-old woman, in trouble with her husband, felt sleepy for 24 h after having consumed a coffee at home. Blood sample, collected 20 h after absorption, revealed the presence of 51 ng/ml of bromazepam, whereas hair sampled at the same time was bromazepam-free. Another strand of hair was collected 1 month after the event, and the proximal 2-cm-long segment was positive for bromazepam at 10.3 pg/mg, while the other segments (2 to 4 and 4 to 6 cm) remained negative. These results are consistent with a single exposure to this drug. The analysis of the residue in the cup of coffee (positive for bromazepam) and the husband's declaration did not challenge the biological conclusions.

12.3.9 Case 9

A young woman was the victim of a sexual assault in a highway station. She declared that the perpetrator forced her to absorb a white quadri-divisible tablet before abusing her. Blood sample, collected 18 h after the offense, revealed the presence of 151 ng/ml of bromazepam. A strand of hair was collected 3 weeks after the event, and the proximal segment (0 to 2 cm) was positive for bromazepam at 5.7 pg/mg (Figure 12.2); the consecutive segment (2 to 4 cm) was positive at 0.9 pg/mg; and the last segment remained bromazepam-free. As it was also described for cocaine (13), there is considerable variability in the area over which incorporated drug can be distributed in the hair shaft and in the rate of axial distribution of drug along the hair shaft. This can explain why a small amount of bromazepam, as compared with the concentration in the proximal segment, was measured in the second segment, as a result of an irregular movement. These results are in accordance with a single exposure to this drug.

12.3.10 Case 10

A man was sexually assaulted and robbed by two other men. The offense occurred at his own home during a rendezvous arranged a few hours before through an erotic phone service. The perpetrators forced him to drink an unknown mixture and requested the confidential number of his credit card. Blood and urine, sampled 6 h after the offense, revealed the presence of bromazepam at 10.4 and 18.0 ng/ml, respectively. On the request of the judge, head and pubic hairs were collected 19 weeks after the event. Head hair length (<4 cm) did not permit analyzing for the corresponding period, but 4.1 pg/mg of bromazepam were quantified in the victim's pubic hair, clearly demonstrating exposure to the drug. However, it is obvious that this result cannot be correlated with the putative time of exposure.

12.3.11 Case 11

A 30-year-old man was admitted to the hospital after having consumed several beers at home the previous night. The glycemia measured at home by the emergency unit at home was 0.33 g/l. The emergency unit treated him with a perfusion of diazepam and 30% glucose, but hypoglycemia persisted at 0.40 g/l. Despite intensive resuscitation attempts, vegetative coma occurred rapidly. Five months later, the patient was pronounced dead. Blood sample, collected at the admission, revealed the presence of 41 ng/ml of glibenclamide. To discriminate between a single administration or repetitive administration, our laboratory was requested to analyze a hair strand (19). A 4-cm hair was divided into two 2-cm segments that both tested positive at 23 pg/mg and 31 pg/mg. The chromatogram of the proximal segment of hair is given in Figure 12.6. The measured concentrations are in accordance with repetitive exposures during the last 4 months.

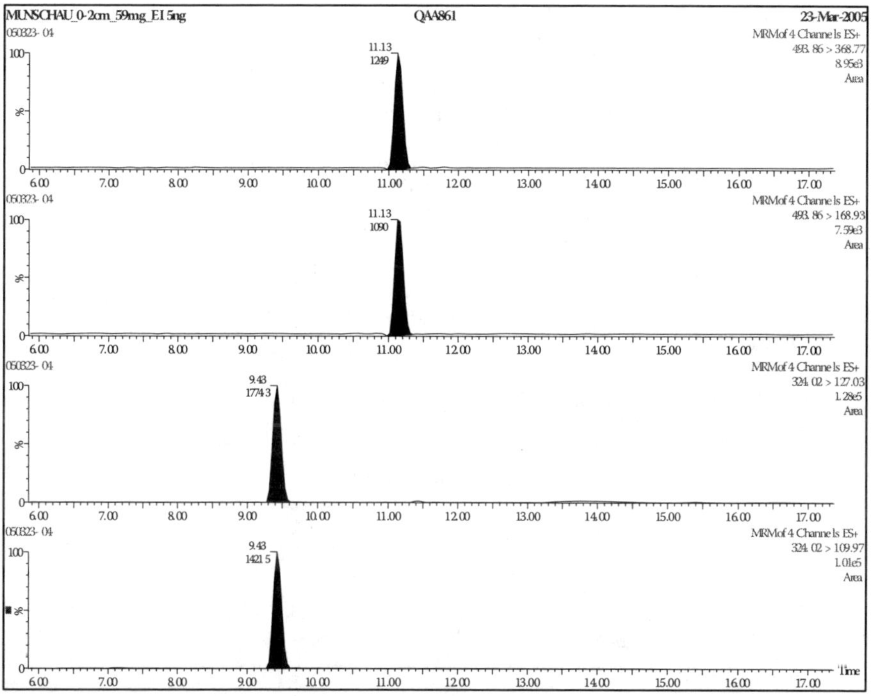

FIGURE 12.6 Chromatogram of the proximal hair segment from a victim of poisoning. Glibenclamide concentration was 23 pg/mg. From the top to the bottom: the two transitions of glibenclamide and the two transitions of gliclazide (IS).

12.3.12 CASE 12

This is a special case, with multiple hair collection to document, at best, zolpidem exposure. Three strands of hair — collected 6 days, 6 weeks, and 6 months after the alleged crime — were tested for hypnotics. The results are given Table 12.3.

In the first analyzed strand (collected 6 days after the event), low concentrations were found in the three segments, demonstrating a therapeutic and an occasional use of zolpidem during the 6 months before sampling. Due to the short time between the event and the hair collection, this analysis was not relevant to the time period of the event.

Therefore, we requested a second strand, collected about 6 weeks later. Four segments were analyzed, and the proximal segment, corresponding to the period of the event, had an elevated concentration in zolpidem. Results in the three other segments were equivalent to those found in the first analyzed strand. Our findings were an increase in the therapeutic treatment or a massive absorption of the drug (for sedation while raped) during the period of the event.

To discriminate these two hypotheses, the judge sent us a third strand of hair, collected 6 months later. Hypnotics were tested in six segments of 1 cm. Concentration of zolpidem was high in the segment corresponding to the period of the event

TABLE 12.3
Zolpidem Concentrations in Hair after Various Collection Time

	Zolpidem (pg/mg)
A. Collection after 6 Days	
0–2 cm	1.9
2–4 cm	2.2
4–6 cm	5.6
B. Collection after 6 Weeks	
0–2 cm	68.0
2–4 cm	1.9
4–6 cm	2.8
6–8 cm	2.7
C. Collection after 6 Months	
0–1 cm	1.2
1–2 cm	1.8
2–3 cm	3.9
3–4 cm	7.4
4–5 cm	18.5
5–6 cm	50.0

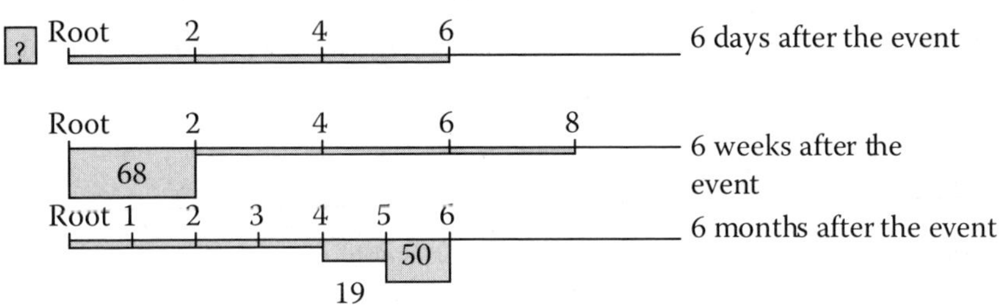

FIGURE 12.7 Concentrations of zolpidem in the three analyzed strands. All of the concentrations are in pg/mg; when not indicated, zolpidem concentrations were positive but lower than 10 pg/mg.

and lower in the segments corresponding to more recent periods. We were therefore able to document the therapeutic use of zolpidem before and after the assault and a massive absorption during the period of the event.

Figure 12.7 represents the different results on a time scale. It was concluded that hair analysis provides a basis for differentiating therapeutic treatment from a massive absorption of zolpidem and then to document a DFSA involving a compound used in therapeutic use.

12.3.13 Case 13

A 5-month-old Caucasian girl was found in respiratory depression after having received from her mother, some hours before, half a spoon of methadone syrup,

TABLE 12.4
Antemortem Concentrations of Methadone and Its Metabolite and Hair Results

Specimen	Methadone	EDDP
Blood	142 ng/ml	38 ng/ml
Urine	466 ng/ml	270 ng/ml
Hair (segment 0 to 1 cm)	1.0 ng/mg	<0.2 ng/mg
Hair (segment 1 to 2 cm)	1.6 ng/mg	<0.2 ng/mg
Hair (segment 2 to 3 cm)	2.3 ng/mg	<0.2 ng/mg
Hair (segment 3 to 5 cm)	21.3 ng/mg	5.2 ng/mg

corresponding to about 10 mg of drug. The mother (26 years old) was a heroin addict, maintained with methadone for several years. She was using methadone during pregnancy and, at delivery time, the baby experienced a withdrawal syndrome. After transfer to a pediatric unit, the baby rapidly developed convulsions and intracranial hypertension associated with hemodynamic problems. Blood and urine were sampled some hours after arrival. The baby was pronounced dead 11 days later, in cardiac distress. Autopsy was unremarkable, and, except for hair, no biological specimen was collected. Antemortem blood analysis (Table 12.4) revealed methadone exposure some hours before specimen collection. This concentration can be considered as an overdosage, with clinical signs including stupor, pupillary constriction, respiratory depression, hypotension, and finally circulatory collapse. Segmental analysis demonstrated repetitive exposure during lifetime as well as *in utero* exposure, as documented by the high concentration in the distal segment. Police examinations revealed that the aim of the methadone administration was just to induce sedation and to stop crying, and that there was no intent to poison the baby, even in the case of repetitive administration. The perpetrator was the mother, using the drug as a substitute of heroin. She was charged with homicide, due to the administration of a fatal feeding. Although not yet judged by a court, the sentence can be up to 30 years of jail, according to the French law. The surreptitious administration of methadone to obtain sedation was considered as a drug-facilitated crime, even in an intrafamilial situation. The drug can be considered as a chemical weapon.

12.3.14 Case 14

A 42-year-old man was offered a drink by a relative during a party. Several hours later, he noticed that his money was lost, with no recollection of the event during the previous period. He went to the police, but no specimen was collected at that time. After several similar cases in the same region of France, the judge in charge of the case asked us to perform a hair test. 7-Amino-flunitrazepam, the major metabolite of flunitrazepam and its marker in hair, was detected in the corresponding segment of hair at 31.7 pg/mg, while the distal segment was negative.

12.3.15 Case 15

A 21-year-old girl was confined illegally for 12 days and continuously raped by three men. To the police, she claimed having no recollection of the event, incoherent behavior, and excessive sedation. Analysis of the proximal segment (root to 3 cm) of a strand of her hair demonstrated exposure to clonazepam, an antiepileptic drug with sedative and amnesic properties, through the identification of 7-aminoclonazepam, its marker, at 135 pg/mg, while the distal segment (3 to 6 cm) remained negative.

12.4 DISCUSSION

Despite late sampling or even lack of collection of traditional biological fluids, such as blood or urine, results for hair testing can be used to document the use of drugs in drug-facilitated crimes (DFC).

Data from the literature are scarce. Frison et al. (20) detected thiopental (150 to 300 pg/mg) and its metabolite pentobarbital (200 to 400 pg/mg) in three different proximal segments, corresponding to the time of the assault, while distal segments remained negative. In two separate cases, Pépin et al. (21) detected 7-aminoflunitrazepam (19 pg/mg) and zopiclone (13 pg/mg). The same authors (13) demonstrated GHB exposure by comparing the concentrations along the hair shaft. Basal GHB concentrations were about 0.7 ng/mg, in comparison with a 5.3-ng/mg concentration in the segment corresponding to the time of the assault.

From our data and the literature, it is obvious that the target concentrations in hair after a single exposure are in the range of few pg/mg. To obtain the requested ultralow limits of detection together with suitable mass spectrometry information, tandem mass spectrometry appears to be a prerequisite. Selectivity and sensitivity are extraordinarily increased by almost completely suppressing the noise level. In comparison with the concentrations that are measured with drugs of abuse, such as heroin or cocaine, in the case of DFCs, the concentrations are at least 1000 times lower.

As it is the case with other applications (survey of addicts, doping control, regranting of driving license, etc.), hair testing is a valuable approach to increase the window of drug detection. Embarrassment associated with urine collection, particularly after sexual assault, can be greatly mitigated through hair analysis. It is always possible to obtain a fresh, identical hair sample if there is any trouble during analysis, a claim of specimen mix-up, or a breach in the chain of custody. This makes hair analysis essentially fail-safe, in contrast to blood or urine analysis, since an identical blood or urine specimen cannot be obtained at a later date. The discrimination between a single exposure and long-term use can be documented by multisectional analysis of hair. With the concept of absence of migration along the hair shaft, a single spot of exposure must be present within the segment corresponding to the period of the alleged event, using a growth rate for hair of 1 cm/month. As this growth rate can vary from 0.7 to 1.4 cm/month, the length of the hair section must be calculated accordingly. A delay of 4 to 5 weeks between the offense and hair collection and sectional analysis of 2-cm sections was considered as satisfactory to have the hair shaft including the spot of exposure. The hair must be cut as close as possible to the scalp. Particular care is also required to ensure that the individual's hair in the strand retains the position it originally had beside another hair shaft.

The unique possibility to demonstrate a single drug exposure through hair analysis has some additional interests. In the case of late crime declaration, positive hair findings are of paramount importance for a victim to start, under suitable conditions, a psychological follow-up. It can also help in the discrimination of false report of assault, for example in the case of revenge. These cases are often sensitive, with little other forensic evidence. Tedious interpretations, in the case of concomitant intake of hypnotics as a therapy for sleeping disorders, are avoided when investigations are done using hair in addition to urine.

12.5 CONCLUSION

It appears that the value of hair analysis for the identification of drug users is steadily gaining recognition. This can be seen from its growing use in preemployment screening, in forensic sciences, and in clinical applications. Hair analysis may be a useful adjunct to conventional drug testing in toxicology. Specimens can be more easily obtained with less embarrassment, and hair can provide a more accurate history of drug use.

Although there are still controversies on how to interpret the results, particularly concerning external contamination, cosmetic treatments, ethnic bias, or drug incorporation, pure analytical work in hair analysis has reached a sort of plateau, having solved almost all of the analytical problems.

Although GC-MS is the method of choice in practice to test for drugs of abuse, GC-MS/MS or LC-MS/MS are today used for routine cases, particularly to target drugs with low concentrations. In the case of drug-facilitated crimes, hair testing should be used to complement conventional blood and urine analysis, as it increases the window of detection and permits differentiation, by segmentation, of long-term therapeutic use from a single exposure. Selectivity and sensitivity of MS/MS are prerequisites.

REFERENCES

1. Wells, D., Drug administration and sexual assault: sex in a glass, *Sci. Justice*, 41, 197–199, 2001.
2. LeBeau, M., Andollo, W., Hearn, W.L. et al., Recommendations for toxicological investigations of drug-facilitated sexual assaults, *J. Forensic Sci.*, 44, 227–230, 1999.
3. Kintz, P., Cirimele, V., Villain, M. et al., Soumission chimique: approches pratiques en toxicologie médico-légale, *Ann. Toxicol. Anal.*, 14, 361–364, 2002.
4. Hindmarch, I., El Sohly, M., Gambles, J. et al., Forensic urinalysis of drug use in cases of alleged sexual assault, *J. Clin. Forensic Med.*, 8, 197–205, 2001.
5. Deveaux, M., Chèze, M., Duffort, G. et al., Etude de 128 cas de soumission chimique en région parisienne (juin 2003-mai 2004): analyses toxicologiques dans les cheveux par chromatographie liquide-spectrométrie de masse en tandem, *J. Med. Leg. Droit Med.*, 47, 351–356, 2004.

6. Kintz, P., La soumission chimique: aspects analytiques et expertises médico-légales, *Ann. Toxicol. Anal.*, 13, 120–121, 2001.
7. Verstraete, A., Fenêtre de détection des xénobiotiques dans le sang, les urines, la salive et les cheveux, *Ann. Toxicol. Anal.*, 14, 390–394, 2002.
8. Rollins, D.E., Wilkins, D.G., and Kruegger, G.G., Codeine disposition in human hair after single and multiple doses, *Eur. J. Clin. Pharmacol.*, 50, 391–397, 1996.
9. Henderson, G.L., Harkey, M.R., Zhou, C. et al., Incorporation of isotopically labeled cocaine and metabolites into human hair, 1: dose response relationships, *J. Anal. Toxicol.*, 20, 1–12, 1996.
10. Negrusz, A., Moore, C.M., Hinkel, K.B. et al., Deposition of 7-aminoflunitrazepam and flunitrazepam in hair after a single dose of Rohypnol, *J. Forensic Sci.*, 46, 1–9, 2001.
11. Negrusz, A., Bowen, A.M., Moore, C. et al., Deposition of 7-aminoclonazepam and clonazepam in hair following a single dose of Klonopin, *J. Anal. Toxicol.*, 26, 471–478, 2002.
12. Chèze, M., Villain, M., and Pépin, G., Determination of bromazepam, clonazepam and metabolites after a single intake in urine and hair by LC-MS/MS: application to forensic cases in drug facilitated crimes, *Forensic Sci. Int.*, 145, 123–130, 2004.
13. Goullé, J.P., Chèze, M., and Pépin, G., Determination of endogenous levels of GHB in human hair: are there possibilities for the identification of GHB administration through hair analysis in case of drug-facilitated sexual assault? *J. Anal. Toxicol.*, 27, 574–580, 2003.
14. Villain, M., Chèze, M., Tracqui, A. et al., Windows of detection of zolpidem in urine and hair: application to two drug facilitated sexual assaults, *Forensic Sci. Int.*, 143, 157–161, 2004.
15. Villain, M., Chèze, M., Tracqui, A. et al., Testing for zopiclone in hair application to drug-facilitated crimes, *Forensic Sci. Int.*, 145, 117–121, 2004.
16. Villain, M., Chèze, M., Dumestre, V. et al., Hair to document drug-facilitated crimes: four cases involving bromazepam, *J. Anal. Toxicol.*, 28, 516–519, 2004.
17. Kintz, P., Cirimele, V., Jamey, C. et al., Testing for GHB in hair by GC/MS/MS after a single exposure: application to document sexual assault, *J. Forensic Sci.*, 48, 195–200, 2003.
18. Villain, M., Concheiro, M., Cirimele, V. et al., Screening method for benzodiazepines and hypnotics in hair at pg/mg level by LC-MS/MS, *J. Chromatogr. B*, 825, 72–78, 2005.
19. Villain, M., Tournoud, C., Flesch, F. et al., Hair to document exposure to glibenclamide, *J. Chromatogr. B*, in press.
20. Frison, G., Favretto, D., Tedeschi, L. et al., Detection of thiopental and pentobarbital in head and pubic hair in a case of drug-facilitated sexual assault, *Forensic Sci. Int.*, 133, 171–174, 2003.
21. Pépin, G., Chèze, M., Duffort, G. et al., De l'intérêt des cheveux et de la spectrometrie de masse en tandem pour la soumission chimique: à propos de neuf cas, *Ann. Toxicol. Anal.*, 14, 395–406, 2002.

13 Application of Hair in Driving-License Regranting

Manfred R. Moeller, Hans Sachs, and Fritz Pragst

CONTENTS

13.1 INTRODUCTION

The death toll of more than 1 million people per year worldwide in motor vehicle accidents is basically not the result of technical failure of vehicles, but to human error. The most important avoidable cause of human failure is driving under the influence of alcohol (DUI) or drugs (DUID). Legal requirements are in place in most countries for the detection of impairment and to prove and sanction DUI and DUID laws. Additionally, there are "per se" laws, or "zero-tolerance" laws in a number of countries (Belgium, Finland, France, Germany, Sweden, Switzerland), where impairment is not the only possibility for sanctions. Toxicological analysis and detection of drugs are sufficient for a conviction.

In June 2003, the European Database on Drugs [1] published a study comparing the legal situation in 16 European states. The chapters are on classification of controlled drugs, consumption, possession and trafficking of illegal drugs, as well as treatment alternatives to prosecution or prison, legal status of cannabis, legal framework of needle and syringe programs, and supplying illicit drugs for medical purposes.

TABLE 13.1
Overview of the Laws in European Countries Governing Driving under the Influence of "Other Intoxicating Substances"

Country	Type	Administrative/ Criminal	Fine (€)	Prison (days)	License Withdrawal (months)
Austria	impairment	administrative	581–3,633	—	1
Belgium	per se impairment	criminal	1,000–10,000	15–180	possible
Denmark	impairment	criminal	fine	365	—
Finland	per se	criminal	fine	182	max. 60
	impairment		60 day fines	700	
France	per se	criminal	4,500	730	36
Germany	per se	administrative	250		1
	impairment	criminal	fine	365–1825	1–3
Greece	impairment	criminal	147	60	3–6
Ireland	impairment	criminal	1,270	180	24
Italy	impairment	criminal	260–1,030	30	0.5–3
Luxembourg	impairment	criminal	250–5,000	8–1095	possible
Netherlands	impairment	criminal	accident: 11,250	1095	60
			fatal: 45,000	3285	
Norway	impairment	criminal	—	365	12
Portugal	impairment	criminal	360–1,800	365	2–24
Spain	per se	administrative	302–602		3
	impairment	criminal		56–84	12–48
Sweden	per se	criminal	day fines	730	1–36
United Kingdom	impairment	criminal	7,000	180	at least 12

However, provisions about DUID are not included in that study. Verstraete [2] and Walsh [3] published overviews on the European DUID legislation and on DUID laws in the U.S., respectively. Table 13.1 shows the survey on European legislation [2]. It is needless to say that the EU is far from any kind of harmonization in this field, and it is obvious that there is a North-South divide in the sanctions. Furthermore, general rules on restoration (regranting) of a driver's license after withdrawal in cases of illegal drug usage do not exist either. Typically, repeated urine samples, staggered over a period of several months, are used to control drug abstinence before the driver's license is restored. However, over the past decade, other body samples have increasingly been used to test recent drug consumption [4–7].

13.2 SENSITIVITY OF DRUG ABUSE DETECTION: COMPARISON BETWEEN URINE AND HAIR ANALYSIS

The probability for a positive result in case of drug abuse depends on the sensitivity of the analysis and on the time window of drug detection in the matrix investigated.

TABLE 13.2
Synopsis of Urine and Hair as Specimen for Drugs of Abuse Testing

Parameter	Urine	Hair
Accepted in court	yes	yes
Complete drug spectrum	yes	yes
Analytical techniques	immunoassays, GC-MS, LC-MS, LC-MS/MS	GC-MS, LC-MS, LC-MS/MS
Detection window	2–5 days	several months
Adulteration	possible	very difficult
Sampling	invasive	not invasive
Conservation	+4°C or –20°C	room temperature
Analysis focused on	metabolites	mother compounds
Second identical sample possible	no	yes
Type of measurement	incremental	cumulative
Risk of false negatives	elevated	weak
Risk of false positives	theoretically zero	theoretically zero

TABLE 13.3
Sensitivity of Drug Detection in Urine and Hair for Different Levels of Drug Abuse

Heavy consumption (several times per day)
→ Detected in hair and urine in all cases
Habitual consumption (daily or almost daily, the subjects are to a certain degree able to control the consumption)
→ Hair analysis leads to positive results for all drugs, with a high probability.
→ Urine analysis leads to negative results in most cases for opiates, cocaine, amphetamines, and ecstasy. Therefore, hair analysis is indispensable.
→ Urine analysis for cannabinoids in repeated tests leads to positive results, with high probability.
Occasional or intermittent consumption (several times per months, but by far not daily)
→ Hair analysis leads to positive results, with medium probability.
→ Urine analysis after short-term request (3 to 5 days) leads to negative results in most cases for opiates, cocaine, amphetamines, and ecstasy. Therefore, hair analysis is indispensable.
→ Urine analysis for cannabinoids leads to a positive result, with medium probability at least in one of four tests.
Experimental consumption (once or a few doses)
→ Not detected in hair or urine

In Table 13.2, a synopsis is given on the strengths and weaknesses of urine and hair for testing drugs of abuse [8].

Direct comparisons between urine and hair have been made [9–12] showing that, except for cannabis [13], hair analysis can be better used to prove occasional and chronic drug abuse than urine. Single use, however, can only be detected in hair in special cases [14]. Sachs and Pragst [15] have defined different levels of drug abuse (Table 13.3) and compared the usefulness of urine and hair for this purpose.

Here they show that, in cases where the subjects are able to control their consumption to a certain extent and where the drug control is announced several days in advance, hair analysis is indispensable.

13.3 HAIR SAMPLING FOR DRUG ANALYSIS

In 1997 the Society of Hair Testing (SoHT) published a general statement concerning the examination of drugs in human hair that was further specified in 2003. This statement made the following demands on the collection of hair samples [6]:

> Sample collection should be performed by a responsible authority respecting the legal, ethical and human rights of the person to be tested for drugs of abuse. Hair samples should be obtained in a nondrug-contaminated environment by an appropriately trained individual, not necessarily a physician. A sufficient amount of sample should be collected so that a repeat analysis or a confirmation analysis by another laboratory can be performed, should it be needed.

To fulfill these demands, hair collection is performed obeying the following rules [6, 16]:

1. Hair sampling must not be performed in the neighborhood of street drugs and not by persons who were in contact with those drugs.
2. To obtain comparable results, hair should be collected from the posterior vertex region of the scalp. If this is not possible, the place from which the sample was taken has to be documented.
3. In order to maintain a statistical significance of the sample and/or to perform a screening test as well as a confirmation test, the weight of the specimen should be approximately 200 mg (a suitable amount of sample could be estimated by comparison with the diameter of a pencil).
4. The hair strand has to be cut close to the skin. The length of remaining hair has to be documented.
5. For shipment and storage, the hair sample should be wrapped in aluminum foil to maintain integrity and to avoid contamination. (Long hair strands can be tied together with a piece of string or of dental floss before being cut.)
6. Hair tip and the cut end of the samples have to be labeled on the aluminum foil.
7. Specimens can be stored under dry conditions at room temperature.

However, although the advantage of hair analysis for long-term or chronic use has been demonstrated, driving-license authorities accept hair analysis as a tool for controlling drug consumption or abstinence only in France, Germany, and Italy so far.

13.4 MANIPULATION OF DRUG CONCENTRATIONS IN HAIR

The drug concentrations in healthy hair are only to a minor extent decreased by shampooing two or three times per week over a longer time. Special advertised and

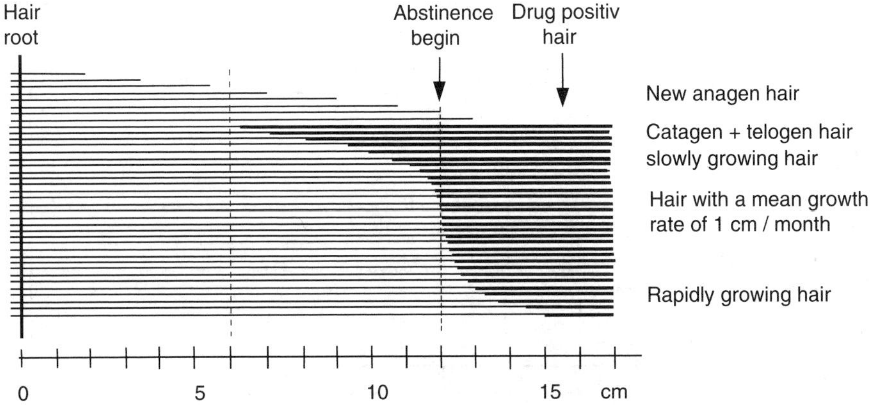

FIGURE 13.1 Theoretical transition from the drug-containing hair region (bold lines) to the drug-free region (thin lines) in a hair tuft collected 12 months after abstinence began. A negative result is only found in the 0- to 6-cm segment.

To prepare the medical statement or to support a psychomedical examination, a drug test is usually performed by either several urine tests or a hair analysis. A hair analysis of a 6-cm strand is sufficient to fulfill the requirements, because there is no strong relationship between the distance of a hair segment from the root and the age of the segment [18]:

- The growth rate of the single hair in a hair tuft can vary by up to 50% of the mean value.
- Approximately 10 to 20% of the hair is in the catagen or telogen stage, which means that they are not growing and that a part of them have not grown in the last (up to 6) months.
- After ending heavy drug consumption, the incorporation of the drug from tissue depots into hair may continue for a certain time (e.g., 2 months).
- The mean hair growth rate of the subject under investigation can strongly differ from the interindividual mean value of 1.1 ± 0.2 cm/month.

Therefore, there is no abrupt change from positive to negative within a sample corresponding to a cessation of drug consumption, but there is a transition zone of, e.g., 6 to 8 cm. This is schematically shown in Figure 13.1 for an individual who stopped drug consumption 12 months before sampling. Only the proximal 6 cm are completely free of drugs (Figure 13.1).

It can be seen that after heavy cocaine consumption (Figure 13.2), even segments grown 2 months after the end of the consumption contain cocaine. Not surprisingly, bundles that are taken several months after the end of consumption carry the drug in the proximal sections because 10 to 20% are in the telogen stage, which means that they stopped growing months before and contain cocaine of former times. Possibly in this case the drug is liberated from tissue depots. As a special observation, this was already reported in 1993 for methadone [9]. For the more lipophilic cannabinoids,

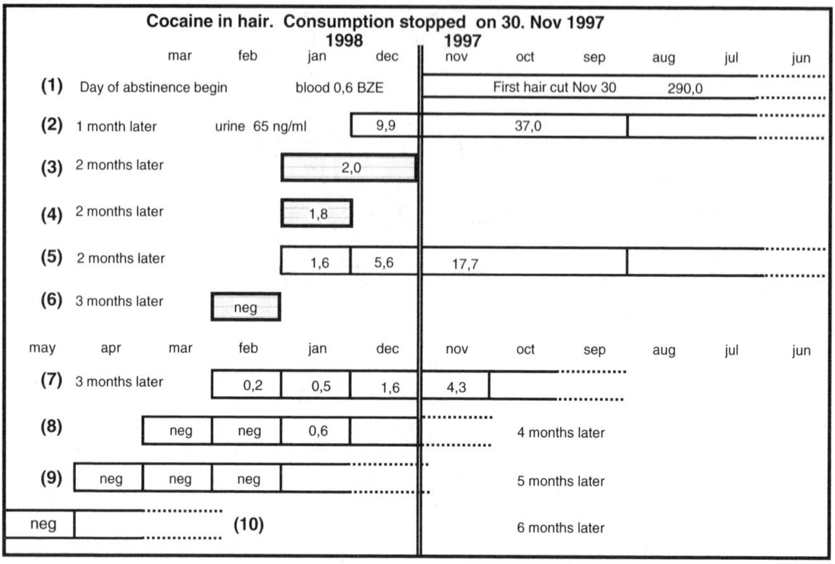

FIGURE 13.2 Cocaine concentrations in hair segments of a cocaine addict. Altogether, ten samples were collected. Samples 3, 4, and 6 were cut at the same sites as samples 1, 2, and 5 and therefore contain only hair grown after the first sampling.

which are known to be stored in fat tissue, the delayed incorporation should be even more pronounced.

Regarding these particularities of hair growth and drug incorporation, the results from a 6-cm proximal hair segment can be interpreted in the following way without any discrimination against the subject:

Positive result: there was a drug consumption within the last 12 months.
Negative result: there is no proof of a drug consumption within the last 6 months.

Shorter hair samples lead to an essential decrease of the time period controlled, and the time and length of the last haircut at the hair dresser becomes important. For instance, if a subject had shaved his head two weeks after abstinence began and after that has let it grow for three months, the hair sample represents only the last three months, since the catagen and telogen hair was also removed. On the other hand, if long hair is shortened to a length of 3 cm at the day of sampling, drug consumption up to 9 months back can lead to a positive result, since the sample still contains the telogen and catagen hair.

Because of a much higher portion of telogen hair (e.g., 50%), the interpretation of results from pubic hair and axillary hair is even more difficult. A 4-cm-long pubic hair sample can represent a time period of more than a year, if the hair was not cut during this period. A negative result means also in this case no proof for drug consumption, whereas a positive result is difficult to assign to a certain time period of consumption.

Following the text of the FeV § 14 (driving permit act) and its interpretation by the driving-license authorities, opiates, cocaine, and amphetamines have to be detected only qualitatively. The consumption of heroin is proved by the detection of 6-acetylmorphine. Morphine is also found, but the ratios of concentrations depend on the extraction method. Due to the presence of acetylcodeine in heroin samples, codeine is also found, but only in lower concentrations unless codeine was taken as a substitute. Dihydrocodeine also leads to a positive pretest, but the GC-MS confirmation distinguishes between the heroin consumption and a possible "substitution therapy." But this therapy also excludes the permission to drive.

Cocaine consumption is proved by detecting the parent drug itself. Benzoylecgonine or ecgonine methyl ester are sometimes also found, depending on the extraction. The detection of cocaethylene shows clearly that the person does not only have an exclusive problem with cocaine, but also with alcohol consumption.

Amphetamine consumption can easily be proved by detecting the parent drugs amphetamine, methamphetamine, 3,4-methylenedioxymethamphetamine (MDMA), or 3,4-methylenedioxyethylamphetamine (MDE). The concentration is not of special interest concerning the withdrawal of the license.

Hashish or marijuana consumption does not automatically lead to a withdrawal of the license. If the person consumes the drug very seldom and strictly separates the activities of consumption and driving a car, a psychomedical examination is not essential. The person is allowed to drive.

Furthermore, It is necessary to distinguish between an "experimental" and a regular consumption. But what is the definition of "experimental," "rare," or "regular" consumption? In a decision of the competent Bavarian state court (BayVGH) the following categories are defined:

- Experimental consumption (once or very few intakes)
- Occasional or intermittent (several times per month, but not daily — not even almost daily)
- Habitual (daily or almost daily)
- Heavy (several times per day)

In driving-ability examination, regular and occasional cannabis use should lead to positive hair results [19]. The cutoff value should eliminate single (experimental) use and analytically false-positive results. Until now, there are no reliable (e.g., prospective) studies known for evaluation of the consumption frequency with respect to establishing a cutoff. It follows from statistical considerations of consumption behavior and hair concentrations that a considerable portion of occasional users are not detected with a cutoff of 0.1 ng/mg THC in hair. Therefore, lower cutoffs of 0.05 or even 0.02 ng/mg THC in hair are discussed. A prerequisite is that the method be sufficiently sensitive. The detection of cannabidiol (CBD) and cannabinol (CBN) should be used for confirmation of the results.

The driving-license authorities ask for a psychomedical examination if the frequency is occasional or higher. As experimental consumption does not lead to a positive THC result, the psychomedical examination is ordered in all positive cases.

13.5.3 Italy

In Italy, hair analysis can also be used to withdraw and restore driver's licenses [20, 21]. In Lombardy [22], decisions are based on street traffic law from April 30, 1992, and additional Décret no. 9 from January 15, 2002. It is stated that a driver's license cannot be granted if the person is physically or psychically unable. The local medical services decide on the individual's ability.

Driving under the influence of drugs of abuse is forbidden. Additionally, drug-dependent subjects or registered drug consumers are not allowed to drive. If the drug dependence is deemed to have been overcome, the commission can make a medical opinion to regrant the driver's license. The commission is authorized to order regular examinations and analyses (urine, hair). The analyses may be performed in special laboratories. Hair analyses can be conducted for opiates, cannabis, cocaine, amphetamines, and others.

In positive cases (hair or urine), the restriction on driving privileges is limited to 6 months, with the license to drive restored upon passing a new examination. In the case of a positive urine sample and a negative hair sample, restriction of driving privileges can be limited to 3 months, with driving privileges restored upon passing a new hair analysis, where hair length must be at least 3 cm.

In cases of negative urine and hair analysis, three controls, after 1, 2, and 3 years have to follow. Further analyses can be ordered. In cases of drug-positive analyses, the procedure has to be repeated as above.

13.6 REGULATIONS IN OTHER COUNTRIES

In a survey at the workshop of the Society of Hair Testing in Berlin in 2002, H. Sachs and F. Pragst asked colleagues from abroad about the regulations in their respective countries. The answers are listed in Table 13.6. In the Netherlands, there are no regulated activities to use hair analysis for drug detection (J. Weijers, Amsterdam).

The questionnaire was answered by: H.-J. Battista (Salzburg), O. Drummer (Victoria, Australia), H. Frison and L. Tedeschi (Padova), C. Jurado (Sevilla), H. Käferstein (Cologne), G. Kauert (Frankfurt), P. Kintz (Strasbourg), R. Kronstrand (Linköping), S. Lohr-Schwaab (Stuttgart), F. Musshoff (Bonn), C. Moore (Chicago), S. Paterson (London), F. Pragst (Berlin), H. Sachs (Munich), A. Schmoldt (Hamburg), Ch. Staub (Genève), A. Verstraete (Belgium), and R. Wennig (Luxembourg).

13.7 CONCLUSIONS

Hair analysis is a powerful tool for detecting drug consumption in cases of regular and occasional use. Even a single use can be detected under certain circumstances. However, it is obvious from the presented tables that there are large differences in the legal approaches taken by different countries. Furthermore, it follows from the answers to the questionnaire that there is not always a clear distinction between driving ability and driving liability or driver's aptitude. These terms have varying definitions in the different countries. There is no question that the activities of the scientific societies are helpful in installing useful procedures on national levels. This

TABLE 13.6
Answers to the Questionnaire on Hair Analysis and Driving Liability

Country	Legal Regulation	Material Used	Cannabis Different	Hair Samples (per year)	Screening or Specific	Drugs Investigated
Australia	yes	not regulated	no	0	specific	all drugs capable of impairing
Austria	yes	not regulated	no	very few	screening	all drugs of abuse listed in the "Suchtmittelregister"
Belgium	yes	not regulated (urine)	no	0	both	—
England (UK)	yes	urine	no	0	screening	amphetamine, ecstasy drugs, cannabinoids, cocaine, heroin, morphine, methadone
France	yes	blood, hair [a]	no	0	specific	amphetamines, ecstasy, cannabinoids, cocaine, opiates; only in all fatal traffic accidents
Germany	yes	urine, hair, (blood)	yes	3.000–4.000	screening	psychoactive drugs
Italy	yes	urine, hair	no	5.000–10.000	screening	stupefying and psychotropic substances
Luxembourg	no	not regulated	no	0	screening	—
Spain	yes	not regulated	no	0	—	all drugs that can affect driving ability
Sweden	yes	blood, urine	no	0	screening	all drugs classified as narcotic drugs
Switzerland	yes	not regulated	no	0	—	all drugs mentioned in the federal law on drugs of abuse
U.S. [b]	yes	blood	no	0	specific	general wording to allow prosecution of DUID

[a] Changed since 2002.
[b] Different rules in the 50 states.

can be seen by the French example, where proposals of the SFTA have been adopted into legal regulations. However, on an international level, there is no harmonization in sight.

REFERENCES

1. European Database on Drugs; available on-line at http://eldd.emcdda.eu.int/.
2. Verstraete, A., Survey of DUID Legislation; available on-line at www.icadts.org/coreport/duidreport.pdf, 2003.
3. Walsh, M.J., A Survey of DUID Laws in the U.S.; available on-line at www.icadts.org/coreport/duidreport.pdf, 2003.
4. Sachs, H. and Kintz, P., Testing for drugs in hair: critical review of chromatographic procedures since 1992, *J. Chromatogr. B*, 173, 147, 1998.
5. Pragst, F., Rothe, M., Spiegel, K., and Sporkert, F., Illegal and therapeutic drug concentrations in hair segments: a timetable of drug exposure? *Forensic Sci. Rev.*, 10, 81, 1998.
6. Society of Hair Testing, Statement of the Society of Hair Testing concerning the examination of drugs in human hair, *Forensic Sci. Int.*, 84, 3, 1997; SoHT recommendations for hair testing in forensic cases, *Forensic Sci. Int.*, 145, 83, 2004.
7. United Nations, Guidelines for Testing Drugs under International Control in Hair, Sweat, and Saliva, United Nations Publication, Sales no. E.99.XI.14, 1999.
8. Kintz, P., Villain, M., Cirimele, V., Janey, C., and Ludes, B., Décret no 2003-293 du 31 mars 2003, Restitution de permis de conduire à partir d'analyses de cheveux (Hair as a discrimination tool of applicants for driving license), *Ann. Toxicol. Anal.*, 15, 117, 2003.
9. Moeller, M.R., Fey, P., and Wennig, R., Simultaneous determination of drugs of abuse (opiates, cocaine and amphetamine) in human hair by GC/MS and its application to a methadone treatment program, *Forensic Sci. Int.*, 61, 185, 1993.
10. Du Pont, R.L. and Baumgartner, W.A., Drug testing by urine and hair analysis: complementary features and scientific issues, *Forensic Sci. Int.*, 70, 63, 1995.
11. Kintz, P., Drug testing in addicts: a comparison between urine, sweat and hair, *Ther. Drug Monit.*, 18, 450, 1996.
12. Iversen, S., Schmoldt, A., Lewerenz, H., and Püschel, K., Stellenwert der toxikologischen Urin- und Haaranalyse bei der Fahreigungsbegutachtung von Kraftfahrern, *Blutalkohol*, 35, 1, 1998.
13. Uhl, M., Chapter 5 of this book.
14. Villain, M., Chapter 12 of this book.
15. Sachs, H. and Pragst, F., Hair Analysis and Driving Availability Examination, presented at Workshop of the Society of Hair Testing, Berlin, May 26–28, 2002.
16. Pragst, F., Sachs, H., and Sporkert, F., Zum gegenwärtigen Stand der Haaranalyse auf illegale Drogen im Rahmen der Fahreignungsprüfung, *Berichte der Bundesanstalt für Straßenwesen: Mensch und Sicherheit*, 111, 21, 1999.
17. Restitution du permis de conduire: Examen biologiques à partir de cheveaux: Consensus de la Société Française de Toxicologie Analytique du décembre 2004, *Ann. Toxicol. Anal.*, 16, 229, 2004.
18. Kronstrand, R., Chapter 1 of this book.
19. Pragst, F. and Nadulski, T., Cut-off in hair in context of driving ability, *Ann. Toxicol. Anal.*, 17, 237, 2006.

20. Tagliaro, F., De Battisti, Z., Lubli, G., Neri, C., Manetto, G., and Marigo, M., Integral use of hair analysis to investigate the physical fitness to obtain the driving license: a case-work study, *Forensic Sci. Int.*, 84, 129, 1997.
21. Ricossa, M.C., Bernini, M., and De Ferrari, F., Hair analysis for driving license in cocaine and heroin use, an epidemiological study, *Forensic Sci. Int.*, 107, 301, 2000.
22. Pichini, S., personal communication, Dec. 2005.

14 Alcohol Markers in Hair

Fritz Pragst and Michel Yegles

CONTENTS

14.1 GENERAL PROBLEMS IN DETECTION OF CHRONIC ALCOHOL ABUSE

Compared with some other substances, the detection of alcohol abuse by hair analysis has some particularities. Alcohol is consumed in much higher amounts by a much higher portion of the population in almost all countries. For instance, the mean daily dose per person is nearly 28 g in Luxembourg, about 23 g in France and in Germany, and about 14 g in the U.S. [1]. However, there is a large variation in the drinking behavior of the individuals. As an example, in Germany, 17 to 23% of the population are abstinent, about 40% are weak drinkers (1 to 10 g/day), 32 to 38% are social drinkers (11 to 60 g/day), and 4 to 5% heavily abuse alcohol or are dependent on alcohol (61 to more than 400 g/day) [2]. Alcohol is socially well accepted and is an essential economic factor in most countries, despite its immense risks for health, its high addictive potential, as well as the increased risk of accidents and the large number of offenses that occur under its influence.

This ambiguous role of the legal drug ethanol leads to a considerable demand for reliable alcohol markers from the forensic as well as the medical points of view to discriminate between social drinking and alcohol abuse or to verify claims of abstinence after previous harmful drinking. Therefore, extensive research has been performed to develop and evaluate such laboratory markers with respect to sensitivity, specificity, and time window of detection. The progress in this field was described in several reviews [3–12]. An overview is given in Figure 14.1. Generally, there is a distinction between "trait markers" that are indicative of a genetic predisposition to alcohol addiction and "state markers" that should characterize the drinking behavior.

The laboratory markers used in practice until present are state markers, which can be subdivided into direct and indirect alcohol markers. Depending on the lifetime in the organism, they can indicate either an actual drinking event or a chronic high alcohol consumption. Direct alcohol markers are chemically derived from the ethanol molecule and contain still the two carbon atoms of ethanol. These are ethanol itself or metabolites of ethanol such as fatty acid ethyl esters (FAEE), ethylglucuronide (EtG), or phosphatidylethanol, as well as follow-up products of the primary metabolite acetaldehyde such as salsolinol. Indirect markers originate from pathogenic changes in the biochemistry and metabolism after chronically excessive alcohol consumption. All clinical parameters at the time routinely used for diagnosis of chronically high alcohol consumption are indirect markers, such as the liver enzymes gamma-glutamyltransferase (GGT), aspartate aminotransferase (ASAT), alanine aminotransferase (ALAT), mean corpuscular erythrocyte volume (MCV), or carbohydrate-deficient transferrine (CDT). Most of them are measured in blood (serum or plasma) and are not suitable for any other sample material including hair. However, there are also some low-molecular-weight indirect markers, the concentration of which is known to be changed by excessive ethanol consumption such as the ratio of 5-hydroxytryptophol/5-hydroxyindolylacetic acid or dolichol.

Despite the considerable progress in using single markers and particularly combinations of two or several markers [13], the situation is still not satisfactory, since the indirect blood or serum markers have deficiencies in specificity or sensitivity,

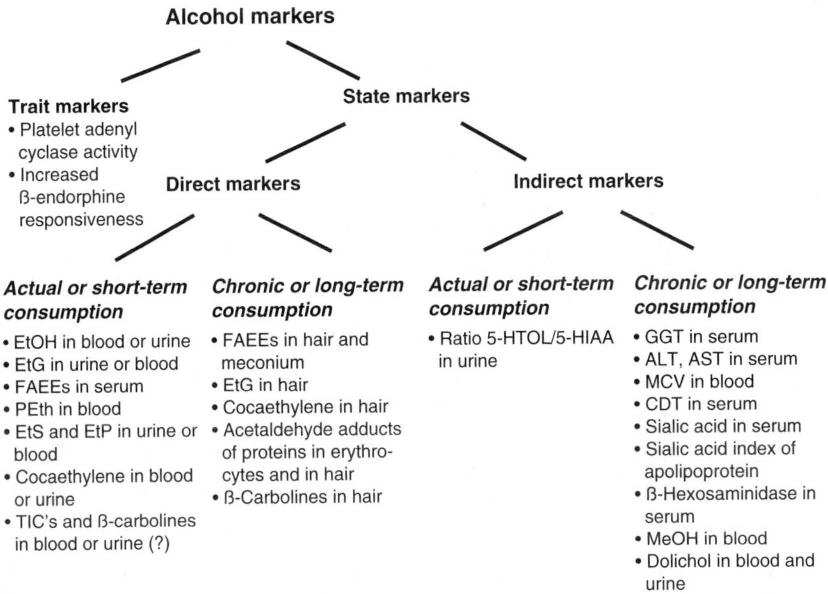

FIGURE 14.1 Classification of markers for alcohol abuse. (Abbreviations: ALT = alanine aminotransferase; AST = aspartate aminotransferase; EtG = ethylglucuronide; CDT = carbohydrate-deficient transferrine; EtOH = ethanol; EtP = ethyl phosphate; EtS = ethyl sulfate; FAEE = fatty acid ethyl ester; GGT = gamma-glutamyltranspeptidase; 5-HIAA = 5-hydroxyindolylacetic acid; 5-HTOL = 5-hydroxytryptophol; MCV = mean corpuscular volume; MeOH = methanol; PEth = phosphatidyl ethanol; TIC = tetrahydroisoquinoline.)

and the upcoming direct markers have a too short detection window in blood or urine. Using hair, the last drawback could be avoided by a durable incorporation of the markers into the hair matrix. In principle, the advantages of hair analysis for the retrospective detection of drug intake and for a time-resolved investigation of the consumption history should also be valid for alcohol.

The possibilities for the detection of chronically elevated alcohol consumption by hair analysis were reviewed by Pragst et al. [14]. Unfortunately, ethanol itself is unsuitable because of its high volatility and because it is reversibly absorbed in hair from external sources, e.g., in pubs or laboratories. However, it can be assumed that ethanol could be chemically bound to free carboxylic groups of the hair proteins or that hydrolyzable esters are formed and incorporated into hair after alcohol consumption. Therefore, hair samples from alcoholics, social drinkers, and teetotalers (children) were investigated by headspace gas chromatography (GC) after hydrolysis with 30% NaOH for ethanol liberated from such ester groups [14]. Furthermore, hair extracts prepared by treatment with methanol or a chloroform/methanol mixture and evaporation of the solvent were hydrolyzed in the same way. The results are shown in Figure 14.2. The samples from the children revealed clearly the lowest values, but there was no unambiguous difference between the samples from social drinkers and from alcoholics. Obviously, such a simple cumulative determination of hydrolyzable ethyl esters from the hair matrix cannot be used as a measure of the

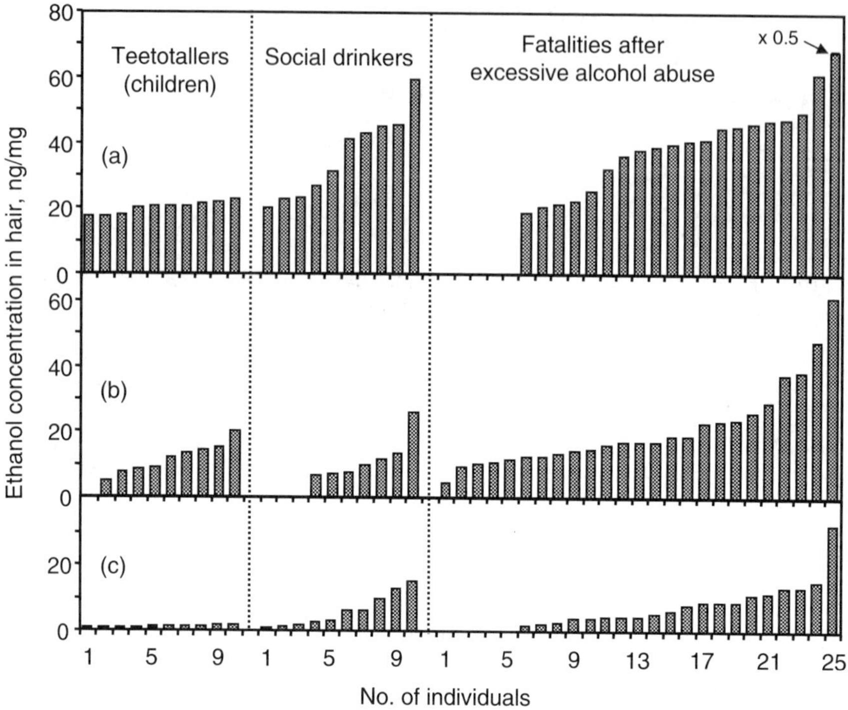

FIGURE 14.2 Ethanol concentration in hair or hair extracts liberated by hydrolysis with 30% NaOH and measured by headspace gas chromatography [14]. (a) Total hair. (b) Hair extracts with $CHCl_3$/MeOH (4:1 v/v). (c) Hair extract with methanol. The individuals in the three series are not identical and are independently arranged in the order of increasing ethanol concentration. (From Pragst, F. et al., *Forensic Sci. Int.*, 107, 201, 2000.With permission.)

extent of alcohol consumption, since other constituents from external sources such as diethyl phthalate and ethyl 4-hydroxybenzoate, which were detected in the same study, dominate and lead to false positive results.

Therefore, the use of hair analysis for detection of alcohol consumption is bound to the analysis of definite alcohol markers. In recent years, some progress was achieved with fatty acid ethyl esters and ethylglucuronide, which will be described in greater detail. Furthermore, benzoylecgonine ethyl ester (cocaethylene) as a mixed metabolite of cocaine and ethanol will be included. Finally, some further attempts based on other markers will be reviewed.

14.2 FATTY ACID ETHYL ESTERS (FAEE)

14.2.1 Formation, Distribution, and Elimination of FAEE in Humans

Fatty acid ethyl esters (FAEE) are a group of more than 20 substances. The enzymatic formation of FAEE after alcohol intake was described for the first time by Lange

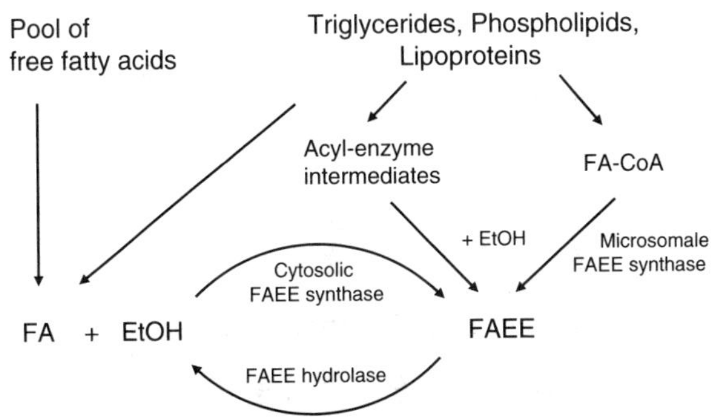

FIGURE 14.3 Formation routes and hydrolysis of fatty acid ethyl esters (FA = fatty acids).

et al. in 1981 [15] and later thoroughly investigated in cell homogenates, animal experiments, and human studies by several groups as reviewed in the literature [16–20]. They are formed in presence of alcohol from free fatty acids, triglycerides, lipoproteins, or phospholipids by specific cytosolic FAEE synthases as well as by nonspecific enzymes such as carboxylesterase, lipoprotein lipase, carboxylester lipase, or cholesterol esterase in blood and almost all tissues (Figure 14.3). The elimination from blood occurs in an at least two-phase kinetics, with a primary half-life of about 3 h and a terminal half-life of about 11 h, by distribution into tissues or hydrolysis under the action of FAEE hydrolases [21]. The hydrolyses occurs mainly in the blood cells and only to a small extent in plasma [22]. They are detectable in blood at least 24 h after cessation of drinking [23]. FAEE concentrations measured in human samples are shown in Table 14.1. An accumulation in tissues can be assumed from the high concentrations in liver, heart muscle, and fat. Therefore, FAEEs are believed to play a role in the pathogenesis of alcohol-induced tissue damage [33].

The use of FAEEs as alcohol markers in blood is limited to the detection of recent consumption up to 44 h after consumption [34]. In adipose or liver tissue, they are particular useful in postmortem cases [27, 28]. However, apart from hair, a real practical application was only achieved in FAEE determination in meconium as a biomarker of fetal exposure to alcohol [29, 30].

14.2.2 Analysis of FAEE in Hair

The methods used for analysis of FAEE from blood (serum or plasma), tissue homogenates, or meconium (as a rule 1 ml or 1 g sample material) are based on liquid extraction by acetone/n-hexane mixtures followed by solid-phase extraction on aminopropyl-silica columns [28, 34–39]. Gas chromatography-mass spectrometry (GC-MS) was generally applied for the quantitative determination, and ethyl heptadecanoate (E17:0) was used as the internal standard. These methods appeared to be unsuitable for hair samples because of insufficient sensitivity for the lower sample amount (10–30 mg) and high chromatographic background caused by other lipids in the extract. Furthermore, E17:0 could not be used as the internal standard, since it was found to be a constituent of the samples.

TABLE 14.1
Data about Concentrations of Fatty Acid Ethyl Esters in Human Sample Material Described in the Literature

Sample Material	Individual FAEE Included[a]	FAEE Concentration	Remarks[b]	Ref.
Serum (vital)	E16:0, E16:1, E18:0, E18:1, E18:2, E20:4	1.2–3.0 μmol/l	BAC = 1 mg/g	[24]
Serum (vital)	E16:0, E18:0, E18:1, E18:2, E20:4, E20:5, E22:6	6.0–12.5 μmol/l	BAC = 0.5–0.7 mg/g	[25]
Full blood (vital)	E16:0, E18:1	4.2–15.1 μg/ml	BAC > 3.0 mg/g	[26]
Heart tissue (postmortem)	E16:0, E18:0, E18:1, E18:2, E20:0, E20:4	386 ± 94 nmol/g	alcohol abuser	[27]
Brain tissue (postmortem)	E16:0, E18:0, E18:1, E18:2, E20:0, E20:4	365 ± 100 nmol/g	alcohol abuser	[27]
Adipose tissue (postmortem)	E16:0, E18:0, E18:1, E18:2, E20:4, E20:5, E22:6	3–94 nmol/g	alcohol abuser	[28]
Meconium	E16:0, E16:1, E18:0, E18:1, E18:2, E18:3, E20:4	0–62 μg/g	725 neonates, 108 positive	[29]
Meconium	E12:0, E14:0, E16:0, E16:1, E18:0, E18:1, E18:2, E18:3, E20:2	2–262 nmol/g	20 positive neonates	[30]
Hair	E14:0, E16:0, E18:0, E18:1	1–30 ng/mg	alcoholics	[31]
Skin surface lipids	E14:0, E16:0, E18:0, E18:1	24–240 ng/mg[c]	alcoholics	[32]

[a] E12:0 = ethyl laurate, E14:0 = ethyl myristate, E16:0 = ethyl palmitate, E16:1 = ethyl palmitoleate, E18:0 = ethyl stearate, E18:1 = ethyl oleate, E18:2 = ethyl linolate, E18:3 = ethyl linolenate; E20:0 = ethyl arachidate, E20:4 = ethyl arachidonate, E20:5 = ethyl eicosapentaenoate, E22:5 = ethyl clupanodonate, E22:6 = ethyl docosahexanoate. In all cases, from References 24–30, E17:0 (ethyl heptadecanoate) was used as internal standard.

[b] BAC = blood alcohol content.

[c] Calculated from the C_{FAEE}/C_{SQ} ratios given in [32] with a squalene (SQ) concentration in sebum of 10%.

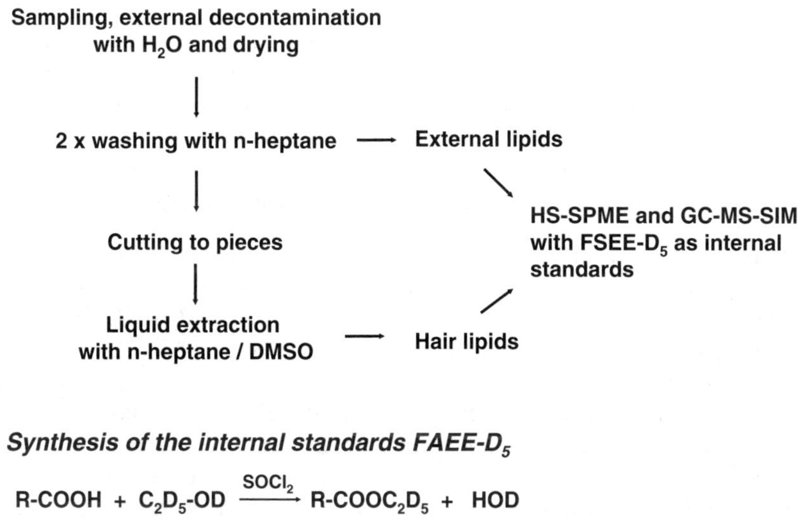

FIGURE 14.4 Practical steps of the hair analysis for FAEE. (From Auwarter, V. et al., *Clin. Chem.*, 47, 2114, 2001; and Pragst, F. et al., *Forensic Sci. Int.*, 121, 76, 2001. With permission.)

Therefore, a method was developed based on liquid extraction of the hair sample, subsequent headspace solid-phase microextraction (HS-SPME) and GC MS in selected-ion monitoring mode (SIM) using deuterated standards [40]. Because of known toxic hazards, n-hexane used primarily as a solvent in the extraction mixture was later displaced by n-heptane [31]. The routine method was limited to ethyl myristate (E14:0), ethyl palmitate (E16:0), ethyl stearate (E18:0), and ethyl oleate (E18:1). The deuterated standards were prepared from the corresponding fatty acids and C_2D_5OD, as described by Pragst et al. [40]. The steps of the procedure are shown in Figure 14.4. All operations were performed in glass vessels.

14.2.2.1 Sample Pretreatment, Decontamination, and Isolation of External Lipids

If available, the proximal hair segment 0 to 6 cm was analyzed. For external decontamination, the sample was washed with water and air-dried. Then, it was cut to pieces of 1 to 2 mm length and 20 to 30 mg that were exactly weighed. The external lipids originating from recent sebum excretion or from hair cosmetics were removed by washing two times for 1 min with n-heptane. The washings were united in 10-ml headspace vials and, after addition of the deuterated standards, evaporated and analyzed for the FAEE by HS-SPME and GC-MS as described below.

14.2.2.2 Hair Extraction

The externally degreased hair samples were extracted for 15 hours at 25°C by a two-phase mixture of 0.5 ml dimethylsulfoxide (DMSO) and 2 ml n-heptane containing each 40 ng of the deuterated FAEE as internal standards. From a series of solvents or solvent mixtures, this aprotic solvent mixture appeared to be most suitable because of the highest extraction yields and the avoidance of ester hydrolysis or transesterification in presence of methanol or other alcohols. After centrifugation, the n-heptane layer was separated into 10-ml headspace vials, the solvent was evaporated in a nitrogen stream, and the residue was used for the analysis.

14.2.2.3 Headspace Solid-Phase Microextraction (HS-SPME)

After optimization of all parameters, the following conditions were used. To the residues of the n-heptane washings and of the hair extract in the headspace vials, 1 ml phosphate buffer (0.1*M*, pH 7.4) and 0.5 g NaCl were added. All further steps were automatically performed by a Multipurpose Sampler (MPS 2, Gerstel, Mühlheim/Ruhr, Germany). After 5 min preheating at 90°C the extraction was performed with a 65-μm polydimethylsiloxane/divinylbenzene (PDMS/DVB) fiber at the same temperature for 30 min with controlled agitation of the sample. The absolute extraction yields were between 30 and 40% at a sample amount of 10 mg. For the desorption in the injection port of the GC, 5 min at 260°C appeared to be sufficient.

14.2.2.4 Gas Chromatography-Mass Spectrometry (GC-MS)

The mass spectra of all FAEE displayed relatively intense molecular ion peaks that were used for quantification, whereas the peaks of the McLafferty rearrangement (CH_2=COH-$OC_2H_5^+$ and CH_2=COH-$OC_2D_5^+$, respectively, m/z = 88 and 93), the peaks of the β-cleavage (CH_2-CH_2-CO-$OC_2H_5^{+\cdot}$ and CH_2-CH_2-CO-$OC_2D_5^{+\cdot}$, m/z = 101 and 106) as well as the peaks m/z = 157 and 162 (C_6H_{12}-$COOC_2H_5^{+\cdot}$ and C_6H_{12}COO-$C_2D_5^{+\cdot}$, respectively) were used as the qualifier ions. In the validation of the method, limits of detection (LOD) between 0.015 ng/mg and 0.04 ng/mg and limits of quantification (LOQ) between 0.05 ng/mg and 0.12 ng/mg were determined for the four esters. A typical chromatogram is shown in Figure 14.5.

The method was extended to 32 FAEE and their deuterated analogs to explore the composition of the FAEE mixture in hair [41]. Besides linear and unsaturated fatty acids, iso- and anteiso-fatty acids (branched in ω-1 and ω-2 position) were also included, which are typical for sebum. A chromatogram obtained by this extended method from a hair sample of an alcoholic in which 15 FAEE were detected is shown in Figure 14.6. Although, in HS-SPME/GC-MS, the peak intensity is not directly related to the abundance of the FAEE in hair, it is seen that also branched FAEE and saturated FAEE with an odd number of carbon atoms are present in well measurable concentrations. The four esters E14:0, E16:0, E18:0, and E18:1 were chosen for the routine method because they were regularly found in all hair samples and appeared to be stable in the hair matrix. Esters with more double bonds, such as E18:2, E18:3, and E20:4, were excluded because of their sensitivity to oxygen. In contrast to the determination in serum or meconium, where these esters represent a considerable part of the FAEE [29, 30], they do not fulfill the requirements on stability in hair because of the much longer exposure to air and light.

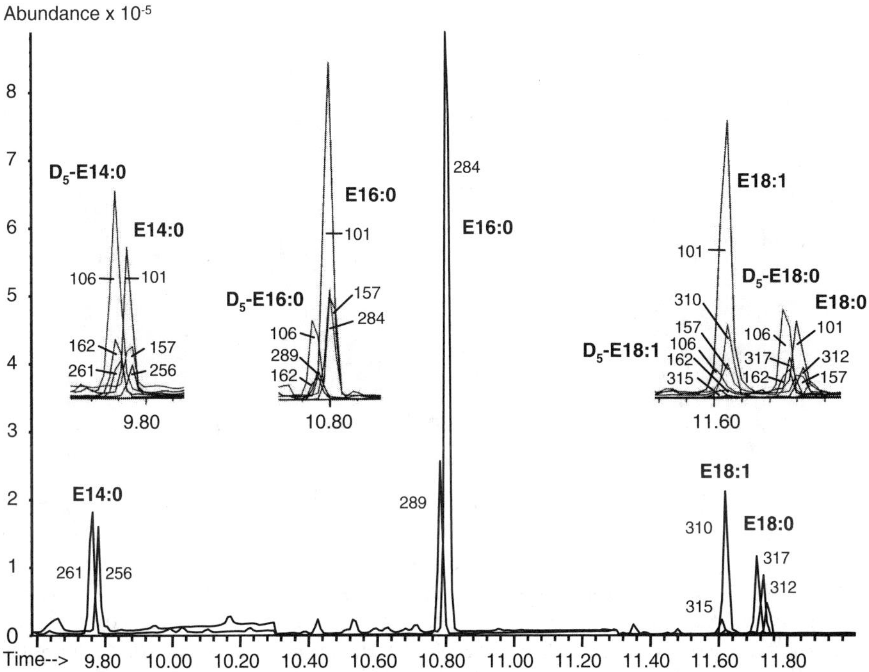

FIGURE 14.5 GC-MS-SIM chromatogram of the hair extract of a death case with known previous alcohol abuse analyzed for FAEE according to the routine procedure. Concentrations: ethyl myristate (E14:0) 0.91 ng/mg; ethyl palmitate (E16:0) 3.23 ng/mg; ethyl oleate (E18:1) 6.39 ng/mg; ethyl stearate (E18:0) 0.31 ng/mg.

An alternative method for determination of FAEE in hair was described recently by Caprara et al. [42], based on the same hair extraction procedure but using SPE on amino columns for cleanup and direct injection in hexane solution instead of HS-SPME. Ethyl laurate (E12:0) and ethyl palmitoleate (E16:1) were included additionally to the four esters described above, and ethyl heptadecanoate (E17:0) was used as internal standard. The measurements were performed on a GC-MS/MS instrument. The LODs of the individual esters were determined to be between 0.003 and 0.010 ng/mg.

14.2.3 Incorporation and Elimination of FAEE in Hair

In the case of incorporation of FAEEs into the hair matrix only within the hair root, the drinking history of an individual should be displayed by their concentrations along the hair length [43]. Therefore, segmental analyses for FAEE were performed in a larger number of cases and compared with the time course of the alcohol consumption in the months before sampling [31]. Besides the hair extract, the external lipids in the washings were also analyzed. A typical example of a patient admitted to a hospital for withdrawal treatment is shown in Figure 14.7. Despite the nearly constant daily drinking behavior during the last 6 months before sampling,

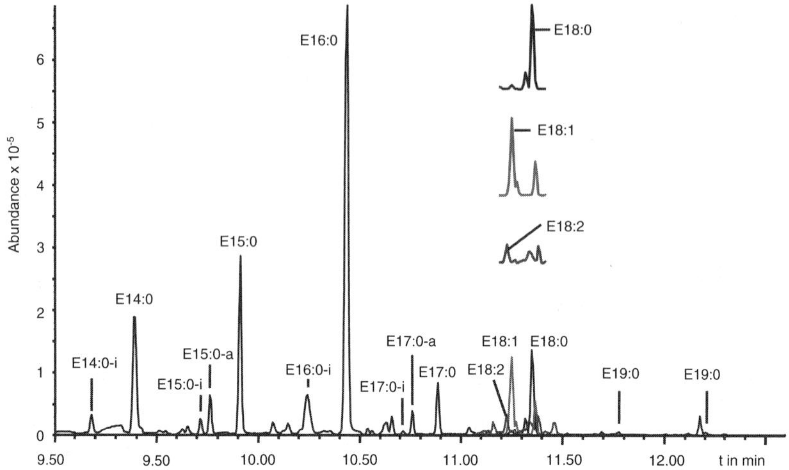

FIGURE 14.6 GC-MS-SIM chromatogram of the postmortem hair sample from an alcoholic (age 50, male, postmortem BAC 3.2 mg/g) screened for 32 fatty acid ethyl esters. For reasons of clarity, only the molecular ion traces are shown. The following concentrations were determined: ethyl 12-methyltrideanoate (E14:0-i) 0.73 ng/mg; ethyl myristate (E14:0) 3.42 ng/mg; ethyl 13-methylmyristate (E15:0-i) 0.14 ng/mg; ethyl 12-methylmyristate (E15:0-a) 0.63 ng/mg; ethyl pentadecanoate (E15:0) 1.32 ng/mg; ethyl 14-methylpentadecanoate (E16:0-i) 0.60 ng/mg; ethyl palmitate (E16:0) 6.37 ng/mg; ethyl 15-methylpalmitate (E17:0-i) 0.02 ng/mg; ethyl 14-methylpalmitate (E17:0-a) 0.20 ng/mg; ethyl heptadecanoate (E17:0) 0.41 ng/mg; ethyl linolate (E18:2) 0.80 ng/mg; ethyl oleate (E18:1) 7.39 ng/mg; ethyl stearate (E18:0) 1.61 ng/mg; ethyl nonadecanoate (E19:0) ≈ 0.02 ng/mg; ethyl arachidate (E20:0) 0.12 ng/mg.

a strong increase of the concentrations from proximal to distal is seen for the corresponding segments. More distally, the concentrations again decrease. The abstinence period between 6 and 9 months before sampling was not recognizable. An agreement between distribution of the FAEE along the hair lengths and periods of drinking and abstinence also was not found in other cases. The FAEE in the external lipids displayed a very similar course. However, there was a higher portion of ethyl oleate as compared with the saturated esters. Since these external concentrations are also related to the hair weight and not to the lipid weight, the FAEE concentrations in the lipid layer on the hair surface were estimated to be one to two orders of magnitude higher than in hair. The much higher concentration of ethyl oleate in the external lipids in comparison with the hair matrix is obviously caused by the higher sensitivity of this unsaturated compound to degradation. For this reason, it is destroyed to a higher degree before entering the hair matrix.

It was concluded from these results that the FAEE are incorporated into hair mainly from sebum steadily produced by the sebaceous glands attached to every hair root. This steady fatting leads to an accumulation that increases with the age of the hair and explains the typical increase from proximal to distal. This accumulation was directly observed in cases where a second hair sample was collected from the same subject two month after the first [41]. During the two months between both samplings, the previous segment 0 to 1 cm had been shifted to the position

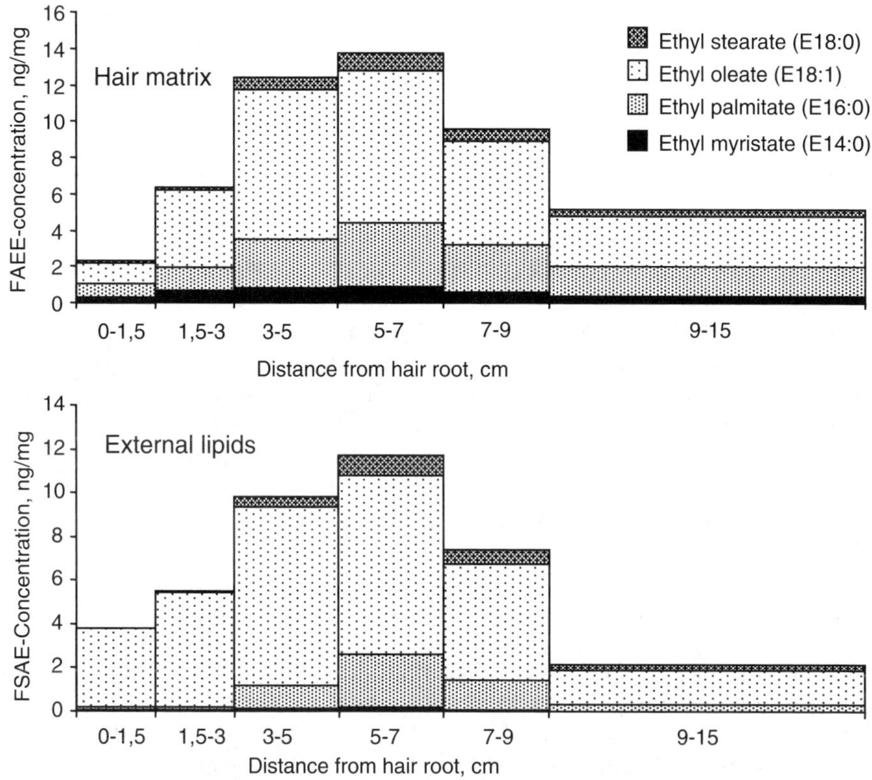

FIGURE 14.7 Segmental analysis of the hair sample of a patient in withdrawal treatment (age 47, female) for FAEE. Sampling 4 days after admission in hospital. Self-reported drinking history: in the last half year before sampling, daily 200 ml brandy or 1.5 l beer; before that, 3 months' abstinence. Shampooing three times per week, last time 5 days before sampling. The concentrations in the external lipids are also related to the hair weight.

2 to 3 cm due to the hair growth of about 1 cm per month. At the same time, the FAEE concentration in this segment more than doubled.

Further evidence for this incorporation mechanism was obtained by the detection of FAEE in skin-surface lipids collected, e.g., from the forehead in a patch or a wipe test [32]. Since, in the holocrine mechanism of the sebaceous glands, a diversity of specific sebum lipids are produced directly in the gland cells [44–46], it was assumed that the FAEEs are also enzymatically formed at this place from ethanol diffusing from the blood circulation to the glands. This assumption was supported by strongly increased FAEE concentrations in hair after daily treatment for 2 months of the corresponding head skin area with a hair lotion containing 62.5% ethanol [47].

The regular treatment with alcohol-containing hair-care products is therefore a serious reason for false-positive results. A systematic study of the effects of other products and procedures of hair care and hair cosmetics on the FAEE concentrations showed that 20 times usual shampooing of the hair sample of an alcoholic did not significantly decrease the concentration in the hair matrix [47]. It was shown that many hair-care products contain traces of FAEE which, however, were without effects after usual application. No substantial decrease of the FAEE concentration in the hair matrix was found after bleaching, shading, and permanent wave. A decrease (64%) was observed only in a dyeing experiment with alkaline reagents (pH = 11). However, the FAEEs on the hair surface measured in the n-heptane washings were strongly decreased by all kinds of hair treatment. Since, as shown above, the external sebum layer is the main source of the FAEE in the hair matrix, it can be expected that for socially adapted individuals with frequent shampooing, lower FAEE concentrations would be found than for antisocial drinkers with less frequent shampooing and the same alcohol consumption.

It was generally observed that the FAEE concentrations in hair slowly decrease. This was seen from the lower concentrations in distant segments of long samples (Figure 14.7) as well as after longer storage of the samples in air. The main processes of elimination are assumed to be hydrolysis and evaporation for all esters and autoxidation of the unsaturated species. Therefore, storage of the dry samples in aluminum foil is the best way to avoid degradation between sampling and measurement.

14.2.4 FAEE Concentrations in Hair and Drinking Behavior

As a consequence of the incorporation mechanism from sebum, a time-resolved investigation of the drinking history by segmental hair analysis for FAEE is not possible. Of course, no further FAEEs are synthesized and deposited in newly grown hair after abstinence begins. However, a lower concentration in proximal segments, as shown in Figure 14.7, was generally observed and is not an unambiguous proof for decreased alcohol consumption, but is caused by a shorter time of accumulation. Therefore, there is only the possibility of using the FAEE concentration as an indicator of the general drinking behavior in the time before sampling without reference to a certain time period.

The method described in Section 14.2.2 was applied to hair samples of teetotalers, moderate social drinkers, patients in alcohol withdrawal treatment, and death cases with known alcohol abuse or alcohol addiction. For interpretation with respect to the drinking behavior, the concentration sum of four esters — ethyl myristate, ethyl palmitate, ethyl oleate, and ethyl stearate — C_{FAEE} was used. In the case of sufficiently long hair, the segment 0 to 6 cm was analyzed. The total length was investigated for hair samples shorter than 6 cm. Some data for these four groups are shown in Figure 14.8 and Figure 14.9.

14.2.4.1 Teetotalers

Surprisingly, in the hair of strict teetotalers, a small C_{FAEE} between 0.06 and 0.37 ng/mg (mean 0.17 ng/mg, $n = 17$ [31, 48]) was measured (Figure 14.8a). The reasons are not yet clear. In principle, the specific metabolism of the sebaceous gland cells should be able to form ethanol from acetate intermediates in analogy to fat alcohols occurring in sebum waxes. Another possibility is the use of hair cosmetics containing

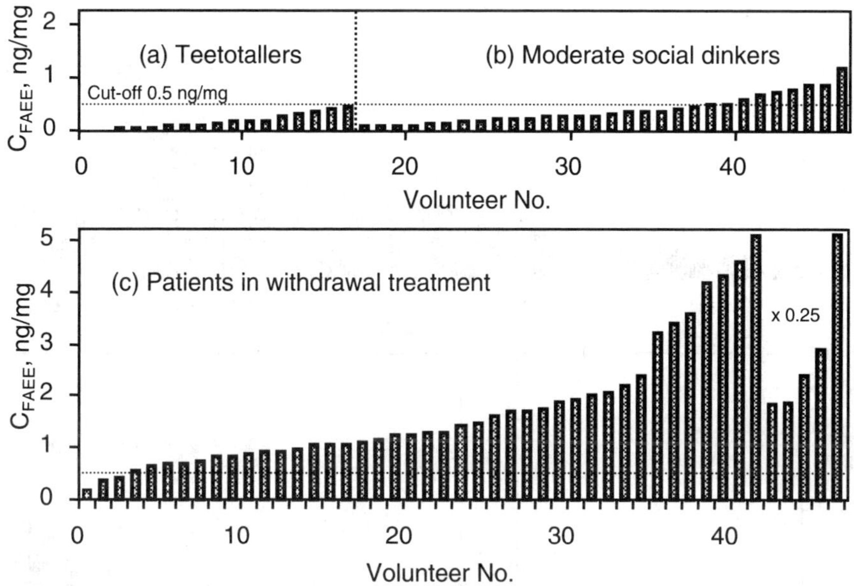

FIGURE 14.8 C_{FAEE} in hair samples from (a) teetotalers, (b) moderate social drinkers, and (c) alcoholics, patients in alcohol withdrawal treatment. The optimum cutoff for excessive alcohol consumption in this clientele was determined at $C_{FAEE} = 0.5$ ng/mg.

ethanol. Since similarly low concentrations were sometimes found for moderate social drinkers, absolute abstinence cannot be controlled using this marker.

14.2.4.2 Moderate Social Drinkers

In the hair of social drinkers with self-reported consumption between 2 and 20 g ethanol per day, between 0.08 and 0.87 ng/mg were determined ($n = 20$, mean 0.40 ng/mg [31, 48]). A correlation between alcohol consumption and C_{FAEE} was not found. Cases with $C_{FAEE} > 1.0$ ng/mg could be explained by use of hair lotions containing ethanol and were excluded. It can be concluded from the data measured until now that normal drinking does not lead to C_{FAEE} above 1.0 ng/mg.

14.2.4.3 Patients in Alcohol Withdrawal Treatment

The results for a total of 47 patients were published in three studies [31, 48, 49]. The samples were collected between 2 and 60 days after beginning abstinence. According to the self-reports, the patients had consumed between 50 and 400 g ethanol per day [31, 48] or between 960 and 7600 g ethanol in the last month before sampling [49]. As shown in Figure 14.8c, C_{FAEE} ranged from 0.2 to 20.5 ng/mg (mean 2.7 ng/mg). A relationship between alcohol consumption and C_{FAEE} also was not seen in these cases. The very low concentrations in two cases (0.20 and 0.37 ng/mg) were explained by a lower alcohol consumption (60 to 80 g/day) and 2 months of abstinence before sampling or by unusual properties of the hair sample [31].

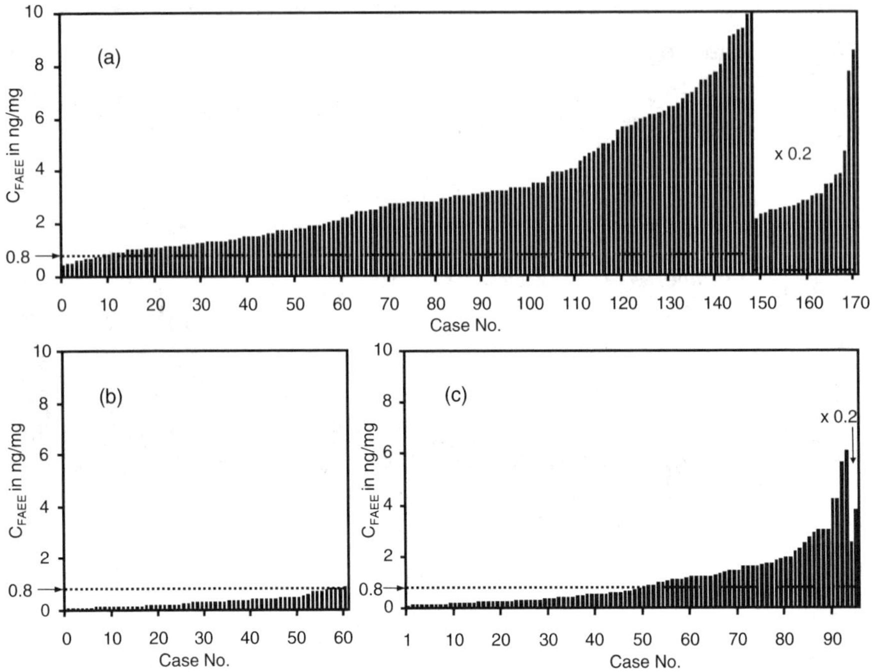

FIGURE 14.9 C_{FAEE} in postmortem hair samples. (a) Cases with known excessive alcohol consumption at lifetime. (b) Cases in which alcohol abuse is excluded. (c) Cases without data about the drinking behavior. The optimum cutoff for excessive alcohol consumption in postmortem cases is C_{FAEE} = 0.8 ng/mg (cf. Figure 14.10).

14.2.4.4 Death Cases

Hair samples of 328 postmortem cases that were investigated in the Institute of Legal Medicine of the University Hospital Charité Berlin were analyzed for FAEE [50]. In 171 of these cases, alcohol addiction or chronic excessive alcohol abuse were known from police reports and were confirmed by the corresponding autopsy findings. Alcohol abuse could clearly be excluded in 61 cases. In the residual 96 cases, the drinking behavior was not known. The results are shown in Figure 14.9. C_{FAEE} of 0.4 to 42 ng/mg (n = 171, mean 5.0 ng/mg) was determined in the alcohol-abuse cases. As a mean, the values in this group were clearly higher than in the group of the withdrawal patients. Presumably, these individuals had even higher alcohol consumption. Furthermore, a higher proportion of these individuals came from an antisocial environment and had neglected hair care. This may have favored the deposition of FAEE from the external lipid layer, which was more seldom removed by shampooing.

C_{FAEE} was clearly lower for the death cases in which alcohol abuse was excluded (0.03 to 0.89 ng/mg, mean 0.32 ng/mg, n = 61). The data were in the same range as for teetotalers and moderate social drinkers. In the cases with unknown drinking behavior, the whole range from 0.08 ng/mg to 18.9 ng/mg was measured.

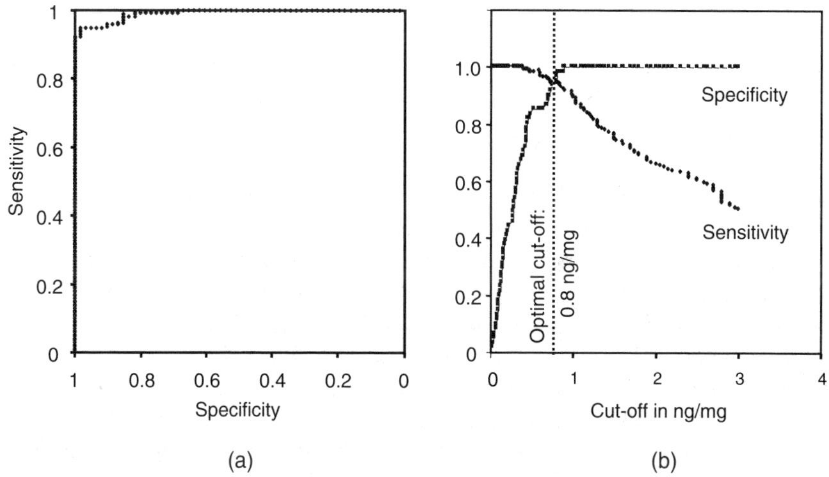

FIGURE 14.10 ROC analysis of the C_{FAEE} in postmortem hair samples presented in Figure 14.9a,b. (a) AUC = 0.989 of the left graph shows that the discrimination power of the method is highly accurate. (b) The optimum between specificity and sensitivity is attained at a cutoff of 0.8 ng/mg in postmortem cases.

14.2.4.5 Cutoff Values

It is obvious from the FAEE concentrations presented above that teetotalers and social drinkers cannot be distinguished by this marker. However, a discrimination between abstinence and moderate social drinking, on the one hand, and excessive alcohol consumption on the other should be possible. For statistical evaluation of the data with respect to cutoff values, the ROC (receiver-operating characteristic) analysis was applied [51]. Using this technique, the discrimination power of the method is characterized by the area under the ROC curve (AUC), and the specificity and selectivity can be plotted as a function of the cutoff. The results of the ROC analysis of the 171 positive and 61 negative death cases are shown in Figure 14.10. From AUC = 0.989 of the ROC curve in Figure 14.10a, it follows that C_{FAEE} has a highly accurate discrimination power between these two groups. The optimal cutoff for death cases is 0.80 ng/mg, with a selectivity of 95% and a specificity of 95% (Figure 14.10b). With a cutoff of 1.0 ng/mg as described in previous papers [31], practically no false-positive cases occur, but the sensitivity is lower, with more than 10% false-negative results.

The situation is more difficult for discrimination between abstinence or moderate social drinking and alcohol abuse of living individuals, where C_{FAEE} shall be used in driving license cases. As shown above, the C_{FAEE} is generally somewhat lower in hair samples of socially integrated cases as compared with death cases. The ROC analysis of all actual data about this clientele led to AUC = 0.935 (highly accurate discrimination power) and an optimal cutoff of 0.5 ng/mg, with a specificity of 90% and a selectivity of 90% [50]. Further investigations for evaluation of the method with a larger number of individuals and inclusion of traditional alcohol markers are in progress [49]. The main problem of these retrospective studies is obtaining realistic data about drinking behavior.

14.2.4.6 Relative FAEE Concentrations with Squalene as Natural Reference Substance

The use of C_{FAEE} as a marker for excessive alcohol consumption is complicated by interindividual differences of the activity of the sebum glands and of elimination by hair care and hair cosmetics. A further source of error is the influence of the investigated hair length caused by increasing accumulation from proximal to distal. An attempt to avoid these errors was made by relating C_{FAEE} to squalene (SQ), which is contained in sebum at levels of 10 to 20% [48]. The squalene concentration (C_{SQ}) in 37 hair samples was determined by high-performance liquid chromatography (HPLC) and ranged from 0.02 to 1.97 μg/mg (mean 0.67 μg/mg). It was shown that SQ can improve the interpretation by correction of the results in cases with deviations from the usual lipid content in hair. However, the relative concentrations C_{FAEE}/C_{SQ} cannot completely replace the absolute concentrations, obviously because of a different kinetics of incorporation and elimination of SQ in hair.

14.2.4.7 Pubic, Axillary, Beard, and Body Hair

The possibility of using hair samples other than scalp hair was examined using 1 teetotaler, 5 moderate social drinkers, and 22 fatalities [52]. Although there were large differences between the C_{FAEE} in hair from the different sites in the same individual, cases of chronic excessive alcohol consumption were characterized by $C_{FAEE} > 1.0$ ng/mg in almost all samples. Therefore, pubic, axillary, beard, or body hair can be used if scalp hair is not available or to confirm scalp hair results and to avoid errors in interpretation caused by the use of hair cosmetics.

14.2.5 Practical Applications

The determination of C_{FAEE} was applied as a marker of the drinking behavior in cases of driving-ability examination (driving under the influence of alcohol, DUI cases) and in postmortem cases. The application to DUI cases will be presented together with ethyl glucuronide in Section 14.4. Furthermore, some initial experiments to include FAEE into neonatal hair testing are described.

In postmortem investigations, the certainty about the chronic drinking behavior is frequently important for the interpretation of the cause or the circumstances of death. The typical pathologic symptoms are not always present or could originate from other reasons. In strongly putrefied or skeletonized corpses, such a morphologic diagnosis is even impossible. The data obtained from the criminal case reports, e.g., based on statements of neighbors, are frequently incomplete or questionable. Furthermore, the traditional alcohol markers such as GGT, MCV, or CDT are not applicable to postmortem blood. Hair analysis for FAEE proved to be a reliable possibility to fill this gap, as shown in many of the cases of Figure 14.9c.

Examples for the use of FAEE in death cases include:

Clearing of reasons for morphologic findings such as the damage of liver or pancreas
Support or exclusion of the diagnosis of death caused by alcohol withdrawal
Contribution to identification of unknown corpses
Investigation of circumstances in traffic or workplace accidents
Clearing of circumstances in murder or homicide cases
Alcohol problems as a reason of suicide

Some typical cases are shown in Table 14.2.

The possibility of revealing alcohol abuse during pregnancy by determination of FAEE in hair of the mothers as well as of the babies was described by Chan et al. [30] and Klein et al. [53]. In the hair of a woman who admitted social drinking during pregnancy, 2.6 pmol/mg FAEE were detected, whereas 0.4 pmol/mg were found in the hair of the infant.

14.3 ETHYLGLUCURONIDE (ETG)

14.3.1 Formation, Distribution, and Elimination of EtG in Human Organism

About 90 to 95% of alcohol is eliminated by oxidation to acetaldehyde, mainly in the liver, whereas only approximately 0.02 to 0.06% is eliminated as ethyl glucuronide (ethyl-β-D-6 glucuronic acid [EtG]) [54, 55]. The conjugation of ethanol occurs in the endoplasmatic reticulum of liver cells and, to a minor extent, in cells of the intestine mucosa and of the lung [56]. The biotransformation requires activated glucuronic acid (UDP-GA) and is catalyzed by the enzyme UDP-glucuronosyl transferases (UGT) (Figure 14.11) with UGT 1A1 and UGT 7B2 as the most active isoforms in liver microsomes [57].

Glucuronidation of alcohol was already reported by Neubauer in 1901 [58]. This direct metabolite of ethanol is a nonvolatile water-soluble substance (structure in Figure 14.11) that was first detected in urine by Jaakonmaki et al. [59] and Kozu [60]. The preparative synthesis, the analytical data and the quantification in serum and urine of EtG were described by Schmitt et al. using GC-MS [61]. The same authors also investigated the kinetic profile of ethyl glucuronide in serum [62, 63]: EtG peaked 2 to 3.5 h later than ethanol and was eliminated with a terminal half-life of 2 to 3 h. EtG could still be determined in serum up to 8 h after complete ethanol elimination. In urine EtG is still detectable up to 80 h after heavy alcohol intake. Thus EtG in body fluids can be used as a short-time marker for alcohol consumption, detectable even after complete elimination of ethanol [64].

The concentration of EtG was determined in several body fluids and tissues using GC-MS or liquid chromatography-mass spectrometry (LC-MS) [65–72]. Some of the data are given in Table 14.3. The highest concentrations were measured in urine, followed by liver, bile, and serum. Muscle and fat tissues had the lowest

TABLE 14.2
FAEE Concentrations in Scalp Hair of Death Cases with Unknown Drinking History

Case No.	Age, Gender	Case History	Autopsy Result	BAC (mg/g)	C_{FAEE} (ng/mg)	Interpretation
01-051	21, f	mummified unknown corpse, found in abandoned building	no known cause of death	—	0.07	no indication of alcohol abuse
02-094	67, m	pedestrian, ignored red traffic light, run over by truck, died immediately	lethal traumatic injuries	0.8	3.0	chronic alcohol abuse
02-171	37, m	death in hospital, AIDS and hepatitis, previous alcoholic	pneumonia	0.0	0.29	no indication of alcohol abuse in last 6 months
02-369	56, m	decomposed body, lived very secluded	no known cause of death	1.3 [a]	2.74	chronic alcohol abuse
02-463	35, m	found dead in apartment, victim of murder by stabbing	bled to death	0.0	1.8	chronic alcohol abuse
02-560	31, m	death 6 h after a car accident caused by himself	lethal traumatic injuries	0.0	0.29	no indication of chronic alcohol abuse
03-185	43, m	alcoholic, found dead in apartment, decided to stop drinking the same morning	no known cause of death	0.0	12.6	heavy drinker, death due to alcohol withdrawal
03-329	59, f	found dead in apartment, alcohol problems and withdrawal treatments in the past known	no known cause of death	0.0	1.49	chronic alcohol abuse, death due to withdrawal not excluded
04-007	64, m	sudden collapse in a pub after 2 glasses of vodka	heart disease	0.0	0.18	no indication of alcohol abuse
04-026	57, f	death in hospital after multiple organ failure, psychosomatic disorders	liver necrosis	0.2	2.25	chronic alcohol abuse
04-377	24, m	suicide, jumped from balustrade, height 18 m, smelled of alcohol	lethal traumatic injuries	1.3	0.53	no indication of chronic alcohol abuse, social drinker
04-410	58, m	work accident, fell from roof, died within several minutes, previous alcoholic	lethal traumatic injuries	0.0	0.03	no indication of alcohol abuse, teetotaler or moderate social drinker

[a] Muscle alcohol concentration, blood not available.

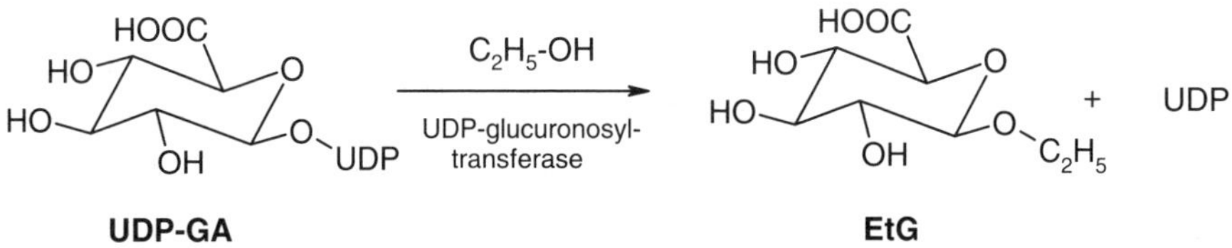

FIGURE 14.11 Formation of ethyl glucuronide (EtG) from activated glucuronic acid (UDP-GA) and ethanol, catalyzed by UDP-glucuronosyl transferases (UGT).

TABLE 14.3
Concentrations of Ethyl Glucuronide in Human Body Fluids and Tissues after Alcohol Consumption

Sample Material	EtG Concentration (μg/ml or μg/g)	Remarks	Ref.
Serum	3.2–13.7	drunk drivers	[61]
Urine	3.0–130	drunk drivers	[61]
Urine	3.6–710	withdrawal patients	[65]
Urine	5.1–1790	drunk drivers	[66]
Muscle	0.13–1.75	fatalities with alcohol history	[67]
Fat	0.18–1.19	fatalities with alcohol history	[67]
Liver	7.9–76.7	fatalities with alcohol history	[67]
Bile	1.10–42.3	fatalities with alcohol history	[67]
Bone marrow	0.52–9.4	fatalities with alcohol history	[67]
Hair	0.025–13.2	alcohol abuser	[68–72]

concentrations. Considering the hydrophilic structure of EtG, this distribution is comprehensible. The possibilities of using EtG as a marker for alcohol abuse were reviewed by Wurst et al. [64].

14.3.2 Analysis of EtG in Hair

The first study reporting the detection of this minor metabolite was done by Sachs in 1993 [73]. Since then, different methods using GC-MS or LC-MS have been described in the literature for the determination of EtG in hair [68–72, 76–79]. An overview of the experimental conditions is given in Table 14.4. Relatively high EtG concentrations were also found in the hair of social drinkers in the first studies [73, 74]. Therefore, these first EtG detection methods were probably not fully optimized for a correct interpretation of EtG findings in hair. In the methods used at present, the decontaminated samples are either pulverized or cut into small pieces. The hair extraction is generally performed with water by incubation or ultrasonication or combinations of both. It was shown by Jurado et al. [72] that this solvent is superior to methanol, methanol/water mixtures, or aqueous trifluoroacetic acid. The commercially available D_5-EtG is generally used as the internal standard. For

TABLE 14.4
Methods for EtG Determination in Hair

Decontamination	Hair Treatment	Cleanup Derivatization	Internal Standard Detection Method	LOD (pg/mg)	Ref.
No indication	no indication	silylation	no internal standard GC-MS-EI	—	[73]
Methanol	pulverization MeOH/water 1:1 (v/v) 4h at 40°C	no cleanup acetylation	no internal standard GC-MS	1000	[74]
Ether/acetone	pulverization 0.25 ml H_2O/1 ml MeOH incubation (5 h) ultrasonication (3 h)	filtration MSTFA	methyl glucuronide GC-MS-EI	2200	[75]
Methanol/acetone	hair cut to 1 mm segments 2 ml H_20 ultrasonication (2 h)	no cleanup BSTFA/pyridine	D_5-EtG GC-MS-EI	—	[68]
Water/acetone	pulverization 2 ml MeOH/H_2O 1:1 (v/v) overnight incubation	no cleanup PFPA/PFPOH	D_5-EtG GC-MS-NCI	31	[69]
Methanol/acetone	hair cut to 1 mm segments 1.5 ml H_2O ultrasonication (3 h)	SFP with aminopropyl columns	D_5-EtG LC-MS/MS	50	[70]
Water/acetone	pulverization 2 ml H_2O ultrasonication (2 h)	SFP with aminopropyl columns PFPA/PFPOH	D_5-EtG GC-MS-NCI	2	[71, 76]
Water/acetone	hair cut to 1 mm segments 2 ml H_2O ultrasonication (2 h) overnight incubation	no cleanup PFPA	D_5-EtG GC-MS-EI	25	[72]
Dichloromethane/ methanol	hair cut to 1 mm segments 700 µl H_2O 20 µl MeOH overnight incubation ultrasonication (2 h)	no cleanup	D_5-EtG LC-ESI-MS-MS in negative ion mode	2	[77]
Water/acetone/ methanol	pulverization 1.5 ml H_2O 3.5 ml MeCN incubation at 45°C (12 h) ultrasonication (1 h)	SFP with aminopropyl columns	D_5-EtG LC-APCI-MS	40	[78]

Note: SPE = solid phase extraction.

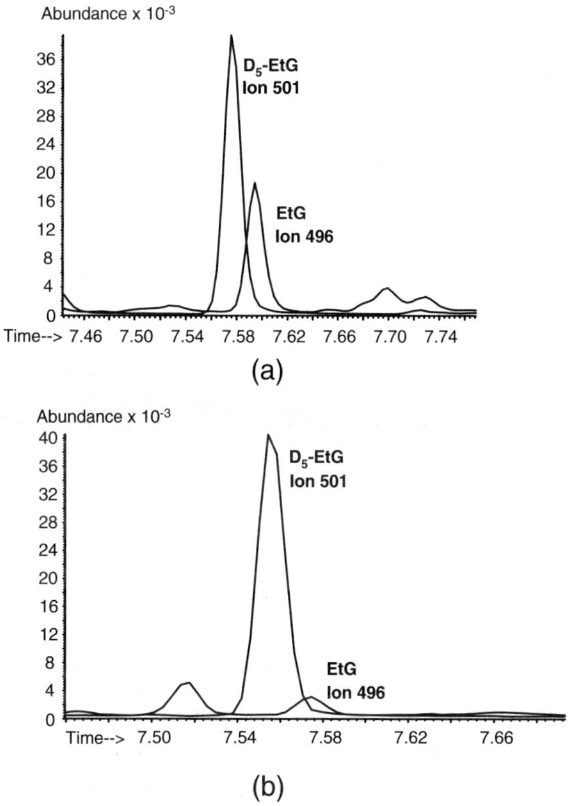

FIGURE 14.12 Determination of ethyl glucuronide in hair samples by GC-MS-NCI after derivatization with PFPA. (a) C_{EtG} 120 pg/mg. (b) Social drinker, C_{EtG} 24.5 pg/mg. (From Yegles, M. et al., *Forensic Sci. Int.*, 145, 167, 2004; and Appenzeller, B. et al., Ethyl Glucuronide Determination in Segmental Hair Analysis of Alcoholics, presented at Communication XIIIème congrès annuel de la Société Française de Toxicologie Analytique, Pau, France, June 8–10, 2005. With permission.)

the GC-MS methods, a cleanup by solid-phase extraction on aminopropyl columns has increased the sensitivity by about one order of magnitude. For GC-MS-EI, the derivatization with pentafluoropropionic anhydride (PFPA) proved to be more favorable compared with heptafluorobutyric anhydride HFBA) and bistrimethylsilyltrifluoroacetamide/trimethylchlorosilane (BSTFA/TMSCl, 99:1) [72]. However, using GC-MS-NCI after derivatization with a mixture of pentafluoropropionic anhydride/pentafluoropropanol (PFPA/PFPOH, 100:70 v/v), the sensitivity could be improved to a detection limit of 2 pg/mg [71]. Typical chromatograms from the sample of an alcoholic and a social drinker obtained by this method are shown in Figure 14.12. Neither a cleanup nor a derivatization was necessary for LC-MS/MS methods [68, 77]. With an up-to-date instrument, a detection limit of 2 ng/mg is obtained simply by injection of the aqueous hair extract into the LC-ESI-MS/MS device [77].

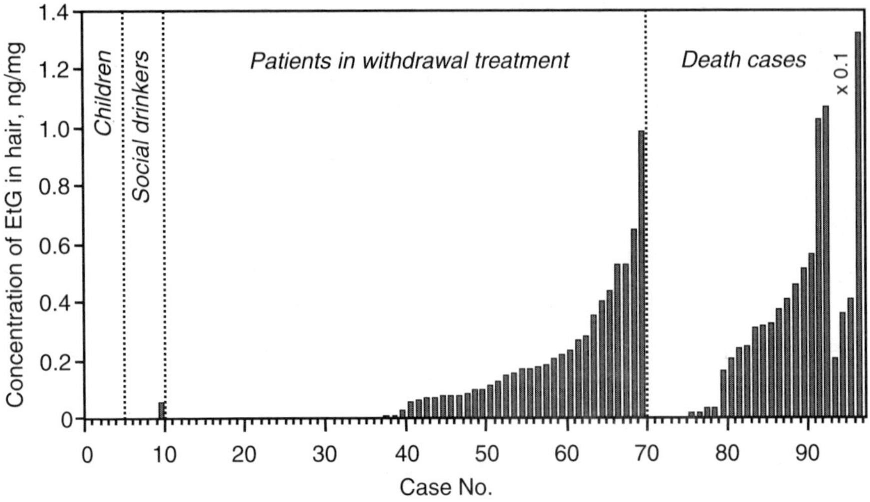

FIGURE 14.13 Concentrations of ethyl glucuronide in 97 hair samples of children, social drinkers, patients in withdrawal treatment, and death cases with known chronic alcohol abuse. (Data from Janda, I. et al., *Forensic Sci. Int.*, 128, 59, 2002. With permission.)

14.3.3 EtG Concentrations in Hair and Drinking Behavior

Skopp et al. [75] detected EtG with concentrations up to 13.8 ng/mg in two of four hair specimens from alcohol abusers and near the detection limit of 2.2 ng/mg in four of seven hair specimens from social drinkers. Such high concentrations for social drinkers could not be confirmed by other authors. In a study by Alt et al. [68] using deuterium-labeled d_5-EtG as internal standard, no EtG could be detected in hair of children and social drinkers, whereas in 23 of 25 hair specimens from alcohol abusers, EtG could be determined with concentration ranges from 0.119 to 4.025 ng/mg EtG [68].

Yegles et al. [69] confirmed the absence of EtG in hair of social drinkers ($n = 6$) using GC-MS-NCI. In 9 of 17 hair specimens from autopsy cases where alcohol was found in serum or gastric content, EtG was determined in hair with concentrations varying between 0.062 and 5.8 ng/mg hair. Furthermore, in all the autopsy cases ($n = 4$) in which alcohol abuse was reported, EtG findings were positive in hair [69].

Janda et al. [70] determined EtG in 97 hair specimens that were taken at autopsies from individuals with known alcoholism or were obtained from alcoholics who were hospitalized for ethanol withdrawal, from social drinkers, and from children who had not consumed any alcohol. The data are shown in Figure 14.13. In 49 of 87 hair specimens of alcoholics, EtG concentrations varied between 0.05 and 13.2 ng/mg. Similar to FAEE (see Section 14.2.4), the concentrations were higher in the death cases than for the withdrawal patients. Only in one of five hair samples of "social drinkers," the EtG concentration was above the detection limit (0.051 ng/mg). No EtG has been detected in the hair of children.

In further studies by Yegles et al. [69, 71], EtG could be determined in all the hair specimens from alcoholic patients (n = 10), with EtG varying between 0.030 and 0.415 ng/mg, and from fatalities with alcohol history (n = 11), with EtG varying between 0.072 and 3.380 ng/mg. In hair specimens of children (n = 3) and of social drinkers (n = 4), no EtG could be detected. Jurado et al. [72] determined EtG in hair specimens of seven alcoholics, with concentrations ranging between 50 and 700 pg/mg hair. No hair samples of social drinkers or teetotalers were investigated in this study.

After optimizing the GC-MS-NCI method by using an HP-5MS capillary column instead of the Ultra-2, EtG was also found in hair of social drinkers (n = 5), with concentration ranging between 9 and 15 pg/mg, whereas in hair of children (n = 3), EtG concentrations were below the lowest limit of quantification of 8 pg/mg [79]. Considering these results, Yegles and Pragst [79] proposed the following preliminary cutoffs using GC-MS-NCI:

C_{EtG} < 8 pg (LLOQ): teetotalers
C_{EtG} > 8 pg/mg and < 25 pg/mg: social drinkers
C_{EtG} > 25 pg/mg: chronic alcohol abuser

Of course, these data need confirmation by a much larger number of samples. Using liquid chromatography-electrospray ionization-tandem mass spectrometry (LC-ESI-MS/MS), Morini et al. [77] also detected EtG in hair of social drinkers in similar concentrations.

The more recent results show that, by using EtG determination in hair, it may be possible to discriminate between teetotalers, social drinkers, and heavy drinkers. EtG concentrations below the limit of quantification may indicate weak social drinkers or teetotalers, but do not completely exclude alcohol abuse. One reason for a negative EtG result after heavy alcohol consumption may be the cosmetic treatment of hair, as bleaching decreases EtG concentration in hair by 78% [71]. Since ethanol is efficiently extracted from hair by incubation with water, it may be washed out by frequent shampooing or hot shower, particularly from hair with cuticle damaged by dyeing, bleaching, or permanent wave. On the other hand, a positive EtG result may be taken as strong evidence for moderate or excessive drinking behavior.

In both studies of Janda et al. [70] and Yegles et al. [71], no correlation was found between the amount of alcohol consumed and the EtG concentration in hair. This is not surprising, considering the variability of the concentrations in serum and the possible elimination by hair care and hair cosmetics. Furthermore, the self-reported data about alcohol consumption may not be sufficiently reliable. Finally, there is experimental evidence that EtG is also eliminated by sweat [80], which can to a different degree contribute to the concentrations in hair.

A relatively good agreement between the self-reported history of alcohol consumption and EtG concentration was found after segmental analysis of EtG in hair from 15 patients included in an alcohol-withdrawal treatment program [76]. Three examples are shown in Figure 14.14. Thus, the cessation of alcohol consumption some months before sampling was in most cases indicated by low concentrations

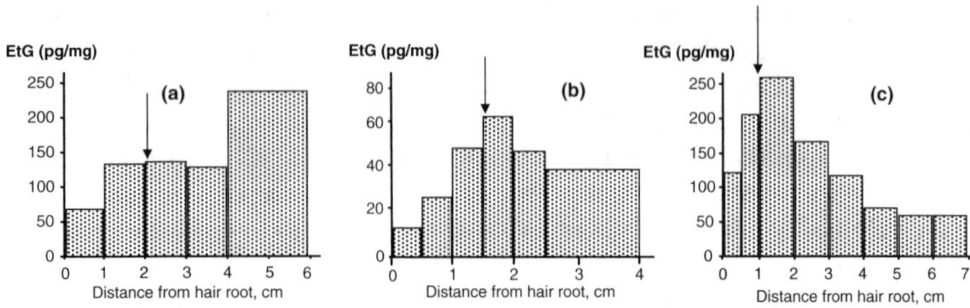

FIGURE 14.14 EtG concentrations in hair segments and drinking history of three patients in withdrawal treatment. The arrows that indicate the time of abstinence are based on the assumption of a hair growth rate of 1 cm/month. (a) Man (44 years): elevated consumption for 2 years (300 ml EtOH per day), then decrease of consumption 2 months before withdrawal. (b) Man (55 years): regular consumption of EtOH (180 ml EtOH per day). (c) Man (33 years): about 500 ml EtOH per day for more than 5 months before withdrawal, then progressive increase up to 700 ml EtOH per day until withdrawal.

in the proximal segment and higher positive results in the corresponding distal segments (Figure 14.14a,b). In another case after a regular consumption of alcohol 5 months before withdrawal, a progressive alcohol consumption increase until withdrawal could be confirmed by EtG hair analysis (Figure 14.14c). Furthermore, after discarding five unreliable subjects (bleached hair, inconstant alcohol intake, and unreliable self-reported consumption), a significant correlation was found between EtG findings in hair corresponding to the period just before withdrawal and the amount of alcohol consumed ($p < 0.01$).

14.4 COMBINED USE OF FAEE AND ETG

As shown in the previous sections, both FAEE and EtG in hair are suitable direct markers for chronic alcohol consumption based on different biochemical origin. However, in general, no significant quantitative relationship to alcohol consumption was found for either marker. For this reason, the interpretation is particularly difficult in borderline cases at the lower level of harmful drinking. Therefore, it was investigated whether the combined use of both hair markers leads to an improved interpretation.

In a first study, the concentrations of both markers were determined in the hair samples of three strict teetotalers, four moderate social drinkers, 10 patients in withdrawal treatment, and 11 fatalities with documented excessive alcohol consumption [71]. The data are shown in Figure 14.15. All cases with alcohol abuse were indicated by both markers. However, there was no proportionality between C_{FAEE} and C_{EtG} in the positive cases. This is not surprising, since both markers have quite different properties and are formed, deposited in hair, and eliminated from hair by completely different mechanisms.

This difference is not necessarily a disadvantage. Therefore, the combined application of FAEE and EtG was examined in 40 cases of driving-ability examination [80]. In all of these cases, the probationers had lost their licenses because of drunken

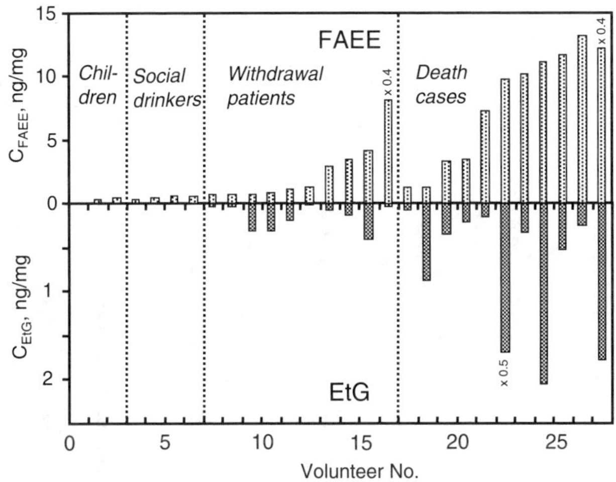

FIGURE 14.15 Comparison of FAEE and EtG in hair of three strict teetotalers, four moderate social drinkers, ten patients in withdrawal treatment, and 11 fatalities with documented excessive alcohol consumption. Cases arranged in the order of increasing C_{FAEE}. (Data from Yegles, M. et al., *Forensic Sci. Int.*, 145, 167, 2004. With permission.)

driving and had applied for reissuing. A prerequisite was strict abstinence from alcohol for at least 1 year. In the cases selected for hair analysis, some doubt about the abstinence remained after the psychological tests as well as the use of the traditional alcohol markers.

The results are shown in Figure 14.16. No indication for alcohol use was certified if $C_{FAEE} \leq 0.4$ ng/mg and $C_{EtG} \leq 8$ pg/mg. From the 40 cases, both results were positive in nine cases, one of either C_{FAEE} or C_{EtG} was positive in 12 cases, and both were negative in 19 cases. As a rule, the final decision of the examining forensic psychologist who considered all other evidence in the case was against reissuing the driving license if at least one of both markers was above the cutoff.

14.5 BENZOYLECGONINE ETHYL ESTER (COCAETHYLENE, BE-ET)

Benzoylecgonine ethyl ester (BE-Et) is one of the metabolites of cocaine regularly determined in hair analysis for cocaine abuse, as described in Chapter 4. Therefore, in this section, only the aspects concerning alcohol shall be considered. According to several *in vitro* and *in vivo* experiments as well as human studies [82–86], BE-Et is formed from cocaine by transesterefication catalyzed by a non-specific carboxylesterase that is located in the endoplasmatic reticulum of liver and kidney cells and also catalyzes the hydrolysis of cocaine to benzoylecgonine (Figure 14.17). It was shown that n-propanol or isopropanol react in the same way to form benzoylecgonine propyl or isopropyl esters [87, 88]. A quantitative study with ten volunteers showed that after coadministration of cocaine and 1 g/kg ethanol, 17 ± 6% of the cocaine was converted to BE-Et [86]. Additional alcohol-specific

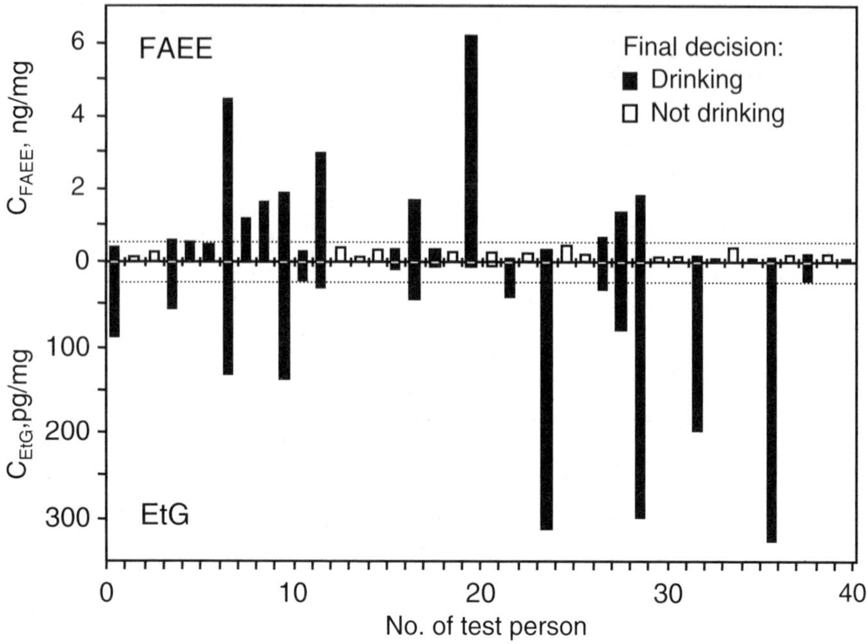

FIGURE 14.16 Comparison of FAEE and EtG in hair of test persons in examination for reissuing a driving license after drunk driving. The decision about drinking behavior is based on all data obtained in medical psychological examination. Dotted lines: cutoff values for heavy drinking $C_{FAEE} = 0.5$ ng/mg and $C_{EtG} = 25$ pg/mg. The test persons are arranged in the order as they were investigated.

metabolites ecgonine ethyl ester and nor-benzoylecgonine ethyl ester were also detected [84, 89]. Therefore, the analysis of BE-Et in hair is an efficient possibility to prove frequent combined use of cocaine and alcohol.

Examples of BE-Et concentrations ($C_{BE\text{-}Et}$) in hair described in the literature [90–96] are given in Table 14.5. For comparison, the corresponding cocaine concentrations (C_{COC}) are also shown. $C_{BE\text{-}Et}$ up to 30 ng/mg was detected. The ratio $C_{BE\text{-}Et}/C_{COC}$ ranges from 0.4 to 60%. Only in some exceptional cases was $C_{BE\text{-}Et}$ higher than C_{COC}. No data about the habits and doses of alcohol and cocaine consumption of the individuals was reported in the studies.

Investigations about the incorporation rate of BE-Et in hair are not known. However, an incorporation rate similar to that of cocaine should be expected from the small structural difference. Therefore, the ratio $C_{BE\text{-}Et}/C_{COC}$ in hair should approximately represent the mean ratio of both compounds in blood during consumption. According to kinetic studies [85], this ratio should essentially be determined by the blood alcohol concentration (BAC) during cocaine use and only to a much lower extent by the cocaine consumption frequency. Since blood alcohol concentrations between 0.1 and 3.0 mg/g are quite usual in practice, this could explain a more than tenfold variation of this ratio. Furthermore, cocaine need not always have been consumed in combination with alcohol.

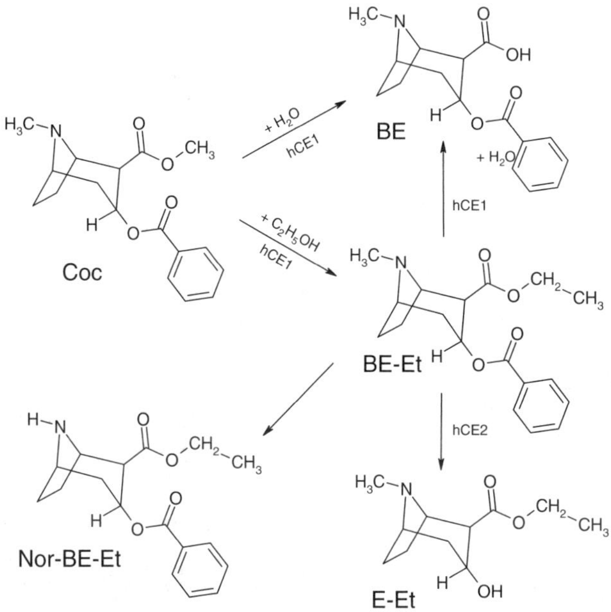

FIGURE 14.17 Hydrolysis and transesterefication of cocaine (Coc) to benzoylecgonine (BE) and benzoylecgonine ethyl ester (BE-Et) are catalyzed by the same carboxylesterase hCE1. BE-Et is metabolized to the further alcohol-specific products ecgonine ethyl ester (E-Et) by another carboxylesterase hCE2, and to nor-benzoylecgonine ethyl ester (Nor-BE-Et).

Therefore, besides $C_{BE\text{-}Et}$, the ratio $C_{BE\text{-}Et}/C_{COC}$ in hair should also be considered for interpretation of the abuse behavior. The detection of BE-Et only shows that cocaine and alcohol were used in combination. Beyond that, and independently of the absolute value of $C_{BE\text{-}Et}$, a ratio $C_{BE\text{-}Et}/C_{COC}$ in the upper range of the data given in Table 14.5 should indicate that the drug was used regularly in combination with high alcohol levels. On the other hand, a $C_{BE\text{-}Et}/C_{COC}$ in the lower range should show that alcohol was present only occasionally or in low concentrations during cocaine use. In this way, information about the general drinking behavior can be obtained from the ratio $C_{BE\text{-}Et}/C_{COC}$ rather than from the absolute value of $C_{BE\text{-}Et}$.

14.6 FURTHER POSSIBILITIES

Compared with illicit or therapeutic drugs, alcohol is consumed in much higher doses and leads to a variety of more-or-less characteristic changes in human metabolism that should also leave their marks in hair. Some of theses further possibilities to detect chronic alcohol consumption by hair analysis are reviewed in this section.

14.6.1 1-Methyl-1,2,3,4-tetrahydro-ß-carboline

Tetrahydroisoquinolines and tetrahydro-β-carbolines are condensation products of endogenic catecholamines (dopamine, noradrenaline, adrenaline) or β-indolylamines

TABLE 14.5
Concentrations of Benzoylecgonine Ethyl Ester BE-Et and Cocaine COC in Hair after Combined Use of Cocaine and Alcohol

Individuals[a]	Positive for BE-Et	C_{BE-Et}, ng/mg Range (mean)	C_{COC}, ng/mg Range (mean)	C_{BE-Et}/C_{COC}, % Range (mean)	Ref.
10 cocaine users	6	0.3–2.6 (0.7)	6.4–19.2 (10.8)	5.3–26.8 (12.4)	[90]
15 pregnant women	15	2.5–30.3 (8.2)	6.6–268.6 (59.9)	5.3–35.3 (16.2)	[91]
9 drug users or drug-related deaths	6	0.03–0.64 (0.20)	0.03–4.11 (2.0)	3.4–15.8 (9.03)	[92]
30 drug abusers	19	0.03–10.9 (1.59)	1.25–35.5 (10.35)	0.4–40 (13.69)	[93]
75 cocaine users	55	0.01–12.79 (1.21)	0.03–227 (54.9)	0.01–43 (5.4)	[94]
15 drug abusers	15	0.42–2.32 (1.11)	0.43–8.98 (5.39)	8.0–247 (51.4)	[95]
74 drug abusers	10	0.05–1.26 (0.27)	0.01–8.37 (2.61)	1.9–59 (17.6)	[96]

Note: Only studies with data of the individual cases were involved.

[a] From each study, only the cases with a positive cocaine result were considered.

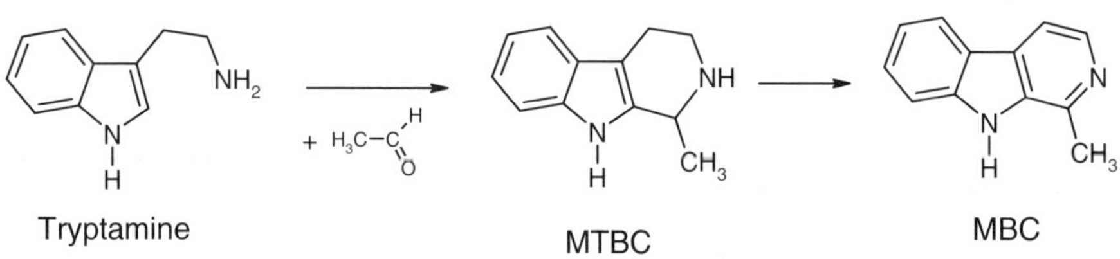

FIGURE 14.18 Formation of 1-methyl-1,2,3,4-tetrahydro-β-carboline (MTBC) and 1-methyl-β-carboline (MBC) by condensation of tryptamine and acetaldehyde.

(tryptamine, serotonine) with aliphatic aldehydes. The substances formed from acetaldehyde as the primary oxidation product of alcohol were frequently seen in the context of alcohol-addiction mechanism as well as of markers for alcohol abuse [97–99]. A method for quantitative analysis of 1-methyl-1,2,3,4-tetrahydro-β-carboline (MTBC) and the corresponding dehydrogenation product 1-methyl-β-carboline (MBC) (Figure 14.18) in hair by HPLC with fluorescence detection after enzymatic digestion was developed by Tsuchiya [100]. MBC was found in samples from five alcoholics in higher concentrations (1.07 to 2.94 ng/mg) than in samples from five nonsmokers without alcohol drinking habits (0.40 to 0.71 ng/mg). The primary condensation product MTBC was not detected. The most frequently investigated substance of this group, salsolinol, was not yet described in hair. The use of these condensation products as alcohol markers is generally limited by the fact that they

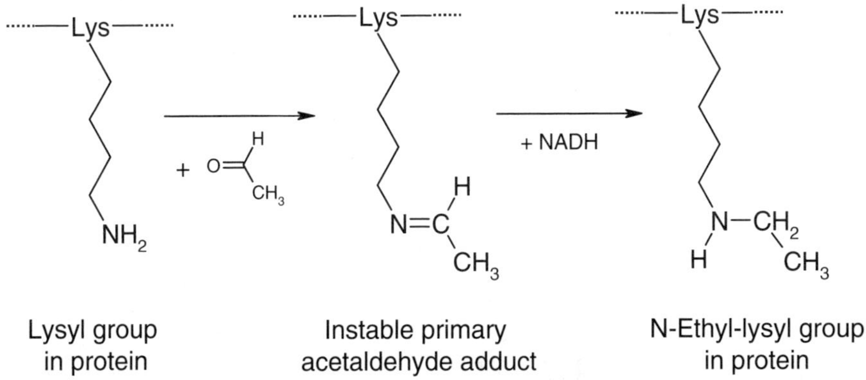

FIGURE 14.19 Acetaldehyde-protein condensation products. (From Sorrell, M.F. and Tuma, D.J., *Ann. N.Y. Acad. Sci.*, 492, 50, 1987. With permission.)

may also originate from pyruvic acid as an intermediate of the carbohydrate metabolism instead of acetaldehyde.

14.6.2 Acetaldehyde-Modified Hair Proteins

Acetaldehyde reacts with free amino groups of proteins to form stable condensation products (Figure 14.19). It was demonstrated more than 10 years ago that these modified proteins in hemoglobin could be useful alcohol markers [101–103]. Only animal experiments were performed to prove their presence in hair [104, 105]. Jelinkova et al. [104] detected two signals in hair of alcohol-fed rats after incubation with 1*M* NaOH and capillary zone electrophoresis that were missing in hair of abstinent rats. Watson et al. [105] developed a direct enzyme-linked immunosorbent assay (ELISA) test specific for acetaldehyde adducts in hair proteins. The test was applied to hair of mice fed with ethanol for 8 weeks. The hair was treated with 0.2*M* mercaptoethanol/8*M* urea at pH 10.5 to 11 overnight at room temperature. The dissolved proteins were purified by 24-h dialysis and then tested by the ELISA, leading to significantly increased signals in comparison with controls.

Although these first experiments were not continued in the last 10 years, the determination of amino acids modified by covalently bound acetaldehyde in hair proteins should be a very promising project for future research, particularly because of their exclusive formation in the hair root and their expected durability and insensitivity to hair treatment or other external interferences.

14.6.3 Other Minor Metabolites of Ethanol

The ethyl group is bound to several other endogenous or exogenous substances in the pathways of ethanol metabolism. An example increasingly considered as an alcohol marker in blood is phosphatidylethanol [106–108], a group of phospholipids in which the aminoalcohol is replaced by ethanol (Figure 14.20). Two very hydrophilic metabolites mainly found in urine are ethyl sulfate [109, 110] and ethyl phosphate [111]. None of these compounds was detected in hair until recently.

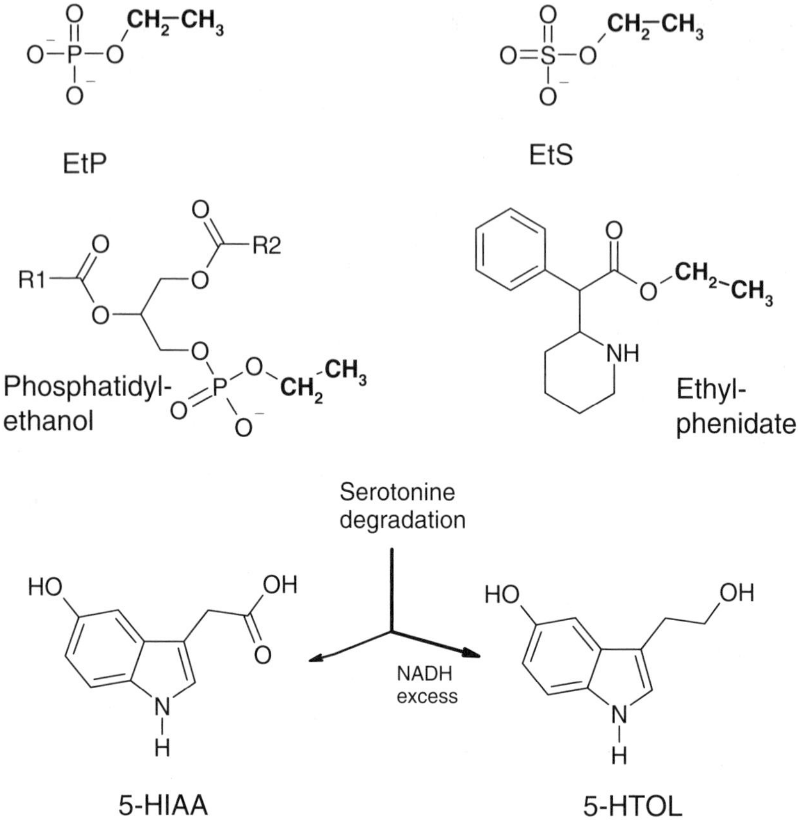

FIGURE 14.20 Structure of further alcohol markers expected in hair. Minor metabolites: ethyl phosphate (EtP), ethyl sulfate (EtS), phosphatidyl ethanol, ethylphenidate. Indirect marker: 5-hydroxytryptophol 5-(HTOL) preferentially formed instead of 5-hydroxyindolylacetic acid (5-HIAA) in the metabolic degradation of serotonine in presence of excessive alcohol.

Similar to the fatty acid ethyl esters and benzoylecgonine ethyl ester, other endogenous or exogenous acids should also be transformed into their ethyl esters during ethanol metabolism. A systematic search including the esters of benzoic acid, phenylacetic acid, hippuric acid, indolyl acetic acid, 5-hydroxyindolylacetic acid, tyrosine, and tryptophane in hair was performed by Spiegel [112]. With detection limits between 0.007 and 0.04 ng/mg of the GC-MS methods used, none of these esters was found. Obviously, the esterification of free acids does not occur to a higher extent. However, the transesterification of methyl esters by carboxylesterases as seen in the case of cocaine seems to be a general process. An example is the formation of ethylphenidate after coingestion of methylphenidate and alcohol [112–114].

14.6.4 Indirect Alcohol Markers

After alcohol intake, increased levels of 5-hydroxytryptophol (5-HTOL) are observed in urine, which in relation to 5-hydroxyindolylacetic acid (5-HIAA) is used as marker of recent alcohol consumption [11]. The biochemical basis is the elevated NADH/NAD^+ ratio during ethanol metabolism, which shifts the degradation of serotonine to the reduction product 5-HTOL instead of the usually dominating 5-HIAA. No investigations to determine the concentration of 5-HTOL or the ratio 5-HTOL/5-HIAA in hair were described in the literature. Higher hair zinc and copper values in 43 male alcoholics than in 39 controls were determined by Gonzales-Reimers et al. [115]. Hair copper was significantly related to the amount of ethanol consumed. As a reason, malnutrition, frequently associated with chronic alcohol abuse, was assumed.

14.7 CONCLUSIONS

There is great demand to include alcohol in the routine of hair analysis for substance abuse. Alcohol itself cannot be used as the analyte for this purpose because of its high volatility. However, there are several suitable minor metabolites of ethanol, notably fatty acid ethyl esters (FAEE) and ethyl glucuronide (EtG), both of which have been thoroughly investigated and are on the verge of a broad practical application. Both FAEE and EtG in hair can discriminate between moderate social drinking and chronic alcohol abuse with a high selectivity and sensitivity that can be further improved by their combined application. However, neither marker can prove absolute abstinence, and they cannot be used for a quantitative retrospective estimation of alcohol consumption.

Benzoylecgonine ethyl ester in hair indicates the combined abuse of alcohol and cocaine and, therefore, is limited to cocaine users. However, in these cases, information about the general drinking habits can be obtained from the concentration ratio of benzoylecgonine ethyl ester to cocaine. Other minor metabolites of alcohol such as phosphatidyl ethanol, ethyl sulfate, ethyl phosphate, 1-methyl-1,2,3,4-tetrahydroisoquinoline, or 1-methyl-1,2,3,4-tetrahydro-β-carboline have not yet been studied in hair or are only in the preliminary stage of study, but these are not expected to be superior to the use of FAEE or EtG as markers. Acetaldehyde-modified hair proteins could be a promising alternative and should be investigated more thoroughly with appropriate techniques of protein and amino acid analysis.

REFERENCES

1. WHO, Global Status Report on Alcohol 2004, World Health Organization, Geneva, 2004.
2. Report of the German Council of Alcohol and Addiction: Verbrauch, Missbrauch, Abhängigkeit — Zahlen und Fakten, Bonn, April 12, 2005; available on-line at http://www.sucht.de.
3. Aderjan, R., *Marker des missbräuchlichen Alkoholkonsums*, Wissenschaftliche Verlagsgesellschaft mbH, Stuttgart, 2000.
4. Conigrave, K.M. et al., Traditional markers of excessive alcohol use, *Addiction*, 98, Suppl. 2, 31–43, 2003.
5. Javors, M.A. and Johnson, B.A., Current status of carbohydrate deficient transferrin, total serum sialic acid, sialic acid index of apolipoprotein J and serum beta-hexosaminidase as markers for alcohol consumption, *Addiction*, 98, Suppl. 2, 45–50, 2003.

6. Wurst, F.M. et al., Emerging biomarkers: new directions and clinical applications, *Alcohol Clin. Exp. Res.*, 29, 465–473, 2005.
7. Helander, A., Biological markers in alcoholism, *J. Neural. Transm. Suppl.*, 66, 15–32, 2003.
8. Hoffman, P.L., Glanz, J., and Tabakoff, B., Platelet adenylyl cyclase activity as a state or trait marker in alcohol dependence: results of the WHO/ISBRA Study on State and Trait Markers of Alcohol Use and Dependence, *Alcohol Clin. Exp. Res.*, 26, 1078–1087, 2002.
9. Ratsma, J.E., Van Der Stelt, O., and Gunning, W.B., Neurochemical markers of alcoholism vulnerability in humans, *Alcohol Alcohol.*, 37, 522–533, 2002.
10. Porjesz, B. et al., The utility of neurophysiological markers in the study of alcoholism, *Clin. Neurophysiol.*, 116, 993–1018, 2005.
11. Beck, O. and Helander, A., 5-hydroxytryptophol as a marker for recent alcohol intake, *Addiction*, 98, Suppl. 2, 63–72, 2003.
12. Musshoff, F. and Daldrup, T., Determination of biological markers for alcohol abuse, *J. Chromatogr. B, Biomed. Sci. Appl.*, 713, 245–264, 1998.
13. Brinkmann, B. et al., ROC analysis of alcoholism markers: 100% specificity, *Int. J. Legal Med.*, 113, 293–299, 2000.
14. Pragst, F. et al., Are there possibilities for the detection of chronically elevated alcohol consumption by hair analysis? A report about the state of investigation, *Forensic Sci. Int.*, 107, 201–223, 2000.
15. Lange, L.G., Bergmann, S.R., and Sobel, B.E., Identification of fatty acid ethyl esters as a product of rabbit myocardial ethanol metabolism, *J. Biol. Chem.*, 256, 12968–12973, 1981.
16. Laposata, E.A. and Lange, L.G., Presence of nonoxidative ethanol metabolism in human organs commonly damaged by ethanol abuse, *Science*, 231, 497–499, 1986.
17. Laposata, M., Szczepiorkowski, Z.M., and Brown, J.E., Fatty acid ethyl esters: non-oxidative metabolites of ethanol, *Prostaglandins Leukot. Essent. Fatty Acids*, 52, 87–91, 1995.
18. Laposata, M., Fatty acid ethyl esters: ethanol metabolites which mediate ethanol-induced organ damage and serve as markers of ethanol intake, *Prog. Lipid Res.*, 37, 307–316, 1998.
19. Laposata, M., Fatty acid ethyl esters: nonoxidative ethanol metabolites with emerging biological and clinical significance, *Lipids*, 34, 281–285, 1999.
20. Laposata, M. et al., Fatty acid ethyl esters: recent observations, *Prostaglandins Leukot. Essent. Fatty Acids*, 67, 193–196, 2002.
21. Doyle, K.M. et al., Fatty acid ethyl esters are present in human serum after ethanol ingestion, *J. Lipid Res.*, 35, 428–437, 1994.
22. Saghir, M., Blodget, E., and Laposata, M., The hydrolysis of fatty acid ethyl esters in low-density lipoproteins by red blood cells, white blood cells and platelets, *Alcohol*, 19, 163–168, 1999.
23. Dan, L. and Laposata, M., Ethyl palmitate and ethyl oleate are the predominant fatty acid ethyl esters in the blood after ethanol ingestion and their synthesis is differentially influenced by the extracellular concentrations of their corresponding fatty acids, *Alcohol Clin. Exp. Res.*, 21, 286–292,1997.
24. Doyle, K.M. et al., Fatty acid ethyl esters in the blood as markers of ethanol intake, *JAMA*, 276, 1152–1156, 1996.
25. Soderberg, B.L. et al., Preanalytical variables affecting the quantification of fatty acid ethyl esters in plasma and serum samples, *Clin. Chem.*, 45, 2183–2190, 1999.

26. Kaphalia, B.S. et al., Fatty acid ethyl esters: markers of alcohol abuse and alcoholism, *Alcohol*, 34, 151–158, 2004.
27. Yamazaki, K. et al., Nonoxidative ethanol and methanol changes in the heart and brain tissue of alcohol abusers, *Jpn. J. Legal Med.*, 51, 380–387, 1997.
28. Refaai, M.A. et al., Liver and adipose tissue fatty acid ethyl esters obtained at autopsy are postmortem markers for premortem ethanol intake, *Clin. Chem.*, 48, 77–83, 2002.
29. Moore, C. et al., Prevalence of fatty acid ethyl esters in meconium specimens, *Clin. Chem.*, 49,133–136, 2003.
30. Chan, D. et al., Recent developments in meconium and hair testing methods for the confirmation of gestational exposures to alcohol and tobacco smoke, *Clin. Biochem.*, 37, 429–438, 2004.
31. Auwarter, V. et al., Fatty acid ethyl esters in hair as markers of alcohol consumption: segmental hair analysis of alcoholics, social drinkers, and teetotalers, *Clin. Chem.*, 47, 2114–2123, 2001.
32. Pragst, F. et al., Wipe-test and patch-test for alcohol misuse based on the concentration ratio of fatty acid ethyl esters and squalene C_{FAEE}/C_{SQ} in skin surface lipids, *Forensic Sci. Int.*, 143, 77–86, 2004.
33. Beckemeier, M.E. and Bora, P.S., Fatty acid ethyl esters: potentially toxic products of myocardial ethanol metabolism, *J. Mol. Cell Cardiol.*, 30, 2487–2494, 1998.
34. Borucki, K. et al., In heavy drinkers fatty acid ethyl esters in the serum are increased for 44 hr after ethanol consumption, *Alcohol Clin. Exp. Res.*, 28, 1102–1106, 2004.
35. Kaluzny, M.A. et al., Rapid separation of lipid classes in high yield and purity using bonded phase columns, *J. Lipid Res.*, 26, 135–140, 1985.
36. Bernhardt, T.G. et al., Purification of fatty acid ethyl esters by solid-phase extraction and high-performance liquid chromatography, *J. Chromatogr. B Biomed. Appl.*, 675, 189–196, 1996.
37. Salem, R.O. et al., Effect of specimen anticoagulant and storage on measurement of serum and plasma fatty acid ethyl ester concentrations, *Clin. Chem.*, 47, 126–127, 2001.
38. Zybko, W.C., Cluette-Brown, J.E., and Laposata, M., Improved sensitivity and reduced sample size in serum fatty acid ethyl ester analysis, *Clin. Chem.*, 47, 1120–1121, 2001.
39. Dan, L. et al., Quantitation of the mass of fatty acid ethyl esters synthesized by Hep G2 cells incubated with ethanol, *Alcohol Clin. Exp. Res.*, 22, 1125–1131, 1998.
40. Pragst, F. et al., Analysis of fatty acid ethyl esters in hair as possible markers of chronically elevated alcohol consumption by headspace solid-phase microextraction (HS-SPME) and gas chromatography-mass spectrometry (GC-MS), *Forensic Sci. Int.*, 121, 76–88, 2001.
41. Pragst, F. et al., Fettsäureethylester im Haar und im Sebum als Marker für chronisch exzessiven Alkoholkonsum, in *Beiträge des wissenschaftlichen Symposiums Rechtsmedizin am 11 Juli 2003, Festschrift für Gunther Geserick zum 65, Geburtstag*, Strauch, H. and Pragst, F. Eds., Verlag Dr. Dieter Helm, Heppenheim, 2003, pp. 61–97.
42. Caprara, D.L. et al., A guinea pig model for the identification of *in utero* alcohol exposure using fatty acid ethyl esters in neonatal hair, *Pediatr. Res.*, 58, 1158–1163, 2006.
43. Pragst, F. et al., Illegal and therapeutic drug concentrations in hair segments: a timetable of drug exposure? *Forensic Sci. Rev.*, 10, 81–111, 1998.
44. Thody, A.N. and Shuster S., Control and function of sebaceous glands, *Physiol. Rev.*, 69, 383–416, 1989.
45. Steward, M.E., Sebaceous gland lipids, *Seminars Dermatol.*, 11, 100–105, 1992.

46. Downing, D.T. et al., Skin lipids: an update, *J. Invest. Dermatol.*, 88, 2s–6s, 1987.
47. Hartwig, S., Auwarter, V., and Pragst, F., Effect of hair care and hair cosmetics on the concentrations of fatty acid ethyl esters in hair as markers of chronically elevated alcohol consumption, *Forensic Sci. Int.*, 131, 90–97, 2003.
48. Auwarter, V., Kiessling, B., and Pragst, F., Squalene in hair: a natural reference substance for the improved interpretation of fatty acid ethyl ester concentrations with respect to alcohol misuse, *Forensic Sci. Int.*, 145, 149–159, 2004.
49. Wurst, F.M. et al., Concentration of fatty acid ethyl esters in hair of alcoholics: comparison to other biological state markers and self-reported ethanol intake, *Alcohol Alcohol.,* 39, 33–38, 2004.
50. Pragst, F., unpublished data, 2005.
51. Greiner, M., Pfeiffer, D., and Smith, R.D., Principles and practical application of the receiver-operating characteristic analysis for diagnostic tests, *Prev. Vet. Med.*, 45, 23–41, 2000.
52. Hartwig, S., Auwarter, V., and Pragst, F., Fatty acid ethyl esters in scalp, pubic, axillary, beard and body hair as markers for alcohol misuse, *Alcohol Alcohol.*, 38, 163–167, 2003.
53. Klein, J., Chan, D., and Koren, G., Neonatal hair analysis as a biomarker for *in utero* alcohol exposure, *N. Engl. J. Med.*, 347, 2086, 2002.
54. Dahl, H. et al., Comparison of urinary excretion characteristics of ethanol and ethyl glucuronide, *J. Anal. Toxicol.*, 26, 201–204, 2002.
55. Goll, M. et al., Excretion profiles of ethyl glucuronide in human urine after internal dilution, *J. Anal. Toxicol.*, 26, 262–266, 2002.
56. Manautou, J.E. and Carlson, G.P., Comparison of pulmonary and hepatic glucuronidation and sulphation of ethanol in rat and rabbit *in vitro*, *Xenobiotica*, 22, 1309–1319, 1992.
57. Foti, R.S. and Fisher, M.B., Assessment of UDP-glucuronosyltransferase catalyzed formation of ethyl glucuronide in human liver microsomes and recombinant UGTs, *Forensic Sci. Int.*, 153, 109–116, 2005.
58. Neubauer, O., Ueber Glucuronsäurepaarung bei Stoffen der Fettreihe, *Archiv für expirimentelle Pathologie und Pharmakologie*, 46, 135–154, 1901.
59. Jaakonmaki, P.I. et al., The characterization by gas-liquid chromatography of ethyl beta-D-glucosiduronic acid as a metabolite of ethanol in rat and man, *Eur. J. Pharmacol.*, 1, 63–70, 1967.
60. Kozu, T., Gas chromatographic analysis of ethyl-β-D-glucuronide in human urine, *Shinzu Igaku Zasshi*, 21, 595–601, 1973.
61. Schmitt, G. et al., Ethyl glucuronide: an unusual ethanol metabolite in humans: synthesis, analytical data, and determination in serum and urine, *J. Anal. Toxicol.*, 19, 91–94, 1995.
62. Schmitt, G. et al., Ethyl glucuronide concentration in serum of human volunteers, teetotalers, and suspected drinking drivers, *J. Forensic Sci.*, 42, 1099–1102, 1997.
63. Droenner, P. et al., A kinetic model describing the pharmacokinetics of ethyl glucuronide in humans, *Forensic Sci. Int.*, 126, 24–29, 2002.
64. Wurst, F.M., Skipper, G.E., and Weinmann, W., Ethyl glucuronide: the direct ethanol metabolite on the threshold from science to routine use, *Addiction*, 98 Suppl. 2, 51–61, 2003.
65. Wurst, F.M. et al., Ethyl glucuronide: a marker of alcohol consumption and a relapse marker with clinical and forensic implications, *Alcohol Alcohol.*, 34 71–77, 1999.
66. Bergstrom, J., Helander, A., and Jones, A.W., Ethyl glucuronide concentrations in two successive urinary voids from drinking drivers: relationship to creatinine content and blood and urine ethanol concentrations, *Forensic Sci. Int.*, 133, 86–94, 2003.

67. Schloegl, H. et al., Distribution of ethyl glucuronide in rib bone marrow, other tissues and body liquids as proof of alcohol consumption before death, *Forensic Sci. Int.*, 156, 213–218, 2006.
68. Alt, A. et al., Determination of ethyl glucuronide in hair samples, *Alcohol Alcohol.*, 35, 313–314, 2000.
69. Yegles, M. et al., Determination by GC-MS/NCI of ethyl glucuronide in hair, in *Proceedings of GTFCh Symposium*, April 26–28, Mosbach/Baden, Pragst, F. and Aderjan, R., Eds., Verlag Dr. Dieter Helm, Heppenheim, 2001, 299–303.
70. Janda, I. et al., Determination of ethyl glucuronide in human hair by SPE and LC-MS/MS, *Forensic Sci. Int.*, 128, 59–65, 2002.
71. Yegles, M. et al., Comparison of ethyl glucuronide and fatty acid ethyl ester concentrations in hair of alcoholics, social drinkers and teetotalers, *Forensic Sci. Int.*, 145, 167–173, 2004.
72. Jurado, C. et al., Diagnosis of chronic alcohol consumption: hair analysis for ethyl-glucuronide, *Forensic Sci. Int.*, 145, 161–166, 2004.
73. Sachs, H., Drogennachweis in Haaren, in *Das Haar als Spur, Spur der Haare*, Kijewski, H., Ed., Schmidt-Römhild, Lübeck, 1997, pp. 119–133.
74. Aderjan, R., Besserer, K., and Sachs, H., Ethyl glucuronide: a non-volatile ethanol metabolite in human hair, in *Proceedings of the 1994 Joint TIAFT/SOFT International Meeting*, Spiehler, V., Ed., DABFT, Newport Beach, CA, 1994, pp. 39–45.
75. Skopp, G. et al., Ethyl glucuronide in human hair, *Alcohol Alcohol.*, 35, 283–285, 2000.
76. Appenzeller, B. et al., Ethyl Glucuronide Determination in Segmental Hair Analysis of Alcoholics, presented at Communication XIIIème congrès annuel de la Société Française de Toxicologie Analytique, Pau, France, June 8–10, 2005.
77. Morini, L. et al., Direct Determination of Ethyl Glucuronide in Hair Samples by Liquid Chromatography Electrospray Tandem Mass Spectrometry, presentation at the Workshop of the Society of Hair Testing, Strasbourg, 28–30 Sept. 2005.
78. Klys, M. et al., A fatal clomipramine intoxication case of a chronic alcoholic patient: application of postmortem hair analysis method of clomipramine and ethyl glucuronide using LC/APCI/MS, *Leg. Med. (Tokyo)*, 7, 319–325, 2005.
79. Yegles. M. and Pragst, F., Cut-Offs for the Detection of Alcohol Abuse by Measurement of Fatty Acid Ethyl Esters and Ethyl Glucuronide in Hair, presented at the Workshop of the Society of Hair Testing, Strasbourg, 28–30 Sep. 2005.
80. Yegles, M., unpublished data, 2005.
81. Pragst, F., Yegles, M., and Volmerhaus, R., unpublished data, 2005.
82. Boyer, C.S. and Petersen, D.R., Enzymatic basis for the transesterification of cocaine in the presence of ethanol: evidence for the participation of microsomal carboxylesterases, *J. Pharmacol. Exp. Ther.*, 260, 939–946, 1992.
83. Dean, R.A. et al., Human liver cocaine esterases: ethanol-mediated formation of ethylcocaine, *FASEB*, 5, 2735–2739, 1991.
84. Dean, R.A. et al., Effects of ethanol on cocaine metabolism: formation of cocaethylene and norcocaethylene, *Toxicol. Appl. Pharmacol.*, 117, 1–8, 1992.
85. Perez-Reyes, M. and Jeffcoat, A.R., Ethanol/cocaine interaction: cocaine and cocaethylene plasma concentrations and their relationship to subjective and cardiovascular effects, *Life Sci.*, 51, 553–563, 1992.
86. Harris, D.S. et al., The pharmacology of cocaethylene in humans following cocaine and ethanol administration, *Drug Alcohol Depend.*, 72, 169–182, 2003.
87. Bailey, D.N., Cocapropylene (propylcocaine) formation by human liver *in vitro*, *J. Anal. Toxicol.*, 19, 1–4, 1995.

88. Bailey, D.N., Formation of cocaisopropylene (isopropylcocaine) by human liver *in vitro*, *J. Anal. Toxicol.*, 19, 205–208, 1995.
89. Wu, A.H. et al., Alcohol-specific cocaine metabolites in serum and urine of hospitalized patients, *J. Anal. Toxicol.*, 16, 132–136, 1992.
90. Cone, E.J. et al., Testing human hair for drugs of abuse, II: identification of unique cocaine metabolites in hair of drug abusers and evaluation of decontamination procedures, *J. Anal. Toxicol.*, 15, 250–255, 1991.
91. DiGregorio, G.J. et al., Prevalence of cocaethylene in the hair of pregnant women, *J. Anal. Toxicol.*, 17, 445–446, 1993.
92. Pichini, S. et al., Determination of opiates and cocaine in hair as trimethylsilyl derivatives using gas chromatography-tandem mass spectrometry, *J. Anal. Toxicol.*, 23, 343–348, 1999.
93. Bourland, J.A. et al., Quantitation of cocaine, benzoylecgonine, cocaethylene, methylecgonine, and norcocaine in human hair by positive ion chemical ionization (PICI) gas chromatography-tandem mass spectrometry, *J. Anal. Toxicol.*, 24, 489–495, 2000.
94. Cairns, T. et al., Levels of cocaine and its metabolites in washed hair of demonstrated cocaine users and workplace subjects, *Forensic Sci. Int.*, 145, 175–181, 2004.
95. Bermejo, A.M. et al., Solid-phase microextraction for the determination of cocaine and cocaethylene in human hair by gas chromatography-mass spectrometry, *Forensic Sci. Int.*, 2005, in press.
96. Lachenmeier, K., Musshoff, F., and Madea, B., Determination of opiates and cocaine in hair using automated enzyme immunoassay screening methodologies followed by gas chromatographic-mass spectrometric (GC-MS) confirmation, *Forensic Sci. Int.*, 2005, in press.
97. Haber, H. and Melzig, M., Tetrahydroisochinoline: endogene Produkte nach chronischen Alkoholmmissbrauch, *Pharmazie*, 47, 3–7, 1992.
98. Musshoff, F., Chromatographic methods for the determination of markers of chronic and acute alcohol consumption, *J. Chromatogr. B Anal. Technol. Biomed. Life Sci.*, 781, 457–480, 2002.
99. Tsuchiya, H. et al., Urinary excretion of tetrahydro-beta-carbolines relating to ingestion of alcoholic beverages, *Alcohol Alcohol.*, 31, 197–203, 1996.
100. Tsuchiya, H., High-performance liquid chromatographic analysis of beta-carbolines in human scalp hair, *J. Chromatogr. A*, 1031, 325–330, 2004.
101. Sillanaukee, P. et al., Acetaldehyde-modified hemoglobin as a marker of alcohol consumption: comparison of two new methods, *J. Lab. Clin. Med.*, 120, 42–47, 1992.
102. Sorrell, M.F. and Tuma, D.J., The functional implications of acetaldehyde binding to cell constituents, *Ann. N.Y. Acad. Sci.*, 492, 50–62, 1987.
103. Lin, R.C. et al., Measurement of hemoglobin-acetaldehyde adduct in alcoholic patients, *Alcohol Clin. Exp. Res.*, 17, 669–674, 1993.
104. Jelinkova, D. et al., Capillary electrophoresis of hair proteins modified by alcohol intake in laboratory rats, *J. Chromatogr. A*, 709, 111–119, 1995.
105. Watson, R.R. et al., Detection of ethanol consumption by ELISA assay measurement of acetaldehyde adducts in murine hair, *Alcohol*, 16, 279–284, 1998.
106. Gustavsson, L., ESBRA 1994 Award Lecture: phosphatidylethanol formation — specific effects of ethanol mediated via phospholipase D, *Alcohol Alcohol.*, 30, 391–406, 1995.
107. Hansson, P. et al., Blood phosphatidylethanol as a marker of alcohol abuse: levels in alcoholic males during withdrawal, *Alcohol Clin. Exp. Res.*, 21, 108–110, 1997.

108. Aradottir, S. and Olsson, B.L., Methodological modifications on quantification of phosphatidylethanol in blood from humans abusing alcohol, using high-performance liquid chromatography and evaporative light scattering detection, *BMC Biochem.*, 6, 18, 2005.
109. Dresen, S., Weinmann, W., and Wurst, F.M., Forensic confirmatory analysis of ethyl sulfate — a new marker for alcohol consumption — by liquid-chromatography/electrospray ionization/tandem mass spectrometry, *J. Am. Soc. Mass. Spectrom.*, 15, 1644–1648, 2004.
110. Helander, A. and Beck, O., Ethyl sulfate: a metabolite of ethanol in humans and a potential biomarker of acute alcohol intake, *J. Anal. Toxicol.*, 29, 270–274, 2005.
111. Halter, C.C. et al., Ethyl Phosphate: Another Marker for Ethanol Consumption beside Ethyl Glucuronide and Ethyl Sulfate — Detected by LC-MS/MS in Urine, Abstracts of 43rd TIAFT Meeting, Aug. 29–Sep. 2, 2005, Seoul, p. 71.
112. Spiegel, K., Untersuchungen zum Nachweis alkoholspezifisch metabolisierter Substanzen aus menschlichen Haaren mittels Gaschromatographie-Massenspektrometrie, dissertation, Mathemathisch-Naturwissenschaftliche Fakultät I, Humboldt-Universität, Berlin, 1996.
113. Markowitz, J.S. et al., Detection of the novel metabolite ethylphenidate after methylphenidate overdose with alcohol coingestion, *J. Clin. Psychopharmacol.*, 19, 362–366, 1999.
114. Markowitz, J.S. et al. Ethylphenidate formation in human subjects after the administration of a single dose of methylphenidate and ethanol, *Drug Metab. Dispos.*, 28, 620–624, 2000.
115. Gonzalez-Reimers, E. et al., Hair zinc and copper in chronic alcoholics, *Biol. Trace Elem. Res.*, 85, 269–275, 2002.

15 Workplace Drug Testing Using Hair Samples

Thomas Cairns, Michael Schaffer, and Virginia Hill

CONTENTS

15.1 INTRODUCTION

Testing for drug use by employees and applicants for employment is a common practice in the U.S., where corporations often model their drug programs after the federal Drug Free Workplace programs. In 2004, the U.S. Department of Health and Human Services Substance Abuse and Mental Health Services Administration (DHHS/SAMHSA) published its Proposed Revisions to Mandatory Guidelines for Federal Workplace Drug Testing Programs,[1] which included the alternative matrices hair, oral fluid, and sweat in addition to urine. Of these matrices, hair offers features that contrast sharply with the others. Some of the unique features of hair as a matrix include its wide window of detection; its ease and noninvasiveness of collection;

ease of storage due to its dry state, which provides stability of the analytes at ambient temperatures; and the presence of multiple metabolites for some drugs to clarify interpretation of results. The wider window of detection of hair analysis provides increased detection of drug use relative to urine and oral fluid testing and an optimum matrix for detecting heroin, phencyclidine (PCP), and ecstasy use. With hair analysis, the ingestion of poppy seeds, codeine, or nasal inhalants does not confound interpretation of results.[2]

Workplace drug testing has the somewhat conflicting demands of simultaneously requiring high-volume testing while necessitating forensic standards, including a well-documented chain of custody for each sample, beginning with sample collection and continuing throughout the entire testing process. Another aspect of workplace testing is the need for effective and efficient screening devices to quickly report negatives and select true drug-positive samples for further testing. In the U.S., there are federal regulations requiring that a screening test for use in most workplace testing be cleared by the U.S. Food and Drug Administration (FDA) as being a safe and effective *in vitro* diagnostic device.[3] While the FDA has not acted to enforce these regulations under the current administration, the existence of the requirement can raise compliance issues in litigation. In light of the above considerations, testing laboratories should utilize screening assays in workplace testing that have received FDA clearance for hair. This chapter will discuss some performance criteria of an effective screening assay, some of which may have variations unique to hair analysis or workplace screening.

Following selection of positive samples by the screening assay, a second process begins, which includes reweighing of a second aliquot of the sample, washing of the sample, extraction of the drug, and analysis — by liquid chromatography-tandem mass spectrometry (LC-MS/MS) for cocaine, opiates, and amphetamines; by gas chromatography-mass spectrometry (GC-MS) for PCP; or by gas chromatography-tandem mass spectrometry (GC-MS/MS) for marijuana — to confirm the true identification of the compound. The impact on interpretation of results by decontamination methods, which still lack uniformity among practitioners in the hair-testing community, will be emphasized in this chapter.

15.2 SAMPLE COLLECTION

Before collecting a hair specimen, a trained collector explains the procedure to the donor, asks the donor to read any instructions provided in the chain of custody form (CCF), and answers any questions the donor may have regarding the collection procedure. The collector requests identification, which is usually a driver's license or other picture ID. The collecting scissors are first cleaned with isopropanol in the donor's presence. The collector cuts the donor's head hair at the posterior vertex of the head and as close to the scalp as possible. The amount of hair collected in this manner is such that a 3.9-cm-long sample should weigh between 30 to 50 mg, an amount equal to the thickness of a shoelace tip. (Proposed federal employee testing regulations require 100 mg total for a split-sampling routine.) If the hair length is less than 3.9 cm, a correspondingly thicker sample of hair should be collected. In our laboratory's procedure, the hair is placed in a folded aluminum foil sample holder with the root end of the hair protruding beyond the designated edge of the foil. The aluminum foil is bent over the sample, locking the hair specimen firmly into place. The foil is placed in a sample-acquisition-card envelope marked with a number matching that of the test-request form, and the envelope is then sealed with a tamper-evident seal. The donor is required to initial the seal and the card, acknowledging that the sample sealed in the container is his or hers. The sample-acquisition-card envelope is placed into another tamper-evident pouch along with the test-request forms. This pouch is also sealed and initialed by the donor and signed by the collector. Hair specimens are maintained at ambient temperature in a secure location until they are shipped without refrigeration to the laboratory.

At the collection site, to ensure security, the collector must not allow unauthorized personnel to interfere in the collection in any way, must perform only one collection at a time, and must ensure that he or she is the only person other than the donor to handle the unsealed specimen. Since specimens are sealed in tamper-evident packaging for shipment, there is no requirement that courier or postal personnel document chain of custody during transit.

15.3 SCREENING PROCEDURES

Clear differentiation between negative (nonusers) and positive (users) populations is the goal of the screening assay. How well an assay achieves this goal depends on such factors as the sensitivity of the assay, matrix effects, interfering compounds, and cross reactivity. These factors will affect the limit of detection (LOD) or sensitivity, precision (inter-assay and intra-assay), and specificity of the assay. Preparing a liquid sample of a hair specimen, the first step in the screening assay, plays a major role in controlling matrix effects. Enzymatic digestion of samples for testing in biological assays, a patented procedure,[4] is used in the authors' laboratory. This method has the great advantage of quick, complete, and mild dissolution of the hair, enabling complete release of the drug from the hair. Solvent extraction methods, used in a number of laboratories, can present serious challenges — specifically, the solvent extract of hair will not contain keratin, but it will contain a significant and likely variable amount of lipid. When the solvent is evaporated, the lipid must be partially solubilized or suspended in an aqueous medium added to the dried extracts. Detergents added to the extract may aid in the solubilization of the lipid, but this needs to be carefully monitored and controlled to avoid damaging the antibodies or enzymes in the subsequent immunoassay. Variations in amounts of lipid among different hair samples and in micelle formation when reconstituting samples in aqueous medium can cause great variability (matrix effects) among samples. Another extraction method for screening assays has used low-pH aqueous extraction. While this method has not been evaluated by the authors of this chapter, the issues to be addressed would include the completeness of extraction and the reproducibility of the neutralization step after extraction and prior to the immunoassay.

As an illustration of matrix effects in an assay of enzymatically digested samples, Figure 15.1 shows the distribution of a population of 100 different hair samples with no drug and with drug at the cutoff concentration in a methamphetamine radioimmunoassay (RIA) used in the authors' laboratory. The distribution of 100 different

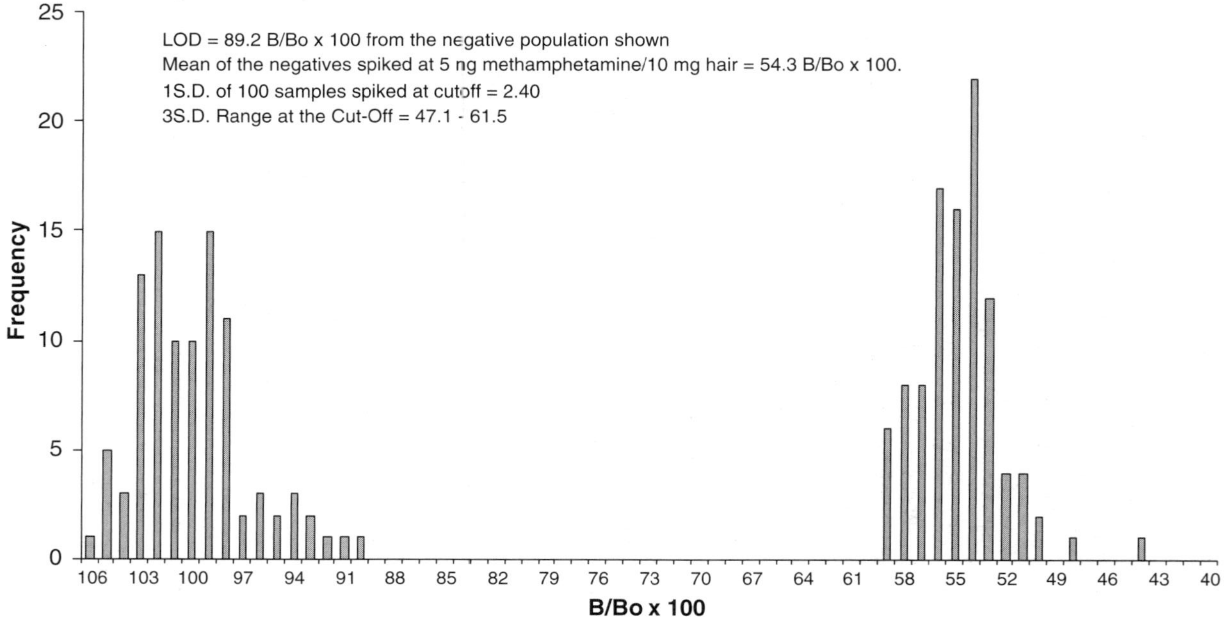

FIGURE 15.1 Distribution of a population of 100 different hair samples with no drug and with drug at the cutoff concentration in a methamphetamine RIA.

TABLE 15.1
Intra-Assay Precision of RIA for Methamphetamine

Percent of Cutoff Concentration:	**−50**	**−25**	**100**	**+25**	**+50**
Methamphetamine (ng/10 mg hair):	**2.5**	**3.75**	**5.0**	**6.25**	**7.5**
RIA Response (% B/B_0)					
Mean	64.9	57.5	54.1	50.8	48.4
SD	1.12	1.07	1.09	1.23	1.29
CV (%)	1.73	1.87	2.01	2.41	2.67

digested hair samples is shown in the histogram nearest the *y*-axis, while the distribution of these same negatives spiked with methamphetamine at the cutoff concentration is shown to the right in the figure. If there is a great variability in the responses of negative samples (termed the B_0, which is the amount of binding in the absence of nonradioactive drug, i.e., of drug in the sample), this variability will likely also occur at the cutoff, creating greater uncertainty in the correct identification of samples containing the cutoff concentration of cocaine. In this assay, the mean of the samples at the cutoff was 54.3% B/B_0, with a standard deviation (SD) of 2.4. (The value "% B/B_0" is the response of the unknown divided by the negative or B_0 reference, expressed as a percent.) The spread of such a population of samples is due not just to matrix effects, of course, but also to the many factors that affect precision. The contribution of matrix differences among different samples to this spread can be estimated by comparing the precision of replicates of the same sample (Table 15.1) with the population of spiked samples (Figure 15.1). In this case, the mean of 20 replicates of one sample at the cutoff of 5 ng/10 mg hair had a mean of 54.1% B/B_0 and a SD of 1.09 (Table 15.1), about half of the SD for the population of 100 different samples.

Figure 15.1 also illustrates another desirable feature of a screening assay: a clear separation between the negative population and the population at or beyond the cutoff. In this case, the separation was over 30% B/B_0 units between the lowest values of the range for the zero-drug population and the highest values of the range for the samples at the cutoff. In this figure, the limit of detection (LOD), which is the lowest dose that can be distinguished from the noise around the zero, can be estimated to be at 89% B/B_0, or 3 SDs from the mean of the negative population. However, a sizable separation between the negatives (zero drug) and the cutoff must not be achieved at the expense of operating within the optimal region of the assay. An assay usually has a working range for quantitation purposes of one to two orders of magnitude at best, with the optimum precision in the steeper part of the curve (in the case of a competitive RIA or enzyme immunoassay [EIA]). Although assays using only a cutoff calibrator do not require a full dose-response curve, knowing the nature of such a curve is helpful in determining the optimum point for the cutoff. Placement of the cutoff in the most linear region of the curve facilitates achieving maximal precision at and around the cutoff. While the RIA assays in this laboratory have readily achieved good precision at doses of 25 and 50% above and below the cutoff, this remains an elusive goal for EIA applications for hair at this time, which generally have been able to demonstrate separation between the cutoff only at 100% or even 200% of the cutoff.

Assuming that an antibody with adequate characteristics is being employed, control of matrix effects generally ensures that creating an immunoassay of sufficient sensitivity, which includes precision issues, for hair analysis is not a problem, although an additional limiting factor in enzymatic immunoassays that is not usually a problem for RIA is that of achieving sufficient signal. Specificity issues, especially cross reactivity with metabolites or other compounds related to the target analyte, are not as critical in workplace screening tests as in clinical diagnostic assays. This is because all screen-positive results in workplace testing are followed by the second and specific confirmatory test on a second aliquot of the sample, whereas in clinical testing there is usually no second test for the same analyte. Thus false positives in the workplace testing screening assay are primarily an expense to the laboratory in the form of unnecessary confirmation testing rather than a danger to the subject. Interference in the assays by, for example, hair products or other compounds or preparations has not been demonstrated to occur for hair-screening assays.

15.4 SAMPLE PREPARATION: WASHING AND EXTRACTION METHODS

15.4.1 Washing Methods for Removal of External Drug from Hair Samples

Once a sample has been determined by the screening assay to be greater than or equal to the cutoff concentration, a second aliquot is weighed for confirmatory testing. Results of this confirmatory test are used to interpret whether any drug present is due to ingestion by the subject. Cutoff levels for parent drugs and required presence of metabolites have been established for this purpose. However, for these tools of interpretation to be valid, sources of drug other than from ingestion must be accounted for, either by removal, detection, or presence of a metabolite that cannot be on the hair from environmental contamination. Thus the first step of confirmation testing is usually some method of washing the hair; methods used to wash hair, however, are not uniform among hair testing laboratories. There is consensus that drug is deposited in the developing hair from capillaries feeding the hair follicle.[5,6] This internally deposited drug is directly related to the ingested dose.[7] When the hair then emerges from the scalp, after 4 to 7 days, it can be exposed to other sources of drugs — either environmental contamination completely unrelated to ingestion, or drugs in the subject's own sweat, if the person is a drug user — and this, although related to ingestion and not a false positive in terms of the subject having used drugs, is not related to drug *dose*. Use of a sweat patch allows collection of sweat as a recognized matrix for identifying drug use.[8] However, in the context of hair analysis, the drug in sweat is unrelated to dose because no control has been applied to account for the subjects' variable hygiene or cosmetic practices that remove the drug to variable degrees. Both of these types of externally deposited drug — contamination and drug in sweat of users — are important to recognize as "avoidable pitfalls" in hair testing, depending on the information sought, but the impact of these can be successfully managed with extended aqueous washing.[9,10] The importance of an extended aqueous wash for removal of both types of external drug has not been fully appreciated by many investigators, leading to many misleading results and conjectures as to mechanisms of incorporation of drugs in hair.[11,12]

Early investigations showed that cocaine vapors, for example, could readily be removed by short exposure to organic solvents, essentially with just a few rinses.[13–15] This fact led many investigators to adopt such "rinsing" procedures as methods of decontamination.[13] However, others showed that drugs in the presence of water could penetrate the hair further,[16,17] but they did not thoroughly pursue methods of removing such drugs. From the early 1990s, Baumgartner and Hill[18] studied such aqueous penetration of drugs, using both samples contaminated by soaking and samples from drug users. From these studies, it was shown empirically, and in agreement with known hair chemistry,[19] that there are regions in the hair that are readily entered by water. It was also shown with thousands of hair samples from users that washing with aqueous medium usually removed external contaminating drugs in three 30-min washes, reaching a plateau after that, with little further removal from more washing. Thus the longer washing did not remove drugs deposited by the capillaries in the follicle of the growing hair, i.e., from the regions where water does not enter under normal hygienic and environmental conditions. In contrast, with samples contaminated with drugs by soaking in concentrated solutions, such aqueous washing removed nearly all the contaminating drug. Further, a contaminated hair could be distinguished from a user's hair sample by measuring the drug in the successive washes and observing the attainment of a plateau in the case of a decontaminated user's hair as opposed to continued gradual loss of drug to the washes in the case of contaminated samples. Upon completion of the washing, the user's hair still contains a large amount of drug relative to the washes.[20,21] This difference in wash characteristics of hair with external contamination versus hair with drug deposited in the follicle during ingestion ("internal" deposition) provided an empirical basis for the development of wash methods and of a calculated "wash criterion."[9,10]

Development of the wash criterion, using the wash procedure of our laboratory, was essential because it renders unnecessary the complete removal of contaminating drug, which is not always possible. The wash criterion was developed empirically to detect when a sample is highly contaminated. The wash procedure is as follows. First, dry isopropanol (2 ml) is added to about 12 mg of hair in 12 × 75-mm tubes, and the tubes are shaken vigorously at 37°C for 15 min; after 15 min, the isopropanol is removed and discarded. Then 2 ml of 0.01*M* phosphate buffer/0.1% BSA (bovine serum albumin), pH 6, are added to the hair samples in the tubes, and the tubes are shaken vigorously for 30 min at 37°C, after which the buffer is removed and discarded. This 30-min wash is repeated twice more, followed by two 60-min washes using the same conditions. However, the final (fifth) phosphate buffer wash is saved and assayed by quantitative RIA. The "wash criterion" is determined as follows: the amount of drug per 10 mg hair in the last wash is multiplied by 5, and this result is subtracted from the values obtained by MS confirmation for the amount of parent drug per 10 mg hair in the hair after washing. The result of subtracting the indicated multiple of the last-wash drug value from the washed-hair value is termed the "wash criterion" and is an overestimate of the amount of drug that would be removed from the hair if further washing were to be applied — 5 additional 1-h washes in the cases of cocaine, morphine, and PCP, and 3.5 additional hours of washing in the case of methamphetamine. If the result after subtraction is less than the cutoff for the parent drug, the result is considered negative for drug use.

The wash criterion has been evaluated in our laboratory using a number of experimental contaminations, including soaking in aqueous drug solution for an hour, coating with drug followed by 6 h of exposure to drug in sweat, or soaking followed by 16 days of storage and multiple shampoos after soaking.[9,10] Soaking hair in aqueous drug is the most penetrating form of contamination. When water comes into contact with hair, it causes rapid swelling of the hair fiber, with an accompanying increase in weight of approximately 30%. Water penetrates the entire hair shaft and occupies the interstitial spaces between the cells or macromolecular protein structures constituting the hair shaft. This structurally incorporated water is rapidly lost (within 15 min) when towel-dried swollen hair is exposed to air at room temperature. However, if the aqueous solution contains drugs, then the drugs can be retained in the interstitial spaces of hair when this has regained its dry weight.[22] However, the above-cited experiments plus years of empirical evidence acquired in our laboratory have revealed that water does not readily penetrate certain region(s) of hair, whether in the course of people's normal living habits or in a test tube. Aqueous washing removes exactly that drug that can be deposited by normal exposure — sometimes in water, sometimes not. When no water is present to swell the hair, the drug remains on the surface and can be removed with a non-hair-swelling agent such as dry isopropanol. In addition, hair of varying porosities and colors soaked in extremely high concentrations of cocaine (1, 10, and 50 μg/ml) have been shown to obey these same rules and to be identified by our wash procedures as contaminated.[10]

An additional consideration regarding contamination of a nonuser's hair is the likelihood that a contaminating drug will be limited and randomly distributed on the hair, i.e., a second sample taken from the same subject will most likely test negative. Essentially, by definition, contamination of nonusers is random and limited. Therefore, lack of reproducibility of results with multiple samples can be an indicator of environmental contamination.

In the case of drug users, drug in sweat on the surface of the skin does not cause *false* positives, since presence of drug is consistent with the drug use, but measurement of such sweat-derived drug needs to be minimized for *quantitative* drug testing. Variabilities in perspiration rates due to differences among subjects in physiology, activities, and environmental conditions cause large variations in exposure of the hair to drug-containing sweat. Furthermore, widely varying cosmetic and hygiene practices among subjects create variation both in the amount of surface drug that can penetrate the hair as well as the amount of drug left on or in the hair when it reaches the laboratory. This externally derived drug, although coming from the subject, needs to be largely removed for correct interpretation of hair analysis results. For example, hair of a drug user with porous hair, in a hot climate, performing manual labor outdoors could well have a different contribution from drug in sweat than a person with nonporous hair rarely venturing out of air-conditioned environments. Although the ingested doses may be similar without washing, the hair samples from the two subjects may appear to contain different hair concentrations of drug. However, with the application of extended aqueous washing, our laboratory has demonstrated that contamination by exogenous environmental sources can be removed or identified, and drugs deposited on hair by the sweat of users can be largely removed to avoid erroneous estimations of drug use.

Reasons to utilize effective washing procedures are (1) to allow the valid use of cutoffs, both for parent drugs and metabolites, which can only be meaningful if applied to hair that is largely cleansed of external contamination, and (2) to allow valid use of metabolites to distinguish use from contamination. Two metabolites that are definitive indicators of use because they are formed *in vivo* are cocaethylene (CE) in the case of ingestion of ethanol along with cocaine[23] and carboxy-THC (tetrahydrocannabinol) from the use of cannabinoids.[24] Other metabolites, however, such as benzoylecgonine (BE) and 6-monoacteylmorphine (6-MAM) can form on the hair from parent drug by nonmetabolic processes.[9,20] The policy of requiring the presence of BE as an indicator of use is meaningful, provided that the sample has been adequately washed. Finally, a third reason for effective washing is to utilize the ability of hair analysis to provide information about the amount of drug ingested over a period of time, which requires the exclusion from the quantitation any drug that is *not* due to ingestion, i.e., drugs deposited externally by sweat on the hair shaft after it has emerged from the skin. And this, of course, also applies to segmental analysis for the purpose of following the pattern of use over a period of time.

A number of studies on the use of hair analysis to identify drug use have failed to employ extensive aqueous washing in their procedures, seriously compromising any conclusions that might have been drawn from the work.[11,12] Besides the high probability of external environmental contamination on the hair of drug users, the wide range of cosmetic and hygienic practices applied to different types of hair (or by females versus males) demands normalization of the variable of drug in sweat of users. As one example, it is known that some hair of African Americans is readily damaged by excessive shampooing, with only weekly or biweekly shampooing being a standard practice. Yet a number of publications have concluded that there is a color or ethnic bias in hair testing after having tested hair without using an extended aqueous wash procedure to remove externally deposited drugs that can enter hair via aqueous diffusion. These publications simply fail to account for the differences created by sweat-deposited drugs. Thus, the reported pitfalls of environmental contamination and hair color bias are avoided largely by effective cleansing of the sample prior to analysis.

15.4.2 Extraction of Drug from Hair Samples Prior to Confirmation by MS Procedures

The next critical component of sample preparation after washing of the hair is the use of an extraction method that recovers uniformly and completely the remaining drug in the hair that is present due to ingestion. Dissolution of the hair in strong base KOH can be used with good results for drugs such as carboxy-THC. For other drugs, this laboratory uses an enzymatic digestion procedure that completely releases the drug from the hair.[7] Other methods, such as solvent extractions, usually in combination with heat or sonication, are often used. These latter procedures especially require careful examination to test for complete recoveries with all types of hair. Uniformity and completeness of recovery from all types of samples are essential for the valid use of the cutoff and metabolite criteria proposed for workplace testing.

15.4.3 Impact of Sample Preparation Methods on Results, Conclusions, and Interpretations in Hair Analysis

The laboratory should employ washes extensively, as described above, and include the results of the wash analysis, by applying a wash criterion, in interpreting results. Thus extensive washing, analysis of the wash to produce the wash criterion, and complete recovery of analytes are used in combination with the cutoff and metabolite criteria in producing the hair analysis results. Failure to optimize any of these components is likely to produce misleading results.

15.4.3.1 Effects of Cosmetic Treatments on Hair Drug Content

One example where sample preparation methods will produce misleading results is that of the effects of cosmetic treatments such as perming, dyeing, straightening, and bleaching on the hair content of drugs.[17] Related to these are products, often offered via the Internet, purported to remove drugs from hair in anticipation of a hair drug test.[25] Studies to test the effects of these products on hair drug content must be performed on hair only after it has been thoroughly washed by procedures such as described above. If this washing is not performed, instead of revealing how little actual drug *in* the hair is removed, the results may falsely suggest a very large removal of drug in those cases where there is large contamination *on the surface* of the hair. Removal of external contamination on the surface of hair by these products is not surprising, but it does not disturb the quantitation of drug internally deposited by ingestion.[12] Further, if failure to wash the sample is also followed with failure to completely extract the drug deposited by ingestion, the apparent result of cosmetic treatment may be highly exaggerated and give the appearance of a much larger effect of a product on hair drug content than is the case.

15.4.3.2 Hair Testing and Claims of Racial or Color Bias

Claims of "race bias" in drug testing have been brought from time to time against hair as well as urine testing. These claims have not been successful against either matrix. From a legal perspective, these claims generally get dismissed on motions for summary judgment. Obviously, there is no evidence to support a claim that people would spontaneously create cocaine in their bodies because of their race. Likewise, there is no "genetic propensity" to produce cocaine-positive results. Variations of the claim involving the use of "products" or "environmental factors" that somehow affect only one race are equally unsupportable.

Claims that the presence of melanin and serotonin in urine would racially skew urine results for marijuana were raised by researchers in the mid-1980s. Subsequent research proved these claims to be inaccurate. In the context of hair testing, the issue arose 15 years ago when a researcher theorized that if cocaine would preferentially bind with melanin in hair, a correction factor may need to be applied to normalize *quantitative* results for cocaine based on hair color. There was never any suggestion that cocaine was not, in fact, present in the tested samples or that positive results were "false." However, "race" was later used as a substitute for "hair color" in several media publications misreporting the melanin-binding theory, and the hair "race bias" theory was created.

A number of publications then began attempting to demonstrate a hair color bias in various ways, including *in vitro* and rodent experiments, and small human experiments. Critical reviews of this work suggest little relevance to workplace drug testing of human hair[11] and/or no statistically significant demonstration of hair color (or "racial") bias.[30]

On the other hand, large scale population studies of drug testing with hair to date have concluded that hair color or race factors do not lead to any statistically significant variations that would create a "bias." Several studies utilizing this laboratory's methodology (extensive washing of the sample, enzymatic digestion, and metabolite criteria) have established that there is no systematic bias occurring with this specific technology.[11,26,27,31,32]

For example, a large study on the issue of possible racial bias and drug testing, involving 1200 real-world cases, showed that with all three methods of reporting utilized (self-reports, urine testing, and hair analysis), the same positive percentage ratio between Caucasians and African-Americans was achieved.[26] These results demonstrated no racial bias when hair was compared with urine and self-reports.

Another large study, published in July 1999 by Dr. Benjamin Hoffman, compared the 1997 results of hair and urine tests on over 1800 black and white candidates for a large municipal police force.[27] Again, no racial bias was found comparing hair testing with urine testing. A 1999 study concluded from the analysis of numerous data sets that any effect of hair color or race would be negligible as a factor in the outcome of a hair test.[28] The authors of the study reported that in side-by-side comparison with hair, urine, and self-reports, the racial differential in positive rates compared with self-reports was actually greater in *urine* than in hair analysis.

Mieczkowski and Newel performed a meta-analysis of all available published studies matching drug test results to race or hair color.[29] Various approaches were used in the reviewed studies, including dosing with known quantities of drugs. In no instance, in any study, was a statistical bias shown to exist. The same author published an analysis of over 56,000 cases showing no significant relationship between hair color and a likelihood to test positive for cocaine.[30]

A 2002 study reported in *Criminal Justice Review* compared hair and urine results of 40,000 police officers at a major metropolitan police department.[31] No bias was found to exist. In another study, an extremely large set of data from 130,000 subjects who had been administered hair and urine tests showed no evidence of bias with hair testing, corroborating other studies.[31,32]

This laboratory has performed analyses of large populations of its own hair results positive for carboxy-THC, cocaine, benzoylecgonine, morphine, codeine, and 6-MAM, attempting to demonstrate a color difference between drug concentrations in black and non-black hair.[11] The result was that no bias associated with hair color could be demonstrated. These results were produced with a particular set of methods that included extensive washing followed by enzymatic digestion of the hair for confirmation. The washing removes drug present due to external sources and digestion achieves complete extraction of the metabolically deposited drug—two features likely required for results free of apparent color bias or other artifacts.

Of particular note also in regard to hair color bias is the requirement for the presence of metabolites in reporting positive workplace hair testing results. There is consensus, for example, that acidic compounds, such as benzoylecgonine and carboxy-THC, do not show a color bias. Therefore, the presence of such a metabolite (e.g., benzoylecgonine) in a hair sample positive for its parent drug (cocaine) argues against the sample's being positive due to color bias for the parent drug.

15.5 CONFIRMATION BY MASS SPECTROMETRY

Parent drugs and metabolites of interest for cocaine, opiates, and carboxy-THC together with their spiked corresponding deuterated internal standards, are extracted from the digested hair matrix using a solid-phase extraction (SPE) process. Amphetamines and PCP are extracted using a liquid/liquid method. The extract is concentrated, reconstituted, and then analyzed. The confirmation and quantification involve either GC-MS (gas chromatography-mass spectrometry) or LC (liquid chromatography) or GC-combined with tandem mass spectrometry (MS/MS) using a triple-stage quadrupole instrument in the product ion mode.[2,33,34]

15.5.1 Criteria for a Positive Cocaine Sample

In our laboratory, a specimen can be reported as positive if it meets one of the following criteria:

1. The cocaine assay result is ≥5 ng/10 mg hair and the BE assay result is ≥5% of the cocaine result (with an administrative cutoff of 0.5 ng) while also passing the wash criterion.
2. The cocaine assay result is ≥5 ng/10 mg hair BE is present ≥ LOD and the cocaethylene assay on-column result is ≥0.5 ng/10 mg hair.
3. The cocaine assay result is ≥5 ng/10 mg hair, BE is present ≥ LOD, and the norcocaine assay result is ≥0.5 ng/10 mg hair, while passing the wash criterion.
4. Any cocaine specimen that quantitates at >15 ng/10 mg hair cocaine BE is ≥ LOD or 0.5 ng cocaethylene.

15.5.2 Criteria for a Positive Opiate Sample

In our laboratory, a specimen can be reported as positive if it meets one of the following criteria in addition to the wash criterion:

1. The codeine is ≥2 ng/10 mg hair.
2. The morphine is ≥2 ng/10 mg hair.
3. If the 6-MAM, a heroin metabolite, is ≥2 ng/10 mg hair and morphine is present, the sample indicates heroin use.

TABLE 15.2
Confirmation Criteria for Drugs of Abuse in Hair

Parent Drug	Screening Cutoff	Metabolites and Related Analytes	MS Cutoff Confirmation (ng/10 mg hair)	Follow-Up LOD Cutoff (ng/10 mg hair)
Cocaine	5 ng/10 mg hair		5	0.2
		BE	0.5	
		CE	0.5	
		NCOC	0.5	
Opiates	2 ng/10 mg hair		2	
		codeine	2	0.5
		morphine	2	0.5
		6-MAM	2	0.5
		oxycodone	2	0.5
PCP	3 ng/10 mg hair		3	1
Amphetamines	5 ng/10 mg hair		5	0.25
		METH	5	1
		MDMA	5	1
		MDEA	5	1
THC	2 ng/gm hair		1 pg/10 mg hair	0.2 pg/10 mg hair

15.5.3 Criteria for Positive Amphetamine, PCP, or Marijuana

In our laboratory, a sample if a sample passes the wash criterion, it is positive for amphetamines when the wash criterion is met and the concentration of amphetamine, methamphetamine, 3,4-methylenedioxymethamphetamine (MDMA), or 3,4-methylenedioxyethylamphetamine (MDEA). Additionally, a positive methamphetamine sample must also contain the metbaolite amphetamine at 0.5 ng/10 mg hair, and a positive MDMA or MDEA must contain MDA at 0.3 ng/10 mg hair. D & L-Methamphetamine determinations are performed for methamphetamine-positive samples upon request.

A sample is positive for PCP when the wash criterion is met and the content is ≥3 ng/10 mg hair, and it is positive for marijuana when the concentration of C-THC is ≥1 pg/10 mg hair.

Table 15.2 summarizes the cutoffs for the five drugs of abuse (expressed in units of ng/10 ng hair, with the exception of C-THC, which is expressed in units of pg/10 mg hair) used in our laboratory.

15.6 Testing Body Hair Samples in Workplace Testing

Most workplace testing is performed with head-hair samples up to 1.5 in. in length. With a growth rate of approximately 0.5 in./month, this represents a window of

TABLE 15.3
Analysis of Cocaine in Head and Body Hair

Subject No.	Hair Site	Cocaine	Benzoylecgonine	Cocaethylene	Norcocaine
		(ng/10 mg hair)			
1	Head	263.1	23.8	0.41	5.5
	Underarm	284.7	17.7	0.51	7.3
	Leg	144.7	6.9	0.38	4.2
2	Head	625.0	57.7	5.7	15.6
	Chest	369.6	39.2	11.5	8.0
	Underarm	60.8	8.2	3.7	3.3
	Leg	139	19	6.7	4.8
3	Head	18.7	1.4	0.3	—
	Underarm	16.6	1.4	0.0	0.36
	Leg	14.4	1.1	0.77	0.3
4	Head	181.5	10.9	0.4	7.4
	Leg	172.7	11.7	0.26	7.7
5	Head	30.8	1.98	0.25	0.5
	Chest	53.2	4.2	0.47	1.1
	Underarm	2.5 [a]	0.45	0	0.06
	Leg	43.4	2.7	0.29	1.0
6	Head	53.2	9.4	1.1	1.2
	Underarm	12.8	3.6	0.3	0.48
	Leg	15.7	2.9	0.86	0.62
7	Head	3.7 [a]	0.4	0.25	0.1
	Underarm	7.5	1.2	0.0	0.22
	Leg	5.8	0.43	0.1	0.24

[a] While the concentration fell below the cutoff level, cocaine was present.

about 3 months. When head hair is unavailable, body hair can be substituted. Growth rates of hair from the body sites leg, chest, and axilla average 0.2, 0.4, and 0.3 in./month, respectively, reflective of variations in the length of time that each hair type spends in anagen, catagen, and telogen growth phases.[35–39] Generally, therefore, hair from a body site other than the head represents a longer time frame than an equivalent length of head hair. The percentage of body hair in the dormant phase (i.e., catagen phase) is greater than with head hair, and therefore the time frame of use derived from body hair testing is difficult to establish. It can be assumed, however, that the use occurs within the total life cycle of the hair.

Some comparisons of drug content of body hair relative to head hair of the same subjects are provided in Table 15.3, Table 15.4, and Table 15.5. For cocaine (Table 15.3), seven male subjects with positive urine results provided the indicated body-hair samples. Results of confirmation for cocaine and its metabolites are shown. Five subjects (Table 15.4) with methamphetamine-positive head hair provided the indicated body-hair samples, and ten subjects (Table 15.5) provided carboxy-THC-positive head and body hair.

TABLE 15.4
Analysis of Amphetamines in Head and Body Hair

Subject No.	Hair Site	Methamphetamine (ng/10 mg hair)	Amphetamine (ng/10 mg hair)
1	Head	38.6	3.2
	Underarm	116.2	13.8
	Leg	97.7	12.8
2	Head	7	0.17
	Chest	14.7	0.24
	Underarm	16.8	0.3
	Leg	8.8	0.25
3	Head	21.1	1.45
	Chest	45.6	3.4
	Underarm	56.1	5.8
	Leg	23.5	2.2
4	Head	38.2	2.1
	Underarm	20.3	1.3
	Leg	80.9	7.6
5	Head	189	31
	Chest	114.6	17.5
	Underarm	91.5	14.7
	Leg	80.7	12.6

TABLE 15.5
Analysis of Marijuana Metabolite in Head and Body Hair

Subject No.:	1	2	3	4	5	6	7	8	9	10
	pg carboxy-THC/10 mg hair									
Head	15.49	2.97	1.89	6.4	40.85	127.4	7.2	14.2	3.3	—[a]
Chest	—	—	—	3.8	—	14.5	10.9	—	4.0	—
Underarm	14.8	—	1.5	1.3	41.9	—	11.2	4.4	10.0	2.2
Leg	12.2	2.0	2.3	4.2	48.9	9.1	23	6.8	5.9	2.3

[a] No analysis performed.

While the drug content of samples from different body sites may show quantitative variability, all of the results show within-subject agreement with respect to presence of drug. Quantitative variability may be due to length of hair tested and dormancy features. Body-hair samples are analyzed with all the same procedures as for head hair and interpreted using the same confirmation criteria. The results demonstrate the validity of analyzing body-hair samples for quantitative drug use when there is a need to do so, provided the interpretation includes consideration of variations in growth rates.

15.7 CONCLUSION

When establishing the procedures used for workplace drug testing, laboratories should follow the processes described in this chapter from beginning to end — from sample collection to result reporting and interpretation. Washing of the hair sample is an extremely critical component of quantitative hair testing, both for removal of contamination and of drug in sweat in the case of drug users. The use of the parent-drug cutoffs and the metabolite criteria are without probative value unless external sources of drug are addressed and the extraction methods extract drug uniformly from all types of hair samples. Assuming good laboratory practice in general, the reported pitfalls of hair testing, including external contamination and hair color bias issues, are readily managed or avoided by diligent attention to these sample-preparation steps, and the testing has been shown to withstand legal scrutiny.

REFERENCES

1. SAMHSA, U.S. Department of Health and Mental Services, Substance Abuse and Mental Health Services Administration, Proposed Revisions to Mandatory Guidelines for Federal Workplace Drug Testing Programs, *Federal Register*, 69, no. 71, 19673–19732 (13 April 2004).
2. Hill, V., Cairns, M., Cheng, C.C., and Schaffer, M., Multiple aspects of hair analysis for opiates: methodology, clinical and workplace populations, and poppy seed ingestion, *J. Anal. Toxicol.*, 29, 696, 2005.
3. FDA, In Vitro Diagnostic Devices: Guidance for the Preparation of 510(k) Submissions, publication FDA 97-4224, U.S. Department of Health and Human Services, Food and Drug Administration, Washington, DC.
4. Baumgartner, W.A. Ligand Assays of Enzymatic Hair Digests, U.S. pat. 5,324,642, 28 June 1994.
5. Ruth, J.A. and Stout, P.R., Mechanisms of drug deposition in hair and issues for hair testing, *Forensic Sci. Rev.*, 16, 115, 2004.
6. Pragst, F., Rothe, M., Spiegel, K., and Spokert, F., Illegal and therapeutic drug concentrations in hair segments: a timetable of drug exposure, *Forensic Sci. Rev.*, 10, 81, 1998.
7. Baumgartner, W.A. and Hill, V.A., Hair analysis for drugs of abuse, *J. Forensic Sci.*, 1433, 1989.
8. Cone, E.J., Hillgrove, M.J., Jenkins, A.J., Keenan, R.M., and Darwin, W.D., Sweat testing for heroin, cocaine, and metabolites, *J. Anal. Toxicol.*, 18, 298, 1994.
9. Cairns, T., Hill, V., Schaffer, T., and Thistle, W., Removing and identifying drug contamination in the analysis of human hair, *Forensic Sci. Int.*, 145, 97, 2004.
10. Schaffer, M., Hill, V., and Cairns, T., Hair analysis for cocaine: the requirement for effective wash procedures and effects of drug concentration and hair porosity in contamination and decontamination, *J. Anal. Chem.*, 29, 1, 2005.
11. Hill, V., Schaffer, M., and Cairns, T., Absence of hair color effects in hair analysis results in large workplace populations, *Annales de Toxicologie Analytique*, 17: 285–297, 2005.
12. Schaffer, M., Hill, V., and Cairns, T., Morphine and 6-monacetylmorphine in hair of heroin users: use of invalid extraction procedures generates erroneous conclusions, *J. Anal. Toxicol.*, 29, 76, 2005.

13. Kintz, P., Bundeli, P., Brenneisen, R., and Ludes, B., Dose concentration relationships in hair from subjects in a controlled heroin-maintenance program, *J. Anal. Toxicol.*, 22, 231, 1998.
14. Koren, G., Klein, J., Forman, R., and Graham, K., Hair analysis of cocaine: differentiation between systemic exposure and external contamination, *J. Clin. Pharmacol.*, 31, 671, 1992.
15. Wand, W.L. and Cone, E.J., Testing human hair for drugs of abuse, IV: environmental cocaine contamination and washing effects, *Forensic Sci. Int.*, 70, 39, 1995.
16. DeLauder, S. and Kidwell, D.A., The incorporation of dyes into hair as a model for drug binding, *Forensic Sci. Int.*, 107, 93, 2000.
17. Skopp, G., Ptosch, L., and Moeller, M.R., On cosmetically treated hair: aspects and pitfalls of interpretation, *Forensic Sci. Int.*, 84, 43, 1997.
18. Baumgartner, W.A. and Hill, V.A., Hair analysis for drugs of abuse: decontamination issues, in *Recent Developments in Therapeutic Drug Monitoring and Clinical Toxicology*, I. Sunshine, Ed., Marcel Dekker, New York, 1992, pp. 577–597.
19. Robbins, C.R., *Chemical and Physical Behavior of Human Hair*, 3rd ed., Springer-Verlag, New York, 2004.
20. Baumgartner, W.A. and Hill, V.A., *Hair Analysis for Organic Analytes: Drug Testing in Hair*, Kintz, P., Ed., CRC Press, Boca Raton, FL, 1996, pp. 223–265.
21. Baumgartner, W.A. and Hill., V.A., Sample preparation techniques, *Forensic Sci. Int.*, 63, 121, 1993.
22. Baumgartner, W.A., Hill, V.A., and Kippenberger, D., Workplace drug testing by hair analysis: advantages and issues, in *Drug Testing Technology*, Mieczkowski, T., Ed., CRC Press, Boca Raton, FL, 1999, pp. 283–311.
23. Cone, E.J., Yousenfnejad, D., Darwin, W.D., and Maguire T., Testing human hair for drugs of abuse, II: identification of unique cocaine metabolites in hair of drug abusers and evaluation of decontamination procedures, *J. Anal. Toxicol.*, 15, 250, 1991.
24. Kintz, P., Cirimele, V., and Mangin, P., Testing human hair for cannabis, II: identification of THC-COOH by GC-MS-NCI as a unique proof, *J. Forensic Sci.*, 40, 619, 1995.
25. Schaffer, M., Hill, V., and Cairns, T., Internet-advertised drug-removal products: effects on cocaine, opiates and carboxy-THC in hair, Abstract, presented at 57th Annual Meeting of the Am. Assoc. Forensic Toxicology, New Orleans, LA, Feb. 21–26, 2005.
26. Mieczkowski, T. and Newel, R., Evaluation of Patterns of Racial Bias in Hair Assays for Cocaine: Black and White Arrestees Compared, *Forensic Sci. Int.*, 63, 85, 1993.
27. Mieczkowski, T. and Newel, R., An analysis of the racial bias controversy in the use of hair assays, in *Drug Testing Technology*, Mieczkowski, T., Ed., CRC Press, Boca Raton, FL, 1999.
28. Hoffman, B., Analysis of race effects on drug testing results, *J. Occup. Environ. Med.*, 41, 612, 1999.
29. Mieczkowski, T. and Newel, R., Statistical examination of hair color as a potential biasing factor in hair analysis, *Forensic Sci. Int.*, 107, 13, 2000.
30. Mieczkowski, T. and Kruger, M., Assessing the effect of hair color on cocaine-positive outcomes in a large sample: a logistic regression in 56,445 cases using hair analysis, *Bull. Int. Assoc. Forensic Toxicol.*, 31, 9, 2001.
31. Mieczkowski, T. and Lersch, K., Drug testing police officers and police recruits: the outcome of urinalysis and hair analysis compared, *Policing: Int. J. Police Strategies Manage.*, 25, 581, 2002.
32. Mieczkowski, T., Lersch, K., and Kruger, M., Police drug testing, hair analysis and the issue of race bias, *Criminal Justice Rev.*, 27, 124, 2002.

33. Cairns, T., Hill, V., Schaffer, M., and Thistle, W., Levels of cocaine and its metabolites in washed hair of demonstrated cocaine users and workplace subjects, *Forensic Sci. Int.*, 145, 175, 2004.
34. Cairns, T., Hill, V., Schaffer, M., and Thistle, W., Amphetamines in washed hair of demonstrated users and workplace subjects, *Forensic Sci. Int.*, 145, 137, 2004.
35. Paus, R. and Cotsarelis, G., Mechanisms of disease: the biology of hair follicles, *New England J. Med.*, 341, 491, 1999.
36. Saitoh, M., Uzuka, M., Sakamoto, M., and Kobori, T., Rate of hair growth, in *Hair Growth*, Montagna, M. and Dobson, Eds., Advances in Biology of Skin Series, Vol. 9, Pergamon Press, Oxford, 1969, pp. 183–201.
37. Saitoh, M., Uzuka, M., and Sakamoto, M., Human hair cycle, *J. Invest. Dermatol.*, 54, 65, 1970.
38. Valkovic, V., *Human Hair*, Vol. I, *Fundamentals and Methods for Measurement of Elemental Composition*, CRC Press, Boca Raton, FL, 1988.
39. Chase, H.B., Growth of hair, *Physiol. Rev.*, 34, 113, 1954.

16 Metals

Jean-Pierre Goullé

CONTENTS

16.1 INTRODUCTION

Using a Medline search, we retrieved 1323 papers (1300 English, 23 French) published from 1980 through August 14, 2005. Among these were 138 reviews (130 English, 8 French). The keywords used were "hair" and "metals." Our research was limited to humans and papers with abstracts. After considering the abstract edition, we thoroughly assessed 151 papers. The most abundant documentation referred to lead, mercury, cadmium, and arsenic. The interest of metal and metalloid determination in hair is not recent, but the new technological developments of inductively coupled plasma spectrometry (ICP-MS) are very promising. Furthermore, hair multielementary analysis and the new speciation analysis offer an original challenge and interesting future applications.

The use of hair samples in an assessment of environmental and occupational metal exposure has received a great deal of attention in the literature [1–9]. This approach is usually based on a comparison with normal or reference concentration ranges for an unexposed population [1]. Except for a few elements, large variations are common in reported normal ranges for hair. This diversity reflects a variation in factors affecting element content in these matrices, including dietary habits, lifestyle, and geochemical environment. Concentrations of some elements in hair may depend on age, sex, hair color, and smoking habits, although information on this subject is scarce and inconsistent. Moreover, it has been demonstrated that for certain elements the data obtained were primarily dependent not only on the hair washing procedure, but also on the analytical method used, which further complicates comparison of different sets of data. In a recent paper, Shamberger [10] reinvestigated the 2001 study of Seidel [11], who found that hair mineral testing submitted for analysis to six different commercial U.S. laboratories was in fact unreliable. A hair extract, which was obtained using a method that avoided the washing step, was compared among five laboratories. Although accurate results were achieved, this nevertheless indicates that the various washing steps used by the laboratories were probably the source of significant variance. Hence it is important that the establishment of reference ranges for a population should be based on well-defined subgroups by using reliable hair washing and analytical procedures.

16.2 HAIR METAL INCORPORATION

In regard to the detection of drugs and drugs of abuse, incorporation of external metal pollution into hair is a major problem. Under most conditions, metal pollution from external air is so embedded that it cannot be efficiently removed with a washing procedure. Furthermore, hair metal concentration is the sum of biological incorporation

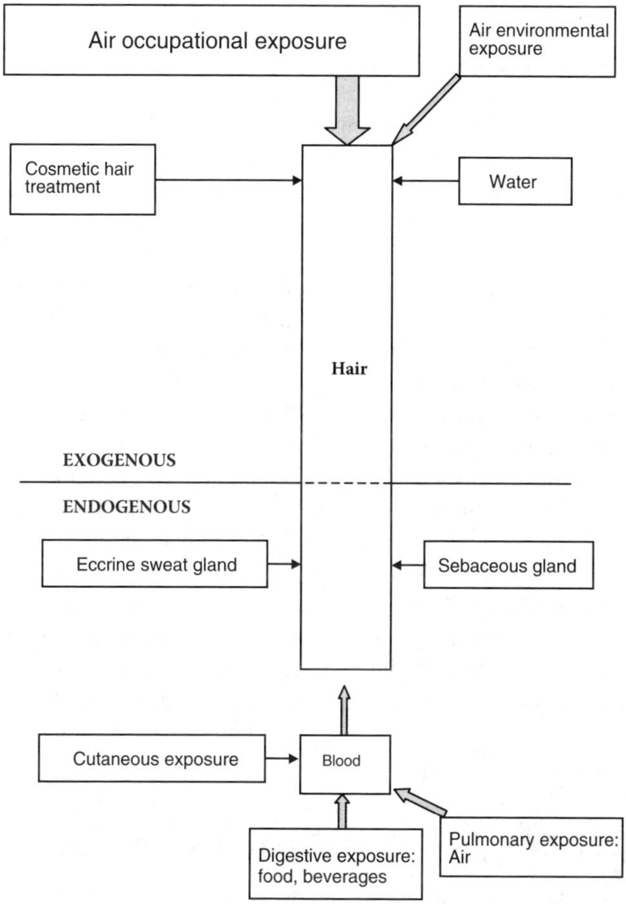

FIGURE 16.1 Flowchart of metals in scalp hair sources.

through digestive, pulmonary, cutaneous exposures, and external pollution (Figure 16.1). Hair provides an effective medium for binding materials such as dust that may contain huge amounts of metals. In a 1988 study, the sources of external metal contamination were examined experimentally by exposing hair samples to soil, to hot water from a water boiler for domestic use, and to household dust and fumes in a kitchen, leading to erroneous determinations of Cu, Fe, and Zn [12]. Much more than drugs and drugs of abuse, there are many sources of contamination including dust, sweat, sebaceous secretions, soaps, shampoos, conditioners, permanent-wave products, bleaches, and hair spray. The adsorption of many metals on hair is dependent on the acidity of the hair or the medium in which the hair sample is immersed, suggesting that hair is an ion exchanger [13]. The pKa is estimated to be between 4.5 and 5.0. Most heavy metals have a high affinity for sulfhydryl groups, so they are easily incorporated into hair, which has a high content of sulfhydryl groups [14]. However, it has also been suggested that the binding sites in hair for metals are also located on functional groups like carboxyl groups and not only on sulfhydryl groups [13].

16.3 HAIR WASHING PROCEDURE AND SAMPLE PREPARATION

Several washing procedures have been proposed. They include the use of deionized water, solvents (acetone and carbon tetrachloride), nonionic detergent, ionic detergent as sodium laurylsulfate, chelating agent as EDTA-2Na, rinses with deionized water, hot solutions, dilute acid, and cold distilled water [15] as well as ultrasonic and combinations of these agents [16]. According to Harrison and Tyree [17], detergent washing reduced the element concentrations more than the organic solvent washing. However, for heavy metals, washing procedures do not essentially influence their concentrations because of the strong complex with the disulfide groups in the keratin proteins [18]. In 1978 and again in 1985, the International Atomic Energy Agency (IAEA) recommended a procedure for hair washing with acetone-water-water-acetone [19–21]. This washing method was further evaluated by Mikasa et al. [13], and their studies showed that there was no loss of heavy metals during washing with acetone. After the washing procedure, hair is usually mineralized with nitric acid at 70°C and then diluted [22]. Decomposition of organic matter is an important part of the determination of metal and metalloid in hair. To decompose the matrix, a mixture of nitric acid with hydrogen peroxide or nitric acid alone in a closed vessel is sufficient [18, 23, 24]. Open-beaker acid digestion is not recommended for ICP-MS due to contamination by airborne particles, loss of volatile elements, and the considered hazardousness of the method [25]. In some cases, treatment of hair samples includes a closed-system microwave-assisted digestion with nitric acid as the matrix solubilization medium followed with appropriate dilution with deionized water [26]. Some particular hair washing procedures are reported in Section 16.9, Elements.

16.4 HAIR ELEMENTS ANALYTICAL METHODS

Although many analytic procedures have been described: graphite furnace atomic absorption spectrometry (GFAAS), neutronic activation analysis (NAA), and inductively coupled plasma spectrometry (ICP) — coupled to atomic emission spectrometry (ICP-AES) or to mass spectrometry (ICP-MS) — are the most popular methods. ICP-MS in particular is a fast and reliable metal and metalloid analytical method. It is the preferred technique due to its multielement analysis capability in a single run, with high-sensitivity detection and the ability to measure a large range of concentrations. It has also been shown to be more sensitive at detecting the lower limits of trace elements and less likely to provide discrepant reference levels than ICP-AES [27]. Except for aluminum, the ICP-MS method is much more sensitive than GFAAS. It is also the only way to routinely assess the rare earth elements and the halogens. Our research has developed and validated a multielementary procedure to simultaneous quantify 32 elements in a 25-mg hair sample: Li, Be, B, Al, V, Cr, Mn, Co, Ni, Cu, Zn, Ga, Ge, As, Se, Rb, Sr, Mo, Pd, Ag, Cd, Sn, Sb, Te, Ba, W, Pt, Hg, Tl, Pb, Bi, U [22].

We use the following analytical procedure: a Thermo Elemental X7CCT benchtop series with PlasmaLab® software and without a dynamic reaction cell (Thermo Optek, Courtaboeuf, France) was used for multielementary determinations. Plasma torch argon purity was higher than 99.999% (Linde Gas, Gargenville, France). Water was purified with a MilliQ$_{PLUS}$ 185 system (Millipore, St Quentin-en-Yvelines, France). Suprapur® nitric acid 65%, triton X100, and multielement standard solutions (30 elements) were obtained from Merck (Darmstadt, Germany). Seven other elements (W, Pd, Pt, Sn, Ge, Hg, Sb) and the rhodium internal standard solution were obtained from CPI international (Amsterdam, Holland). Global performance was assessed using a quality control program. Our laboratory is a registered participant of the Institut National de Santé Publique du Québec (Sainte-Foy, Canada) interlaboratory comparison program for whole blood, urine, and beard hair of nonoccupationally exposed individuals spiked with selected elements. After warm water and acetone decontamination, 25 mg of hair was mineralized with 0.25 ml nitric acid at 70°C for 1 h. A quantity of 0.1 ml of this solution was diluted into 3.9 ml (0.5%, v/v, butanol; 0.65%, w/v, nitric acid; 0.01%, v/v, triton with Rh [1 ppb] as internal standard). A calibration curve from limit of detection to 25 ng/ml or 250 ng/ml, depending on the element, was prepared. Intra-essay inaccuracy ranged from 0.4 to 6.7%. Inter-essay inaccuracy was also considered satisfactory. Quantification limits ranged from 0.2 pg/mg (Tl) to 0.5 ng/mg (B) for hair (Table 16.I).

16.5 METAL HAIR REFERENCE VALUES

The use of hair samples in assessments of environmental and occupational metal exposure has received a great deal of attention in the literature. Major variations are common in published normal ranges [1, 27, 28]. This diversity reflects variation due to many factors:

- Changes in analytical methods. The effect of the development of analytical techniques on reported mean concentrations in hair can be demonstrated using cadmium as an example [1]. In 1973 the first reported mean values in human hair were between 2 and 3 ng/mg. During the two next decades they were approximately 1 ng/mg. In the 1990s, reported mean concentrations for unexposed populations decreased to less than 0.30 ng/mg. Fifteen years later, a median value of 0.01 ng/mg has been established with ICP-MS [22].
- Variation in element content due to regional or local dietary habits, lifestyle, or geochemical environment.
- Individual variation due to age, sex, hair color, smoking habits, and cosmetic treatments.

As interlaboratory agreement on normal values is limited, each laboratory has to establish its own hair reference ranges. Using the analytical procedure previously described [22], reference values with median and reference ranges from 5th to 95th percentile were determined in hair based on healthy volunteers (n = 45) [22]. The results are reported in Table 16.2. Rodushkin and Axelsson have compared mean hair concentrations with mean whole blood (Table 16.3). Except for some elements, hair contains significantly higher concentrations of metals as compared with blood [1], in agreement with our findings [22].

TABLE 16.1
Hair Multielementary ICP-MS Analytical Validation

Compound	r	LOD	LOQ	CV % (1)	CV % (2)
Lithium	0.9999	0.002	0.007	6.5	6.1
Beryllium	0.9998	0.002	0.007	3.9	8.8
Boron	0.9991	0.14	0.46	3.6	8.9
Aluminum	0.9993	0.02	0.08	2.3	7.7
Vanadium	0.9998	0.001	0.003	1.7	9.0
Chromium	0.9999	0.06	0.20	3.5	9.3
Manganese	0.9996	0.001	0.004	1.7	6.6
Cobalt	0.9998	0.0003	0.001	2.3	7.9
Nickel	0.9998	0.01	0.05	1.8	6.4
Copper	0.9999	0.01	0.03	1.3	10.4
Zinc	0.9996	0.01	0.04	1.1	8.1
Gallium	0.9998	0.0003	0.0009	2.2	8.9
Germanium	0.9999	0.001	0.002	1.8	7.6
Arsenic	0.9997	0.01	0.02	3.5	6.4
Selenium	0.9997	0.02	0.06	2.6	7.8
Rubidium	0.9995	0.0003	0.001	2.0	5.8
Strontium	0.9995	0.0002	0.0007	1.0	7.0
Molybdenum	0.9998	0.0004	0.001	3.9	8.2
Palladium	0.9995	0.001	0.003	2.9	22.3
Silver	0.9998	0.0005	0.002	0.7	9.9
Cadmium	0.9998	0.0003	0.0009	0.7	5.9
Tin	0.9998	0.001	0.002	1.0	5.9
Antimony	0.9998	0.0003	0.001	1.0	5.2
Tellurium	0.9997	0.0006	0.002	6.7	6.1
Barium	0.9998	0.001	0.003	0.8	5.5
Tungsten	0.9998	0.0002	0.001	2.1	7.2
Platinum	0.9999	0.0001	0.0002	1.5	6.2
Mercury	0.9986	0.004	0.013	0.4	9.5
Thallium	0.9995	0.00005	0.0002	3.7	4.7
Lead	0.9997	0.0003	0.001	0.7	4.4
Bismuth	0.9997	0.0008	0.003	1.4	5.3
Uranium	0.9998	0.00004	0.0002	2.0	7.2

Note: r = correlation coefficient; LOD = limit of detection (ng/mg); LOQ = limit of quantification (ng/mg); CV % (1) = intra-essay imprecision; CV % (2) = inter-essay imprecision.

Source: Goullé, J.P. et al., *Forensic Sci. Int.*, 153, 39, 2005. With permission.

16.6 HAIR METAL ANALYSIS INTERPRETATION

Metal hair analyses indicate past exposure, but they are not always reflective of body burden [14, 29]. Many pitfalls of hair analysis for metal toxicant in clinical practice have been reported [11, 30, 31]. Despite a 20-year-old study that found poor reliability for many minerals, it is still currently being used as the only biological

TABLE 16.2
Hair Multielementary ICP-MS Reference Ranges (n = 45)

Compound	Median	Reference Range (5th–95th percentile)
Lithium	0.016	0.003–0.042
Beryllium	0.007	0.003–0.012
Boron	0.54	0.26–1.87
Aluminum	1.63	0.26–5.30
Vanadium	0.016	0.001–0.051
Chromium	0.20	0.11–0.52
Manganese	0.067	0.016–0.57
Cobalt	0.023	0.004–0.14
Nickel	0.23	0.08–0.90
Copper	20.3	9.0–61.3
Zinc	162	129–209
Gallium	0.011	0.002–0.068
Germanium	0.004	0.001–0.039
Arsenic	0.05	0.03–0.08
Selenium	0.54	0.37–1.37
Rubidium	0.006	0.003–0.03
Strontium	0.89	0.17–4.63
Molybdenum	0.021	0.01–0.028
Palladium	0.01	0.004–0.049
Silver	0.08	0.02–1.31
Cadmium	0.011	0.004–0.17
Tin	0.046	0.007–0.34
Antimony	0.008	0.003–0.13
Tellurium	0.0003	0.0003–0.001
Barium	0.28	0.05–1.58
Tungsten	0.0013	0.0001–0.007
Platinum	0.00035	0.0004–0.0008
Mercury	0.66	0.31–1.66
Thallium	0.0002	0.0001–0.0004
Lead	0.41	0.13–4.57
Bismuth	0.009	0.0004–0.14
Uranium	0.009	0.002–0.03

Note: Median and reference ranges are expressed in ng/mg or ppm.

Source: Goullé, J.P. et al., *Forensic Sci. Int.*, 153, 39, 2005. With permission.

material by health-care practitioners and promoted by laboratories as a clinical assessment tool as well as to identify toxic exposures. A split hair sample taken from near the scalp of a single healthy volunteer was submitted for analysis to six commercial U.S. laboratories [11]. The differences in highest and lowest reported mineral concentrations for the same sample exceeded tenfold for 12 minerals. The hair washing procedures were also different. Moreover, these laboratories also provided conflicting dietary and nutritional supplement recommendations based on their

TABLE 16.3
Comparison of Average Element Concentrations in Hair (μg/g) and Whole Blood (mg/l)

Ratio (hair concentration)/ (blood concentration)	Elements
<1	Fe, Rb, Na, Cl, Cs, P, K
1–10	Mg, Ba, Br, Se, Li, Ca, I, Hf
10–100	Si, Be, Th, Tl, Re, Zn, Cu, Pt, Ir, Mo, Zr, As, Mn, Sc, Nb, Pb, B, Sb, Sr, Ga
100–1000	Ta, Hg, Co, W, Ni, Y, Al, Cr, Cd, Sn, V, REE, Ti
>1000	Au, Bi, Ag, U

Source: Rodushkin, I. and Axelsson, M.D., *Sci. Total Environ.*, 262, 21, 2000. With permission.

results. Adult [31] and pediatric [30] cases of suspected heavy metal poisoning have also been reported. They most often presented nonspecific multisystemic symptoms: joint pain, muscle aches, fatigue, flu-like symptoms, constipation, loss of appetite, headache, etc. Hair results showed abnormal levels of many elements, including heavy metals. A diagnosis of heavy metal poisoning was concluded, and chelating therapy was proposed for each patient. Some patients also had amalgam fillings removed and replaced. The original diagnosis of heavy metal poisoning was therefore not substantiated. The patients did not have any previous history of exposure to heavy metals or specific clinical characteristics of heavy metal poisoning. Moreover, blood and urine determinations were normal or within normal range. Additional tests such as chelating were also within normal limits or difficult to interpret.

However, it should be noted that hair analysis can be useful in certain settings. Mercury, arsenic, and thallium poisoning have been largely documented with the use of hair analysis. It is important to distinguish the use of hair metal analysis in a research setting from the use of a panel of hair metal measurements to make a diagnosis in an individual patient. This is particularly true with patients whose symptoms and exposure history may suggest a low likelihood of metal toxicity. Research studies using validated methods can effectively assess methylmercury (MeHg) levels of a population, as in the Seychelles study [32]. For MeHg, critical limit values have been fixed in hair by the World Health Organization (WHO).

16.7 HAIR METAL ANALYSIS RESULTS

16.7.1 Influence of Gender, Age, and Smoking Habits

Wolfsperger et al. [33] have measured significant hair differences for smokers when compared with nonsmokers for many elements: As, Cd, Co, Cr, Pb, Ni [33]. Some differences were also observed between males and females. Other studies have demonstrated metal hair differences between genders, age, or smoking habits [1, 34–38]. For Khalique et al. [34], no appreciable change in metal hair concentration was observed as a function of age for both sexes.

16.7.2 Influence of Environmental Exposure

On June 12–13 2001, the Agency for Toxic Substances and Disease Registry (ATSDR) convened a seven-member panel in Atlanta, GA, to review and discuss the current state of the science related to hair analysis, specifically its use in assessing environmental exposures in support of the agency's public evaluation activities. The principal lesson learned from the meeting was that, for most substances, data are insufficient to predict health effects from the concentration of the substance in hair. The presence of a substance in hair may indicate the source of exposure (both internal and external), but it does not necessarily indicate the source of exposure [39].

Pereira et al. [40] have reported the metal hair content of a human population living near an abandoned cupric pyrite mine. Higher concentrations and subsequently higher ranges of Cd, Cu, and As were recorded in individuals living near the mine, in contrast to individuals living several kilometers away. In another study, hair samples were randomly collected from 42 children (aged 6 to 18 years) representing rural and urban areas of the United Arab Emirates. Metal hair content revealed significant differences between levels of some metals from rural and urban areas [41]. Rosborg et al. [42] have demonstrated the importance of intake from minerals in water, as positive correlations were found between the concentrations in hair and water for many elements ($p \leq 0.001$) in 47 females from an acid region in Southern Sweden when compared with 43 females from an alkaline area. In another reported series, Nowak and Chmielnicka [43] have evaluated the environmental exposure to lead and cadmium during 1990–1997 in inhabitants of an area of high environmental exposure to lead and cadmium in Poland. Lead concentrations in the hair of subjects from the exposed group differed from those of the control group ($p < 0.005$), but there were no statistically significant differences in cadmium concentrations in hair between the groups. Other authors have studied the correlation of metals in hair according to the metal concentration in the environment [2, 5, 19, 36, 44–58]. The major influences of environmental exposure for arsenic in Bangladesh and West Bengal, India, and for mercury in the Brazilian Amazon are discussed in Section 16.9, Elements.

16.7.3 Influence of Occupational Exposure

Franzblau et al. [29] screened ten metals in blood and hair for trace metal exposures in an industrial population. They found that the levels in blood and hair were not well correlated. Therefore, subsets of the population with high metal burdens could not be identified on the basis of self-reported occupational exposure histories. Many elements have also been evaluated during occupational exposures [3, 5, 7, 20, 29, 59–74]. However, the interpretation remains controversial.

16.7.4 Rare Earth Elements

Distribution characteristics of 16 rare earth elements (REEs) in children's scalp hair from a REE mining area in Southern China have been measured and compared with those of a free REEs reference area by Tong et al. [75]. The results were significantly higher for those from the mining area than for those from the reference area: La = 0.14–6.93 μg/g versus 0.04–0.40 μg/g; Nd = 0.09–5.27 μg/g versus 0.04–0.32 μg/g; Gd = 12.2–645.6 μg/g versus 8.3–64.6 μg/g; Lu = 0.2–13.3 ng/g versus 0.4–3.3 ng/g; Y = 0.03–1.27 μg/g versus 0.03–0.29 μg/g; and Se = 0.05–0.30 μg/g versus 0.11–0.36 μg/g, respectively. The distribution pattern of REEs in scalp hair from the mining area was very similar to that of REEs in the mine and the atmosphere surrounding that area. They concluded that the scalp hair REEs contents may indicate not only quantitatively but also qualitatively (distribution pattern) the absorption of REEs from environmental exposure into the human body.

16.7.5 Influence of Metal Implants

Metal concentrations in the serum and hair of patients with titanium alloy spinal implants have been studied by Kasai et al. [76]. These authors concluded that approximately one-third of patients with titanium alloy spinal implants exhibited abnormal serum or hair metal concentrations at a mean time of 5.1 years after surgery. This was due to titanium or aluminum that can travel to distal organs after dissolution of metals from the spinal implants.

16.7.6 Influence of Various Diseases

Various studies have attempted to correlate metal hair content and various disorders or diseases: hypertension, coronary heart disease, Alzheimer's disease, neurological disorders. However, the results were not consistent when applied to individuals [77–80].

16.7.7 Oligo-Element Status

Guillard et al. [81] have shown in a case of congenital hypomagnesemia that hair magnesium does not constitute an adequate measure of magnesium status, as the level in hair was higher than in healthy subjects. Other oligo-elements have been correlated with various diseases and nutritional status. They have been shown to be of limited interest.

16.8. METAL HAIR CERTIFIED REFERENCE MATERIAL

The need for hair certified reference materials (CRM) in elemental composition has rapidly increased in laboratories engaged in chemical analyses of such matrices. To meet the ever-increasing demand, international organizations and government-supported bodies are actively involved in the issuance of these certified reference materials. It is more than 20 years since human hair powder has been prepared and certified as a reference material to assist in the validation of analytical procedures used in clinical and environmental laboratories. Trace-element analysis of human hair has been carried out in laboratories throughout the world for the purpose of assessing the nutritional and toxicological status of individuals. However, the reliability of data provided by laboratories engaged in hair analysis is subject to question with regard to the reference method of analysis as well as the appropriate CRM. In 1982, the IAEA was the first to prepare human hair reference material for interlaboratory study of trace and other elements [82]. Later, many CRMs were prepared by the National Institute for Environmental Studies (NIES) in Japan by using the data obtained by various analytical techniques: atomic absorption spectrometry, flame emission spectrometry, inductively coupled plasma atomic emission spectrometry, isotope dilution mass spectrometry, neutron activation analysis, spectrophotometry, atomic fluorescence spectrometry, and microwave-induced plasma emission spectrometry [83]. Chinese CRMs (GBW 07601 or GBW 09101, from China National Analysis Center for Iron and Steel, Beijing, China) are available [79, 84]. Therefore, ICP-MS is a suitable analytical technique due to its multielement analysis capability in a single run, with high-sensitivity detection and the ability to measure a large range of concentrations. So, ICP-MS is a technique of choice for determining metals and metalloids in CRM. Nevertheless, radiochemical neutron activation analysis (RNAA) has been proven to be a reliable technique for ultratrace analysis, particularly in the certification of some ultratrace elements like REEs [84].

16.9 ELEMENTS

Hair analysis is a promising tool for routine clinical screening and diagnosis of a very limited number of element exposures in the human body. Although exposure or systemic intoxications have been recognized by abnormally high values of As, Th, Hg, Cd, Co, Ge, Pb, Li, Mn, and Ni in hair, only As, Th, and Hg are not controversial. Evidence of toxicity could not be found by measuring hair aluminum or vanadium. For essential trace elements, deficiencies or excesses of elements such as Ca, Zn, Se, Cu, and Cr in hair have been correlated with diseases and nutritional status, and other elements are of very limited interest.

16.9.1 Essential and Other Elements

Among these elements, many have also been monitored in hair: Li, Na, K, P, B, Ca, Mg, V, Cr, Fe, Mn, Cu, Zn, Mo, Sr, Se, Au, Ge, and Co.

16.9.2 Toxic Elements

16.9.2.1 Aluminum

Many toxic elements such as Pb, Hg, Cd, Ag, Ba, As, Sb, Sn, Al, Ni, Bi, and Th have also been assessed. Most of them are of limited interest in an individual where no urine or blood collection has been performed. In hemodialyzed patients, the risk of toxicity attributed to the body accumulation of aluminum justifies the need for monitoring aluminum in various human media. However, it has been concluded that hair aluminum analysis is of no value as an indicator of body aluminum accumulation [85–87].

16.9.2.2 Antimony

Antimony accumulation in hair during treatment of Leishmaniasis has been reported (hair antimony median for patients being treated was 2.9 μg/g versus 0.4 μg/g for controls). ICP-MS antimony in hair samples of patients treated for Leishmaniasis has shown concentrations up to 24 μg/g [88]. In the case of a strongly elevated soil contamination with antimony, the rate of transfer of antimony from the soil to human appeared to be very low, as antimony in urine, blood, and scalp hair were within the normal range [89].

16.9.2.3 Silver

Biological monitoring of workers exposed to silver (smelting and refining) was performed in blood, urine, feces, and hair samples. The concentration of silver in hair was markedly higher for the silver workers than for controls (130 ± 160 μg/g versus 0.57 ± 0.56 μg/g) as compared with feces, blood, and urine (respectively ten times higher, two times higher, and identical to the controls) [90]. The importance of the silver hair findings can be attributed to airborne particles of silver that can bind to hair and lead to very high values.

16.9.2.4 Cadmium

A number of studies have been assessed regarding the significance of cadmium in hair as an indicator of environmental or occupational exposure to the metal [2, 36, 40, 43, 64]. The most important health effect of cadmium in environmental medicine is kidney damage and occupational inhalation exposure, which may cause lung cancer. All of these findings suggest that blood or renal cortex cadmium are effective indicators of a cumulative dose after environmental exposure to the metal, but hair cadmium is weakly or moderately correlated with body burden [52, 91]. For occupational exposure, the determination of cadmium concentration in hair is of limited value because in humans it is difficult to distinguish between externally deposited and endogenous cadmium [92]. If scalp hair analysis has been described as a tool in assessing human exposure to some heavy metals as cadmium (S. Domingo's mine, Portugal) [40], this determination is only suitable as a screening method based on a large population [55]. Hair cadmium is not suitable to reflect the individual cadmium load.

16.9.2.5 Chromium

For chromium, none of the blood, urine, or hair levels accurately reflect chromium body stores [93]. It has been shown that the median hair chromium concentrations for tannery workers (0.55 μg/g) were significantly higher ($p = 0.0001$) than for the controls (0.12 μg/g) [71]. A significant positive correlation was demonstrated between hair chromium and urinary chromium related to creatinine from tannery workers [71, 72]. Hair, serum, and urine chromium concentrations in former employees of the leather tanning industry were significantly lower than the corresponding values obtained during their employment, suggesting that chromium III accumulated from employment period in this industry does not result in long-term elevation of chromium concentrations in the body [69].

16.9.2.6 Germanium

Germanium is not considered of major interest, but even if germanium intoxication is rare, due to chronic exposure to large quantities of inorganic germanium contained in natural remedies like ginseng, it can be severe and includes such symptoms as renal dysfunction, anemia, nausea, vomiting, and anorexia [94, 95]. More than 30 cases have been reported, and a considerable amount of germanium was detected in the hair (ranging from 1.6 μg/g to 192.3 μg/g) and in the nails [94–96]. Analytical methods have also been evaluated for germanium: ICP-MS is approximately 100 times more sensitive than GFAAS [97].

16.9.2.7 Manganese

Biomonitoring of manganese in blood, urine, and axillary hair following low-dose exposure during the manufacture of dry-cell batteries has been assessed [65]. It was concluded that the suitability of manganese analysis in hair for biomonitoring purposes suffers from a relative background variation and is controversial with industrially exposed individuals, who had significantly higher levels of manganese in blood and hair than the control group, respectively 7.6 and 3.2 times higher [98]. A very rare case of potassium permanganate ingestion (10 g) within 4 weeks was responsible for an increased manganese level in hair (1.6 μg/g) compared 83 healthy individuals (0.35 ± 0.27 μg/g) [99]. A chronic manganese exposure from drinking water (1.21 ppm instead of <0.05 ppm specified by the U.S. Environmental Protection Agency [EPA]) was responsible for elevated manganese concentrations in whole blood, urine, and hair [100]. The determination of manganese in biological materials by GFAAS is problematic, as sensitivity is not sufficient compared with ICP-MS [101].

16.9.2.8 Nickel

Gammelgaard and Veien [102] measured the concentrations of nickel in nails (fingernails and toenails), plasma, and hair from 71 nickel-hypersensitive women and 20 nonhypersensitive women. The 71 nickel-hypersensitive women had significantly higher levels of nickel in toenail, plasma, and hair compared with control subjects. The median hair nickel averages were 0.34 ng/mg (ranging from 0.02 to 1.74 ng/mg) and 0.15 ng/mg (ranging from 0.02 to 0.95 ng/mg), respectively.

16.9.2.9 Uranium

Karpas et al. [103] have evaluated urine, hair, and nails as indicators for ingestion of uranium in drinking water. The uranium daily intake from drinking water ranged from 0.03 to 2,775 μg/day. As expected, the concentration of uranium in hair had a wide distribution, ranging from 0.006 to 250 ng/mg. The log-log plot of the daily uranium excretion by hair, as a function of the intake in drinking water for each of the subjects that ingested 10 μg/day or more, proved a marked correlation between daily intake and amount of uranium accumulated in hair. The slope of the regress line indicates that the ratio between the intake of uranium and removed through hair growth is 0.37%. This study clearly demonstrated that the content of uranium in hair reflects the body burden of uranium in the steady-state exposure. The concentration of uranium in hair is on average eight times its concentration in urine. These authors conclude that analyzing the uranium content in hair a single time may be an acceptable substitute for analyzing several samples over a lengthy period to estimate the exposure.

16.9.2.10 Cobalt, Tantale, and Tungsten

Biological monitoring of cobalt, tantale, and tungsten was carried out on the urine, blood, and pubic hair and toenails of 251 subjects occupationally exposed to hard metal dusts. Cobalt, tantale, and tungsten pubic hair can only be used as indicators proving qualitative hard metal exposure [68]. An accidental case of severe acute tungsten intoxication in a military man has been reported by Marquet et al. [104]. Tungsten biological fluids determination revealed very high concentrations. The level in hair was 4.26 μg/g (N = 0.1 μg/g).

16.9.2.11 Lead

Lead is one of the most extensively studied substances in hair. Neurological effects of lead exposure to the developing nervous system of the fetus and infant are of major importance in environmental medicine. Hair analysis has been proposed as a calendar of events in lead poisoning by Grandjean [105]. This author reported a lead nitrate poisoning over an extended time period (>6 months). Despite the extremely high blood lead levels and the severe clinical lead poisoning, lead concentrations in hair were relatively low in comparison with the concentrations found in the hair of workers exposed to high levels of airborne lead. Nevertheless, the hair lead concentrations exhibited rapid changes and normalized shortly after chelating treatment had been instituted. This observation suggests that a large proportion of the lead content of hair from individuals with respiratory lead exposure may be exogenous. Many studies have shown a group correlation between lead concentrations in hair and blood, particularly in occupationally exposed subjects for whom Foo et al. [106] reported a high correlation ($r = 0.85, p < 0.0001, n = 209$). There is also a good similarity with respect to influencing variables on lead levels in blood and hair for these subjects [107]. Synchrotron X-ray fluorescence has been used to study the distribution of lead in a hair sample collected from a lead smelter worker [60]. These results suggest that the lead originates both from ingestion and environmental exposure; however, direct deposition from the environment was the more important source of lead in head hair and confirms the findings of Grandjean et al. [105]. Therefore, for this element, the type of washing method employed is very important.

Sen and Das Chaudhuri [108] have determined lead in human scalp hair based on three methods of hair washing. The best results were obtained with nonionic detergent-acetone (Pb = 5.7 ± 1.8 ng/mg) versus ethanol-acetone (Pb = 6.9 ± 2.0 ng/mg) and distilled water (Pb = 13.1 ± 3.3 ng/mg). However, many studies have shown that lead hair was not a reliable test to measure individual lead exposure. In 1994, Tracqui et al. [109] reported the lack of relationship between hair lead levels and some common markers such as blood lead levels. More recently, the U.S. Centers for Disease Control and Prevention (CDCP) have compared hair and blood samples from 189 children to assess the accuracy of hair analysis in screening for lead poisoning. This method had 57% sensitivity and an 18% false-negative rate. The investigators concluded that measurement of lead content in hair is not an adequate method of screening for childhood lead poisoning, but it is necessary to assess the whole blood lead level to obtain a reliable measure of individual lead exposure [97]. Therefore, individual diagnosis based on hair lead determination should be interpreted with caution and must be validated by blood analysis.

16.9.2.11.1 Lead Isotopes

Lead isotopic ratios ($^{206}Pb/^{207}Pb$ and $^{208}Pb/^{207}Pb$) can be used for tracing out the source of lead exposure. In a recent study Rodushkin and Axelsson found that lead hair and lead nail concentrations for one subject were higher than mean concentrations by two orders of magnitude [1]. The lead isotopic ratios in hair and nail samples were very similar to that of a suspected red color paint from the 1950s removed by burnishing in the process of restoration of old furniture.

16.9.2.12 Arsenic and Thallium

These elements have been classically used for a number of years as a means of criminal poisoning. Although both manifest characteristically with peripheral neuropathies, thallium is mainly associated with alopecia and arsenic with gastrointestinal symptoms. Rusyniak et al. [110] have described the symptoms, physical findings, diagnostic test results, and outcomes in a group of men poisoned with thallium and arsenic in a small Midwestern American town.

16.9.2.12.1 Arsenic

Humans are exposed to various arsenic compounds, both inorganic and organic, which differ substantially with respect to chemical and toxicological properties. Long-term effects of oral exposure to inorganic arsenic, mainly from the drinking water in many countries, has been associated with characteristic skin changes (hyperkeratosis, skin cancer), while inhalation may cause lung cancer [55]. Due to its high affinity to sulfhydryl groups, arsenic is readily incorporated by hair, and arsenic concentrations in hair are consequently higher compared with those in other tissues. This is also due to the very slow drop in arsenic levels in biological fluids after mineral arsenic exposure. In fact, as soon as an individual is isolated from exposure, hair values return to normal within several weeks [10]. It also explains why most of the arsenic in hair occurs in the trivalent inorganic form [111]. In contrast, organic arsenic compounds via seafood are rapidly cleared from the body, so intake of organic arsenic compounds via seafood is not reflected by the hair [55].

In cases of human arsenic poisoning, the distribution of this element along the length of a hair can be used to distinguish between chronic and acute exposure [112, 113]. Analysis of 1.0-cm segments provides a pattern of monthly exposure [114]. Typical results after a double fatal human arsenic poisoning are reported in Table 16.4. Hair arsenic is useful as a confirmatory feature in chronic poisoning, provided that external contamination by arsenic can be excluded [115]. As regards occupational health in cases of high arsenic air contamination, monitoring exposure by determining arsenic in hair is considered to be of value only when used for environmental monitoring rather than for biological monitoring [70].

TABLE 16.4
Arsenic Concentration in Hair of Poisoned Couple

	Hair As (ng/mg)	
	Wife	Husband
1 cm (root)	108.7	293.6
1 cm		142.9
1 cm	6.5	43.3
1 cm		27.6
1 cm	1.0	21.4
2 cm		18.1
2 cm	1.3	13.0
2 cm (end)	—	13.4

Note: Normal range is 0.1 to 1.0 ng/mg.

Source: Goullé, J.P., Mahieu, L., and Kintz, P., *Ann. Toxicol. Anal.*, 17, 243, 2005. With permission.

Studying urinary excretion of arsenic after exposure to arsenic present in drinking water, Kurttio et al. [116] established that the arsenic content of hair correlated well with the past and chronic exposure. An increase of 10 µg/l in the arsenic concentration of the drinking water or an increase of 10 to 20 µg/day of the mineral arsenic exposure corresponded to a 0.1 ng/mg increase in hair arsenic. Arsenic hair contents of workers applying the herbicide monosodium methane arsenate were increased during the spraying season and returned to preseason levels once herbicide application ceased [117]. In contrast, studies of employees at a semiconductor plant showed that nonoccupational factors such as sex, tap-water quality, and dietary habits contributed more to hair arsenic levels than the contamination from the workplace [118].

Since 1983, a large number of people have experienced arsenic toxicity due to drinking of arsenic-contaminated water in India, particularly in West Bengal. According to Mazumder et al. [119] it is "the worst calamity in the world." These authors found no correlation between the quantities of arsenic taken through water and the level of arsenic in hair. When studying chronic arsenic toxicity in Bangladesh and West Bengal, India, Rahman et al. [120] reported that the diagnosis of subclinical arsenicosis was made in 83, 93, and 95% of hair, nail, and urine samples in Bangladesh; and in 57, 83, and 89% of hair, nail, and urine samples in West Bengal, respectively. Approximately 90% of children below 11 years of age living in the affected areas showed hair and nail arsenic above the normal level. Recently and for the first time, Samanta et al. [19] analyzed hair, nails, and skin scales of arsenic victims from the arsenic-affected area of West Bengal for ten trace elements. This study revealed the higher levels of the toxic elements arsenic, manganese, lead, and nickel in the tissue samples; hair results are reported in Table 16.5.

TABLE 16.5
Concentrations of Arsenic (μg/g) in Hair Collected in Arsenic-Affected Areas

	Hair (*n* = 44)		
Elements	**Geo. Mean (SEM)**	**Median**	**Range**
As	3.43 (0.73)	2.29	0.17–14.39
Se	0.87 (0.05)	0.88	0.41–1.64
Hg	0.88 (0.08)	0.82	0.19–3.0
Zn	152.42 (7.21)	140.05	82.52–339.64
Pb	8.03 (1.56)	4.65	0.57–41.71
Ni	1.59 (0.18)	1.17	0.45–12.45
Cd	0.40 (0.17)	0.13	0.008–2.14
Mn	15.48 (2.25)	10.79	1.85–43.56
Cu	14.76 (1.11)	11.72	4.2–55.29
Fe	69.50 (7.44)	55.60	15.53–304.49

Source: Samanta, G. et al., *Sci. Total Environ.*, 326, 33, 2004. With permission.

16.9.2.12.1.1 Arsenic Speciation

Using HPLC-ICP-MS, speciation of arsenic in human hair has been successfully achieved by Mandal et al. [121, 122] as a biomarker for arsenic exposure. Hair samples were collected from polluted areas in Bengal. Hair contained mainly arsenite iAs (III) and arsenate iAs (V), approximately 60 and 34% respectively, and monomethylarsonic acid MMA (V) and dimethylarinic acid DMA (V), approximately 3% of each. HPLC-ICP-MS has also been applied by Ginet and Kintz to Napoleon's hair to prove mineral arsenic exposure [123] after the confirmation of elevated total arsenic in five strands of the Emperor's hair [124].

16.9.2.12.2 Thallium

Subsequent inorganic thallium poisonings with suicidal [113, 125] or homicidal intent [113, 126] have been reported. The use of thallium in an attempted assassination of four members of a political organization was described by McCormack and McKinney [127]. The authors found elevated thallium levels in the serum, urine, hair (ranging from 1.46 to 12.69 ng/mg), and nail samples from the victims, who complained of abdominal pain within two days after eating a snack prepared by their hosts. Painful peripheral neuropathy occurred within one week, and loss of hair within three weeks. A probable case of chronic occupational thallium poisoning in a glass factory has been reported previously by Hirata et al. [66]: a male worker who handled thallium-containing raw material for glass manufacturing complained of alopecia, abdominal pain, diarrhea, and tingling in all four limbs. The thallium content of the hair (ICP-MS) was 0.02 ng/mg for these patients and 0.58 ng/mg for subsequent workers over a period of 32 months and 13 months, respectively, after they had ceased glasswork production. These levels of thallium exposure were considered to be very high [22]. Hair thallium levels of 1,163 subjects living in the vicinity of a cement plant emitting thallium-containing dust were assessed by Brockhaus et al. [57]. They were found to be markedly increased (mean 0.0095 ng/mg). The major route of the population's increased intake of thallium was ascertained to be the consumption of vegetables and fruit grown in the vicinity of the cement plant. The pulmonary route of reuptake, as well as other sources, did not seem to play a significant role in the population's exposure to thallium. Polyneuritic symptoms, sleep disorders, headache, fatigue, and other signs of psychasthenia were found to be the major health effects associated with increased thallium levels in urine and hair. However, no positive correlation was found between the thallium levels in hair and urine and the prevalence of skin alterations, hair loss, and gastrointestinal dysfunction.

16.9.2.13 Mercury

This element occurs in several forms: inorganic, elemental, and organic mercury. The liquid-metal elemental form is not at all toxic when ingested. In contrast, inorganic salts are relatively toxic (1.5 g of mercury chloride is lethal). The mercury vapors are even more toxic, and the organic form is the most toxic form (0.1 g of methylmercury is lethal).

16.9.2.13.1 Elemental Mercury

For the general population, the main elemental mercury source is the atmosphere due to the high volatility of the element. Elemental mercury is dispersed through natural volcanic activity and, human activity (final recovery of the gold particles extracted by burning or heating the amalgam, waste incinerator). Health risks of the elemental mercury vapor from dental amalgam have been debated in the past few years [128]. The French Agence Française de Sécurité Sanitaire des Produits de Santé (AFSSAPS) recently established in its report that mercury vapor from dental amalgam was safe [129]. In cases of occupational exposure to mercury vapor, mercury in hair is also an indicator of mercury exposure [3, 74]. At exposure levels ranging from 50 to 200 $\mu g/m^3$ in a thermometer factory, the mean hair (1 cm from base) mercury levels respectively ranged from 0.8 to 2.5 ng/mg [74]. In contrast, a longitudinal study with workers exposed to mercury vapor at low concentrations showed no changes of hair mercury concentrations, even after 23 months of exposure [67]. In the absence of increased mercury levels in the air and at steady-state conditions, mercury in hair seems to be suitable to indicate the amount of incorporated inorganic mercury [3].

16.9.2.13.2 Inorganic Mercury

Inorganic mercury exposure is generally due to accidental or suicidal ingestion of mercuric chloride [113]. After acute mercuric mercury poisoning, chemical speciation of hair mercury shows a peak of inorganic mercury value, with total hair mercury ranging from 6.1 to 13.1 ng/mg [130]. Widespread use of skin-lightening preparations containing mercury may cause mercury poisoning [131, 132]. A mean value of 156 ng/mg mercury in scalp hair was measured in an epidemiological study from 20 Senegalese women using mercurial cosmetics for skin depigmentation [132]. Recently, Harada et al. [131] reported the case of Kenyan subjects using skin-lightening soap containing mercury iodide. All of the subjects with a high hair mercury level (>36.1 ng/mg) had applied this soap for daily use, which subsequently produced various symptoms suggesting inorganic-mercury poisoning. However, urine, not hair, remains the most practical and sensitive means of monitoring low-level occupational exposure to inorganic mercury [62]. Although the major source of mercury in polluted mining areas is inorganic mercury, it was observed that active transformation of inorganic mercury to organic mercury species (MeHg) takes place in water, sediment, and soils [133]. The percentage of mercury as MeHg varied from 5 to 83% in these elements [133]. Moreover, MeHg is easily accumulated into the body and concentrates in the hair.

16.9.2.13.3 Organic Mercury

The most valid conclusions of hair trace element analysis can be obtained for MeHg. A comprehensive evaluation revealed a basic correlation between hair mercury levels and the frequency of fish consumption [44–46, 48, 50, 56, 134–136]. From outbreaks of MeHg poisoning, primarily in Minamata, Japan, and Iraq, there were major dose-response relations available that are based on mercury concentrations in hair [54, 137, 138]. Minamata disease (M.d.) was discovered in 1956. It was MeHg poisoning that occurred in humans who ingested fish and shellfish contaminated by MeHg from mercury chloride discharged in wastewater from a chemical plant. The marine products in Minamata Bay displayed high levels of mercury contamination (5.6 to 35.7 ppm) [58]. The mercury content in hair of patients, their family, and inhabitants of the bay were detected at high or very high levels of mercury (max. 705 ng/mg, i.e., 705 ppm) [58]. More than 2200 patients have been officially recognized as having M.d., and 1043 have died [58]. The present mercury contents of scalp hair and clinical symptoms in inhabitants of the Minamata area revealed a normal total mercury in hair (<10 ng/mg) [54]. The Seychelles population has among the highest fish consumption in the world, nearly 200 g/day, the majority being predatory species with elevated MeHg content. Hair mercury concentrations for this population have reached levels as high as 12 ng/mg [139]. Hansen et al. [140] showed chronic systemic mercury intoxication in Greenlanders who ate a mercury-contaminated seal. Sherlock [141] found a correlation of 0.92 between the concentration of mercury in the hair and blood of an exposed population. When organic mercury exposure occurred, the mean ratio of total mercury concentrations observed in hair compared with total mercury in blood was approximately 250 [142–144]. A mercury content of 24 μg/l in whole blood is typically associated with 6 ng/mg total mercury in the hair. For Lindberg et al. [47], the total mercury in hair was significantly associated with the MeHg in blood ($r^2 = 0.89$, $p < 0.001$), but not with the inorganic mercury in blood. Therefore, the total mercury in hair appears to reflect MeHg exposure and not inorganic Hg exposure, even in persons with no fish intake.

In populations that consume large amounts of fish and fish products (100 g/day), the WHO recommends monitoring MeHg levels in the hair of women of child-bearing age [138]. Furthermore, the WHO accepts human hair as the optimal indicator for the assessment of contaminations in populations exposed to methylmercury. According to a WHO report [138], based on the neurotoxicity data in Japan and Iraq, the nonobserved adverse effects level (NOAEL) was estimated to be 50 ng/mg in hair. A NOAEL of 10 ng/mg in hair associated with fetus neurotoxicity has been proposed by Grandjean et al. [145].

16.9.2.13.4 Mercury Speciation

Hair inorganic mercury is usually 10% of the total hair mercury content, and methylmercury is generally 90% of the total mercury. After a single mineral exposure, Suzuki et al. [130] found 40% for the mercury inorganic part. In the Amazon, where occupational exposure includes inorganic mercury used in gold amalgamation at mining sites or refining activities, most of the mercury in the hair was inorganic [146]. In certain areas, entire families may be exposed to elemental mercury vapors from the occupational burning of a mercury-gold amalgam or to MeHg through the consumption of fish from mercury-contaminated local waterways [147]. Urine samples were used to determine the inorganic mercury burden, while hair samples were used as an index of MeHg exposure from consumption of mercury-contaminated fish [147]. Barbosa et al. [148] have assessed hair mercury speciation in inhabitants of a polluted area in the Brazilian Amazon. Total mercury ranged from 1.5 to 59.0 ng/mg, with only 21% of the sampled population having mercury concentration of less than 10 ng/mg hair. The mean percentage of MeHg was 71.3% (ranging from 34 to 100%) of the total mercury in hair. The authors of this paper [148] also have summarized studies comparing total mercury and MeHg in hair. Trace metals in ancient hair (400–800 years) from an archaeological site in Alaska demonstrated that MeHg levels were less than 2% of the total mercury in these hair samples, characterizing the extent of changes in MeHg exposures from preindustrial to modern times [53]. These findings were confirmed by the determination of hair mercury levels of Japanese women during the period 1881 to 1968 [149]. The increase of inorganic mercury levels in unwashed hair samples from the 1920s was suspected to be due to mercury contamination of hair cosmetics, and increased organic mercury levels in the hair from the 1960s can be explained by elevated consumption of methylmercury-contaminated fish.

16.10 CONCLUSION

Despite the external contamination and lack of standardized methodology, the World Health Organization, the U.S. Environmental Protection Agency, and the International Atomic Energy Agency have recommended the use of hair samples as an important biological material for worldwide environmental monitoring [150, 151].

ACKNOWLEDGMENTS

I am grateful for the valuable advice of Richard Medeiros, Rouen University Hospital medical editor, in the editing of the manuscript.

REFERENCES

1. Rodushkin, I. and Axelsson, M.D., Application of double focusing sector field ICP-MS for multielemental characterization of human hair and nails, part II: a study of the inhabitants of northern Sweden, *Sci. Total Environ.*, 262, 21, 2000.

2. Nowak, B. and Kozlowski, H., Heavy metals in human hair and teeth: the correlation with metal concentration in the environment, *Biol. Trace Elem. Res.*, 62, 213, 1998.
3. Wilhelm, M., Muller, F., and Idel, H., Biological monitoring of mercury vapour exposure by scalp hair analysis in comparison to blood and urine, *Toxicol. Lett.*, 88, 221,1996.
4. Batzevich, V.A., Hair trace element analysis in human ecology studies, *Sci. Total Environ.*, 164, 89, 1995.
5. Bencko, V., Use of human hair as a biomarker in the assessment of exposure to pollutants in occupational and environmental settings, *Toxicology*, 101, 29, 1995.
6. Ali, M. et al., Trace element concentration in hair of Bangladesh children under normal and malnutrition conditions, *J. Radioanal. Nucl. Chem.*, 219, 81, 1997.
7. Teresa, M., Vasconcelos, S.D., and Tavares, H.M.F., Trace element concentrations in blood and hair of young apprentices of a technical-professional school, *Sci. Total Environ.*, 205, 189, 1997.
8. Foo, S.C. and Tan, T.C., Elements in the hair of south-east Asian islanders, *Sci. Total Environ.*, 209, 185, 1998.
9. Kuangfei, L. et al., Metallic elements in hair as a biomarker of human exposure to environmental pollution: a preliminary investigation in Hubei Province, *Crit. Rev. Plant. Sci.*, 18, 417, 1999.
10. Shamberger, R.J., Validity of hair mineral testing, *Biol. Trace Elem. Res.*, 87, 1, 2002.
11. Seidel, S. et al., Assessment of commercial laboratories performing hair mineral analysis, *JAMA*, 285, 67, 2001.
12. Doi, R. et al., A study of the sources of external metal contamination of hair, *Sci. Total Environ.*, 77, 153, 1988.
13. Mikasa, H. et al., Adsorption and elution of metals on hair, *Biol. Trace Elem. Res.*, 16, 59, 1988.
14. Bush, V.J. et al., Essential and toxic element concentrations in fresh and formalin-fixed human autopsy tissues, *Clin. Chem.*, 41, 284, 1995.
15. Taylor, A., Usefulness of measurements of trace elements in hair, *Ann. Clin. Biochem.*, 23, 364, 1986.
16. Raghupathy, L. et al., Methods of removing external metal contamination from hair samples for environmental monitoring, *Sci. Total Environ.*, 77, 14, 1988.
17. Harrison, W.W. and Tyree, A.B., The determination of trace elements in human fingernails by atomic absorption spectroscopy, *Clin. Chim. Acta*, 31, 63, 1971.
18. Chen, K.L., Amarasiriwardena, C.J., and Christiani, D.C., Determination of total arsenic concentrations in nails by inductively coupled plasma mass spectrometry, *Biol. Trace Elem. Res.*, 67, 109, 1999.
19. Samanta, G. et al., Arsenic and other elements in hair, nails, and skin-scales of arsenic victims in West Bengal, India, *Sci. Total Environ.*, 326, 33, 2004.
20. Kucera, J. et al., Monitoring of occupational exposure in manufacturing of stainless steel constructions, part I: chromium, iron, manganese, molybdenum, nickel and vanadium in the workplace air of stainless steel welders, *Cent. Eur. J. Public Health*, 9, 171, 2001.
21. IAEA (International Atomic Energy Agency), Report on the Second Research Coordination Meeting of IAEA, Neuherberg, Germany, October 1985.
22. Goullé, J.P. et al., Metal and metalloid multi-elementary ICP-MS validation in whole blood, plasma, urine and hair, reference values, *Forensic Sci. Int.*, 153, 39, 2005.
23. Samanta, G. et al., Flow injection hydride generation atomic absorption spectrometry for determination of arsenic in water and biological samples from arsenic-affected districts of West Bengal, India and Bangladesh, *Microchem. J.*, 62, 174, 1999.

24. Puchyr, R.F. et al., Preparation of hair for measurement of elements by inductively coupled plasma-mass spectrometry (ICP-MS), *Biol. Trace Elem. Res.*, 62, 174, 1999.
25. Monaster, A. and Golightly, D.W., Inductively coupled plasma, in *Analytical Atomic Spectroscopy*, NCA Publisher, New York, 1987, 338.
26. Razagui, I.B. and Haswell, S.J., The determination of mercury and selenium in maternal and neonatal scalp hair by inductively coupled plasma-mass spectrometry, *J. Anal. Toxicol.*, 21, 149, 1997.
27. Miekeley, N. et al., How reliable are human hair reference intervals for trace elements? *Sci. Total Environ.*, 218, 9, 1998.
28. Klevay, L.M., Christopherson, D.M., and Shuler, T.R., Hair as a biopsy material: trace element data on one man over two decades, *Eur. J. Clin. Nutr.*, 58, 1359, 2004.
29. Franzblau, A., Rosenstock, L., and Eaton, D.L., Use of inductively coupled plasma-atomic emission spectroscopy (ICP-AES) in screening for trace metal exposures in an industrial population, *Environ. Res.*, 46, 15, 1988.
30. Poon, W.T. et al., Use of hair analysis in the diagnosis of heavy metal poisoning: report of three cases, *Hong Kong Med. J.*, 10, 197, 2004.
31. Frisch, M. and Schwartz, B.S., The pitfalls of hair analysis for toxicants in clinical practice: three case reports, *Environ. Health Perspect.*, 110, 433, 2002.
32. Davidson, P.W. et al., Effects of prenatal and postnatal methylmercury exposure from fish consumption on neurodevelopment: outcomes at 66 months of age in the Seychelles Child Development Study, *JAMA*, 280, 701, 1998.
33. Wolfsperger, M. et al., Heavy metals in human hair samples from Austria and Italy: influence of sex and smoking habits, *Sci. Total Environ.*, 156, 235, 1994.
34. Khalique, A. et al., A comparative study based on gender and age dependence of selected metals in scalp hair, *Environ. Monit. Assess.*, 104, 45, 2005.
35. Benes, B. et al., Determination of normal concentration levels of Cd, Cr, Cu, Hg, Pb, Se and Zn in hair of the child population in the Czech Republic, *Cent. Eur. J. Public Health*, 11, 184, 2003.
36. Chlopicka, J. et al., Lead and cadmium in the hair and blood of children from a highly industrial area in Poland, *Biol. Trace Elem. Res.*, 62, 229, 1998.
37. Meng, Z., Age- and sex-related differences in zinc and lead levels in human hair, *Biol. Trace Elem. Res.*, 61, 79, 1998.
38. Ashraf, W., Jaffar, M., and Mohammad, D., Age and sex dependence of selected trace metals in scalp hair of urban population of Pakistan, *Sci. Total Environ.*, 111, 576, 2003.
39. Harkins, D.K. and Susten, A.S., Hair analysis: exploring the state of the science, *Environ. Health Perspect.*, 111, 576, 2003.
40. Pereira, R., Ribeiro, R., and Gonçalves, F., Scalp hair analysis as a tool in assessing human exposure to heavy metals (S. Domingos mine, Portugal), *Sci. Total Environ.*, 327, 81, 2004.
41. Hasan, M.Y. et al., Trace metal profiles in hair samples from children in urban and rural regions of the United Arab Emirates, *Vet. Hum. Toxicol.*, 46, 119, 2004.
42. Rosborg, I., Nihlgard, B., and Gerhardsson, L., Hair element concentrations in females in one acid and one alkaline area in southern Sweden, *Ambio*, 32, 440, 2003.
43. Nowak, B. and Chmielnicka, J., Relationship of lead and cadmium to essential elements in hair, teeth, and nails of environmentally exposed people, *Ecotoxicol. Environ. Saf.*, 46, 265, 2000.
44. Ip, P. et al., Environmental mercury exposure in children: South China's experience, *Pediatr. Int.*, 46, 715, 2004.
45. Agusa, T. et al., Mercury contamination in human hair and fish from Cambodia: levels, specific accumulation and risk assessment, *Environ. Pollut.*, 134, 79, 2005.

46. Weihe, P., Grandjean, P., and Jorgensen, P.J., Application of hair-mercury analysis to determine the impact of a seafood advisory, *Environ. Res.*, 96, 28, 2004.
47. Lindberg, A. et al., Exposure to methylmercury in non-fish-eating people in Sweden, *Environ. Res.*, 96, 28, 2004.
48. Dorea, J. et al., Mercury in hair and in fish consumed by Riparian women of the Rio Negro, Amazon, Brazil, *Int. J. Environ. Health Res.*, 13, 239, 2003.
49. Mortada, W.I. et al., Reference intervals of cadmium, lead, and mercury in blood, urine, hair, and nails among residents in Mansoura city, Nile delta, Egypt, *Environ. Res.*, 90, 104, 2002.
50. Santos, E.C. et al., A contribution to the establishment of reference values for total mercury levels in hair and fish in Amazonia, *Environ. Res.*, 90, 6, 2002.
51. Saad, A. and Hassanien, M.A., Assessment of arsenic level in the hair of the non-occupational Egyptian population: pilot study, *Environ. Int.*, 27, 471, 2001.
52. Liu, X.J. et al., Significance of cadmium concentrations in blood and hair as an indicator of dose 15 years after the reduction of environmental exposure to cadmium, *Toxicol. Lett.*, 123, 135, 2001.
53. Egeland, G.M. et al., Trace metals in ancient hair from the Karluk archaeological site, Kodiak, Alaska, *Int. J. Circumpolar. Health*, 58, 52, 1999.
54. Harada, M. et al., The present mercury contents of scalp hair and clinical symptoms in inhabitants of the Minamata area, *Environ. Res.*, 77, 160, 1998.
55. Wilhelm, M. and Idel, H., Hair analysis in environmental medicine, *Zentralbl. Hyg. Umweltmed.*, 198, 485, 1996.
56. Airey D., Total mercury concentrations in human hair from 13 countries in relation to fish consumption and location, *Sci. Total Environ.*, 31, 157, 1983.
57. Brockhaus, A. et al., Intake and health effects of thallium among a population living in the vicinity of cement plant emitting thallium containing dust, *Int. Arch. Occup. Environ. Health*, 48, 375, 1981.
58. Harada, M., Minamata disease: methylmercury poisoning in Japan caused by environmental pollution, *Crit. Rev. Toxicol.*, 25, 1, 1995.
59. Violante, N. et al., Assessment of workers' exposure to palladium in a catalyst production plant, *J. Environ. Monit.*, 7, 463, 2005.
60. Martin, R.R. et al., Preliminary synchrotron analysis of lead in hair from a lead smelter worker, *Chemosphere*, 58, 1385, 2005.
61. Petrucci, F. et al., Biomonitoring of a worker population exposed to platinum dust in a catalyst production plant, *Occup. Environ. Med.*, 62, 27, 2005.
62. Morton, J. et al., Comparison of hair, nails and urine for biological monitoring of low level inorganic mercury exposure in dental workers, *Biomarkers*, 9, 47, 2004.
63. Gerhardsson, L. et al., Cadmium, copper and zinc in tissues of deceased copper smelter workers, *J. Trace Elem. Med. Biol.*, 16, 261, 2002.
64. Vishwanathan, H. et al., Trace metal concentration in scalp hair of occupationally exposed autodrivers, *Environ. Monit. Assess.*, 77, 149, 2002.
65. Bader, M. et al., Biomonitoring of manganese in blood, urine and axillary hair following low-dose exposure during the manufacture of dry cell batteries, *Int. Arch. Occup. Environ. Health*, 72, 521, 1999.
66. Hirata, M. et al., Probable case of chronic occupational thallium poisoning in a glass factory, *Ind. Health*, 36, 300, 1998.
67. Ishihara, N. and Urushiyama, K., Longitudinal study of workers exposed to mercury vapour at low concentrations: time course of inorganic and organic mercury concentrations in urine, blood, and hair, *Occup. Environ. Med.*, 51, 660, 1994.

68. Sabbioni, E. et al., Metal determinations in biological specimens of diseased and non-diseased hard metal workers, *Sci. Total Environ.*, 150, 41, 1994.
69. Simpson, J.R. and Gibson, R.S., Hair, serum, and urine chromium concentrations in former employees of the leather tanning industry, *Biol. Trace Elem. Res.*, 32, 155, 1992.
70. Yamauchi, H. et al., Biological monitoring of arsenic exposure of gallium arsenide and inorganic arsenic-exposed workers by determination of inorganic arsenic and its metabolites in urine and hair, *Am. Ind. Hyg. Assoc. J.*, 50, 606, 1989.
71. Randall, J.A. and Gibson, R.S., Hair chromium as an index of chromium exposure of tannery workers, *Br. J. Ind. Med.*, 46, 171, 1989.
72. Saner, G., Yuzbasiyan, V., and Cigdem, S., Hair chromium concentration and chromium excretion in tannery workers, *Br. J. Ind. Med.*, 41, 263, 1984.
73. Bencko, V., Nickel: a review of its occupational and environmental toxicology, *J. Hyg. Epidemiol. Microbiol. Immunol.*, 8, 161, 1982.
74. Richter, E.D., Peled, N., and Luria, M., Mercury exposure and effects at a thermometer factory, *Scand. J. Work. Environ. Health*, 8, 161, 1982.
75. Tong, S.L. et al., Distribution characteristics of rare earth elements in children's scalp hair from a rare earths mining area in southern China, *J. Environ. Sci. Health A. Tox. Hazard Subst. Environ. Eng.*, 39, 2517, 2004.
76. Kasai, Y., Iida, R., and Uchida, A., Metal concentrations in the serum and hair of patients with titanium alloy spinal implants, *Spine*, 28, 1320, 2003.
77. Yenigun, A. et al., Hair zinc level in Downs syndrome, *Downs Syndr. Res. Pract.*, 9, 53, 2004.
78. Tang, Y.R. et al., Studies of five microelement contents in human serum, hair, and fingernails correlated with aged hypertension and coronary heart disease, *Biol. Trace Elem. Res.*, 92, 97, 2003.
79. Lech, T. et al, Lead, copper, zinc, and magnesium content in hair of children and young people with some neurological diseases, *Biol. Trace Elem. Res.*, 85, 111, 2002.
80. Kobayashi, S. et al., Hair aluminium in normal aged and senile dementia of Alzheimer type, *Prog. Clin. Biol. Res.*, 317, 1095, 1989.
81. Guillard, O. et al., Congenital hypomagnesemia: alternatives to tissue biopsies for monitoring body magnesium status, *Clin. Biochem.*, 69, 171, 1982.
82. M'Baku, S.B. and Parr, R.M., Interlaboratory study of trace and other elements in the IAEA powdered human hair reference material, HH-1, *J. Radioanal. Chem.*, 69, 171, 1982.
83. 83. Okamoto, K. et al., Preparation and certification of human hair powder reference material, *Clin. Chem.*, 31, 1592, 1985.
84. Cao, L. et al., Radiochemical neutron-activation analysis of uncertified ultra-trace rare earth elements in two biological certified reference materials, *Anal. Bioanal. Chem.*, 372, 397, 2002.
85. Pineau, A. et al., An evaluation of the biological significance of aluminium in plasma and hair of patients on long-term hemodialysis, *Eur. J. Pharmacol.*, 228, 263, 1993.
86. Chappuis, P. et al., Relationship between hair, serum and bone aluminium in hemodialyzed patients, *Clin. Chim. Acta*, 179, 271, 1989.
87. Chappuis, P. et al., Analytical problems encountered in determining aluminium status from hair in controls and hemodialyzed patients, *Clin. Chem.*, 34, 2253, 1988.
88. Miekeley, N., Mortari, S.R., and Schubach, A.O., Monitoring of total antimony and its species by ICP-MS and on-line ion chromatography in biological samples from patients treated for Leishmaniasis, *Anal. Bioanal. Chem.*, 372, 495, 2002.

89. Gebel, T., Claussen, K., and Dunkelberg, H., Human biomonitoring of antimony, *Int. Arch. Occup. Environ. Health*, 71, 221, 1998.
90. DiVincenzo, G.D., Giordano, C.J., and Schriever, L.S., Biologic monitoring of workers exposed to silver, *Int. Arch. Occup. Environ. Health*, 56, 207, 1985.
91. Hac, E., Krzyzanowski, M., and Krechniak, J., Cadmium content in human kidney and hair in the Gdansk region, *Sci. Total Environ.*, 224, 81, 1998.
92. Lauwerys, R.R. et al., Cadmium: exposure markers as predictors of nephrotoxic effects, *Clin. Chem.*, 40, 1391, 1994.
93. Dubois, F. and Belleville, F., Chrome: rôle physiologique et intérêt en pathologie humaine, *Pathologie Biologie*, 39, 801, 1991.
94. Asaka, T. et al., Germanium intoxication with sensory ataxia, *J. Neurol. Sci.*, 130, 220, 1995.
95. Obara, K. et al., Germanium poisoning: clinical symptoms and renal damage caused by long-term intake of germanium, *Jpn. J. Med.*, 30, 67, 1994.
96. Morita, H. et al., Determination of germanium and some other elements in hair, nail, and toenail from persons exposed and unexposed to germanium, *Sci. Total Environ.*, 58, 237, 1986.
97. Esteban, E. et al., Hair and blood as substrates for screening children for lead poisoning, *Arch. Environ. Health*, 54, 436, 1999.
98. Luse, I. et al., Risk assessment of manganese, *Cent. Eur. J. Public Health*, 8, 51, 2000.
99. Holzgraefe, M. et al., Chronic enteral poisoning caused by potassium permanganate: a case report, *J. Toxicol. Clin. Toxicol.*, 24, 235, 1986.
100. Woolf, A. et al., A child with chronic manganese exposure from drinking water, *Environ. Health Perspect.*, 110, 613, 2002.
101. Baruthio, F. et al., Determination of manganese in biological materials by electrothermal atomic absorption spectrometry: a review, *Clin. Chem.*, 34, 227, 1988.
102. Gammelgaard, B. and Veien, N.K., Nickel in nails, hair and plasma from nickel-hypersensitive women, *Acta Derm. Venereol.*, 70, 417, 1990.
103. Karpas, Z. et al., Urine, hair, and nails as indicators for ingestion of uranium in drinking water, *Health Phys.*, 88, 229, 2005.
104. Marquet, P. et al., Tungsten determination in biological fluids, hair and nails by plasma emission spectrometry in a case of severe acute intoxication in man, *J. Forensic. Sci.*, 42, 527, 1997.
105. Grandjean, P., Lead poisoning: hair analysis shows the calendar of events, *Hum. Toxicol.*, 3, 223, 1984.
106. Foo, S.C. et al., Metals in hair as biological indices for exposure, *Int. Arch. Occup. Environ. Health*, 65, 83, 1995.
107. Wilhelm, M. et al., Hair lead levels in young children from the F.R.G., *J. Trace Elem. Electrolytes Health Dis.*, 3, 165, 1989.
108. Sen, J. and Das Chaudhuri, A.B., Brief communication: choice of washing method of hair samples for trace element analysis in environmental studies, *Am. J. Phys. Anthropol.*, 115, 289, 2001.
109. Tracqui, A. et al., Lack of relationship between hair lead levels and some usual markers (blood lead levels, ZPP, urinary ALA-D) in occupationally exposed workers, *Ann. Biol. Clin.*, 52, 769, 2001.
110. Rusyniak, D.E., Furbee, R.B., and Kirk, M.A., Thallium and arsenic poisoning in a small Midwestern town, *Ann. Emerg. Med.*, 39, 307, 2002.
111. Hopps, H.C., The biological bases for using hair and nail for analyses of trace elements, *Sci. Total Environ.*, 7, 71, 1977.

112. Koons, R.D. and Peters, C.A., Axial distribution of arsenic in individual human hairs by solid sampling graphite furnace AAS, *J. Anal. Toxicol.*, 18, 36, 1994.
113. Goullé, J.P., Métaux, in *Toxicologie et Pharmacologie Médicolégales*, Kintz, P., Ed., Elsevier, Amsterdam, 1998, p. 189.
114. Goullé, J.P., Mahieu, L., and Kintz, P., The murder weapon was found in the hair! *Ann. Toxicol. Anal.*, 17, 243, 2005.
115. Hindmarsh, J.T., Caveats in hair analysis in chronic arsenic poisoning, *Clin. Biochem.*, 35, 1, 2002.
116. Kurttio, P. et al., Urinary excretion of arsenic species after exposure to arsenic present in drinking water, *Arch. Environ. Contam. Toxicol.*, 34, 297, 1998.
117. Abdelghani, A.A. et al., Arsenic levels in blood, urine, and hair of workers applying monosodium methanearsonate (MSMA), *Arch. Environ. Health*, 41, 163, 1995.
118. DePeyster, A. and Silvers, J.A., Arsenic levels in hair of workers in a semiconductor fabrication facility, *Am. Ind. Hyg. Assoc. J.*, 56, 377, 1995.
119. Mazumder, D.N. et al., Chronic arsenic toxicity in west Bengal: the worst calamity in the world, *J. Indian Med. Assoc.*, 96, 4, 1998.
120. Rahman, M.M. et al., Chronic arsenic toxicity in Bangladesh and West Bengal India: a review and commentary, *J. Toxicol. Clin. Toxicol.*, 39, 683, 2001.
121. Mandal, B.K. et al., Speciation of arsenic in biological samples, *Toxicol. Appl. Pharmacol.*, 198, 307, 2004.
122. Mandal, B.K., Ogra, Y., and Suzuki, K.T., Speciation of arsenic in human nail and hair from arsenic-affected area by HPLC-inductively coupled argon plasma mass spectrometry, *Toxicol. Appl. Pharmacol.*, 189, 73, 2003.
123. Ginet, M. and Kintz, P., Multi-elementary screening by ICP-MS and speciation of arsenic by HPLC-ICP-MS in Napoleon's hair, *Ann. Toxicol. Anal.*, 17, 123, 2005.
124. Kintz, P. et al., A new series of hair analysis from Napoleon confirms chronic exposure to arsenic, *J. Anal. Toxicol.*, 26, 584, 2002.
125. Koshy, K.M. and Lovejoy, F.H., Thallium ingestion with survival: ineffectiveness of peritoneal dialysis and potassium chloride diuresis, *Clin. Toxicol.*, 118, 521, 1981.
126. Rasmussen, O.V., Thallium poisoning: an aspect of human cruelty, *Lancet*, 1, 1164, 1981.
127. McCormack, J. and McKinney, W., Thallium poisoning in group assassination attempt, *Postgrad. Med.*, 74, 239, 1983.
128. WHO (World Health Organization), Inorganic mercury, in *Environmental Health Criteria*, Geneva, 1991, p. 118.
129. Anon., Mercury amalgam report summary, Oct. 2005; available on-line at http://afssaps.sante.fr/htm/10/dentaire/sommaire.htm
130. Suzuki, T. et al., An acute mercuric mercury poisoning: chemical speciation of hair mercury shows a peak of inorganic mercury value, *Hum. Exp. Toxicol.*, 11, 53, 1992.
131. Harada, M. et al., Wide use of skin-lightening soap may cause mercury poisoning in Kenya, *Sci. Total Environ.*, 269, 183, 2001.
132. Gras, G. and Mondain, J., Problème posé par l'utilisation des cosmétiques mecuriels au Sénégal, *Toxicol. European Res.*, 3, 175, 1981.
133. Horvat, M. et al., Total mercury, methylmercury and selenium in mercury polluted areas in the province Guizhou, China, *Sci. Total Environ.*, 304, 231, 2003.
134. Dorea, J.G. et al., Hair mercury (signature of fish consumption) and cardiovascular risk in Munduruku and Kayabi Indians of Amazonia, *Environ. Res.*, 97, 209, 2005.
135. McDowell, M.A. et al., Hair mercury levels in U.S. children and women of childbearing age: reference range data from NHANES 1999–2000, *Environ. Health Perspect.*, 112, 1165, 2004.

136. Yasutake, A. et al., Current hair mercury levels in Japanese: survey in five districts, *Tohoku J. Exp. Med.*, 199, 161, 2003.
137. Greenwood, M.R., Methylmercury poisoning in Iraq: an epidemiological study of the 1971–1972 outbreaks, *J. Appl. Toxicol.*, 5, 148, 1985.
138. WHO (World Health Organization), Methylmercury, in *Environmental Health Criteria*, Geneva, 1990, p. 101.
139. Matthews, A.D., Mercury content of commercially important fish of the Seychelles and hair mercury levels of a selected part of the population, *Environ. Res.*, 30, 305, 1983.
140. Hansen, J.C. et al., Human exposure to heavy metals in East Greenland, I: mercury, *Sci. Total Environ.*, 26, 233, 1983.
141. Sherlock, J.C. et al., Duplication diet study on mercury intake by fish consumers in the United Kingdom, *Arch. Environ. Health*, 37, 271, 1982.
142. Johnsson, C., Schutz, A., and Sallsten, G., Impact of consumption of freshwater fish on mercury levels in hair, blood, urine, and alveolar air, *J. Toxicol. Environ. Health*, 68, 129, 2005.
143. Budtz-Jorgensen, E. et al., Association between mercury concentrations in blood and hair in methylmercury-exposed subjects at different ages, *Environ. Res.*, 95, 385, 2004.
144. Grandjean, P., Weihe, P., and Nielsen, J.B., Methylmercury: significance of intrauterine and postnatal exposures, *Clin. Chem.*, 40, 1395, 1994.
145. Grandjean, P. et al., Methylmercury neurotoxicity in Amazonian children: downstream from gold mining, *Environ. Health Perspect.*, 107, 587, 1999.
146. Akagi, H. et al., Human exposure to mercury due to gold mining in the Tapajós River Basin, Amazon, Brazil-speciation of mercury human hair, blood and urine, *Water Air Soil Poll.*, 80, 85, 1995.
147. Counter, S.A., Buchanan, L.H., and Ortega, F., Mercury levels in urine and hair of children in an Andean gold-mining settlement, *Int. J. Occup. Environ. Health*, 11, 132, 2005.
148. Barbosa, A.C. et al., Hair mercury speciation as a function of gender, age, and body mass index in inhabitants of the Negro River basin, Amazon, Brazil, *Arch. Environ. Contam. Toxicol.*, 40, 439, 2001.
149. Suzuki, T., Hongo, T., and Yamamoto, R., Hair mercury levels of Japanese women during the period 1881 to 1968, *J. Appl. Toxicol.*, 4, 101, 1984.
150. Druyan, M.E. et al., Determination of reference ranges for elements in human scalp hair, *Biol. Trace Elem. Res.*, 62, 183, 1998.
151. Morton, J., Carolan, V.A., and Gardiner, P.H.E., Removal of exogenously bound elements from human hair by various washing procedures and determination by inductively coupled plasma mass spectrometry, *Anal. Chim. Acta*, 455, 23, 2002.

Index

A

B

C

D

E

I

J

K

L

M

N

O

P

Q

R

S

U

V

W

X

Z

20